UNLOCKING THE

DOCTRINE AND COVENANTS

UNLOCKING THE
DOCTRINE AND COVENANTS

A SIDE-BY-SIDE COMMENTARY

ED J. PINEGAR · RICHARD J. ALLEN

Covenant Communications, Inc.

Cover image: Joseph's Nauvoo @ Al Rounds. www.alrounds.com
Cover and book design © 2008 by Covenant Communications, Inc.

Published by Covenant Communications, Inc.
American Fork, Utah

Printed in U.S.A.
First Printing: October 2008

15 14 13 12   10 9 8 7 6 5 4

ISBN-13 978-1-59811-698-4
ISBN-10 1-59811-698-3

INTRODUCTION

The study of the Doctrine and Covenants is the study of light, life, the divine restoration of covenant principles and keys, and the unfolding of the dispensation of the fullness of times through modern-day prophets. The Apostle Peter looked forward to a time when the gospel would be restored—unfolding and expanding beneath the canopy of modern revelation: "Repent ye therefore, and be converted, that your sins may be blotted out, when the times of refreshing shall come from the presence of the Lord; And he shall send Jesus Christ, which before was preached unto you: Whom the heaven must receive until the times of restitution of all things, which God hath spoken by the mouth of all his holy prophets since the world began" (Acts 3:19–21).

These predicted times of refreshing dawned during the spring of 1820 when the young Joseph Smith experienced, amidst effulgent rays of glory, the vision of the Father and the Son, declaring once again the word of truth to a world hungering for pure light. As the Restoration of the gospel unfolded through divine intervention in modern times, blessing after blessing emerged to grace the lives of all those willing to respond with faith and humility to the call to become "fellowcitizens with the saints, and of the household of God" (Eph. 2:19). The Book of Mormon whispered from the dust—this "marvellous work and a wonder" foretold by Isaiah (Isa. 29:14)—to restore the fulness of the gospel in the form of another witness for Jesus Christ. Line upon line, precept upon precept, the pages of the Doctrine and Covenants brought forth the essence of covenant wisdom and priesthood power, allowing the Church and kingdom of God to arise "out of obscurity and out of darkness, the only true and living church upon the face of the whole earth, with which I, the Lord, am well pleased . . ." (D&C 1:30).

From the squalor of his confinement in Liberty Jail, the Prophet Joseph Smith was buoyed up on the wings of inspiration to celebrate the triumph of the spirit of faith and virtue within the hearts and souls of the obedient of Zion: "Let thy bowels also be full of charity towards all men, and to the household of faith, and let virtue garnish thy thoughts unceasingly; then shall thy confidence wax strong in the presence of God; and the doctrine of the priesthood shall distil upon thy soul as the dews from heaven. The Holy Ghost shall be thy constant companion, and thy scepter an unchanging scepter of righteousness and truth; and thy dominion shall be an everlasting dominion, and without compulsory means it shall flow unto thee forever and ever" (D&C 121:45–46).

It is through such passages that the vitality of the gospel of Jesus Christ is confirmed to the honest at heart in our time, resonating with hope and faith, edifying those who seek to embrace the principles and ordinances of salvation and learn to cultivate the "godly walk and conversation" ordained as a way of life for the Saints of God (D&C 20:69).

The study of the Doctrine and Covenants is a study of God's love for His children. In these pages are laid down with clarity the principles and procedures for building Zion—as both a pattern of righteous living and a place where God can dwell with His people. This new canon grew segment by segment and edition by edition until it became the fundamental handbook of Church governance in our day. By far the most important edition of the Doctrine and Covenants is the "edition" that resides in the heart and soul of each sincere and willing reader as a living testament of devotion to the Lord and His covenant plan of redemption. Alma taught: ". . . and he that will not harden his heart, to him is given the greater portion of the word, until it is given unto him to know the mysteries of God until he know them in full" (Alma 12:10). How much of the word is "found in us," as Alma put it (Alma 12:13), is a measure of the quality of our hearts as receptacles of truth and our willingness to seek the confirmation of the Holy Spirit.

The Lord spoke of the scriptures as residing in His own bosom: "And a commandment I give unto thee [Sidney Rigdon]—that thou shalt write for him [the Prophet Joseph Smith]; and the scriptures shall be given, even as they are in mine own bosom, to the salvation of mine own elect" (D&C 35:20). It is our sacred commission to accept the word of God, "line upon line, precept upon precept" (2 Ne. 28:30; D&C 98:12; see also Isa. 28:13), and write it within our bosom, just as it comes from the bosom of Christ. Paul spoke of the Saints of God in terms of living epistles: "Ye are our epistle written in our hearts, known and read of all men: Forasmuch as ye are manifestly declared to be the epistle of Christ ministered by us, written not with ink, but with the Spirit of the living God; not in tables of stone, but in fleshly tables of the heart" (2 Cor. 3:2–3). In writing the word of truth upon our own hearts through the prayerful study of the scriptures, we emulate the Father, in whose image we are created, and by whom we shall be judged through His Son: "And behold, all things are written by the Father; therefore out of the books which shall be written shall the world be judged" (3 Ne. 27:26).

The authors offer this commentary as an adjunct to the systematic process of acquiring increased understanding of the word of God—especially as it pertains to the Doctrine and Covenants and the history of the Restoration. The approach used is to include every verse of the Doctrine and Covenants—from the beginning to the end—accompanied by commentaries and insights on sequential segments. Where appropriate and relevant, quotations are included from General Authorities (especially presidents of the Church), scholars, historians, and other commentators. Background summaries of the historical settings and circumstances are included. Cross-references to other standard works are also regularly given. Short profiles of many of the contemporaries of the Prophet Joseph Smith named in the Doctrine and Covenants have been added. In this regard, the authors recognize with appreciation the usefulness of the reference book *Who's Who in the Doctrine & Covenants* (Salt Lake City: Bookcraft, 1997), by Susan Easton Black, which served as a helpful source of facts. The emphasis throughout *Unlocking the Doctrine and Covenants* is on the doctrines and principles of the gospel of Jesus Christ, and on the manner of daily living that will conform to the commandments and teachings of the Redeemer in order to sustain hope, build testimony, magnify faith, and bring a higher degree of discipleship into our lives. The readers are encouraged to "liken" the scriptures unto themselves for "profit and learning," as Nephi counseled (1 Ne. 19:23).

The authors also wish to express sincere appreciation for the committed support of the staff of Covenant Communications and their devoted interest in this project. Special thanks to the managing editor, Kathryn Jenkins, and to her colleagues for their service in the production of this book. Special thanks also to Pat Pinegar, wife of Ed Pinegar, and Carol Lynn Allen, wife of Richard Allen, for their support and encouragement as this work progressed completion.

Ed J. Pinegar
Richard J. Allen

CITATIONS USED IN THIS BOOK

AF James E. Talmage, *Articles of Faith* (Salt Lake City: Deseret Book, 1984)

APPP Parley P. Pratt, *Autobiography of Parley P. Pratt,* ed. by his son Parley P. Pratt (Salt Lake City: Deseret Book, 1985)

AQDC Richard O. Cowan, *Answers to Your Questions About the Doctrine and Covenants* (Salt Lake City: Deseret Book, 1996)

ASA Joseph Fielding McConkie, *Answers: Straightforward Answers to Tough Gospel Questions* (Salt Lake City: Deseret Book, 1998)

CHC B. H. Roberts, *Comprehensive History of the Church of Jesus Christ of Latter-day Saints,* 6 vols. (Provo, Utah: Brigham Young University Press, 1965)

CHFT *Church History in the Fulness of Times,* rev. ed. (Salt Lake City: Corporation of the President of The Church of Jesus Christ of Latter-day Saints, 1993)

CHMR Joseph Fielding Smith, *Church History and Modern Revelation,* 4 vols. (Salt Lake City: Deseret Book, 1947–1950)

CR Conference Report

CYSNT Daniel H. Ludlow, *A Companion to Your Study of the New Testament: The Four Gospels* (Salt Lake City: Deseret Book. 1982)

DBY Brigham Young, *Discourses of Brigham Young,* selected and arranged by John A. Widtsoe (Salt Lake City: Deseret Book, 1954)

DCBM Joseph Fielding McConkie and Robert L. Millet, *Doctrinal Commentary on the Book of Mormon,* 4 vols. (Salt Lake City: Bookcraft, 1987–1992)

DCC Hyrum M. Smith and Janne M. Sjodahl, *Doctrine and Covenants Commentary* (Salt Lake City: Deseret Book, 1978)

DCE Hoyt W. Brewster, Jr., *Doctrine and Covenants Encyclopedia* (Salt Lake City: Bookcraft, 1996)

DCOMS Richard O. Cowan, *The Doctrine and Covenants: Our Modern Scripture* (Salt Lake City: Bookcraft, 1984)
Doxey Roy W. Doxey, *The Doctrine and Covenants Speaks,* 2

vols. (Salt Lake City: Deseret Book, 1964–1970)

DE Susan Easton Black et al., *Doctrines for Exaltation: The Sperry Symposium on the Doctrine and Covenants*, ed. (Salt Lake City: Deseret Book, 1989)

DNTC Bruce R. McConkie, *Doctrinal New Testament Commentary*, 3 vols. (Salt Lake City: Bookcraft, 1973)

DS Joseph Fielding Smith, *Doctrines of Salvation*, 3 vols. (Salt Lake City: Bookcraft, 1954–1956)

EM *Encyclopedia of Mormonism*, ed. Daniel H. Ludlow, 4 vols. (New York: Macmillan, 1992)

ER John R. Widtsoe, *Evidence and Reconciliations* (Salt Lake City: Bookcraft, 1960)

FAR Kent P. Jackson, *From Apostasy to Restoration* (Salt Lake City: Deseret Book, 1996)

FPM Spencer W. Kimball, *Faith Precedes the Miracle* (Salt Lake City: Deseret Book, 1972)

HJS Lucy Mack Smith, *History of Joseph Smith by His Mother* (Salt Lake City: Stevens & Wallis, Inc., 1945)

HO Byron R. Merrill et al., comps., *The Heavens Are Open: The 1992 Sperry Symposium on the Doctrine and Covenants and Church History* (Salt Lake City: Deseret Book, 1993)

HR *Heroes of the Restoration* (Salt Lake City: Bookcraft, 1997)

IE *Improvement Era*

JS John A. Widtsoe, *Joseph Smith—Seeker After Truth, Prophet of God* (Salt Lake City: Bookcraft, 1951)

LB Robert L. Millet and Joseph Fielding McConkie, *The Life Beyond* (Salt Lake City: Bookcraft, 1986)

LDPDC Roy W. Doxey, comp., *Latter-day Prophets and the Doctrine and Covenants*, 4 vols. (Salt Lake City: Deseret Book, 1978)

LJSP George Q. Cannon, *The Life of Joseph Smith, the Prophet* (Salt Lake City: Deseret Book, 1986)

Ludlow Daniel H. Ludlow, *A Companion to Your Study of the Doctrine and Covenants*, 2 vols. (Salt Lake City: Deseret Book, 1978)

MD Bruce R. McConkie, *Mormon Doctrine*, 2nd ed. (Salt Lake City: Bookcraft, 1966)

MF Spencer W. Kimball, *The Miracle of Forgiveness* (Salt Lake City: Bookcraft, 1969)

MMSC Bruce R. McConkie, *The Millennial Messiah: The Second Coming of the Son of Man* (Salt Lake City: Deseret Book, 1982)

NWAF Bruce R. McConkie, *A New Witness for the Articles of Faith* (Salt Lake City: Deseret Book, 1985)

PC John A. Widtsoe, *Program of the Church* (1938)

PMFCC Bruce R. McConkie, *The Promised Messiah: The First Coming of Christ* (Salt Lake City: Deseret Book, 1978)

PPRG Victor L. Ludlow, *Principles and Practices of the Restored Gospel* (Salt Lake City: Deseret Book, 1992)

PWJS Dean C. Jessee, ed. and comp., *The Personal Writings of Joseph Smith* (Salt Lake City: Deseret Book, 1984)

RL Truman G. Madsen, *The Radiant Life* (Salt Lake City: Bookcraft, 1994)

SNT Orson F. Whitney, *Saturday Night Thoughts* (1921)

SSDC Robert L. Millet and Kent P. Jackson, ed., *Studies in Scripture, Volume 1: The Doctrine and Covenants* (Salt Lake City: Deseret Book, 1989)

STDC Leaun G. Otten and C. Max Caldwell, *Sacred Truths of the Doctrine and Covenants*, 2 vols. (Salt Lake City: Deseret Book, 1982–1983)

TGBH Gordon B. Hinckley, *Teachings of Gordon B. Hinckley* (Salt Lake City: Deseret Book, 1997)

THBL Harold B. Lee, *Teachings of Harold B. Lee*, edited by Clyde J. Williams (Salt Lake City: Bookcraft, 1996)

TPJS Joseph Smith, *Teachings of the Prophet Joseph Smith* (Salt Lake City: Deseret Book, 1976)

UR John A. Widtsoe, *An Understandable Religion* (Independence, Missouri: Zion's Printing and Publishing Co., 1944)

VM James E. Talmage, *The Vitality of Mormonism* (Boston: Gorham Press, 1919)

All photographs were taken by and are used by permission of Kenneth Mays.

How to Use This Book

The left column on each page contains the actual text of the Doctrine and Covenants without chapter headings or footnotes. The Doctrine and Covenants text in this book appears on page numbers that correspond exactly to the page numbers in the Doctrine and Covenants, making this book ideal for classroom use.

The right column on each page contains commentary that corresponds with the Doctrine and Covenants text to its left.

The background to each section contains a brief description of when and where each revelation was received as well as a little about the circumstances.

Unless otherwise noted, each revelation was received through the Prophet Joseph Smith.

Boxes that provide biographical information on the people found in the Doctrine and Covenants were written by Ed J. Pinegar and Richard J. Allen, who used as a reference the book *Who's Who in the Doctrine & Covenants* (Salt Lake City: Bookcraft, 1997) by Susan Easton Black.

Information in other boxes was written by or based on the writings of Leaun G. Otten and C. Max Caldwell as found in volumes 1 and 2 of *Sacred Truths of the Doctrine and Covenants* (Springville, Utah: LEMB, Inc., 1983). Where references are not provided, the information was written by the editor.

All interior photographs are taken and copyrighted by Kenneth Mays. Photo captions were written by the editor.

SECTION 1

1. Hearken, O ye people of my church, saith the voice of him who dwells on high, and whose eyes are upon all men; yea, verily I say, hearken ye people from afar and ye that are upon the islands of the sea, listen together.
2. For verily the voice of the Lord is unto all men, and there is none to escape, and there is no eye that shall not see, neither ear that shall not hear, neither heart that shall not be penetrated.
3. And the rebellious shall be pierced with much sorrow, for their iniquities shall be spoken upon the housetops, and their secret acts shall be revealed.
4. And the voice of warning shall be unto all people, by the mouths of my disciples, whom I have chosen in these last days.
5. And they shall go forth and none shall stay them, for I the Lord have commanded them.
6. Behold, this is mine authority, and the authority of my servants,

The John Johnson Home in Hiram, Ohio, and the room where the Prophet Joseph Smith translated the Bible. The Prophet and his family were staying at this home, where five conferences were held November 1–13, 1831, to prepare the revelations for publication. (Hiram is spelled the way it is because it is named after Hiram, the Biblical king of Tyre.) It was while living and working here that the Prophet received the revelation that became Section 1 of the Doctrine and Covenants, the only book preface in the world written by the Lord Himself and the Lord's validation that the revelations are worthwhile.

Section 1 Background—Given at a special conference of the priesthood on November 1, 1831, in Hiram, Portage County, Ohio.

President Ezra Taft Benson pointed out: "The Doctrine and Covenants is the only book in the world that has a preface written by the Lord Himself" ("The Gift of Modern Revelation," *Ensign,* Nov. 1986, 78).

Known as the "Lord's Preface," this revelation was such a moving experience to the ten men present—Joseph Smith, Oliver Cowdery, David Whitmer, John Whitmer, Peter Whitmer, Jr., Sidney Rigdon, William E. McLellan, Orson Hyde, Luke S. Johnson, and Lyman E. Johnson—that they prepared a statement testifying to the world that they knew that the revelations were of the Lord. Originally, it was intended that this testimony be published at the front of the book.

First published in the *Evening and Morning Star* in March 1833, Section 1 was included in the Book of Commandments in 1833. If the Doctrine and Covenants is the scriptural overture of the heavenly campaign to prepare God's children for the Second Coming, then Section 1 is the preface to this magnificent opus.

D&C 1:1—The Lord's voice of warning makes clear the sober and compelling truth that the latter-day work is the ultimate directive to all mankind to repent and come unto the Lord Jesus Christ, that He might heal the wounds of the faithful and penitent and teach them how to abide the day of His coming.

D&C 1:5—The Lord's servants during the dispensation of the fullness of times have the responsibility to warn the world and prepare the people for the Second Coming of the Lord and Savior Jesus Christ. We should seek by example and precept to invite all to come unto Christ; indeed, every member *is* a missionary. Without exception, we can all contribute to the growth of the kingdom of God by embarking with faith, devotion, and courage upon the pathway of missionary service. The degree of our commitment to this covenant principle will in large measure determine our worthiness before the Lord of grace and mercy when the hour of accountability arrives.

D&C 1:6—The revelations in some sixty-five sections of the current edition of the Doctrine and Covenants predated Section 1. A compilation of the early revelations known as *A Book of Commandments for the Government of the Church of Christ* was in the process of being printed in Missouri in 1833 when a mob destroyed the press. Only a few copies of the work were rescued and preserved. An expanded version of the book was published in 1835 under the title *Doctrine and Covenants of the Church of the Latter Day Saints*—some three years before the Lord revealed the ultimate and full name of His church (see D&C 115:4).

and my preface unto the book of my commandments, which I have given them to publish unto you, O inhabitants of the earth.

7. Wherefore, fear and tremble, O ye people, for what I the Lord have decreed in them shall be fulfilled.

8. And verily I say unto you, that they who go forth, bearing these tidings unto the inhabitants of the earth, to them is power given to seal both on earth and in heaven, the unbelieving and rebellious;

9. Yea, verily, to seal them up unto the day when the wrath of God shall be poured out upon the wicked without measure,

10. Unto the day when the Lord shall come to recompense unto every man according to his work, and measure to every man according to the measure which he has measured to his fellow man.

11. Wherefore the voice of the Lord is unto the ends of the earth, that all that will hear may hear:

12. Prepare ye, prepare ye for that which is to come, for the Lord is nigh;

13. And the anger of the Lord is kindled, and his sword is bathed in heaven, and it shall fall upon the inhabitants of the earth,

14. And the arm of the Lord shall be revealed; and the day cometh that they who will not hear the voice of the Lord, neither the voice of his servants, neither give heed to the words of the prophets and apostles, shall be cut off from among the people;

15. For they have strayed from mine ordinances, and have broken mine everlasting covenant;

16. They seek not the Lord to establish his righteousness, but every man walketh in his own way, and after the image of his own God, whose image is in the likeness of the world, and whose substance is that of an idol, which waxeth old and shall perish in Babylon, even Babylon the great, which shall fall.

17. Wherefore, I the Lord, knowing

The Hill Cumorah, outside Palmyra, New York, where Joseph Smith obtained the plates from the Angel Moroni.

D&C 1:7—To fear the Lord means to hearken in humility to His counsel.

D&C 1:8—Under the aegis of the Abrahamic covenant (see Abraham 2:9–11), the servants of the Lord are to preach the gospel to the ends of the earth and bring the blessings of heaven to all who will listen (see Matt. 28:19–20)—a divine decree renewed and reactivated as part of the latter-day restoration of the gospel with its associated priesthood powers. The emissaries of the Lord act under priesthood authority to prepare the way for the Lord's return in power to judge the world. In this sense, the missionaries of the Lord "seal" the unbelieving and rebellious against the hour of accountability for their impenitent deeds and actions.

D&C 1:12–16—Apostasy and wickedness are to precede the Second Coming. James E. Talmage asked the following penetrating questions of conscience: "Are we worshipping the true and living God, or are we going idolatrously after the gods of gold and silver, of iron and wood, and brass, diamonds and other idols of wealth? Are we worshipping our farms, our cattle and sheep? Who is our God? To whom are we yielding homage, allegiance and worship? Not worship by means of words only, in ritualistic form, but worship in action, devotion, and sacrificial service?" (CR, Oct. 1930, 72).

In response to such questions, should we not carefully guard and preserve our own lives and those of our children lest, through carelessness or the "easiness of the way" (Alma 37:46), we stumble and fall into darkness? An understanding of the great and damaging sweep of apostate trends in the history of mankind should sharpen our understanding of the need to preserve the light of the gospel in our own lives at all costs and avoid being participants in the inexorable fall of Babylon.

D&C 1:17—Regarding calamity, a little more than a year and a half prior to the issuance of Section 1, the Book of Mormon was published, providing dramatic evidence of the tragic outcomes that befall a people who altogether turn away from God and break the everlasting covenant. The Lord foresaw that the same calamity would encompass all of His children—except for the renewal and reestablishment in the latter days of the holy covenant of salvation and exaltation, with power to recover and bless the faithful and obedient. This vision of impending calamity was foreseen by the prophets of old (see Isa. 24:4–5; Amos 8:11–12; and the words of Christ in Matt. 24:11–12).

the calamity which should come upon the inhabitants of the earth, called upon my servant Joseph Smith, jun., and spake unto him from heaven, and gave him commandments;

18. And also gave commandments to others, that they should proclaim these things unto the world; and all this that it might be fulfilled, which was written by the prophets,

19. The weak things of the world shall come forth and break down the mighty and strong ones, that man should not counsel his fellow man, neither trust in the arm of flesh,

20. But that every man might speak in the name of God the Lord, even the Savior of the world;

21. That faith also might increase in the earth;

22. That mine everlasting covenant might be established;

23. That the fulness of my gospel might be proclaimed by the weak and the simple unto the ends of the world, and before kings and rulers.

24. Behold, I am God and have spoken it: these commandments are of me, and were given unto my servants in their weakness, after the manner of their language, that they might come to understanding.

25. And inasmuch as they erred it might be made known:

26. And inasmuch as they sought wisdom they might be instructed:

27. And inasmuch as they sinned they might be chastened, that they might repent:

28. And inasmuch as they were humble they might be made strong, and blessed from on high, and receive knowledge from time to time:

29. And after having received the record of the Nephites, yea, even my servant Joseph Smith, jun., might have power to translate through the mercy of God, by the power of God, the Book of Mormon.

30. And also those to whom these commandments were given, might have power to lay the foundation of this church, and to bring it forth out of obscurity and out of darkness, the only true and living church upon the face of the whole earth, with which I, the Lord, am well pleased, speaking unto the church collectively and not individually—

31. For I the Lord cannot look upon sin with the least degree of allowance;

32. Nevertheless, he that repents and does the commandments of the Lord shall be forgiven;

The Smith log home in Palmyra, New York (it is called a "home" rather than a "cabin" because it had a wood floor intead of a dirt floor). This home has been rebuilt on its original site; the line between Palmyra and Manchester went down the middle of the Smith farm between this log home and the Smith family frame home. When President Gordon B. Hinckley dedicated this rebuilt home in 1998, he verified that the Angel Moroni appeared to Joseph Smith three successive times in the upstairs room here on the night of September 21–22, 1823.

D&C 1:19—How is it that an unlearned young man distinguished by no honors or credentials of the world, a "weak thing of the world," could inaugurate the single most important preparatory initiative for the Second Coming of Christ? Because he was called of God and endowed with power and authority to act according to the Spirit of truth and light for the blessing of all mankind.

D&C 1:21—Faith is the principle of the gospel that moves us to action (see James 2:18–20) and gives us power to do all things (see Ether 12:11–30). It is through obedience to the sacred priesthood covenants of the Restoration that faith can flourish and be magnified.

D&C 1:24—Promising that we "might come to an understanding," the Lord will make us equal to the task by providing us a way to accomplish His commandments. He will go before our face, and be on our right hand and left hand. His Spirit will be in our hearts and His angels round about to bear us up. As we exercise our faith He will give us understanding and fortitude to accomplish the task.

D&C 1:30—The position that The Church of Jesus Christ of Latter-day Saints is the only true Church upon the face of the earth is fundamental. . . . Now to those who think us uncharitable, we say that it was not devised by us; it was declared by Him [see D&C 1:30]. . . . Now this is not to say that the churches, all of them, are without some truth. They have some truth—some of them very much of it. They have a form of godliness. Often the clergy and adherents are not without dedication, and many of them practice remarkably well the virtues of Christianity. They are, nonetheless, incomplete (*Ludlow*).

D&C 1:30—Through the comprehensive missionary program of the Church, the kingdom of God is indeed being "brought forth out of obscurity and out of darkness." The number of missionaries sent out since the unfolding of the Restoration exceeds one million, and technology has made Church programs and doctrines accessible to countless millions in all parts of the world.

D&C 1:31–32—There can be no allowance for sin because the law of justice must be satisfied. Nevertheless, God does make allowance for the sinner who repents. The infinite and perfect love of God the Father is expressed through His Beloved Son and our Savior Jesus Christ, and the plan of salvation is centered in His Atonement. When we confess and forsake our sins, the Lord will remember them no more (see D&C 58:42–43) and our guilt will be swept away (see Enos 1:6). Mercy is provided for the faithful and penitent through the Atonement of the Lord Jesus Christ—through which the law of justice can then be satisfied. If we fail to repent, we must suffer even as the Lord did suffer (see D&C 19:15–19). And when we fail to keep the commandments, we lose the light of the Lord (see D&C 60:3) and the Spirit is taken away (see Mormon 1:13–14).

33. And he that repents not, from him shall be taken even the light which he has received, for my Spirit shall not always strive with man, saith the Lord of Hosts.

34. And again, verily I say unto you, O inhabitants of the earth, I the Lord am willing to make these things known unto all flesh,

35. For I am no respecter of persons, and will that all men shall know that the day speedily cometh; the hour is not yet, but is nigh at hand, when peace shall be taken from the earth, and the devil shall have power over his own dominion,

36. And also the Lord shall have power over his saints, and shall reign in their midst, and shall come down in judgment upon Idumea, or the world.

37. Search these commandments, for they are true and faithful, and the prophecies and promises which are in them shall all be fulfilled.

38. What I the Lord have spoken, I have spoken, and I excuse not myself: and though the heavens and the earth pass away, my word shall not pass away, but shall all be fulfilled, whether by mine own voice or by the voice of my servants, it is the same;

39. For behold, and lo, the Lord is God, and the Spirit beareth record, and the record is true, and the truth abideth forever and ever. Amen.

D&C 1:35—The Lord, who is no respecter of persons, invites every mortal to come unto Him: ". . . he inviteth them all to come unto him and partake of his goodness; and he denieth none that come unto him, black and white, bond and free, male and female; and he remembereth the heathen; and all are alike unto God, both Jew and Gentile" (2 Ne. 26:33).

D&C 1:36—We are emissaries of peace, even though peace will be taken from the earth; we are facilitators of the spirit of peace, even though Satan will rage across the landscape in the latter days. That is the dichotomy of our existence: to strive endlessly to bring the peace of the gospel into the hearts of our neighbors as they yearn to overcome the stress and turmoil of the mortal sphere.

D&C 1:37–38—Declared John A. Widtsoe: "The most important prophet in any age for the people of that age, is the living prophet. . . . To follow the living prophet, the interpreter of the past, and the foreteller of the future, is the essence of wisdom. The very strength of the Church restored through the instrumentality of Joseph Smith lies in the doctrine of continuing revelation through a living prophet" (JS, 288). The Doctrine and Covenants is a testament to the perpetuity and eternal nature of God's covenants. What He has promised to the obedient and faithful of the flock will be fulfilled—"whether by mine own voice or by the voice of my servants, it is the same" (D&C 1:38).

Five early editions of the Book of Mormon, dating from 1830 to 1842 and spanning the areas from Palmyra and Kirtland to Nauvoo. One of the editions was carried on a mission to Europe by Willard Bean.

SECTION 2

1. Behold I will reveal unto you the Priesthood, by the hand of Elijah the prophet, before the coming of the great and dreadful day of the Lord;
2. And he shall plant in the hearts of the children the promises made to the fathers, and the hearts of the children shall turn to their fathers;
3. If it were not so, the whole earth would be utterly wasted at its coming.

SECTION 3

1. The works, and the designs, and the purposes of God cannot be frustrated, neither can they come to naught,
2. For God doth not walk in crooked paths,
neither doth he turn to the right hand nor to the left, neither doth he vary from that which he hath said, therefore his paths are straight, and his course is one eternal round.
3. Remember, remember that it is not the work of God that is frustrated, but the work of men;
4. For although a man may have many revelations, and have power to do many mighty works, yet if he boasts in his own strength, and sets at naught the counsels of God, and follows after the dictates of his own will and carnal desires, he must fall and incur the vengeance of a just God upon him.
5. Behold, you have been entrusted with these things, but how strict were your commandments; and remember, also the promises which were made to you, if you did not transgress them;
6. And behold, how oft you have

MARTIN HARRIS

Martin Harris was born in 1783 at Easttown, Saratoga County, New York. A farmer of some respect in Palmyra, he became intrigued with the mission of the young Prophet Joseph Smith. Martin served as scribe for the translation of the early part of the record in 1828 (the Book of Lehi) but was responsible for the loss of the first 116 pages of manuscript. After repenting, Martin became one of the three witnesses to the Book of Mormon in June 1829. He mortgaged his farmland to finance the publication of the Book of Mormon. On April 6, 1830, he was baptized by Oliver Cowdery. In 1832 he served a mission for the Church in New York and later participated in Zion's Camp. He was one of the three to choose the Quorum of the Twelve Apostles in 1835 and served on the High Council in Kirtland. Soon thereafter he became estranged from the Church through his prideful lapses. Brigham Young later helped him move to Utah. He was rebaptized on September 17, 1870, and he reconfirmed his testimony just before he passed away in 1875 at Clarkston, Cache Valley, Utah.

Section 2 Background—An extract from the words of the Angel Moroni given on the evening of September 21, 1823, to the Prophet Joseph Smith in Manchester, Ontario County, New York. Moroni made three appearances to Joseph in his bedroom during the night, instructing him that the Lord had a work for him to do in translating an ancient record containing an account of the former inhabitants of America.

D&C 2:1–2—The words of Moroni, citing Malachi, were fulfilled on April 3, 1836, with the appearance of Elijah in the Kirtland Temple and the restoration of the keys and blessings of eternal families (see D&C 110:13–16). The Prophet Joseph Smith said, "The greatest responsibility in this world . . . is to seek after our dead" (*TPJS*, 356.) Who is accountable for that work? We are. We are the saviors on Mount Zion.

Section 3 Background—Joseph had been entrusted by Moroni with the sacred plates three months earlier and had begun the inspired translation. Martin Harris, a prosperous Palmyra farmer, had acted as scribe. Between April 12 and June 14, 1828, the first 116 pages of the manuscript were completed, then subsequently lost by Martin Harris. George Q. Cannon describes the Prophet's anguish: "The sorrow and humiliation which Joseph felt were beyond description. The Lord's rebukes for his conduct pierced him to the center. He humbled himself in prayer and repentance; and so true was his humility that the Lord accepted it as expiation and the treasures were restored to his keeping (*LJSP*, 55). In Section 3, the Lord explains the serious nature of this disloyalty.

D&C 3:1–2—What joy we should feel knowing that the plan of salvation cannot be frustrated by the devil or by evil and conspiring men! God knows all things (see 2 Ne. 9:20), and all things are present before Him (see D&C 38:2). Remember that the work of Heavenly Father and our Savior is our immortality and eternal life (see Moses 1:39)—a work of vast scope and significance involving billions upon billions of sons and daughters of God.

D&C 3:4—This passage is a jewel of divine wisdom to all of God's children—even those who at the moment seem to be at the apex of spiritual strength and appear unshakeable in their station of power. No one is beyond temptation; all are cautioned to set aside any boastful or prideful infatuation with their own perceived gifts and strengths—all of which, without exception, come from God.

transgressed the commandments and the laws of God, and have gone on in the persuasion of men;

7. For, behold, you should not have feared man more than God, although men set at naught the counsels of God, and despise his words;

8. Yet you should have been faithful, and he would have extended his arm and supported you against all the fiery darts of the adversary; and he would have been with you in every time of trouble.

9. Behold, thou art Joseph, and thou wast chosen to do the work of the Lord, but because of transgression, if thou art not aware thou wilt fall;

10. But remember God is merciful; therefore, repent of that which thou hast done which is contrary to the commandment which I gave you, and thou art still chosen, and art again called to the work;

11. Except thou do this, thou shalt be delivered up and become as other men, and have no more gift.

12. And when thou deliveredst up that which God had given thee sight and power to translate, thou deliveredst up that which was sacred into the hands of a wicked man,

13. Who has set at naught the counsels of God, and has broken the most sacred promises which were made before God, and has depended upon his own judgment, and boasted in his own wisdom,

14. And this is the reason that thou hast lost thy privileges for a season,

15. For thou hast suffered the counsel of thy director to be trampled upon from the beginning.

16. Nevertheless my work shall go forth, for inasmuch as the knowledge of a Savior has come unto the world, through the testimony of the Jews, even so shall the knowledge of a Savior come unto my people,

17. And to the Nephites, and the Jacobites, and the Josephites, and the Zoramites, through the testimony of their fathers—

18. And this testimony shall come to the knowledge of the Lamanites, and the Lemuelites and the Ishmaelites, who dwindled in unbelief because of the iniquity of their fathers, whom the Lord has suffered to destroy their brethren the Nephites, because of their iniquities and their abominations;

19. And for this very purpose are these plates preserved, which contain these records—that the promises of the Lord might be fulfilled, which he made to his people;

D&C 3:7–8—Our trust and faith can and must be only in God. To trust the arm of flesh in matters of an eternal nature is to put your life in jeopardy, and yielding to peer pressure and to the praise of the world will always lead one off the strait and narrow path that leads to eternal life.

D&C 3:9–10— In this brief span of words we see reflected the essence of the whole cosmos of the plan of redemption. When the chosen individual—whose name is known to the Lord in every case—falls into the shadows, he is immediately illuminated with the light and mercy of the Redeemer. Through repentance, the chosen one is still chosen. He knows us personally. He calls us by name. He will be with us, as He said, "in every time of trouble" (verse 8).

D&C 3:14—Joseph lost the gift of translation for a time because he set aside the counsel of the Lord.

D&C 3:16—The Lord speaks about the two witnesses of His divine calling as Redeemer—the Bible and the Book of Mormon—that should in the latter days come together as a combined witness of the truth (see Ezek. 37:15–17). The design of the Lord was to gather all things in one during the dispensation of the fullness of times (see Eph. 1:10; D&C 27:13; 29:8; 84:100). Thus the Prophet of the Restoration, Joseph Smith, was commissioned of the Lord and was prepared, tutored, and schooled by heavenly beings for the work of the ministry—step by step, line upon line—until he was ready to complete the magnificent work to which he was called.

D&C 3:19—From similar language in the Title Page of the Book of Mormon we learn the purpose of that magnificent record: "Which is to show unto the remnant of the House of Israel what great things the Lord hath done for their fathers; and that they may know the covenants of the Lord, that they are not cast off forever—And also to the convincing of the Jew and Gentile that JESUS is the CHRIST, the ETERNAL GOD, manifesting himself unto all nations." This testament and witness of Christ is explained in the introduction to the Book of Mormon in the words of the Prophet Joseph Smith as follows: "I told the brethren that the Book of Mormon was the most correct of any book on earth, and the keystone of our religion, and a man would get nearer to God by abiding by its precepts, than by any other book."

The frame house where the Prophet Joseph Smith began the translation of the plates with the assistance of Martin Harris, who acted as scribe. At right is the kitchen of the home, where Joseph learned of the loss of the 116 pages of the manuscript. According to historian Larry Porter, the pages were likely stolen by Martin's wife, Lucy Harris, and his son-in-law, Flanders Dyke.

20. And that the Lamanites might come to the knowledge of their fathers, and that they might know the promises of the Lord, and that they may believe the gospel and rely upon the merits of Jesus Christ, and be glorified through faith in his name, and that through their repentance they might be saved. Amen.

SECTION 4

1. Now behold, a marvelous work is about to come forth among the children of men;
2. Therefore, O ye that embark in the service of God, see that ye serve him with all your heart, might, mind and strength, that ye may stand blameless before God at the last day;
3. Therefore, if ye have desires to serve God ye are called to the work,
4. For behold the field is white already to harvest, and lo, he that thrusteth in his sickle with his might, the same layeth up in store that he perish not, but bringeth salvation to his soul;
5. And faith, hope, charity and love, with an eye single to the glory of God, qualify him for the work.
6. Remember faith, virtue, knowledge, temperance, patience, brotherly kindness, godliness, charity, humility, diligence.
7. Ask and ye shall receive, knock and it shall be opened unto you. Amen.

The grave markers of Joseph Smith Sr. and Lucy Mack Smith in the Smith Family Cemetery adjacent to the Joseph Smith Homestead at the south end of Main Street in Nauvoo. The matching headstones stand not far from the banks of the Mississippi River. Though the two monuments stand side by side, it is not certain where Joseph Smith Sr. is actually interred (historians do believe he is buried "nearby").

Section 4 Background—Given through the Prophet Joseph Smith to his father, who had been the first to believe the Prophet's story and to encourage him in being faithful to the angel. It is in answer to his father's humble inquiry as to what the Lord would have him do. In seven brief verses, it contains enough for a lifetime of study, and it might well be referred to as the "great anthem scripture" of missionary work.

D&C 4:1—The marvelous work referred to is mentioned several times in the Doctrine and Covenants (see also D&C 6:1; 11:1; 12:1; 14:1; 18:44), and comprises the coming forth of the Book of Mormon, the restoration of the priesthood and associated keys, and the establishment once again of the Church and kingdom of God upon the earth during the dispensation of the fullness of times.

D&C 4:2—Service in the vineyard of the Lord requires focused and devoted preparation. The heart is prepared through the "mighty change" (Mosiah 5:2; Alma 5:13); the mind is prepared through prayerful immersion in the word of God, which aligns one with God's will. Might and strength are cultivated by constantly exercising one's spiritual faculties of faith and hope, depending on the strength and might of the Lord.

D&C 4:3—Righteous desire can empower our lives as we yield our hearts to God (see Hel. 3:35). The desire within us gives us the will to act; we are then called to the work if we are found worthy. Section 4 is not exclusive to full-time missionaries but rather to full-time disciples of the Lord Jesus Christ.

D&C 4:4—Saying that "the field is white already to harvest" (see also D&C 6:3; 11:3; 12:3; 14:3; 33:3, 7) means that many of Heavenly Father's children are ready and willing to come unto Christ. The greatest work we can do and the thing that is of most worth is being an instrument in the hands of the Lord to bring souls unto Him (see D&C 15:6).

D&C 4:5—In order to be a worthy agent in the hands of the Lord, it is essential that we strive with every fiber of our being to possess the qualities and attributes of our Savior Jesus Christ.

D&C 4:7—*Asking* is a fundamental facet of communication between God and man. The principle of asking and seeking understanding is foundational to gaining knowledge in mortality. Throughout the history of the Church, revelations came as circumstances provoked questions that were taken before the Lord in humble and faithful prayer. The Doctrine and Covenants is largely a product of this revelatory process. It was the quest for knowledge that led to the restoration of the priesthood (see D&C 13), to the unfolding of a greater understanding of the post-mortal degrees of glory (see D&C 76), and to insights and guidance for many individuals, such as the Whitmer brothers (see D&C 14; 15; 16). The same thing applies to all of us.

SECTION 5

1. Behold, I say unto you, that as my servant Martin Harris has desired a witness at my hand, that you, my servant Joseph Smith, jun., have got the plates of which you have testified and borne record that you have received of me;

2. And now, behold, this shall you say unto him, he who spake unto you, said unto you, I, the Lord, am God, and have given these things unto you, my servant Joseph Smith, Jun., and have commanded you that you should stand as a witness of these things,

3. And I have caused you that you should enter into a covenant with me, that you should not show them except to those persons to whom I commanded you; and you have no power over them except I grant it unto you.

4. And you have a gift to translate the plates, and this is the first gift that I bestowed upon you, and I have commanded that you should pretend to no other gift, until my purpose is fulfilled in this; for I will grant unto you no other gift until it is finished.

5. Verily, I say unto you, that woe shall come unto the inhabitants of the earth if they will not hearken unto my words;

6. For hereafter you shall be ordained and go forth and deliver my words unto the children of men.

7. Behold, if they will not believe my words, they would not believe you my servant Joseph, if it were possible that you could show them all these things which I have committed unto you.

8. O! this unbelieving and stiffnecked generation, mine anger is kindled against them.

9. Behold, verily I say unto you, I have reserved those things which I have entrusted unto you, my servant Joseph, for a wise purpose in me, and it shall be made known unto future generations;

10. But this generation shall have my word through you;

11. And in addition to your testimony, the testimony of three of my servants, whom I shall call and ordain, unto whom I will show these things, and they shall go forth with my words that are given through you;

12. Yea, they shall know of a surety that these things are true, for from heaven will I declare it unto them.

Section 5 Background—Martin Harris had come to Harmony to seek confirmation that Joseph indeed possessed the sacred plates. In this section, the Lord makes clear His design for witnessing the truth.

D&C 5:1–4—The Lord works through worthy individuals who operate by covenant, using heavenly gifts and powers granted unto them to perform mighty deeds. This pattern applies to all of us.

D&C 5:7—Testimony is not built upon objects or artifacts, but rather upon the witness of the Holy Spirit in response to humble, sincere prayer (see 1 Cor. 12:2; Moroni 10:4–5). It is the whispering of the Spirit that conveys assurance that something is true—not what we hold in our hands or see with our mortal eyes.

D&C 5:9—Regarding the translation of the first 116 pages of the Book of Mormon, the Lord had taken preparatory steps many centuries earlier to ensure the integrity and success of bringing forth His word. The phrase "for a wise purpose" was used by Nephi (see 1 Ne. 9:5) as well as by Mormon (see Words of Mormon 1:7) in regard to preserving a more spiritual account of the early portion of the record of the Nephites than the one found in the "Book of Lehi" (the book from which the 116 pages were translated). This "wise purpose" enabled Joseph to replace the account lost in the original 116 pages of manuscript.

D&C 5:11—The Lord always uses the principle of witnesses, and has declared that "In the mouth of two or three witnesses shall every word be established" (2 Cor. 13:1; see also Matt. 18:16). The testimony of the Three Witnesses to the Book of Mormon—Oliver Cowdery, David Whitmer, and Martin Harris—stands at the beginning of this sacred volume of scripture to confirm the truth of the work.

THE WITNESS PROCESS

The witness process consists of both a physical and spiritual witness. Martin Harris wanted a personal witness of the reality of the plates from which Joseph Smith translated the Book of Mormon (see D&C 5:1), and apparently he thought that physically viewing the plates would constitute such a witness. This type of witness—consistent with the world's view—seems to have a place in the Lord's plan, since He promised Martin a view of the plates (see D&C 5:23–24).

There are limitations to this type of witness, though. While it is supportive, it isn't adequate. The Lord taught Joseph Smith that faith and testimony cannot be built on tangible evidence alone. Speaking of the witnesses of the Book of Mormon, the Lord said, "they shall know of a surety that these things are true" (D&C 5:12). This suggests an irrefutable witness, and that kind of witness must include a "manifestation of my Spirit" (D&C 5:16).

The Lord was willing that Marin Harris should become a witness to the Book of Mormon, but He made it clear that Martin was not yet prepared to be such (see D&C 5:28). Joseph Smith reinforced the need for Martin to repent properly when he said, "Martin Harris, you have got to humble yourself before God this day, that you may obtain a forgiveness of your sins. If you do, it is the will of God that you should look upon the plates in company with Oliver Cowdery and David Whitmer (HC 1:55).

Apparently Martin was unprepared for either a physical or spiritual witness because of his unworthiness (STDC 1:36–37).

Note: At the time this section was received, Martin Harris had already delivered the engravings to Professor Anthon, who had verified their authenticity, and had repented of taking the 116 manuscript pages. Now he wanted actual evidence of the plates.

13. I will give them power that they may behold and view these things as they are;

14. And to none else will I grant this power, to receive this same testimony among this generation, in this the beginning of the rising up and the coming forth of my church out of the wilderness; clear as the moon, and fair as the sun, and terrible as an army with banners.

15. And the testimony of three witnesses will I send forth of my word;

16. And behold, whosoever believeth on my words them will I visit with the manifestation of my Spirit and they shall be born of me, even of water and of the Spirit.

17. And you must wait yet a little while, for ye are not yet ordained;

18. And their testimony shall also go forth unto the condemnation of this generation if they harden their hearts against them;

19. For a desolating scourge shall go forth among the inhabitants of the earth, and shall continue to be poured out from time to time, if they repent not, until the earth is empty, and the inhabitants thereof are consumed away and utterly destroyed by the brightness of my coming.

20. Behold, I tell you these things, even as I also told the people of the destruction of Jerusalem, and my word shall be verified at this time as it hath hitherto been verified.

21. And now I command you my servant Joseph to repent and walk more uprightly before me, and yield to the persuasions of men no more;

22. And that you be firm in keeping the commandments wherewith I have commanded you, and if you do this, behold I grant unto you eternal life, even if you should be slain.

23. And now, again, I speak unto you, my servant Joseph, concerning the man that desires the witness.

24. Behold, I say unto him, he exalts himself and does not humble himself sufficiently before me; but if he will bow down before me, and humble himself in mighty prayer and faith, in the sincerity of his heart, then will I grant unto him a view of the things which he desires to see.

25. And then he shall say unto the people of this generation, behold, I have seen the things which the Lord hath shown unto Joseph Smith, jun., and I know of a surety that they are true, for I have seen them, for they have been shown unto me by the power of God and not of man.

D&C 5:14—In his inspired dedicatory prayer at the Kirtland Temple, the Prophet Joseph used the words of this verse in a slightly different formulation: "That thy church may come forth out of the wilderness of darkness, and shine forth fair as the moon, clear as the sun, and terrible as an army with banners" (D&C 109:73). The image is one of contrast—darkness transformed into light, concealment superseded by revelation, modest beginnings evolving into the army of God as the unfolding ensign of truth for the world.

D&C 5:16—Those who believe in the words of the Lord shall be born again. The first step in the process is to believe in the word of God, which testifies that Jesus is the Christ, the Savior and Redeemer of the world.

D&C 5:18—Even though all three witnesses to the Book of Mormon eventually became estranged from the Church—Oliver Cowdery and Martin Harris, unlike David Whitmer, later returned—each was steadfast to his dying day in confirming his testimony of having seen the plates. Logically, if there had been a fraudulent collusion between these witnesses and the Prophet Joseph, then the witnesses would scarcely have behaved as they did, but would have exposed the fraud when cut off from fellowship in the Church.

D&C 5:21–22—We can humbly take a lesson from the words of the Lord to the Prophet Joseph. If he had need to repent, then how much more reason is there for us all to repent by walking more uprightly before God—that we might also receive the blessing of eternal life, no matter what might befall us in the future. "Even if you should be slain," are the words of the Lord to Joseph, surely a prescient view of his martyrdom to come.

D&C 5:23–25, 28—John A. Widtsoe once described Martin Harris as a willful but honest man who wanted to be certain of everything he undertook. A critical factor, though, is that one must seek the Spirit in order to become converted. Here Martin Harris is promised he can be one of the witnesses *if* he humbles himself. This is an example of a conditional promise; the condition is humility.

D&C 5:24—The Lord gives to Martin Harris the divine formula of preparation and worthiness to receive personal revelation as a prospective witness of the truth—be humble, bow before God, pray, have faith, be sincere.

26. And I, the Lord, command him, my servant Martin Harris, that he shall say no more unto them concerning these things, except he shall say I have seen them, and they have been shown unto me by the power of God, and these are the words which he shall say;

27. But if he deny this, he will break the covenant which he has before covenanted with me, and behold, he is condemned.

28. And now, except he humble himself and acknowledge unto me the things that he has done which are wrong, and covenant with me that he will keep my commandments, and exercise faith in me, behold, I say unto him, he shall have no such views, for I will grant unto him no views of the things of which I have spoken.

29. And if this be the case, I command you, my servant Joseph, that you shall say unto him, that he shall do no more, nor trouble me any more concerning this matter.

30. And if this be the case, behold, I say unto thee Joseph, when thou hast translated a few more pages, thou shalt stop for a season, even until I command thee again; then thou mayest translate again.

31. And except you do this, behold, thou shalt have no more gift, and I will take away the things which I have entrusted with thee.

32. And now, because I foresee the lying in wait to destroy thee, yea, I foresee that if my servant Martin Harris humbleth not himself, and receive a witness from my hand, that he will fall into transgression;

33. And there are many that lie in wait to destroy thee from off the face of the earth, and for this cause, that thy days may be prolonged, I have given unto thee these commandments.

34. Yea, for this cause I have said, stop and stand still until I command thee, and I will provide means whereby thou mayest accomplish the thing which I have commanded thee;

35. And if thou art faithful in keeping my commandments, thou shalt be lifted up at the last day. Amen.

D&C 5:33—These restrictions were given for Joseph's protection. As he hints in verse 22, the Lord knew Joseph would eventually be killed as a result of the work (see D&C 136:39; Heb. 9:16–17).

D&C 5:34–35—In His wisdom, the Lord is preserving the Prophet Joseph so that his mission can proceed to its conclusion. The words of this passage are reminiscent of the famous words of Nephi in the Book of Mormon in response to Father Lehi's directive to return to Jerusalem to obtain the brass plates of Laban: "And it came to pass that I, Nephi, said unto my father: I will go and do the things which the Lord hath commanded, for I know that the Lord giveth no commandments unto the children of men, save he shall prepare a way for them that they may accomplish the thing which he commandeth them" (1 Ne. 3:7). In both cases, the commandment of the Lord was for the purpose of preserving His word and laying the foundation for its promulgation among future generations. All of us can take comfort in knowing that our duties before God are sustained by the promise that He will open the way for us to fulfill the obligations that are placed upon our shoulders.

Martin Harris home, located on what was a 320-acre farm about one mile north of the four-corners churches in Palmyra. Harris learned of the Smith family when he hired some of them as laborers on his farm. He helped finance the printing of the Book of Mormon: first by taking out an 18-month mortgage on his farm to pay the first $3,000 installment on the printing, and later by selling 150 acres for $3,000, which he gave directly to E.B. Grandin Printing. Martin Harris stayed behind for a time after the rest of the Saints left New York so he could personally oversee the binding of the first 5,000 copies of the Book of Mormon, a process that took almost two years.

SECTION 6

1. A great and marvelous work is about to come forth unto the children of men.

2. Behold, I am God, give heed unto my word, which is quick and powerful, sharper than a two-edged sword, to the dividing asunder of both joints and marrow; therefore give heed unto my words.

3. Behold the field is white already to harvest, therefore whoso desireth to reap, let him thrust in his sickle with his might, and reap while the day lasts, that he may treasure up for his soul everlasting salvation in the kingdom of God:

4. Yea, whosoever will thrust in his sickle and reap, the same is called of God;

5. Therefore, if you will ask of me you shall receive; if you will knock it shall be opened unto you.

6. Now, as you have asked, behold, I say unto you, keep my commandments, and seek to bring forth and establish the cause of Zion,

7. Seek not for riches but for wisdom, and behold, the mysteries of God shall be unfolded unto you, and then shall you be made rich. Behold, he that hath eternal life is rich.

8. Verily, verily, I say unto you, even as you desire of me, so it shall be unto you; and if you desire, you shall be the means of doing much good in this generation.

9. Say nothing but repentance unto this generation, keep my commandments, and assist to bring forth my work, according to my commandments, and you shall be blessed.

10. Behold thou hast a gift, and blessed art thou because of thy gift. Remember it is sacred and cometh from above:

11. And if thou wilt inquire, thou shalt know mysteries which are great and marvelous: therefore thou shalt exercise thy gift, that thou mayest find out mysteries, that thou mayest bring many to the knowledge of the truth; yea, convince them of the error of their ways.

12. Make not thy gift known unto any, save it be those who are of thy faith. Trifle not with sacred things.

13. If thou wilt do good, yea, and hold out faithful to the end, thou shalt be saved in the kingdom of God, which is the greatest of all the gifts of God; for there is no gift greater than the gift of salvation.

14. Verily, verily, I say unto thee,

Section 6 Background—Sections 6, 7, 8, and 9 constitute a remarkable manifestation of the process of using the spirit of revelation to receive guidance and truth from the Lord. This material constitutes an exceptionally unique primer on the workings of spiritual communication with the Lord—more detailed and specific than is available elsewhere in holy canon.

D&C 6:2—We are not left alone as we "give heed" unto the word of God. The Lord does not leave us without a lodestar in life, nor without an anchor to secure our souls to His abiding principles and doctrines. By pondering His word with faith and asking in the spirit of hope, we can receive spiritual guidance to transcend the challenges of this probationary state.

D&C 6:3—The expression "the field is white" became a theme of urgency during the early days of the Restoration, being used no fewer than eight times in different variations. During the early days of the Restoration, the unspeakable trials of the Missouri period and the daunting tasks of building up a new city unto God on the banks of the Mississippi were to short-circuit the operation of the worldwide missionary effort not a whit. It is a testimony to the faith and fiber of the early Saints that they were able to achieve such a magnificent harvest of missionary success despite the adversity and tribulations of those years.

D&C 6:8—Pure desire is the foundation of charity. From our righteous desires flow acts of goodness. Elder John A. Widtsoe taught: "If we want something for this Church and Kingdom, or if we want something for our individual lives, we must have a great, earnest, overpowering desire for that thing. We must reach out for it, with full faith in our Heavenly Father that the gift may be given us. Then it would seem as if the Lord himself cannot resist our petition. If our desire is strong enough, if our whole will is tempered and attuned to that which we desire, if our lives make us worthy of the desired gift, the Lord, by his own words, is bound to give us that which we desire, in his own time and in his own manner" (CR, April 1935, 82).

D&C 6:10–13—In this set of pronouncements on behalf of Oliver Cowdery, there emerges a sacred pattern for us all: Gifts come from heaven for the purpose of bringing souls to Christ. Those who use their gifts with honor and selfless service will find that these gifts are edified and sublimated into the greatest of all gifts from the Lord—salvation in the kingdom of God. But we must remember to proceed in faith and obedience, lest we fall away from the pathway (as Oliver Cowdery did) and thus relinquish the blessings of the Holy Spirit.

Homesite of Joseph and Emma Smith in Harmony, Pennsylvania. Oliver Cowdery, then a schoolteacher, was boarding with the Joseph Smith Sr. family almost 100 miles away during the 1828–29 academic year—not unusual at the time, when most teachers were young unmarried men who took on teaching as a temporary job before settling into a career. While living with the Joseph Smith Sr. family, Oliver learned about the Prophet and became convinced of the truthfulness of his mission. Oliver arrived in Harmony to join and assist the Prophet Joseph on June 5, 1829.

blessed art thou for what thou hast done, for thou hast inquired of me, and behold as often as thou hast inquired, thou hast received instruction of my Spirit. If it had not been so, thou wouldst not have come to the place where thou art at this time.

15. Behold, thou knowest that thou hast inquired of me, and I did enlighten thy mind; and now I tell thee these things, that thou mayest know that thou hast been enlightened by the Spirit of truth;

16. Yea, I tell thee, that thou mayest know that there is none else save God that knowest thy thoughts and the intents of thy heart:

17. I tell thee these things as a witness unto thee, that the words or the work which thou hast been writing is true.

18. Therefore be diligent, stand by my servant Joseph, faithfully, in whatsoever difficult circumstances he may be for the word's sake.

19. Admonish him in his faults, and also receive admonition of him. Be patient; be sober; be temperate; have patience, faith, hope and charity.

20. Behold, thou art Oliver, and I have spoken unto thee because of thy desires; therefore treasure up these words in thy heart. Be faithful and diligent in keeping the commandments of God, and I will encircle thee in the arms of my love.

21. Behold, I am Jesus Christ, the Son of God. I am the same that came unto my own, and my own received me not. I am the light which shineth in darkness, and the darkness comprehendeth it not.

22. Verily, verily, I say unto you, if you desire a further witness, cast your mind upon the night that you cried unto me in your heart, that you might know concerning the truth of these things.

23. Did I not speak peace to your mind concerning the matter? What greater witness can you have than from God?

24. And now, behold, you have received a witness, for if I have told you things which no man knoweth, have you not received a witness?

25. And, behold, I grant unto you a gift, if you desire of me, to translate even as my servant Joseph.

26. Verily, verily, I say unto you, that there are records which contain much of my gospel, which have been kept back because of the wickedness of the people;

27. And now I command you, that if you have good desires—a desire to lay up treasures for yourself in

D&C 6:14—The experience of Oliver Cowdery confirms that the Lord stands ready to respond to our prayers and supplications; the Lord has designed the plan of happiness to encompass the principle of personal revelation as an entitlement to His children. Personal revelation does not come through our physical senses, but is revealed to the obedient and valiant through the Holy Ghost.

D&C 6:15—The Lord conducts an intimate dialogue with Oliver Cowdery, confirming to him the process of enlightenment he has experienced by virtue of his sincere inquiry.

D&C 6:16–19—In these remarkable words from God we have a divine witness that the Book of Mormon is true (see also D&C 17:6; 20:7–13). We also have further witness of His love and compassion for us. He gives us fatherly counsel to be patient in our world of care and adversity, and to exercise faith, hope, and charity—the elements of a Christlike life.

D&C 6:20–21—The Savior knows each of us by name. He seeks a personal relationship with us and embraces us with love as we strive diligently to keep His commandments.

D&C 6:22–23—The Lord speaks with Oliver Cowdery and teaches him an unforgettable lesson: Remember the influence of the Spirit in your life. Think back on the miraculous event when you were touched by the Spirit in ways that only you and the Lord are aware of. Recall the feelings of peace that were engendered in your heart by communion with God. Know that God hears and answers prayers. Understand the outcome of this event for what it is: a personal witness from God that the gospel is true and that you are on the right course before your Maker!

D&C 6:24—The Lord told Oliver Cowdery through Joseph Smith of a private spiritual experience that no one could have known about except Oliver. He shared this with Joseph Smith after Section 6 had been given, whereupon the Prophet concluded: ". . . he knew that the work was true, because no being living knew of the thing alluded to in the revelation, but God and himself" (HC 1:35).

D&C 6:27—Oliver is promised a gift, based on his righteous desires, to assist in bringing forth the word of God, hitherto hidden from the world "because of iniquity." The Lord has reserved much of His word in abeyance until His people should demonstrate by their faith and obedience that they are worthy and prepared to receive even more of the holy scriptures. How do we respond to the wonders and glories of the Book of Mormon that we have been privileged already to receive?

heaven—then shall you assist in bringing to light, with your gift, those parts of my scriptures which have been hidden because of iniquity.

28. And now, behold, I give unto you, and also unto my servant Joseph, the keys of this gift, which shall bring to light this ministry; and in the mouth of two or three witnesses shall every word be established.

29. Verily, verily, I say unto you, if they reject my words, and this part of my gospel and ministry, blessed are ye, for they can do no more unto you than unto me;

30. And even if they do unto you, even as they have done unto me, blessed are ye, for you shall dwell with me in glory;

31. But if they reject not my words, which shall be established by the testimony which shall be given, blessed are they, and then shall ye have joy in the fruit of your labors.

32. Verily, verily, I say unto you, as I said unto my disciples, where two or three are gathered together in my name, as touching one thing, behold, there will I be in the midst of them, even so am I in the midst of you.

33. Fear not to do good, my sons, for whatsoever ye sow, that shall ye also reap; therefore, if ye sow good, ye shall also reap good for your reward.

34. Therefore, fear not, little flock, do good; let earth and hell combine against you, for if ye are built upon my Rock, they cannot prevail.

35. Behold, I do not condemn you, go your ways and sin no more, perform with soberness the work which I have commanded you;

36. Look unto me in every thought; doubt not, fear not;

37. Behold the wounds which pierced my side, and also the prints of the nails in my hands and feet; be faithful, keep my commandments, and ye shall inherit the kingdom of heaven. Amen.

OLIVER COWDERY

Oliver was born October 3, 1806, in Wells, Rutland County, Vermont. Having heard of the work of the Prophet Joseph Smith, he came to meet him at Harmony, Pennsylvania, on April 5, 1829, and two days later started to serve as scribe in the translation of the Book of Mormon. With Joseph, he received the Aaronic Priesthood under the hands of John the Baptist on May 15, 1829, and the Melchizedek Priesthood shortly thereafter from Peter, James, and John. Oliver was thus the second elder of the Church. With Joseph, he beheld the Lord Jesus Christ in the Kirtland Temple on April 3, 1836, and there received sacred priesthood keys from Elijah, Elias, and Moses. Over the next few years he became disgruntled with the leadership of the Church and fell into apostasy. In 1848 he sought to renew his fellowship in the Church and was baptized once again. He was true to his witness of the truth of the Book of Mormon to his dying day on March 3, 1850, at Richmond, Ray County, Missouri.

D&C 6:28–31—The Lord operates on the basis of priesthood keys bestowed upon His chosen servants. The keys are administered and empowered through the Holy Spirit, based on the obedience and humble service of the chosen workers. In this case, the keys of bringing forth the Book of Mormon are to be shared by Joseph and Oliver, Joseph being the prophet-leader of the Restoration and the ultimate curator of the sacred keys.

The Lord pronounces a blessing upon Oliver: should the people reject the words, Oliver would be nonetheless blessed for his efforts—even if he should lose his life in the process, just as the Lord lost His life in bringing about the Atonement; conversely, if the people should accept the word of the Lord, how great would be Oliver's joy as an instrument in the process of conversion. The same applies to us all: When we do our best in building up the kingdom of God and spreading the truths of the gospel, we are blessed by the Lord in all cases. Those whom we teach might accept or reject the gospel truths—but in either case we will have joy in the Lord for our valiant service.

D&C 6:32—When we gather together in the name of Christ, we necessarily work toward a unity of mind and heart in regard to our agenda of service in building the kingdom of God. In our own day, the Lord promises to be in our midst as we go forth to preach His gospel.

D&C 6:33–34—The law of the harvest is an eternal verity. If we sow filthiness, we reap filthiness (see Mosiah 7:30–31). If we sow goodness and love, we reap the same. We will be restored, blessed, or condemned, according to what we have sown in regard to our works—good for good and evil for evil.

D&C 6:35–37—What an inspiring and motivating framework for service is provided by the Savior's words: You are forgiven! Go forth! Look unto me! Doubt not! Fear not! I am your Redeemer and Savior! Be faithful and obedient, and you shall inherit the kingdom of heaven! This buoyant and edifying formula for spiritual living enables us to overcome doubt and fear through the atoning sacrifice of the Savior. Let us see in our mind's eye the prints of the nails in the Savior's hands and feet and commit to greater devotion, greater obedience, greater valor in keeping His commandments. Let us conquer fear and doubt and rejoice in the love that God has for us.

SECTION 7

1. And the Lord said unto me, John, my beloved, what desirest thou? For if you shall ask, what you will, it shall be granted unto you.
2. And I said unto him, Lord, give unto me power over death, that I may live and bring souls unto thee.
3. And the Lord said unto me, Verily, verily, I say unto thee, because thou desirest this thou shalt tarry until I come in my glory, and shalt prophesy before nations, kindreds, tongues and people.
4. And for this cause the Lord said unto Peter, If I will that he tarry till I come, what is that to thee? for he desired of me that he might bring souls unto me, but thou desiredst that thou mightest speedily come unto me in my kingdom.
5. I say unto thee, Peter, this was a good desire, but my beloved has desired that he might do more, or a greater work yet among men than what he has before done;
6. Yea, he has undertaken a greater work, therefore I will make him as flaming fire and a ministering angel: he shall minister for those who shall be heirs of salvation who dwell on the earth:
7. And I will make thee to minister for him and for thy brother James; and unto you three I will give this power and the keys of this ministry until I come.
8. Verily, I say unto you, ye shall both have according to your desires, for ye both joy in that which ye have desired.

SECTION 8

1. Oliver Cowdery, verily, verily, I say unto you, that assuredly as the Lord liveth, who is your God and your Redeemer, even so surely shall you receive a knowledge of whatsoever things you shall ask in faith, with an honest heart, believing that you shall receive a knowledge concerning the engravings of old records, which are ancient, which contain those parts

Section 7 Background—Given to the Prophet Joseph Smith and his scribe Oliver Cowdery "when they [Joseph Smith and Oliver Cowdery] inquired through the Urim and Thummim." Oliver was part of the revelatory process at this time, and a difference of opinion had arisen between the two as to whether John the Apostle had died or continued to live.

D&C 7:3–6—The Lord commends Peter for his desire to come unto Him speedily, for surely this was a noble aspiration. But the Lord places even greater commendation upon John, who wants to remain behind to do even more on behalf of the sons and daughters of God than he had hitherto done. Three of the twelve Nephite disciples chosen by the risen Lord in the New World expressed a desire similar to that of John (see 3 Ne. 28:6–8). They are living icons of the commitment to engage with full devotion in the spiritual gathering of God's children.

D&C 7:7—Peter, James, and John form a priesthood leadership presidency—in effect the First Presidency—holding the keys of the ministry of the Lord's gospel. Section 7 was given in April 1829. The following month, on May 15, John the Baptist appeared and bestowed the Aaronic Priesthood on Joseph and Oliver. Soon thereafter, Peter, James, and John appeared and conveyed the Melchizedek Priesthood to Joseph and Oliver.

Section 8 Background—The Lord had bestowed the gift of translating upon Oliver Cowdery as well as upon the Prophet Joseph, and Oliver had a keen interest in pursuing this capacity. In the words of Joseph Smith: "Whilst continuing the work of translation, during the month of April, Oliver Cowdery became exceedingly anxious to have the power bestowed upon him, and in relation to this desire the following revelations were obtained [referring to both Section 8 and 9]" (*HC* 1:35).

D&C 8:1–3—This same gift and spirit of revelation is accessible to all, for, as Paul declared, ". . . no man can say that Jesus is the Lord, but by the Holy Ghost" (1 Cor. 12:3). The key is to live worthy of the Spirit and learn to recognize spiritual manifestations. The Holy Ghost is the Revelator (see Eph. 3:5; Alma 5:46). He bears record of the truth of all things (see Moroni 10:5), will show us all things we should do (see 2 Nephi 32:5), teach us all things and bring all things to our remembrance (see John 14:26), testify of Christ (see John 15:26), and witness of the Father and the Son (see 2 Nephi 31:18). We should seek the Spirit so that we might have the spirit of revelation in our lives to enable us to teach with the power and authority of God (see Alma 17:3). The principle of revelation requires that we grow in this capacity to learn as we strive to understand the will of the Lord by listening to and following divine counsel, observing how it guides us forward with sure and steady steps.

of my scripture of which have been spoken by the manifestation of my Spirit;

2. Yea, behold, I will tell you in your mind and in your heart, by the Holy Ghost, which shall come upon you and which shall dwell in your heart.

3. Now, behold, this is the Spirit of revelation; behold, this is the Spirit by which Moses brought the children of Israel through the Red Sea on dry ground;

4. Therefore this is thy gift; apply unto it, and blessed art thou, for it shall deliver you out of the hands of your enemies, when, if it were not so, they would slay you and bring your soul to destruction.

5. O! remember these words, and keep my commandments. Remember this is your gift.

6. Now this is not all thy gift; for you have another gift, which is the gift of Aaron: behold, it has told you many things;

7. Behold, there is no other power, save the power of God, that can cause this gift of Aaron to be with you;

8. Therefore doubt not, for it is the gift of God, and you shall hold it in your hands, and do marvelous works; and no power shall be able to take it away out of your hands, for it is the work of God.

9. And, therefore, whatsoever you shall ask me to tell you, by that means, that will I grant unto you, and you shall have knowledge concerning it:

10. Remember that without faith you can do nothing, therefore ask in faith. Trifle not with these things; do not ask for that which you ought not:

11. Ask that you may know the mysteries of God, and that you may translate and receive knowledge from all those ancient records which have been hid up, that are sacred, and according to your faith shall it be done unto you.

12. Behold, it is I that have spoken it; and I am the same that spake unto you from the beginning. Amen.

SECTION 9

1. Behold, I say unto you, my son, that because you did not translate according to that which you desired of me, and did commence again to write for my servant, Joseph Smith, jun., even so I would that ye should continue until you have finished this record, which I have entrusted unto him:

D&C 8:4–5—The compassion, love, and benevolence of the Lord are manifest in such a promise—that He will reveal unto us wisdom and understanding for the purpose of our deliverance and safety.

D&C 8:6–9—Aaron, the elder brother of Moses, had the rod of leadership and acted as a spokesman for Moses. In the same way, Oliver was to go before Joseph and often served as his spokesman. There is a further aspect of the "gift of Aaron" that deserves consideration. In the Old Testament, we learn that Aaron was given charge of the Urim and Thummim as part of his priestly duties before the Lord (see Ex. 28:30; Lev. 8:8). Could the "gift of Aaron" also refer to the privilege of using the Urim and Thummim as a tangible instrument for revealing divine knowledge?

D&C 8:10–11—Oliver inaugurated his ministry through the power of faith. He would go on to accomplish many great things as an instrument in the Lord. And yet he did not hearken with enduring valor to the counsel of the Lord, who said to him: "without faith you can do nothing." Eventually, Oliver slipped and fell. His suffering was intense until, humbled, he finally returned to the fold—but not before he lost his gifts. "Without faith you can do nothing" is the lesson of Oliver Cowdery.

Section 9 Background—With the Lord's permission and commission, Oliver Cowdery had started translating the Book of Mormon. However, his faith was insufficient to receive the essential inspiration to accomplish the task, and the Lord instructs him to be content to serve as scribe for the time being.

D&C 9:12—Oliver is commanded to work with Joseph Smith until the Book of Mormon project is finished, then other records may be brought forth for Oliver to help translate. Which other records could be involved? The Book of Mormon makes clear that our current record comprises but a small part of the full historical archive of preserved accounts. How often did the prophet/historians of the Book of Mormon state that not even "a hundredth part" of the records were included? (See for example Jacob 3:13; Words of Mormon 1:5; Hel. 3:14; 3 Ne. 5:8; 26:6; and Ether 15:33.) In some future day—in "the own due time of the Lord" (2 Ne. 27:10)—the complete account will be made available. The Savior explained to the ancient American Saints: "And when they [the remnant of Israel (in the future)] shall have received this [the Book of Mormon], which is expedient that they should have first, to try their faith, and if it shall so be that they shall believe these things then shall the greater things be made manifest unto them" (3 Ne. 26:9; compare Ether 3:22–28; 4:5–7).

2. And then, behold, other records have I, that I will give unto you power that you may assist to translate.

3. Be patient, my son, for it is wisdom in me, and it is not expedient that you should translate at this present time.

4. Behold, the work which you are called to do, is to write for my servant Joseph;

5. And, behold, it is because that you did not continue as you commenced, when you began to translate, that I have taken away this privilege from you.

6. Do not murmur, my son, for it is wisdom in me that I have dealt with you after this manner.

7. Behold, you have not understood; you have supposed that I would give it unto you, when you took no thought, save it was to ask me;

8. But, behold, I say unto you, that you must study it out in your mind; then you must ask me if it be right, and if it is right I will cause that your bosom shall burn within you; therefore, you shall feel that it is right;

9. But if it be not right, you shall have no such feelings, but you shall have a stupor of thought, that shall cause you to forget the thing which is wrong: therefore, you cannot write that which is sacred, save it be given you from me.

10. Now if you had known this, you could have translated; nevertheless, it is not expedient that you should translate now.

11. Behold, it was expedient when you commenced, but you feared and the time is past, and it is not expedient now;

12. For, do you not behold that I have given unto my servant Joseph sufficient strength, whereby it is made up; and neither of you have I condemned.

13. Do this thing which I have commanded you, and you shall prosper. Be faithful, and yield to no temptation.

14. Stand fast in the work wherewith I have called you, and a hair of your head shall not be lost, and you shall be lifted up at the last day. Amen.

D&C 9:7–9—These well-known words remind us to be thankful for the experience of Oliver Cowdery. Because of his misunderstandings and difficulties with the process of inspired translation, we have the benefit of the Lord's counsel concerning how revelation through the Spirit truly operates. Communication through the Spirit is not a passive or routine thing, but requires study, effort, and the formulation of possible resolutions. These can then be taken before the Lord for His confirmation ("your bosom shall burn") or decline ("a stupor of thought"). As children of God, we are endowed with the capacity to reason, ponder, and apply the light of our understanding to challenges. As we do so, investing our time and effort in worthy objectives, the Lord will bless us with the confirmation of the Spirit or direct us away from what is not correct and appropriate.

The burning within our bosom is the feeling that it is right—not some extravagant physical manifestation, but rather a feeling of peace and comfort (see D&C 6:23). Without such feelings of peace, we learn that it is not of the Lord, for we will have a stupor of thought. Said Elder Melvin J. Ballard in this regard: "I know of nothing today that the Latter-day Saints need more than the guidance of the Holy Spirit in the solution of the problems of life" (CR, April 1931, 37–38).

D&C 9:10–13—Fear and passivity dissipate opportunity; courage and faith generate opportunity. Oliver lapsed into the former state and was consigned to complete his work as the scribe, with Joseph in the chair of leadership as seer and translator. The Lord "made up" the loss of productivity on the part of Oliver by increasing the flow of strength to Joseph. That is the divine pattern. Nevertheless, the Lord is patient and forgiving, and the work continued to its completion, giving us today the transcendent blessing of having before us the Book of Mormon.

There is wisdom and joy in learning to recognize the communications of the Spirit. When we humbly seek the will of the Lord always, there are fewer concerns and distractions associated with the sacred process of cultivating and heeding the promptings of the Holy Ghost. Listening with faith and hope is a skill of discipleship. In those instances where answers don't seem to come, we respond with patience and longsuffering and continue waiting on the Lord, who blesses us "in His own due time" (Enos 1:16; 3 Ne. 5:25; Mormon 5:12), according to His wisdom and love. He has stated: "If thou shalt ask, thou shalt receive revelation upon revelation, knowledge upon knowledge, that thou mayest know the mysteries and peaceable things—that which bringeth joy, that which bringeth life eternal" (D&C 42:61).

To-scale model of the home in Harmony, Pennsylvania, where Joseph Smith received Section 9, regarding Oliver Cowdery's desire to translate the plates. According to Elder Neal A. Maxwell, only the Prophet Joseph knew the full translating process, and he did not share it; we don't know the details, but we know the process required exceptional faith. A number of recollected accounts about the method and manner of translating vary in their details, but none are considered official—which is how the Lord intends it, says Elder Maxwell. The Prophet and his scribes consistently produced seven to nine pages of text per day for a period of sixty-three days without using notes, reviews, or reference materials.

SECTION 10

1. Now, behold, I say unto you, that because you delivered up those writings which you had power given unto you to translate, by the means of the Urim and Thummim, into the hands of a wicked man, you have lost them;

2. And you also lost your gift at the same time, and your mind became darkened;

3. Nevertheless, it is now restored unto you again, therefore see that you are faithful and continue on unto the finishing of the remainder of the work of translation as you have begun:

4. Do not run faster, or labor more than you have strength and means provided to enable you to translate; but be diligent unto the end:

5. Pray always, that you may come off conqueror; yea, that you may conquer Satan, and that you may escape the hands of the servants of Satan, that do uphold his work.

6. Behold, they have sought to destroy you; yea, even the man in whom you have trusted, has sought to destroy you.

7. And for this cause I said that he is a wicked man, for he has sought to take away the things wherewith you have been entrusted; and he has also sought to destroy your gift;

8. And because you have delivered the writings into his hands, behold, wicked men have taken them from you:

9. Therefore, you have delivered them up; yea, that which was sacred unto wickedness.

10. And, behold, Satan has put it into their hearts to alter the words which you have caused to be written, or which you have translated, which have gone out of your hands.

11. And, behold, I say unto you, that because they have altered the words, they read contrary from that which you translated and caused to be written;

12. And, on this wise, the devil has sought to lay a cunning plan, that he may destroy this work;

13. For he has put into their hearts to do this, that by lying they may say they have caught you in

Section 10 Background—The Lord reveals that He had already prepared a way to frustrate the evil designs of those into whose hands the first 116 pages of the manuscript had fallen—He would cause Joseph to begin anew the translation from the smaller Plates of Nephi to prevent wicked men from altering the lost section so it would be different from any version that would subsequently be translated.

D&C 10:4—We need to pace ourselves in keeping with our capacities. At the same time, we should pray for victory and remember that the Lord will sustain and support us in our valiant efforts to help build the kingdom of God.

D&C 10:5—The power of prayer is the power to draw upon the powers of Heaven. The Lord has made the commandment of prayer imperative in our lives. We have been exhorted and admonished to pray, ask, cry, and call upon God for all things. Without prayer we are left to ourselves—without the strength of the Lord. We pray to know the truth (see Alma 5:46; Moro. 10:4). We pray to overcome and resist temptation (see Alma 13:28; 3 Ne. 18:18). We pray for strength (see 1 Ne. 7:17). We pray with faith for forgiveness of sins (see Enos 1:4). We pray to be strong in humility and firm in our faith (see Hel. 3:35). We pray to counsel with the Lord in all our doings (see Alma 37:37). We pray with all the energy of our hearts that we might have charity (see Moro. 7:48). And we pray for the Spirit (see D&C 19:38; 42:14). Let us remember that we are to ask in faith with real intent according to the Spirit—and we will receive all things (see D&C 46:30).

D&C 10:9—Joseph is reminded of the tragic consequences of his yielding to the petitions of Martin Harris, "a wicked man" (verse 7), and thus losing the initial segment of the translation. The devil prompted evil men to alter the translation and thus entrap the Prophet and destroy the work of God in exchange for the glory of the world.

Site of Isaac and Elizabeth Hale home.

the words which you have pretended to translate.

14. Verily, I say unto you, that I will not suffer that Satan shall accomplish his evil design in this thing,

15. For, behold, he has put it into their hearts to get thee to tempt the Lord thy God, in asking to translate it over again;

16. And then, behold, they say and think in their hearts, we will see if God has given him power to translate, if so, he will also give him power again;

17. And if God giveth him power again, or if he translates again, or in other words, if he bringeth forth the same words, behold, we have the same with us, and we have altered them:

18. Therefore, they will not agree, and we will say that he has lied in his words, and that he has no gift, and that he has no power:

19. Therefore, we will destroy him, and also the work, and will do this that we may not be ashamed in the end, and that we may get glory of the world.

20. Verily, verily, I say unto you, that Satan has great hold upon their hearts; he stirreth them up to iniquity against that which is good,

21. And their hearts are corrupt, and full of wickedness and abominations, and they love darkness rather than light, because their deeds are evil: therefore they will not ask of me.

22. Satan stirreth them up, that he may lead their souls to destruction.

23. And thus he has laid a cunning plan, thinking to destroy the work of God, but I will require this at their hands, and it shall turn to their shame and condemnation in the day of judgment;

24. Yea, he stirreth up their hearts to anger against this work;

25. Yea, he saith unto them, Deceive and lie in wait to catch, that ye may destroy: behold, this is no harm, and thus he flattereth them, and telleth them that it is no sin to lie, that they may catch a man in a lie, that they may destroy him;

26. And thus he flattereth them, and leadeth them along until he draggeth their souls down to hell; and thus he causeth them to catch themselves in their own snare;

27. And thus he goeth up and down, to and fro in the earth, seeking to destroy the souls of men.

28. Verily, verily, I say unto you, wo be unto him that lieth to deceive, because he supposeth that another lieth to deceive; for such are not exempt from the justice of God.

29. Now, behold, they have altered these words, because Satan saith unto them, He hath deceived you: and thus he flattereth them away

D&C 10:27—The devil's purpose is to make all mankind "miserable like unto himself" (2 Ne. 2:27) and to destroy their souls (see D&C 64:17). He seeks to deceive the children of God (see 3 Ne. 2:2). The devil is "an enemy to God" (Mosiah 16:5) and "to all righteousness" (Alma 34:23). He desires "to have you, that he may sift you as wheat" (3 Ne. 18:18). He rages in the hearts of men to "stir them up to anger against that which is good" (2 Ne. 28:20). The devil is "the father of contention" (3 Ne. 11:29) and seeks to turn our hearts from the truth (see D&C 78:10). But as we live according to the commandments and our covenants, we can take heart in knowing the devil can have no power over the righteous (see Alma 48:17).

ENTRUSTED TO SACRED THINGS

When Martin Harris requested the privilege of showing the manuscript to others, he was certain he could protect it and was willing to make promises before the Lord. As he persisted in that desire, Joseph was apparently convinced that Martin was capable of handling such a sacred document. Joseph pleaded with the Lord, asking that the plans of mortals be given divine approval. Knowing the weakness of men, the Lord allowed them to learn a difficult lesson by simply granting them their desire.

When failure resulted, as the Lord knew it surely would, He proceeded to teach His youthful prophet a significant principle: "For although a man may have many revelations, and have power to do many mighty works, yet if he boasts in his own strength, and sets at naught the counsels of God, and follows after the dictates of his own will and carnal desires, he must fall and incur the vengeance of a just God upon him" (D&C 3:4).

This is a common weakness in all of us. We may fear man more than God and often depend on our own judgment instead of the Lord's counsel. Do we sometimes consider we are an exception and therefore justify our disobedient behavior?

The gravity of Joseph's situation was emphasized when the Lord pointed out another aspect of their transgression: those things that were sacred had been delivered up into the hands of a wicked man (see D&C 3:12; 10:9). Joseph seemingly was not fully aware of the sacred nature of the plates and the translation of them. He apparently hadn't considered all that had been done to bring that ancient record into his hands. Perhaps he hadn't thought about all the spiritual strugglings, hours of labor and toil, days of fasting and praying, and all the worrying involved in properly preparing those records. He may have overlooked how involved the Lord had been in the unnumbered spiritual and sacred experiences in the lives of ancient prophets—and how sacred this book really is (STDC 1:21–23).

to do iniquity, to get thee to tempt the Lord thy God.

30. Behold, I say unto you, that you shall not translate again those words which have gone forth out of your hands;

31. For, behold, they shall not accomplish their evil designs in lying against those words. For, behold, if you should bring forth the same words they will say that you have lied; that you have pretended to translate, but that you have contradicted yourself:

32. And, behold, they will publish this, and Satan will harden the hearts of the people to stir them up to anger against you, that they will not believe my words.

33. Thus Satan thinketh to overpower your testimony in this generation, that the work may not come forth in this generation:

34. But behold, here is wisdom, and because I show unto you wisdom, and give you commandments concerning these things, what you shall do, show it not unto the world until you have accomplished the work of translation.

35. Marvel not that I said unto you, here is wisdom, show it not unto the world, for I said, show it not unto the world, that you may be preserved.

36. Behold, I do not say that you shall not show it unto the righteous;

37. But as you cannot always judge the righteous, or as you cannot always tell the wicked from the righteous, therefore I say unto you, hold your peace until I shall see fit to make all things known unto the world concerning the matter.

38. And now, verily I say unto you, that an account of those things that you have written, which have gone out of your hands, are engraven upon the plates of Nephi;

39. Yea, and you remember it was said in those writings that a more particular account was given of these things upon the plates of Nephi.

40. And now, because the account which is engraven upon the plates of Nephi is more particular concerning the things which, in my wisdom, I would bring to the knowledge of the people in this account;

41. Therefore, you shall translate the engravings which are on the plates of Nephi, down even till you come to the reign of king Benjamin, or until you come to that which you have translated, which you have retained;

42. And behold, you shall publish it as the record of Nephi, and thus I will confound those who have altered my words.

43. I will not suffer that they shall destroy my work; yea, I will show unto them that my wisdom is greater than the cunning of the devil.

44. Behold, they have only got a part, or an abridgment of the account of Nephi.

45. Behold, there are many things engraven on the plates of Nephi which do throw greater views upon my gospel; therefore, it is wisdom in me that you should translate this first part of the engravings of Nephi, and send forth in this work.

46. And, behold, all the remainder of this work does contain all those parts of my gospel which my holy prophets, yea, and also my disciples,

D&C 10:30—Joseph is commanded not to redo the 116 pages that were lost. The Lord knew the conspirators planned to publish their altered version and then impute contradictions to the Prophet, thereby attempting to destroy the faith of the people.

D&C 10:33—From this account, we learn of the majesty of the Lord in overpowering and frustrating the satanic work of those who would destroy the gospel plan. His wisdom reigns supreme. As President Joseph Fielding Smith warned, "Never before in the history of the world has Satan raged more determinedly in the hearts of the people than he is doing today" (CHMR 1:28–29). Let us not slack off. We can be watchful and prayerful. Let us assume that Satan and his minions are committed to our destruction, and that they will employ every device, every tactic, every deception, every subterfuge to thwart the designs of God. Let us therefore renew our commitment to move forward with valor in carrying out our duties and lifting the cause of Zion "in the strength of the Lord" (Alma 20:4).

D&C 10:34—The Lord instructs Joseph in wisdom to translate from the plates of Nephi down to the place where the 116 pages (taken from the Book of Lehi) left off.

D&C 10:40—When the prophet/historian Mormon was completing his work of gathering and abridging the accounts of the people from Lehi down to his own day, he was prompted to add the material from the plates of Nephi that conveyed the parallel, but more spiritual, account down to the time of King Benjamin. His own testimony gives us the reasoning behind this strategy: "But behold, I shall take these plates, which contain these prophesyings and revelations, and put them with the remainder of my record, for they are choice unto me; and I know they will be choice unto my brethren. And I do this for a wise purpose; for thus it whispereth me, according to the workings of the Spirit of the Lord which is in me. And now, I do not know all things; but the Lord knoweth all things which are to come; wherefore, he worketh in me to do according to his will" (Words of Mormon 1:6–7).

D&C 10:42–45—The Lord, in His wisdom, inspired the ancient prophets to prepare for this critical moment in history when Satan would rage but find that his devious plans would be frustrated. Note how Nephi expresses his perspective on the nature of his spiritual writings on the smaller plates: "Wherefore, the Lord hath commanded me to make these plates for a wise purpose in him, which purpose I know not. But the Lord knoweth all things from the beginning; wherefore, he prepareth a way to accomplish all his works among the children of men; for behold, he hath all power unto the fulfilling of all his words" (1 Ne. 9:5–6).

D&C 10:46—In bringing forth the Book of Mormon, the Lord is answering the faithful prayers of the ancient prophets, who desired that these truths would come forth to future generations.

desired in their prayers should come forth unto this people.

47. And I said unto them, that it should be granted unto them according to their faith in their prayers;

48. Yea, and this was their faith, that my gospel, which I gave unto them, that they might preach in their days, might come unto their brethren the Lamanites, and also all that had become Lamanites, because of their dissensions.

49. Now, this is not all—their faith in their prayers was, that this gospel should be made known also, if it were possible that other nations should possess this land;

50. And thus they did leave a blessing upon this land in their prayers, that whosoever should believe in this gospel in this land, might have eternal life;

51. Yea, that it might be free unto all of whatsoever nation, kindred, tongue, or people they may be.

52. And now, behold, according to their faith in their prayers will I bring this part of my gospel to the knowledge of my people. Behold, I do not bring it to destroy that which they have received, but to build it up.

53. And for this cause have I said; if this generation harden not their hearts, I will establish my church among them.

54. Now I do not say this to destroy my church, but I say this to build up my church;

55. Therefore, whosoever belongeth to my church need not fear, for such shall inherit the kingdom of heaven;

56. But it is they who do not fear me, neither keep my commandments, but build up churches unto themselves to get gain, yea, and all those that do wickedly and build up the kingdom of the devil; yea, verily, verily, I say unto you, that it is they that I will disturb, and cause to tremble and shake to the center.

57. Behold, I am Jesus Christ, the Son of God. I came unto my own, and my own received me not.

58. I am the light which shineth in darkness, and the darkness comprehendeth it not.

59. I am he who said, other sheep have I which are not of this fold, unto my disciples, and many there were that understood me not.

60. And I will show unto this people that I had other sheep, and that they were a branch of the house of Jacob;

61. And I will bring to light their marvelous works, which they did in my name;

62. Yea, and I will also bring to light my gospel which was ministered unto them, and, behold, they shall not deny that which you have received, but they shall build it up, and shall bring to light the true points of my doctrine, yea, and the only doctrine which is in me;

63. And this I do that I may establish my gospel, that there may not be so much contention; yea,

D&C 10:48–51—In the latter days the remnants of Israel in America, the Lamanites, were to receive the fullness of the gospel, which would also come to whichever nation would possess the promised land in faith. The blessings of the gospel of Jesus Christ are offered free—"without money and without price" (2 Ne. 9:50; see also Alma 1:20)—to all who seek to come unto Christ and repent in faith and obedience.

D&C 10:55–56—The Lord will establish His Church in the latter days. Those who belong to His Church need not fear, for they will inherit the kingdom of heaven—but the wicked will "tremble and shake to the center" (verse 56).

D&C 10:57–58—In this testimony of His divinity, the Lord expresses the contrast between light and darkness in order to illustrate the power of His message of life and salvation. These words resonate elsewhere in the scriptures as well (see John 1:5; 1 John 2:8; D&C 11:11; 34:2; 39:2; 45:7; 88:49). Through conversion to the gospel of Jesus Christ, the light grows within us and our eye becomes single to the glory of God (see D&C 4:5; 82:19).

D&C 10:59–62—The Savior spoke of "other sheep" to His listeners in Jerusalem (John 10:16) as well as to those in ancient America (see 3 Ne. 15:17–21; 16:1). He characterizes the work of His faithful in the Book of Mormon as "marvelous." Those who receive the light of the fullness of His everlasting gospel will build it up—elevate it, edify it, raise it up as an ensign to the people in order to disseminate and glorify the "true points" of His doctrine contained therein—the only doctrine that He says is "in me." This language anticipates the Lord's words to Sidney Rigdon, who would soon be assisting the Prophet Joseph in his inspired translation of the Bible: "And a commandment I give unto thee—that thou shalt write for him; and the scriptures shall be given, even as they are in mine own bosom, to the salvation of mine own elect" (D&C 35:20). The scriptures—the word of the Lord—are in His bosom. His doctrine is in His bosom. What He reveals to us comes from the innermost part of His being. It is the word of God, representing the will of the Father. It is the key to eternal life, which key He desires for all to have.

D&C 10:63—Those who accept the Book of Mormon as the word of God and another testament of Jesus Christ will have the fullness of His gospel (see D&C 20:9). They will be able to harmonize these truths with those contained in the record of the Jews, the Holy Bible. Multiple witnesses of the same truth mitigate contention and resolve differences. Among the first lessons taught by the Savior to His Saints in America was to resolve disputations concerning points in His doctrine (see 3 Ne. 11:22, 28; 18:34; 27:3).

Satan doth stir up the hearts of the people to contention concerning the points of my doctrine; and in these things they do err, for they do wrest the scriptures and do not understand them;

64. Therefore, I will unfold unto them this great mystery;

65. For, behold, I will gather them as a hen gathereth her chickens under her wings, if they will not harden their hearts,

66. Yea, if they will come, they may, and partake of the waters of life freely.

67. Behold, this is my doctrine: whosoever repenteth and cometh unto me, the same is my church.

68. Whosoever declareth more or less than this, the same is not of me, but is against me; therefore he is not of my church.

69. And now, behold, whosoever is of my church, and endureth of my church to the end, him will I establish upon my rock, and the gates of hell shall not prevail against them.

70. And now, remember the words of him who is the life and light of the world, your Redeemer, your Lord and your God. Amen.

SECTION 11

1. A great and marvelous work is about to come forth among the children of men.

2. Behold, I am God, and give heed to my word, which is quick and powerful, sharper than a two-edged sword, to the dividing asunder of both joints and marrow; therefore give heed unto my word.

3. Behold, the field is white already to harvest, therefore, whoso desireth to reap, let him thrust in his sickle with his might, and reap while the day lasts, that he may treasure up for his soul everlasting salvation in the kingdom of God;

4. Yea, whosoever will thrust in his sickle and reap, the same is called of God;

D&C 10:65–67—The image of the hen gathering her chickens conveys in a natural, understandable way the sense of compassion and concern that the Creator has for His children.

Section 11 Background—Given through the Prophet Joseph Smith for his brother Hyrum in May 1829 at Harmony, Susquehanna County, Pennsylvania, subsequent to the restoration of the Aaronic Priesthood (May 15 of that year) and the baptism of Samuel H. Smith (May 25). Hyrum had arrived in Harmony for a visit and requested that Joseph inquire of the Lord through the Urim and Thummim for guidance. The resulting revelation is now known as Section 11. The two brothers were the closest of friends throughout their lives, and the opportunity for the Prophet to seek a spiritual blessing for Hyrum was a moment of solemn tenderness and joy. Later on in his career, the Prophet Joseph, beset with mounting persecution and difficulties, was to pay this tribute to Hyrum: "There was Brother Hyrum who next took me by the hand—a natural brother. Thought I to myself, Brother Hyrum, what a faithful heart you have got! Oh may the Eternal Jehovah crown eternal blessings upon your head, as a reward for the care you have had for my soul! O how many are the sorrows we have shared together; and again we find ourselves shackled with the unrelenting hand of oppression. Hyrum, thy name shall be written in the book of the law of the Lord, for those who come after thee to look upon, that they may pattern after thy works" (HC 5:107–108).

The grave of Hyrum Smith, left, next to those of Joseph Smith Jr. and Emma Hale Smith in the Smith family cemetery adjacent to the Joseph Smith Homestead in Nauvoo.

5. Therefore, if you will ask of me, you shall receive, if you will knock, it shall be opened unto you.

6. Now, as you have asked, behold, I say unto you, keep my commandments, and seek to bring forth and establish the cause of Zion.

7. Seek not for riches but for wisdom, and, behold, the mysteries of God, shall be unfolded unto you, and then shall you be made rich: behold, he that hath eternal life is rich.

8. Verily, verily, I say unto you, even as you desire of me, so it shall be done unto you: and, if you desire, you shall be the means of doing much good in this generation.

9. Say nothing but repentance unto this generation. Keep my commandments, and assist to bring forth my work, according to my commandments, and you shall be blessed.

10. Behold, thou hast a gift, or thou shalt have a gift if thou wilt desire of me in faith, with an honest heart, believing in the power of Jesus Christ, or in my power which speaketh unto thee;

11. For, behold, it is I that speak; behold, I am the light which shineth in darkness, and by my power I give these words unto thee.

12. And now, verily, verily, I say unto thee, put your trust in that Spirit which leadeth to do good: yea, to do justly, to walk humbly, to judge righteously, and this is my Spirit.

13. Verily, verily, I say unto you, I will impart unto you of my Spirit; which shall enlighten your mind, which shall fill your soul with joy,

14. And then shall ye know, or by this shall you know all things whatsoever you desire of me, which are pertaining unto things of righteousness, in faith believing in me that you shall receive.

15. Behold, I command you, that you need not suppose that you are called to preach until you are called:

16. Wait a little longer, until you shall have my word, my rock, my church, and my gospel, that you may know of a surety my doctrine;

17. And then behold, according to your desires, yea, even according to your faith shall it be done unto you.

18. Keep my commandments, hold your peace, appeal unto my Spirit;

19. Yea, cleave unto me with all your heart, that you may assist in bringing to light those things of which has been spoken; yea, the translation of my work; be patient until you shall accomplish it.

20. Behold, this is your work, to keep my commandments, yea, with all your might, mind, and strength;

D&C 11:7—Hyrum is promised guidance in the work as he keeps the commandments and seeks not the riches of the world but the wisdom of the eternities so that the mysteries of God will be unfolded unto him. Concerning this passage, President Heber J. Grant said: "I do not think I ever read in my life a revelation that made a more profound impression upon me than did this, and I believe that all Latter-day Saints who will read it with a prayerful heart, seeking to God for the light of his Holy Spirit, will have their minds lit up, and the same inspiration that must have come to our beloved patriarch at the time the revelation was given to him, will come to them" (*Millennial Star*, Feb. 12, 1894, 56:102).

D&C 11:9—In all the scriptures and words of the prophets the most often and repeated admonition is to repent.

D&C 11:11–13—The Lord bestows unto Hyrum a wondrous gift—the right and privilege to commune with the Redeemer of mankind and, through His Spirit, to receive enlightenment and an overwhelming abundance of joy. The touchstone of spiritual enlightenment is the outcome that is facilitated: Does it lead to good results? Does it promote humility and righteousness? Does it fill with joy and light? If so, then the Spirit of the Lord is at work. The fourth principle of the gospel—the bestowal of the gift of the Holy Ghost by the laying on of hands—is the means by which God's supreme endowment of truth and light is granted to those who are moved by faith to repent of their sins and enter into a covenant of obedience to His commandments, thus qualifying themselves to have His Spirit always with them for guidance, comfort, enlightenment, learning, and the joyful confirmation of their testimony of the Savior's Atonement. "For by the water ye keep the commandment; by the Spirit ye are justified, and by the blood ye are sanctified" (Moses 6:60).

D&C 11:20—What the Lord says to Hyrum, He says to all of us. Our work is indeed to keep His commandments with our whole heart and strength. His work is to "bring to pass the immortality and eternal life of man" (Moses 1:39). We have the privilege of a grand partnership working with the Lord toward the same goal.

Hyrum, the ever-faithful older brother of Joseph Smith Jr., served as both Patriarch to the Church and the assistant president of the Church (an office no longer found in the organizational structure of the Church). Some historians maintain that as assistant president, Hyrum would have become the next president of the Church. Hyrum had six children by his first wife, Jerusha Barden; following her death, he married Mary Fielding, and they had two children. Their son, Joseph F. Smith, became the sixth president of the Church. Their grandson, Joseph Fielding Smith, became the tenth president of the Church. Hyrum was martyred at Carthage Jail with his brother, Joseph Smith Jr., dying just moments before the Prophet was shot and fell from the jail window.

21. Seek not to declare my word, but first seek to obtain my word, and then shall your tongue be loosed; then, if you desire, you shall have my Spirit and my word, yea, the power of God unto the convincing of men;

22. But now hold your peace, study my word which hath gone forth among the children of men, and also study my word which shall come forth among the children of men, or that which is now translating, yea, until you have obtained all which I shall grant unto the children of men, in this generation, and then shall all things be added thereunto.

23. Behold thou art Hyrum, my son, seek the kingdom of God, and all things shall be added according to that which is just.

24. Build upon my rock, which is my gospel;

25. Deny not the Spirit of revelation, nor the Spirit of prophecy, for wo unto him that denieth these things;

26. Therefore, treasure up in your heart until the time which is in my wisdom that you shall go forth.

27. Behold, I speak unto all who have good desires, and have thrust in their sickle to reap.

28. Behold, I am Jesus Christ, the Son of God. I am the life and the light of the world.

29. I am the same who came unto my own and my own received me not;

30. But verily, verily, I say unto you, that as many as receive me, to them will I give power to become the sons of God, even to them that believe on my name. Amen.

SECTION 12

1. A great and marvelous work is about to come forth among the children of men.

2. Behold, I am God, and give heed to

JOSEPH KNIGHT, SR.

Joseph Knight, Sr., was born November 3, 1772, at Oakham, Worcester County, Massachusetts. He operated a farm and gristmill at Colesville, New York. In 1826 he learned from Joseph Smith about the Restoration of the gospel and allowed Joseph to use his horse and carriage to transport the plates when they were turned over to him by Moroni. Father Knight, as he was known, gave encouragement and financial support to the young Prophet and was baptized on June 28, 1830, by Oliver Cowdery. He and his family later moved to Ohio and then to Jackson County, Missouri, finally relocating to Nauvoo in 1839. He was ever supportive of the Prophet Joseph and the Church. His final years were marked by ill health and feebleness, though he remained strong in the gospel. He died on February 2, 1847, at Mount Pisgah, Harrison County, Iowa.

D&C 11:21—The obligation that rests on every missionary in the Lord's kingdom—and all of us are missionaries—is to obtain His word. That is the rite of passage to the condition where one is ready, through the Spirit, to declare His word. First obtain; then declare. Our attitudes and behavior become more Christlike as the word is internalized within us. We become a new creature, a new being. We partake of His love (see 1 Ne. 11:25), and with this love we begin the process of taking upon us His divine nature (see 2 Peter 1:4).

D&C 11:23–27—The Lord confirms His personal relationship with Hyrum, calling him by name. This dialogue is a patriarchal dialogue—one between the Lord and His son. It is a communion among two individuals—one great and majestic and perfect, and the other striving to become so. What the Lord says to Hyrum, calling him by name, He says to all of us—as we humbly listen for the utterance of our own personal name by the Master, and then feel the spirit of contrition and submissiveness come over our being. We are ready to receive counsel from heaven—just as Hyrum was.

D&C 11:30—Those who receive Christ will be given power to become "the children of Christ, his sons, and his daughters" (Mosiah 5:7).

Section 12 Background—Given through the Prophet Joseph Smith to Joseph Knight, Sr. Of him, the Prophet later wrote this entry in his journal: *"Tuesday, 22* [1842].—I find my feelings . . . towards my friends revived, while I contemplate the virtues and the good qualities and characteristics of the faithful few, which I am now recording in the Book of the Law of the Lord,—of such as have stood by me in every hour of peril, for these fifteen long years past,—say, for instance, my aged and beloved brother, Joseph Knight, Sen., who was among the number of the first to administer to my necessities, while I was laboring in the commencement of the bringing forth of the work of the Lord, and of laying the foundation of the Church of Jesus Christ of Latter-day Saints. For fifteen years he has been faithful and true, and even-handed and exemplary, and virtuous and kind, never deviating to the right hand or the left. . . . may God Almighty lengthen out the old man's days; and may his trembling, tortured, and broken body be renewed, and in the vigor of health turn upon him, if it be Thy will, consistently, O God; and it shall be said of him, by the sons of Zion, while there is one of them remaining, that this man was a faithful man in Israel; therefore his name shall never be forgotten" (HC 5:124–125).

my word, which is quick and powerful, sharper than a two-edged sword, to the dividing asunder of both joints and marrow; therefore, give heed unto my word.

3. Behold, the field is white already to harvest, therefore, whoso desireth to reap, let him thrust in his sickle with his might, and reap while the day lasts, that he may treasure up for his soul everlasting salvation in the kingdom of God;

4. Yea, whosoever will thrust in his sickle and reap, the same is called of God;

5. Therefore, if you will ask of me you shall receive, if you will knock it shall be opened unto you.

6. Now, as you have asked, behold, I say unto you, keep my commandments, and seek to bring forth and establish the cause of Zion.

7. Behold, I speak unto you, and also to all those who have desires to bring forth and establish this work,

8. And no one can assist in this work, except he shall be humble and full of love, having faith, hope, and charity, being temperate in all things, whatsoever shall be entrusted to his care.

9. Behold, I am the light and the life of the world, that speak these words, therefore give heed with your might, and then you are called. Amen.

SECTION 13

1. Upon you my fellow servants, in the name of Messiah, I confer the Priesthood of Aaron, which holds the keys of the ministering of angels, and of the gospel of repentance, and of baptism by immersion for the remission of sins; and this shall never be taken again from the earth, until the sons of Levi do offer again an offering unto the Lord in righteousness.

The Susquehanna River, near Harmony, Pennsylvania; Joseph Smith and Oliver Cowdery were ordained to the Aaronic Priesthood by John the Baptist along its banks on May 15, 1829. Joseph Smith Jr. and Oliver Cowdery had the Melchizedek Prieshood conferred upon them by Peter, James, and John along the banks of the same river somewhere between Colesville, New York, and Harmony, Pennsylvania; the exact date of that ordination is not known. The Hebrew word for hand means "power"; therefore, the laying on of hands means the conferring of power.

D&C 12:9—The message of the Doctrine and Covenants is that the Lord is fulfilling His divine promise, decreed from the foundation of the earth and confirmed by chosen prophets in all ages, to bring light and life to His elect in the last days through the marvel of the Restoration.

Section 13 Background—This section concerns the ordination of Joseph Smith and Oliver Cowdery to the Aaronic Priesthood along the banks of the Susquehanna River, near Harmony, Pennsylvania, on May 15, 1829, under the hands of John the Baptist (see JS–H 1:68–73 for details of this extraordinary event). Some days later Peter, James, and John, the Lord's Apostolic leadership during the meridian of time, also appeared to Joseph and Oliver, as a continuation of the extraordinary process of priesthood restoration, and conferred upon them the Melchizedek Priesthood (see D&C 27:12–13).

D&C 13:1—With the restoration of the keys and powers of the Aaronic Priesthood, the fundamental gateway to authorized membership in the Lord's Church through the gospel of faith, repentance, and baptism was once again instituted. The Aaronic Priesthood is the instrumentality for providing the foundational leadership and ordinances to initiate the admission of the Saints into the Church and kingdom of God by covenant and oversee the regular sacramental reinforcement of covenant vows.

The priesthood of God is the divine agency and vital administering principle by which the Creation was accomplished and the plan of salvation made operational for achieving the "immortality and eternal life of man" (Moses 1:39). The Doctrine and Covenants is the principal scriptural medium in the latter days for codifying, understanding, and applying the principles and policies embodied in the priesthood as it has been restored to the earth once again by divine intervention and blessing. It is especially in the cross-illumination of five extraordinary sections of the Doctrine and Covenants—13, 20, 84, 107, and 121—that much defining light has been shed on the nature and operation of the priesthood of God for the salvation of His children.

D&C 13:1—What is meant by *the ministering of angels?* Elder Bruce R. McConkie clarifies the meaning of this term as follows:

> The Priesthood of Aaron . . . holds "the keys of the ministering of angels," meaning that those who hold it and are faithful have the key whereby they can open the door to the receipt of visitations from heavenly messengers. (D. & C. 13; 84:26–27; 107:20.) Faith, repentance, and baptism—comprising as they do the preparatory gospel—fall within its province. . . . (*MD*, 11.)

D&C 13:1—What is meant by the "sons of Levi," and what are we to understand about their offering in righteousness? Scholar Richard Cowan explains:

SECTION 14

1. A great and marvelous work is about to come forth unto the children of men.

2. Behold, I am God, and give heed to my word, which is quick and powerful, sharper than a two-edged sword, to the dividing asunder of both joints and marrow; therefore give heed unto my word.

3. Behold, the field is white already to harvest, therefore, whoso desireth to reap let him thrust in his sickle with his might, and reap while the day lasts, that he may treasure up for his soul everlasting salvation in the kingdom of God,

4. Yea, whosoever will thrust in his sickle and reap, the same is called of God.

5. Therefore, if you will ask of me you shall receive, if you will knock it shall be opened unto you.

6. Seek to bring forth and establish my Zion. Keep my commandments in all things,

7. And, if you keep my commandments and endure to the end you shall have eternal life, which gift is the greatest of all the gifts of God.

8. And it shall come to pass, that if you shall ask the Father in my name, in faith believing, you shall receive the Holy Ghost, which giveth utterance, that you may stand as a witness of the things of which you shall both hear and see, and also that you may declare repentance unto this generation.

9. Behold, I am Jesus Christ the Son of the living God, who created the heavens and the earth; a light which cannot be hid in darkness;

10. Wherefore, I must bring forth

DAVID WHITMER

David Whitmer was born January 7, 1805, near Harrisburg, Dauphin County, Pennsylvania, the son of Peter Whitmer, Sr. He learned in 1828 of the mission of Joseph Smith and became one of the three witnesses of the Book of Mormon. He was on hand as one of the original six members of the Church at its organization on April 6, 1830, and was ordained an elder that day. He and his family suffered great persecution along with the other Saints in Missouri. He became president of the Clay County high council on July 3, 1834, and a few days later was appointed president of the Church in Missouri. His service for the Church was considerable, but in 1836 he fell prey to feelings of pride and apostasy. On April 13, 1838, he was excommunicated and took up residence in Richmond, Missouri. For the next half-century he pursued a business and community service career in Richmond, where he established a reputation of honesty and respect. Though he remained aloof from the Church, he consistently confirmed his witness of the Book of Mormon, even to his dying day on January 25, 1888, at Richmond, Ray County, Missouri.

The answer to this question may be understood on at least two levels. On the literal level, Joseph Smith explained that the Savior's atonement did not completely end blood offerings. "These sacrifices as well as every ordinance, belonging to the priesthood, will, when the Temple of the Lord shall be built, and the sons of Levi be purified, be fully restored and attended to" (*TPJS*, 173). . . .

On a more figurative level, the Lord promised that faithful bearers of the Melchizedek and Aaronic Priesthood who magnify their callings "become the sons of Moses and of Aaron" respectively (D&C 84:33–34). Because Moses and Aaron were members of the tribe of Levi, faithful latter-day priesthood bearers become the "sons of Levi," and their "offering" is the faithful service they render (see, for example, D&C 128:24) (AQDC, 19).

Section 14, 15, 16 Background—Given through the Prophet Joseph Smith in June 1829 to David Whitmer, John Whitmer, and Peter Whitmer—each in sequence. It was during the spring of 1829 that much of the Book of Mormon was translated, and it was a time of near penury for the Prophet, who depended on the generosity of the Whitmer family for financial support. David Whitmer traveled the 135 miles from Fayette to Harmony to assist in moving the Prophet to the Whitmer home to complete the translation.

D&C 14:6—We have been commanded to establish Zion. Zion is not a dream, but rather a destiny; not a wish, but a commandment of God. God will have a pure and righteous people. Where such people emerge in the strength of the Lord, nourished by the blessings of the Almighty, there is Zion (see D&C 97:21). We can strive to establish Zion by: (1) cultivating purity and humility in thought, desire, and action; (2) working for the cause of Zion by consistently and sincerely inviting others to come unto Christ; (3) establishing and cultivating unified families patterned after a celestial model—the essential building blocks of a Zion society; and (4) being grateful to receive the blessings of a Zion people—happiness, peace, and joy.

D&C 14:7—David Whitmer fell from his position of leadership in the Church and lost an abundance of promised blessings, though he was faithful in confirming his testimony of the Book of Mormon until his dying day. From his wavering example, as well as from the example of his valiant peers who remained faithful by enduring to the end, we can learn powerful lessons that the Lord's word will be fulfilled—to our eternal glory and edification, or to our eternal sorrow and remorse—based on our own choices and agency.

D&C 14:7—Eternal life is the greatest of all the gifts of God (see D&C 6:13; 14:7). How can we partake of the assurance that eternal life will be ours in the future and thus have peace in the mortal realm? Through the confirmation of the Holy Spirit bestowed upon the valiant and the faithful.

the fulness of my gospel from the Gentiles unto the house of Israel.
11. And behold, thou art David, and thou art called to assist; which thing if ye do, and are faithful, ye shall be blessed both spiritually and temporally, and great shall be your reward. Amen.

SECTION 15

1. Hearken, my servant John, and listen to the words of Jesus Christ, your Lord and your Redeemer,
2. For behold, I speak unto you with sharpness and with power, for mine arm is over all the earth,
3. And I will tell you that which no man knoweth save me and thee alone,
4. For many times you have desired of me to know that which would be of the most worth unto you.
5. Behold, blessed are you for this thing, and for speaking my words which I have given you, according to my commandments.
6. And now, behold, I say unto you, that the thing which will be of the most worth unto you, will be to declare repentance unto this people, that you may bring souls unto me, that you may rest with them in the kingdom of my Father. Amen.

SECTION 16

1. Hearken my servant Peter, and listen to the words of Jesus Christ, your Lord and your Redeemer,
2. For behold, I speak unto you with sharpness and with power, for mine arm is over all the earth,
3. And I will tell you that which no man knoweth save me and thee alone,
4. For many times you have desired

The German Reformed Church meetinghouse attended by the Whitmer family in Fayette, New York.

D&C 14:8–11—The pattern expressed by these words is instructive for each of us in these days of urgency prior to the Second Coming. Just as David Whitmer was faithful in his calling as a witness, we too can stand as faithful witnesses to the truthfulness of the gospel of Jesus Christ. In the words of King Benjamin: ". . . I would desire that ye should consider on the blessed and happy state of those that keep the commandments of God. For behold, they are blessed in all things, both temporal and spiritual; and if they hold out faithful to the end they are received into heaven, that thereby they may dwell with God in a state of never-ending happiness" (Mosiah 2:41).

D&C 15:2—"The term *arm of the Lord* suggests 'the power, might, strength, or authority of God.' Thus, the use of the longer term *arm of the Lord to be revealed* in both the introductory and closing sections of the Doctrine and Covenants suggests that in this dispensation the power and authority of the Lord will again be clearly manifested on the earth" (*Ludlow* 2:17).

D&C 15:3–6—The Lord reveals to John Whitmer His intimate knowledge of the individual's quest for divine guidance. He tells John what no one else knows, save the Redeemer and His sincere servant—that John has repeatedly prayed to know what course to pursue in life to be of maximum service. The answer comes in words that have resonated with power in the hearts and minds of more than one million full-time missionaries and countless other Saints since the dawn of the Restoration: the thing that would be of most worth is to preach the gospel and bring souls unto Christ.

JOHN WHITMER

John Whitmer was born August 27, 1802, at Fayette Township, Seneca County, New York, son of Peter Whitmer, Sr. He assisted the Prophet as scribe in the translation of the Book of Mormon. Baptized by Oliver Cowdery, he was one of the eight witnesses of the Book of Mormon. He tirelessly engaged in proselyting for the restored Church and also wrote a segment of the History of the Church. On July 3, 1834, he became a member of the presidency of the Church in Missouri. Later, in Kirtland, he became editor of the *Messenger and Advocate*. Upon his return to Missouri, he purchased tracts of land for the Saints. Because of alleged irregularities in these transactions, an investigation was carried out; John refused to cooperate with Church leaders and was excommunicated on March 10, 1838. Though acrimonious about this action and bitter against the Prophet and the Church, John never recanted his firm testimony of the Book of Mormon. He died on July 11, 1878, at Far West, Caldwell County, Missouri.

of me to know that which would be of the most worth unto you.

5. Behold, blessed are you for this thing, and for speaking my words which I have given unto you according to my commandments.

6. And now, behold, I say unto you, that the thing which will be of the most worth unto you, will be to declare repentance unto this people, that you may bring souls unto me, that you may rest with them in the kingdom of my Father. Amen.

SECTION 17

1. Behold, I say unto you, that you must rely upon my word, which if you do, with full purpose of heart, you shall have a view of the plates, and also of the breast plate, the sword of Laban, the Urim and Thummim, which were given to the brother of Jared upon the mount, when he talked with the Lord face to face, and the miraculous directors which were given to Lehi while in the wilderness, on the borders of the Red Sea;

2. And it is by your faith that you shall obtain a view of them, even by that faith which was had by the prophets of old.

3. And after that you have obtained faith, and have seen them with your eyes, you shall testify of them, by the power of God;

4. And this you shall do that my servant Joseph Smith, jun., may not be destroyed, that I may bring about my righteous purposes unto the children of men in this work.

5. And ye shall testify that you have seen them, even as my servant Joseph Smith, jun., has seen them, for it is by my power that he has seen them, and it is because he had faith;

6. And he has translated the book, even that part which I have commanded

---

PETER WHITMER, JR.

Peter Whitmer, Jr., was born September 27, 1809, at Fayette Township, Seneca County, New York, the son of Peter Whitmer, Sr. Peter became acquainted with the Prophet Joseph Smith in the summer of 1829, when Joseph lived for a time in the family residence. Peter served as a scribe on occasion in the work of translation and became one of the eight witnesses of the Book of Mormon. He was baptized in June 1830 by Oliver Cowdery and was then ordained an elder. In the period 1830–1831 he accompanied Parley P. Pratt, Oliver Cowdery, and Ziba Peterson on a mission among the Lamanites (see D&C 32:2). In Independence he established a trade as a tailor. On October 25, 1831, he was ordained a high priest. Beset by aggressive mob action and persecution in Independence, Peter relocated to Clay County, where he provided charitable service to many, despite his ill health. He died on September 22, 1836, at Liberty, Clay County, Missouri.

D&C 16:6—The Lord counsels Peter about the thing that will be of most worth to him, namely, preaching the gospel and bringing souls unto Christ. This counsel to Peter is now given for the second time in the Doctrine and Covenants (see D&C 15:6), a reminder of the importance of this divine mandate to serve as an emissary of Christ to carry the gospel message to the world.

Section 17 Background—Given through the Prophet Joseph Smith to Oliver Cowdery, David Whitmer, and Martin Harris during the month of June 1829 in Fayette, Seneca County, New York. The Prophet Joseph had learned that three special witnesses were to see the plates from which the Book of Mormon was being translated. At the request of the three men, Joseph asked the Lord if they might be the witnesses.

D&C 17:1–2—The three witnesses acted on faith in order to participate in witnessing holy things. That experience obligated them, under commission from God, to bear their testimonies to the world, confirming the divinity of the work. It is instructive that the Lord authorized the three witnesses to view not only the plates, but the associated sacred artifacts and accoutrements that confirmed and substantiated the cultural and historical reality of the events described in the Book of Mormon.

D&C 17:3—Through the blessings of the Spirit and the exercise of faith we can obtain "greater views" (D&C 10:45) of the Lord's plan of happiness and become edified by the joy of having a spiritual vision, as it were, of the destination of our quest for eternal life. That blessing obligates us, in turn, to share our sincere and fervent testimonies with others at all times. In the case of the three witnesses, their testimony of the remarkable event in which they were privileged to become personal observers of the sacred objects in the presence of the angel Moroni they never recanted or retracted, despite their loss of fellowship in the Church.

D&C 17:4—The Restoration of the gospel and the coming forth of the Book of Mormon were not without accompanying threats and dangers of the most egregious kind. From the beginning, the life of the Prophet was subject to lethal perils—and his work was discredited repeatedly by skeptics and adversaries. It was only through the intervention of the Lord that the Prophet's mission was allowed to proceed to its conclusion. The testimony of the three witnesses provided persuasive evidence of the extraordinary heavenly provenance of the new scripture.

D&C 17:5—This sublime witness by the Lord of the divinity of the Book of Mormon is extended as living proof of the verity of the mission of Joseph Smith as the Prophet of the Restoration. God lives. His work goes forth. The Book of Mormon is true—for the Author thereof is the Lord Himself, through the witness and record of all the holy prophets.

him, and as your Lord and your God liveth it is true.

7. Wherefore you have received the same power, and the same faith, and the same gift like unto him;

8. And if you do these last commandments of mine, which I have given you, the gates of hell shall not prevail against you; for my grace is sufficient for you, and you shall be lifted up at the last day.

9. And I, Jesus Christ, your Lord and your God, have spoken it unto you, that I might bring about my righteous purposes unto the children of men. Amen.

SECTION 18

1. Now, behold, because of the thing which you, my servant Oliver Cowdery, have desired to know of me, I give unto you these words:

2. Behold, I have manifested unto you, by my Spirit in many instances, that the things which you have written are true; wherefore you know that they are true;

3. And if you know that they are true, behold, I give unto you a commandment, that you rely upon the things which are written;

4. For in them are all things written concerning the foundation of my church, my gospel, and my rock;

5. Wherefore, if you shall build up my church, upon the foundation of my gospel and my rock, the gates of hell shall not prevail against you.

6. Behold, the world is ripening in iniquity, and it must needs be that the children of men are stirred up unto repentance, both the Gentiles and also the house of Israel:

7. Wherefore, as thou hast been baptized by the hands of my servant Joseph Smith, jun., according to that which I have commanded him, he hath fulfilled the thing which I commanded him.

8. And now marvel not that I have called him unto mine own purpose,

Site of the Peter Whitmer Farm in Fayette, New York, where The Church of Jesus Christ of Latter-day Saints was organized on April 6, 1830.

D&C 17:7–9—The Lord is beneficent. He grants blessings with abundance and mercy. The three witnesses were given the same power, faith, and gift as the Prophet. By faith, they were introduced, just as the Prophet, into the sacred venue where the plates and other associated objects were revealed through a heavenly manifestation of power as a gift from the Lord.

Section 18 Background—Given in June 1829 in Fayette, New York, to Oliver Cowdery and David Whitmer as a result of supplication for knowledge concerning the promised restoration of the Melchizedek Priesthood (see *HC* 1:60–64). Oliver and David are to "search out the Twelve" (verse 37) that are to be called to the Quorum of Twelve Apostles. Subsequently, the three witnesses of the Book of Mormon did indeed select the Twelve that were then called on February 14–15, 1835.

D&C 18:1–5—The directive to build the Church upon the gospel of Jesus Christ has universal validity—then as now. What is the nature of the "rock" upon which the Church is to be built? The Prophet Joseph Smith clarifies: "Jesus in His teachings says, 'Upon this rock I will build my Church, and the gates of hell shall not prevail against it.' [Matt. 16:18] What rock? Revelation" (*HC* 5:258). The early sections of the Doctrine and Covenants (especially Sections 6, 7, 8, and 9) constitute a unique primer on the process of divine revelation as it relates to the coming forth of the Book of Mormon and the laying of the foundation of the restored Church.

D&C 18:5—In the words of Daniel H. Wells, counselor to President Brigham Young, we have the following explanation: "If we are faithful we shall increase in the things of God. The Devil can claim no right to the blessings of the Lord; for those things belong to the Saints; therefore let us do all we can for the building up of the kingdom of God, and He will furnish us all we need; for all belongs to Him. No part of the human family belongs to the Devil, unless they sell themselves to him. But the Lord cannot consistently bless us, unless He knows that we will serve Him and make a good use of what He bestows" (*JD* 5:43–44).

D&C 18:6—The gospel-anchored observer of human affairs will scarcely fail to discern the erosion of eternal values rampant in our day—"for the devil is come down unto you, having great wrath, because he knoweth that he hath but a short time" (Rev. 12:12). Section 18 of the Doctrine and Covenants emphasizes the need to rise to the challenge of standing firm against the wiles of the devil and remaining strong in the cause of Zion by leading a faithful and penitent life worthy of those who will be "blessed unto eternal life" (verse 8).

which purpose is known in me; wherefore, if he shall be diligent in keeping my commandments, he shall be blessed unto eternal life, and his name is Joseph.

9. And now, Oliver Cowdery, I speak unto you, and also unto David Whitmer, by the way of commandment; for, behold, I command all men everywhere to repent, and I speak unto you, even as unto Paul, mine apostle, for you are called even with that same calling with which he was called.

10. Remember the worth of souls is great in the sight of God;

11. For, behold, the Lord your Redeemer suffered death in the flesh; wherefore he suffered the pain of all men, that all men might repent and come unto him.

12. And he hath risen again from the dead, that he might bring all men unto him, on conditions of repentance;

13. And how great is his joy in the soul that repenteth.

14. Wherefore, you are called to cry repentance unto this people;

15. And if it so be that you should labor all your days in crying repentance unto this people, and bring, save it be one soul unto me, how great shall be your joy with him in the kingdom of my Father?

16. And now, if your joy will be great with one soul that you have brought unto me into the kingdom of my Father, how great will be your joy if you should bring many souls unto me!

17. Behold, you have my gospel before you, and my rock, and my salvation.

18. Ask the Father in my name, in faith believing that you shall receive, and you shall have the Holy Ghost, which manifesteth all things which are expedient unto the children of men.

19. And if you have not faith, hope, and charity, you can do nothing.

20. Contend against no church, save it be the church of the devil.

21. Take upon you the name of Christ, and speak the truth in soberness;

22. And as many as repent, and are baptized in my name, which is Jesus Christ, and endure to the end, the same shall be saved.

23. Behold, Jesus Christ is the name which is given of the Father, and there is none other name given whereby man can be saved;

24. Wherefore, all men must take upon them the name which is given of the Father, for in that name shall they be called at the last day;

The interior of the Whitmer home in Fayette, New York, where the Prophet Joseph Smith completed the translation of the Book of Mormon.

D&C 18:10—These words, among the most resonating in all of holy writ, confirm the universal love of the Savior for all of us. That knowledge, as confirmed by the Holy Spirit, does more to advance our progress along the mortal pathway than almost any other element of truth. To know that we are loved invigorates our faith, empowers our repentance, motivates us to complete the ordinance requirements for all Saints, opens our hearts and minds to the continual guidance of the Holy Ghost, and strengthens us for the supreme commitment of enduring to the end.

D&C 18:13—We realize with astonishment and joy that all that God does is for our benefit. We are His literal children. No wonder that we bring joy to the Lord when He sees us progressing as we repent and move forward with our lives. For all who would wish to make the Savior feel joy the strategy most readily at hand is to repent and be an instrument in His hands to help others to repent as well.

D&C 18:15–16—There is profound joy in missionary service, whether the harvest is small or whether it is great. Missionary work is the venue for joy, not discouragement. The key is to labor in the strength of the Lord. This is our joy and glory: helping people come unto Christ and thus partake of His infinite Atonement.

D&C 18:17–19—In the allegory of Zenos concerning the olive trees, the lord of the vineyard exclaimed in anguish over his faltering trees: "What could I have done more for my vineyard?" (Jacob 5:41). Indeed, the Lord can do no greater work on our behalf than bring to bear the gospel of the Atonement. With great power, the Lord of the Restoration declares unto Oliver and David—together with all of the Saints—that His gospel is before us and His Holy Spirit waits to teach us all the essentials of salvation and exaltation. What more can He do for us than that? It is up to us to respond in the spirit of faith, hope, and charity, to take up our cross and follow Him in devotion and humility.

D&C 18:20–23—The only name whereby man can be saved is that of Jesus Christ (see Mosiah 3:17). Heavenly Father's plan is centered in His Beloved Son, Jesus Christ. Everything is because of our Savior Jesus Christ. The priesthood is after the order of the Lord Jesus Christ (see D&C 107:3). We pray to the Father only in the name of Jesus Christ (see 3 Ne. 18:19–20). All miracles are done in the name of Jesus Christ (see 4 Ne. 1:5). We exercise our faith in and through the Lord Jesus Christ (see Mosiah 3:12; Alma 37:33). We repent because of the atoning sacrifice of the Lord Jesus Christ (see Alma 22:14; D&C 19:15–19). We are baptized and take upon ourselves the name of Jesus Christ when we enter His fold (see 2 Ne. 31:13; D&C 20:37). We receive the Holy Ghost from Heavenly Father because of Jesus Christ (see 2 Ne. 31:12; 3 Ne. 19:22). Everything is centered in our Savior Jesus Christ; it is He alone to whom we look for our salvation (see Alma 15:6; 34:6).

25. Wherefore, if they know not the name by which they are called, they cannot have place in the kingdom of my Father.

26. And now, behold, there are others who are called to declare my gospel, both unto Gentile and unto Jew;

27. Yea, even Twelve, and the Twelve shall be my disciples, and they shall take upon them my name; and the Twelve are they who shall desire to take upon them my name with full purpose of heart;

28. And if they desire to take upon them my name with full purpose of heart, they are called to go into all the world to preach my gospel unto every creature;

29. And they are they who are ordained of me to baptize in my name, according to that which is written;

30. And you have that which is written before you; wherefore you must perform it according to the words which are written.

31. And now I speak unto you, the Twelve—Behold, my grace is sufficient for you: you must walk uprightly before me and sin not.

32. And, behold, you are they who are ordained of me to ordain priests and teachers; to declare my gospel, according to the power of the Holy Ghost which is in you, and according to the callings and gifts of God unto men;

33. And I, Jesus Christ, your Lord and your God, have spoken it.

34. These words are not of men, nor of man, but of me; wherefore, you shall testify they are of me, and not of man;

35. For it is my voice which speaketh them unto you, for they are given by my Spirit unto you, and by my power you can read them one to another, and save it were by my power, you could not have them;

36. Wherefore you can testify that you have heard my voice, and know my words.

37. And now, behold, I give unto you Oliver Cowdery, and also unto David Whitmer, that you shall search out the Twelve, who shall have the desires of which I have spoken;

38. And by their desires and their works you shall know them;

39. And when you have found them you shall show these things unto them.

40. And you shall fall down and worship the Father in my name;

41. And you must preach unto the world, saying, you must repent and be baptized, in the name of Jesus Christ;

42. For all men must repent and be baptized, and not only men, but women, and children who have arrived at the years of accountability.

43. And now, after that you have received this, you must keep my commandments in all things;

44. And by your hands I will work a marvelous work among the children

D&C 18:27–28—With these words the Lord inaugurates the process of training the future Twelve Apostles, who were called in February 1835 from among the men that valiantly participated in Zion's Camp.

D&C 18:33–36—Have we heard the Lord Himself proclaim the words of salvation unto us? Yes, if we search and ponder His words in the canon of scriptures and then experience the power of the Spirit confirming the truth of those words. The Lord taught this principle to the future Twelve—and by this same principle we can intimately know the words of Christ, as if He had spoken them to us in person.

D&C 18:38—The inaugural quality essential for apostleship is a desire to serve with full purpose of heart. The importance of righteous desire among all of God's children is underscored by Elder John A. Widtsoe:

> Righteous desire, backed by a ready will and honest prayer, works wonders in human lives. It reveals truth. It trains the will for righteousness. It leads to increasing accomplishment. It is protection amidst the temptations and storms of life. It places man on the road to abundant joy. In the end it lifts man to a place near the gods.
>
> When such desire is coupled with obedience to law, the gates of heaven are thrown open, and we may, secure of the outcome, advance to our high, eternal destiny.
>
> A man's prayerful desires, were they fully known, are his truest measure. The truest measure of a nation is its national desire, addressed to God. The progression or retrogression of the race is but a reflection of the combined desire of the multitude. As our desires are, so are we. (UR, 70.)

D&C 18:42—The essential core of the gospel of Jesus Christ is repentance and baptism. The Lord's plan for ensuring eternal happiness for His children, through the power of the Atonement, is profoundly simple and glorious, based on just four key steps that open up current vistas and eventual realities of immortality and eternal life to all those who embrace covenant truth with broken hearts and contrite spirits and endure to the end. Man is the offspring of God, and as such, can achieve true happiness and joy only by following the patterns of thought and action that accord with divine truth. These patterns are embodied in the principles of faith, repentance, baptism, and receiving the gift of the Holy Ghost under the hands of the priesthood of God.

D&C 18:44–47—What could be a more clearly articulated message to the world? To the obedient, the Lord gives a blessing more important than any other thing: the opportunity to be agents in fulfilling the miracles of the Lord's design for the salvation of His children. To fail to live up to the great promises given will result in the loss of salvation.

of men, unto the convincing of many of their sins, that they may come unto repentance, and that they may come unto the kingdom of my Father;

45. Wherefore, the blessings which I give unto you are above all things.

46. And after that you have received this, if you keep not my commandments you cannot be saved in the kingdom of my Father.

47. Behold, I, Jesus Christ, your Lord and your God, and your Redeemer, by the power of my Spirit have spoken it. Amen.

SECTION 19

1. I am Alpha and Omega, Christ the Lord; yea, even I am He, the beginning and the end, the Redeemer of the world.

2. I, having accomplished and finished the will of him whose I am, even the Father, concerning me—having done this that I might subdue all things unto myself—

3. Retaining all power, even to the destroying of Satan and his works at the end of the world, and the last great day of judgment, which I shall pass upon the inhabitants thereof, judging every man according to his works and the deeds which he hath done.

4. And surely every man must repent or suffer, for I, God, am endless;

5. Wherefore, I revoke not the judgments which I shall pass, but woes shall go forth, weeping, wailing and gnashing of teeth, yea, to those who are found on my left hand;

6. Nevertheless it is not written that there shall be no end to this torment, but it is written endless torment.

7. Again, it is written eternal damnation; wherefore it is more express than other scriptures, that it might work upon the hearts of the children of men-altogether for my name's glory;

8. Wherefore I will explain unto

Two moments of truth apply to the doctrines and teachings in this section. The first is the singularly sacred and profoundly transforming act of the Atonement itself—those hours of agony on the part of the Redeemer in the garden and on the cross whereby, through His own perfect obedience, He "became the author of eternal salvation unto all them that obey him" (Hebrews 5:9). The second is the very hour, which must of necessity be experienced by every person who seeks to become a disciple of Christ, in which the irreversible personal commitment to rebirth and rejuvenation is made in the depths of one's soul.

Section 19 Background—Martin Harris, who had underwritten the publication of the Book of Mormon at the E. B. Grandin printing establishment in Palmyra, became nervous about his investment and importuned the Prophet Joseph Smith repeatedly to inquire of the Lord for direction. In response, the Lord gave what is now Section 19. The Prophet's exemplary quest to "seek the face of the Lord always" is recorded in unforgettable episodes in the pages of the Doctrine and Covenants. The visions opened up to the Prophet of the Restoration are ample evidence that the worthy and anointed can indeed seek and find the face of the Lord—whose qualities and mission are reflected in exquisite detail throughout this sacred volume of modern scripture.

D&C 19:1—The Savior has achieved victory over all the enemies of righteousness. As such, He is omnipotence personified—one who has unlimited power. We can have immense comfort and hope through the Savior, who has opened the way for the faithful and obedient to follow Him home as they subdue the natural man and become His sons and daughters.

D&C 19:4—God does not will the suffering of sinners; this outcome is according to the eternal law of consequences. Elder Bruce R. McConkie emphasized the principle of universal repentance when he taught that attaining salvation is a "long and grueling process" that consists of continual repentance based on our circumstances and experiences. He further taught that gaining salvation is a process of coming to a unity with the Lord as we become like Him through bridling our passions, overcoming the world, and growing in grace (see NWAF, 221–222).

The E. B. Grandin printing establishment in Fayette, New York, where the first edition of the Book of Mormon was printed. Martin Harris mortgaged his 320-acre farm to pay the first installment, and later sold 180 acres to pay the rest of the printing bill.

you this mystery, for it is meet unto you to know even as mine apostles.

9. I speak unto you that are chosen in this thing, even as one, that you may enter into my rest;

10. For, behold, the mystery of Godliness, how great is it? for, behold, I am endless, and the punishment which is given from my hand, is endless punishment, for endless is my name: Wherefore—

11. Eternal punishment is God's punishment.

12. Endless punishment is God's punishment.

13. Wherefore I command you to repent, and keep the commandments which you have received by the hand of my servant Joseph Smith, jun., in my name;

14. And it is by my almighty power that you have received them;

15. Therefore I command you to repent—repent, lest I smite you by the rod of my mouth, and by my wrath, and by my anger, and your sufferings be sore—how sore you know not! how exquisite you know not! yea, how hard to bear you know not!

16. For behold, I, God, have suffered these things for all, that they might not suffer if they would repent,

17. But if they would not repent, they must suffer even as I,

18. Which suffering caused myself, even God, the greatest of all, to tremble because of pain, and to bleed at every pore, and to suffer both body and spirit; and would that I might not drink the bitter cup and shrink—

19. Nevertheless, glory be to the Father, and I partook and finished my preparations unto the children of men;

20. Wherefore, I command you again to repent, lest I humble you with my almighty power, and that you confess your sins, lest you suffer these punishments of which I have spoken, of which in the smallest, yea, even in the least degree you have tasted at the time I withdrew my spirit.

21. And I command you, that you preach naught but repentance, and show not these things unto the world until it is wisdom in me.

22. For they cannot bear meat now, but milk they must receive; wherefore, they must not know these things lest they perish.

23. Learn of me, and listen to my words; walk in the meekness of my Spirit, and you shall have peace in me.

24. I am Jesus Christ; I came by the will of the Father, and I do his will.

25. And again, I command thee that thou shalt not covet thy

The interior of the E.B. Grandin printing shop, where the Book of Mormon was printed.

D&C 19:11–12—*Endless* and *eternal* are descriptions of the nature of the Lord. The punishment men receive for their sins is not of an endless duration, but is rather a penalty befitting the sin, except in the case of those who have sinned against the Holy Ghost. All other people are redeemed from Hell after their punishment and receive the telestial glory (see D&C 76:84–88).

D&C 19:13–16—The mission of God the Father and His Son Jesus Christ is to "bring to pass the immortality and eternal life of man" (Moses 1:39). Such could not transpire except there should be an infinite Atonement that opened the way for mankind to be saved by obedience through the "merits, and mercy, and grace of the Holy Messiah" (2 Ne. 2:8).

D&C 19:17–19—It is the will of God to spare the penitent from eternal suffering. The Savior loves us and has suffered for us if we will but repent. Said the prophet Alma: "Behold, he sendeth an invitation unto all men, for the arms of mercy are extended towards them, and he saith: Repent, and I will receive you" (Alma 5:33; see also Alma 42:13–15).

D&C 19:20—We all know, from time to time, the feelings of loneliness and isolation when the Holy Ghost is withdrawn, perhaps because of a lapse on our part to hold to the iron rod with full devotion. This verse alludes to a time when Martin Harris experienced the withdrawal of the Spirit of the Lord—and the Lord uses that painful memory as a platform to explain that ultimate judgment for the unrepentant sinner would constitute an unfathomable intensification of that feeling. We have a choice. We can be easily entreated as we are commanded to repent and change our ways—or we can rebel and suffer the consequences. There is allowance for the sinner through the plan of salvation—but not for the sin. If we don't repent, we lose the Spirit as well.

D&C 19:22—We should use prudence and wisdom in teaching the principles of the gospel. Milk comes first, then meat. When the student responds with faith and a sincere hunger for truth, then more is given, even until "it is given unto him to know the mysteries of God until he know them in full" (Alma 12:10).

D&C 19:23—This is among the most cited of the Savior's statements contained in the Doctrine and Covenants. It is, in effect, a covenant statement. It poses a condition and then expresses a promised blessing: If we learn of Christ, listen to His words through the Spirit, and conduct our lives in humility and meekness (which is the essential nature of our Lord), then we receive a state of sanctity and bliss called *peace*.

D&C 19:24—Let us rejoice in the knowledge that each of us—every one of us—has great worth in the eyes of the Redeemer, so much so that He gave His life for us in a divine mission to reclaim each one who would come to Him with a broken heart and a contrite spirit.

neighbor's wife; nor seek thy neighbor's life.

26. And again, I command thee that thou shalt not covet thine own property, but impart it freely to the printing of the Book of Mormon, which contains the truth and the word of God,

27. Which is my word to the Gentile, that soon it may go to the Jew, of whom the Lamanites are a remnant, that they may believe the gospel, and look not for a Messiah to come who has already come.

28. And again, I command thee that thou shalt pray vocally as well as in thy heart; yea, before the world as well as in secret, in public as well as in private.

29. And thou shalt declare glad tidings, yea, publish it upon the mountains, and upon every high place, and among every people that thou shalt be permitted to see.

30. And thou shalt do it with all humility, trusting in me, reviling not against revilers.

31. And of tenets thou shalt not talk, but thou shalt declare repentance and faith on the Savior and remission of sins by baptism and by fire, yea, even the Holy Ghost.

32. Behold, this is a great and the last commandment which I shall give unto you concerning this matter; for this shall suffice for thy daily walk, even unto the end of thy life.

33. And misery thou shalt receive if thou wilt slight these counsels; yea, even the destruction of thyself and property.

34. Impart a portion of thy property; yea, even part of thy lands, and all save the support of thy family.

35. Pay the debt thou hast contracted with the printer. Release thyself from bondage.

36. Leave thy house and home, except when thou shalt desire to see thy family:

37. And speak freely to all: yea, preach, exhort, declare the truth, even with a loud voice, with a sound of rejoicing, crying—Hosanna, hosanna! blessed be the name of the Lord God.

38. Pray always, and I will pour out my Spirit upon you, and great shall be your blessing; yea, even more than if you should obtain treasures of earth and corruptibleness to the extent thereof.

39. Behold, canst thou read this without rejoicing and lifting up thy heart for gladness?

40. Or canst thou run about longer as a blind guide?

41. Or canst thou be humble and meek, and conduct thyself wisely before me? yea, come unto me thy Savior. Amen.

D&C 19:26—Martin Harris mortgaged his farm to support the publication of the Book of Mormon. When he became worried about his indebtedness, the Lord reminded him of the divine purpose for the investment. Let us remember that "things" are of the world and have no eternal value. If our value system is on the vain things of the world we are more likely to succumb to covetousness. Instead of coveting out of greed and avarice, we should "covet earnestly the best gifts" (1 Cor. 12:31) and "covet to prophesy" (1 Cor. 14:39), meaning to seek after the fruits of the Spirit.

D&C 19:27—That they may believe the gospel. The word of God in the Book of Mormon is to be revealed so that the Gentiles and the Jews (including the Lamanites, who are of the blood of Israel) might believe in the Savior and His gospel.

D&C 19:29–31—The counsel of the Lord is clear: teach the principles of the gospel in humility, keep your promises, speak freely but without argumentation to everyone concerning the truth, pray always, and conduct yourself wisely before the Lord.

D&C 19:39—What is our attitude when we approach the word of God and ponder the things of eternity? Do we do so with rejoicing and gladness? Or do we resist opening ourselves up to the visions of glory that await the righteous? Do we, ultimately, humble ourselves in wisdom and come unto the Savior? These are fundamentally important questions of conscience that arise from the example of Martin Harris. The key to worshipping in righteousness, exercising faith, and following our Heavenly Father and Savior is to understand and appreciate Their character, power, and goodness. They are omnipotent (see D&C 19:3, 14, 20; 20:24; 61:1; 93:17), omniscient (see D&C 38:1–2; 2 Ne. 9:20), and omnipresent (personal beings, yet present in all things: see D&C 88:12–13, 41).

The home of Lucy Harris, first wife of Martin Harris, in Palmyra, New York. Lucy eventually left Martin because of his role in the translation and printing of the Book of Mormon. As part of her divorce settlement, she received 80 acres of Martin Harris's farm, on which she built this home. Martin eventually married Caroline Young, the niece of Brigham Young, and they had seven children. Caroline and the children moved to Utah to join the Saints in 1856, but Martin did not follow until 1870.

SECTION 20

1. The rise of the church of Christ in these last days, being one thousand eight hundred and thirty years since the coming of our Lord and Savior Jesus Christ in the flesh, it being regularly organized and established agreeable to the laws of our country, by the will and commandments of God, in the fourth month, and on the sixth day of the month which is called April;

2. Which commandments were given to Joseph Smith, jun., who was called of God, and ordained an apostle of Jesus Christ, to be the first elder of this church;

3. And to Oliver Cowdery, who was also called of God, an apostle of Jesus Christ, to be the second elder of this church, and ordained under his hand;

4. And this according to the grace of our Lord and Savior Jesus Christ, to whom be all glory, both now and for ever. Amen.

5. After it was truly manifested unto this first elder that he had received a remission of his sins, he was entangled again in the vanities of the world;

6. But after repenting, and humbling himself sincerely, through faith God ministered unto him by an holy angel, whose countenance was as lightning, and whose garments were pure and white above all other whiteness;

7. And gave unto him commandments which inspired him;

8. And gave him power from on high, by the means which were before prepared, to translate the Book of Mormon,

9. Which contains a record of a fallen people, and the fulness of the gospel of Jesus Christ to the Gentiles and to the Jews also,

The Whitmer log home in Fayette, New York, where Joseph Smith and Oliver Cowdery lived with the Whitmer family for a time. Because of the intense persecution in Harmony, Pennsylvania, Joseph Smith sought the help of Oliver Cowdery's friend David Whitmer, who subsequently helped Joseph and Oliver make the move to Fayette so they could continue translation of the plates. While here, Oliver met, fell in love with, and married David Whitmer's sister, Elizabeth Ann. Fayette is named for the famous general, Marquis de LaFayette.

Section 20 Background—Known as the "Revelation on Church Organization and Government" (see *HC* 1:64–70), this section served as a kind of constitution for the operation and regulation of the restored Church. The Prophet Joseph Smith wrote: "In this manner did the Lord continue to give us instructions from time to time, concerning the duties which now devolved upon us; and among many other things of the kind, we obtained of Him the following, by the spirit of prophecy and revelation; which not only gave us much information, but also pointed out to us the precise day upon which, according to His will and commandment, we should proceed to organize His Church once more here upon the earth" (*HC* 1:64). Several other sections contain further key references to Church regulation and the operation of the priesthood (see especially Sections 21, 27, 41, 84, 90, 102, 107, 115, and 121).

D&C 20:1—On April 6, 1830, the Lord's Church was organized in this dispensation. The Prophet Joseph recorded the following concerning the organizational meeting:

> "Having opened the meeting by solemn prayer to our Heavenly Father, we proceeded, according to previous commandment, to call on our brethren to know whether they accepted us as their teachers in the things of the kingdom of God, and whether they were satisfied that we should proceed and be organized as a Church according to said commandment which we had received. To these several propositions they consented by a unanimous vote. I then laid my hands upon Oliver Cowdery, and ordained him an Elder of the 'Church of Jesus Christ of Latter-day Saints;' after which, he ordained me also to the office of an Elder of said Church. We then took bread, blessed it, and brake it with them; also wine, blessed it, and drank it with them. We then laid our hands on each individual member of the Church present, that they might receive the gift of the Holy Ghost, and be confirmed members of the Church of Christ. The Holy Ghost was poured out upon us to a very great degree—some prophesied, whilst we all praised the Lord, and rejoiced exceedingly. . . . (*HC* 1:76.)

Among those present at the organizational meeting of the Church were Joseph Smith, Oliver Cowdery, Hyrum Smith, Samuel H. Smith, Peter Whitmer, Jr., and David Whitmer.

D&C 20:2—The Lord ministered to Joseph Smith and prepared him as an Apostle and first elder of the Church, to perform his sacred mission.

10. Which was given by inspiration, and is confirmed to others by the ministering of angels, and is declared unto the world by them,

11. Proving to the world that the Holy Scriptures are true, and that God does inspire men and call them to his holy work in this age and generation, as well as in generations of old,

12. Thereby showing that he is the same God yesterday, to-day, and for ever. Amen.

13. Therefore, having so great witnesses, by them shall the world be judged, even as many as shall hereafter come to a knowledge of this work;

14. And those who receive it in faith, and work righteousness, shall receive a crown of eternal life;

15. But those who harden their hearts in unbelief, and reject it, it shall turn to their own condemnation,

16. For the Lord God has spoken it; and we, the elders of the church, have heard and bear witness to the words of the glorious Majesty on high, to whom be glory forever and ever. Amen.

17. By these things we know that there is a God in heaven, who is infinite and eternal, from everlasting to everlasting the same unchangeable God, the framer of heaven and earth, and all things which are in them;

18. And that he created man, male and female, after his own image and in his own likeness, created he them,

19. And gave unto them commandments that they should love and serve him, the only living and true God, and that he should be the only being whom they should worship.

20. But by the transgression of these holy laws, man became sensual and devilish, and became fallen man.

21. Wherefore, the Almighty God gave his Only Begotten Son, as it is written in those scriptures which have been given of him.

22. He suffered temptations but gave no heed unto them;

23. He was crucified, died, and rose again the third day;

24. And ascended into heaven, to sit down on the right hand of the

JOSEPH SMITH'S PREPARATION AND SPIRITUAL GROWTH

Obviously, searching and understanding the scriptures became the key to Joseph Smith's preparation and spiritual growth. This section of the Doctrine and Covenants delivered up a number of important truths; among other things, he learned:

1. There is a God in heaven (verses 17–19)
2. Jesus atoned for fallen man (verses 20–25)
3. The Holy Ghost testifies of the Father and the Son (verses 26–28)
4. All mankind must repent (verses 5–6, 29)
5. There are principles of justification and sanctification (verses 30–31)
6. Man must endure to the end in faith (verses 25, 29, 32–34)
7. God is unchangeable, the holy scriptures are true, and men will be judged thereby (verses 11–15, 35)

Of these, testified Elder Bruce R. McConkie, the greatest truth known to man is that there is an infinite and eternal God in heaven who ordained and established a plan of salvation so that we might eventually become like Him (STDC 1:85–86).

D&C 20:8–12—The Restoration proceeded to unfold under divine aegis in steps that reflected consummate order—beginning with the effulgent outpouring of truth and light concerning the nature of the Father and the Son (the First Vision), continuing with the bringing forth of the Book of Mormon ("the fulness of the gospel of Jesus Christ"—D&C 20:9), then the establishment of the Kingdom of Heaven on earth (including the authority of the priesthood and all attendant ordinances and offices), and subsequently the ongoing gathering of the Saints to holy places (stakes, temples) as designated through prophetic leadership. All of this rested on the foundation of a true knowledge of Deity as established through the First Vision and confirmed through the witness of the Holy Spirit. It was the Lord Himself who bore witness to the truthfulness of the Book of Mormon in these verses.

D&C 20:14—The Book of Mormon is the canonical text according to which we will be judged. Those who receive it in faith and conduct their lives in keeping with the principles of righteousness will receive "a crown of eternal life"—which is the greatest gift of God (see D&C 14:7). The Prophet Joseph stated: "I told the brethren that the Book of Mormon was the most correct of any book on earth, and the keystone of our religion, and a man would get nearer to God by abiding by its precepts, than by any other book" (HC 4:461).

D&C 20:16–17—Overwhelming evidence is at hand proving the existence of the unchangeable God—including the manifestations of the First Vision and the witness of the Book of Mormon. The name *Jehovah*, in fact, means just that: the Unchangeable One, or the eternal I AM (see Ex. 6:3).

D&C 20:19—The commandments from the beginning have always been to love, worship, and serve our Heavenly Father (see Deut. 6:5; Matt. 22:37–38; Moro. 7:13; D&C 59:5). Love is the center of all things, for it truly fulfills all the law and the prophets (see Matt. 22:36–40) and is the motive for all that Heavenly Father and our Savior do. To worship God is to show Him reverence, honor, devotion, and love. True worship is more than just a feeling or attitude—it is accompanied by an offering of self and service.

D&C 20:20—We do not inherit a fallen or evil state; such a state is the result of our own disobedience and iniquity.

Father, to reign with almighty power according to the will of the Father,

25. That as many as would believe and be baptized in his holy name, and endure in faith to the end, should be saved:

26. Not only those who believed after he came in the meridian of time, in the flesh, but all those from the beginning, even as many as were before he came, who believed in the words of the holy prophets, who spake as they were inspired by the gift of the Holy Ghost, who truly testified of him in all things, should have eternal life,

27. As well as those who should come after, who should believe in the gifts and callings of God by the Holy Ghost, which beareth record of the Father, and of the Son;

28. Which Father, Son, and Holy Ghost are one God, infinite and eternal, without end. Amen.

29. And we know that all men must repent and believe on the name of Jesus Christ, and worship the Father in his name, and endure in faith on his name to the end, or they cannot be saved in the kingdom of God.

30. And we know that justification through the grace of our Lord and Savior Jesus Christ is just and true;

31. And we know also, that sanctification through the grace of our Lord and Savior Jesus Christ, is just and true to all those who love and serve God with all their mights, minds, and strength.

32. But there is a possibility that man may fall from grace and depart from the living God;

33. Therefore let the church take heed and pray always, lest they fall into temptation;

34. Yea, and even let those who are sanctified take heed also.

35. And we know that these things are true and according to the revelations of John, neither adding to, or diminishing from the prophecy of his book, the Holy Scriptures, or the revelations of God which shall come hereafter by the gift and power of the Holy Ghost, the voice of God, or the ministering of angels.

36. And the Lord God has spoken it; and honor, power, and glory, be rendered to his holy name, both now and ever. Amen.

37. And again, by way of commandment to the church concerning the manner of baptism.—All those who humble themselves before God, and desire to be baptized and come forth with broken hearts and contrite spirits, and witness before the church that they have truly repented

D&C 20:30–31—To be justified means that we have been approved of the Lord and absolved of all wrongdoing. We stand guiltless and blameless before the Lord, justified through grace by the Holy Spirit (see Moses 6:60), a process by which the righteous are ratified (see 1 Ne. 16:2). Justification by the Spirit is made possible through the Atonement of the Lord Jesus Christ (see Mosiah 14:11), for it is by the grace of God that we are saved (see D&C 20:30). Because no one obeys the law with perfect performance, it is only through "the merits, and mercy, and grace of the Holy Messiah" (2 Ne. 2:8) that redemption can come to us, based on our penitence and righteousness.

Sanctification is a process of purification before God. We are sanctified when we are in reality purified through the atoning blood of Christ and made innocent and holy. Through the grace of God we can become sanctified in Christ, made clean and pure by the power of the Holy Ghost (see 3 Ne. 27:19–20; Moro. 10:32–33). Sanctification is more than just doing: it is a "becoming" within our soul—a mighty change, a heart yielding to the enticings of the Spirit and to God (see Mosiah 3:19). Being sanctified, we are prepared, made holy, consecrated, and set apart for sacred service.

D&C 20:37—This statement defines the qualities of worthiness for those who want to be accepted into the fold of Christ. Learning to qualify for baptism is a sacred and solemn obligation because of the profound significance of the covenant we make with our Heavenly Father and Savior. When we fail to teach this to our children, we are held responsible (see D&C 68:25–28). Baptism is both for the remission of sins as well as the gateway to the Church and kingdom of God. If we are faithful to our baptismal covenant it can bring entrance to the celestial kingdom (see John 3:3–5; D&C 76:51). We are to be humble—recognizing our relationship with and dependence on God and exhibiting the fruits of discipleship by being submissive, teachable, easily entreated, meek, and showing forth our sacrifice of a broken heart and contrite spirit (see 3 Ne. 9:20). Our desire to be baptized is evidenced by our having repented of our sins. To repent and be baptized is the clarion call from the scriptures, the prophets, and our Savior (see Acts 2:38; 2 Ne. 9:23; 31:11; 3 Ne. 11:37–38). When we take the name of Christ upon us, we covenant to exercise faith in Him, follow Him, keep His commandments, and seek to live a Christ-like life. Through baptism we become His sons and daughters (see Mosiah 5:7). We are born of Him and are called Christians. We are to remain steadfast in Christ and endure to the end, thus qualifying for eternal life (see 2 Ne. 31:20). We are to bear witness to the truth of all things pertaining to the kingdom of God (see Mosiah 18:8–9) and especially the Book of Mormon—the keystone of our religion.

of all their sins, and are willing to take upon them the name of Jesus Christ, having a determination to serve him to the end, and truly manifest by their works that they have received of the Spirit of Christ unto the remission of their sins, shall be received by baptism into his church.

38. The duty of the elders, priests, teachers, deacons, and members of the church of Christ.—An apostle is an elder, and it is his calling to baptize.

39. And to ordain other elders, priests, teachers, and deacons,

40. And to administer bread and wine—the emblems of the flesh and blood of Christ—

41. And to confirm those who are baptized into the church, by the laying on of hands for the baptism of fire and the Holy Ghost, according to the scriptures;

42. And to teach, expound, exhort, baptize, and watch over the church;

43. And to confirm the church by the laying on of the hands, and the giving of the Holy Ghost;

44. And to take the lead of all meetings.

45. The elders are to conduct the meetings as they are led by the Holy Ghost, according to the commandments and revelations of God.

46. The priest's duty is to preach, teach, expound, exhort, and baptize, and administer the sacrament,

47. And visit the house of each member, and exhort them to pray vocally and in secret, and attend to all family duties;

48. And he may also ordain other priests, teachers, and deacons.

49. And he is to take the lead of meetings when there is no elder present;

50. But when there is an elder present, he is only to preach, teach, expound, exhort, and baptize,

51. And visit the house of each member, exhorting them to pray vocally and in secret, and attend to all family duties.

52. In all these duties the priest is to assist the elder if occasion requires.

53. The teacher's duty is to watch over the church always, and be with and strengthen them,

54. And see that there is no iniquity in the church—neither hardness with each other—neither lying, backbiting, nor evil speaking;

55. And see that the church meet together often, and also see that all the members do their duty;

56. And he is to take the lead of meetings in the absence of the elder or priest—

57. And is to be assisted always, in all his duties in the church, by the deacons, if occasion requires;

D&C 20:41—President Harold B. Lee said that receiving the Holy Ghost puts us back in the presence of one of the Godhead—and, because of that, we are spiritually reborn. Receiving the Holy Ghost, in fact, is an essential part of the process of spiritual rebirth; he burns out any iniquity in our souls and justifies us for salvation. As we are justified, the pure spirit triumphs over flesh and governs the flesh, and helps us with all we must do to qualify for exaltation.

D&C 20:45—All meetings are for edifying those present and strengthening their faith. The Holy Ghost will inspire the one responsible—both in advance as well as in the very moment of service—how to proceed: whether to preach, teach, exhort, sing, pray, or supplicate the Lord (see Moro. 6:9). Let us remember that it is the Holy Spirit that will show us all things we are to do (see 2 Ne. 32:5) as well as inspire us in regard to what to teach (see D&C 42:14; 68:3–4). When conducting meetings, one should always seek to be worthy of the Holy Spirit and honor the investment of time and attention of those being served. These precious moments should always be prefaced with the thought: "What would the Lord have me do to bless their lives?"

D&C 20:51—The inspired program of visiting the homes of members in the spirit of charity and service is central to the mission of the Church to nourish and perfect the Saints. Home teaching and visiting teaching are the backbone strategies in this regard. The Aaronic Priesthood bearer under the direction of the bishop and quorum presidencies can have a marvelous effect on his quorum members and the people they serve. It all depends on his vision of the work, his desire to serve, and his worthiness to be an instrument in the hands of the Lord and an agent for accomplishing much good. All priesthood bearers—both Aaronic and Melchizedek—have the responsibility to bless and watch over the Church. The sisters of the Relief Society carry on a parallel work of charity in visiting and sustaining their colleagues in the work of the Lord.

58. But neither teachers nor deacons have authority to baptize, administer the sacrament, or lay on hands:

59. They are, however, to warn, expound, exhort, and teach and invite all to come unto Christ.

60. Every elder, priest, teacher, or deacon, is to be ordained according to the gifts and callings of God unto him; and he is to be ordained by the power of the Holy Ghost, which is in the one who ordains him.

61. The several elders, composing this church of Christ are to meet in conference once in three months, or from time to time as said conferences shall direct or appoint;

62. And said conferences are to do whatever church business is necessary to be done at the time.

63. The elders are to receive their licenses from other elders, by vote of the church to which they belong, or from the conferences.

64. Each priest, teacher, or deacon, who is ordained by a priest may take a certificate from him at the time, which certificate when presented to an elder, shall entitle him to a license, which shall authorize him to perform the duties of his calling, or he may receive it from a conference.

65. No person is to be ordained to any office in this church, where there is a regularly organized branch of the same, without the vote of that church;

66. But the presiding elders, traveling bishops, High Councilors, High Priests, and elders, may have the privilege of ordaining, where there is no branch of the church that a vote may be called.

67. Every President of the High Priesthood (or presiding elder), bishop, High Councilor, and High Priest, is to be ordained by the direction of a High Council or general conference.

68. The duty of the members after they are received by baptism.— The elders or priests are to have a sufficient time to expound all things concerning the church of Christ to their understanding, previous to their partaking of the sacrament and being confirmed by the laying on of the hands of the elders, so that all things may be done in order.

69. And the members shall manifest before the church, and also before the elders, by a Godly walk and conversation, that they are worthy of it, that there may be works and faith agreeable to the Holy Scriptures—walking in holiness before the Lord.

70. Every member of the church of Christ having children, is to bring them unto the elders before the church, who are to lay their hands upon them in the name of Jesus Christ, and bless them in his name.

71. No one can be received into the church of Christ unless he has arrived unto the years of accountability before God, and is capable of repentance.

D&C 20:58–59—This is the word of the Lord in regard to those who have been received into the kingdom of God through baptism. Walking in holiness before the Lord requires that we keep the commandments. From the early sections of the Doctrine and Covenants we have abundant examples of the admonition to keep the commandments (see D&C 6:6, 9, 37; 8:5; 11:6, 9, 18, 20; 12:6; 14:6–7; 18:43, 46; 19:13; 25:15; 35:24; 42:1, 29, 78; and 43:35). Our obedience and worthiness are demonstrated by our faith—which moves us to action and good works. As members we will be known by our fruits (see 3 Ne. 14:20) and by the light that we radiate—showing our good works and thus glorifying our Heavenly Father (see 3 Ne. 12:16).

Interior of the Whitmer home in Fayette, New York, where Oliver Cowdery and Joseph Smith lived with the Whitmer family after enduring intense persecution in Harmony, Pennsylvania.

D&C 20:69—"A godly walk and conversation" is the simple formula the Lord designated as the governing lifestyle of His Saints. If we follow in the footsteps of the Savior, then we are pursuing a "godly walk." If our behavior (our thoughts, our actions, our words, our relationships—"conversation" in the more antique sense of that word) is congruent with the qualities of Christian discipleship, then we are deporting ourselves as Saints, with a hope fixed in Christ, and our minds and hearts attuned to the guidance of the Spirit through channels of personal inspiration and revelation.

D&C 20:70—The regulation of the Church includes, by divine commandment, the blessing of children under the hands of the elders in the name of Jesus Christ. The Lord is our Exemplar in this regard, for He rejoiced in calling little children unto Him and blessing them in love and mercy (see Matt. 19:14; Mark 10:14; Luke 18:16; 3 Ne. 17:21).

72. Baptism is to be administered in the following manner unto all those who repent:

73. The person who is called of God, and has authority from Jesus Christ to baptize, shall go down into the water with the person who has presented himself or herself for baptism, and shall say, calling him or her by name—Having been commissioned of Jesus Christ, I baptize you in the name of the Father, and of the Son, and of the Holy Ghost. Amen.

74. Then shall he immerse him or her in the water, and come forth again out of the water.

75. It is expedient that the church meet together often to partake of bread and wine in the remembrance of the Lord Jesus;

76. And the elder or priest shall administer it; and after this manner shall he administer it—he shall kneel with the church and call upon the Father in solemn prayer, saying—

77. O God, the eternal Father, we ask thee in the name of thy Son, Jesus Christ, to bless and sanctify this bread to the souls of all those who partake of it, that they may eat in remembrance of the body of thy Son, and witness unto thee, O God, the eternal Father, that they are willing to take upon them the name of thy Son, and always remember him and keep his commandments which he has given them, that they may always have his Spirit to be with them. Amen.

78. The manner of administering the wine.—He shall take the cup also, and say—

79. O God, the eternal Father, we ask thee in the name of thy Son, Jesus Christ, to bless and sanctify this wine to the souls of all those who drink of it, that they may do it in remembrance of the blood of thy Son, which was shed for them; that they may witness unto thee, O God, the eternal Father, that they do always remember him, that they may have his Spirit to be with them. Amen.

80. Any member of the church of Christ transgressing, or being overtaken in a fault, shall be dealt with as the scriptures direct.

81. It shall be the duty of the several churches composing the church of Christ, to send one or more of their teachers to attend the several conferences held by the elders of the church,

82. With a list of the names of the several members uniting themselves with the church since the last conference, or send by the hand of some priest, so that a regular list of all the names of the whole church may be kept in a book by one of the elders, whosoever the other elders shall appoint from time to time;

83. And also if any have been expelled from the church, so that their names may be blotted out of the general church record of names.

84. All members removing from the church where they reside, if going to a church where they are not known, may take a letter certifying that they are regular members and in good standing, which certificate may be signed by any elder or priest, if the member receiving the letter is personally acquainted with the elder or priest, or it may be signed by the teachers or deacons of the church.

D&C 20:72—The manner of baptizing the penitent who have reached the age of accountability is outlined, including the specific wording to be used prior to the immersion procedure. President Joseph Fielding Smith reminds us: "The Lord has given to the Church very few forms. In the ordinance of baptism definite words are given which must be used by the priest or elder who officiates" (CHMR 1:90).

D&C 20:73, 77, 79—While all of our prayers should be sincere and heartfelt communication between us and our Heavenly Father, the prayers in these verses—one for baptism and the other two for the sacrament—are set prayers that cannot vary in the least.

D&C 20:75—The method and wording to be used in the administration of the sacrament is given by revelation. The sacramental prayers are covenant-making prayers dictated by the Lord in revelation to the Prophet Joseph as well as to Moroni (see Moro. 4:3; 5:2). We renew our covenants as we partake of the sacrament. We covenant to remember the Lord and His sacrifice, to take upon us the name of our Savior Jesus Christ to remember Him and His commandments—with the promise that we will thus be blessed with the Holy Spirit. This glorious covenant and promise strengthens and reminds us of our sacred duty and the promises made to us from the Lord. Because the hearts of men are unsteady (see Hel. 12:1), this weekly remembering of the Lord and His mercy and grace help us stay on the strait and narrow path. We mortals, with our finite minds, need constant reminders, and the sacrament is Heavenly Father's way of helping us remember His Son's sacrifice. The sacrament is a vital part of Heavenly Father's plan to help us keep the commandments. To realize the importance of the sacrament is to come to know the Lord Jesus Christ. As we make partaking of the sacrament an important part of our life, we will keep the commandments and live by the Spirit.

D&C 20:78—According to President Joseph Fielding Smith, the practice of using wine for the sacrament was originally abandoned because the Prophet had so many enemies that could have adulterated it. Even when wine was used for the sacrament, the Saints had to make it themselves and it had to be "new" (in other words, not fermented).

D&C 20:82—The scriptures are to be used to guide how the Church should deal with members who transgress. Records of membership are to be kept and updated with care.

SECTION 21

1. Behold there shall be a record kept among you, and in it thou shalt be called a seer, a translator, a prophet, an apostle of Jesus Christ, an elder of the church through the will of God the Father, and the grace of your Lord Jesus Christ,

2. Being inspired of the Holy Ghost to lay the foundation thereof, and to build it up unto the most holy faith,

3. Which church was organized and established in the year of your Lord eighteen hundred and thirty, in the fourth month, and on the sixth day of the month, which is called April.

4. Wherefore, meaning the church, thou shalt give heed unto all his words and commandments which he shall give unto you as he receiveth them, walking in all holiness before me;

5. For his word ye shall receive, as if from mine own mouth, in all patience and faith;

6. For by doing these things the gates of hell shall not prevail against you; yea, and the Lord God will disperse the powers of darkness from before you, and cause the heavens to shake for your good, and his name's glory.

7. For thus saith the Lord God, him have I inspired to move the cause of Zion in mighty power for good, and his diligence I know, and his prayers I have heard.

8. Yea his weeping for Zion I have seen, and I will cause that he shall mourn for her no longer, for his days of rejoicing are come unto the remission of his sins, and the manifestations

Seneca Lake.

Section 21 Background—Given on Tuesday, April 6, 1830, in the home of Peter Whitmer, Sr. on the historic occasion of the organization of the Church (see *HC* 1:74–79). The name of the new church was "The Church of Christ."

D&C 21:5—The blessings of following the prophet are like those of following our Savior (see 3 Ne. 12:2; 28:34–35; D&C 84:35–38). We are empowered by our obedience with the blessings of the Spirit. When the prophet speaks, he speaks for the Lord (see D&C 1:38; 68:4). It is imperative to hearken to the prophets, for the consequences are grave if we do not (see 3 Ne. 12:1–2; 28:34–35). We will always be blessed for following the prophet (see D&C 124:45).

D&C 21:6—Here is a failsafe key for enjoying the blessings of security and safety in a world beset with insidious dangers: *simply follow the prophet of God.* Inherent in this policy—which is a covenant arrangement based on a commandment with promise—is the ability, in the strength of the Lord, to see that the powers of darkness are dispersed. The heavens are arrayed and engaged for our good if we simply follow the prophets, through whom we are given the word of God. What greater protection can come to individuals and families than to heed, in righteousness, the words of the living prophet? Storms and challenges are inevitable; enveloping shadows are part of life; but the calming voice of the living prophet dispels doubt and neutralizes the raging of evil in the world—if we but listen and obey. By following the word of God emanating from His prophets and confirmed by the Holy Ghost, we also come alive spiritually. We dispel the darkness before us through the illuminating light of the gospel of Jesus Christ, and the minions of Satan retreat in fear.

D&C 21:7—The guidance system of the kingdom of God is anchored in the divine commission of prophets, seers, and revelators who communicate the Lord's truths under inspiration of the Holy Spirit. By following the Lord's designated prophet, as if we were in fact following the Lord Himself, we move in pathways of light and knowledge that accord with divine will. We observe that modern-day revelation continues to be given by the Lord through His chosen servants in our day, bringing about such significant developments as priesthood correlation, extending the priesthood to all worthy males, publishing improved editions of the scriptures, expanding the scope and activity of the Seventies, and adding to the sacred canon. All of this occurs within the framework laid down as an integral part of the Restoration, whereby the prophet of the Lord holds all the keys and authority of leadership for the Church as a whole (see D&C 43:2–3).

of my blessings upon his works.

9. For, behold, I will bless all those who labor in my vineyard with a mighty blessing, and they shall believe on his words, which are given him through me by the Comforter, which manifesteth that Jesus was crucified by sinful men for the sins of the world, yea, for the remission of sins unto the contrite heart.

10. Wherefore it behooveth me that he should be ordained by you, Oliver Cowdery, mine apostle;

11. This being an ordinance unto you, that you are an elder under his hand, he being the first unto you, that you might be an elder unto this church of Christ, bearing my name,

12. And the first preacher of this church unto the church, and before the world, yea, before the Gentiles; yea, and thus saith the Lord God, lo, lo! to the Jews also. Amen.

SECTION 22

1. Behold, I say unto you, that all old covenants have I caused to be done away in this thing, and this is a new and an everlasting covenant, even that which was from the beginning.

2. Wherefore, although a man should be baptized an hundred times, it availeth him nothing, for you cannot enter in at the strait gate by the law of Moses, neither by your dead works;

3. For it is because of your dead works, that I have caused this last covenant and this church to be built up unto me, even as in days of old.

4. Wherefore, enter ye in at the gate, as I have commanded, and seek not to counsel your God. Amen.

SAMUEL H. SMITH

Samuel H. Smith was born March 13, 1808, at Tunbridge, Orange County, Vermont, son of Joseph Smith Sr. and Lucy Mack. He was convinced of the divine mission of his older brother, Joseph, and was baptized by Oliver Cowdery on May 25, 1829, the third person to be baptized in the new dispensation. He was one of the eight witnesses of the Book of Mormon and one of the six original members of the Church upon its organization. Considered the first missionary of the Church, he performed labors that resulted in the conversion of Heber C. Kimball and Brigham Young. Samuel was tireless in contributing to the building up of the Kingdom in callings that ranged from being a member of the high council in Kirtland to serving as a counselor in Nauvoo to Vinson Knight, presiding bishop of the Church, and later as bishop of the Nauvoo Ward. He was foiled by mobs in his attempt to come to the rescue of Joseph and Hyrum in Carthage, but later accompanied the bodies back to Nauvoo. He passed away in poor health on July 30, 1844.

D&C 21:8–9—The spirit of joy flows from the consummate peace attending the remission of sins. The gospel is a divine system of joy, for "men are that they might have joy" (2 Ne. 2:25). The Prophet Joseph is promised that his colleagues in the newly organized Church will believe in his words that come through the Holy Spirit. Joy will attend this phenomenon of seeing the fruit of his labors in this way. "I have no greater joy," said John the Beloved, "than to hear that my children walk in truth" (3 John 1:4).

D&C 21:12—On Sunday, April 11, 1830, just five days after the organization of the Church in Fayette, New York, Oliver Cowdery preached what Joseph Smith characterized as "the first public discourse that was delivered by any of our number" (HC 1:81). Joseph continues: "Our meeting was held, by previous appointment, at the house of Mr. Peter Whitmer, Sen., Fayette. Large numbers of people attended. . . ." We don't know the topic of Oliver's discourse, but after the meeting, several people came forward and wanted to be baptized "by Oliver Cowdery, in Seneca Lake." One of those would become Oliver's wife.

Section 22 Background—At the meeting on April 6, 1830, in which the Church had been organized, baptism had been a central theme. Some were concerned that since they had already been baptized, though in a different church, they didn't need to be baptized again.

D&C 22:1—The gospel of Jesus Christ encompasses all covenants and obligations relating to exaltation and eternal life, including baptism, priesthood ordinations, and temple marriage. All of the Lord's promises and eternal blessings as revealed and renewed in the dispensation of the fulness of times are administered by covenant under the inclusive title "the new and everlasting covenant."

D&C 22:2–4—During the Restoration of the gospel, when some in the circle of Joseph Smith who had already been baptized were reluctant to be baptized again, Christ commanded that the people complete this ordinance as part of "a new and an everlasting covenant" allowing them to enter in at the strait gate and become part of the fold of Christ in the restored Church and kingdom of God on the earth. The "dead works" mentioned here refers to being baptized without proper authority: being baptized a hundred times without authorized priesthood authority will avail the individual nothing.

D&C 22:4—Jacob said, "Wherefore, brethren, seek not to counsel the Lord, but to take counsel from his hand" (Jacob 4:10). In June 1831, the Lord warned: "Behold, thus saith the Lord unto my people—you have many things to do and to repent of; for behold, your sins have come up unto me, and are not pardoned, because you seek to counsel in your own ways" (D&C 56:14).

SECTION 23

1. Behold, I speak unto you, Oliver, a few words. Behold, thou art blessed, and art under no condemnation. But beware of pride, lest thou shouldst enter into temptation.
2. Make known thy calling unto the church, and also before the world, and thy heart shall be opened to preach the truth from henceforth and forever. Amen.
3. Behold, I speak unto you, Hyrum, a few words: for thou also art under no condemnation, and thy heart is opened, and thy tongue loosed; and thy calling is to exhortation, and to strengthen the church continually. Wherefore thy duty is unto the church for ever, and this because of thy family. Amen.
4. Behold, I speak a few words unto you, Samuel, for thou also art under no condemnation, and thy calling is to exhortation, and to strengthen the church, and thou art not as yet called to preach before the world. Amen.
5. Behold, I speak a few words unto you, Joseph, for thou also art under no condemnation, and thy calling also is to exhortation, and to strengthen the church; and this is thy duty from henceforth and forever. Amen.
6. Behold, I manifest unto you, Joseph Knight, by these words, that you must take up your cross, in the which you must pray vocally before the world as well as in secret, and in your family, and among your friends, and in all places.
7. And, behold, it is your duty to unite with the true church, and give your language to exhortation continually, that you may receive the reward of the laborer. Amen.

SECTION 24

1. Behold, thou wast called and chosen to write the Book of Mormon, and to my ministry; and I have lifted thee up out of thy afflictions, and have counseled thee, that thou hast been delivered

---

JOSEPH SMITH SR.

Joseph Smith Sr. was born July 12, 1771, in Essex County, Massachusetts. He pursued farming and teaching as a profession, moving with his family from location to location in Vermont and New Hampshire, only to find that prosperity remained an elusive goal. In 1816 the family moved to Palmyra, New York. Father Smith had faith in the reports of his son Joseph concerning the events of the Restoration that commenced there and was ever supportive and encouraging in his relationship with the young prophet. Joseph Sr. was one of the eight witnesses of the Book of Mormon. He was baptized on April 6, 1830, the day the Church was organized. On December 18, 1833, he was ordained the first patriarch in the new dispensation. He later served an extended mission in the Eastern States. Suffering from much ill health in his final years in Nauvoo, he left the mortal realm behind on September 14, 1840, and inherited a place "with Abraham" in the eternal realm (D&C 124:19).

Section 23 Background—Given in April 1830 at Manchester, New York, after specific people asked to know their duties.

D&C 23:1—We observe a pattern in the words of the Lord to these brethren: Except in the case of Joseph Knight, Sr., the Lord begins by defining His *current* relationship with his servants—"thou art under no condemnation."

D&C 23:1—Never has an attitude or attribute been so damning to the human soul as pride. It was the pride of the Nephite nation that led to their eventual destruction as a people (see Moro. 8:27). The spacious building in Lehi's vision of the tree of life is a representation of the pride and vain ambitions of the world, and "the fall thereof was exceedingly great" (1 Ne. 11:36). Pride separates one from God, for one seeks his own will instead of the will of the Father. It is pride of heart that can in fact destroy one's soul (see Jacob 2:16).

D&C 23:3—Hyrum was ordained patriarch to the Church on January 24, 1841. The word of the Lord to him in verse 3 may have alluded to this coming blessing (see CHMR 1:112–13).

D&C 23:6—In the case of Joseph Knight, Sr., there is a direct call to repentance ("take up your cross"). According to James E. Talmage:

> The cross to be taken up may be heavy, perhaps to be dragged because too burdensome to be borne. We are apt to assume that self-denial is the sole material of our cross; but this is true only as we regard self-denial in its broadest sense, comprising both positive and negative aspects. One man's cross may consist mostly in refraining from doings to which he is inclined, another's in doing what he would fain escape. One's besetting sin is evil indulgence; his neighbor's a lazy inattention to the activities required by the Gospel of Jesus Christ, coupled perchance with puritanical rigor in other observances.
>
> But the great question, striking home to every thoughtful soul, is that of the Master—"For what is a man profited, if he shall gain the whole world and ose his own soul?" (Matt. 16:26). (VM, 353.)

Section 24 Background—The leaders of the young Church had experienced considerable tribulation and persecution in their travels and service. The voice of the Lord comes in the form of encouragement and confirmation of the great cause in which they are enlisted.

from all thine enemies, and thou hast been delivered from the powers of Satan and from darkness!

2. Nevertheless, thou art not excusable in thy transgressions; nevertheless, go thy way and sin no more.

3. Magnify thine office; and after thou hast sowed thy fields and secured them, go speedily unto the church which is in Colesville, Fayette and Manchester, and they shall support thee; and I will bless them both spiritually and temporally;

4. But if they receive thee not, I will send upon them a cursing instead of a blessing.

5. And thou shalt continue in calling upon God in my name, and writing the things which shall be given thee by the Comforter, and expounding all scriptures unto the church;

6. And it shall be given thee in the very moment what thou shalt speak and write, and they shall hear it, or I will send unto them a cursing instead of a blessing.

7. For thou shalt devote all thy service in Zion; and in this thou shalt have strength.

8. Be patient in afflictions, for thou shalt have many; but endure them, for, lo, I am with thee, even unto the end of thy days.

9. And in temporal labors thou shalt not have strength, for this is not thy calling. Attend to thy calling and thou shalt have wherewith to magnify thine office, and to expound all scriptures, and continue in laying on of the hands and confirming the churches.

10. And thy brother Oliver shall continue in bearing my name before the world, and also to the church. And he shall not suppose that he can say enough in my cause; and lo, I am with him to the end.

11. In me he shall have glory, and not of himself, whether in weakness or in strength, whether in bonds or free,

12. And at all times, and in all places, he shall open his mouth and declare my gospel as with the voice of a trump, both day and night. And I will give unto him strength such as is not known among men.

13. Require not miracles, except I shall command you, except casting out devils, healing the sick, and against poisonous serpents, and against deadly poisons;

14. And these things ye shall not do, except it be required of you by them who desire it, that the scriptures might be fulfilled; for ye shall do according to that which is written.

15. And in whatsoever place ye shall enter, and they receive you not in my name, ye shall leave a cursing instead of a blessing, by casting off the dust of your feet against them as a testimony, and cleansing your feet by the wayside.

16. And it shall come to pass that whosoever shall lay their hands upon you by violence, ye shall command

A country road in Colesville (now Nineveh), New York.

D&C 24:6–8—The Lord gives fatherly counsel to His young servant, whose weaknesses and strengths are known from the heavenly perspective. But the Prophet is not alone, for the Spirit will reveal to him "in the very moment" of need what he is to say and write in fulfilling his divinely appointed calling. The Lord covenants with His emissaries to grant unto them the immediate guidance of the Spirit.

D&C 24:9—The Prophet is promised by the Lord that he would receive a blessing from heaven whereby he would have sufficient resources to accomplish his duties. He did not receive a blessing of temporal acumen or special capability in material productivity, for that was not his calling. He was to be the emissary of the word of God, and as such the Lord would sustain and bless him in his labors.

D&C 24:12—As members, missionaries, and disciples of the Lord Jesus Christ, we have been called to be witnesses at all times and in all places (see Mosiah 18:9) and to "declare his word among his people, that they might have everlasting life" (3 Ne. 5:13). We can do this by letting our light so shine that people might see our good works and glorify our Father in Heaven (see 3 Ne. 12:16). We can do this by opening our mouths to testify of the truth—and they shall be filled (see D&C 33:8–11). We can warn our neighbors in meekness and mildness (see D&C 88:81). We can serve full-time missions. We can serve as ward missionaries. We can serve as Church service missionaries. We can fast and pray for all those who know not God (see Alma 6:6). Let us remember that this is the last time the vineyard will be pruned and it is our responsibility to do it.

D&C 24:12—We are told to preach the gospel with "the voice of a trump." Scholar Hoyt Brewster, Jr., explains this simile: "The righteous resonance in the voices of those called to declare the message of salvation should be as clear as the tones of the trumpet. Just as the sonorous sound of Joshua's trumpeters caused the wicked walls of ancient Jericho to tumble, so should the divine message of God's servants destroy the sanctuaries of sin inhabited by the wicked of our day (Josh. 6). 'For if the trumpet give an uncertain sound, who shall prepare himself . . . ?' (1 Cor. 14:8)" (DCE, 548).

D&C 24:15—When people reject the truth, Joseph and Oliver are to dust off and cleanse their own feet as a ceremonial witness against those who elect to oppose the truth as presented by the Lord's authorized servants (see also D&C 60:15; 75:20; 84:92; 99:4). James E. Talmage comments on this kind of witness: "The responsibility of testifying before the Lord by this accusing symbol is so great that the means may be employed only under unusual and extreme conditions, as the Spirit of the Lord may direct" (JC, 320).

to be smitten in my name; and, behold, I will smite them according to your words, in mine own due time.

17. And whosoever shall go to law with thee shall be cursed by the law.

18. And thou shalt take no purse nor scrip, neither staves, neither two coats, for the church shall give unto thee in the very hour what thou needest for food and for raiment, and for shoes and for money, and for scrip;

19. For thou art called to prune my vineyard with a mighty pruning, yea, even for the last time; yea, and also all those whom thou hast ordained, and they shall do even according to this pattern. Amen.

SECTION 25

1. Hearken unto the voice of the Lord your God, while I speak unto you, Emma Smith, my daughter, for verily I say unto you, all those who receive my gospel are sons and daughters in my kingdom.

2. A revelation I give unto you concerning my will, and if thou art faithful and walk in the paths of virtue before me, I will preserve thy life, and thou shalt receive an inheritance in Zion.

3. Behold, thy sins are forgiven thee, and thou art an elect lady, whom I have called.

4. Murmur not because of the things which thou hast not seen, for they are withheld from thee and from the world, which is wisdom in me in a time to come.

5. And the office of thy calling shall be for a comfort unto my servant, Joseph Smith, jun., thy husband, in his afflictions with consoling words, in the spirit of meekness.

6. And thou shalt go with him at the time of his going, and be unto him for a scribe, while there is no one to be a scribe for him, that I may send my servant, Oliver Cowdery, whithersoever I will.

7. And thou shalt be ordained under his hand to expound scriptures, and to exhort the church,

EMMA HALE SMITH

Emma Hale was born July 10, 1804, in Harmony, Susquehanna County, Pennsylvania, daughter of Isaac Hale and Elizabeth Lewis Hale. Her father withheld consent for her to marry Joseph, so the two eloped and were married in January 1827. She assisted her husband as a scribe in the translation of the Book of Mormon. She was baptized on June 28, 1830, by Oliver Cowdery. She was instrumental in preparing a selection of hymns for the Church. Joseph and Emma had nine children, of whom only four grew to maturity. Her life was filled with abundant tribulation and adversity, but she remained supportive and loyal to her devoted and loving husband. Following the martyrdom, she declined to go West with the Saints. Her second marriage was to Major Lewis Bidamon. She passed away on April 30, 1879, at Nauvoo, Illinois, at the age of 74, and was buried next to the plot where the Prophet Joseph was buried.

D&C 24:18—Concerning resources for completing their mission, Joseph and Oliver are to go without purse or scrip (a container or satchel), and are to depend on the Lord for their subsistence, for He will give them "in the very hour" what they might need to carry on their service in the vineyard of the Lord.

Section 25 Background—This section is a revelation given by a prophet-husband to his beloved wife and partner—a tender moment in which the blessings of the Almighty were pronounced upon "an elect lady" and a sacred commission put into place. Later, in August 1842, Joseph was to write concerning Emma: "How glorious were my feelings when I met that faithful and friendly band, on the night of the eleventh, on Thursday, on the island at the mouth of the slough, between Zarahemla and Nauvoo: with what unspeakable delight, and what transports of joy swelled my bosom, when I took by the hand, on that night, my beloved Emma—she that was my wife, even the wife of my youth, and the choice of my heart. Many were the reverberations of my mind, when I contemplated for a moment the many scenes we had been called to pass through, the fatigues and the toils, the sorrows and sufferings, and the joys and consolations, from time to time, which had strewed our paths and crowned our board. Oh what a commingling of thought filled my mind for the moment, again she is here, even in the seventh trouble—undaunted, firm, and unwavering—unchangeable, affectionate Emma!" (*HC* 5:107).

D&C 25:3—Mother Smith wrote of Emma: "I have never seen a woman in my life, who would endure every species of fatigue and hardship, from month to month, and from year to year, with that unflinching courage, zeal, and patience, which she has ever done; for I know that which she has had to endure—she has been tossed upon the ocean of uncertainty—she has breasted the storms of persecution, and buffeted the rage of men and devils, which would have borne down almost any other woman" (*HJS*, 190–191).

D&C 25:5–6—Joseph and Emma were partners along the pathway of adversity, companions in the storms of life. She was counseled to "go with him" as he completed his mission—and this counsel, as a universal theme of marital togetherness, applies to all the wives of Zion and to their partners as well. They are to *go together* in meeting the challenges of this probationary phase of life, that they may rejoice and look forward to an eternal family relationship in the hereafter, according to the grace and glory of the Father and the Son.

D&C 25:7—The word "ordained" here is used in the sense of "setting apart," or being given special blessing in connection with a Church calling.

according as it shall be given thee by my Spirit:

8. For he shall lay his hands upon thee, and thou shalt receive the Holy Ghost, and thy time shall be given to writing, and to learning much.

9. And thou needest not fear, for thy husband shall support thee in the church; for unto them is his calling, that all things might be revealed unto them, whatsoever I will, according to their faith.

10. And verily I say unto thee that thou shalt lay aside the things of this world, and seek for the things of a better.

11. And it shall be given thee, also, to make a selection of sacred hymns, as it shall be given thee, which is pleasing unto me, to be had in my church;

12. For my soul delighteth in the song of the heart, yea, the song of the righteous is a prayer unto me, and it shall be answered with a blessing upon their heads.

13. Wherefore, lift up thy heart and rejoice, and cleave unto the covenants which thou hast made.

14. Continue in the spirit of meekness, and beware of pride. Let thy soul delight in thy husband, and the glory which shall come upon him.

15. Keep my commandments continually, and a crown of righteousness thou shalt receive. And except thou do this, where I am you cannot come.

16. And verily, verily I say unto you, that this is my voice unto all. Amen.

SECTION 26

1. Behold, I say unto you, that you shall let your time be devoted to the studying of the scriptures, and to preaching, and to confirming the church at Colesville, and to performing your labors on the land, such as is required, until after you shall go to the west to hold the next conference; and then it shall be made known what you shall do.

2. And all things shall be done by common consent in the church, by much prayer and faith, for all things you shall receive by faith. Amen.

Monument at the grave site of John Whitmer.

D&C 25:9–10—This revelation serves to remind all of us to place spiritual things in the highest priority, remain humble, and honor our covenants, so that we may hope in faith and courage for the blessings of the Spirit.

D&C 25:11–13—These words are the source of never-ending inspiration for those among the Saints who give of their musical talents to edify and bless the lives of the Lord's children. All who participate in musical offerings of a spiritual character are uplifted to know that the Lord considers such righteous expressions a prayer that will result in the bestowal of blessings. The Church hymnal, to which Emma contributed her service, along with the assistance of W. W. Phelps, was finally published early in 1836 and contained 90 hymns. Many of the hymns included in Emma's selection are perennial favorites even today: "The Spirit of God like a Fire Is Burning," "Redeemer of Israel," "Gently Raise the Sacred Strain," "Earth with Her Ten Thousand Flowers," "How Firm a Foundation," "He Died! The Great Redeemer Died," and "I Know That My Redeemer Lives."

D&C 25:14—Pride erects a barrier to blessings of the Spirit. Meekness dissolves that barrier and invites an influx of glory and joy that can come only through covenant valor and submission to the will of God.

D&C 25:14—It is the will of the Lord that we cultivate relationships of support and encouragement in our families. The relationship of devotion and love reflected in the example of Joseph and Emma and their children can radiate in our own families as well, provided we cultivate wise spiritual priorities, practice unselfishness and compassion, maintain a productive balance in the allocation of our time and energies, and keep the commandments of God.

Section 26 Background—Given to the Prophet Joseph Smith, Oliver Cowdery, and John Whitmer in July 1830 at Harmony, Susquehanna County, Pennsylvania. John Whitmer was at the time living with Joseph and Emma and assisting in collating and arranging the revelations that had been given to that point.

D&C 26:2—Common consent involved not only sustaining Church leaders, but also giving consent to doctrinal and organizational decisions, such as occurred in relation to the formal organization of the Church on April 6, 1830. This brief revelation on common consent was the scriptural foundation upon which this doctrine was unfolded, line upon line and precept upon precept, in the seasons to come. Common consent confirms and sustains the moral agency of man—anchored in prayer and faith, it ennobles citizenship within the kingdom of God by recognizing the value of each individual in the family of God. When we affirm our sustaining vote for our leaders, we essentially make a solemn covenant with the Lord to extend our loyalty and support to them in the spirit of the united quest to work together in the building up of the kingdom of God.

SECTION 27

1. Listen to the voice of Jesus Christ, your Lord, your God, and your Redeemer, whose word is quick and powerful.

2. For, behold, I say unto you, that it mattereth not what ye shall eat, or what ye shall drink, when ye partake of the sacrament, if it so be that ye do it with an eye single to my glory; remembering unto the Father my body which was laid down for you, and my blood which was shed for the remission of your sins:

3. Wherefore, a commandment I give unto you, that you shall not purchase wine, neither strong drink of your enemies:

4. Wherefore, you shall partake of none, except it is made new among you; yea, in this my Father's kingdom which shall be built up on the earth.

5. Behold, this is wisdom in me: wherefore, marvel not, for the hour cometh that I will drink of the fruit of the vine with you on the earth, and with Moroni, whom I have sent unto you to reveal the Book of Mormon, containing the fulness of my everlasting gospel, to whom I have committed the keys of the record of the stick of Ephraim;

6. And also with Elias, to whom I have committed the keys of bringing to pass the restoration of all things, spoken by the mouth of all the holy prophets since the world began, concerning the last days:

7. And also John the son of Zacharias, which Zacharias he (Elias) visited and gave promise that he should have a son, and his name should be John, and he should be filled with the spirit of Elias;

8. Which John I have sent unto you, my servants, Joseph Smith, jun., and Oliver Cowdery, to ordain you unto this first priesthood which you have received, that you might be called and ordained even as Aaron:

9. And also Elijah, unto whom I

NEWEL KNIGHT

Newel Knight was born September 13, 1800, at Windham County, Vermont, son of Joseph Knight. Newel became acquainted with Joseph Smith when the Prophet was boarding with the Knight family in Colesville, New York, in 1826. During the month of April 1830, Joseph miraculously rescued Newel from the effects of an evil influence—an event the Prophet characterized as "the first miracle that was done in the Church" (HC 1:83). Newel was baptized in May 1830 and remained ever faithful to the Church. Persecution and hardship were his lot during two sojourns in Missouri and later in Nauvoo. His first wife, Sally, died because of the suffering she experienced in Missouri. While en route West with the Saints fleeing from the mobs, Newel, beset with a lung disorder, died in the Iowa Territory on January 11, 1847, leaving his second wife, Lydia, with their seven young children. In speaking of Newel and his brother, Joseph Knight, Jr., the Prophet stated that he had recorded their names "in the Book of the Law of the Lord with unspeakable delight, for they are my friends" (HC 5:125).

Section 27 Background—The Prophet recorded in his journal: "Early in the month of August [1830] Newel Knight and his wife paid us a visit at my place in Harmony, Pennsylvania; and as neither his wife nor mine had been as yet confirmed, it was proposed that we should confirm them, and partake together of the Sacrament, before he and his wife should leave us. In order to prepare for this I set out to procure some wine for the occasion, but had gone only a short distance when I was met by a heavenly messenger, and received the following revelation [Section 27]. . . . In obedience to the above commandment, we prepared some wine of our own making. . . . The Spirit of the Lord was poured out upon us, we praised the Lord God, and rejoiced exceedingly" (HC 1:106, 108).

D&C 27:2—It is wisdom in the Lord that the significance of one's spiritual attitude in partaking of the sacrament overshadows the nature of the emblems to be used. Elder Charles W. Penrose described this attitude in eloquent terms on May 1, 1880, in the Salt Lake Tabernacle:

> . . . we come together to renew our covenants, to make manifest before God and one another our feelings and desires in relation to these matters, to witness to the heavens and the earth that we are called to be Saints, that we have come out of the world, that we have separated ourselves from that which is evil, and dedicated and consecrated ourselves to the service of God . . . that we will place in our estimation first the kingdom of God and his righteousness with the hope and belief that if we do this all other things shall be added unto us as we need them. (JD 22:83.)

D&C 27:5—In an extraordinary view of the glories to come, the Lord opens up to Joseph Smith a vision of the sacramental ordinance as it will occur in some future day—with the Savior presiding in the company of an august throng including all the noble prophets of former times. The lesson of this revelation might be that we think of this vision during the sacrament, from time to time, and imagine how fulfilling it would be if the Savior Himself were present to receive our humble expression of worship and covenant renewal. Then we can remind ourselves that He is, in fact, present through the operation of the Spirit, for He has promised: ". . . and, lo, I am with you alway, even unto the end of the world" (Matt. 28:20; see also D&C 31:13; 100:12; 105:41).

D&C 27:8—It was through the administration of John the Baptist and the Apostles Peter, James, and John that Joseph Smith and Oliver Cowdery were privileged to receive the keys of the Aaronic and Melchizedek priesthoods several months prior to this revelation. Though the exact date of the appearance of these three Apostles is not recorded in the writings of the Church, it most likely occurred prior to the end of May 1829.

have committed the keys of the power of turning the hearts of the fathers to the children, and the hearts of the children to the fathers, that the whole earth may not be smitten with a curse:

10. And also with Joseph and Jacob, and Isaac, and Abraham, your fathers, by whom the promises remain;

11. And also with Michael, or Adam, the father of all, the prince of all, the ancient of days.

12. And also with Peter, and James, and John, whom I have sent unto you, by whom I have ordained you and confirmed you to be apostles, and especial witnesses of my name, and bear the keys of your ministry, and of the same things which I revealed unto them:

13. Unto whom I have committed the keys of my kingdom, and a dispensation of the gospel for the last times; and for the fulness of times, in the which I will gather together in one all things, both which are in heaven, and which are on earth:

14. And also with all those whom my Father hath given me out of the world:

15. Wherefore, lift up your hearts and rejoice, and gird up your loins, and take upon you my whole armor, that ye may be able to withstand the evil day, having done all ye may be able to stand.

16. Stand, therefore, having your loins girt about with truth, having on the breastplate of righteousness, and your feet shod with the preparation of the gospel of peace, which I have sent mine angels to commit unto you,

17. Taking the shield of faith wherewith ye shall be able to quench all the fiery darts of the wicked;

18. And take the helmet of salvation, and the sword of my Spirit, which I will pour out upon you, and my word which I reveal unto you, and be agreed as touching all things whatsoever ye ask of me, and be faithful until I come, and ye shall be caught up, that where I am ye shall be also. Amen.

D&C 27:15—The compelling symbolism in this passage is a reminder that the gospel of Jesus Christ is a defense and a security for the Saints. It also projects onto our minds a unique kind of uniform of valor that equips the individual with the tools of effective missionary work and service. The individual takes upon himself or herself truth, righteousness, the gospel of peace, faith, salvation, the Spirit, and the word of God—all as vital aspects of the "godly walk and conversation" (D&C 20:69) that the children of God are to acquire and demonstrate.

In his epistle to the Ephesians concerning putting on "the whole armour of God" (Eph. 6:11), the Apostle Paul also refers to "loins girt about with truth . . . the breastplate of righteousness . . . feet shod with the preparation of the gospel of peace . . . the shield of faith . . . the helmet of salvation, and the sword of the Spirit" (Eph. 6:14–17). Though we aspire to embrace and live the gospel of peace, we are obliged to ply our course through the valleys of war—for the battle to overcome evil by means of good has been a reality from as early as the premortal sphere. Discipleship is not a passive enterprise. The lifestyle associated with the kingdom of God is one of proactive preparation, training, and service. The Saints of God are ever at war, for the evil one and his minions never sleep and never desist in their dark designs to thwart the plan of salvation. The commission of the Saints is to be ever watchful, ever willing to move forward in the strength of the Lord against the forces that threaten the family and contravene the commitment to live "after the manner of happiness" (2 Ne. 5:27).

The ultimate victory is destined to belong to the Father and Son, who uphold the principles of righteousness, valor, and spiritual liberty forever. Along the pathway to that victory advance the heroes of the covenant who put on the armor of God and move forward in the strength of the Lord. Faith, truth, following the Spirit—these are the mighty weapons of spiritual conquest. Virtue, purity, integrity, godlike discourse and deportment—these are the additional armaments that ensure victory. Ultimately the qualities of discipleship that will prevail over the forces of evil—including overcoming the internal aberrations of worldly pride and self-centeredness—are *inner* qualities, as the Prophet Joseph Smith taught us from the confines of his squalid cell at Liberty Jail:

> Let thy bowels also be full of charity towards all men, and to the household of faith, and let virtue garnish thy thoughts unceasingly; then shall thy confidence wax strong in the presence of God; and the doctrine of the priesthood shall distil upon thy soul as the dews from heaven. The Holy Ghost shall be thy constant companion, and thy scepter an unchanging scepter of righteousness and truth; and thy dominion shall be an everlasting dominion, and without compulsory means it shall flow unto thee forever and ever. (D&C 121:45–46.)

SECTION 28

1. Behold, I say unto thee, Oliver, that it shall be given unto thee, that thou shalt be heard by the church in all things whatsoever thou shalt teach them by the Comforter, concerning the revelations and commandments which I have given.

2. But, behold, verily, verily, I say unto thee, no one shall be appointed to receive commandments and revelations in this church, excepting my servant Joseph Smith, jun., for he receiveth them even as Moses;

3. And thou shalt be obedient unto the things which I shall give unto him, even as Aaron, to declare faithfully the commandments and the revelations, with power and authority unto the church.

4. And if thou art led at any time by the Comforter, to speak or teach, or at all times by the way of commandment unto the church, thou mayest do it.

5. But thou shalt not write by way of commandment, but by wisdom:

6. And thou shalt not command him who is at thy head, and at the head of the church,

7. For I have given him the keys of the mysteries, and the revelations which are sealed, until I shall appoint unto them another in his stead.

8. And now, behold, I say unto you, that you shall go unto the Lamanites and preach my gospel unto them; and inasmuch as they receive thy teachings, thou shalt cause my church to be established among them, and thou shalt have revelations, but write them not by way of commandment.

9. And now, behold, I say unto you, that it is not revealed, and no man knoweth where the city shall be built, but it shall be given hereafter. Behold, I say unto you that it shall be on the borders by the Lamanites.

10. Thou shalt not leave this place until after the conference, and my servant Joseph shall be appointed to preside over the conference by the voice of it, and what he saith to thee thou shalt tell.

11. And again, thou shalt take thy brother, Hiram Page, between him and thee alone, and tell him that those things which he hath written

Section 28 Background—In September 1830, Joseph could no longer depend on the protection of his father-in-law, Isaac Hale, against the rising threat of persecution; he therefore accepted the invitation to live with the Peter Whitmer, Sr., family in Fayette, New York. During this time, the Prophet learned about Hiram Page's claims of receiving revelations by means of a certain stone. Newel Knight described the circumstances in his journal: "[Page] had managed to get up some discussions of feeling among the brethren by giving revelations concerning the government of the Church and other matters, which he claimed to have received through the medium of a stone he possessed. . . . Even Oliver Cowdery and the Whitmer family had given heed to them. . . . Joseph was perplexed and scarcely knew how to meet this new exigency. That night I occupied the same room that he did and the greater part of the night was spent in prayer and supplication. After much labor with these brethren they were convinced of their error, and confessed the same, renouncing [Page's] revelations as not being of God" (*RPJS*, 39–40). Section 28 identifies clearly one of the first principles of remaining on the straight and narrow and deflecting the deceptions of the adversary: follow the prophet.

D&C 28:2–7—By divine calling and design, the Prophet Joseph holds the keys to the mysteries and only he receives revelation for the Church; here it reveals that Joseph Smith is of the same stature as Moses in receiving revelation for the Church of his day. The lesson for Oliver to learn is to expound the revealed word of God in the spirit of wisdom under inspiration from the Comforter. He is not to speak by way of commandment—for this is the divine prerogative of the Lord Himself, acting through the office of His chosen prophet.

D&C 28:8–9—Oliver is to continue with his commission to expound and preach the gospel by undertaking a mission among the Lamanites. The Lord declares that the location of the city of Zion has not yet been revealed to anyone—a reference that refutes the claims of Hiram Page that he has been given this information through revelation. The Lord states only that the city of Zion will be built in the borders by the Lamanites. In a later revelation dated July 20, 1831, the Lord will reveal that the city of Zion is to be built in Missouri (see D&C 57:1–2).

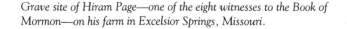

Grave site of Hiram Page—one of the eight witnesses to the Book of Mormon—on his farm in Excelsior Springs, Missouri.

from that stone, are not of me, and that Satan deceiveth him;

12. For, behold, these things have not been appointed unto him, neither shall anything be appointed unto any of this church contrary to the church covenants.

13. For all things must be done in order, and by common consent in the church, by the prayer of faith.

14. And thou shalt assist to settle all these things according to the covenants of the church before thou shalt take thy journey among the Lamanites.

15. And it shall be given thee from the time thou shalt go, until the time thou shalt return, what thou shalt do.

16. And thou must open thy mouth at all times declaring my gospel with the sound of rejoicing. Amen.

SECTION 29

1. Listen to the voice of Jesus Christ, your Redeemer, the Great I AM, whose arm of mercy hath atoned for your sins;

2. Who will gather his people even as a hen gathereth her chickens under her wings, even as many as will hearken to my voice and humble themselves before me, and call upon me in mighty prayer.

3. Behold, verily, verily, I say unto you, that at this time your sins are forgiven you, therefore ye receive these things; but remember to sin no more, lest perils shall come upon you.

4. Verily, I say unto you, that ye are chosen out of the world to declare my gospel with the sound of rejoicing, as with the voice of a trump:

5. Lift up your hearts and be glad, for I am in your midst, and am your advocate with the Father; and it is his good will to give you the kingdom;

6. And as it is written, Whatsoever ye shall ask in faith, being united in prayer according to my command, ye shall receive;

D&C 28:13—It is the pattern of Church governance instituted of the Lord that the prayerful consent of the faithful shall be acknowledged and honored. What is upheld by the vote of the Saints of God is much more likely to be secured within the bounds of propriety that have been set by the Lord. In a 1913 general epistle to the Church, the First Presidency stated:

> From the days of Hiram Page (Doc. and Cov., Sec. 28), at different periods there have been manifestations from delusive spirits to members of the Church. . . . When visions, dreams, tongues, prophecy, impressions or any extraordinary gift of inspiration, convey something out of harmony with accepted revelations of the Church or contrary to the decisions of its constituted authorities, Latter-day Saints may know that it is not of God, no matter how plausible it may appear. . . .
>
> Be not led by any spirit or influence that discredits established authority and contradicts true scientific principles and discoveries, or leads away from the direct revelations of God for the government of the Church. . . . (First Presidency Joseph F. Smith, Anthon H. Lund, Charles W. Penrose, "A Warning Voice," *IE*, September 1913, 16:1148–49.)

D&C 28:15–16—The Doctrine and Covenants gives resounding promises to those proclaiming the gospel that they shall know by the Spirit how to proceed "in the very hour" of need (D&C 24:18; 84:85; 100:6; 124:97)—even "in the very moment" (D&C 24:6; 100:6). The Lord will assist us if we will just open our mouths. The application is clear: Start a conversation and turn it into a teaching moment about the gospel. Remember that the Lord will help you.

Section 29 Background—Given in September 1830 in the presence of six elders, some days before the convening of the second conference of the Church in the home of Peter Whitmer (see *HC* 1:111–115).

D&C 29:1–3—Scarcely six months previous to this revelation the Book of Mormon was published to the world. Therein the words of the resurrected Savior are preserved as He used multiple times the same symbolism for the gathering just expressed: ". . . how oft have I gathered you as a hen gathereth her chickens under her wings. . . ." What is conveyed by this expression? The compassion of a parent; the mercy of a loving care-giver; the call of one who nourishes and protects. What is our role in this scene? To listen; to be humble; to pray; to repent; to come unto the Lord.

D&C 29:4–7—The gathering is fulfilled through the process of missionary work. Missionary work is accomplished by the power of faith. What is asked in faith by the Saints of God—particularly as they are united in purpose as a community of disciples devoted to the purposes of the Lord in building the Kingdom—will be granted. Many people are ready and waiting to be gathered. We are to thrust in our sickle with our might (see D&C 4:4; 31:5).

7. And ye are called to bring to pass the gathering of mine elect, for mine elect hear my voice and harden not their hearts;

8. Wherefore the decree hath gone forth from the Father, that they shall be gathered in unto one place upon the face of this land, to prepare their hearts and be prepared in all things against the day when tribulation and desolation are sent forth upon the wicked;

9. For the hour is nigh and the day soon at hand when the earth is ripe: and all the proud, and they that do wickedly, shall be as stubble, and I will burn them up, saith the Lord of Hosts, that wickedness shall not be upon the earth;

10. For the hour is nigh, and that which was spoken by mine apostles must be fulfilled; for as they spoke so shall it come to pass;

11. For I will reveal myself from heaven with power and great glory, with all the hosts thereof, and dwell in righteousness with men on earth a thousand years, and the wicked shall not stand.

12. And again, verily, verily, I say unto you, and it hath gone forth in a firm decree, by the will of the Father, that mine apostles, the Twelve which were with me in my ministry at Jerusalem, shall stand at my right hand at the day of my coming in a pillar of fire, being clothed with robes of righteousness, with crowns upon their heads, in glory even as I am, to judge the whole house of Israel, even as many as have loved me and kept my commandments, and none else;

13. For a trump shall sound both long and loud, even as upon Mount Sinai, and all the earth shall quake, and they shall come forth: yea, even the dead which died in me, to receive a crown of righteousness, and to be clothed upon, even as I am, to be with me, that we may be one.

14. But, behold, I say unto you, that before this great day shall come, the sun shall be darkened, and the moon shall be turned into blood, and the stars shall fall from heaven, and there shall be greater signs in heaven above, and in the earth beneath;

15. And there shall be weeping and wailing among the hosts of men;

HIRAM PAGE

Hiram Page was born in 1800 in Vermont. In his travels as a medical practitioner, he became acquainted with the Peter Whitmer family in Fayette, New York. He married Peter's oldest daughter, Catherine, on November 10, 1825. Through the Whitmers, Hiram learned of the mission of Joseph Smith and eventually became one of the eight witnesses of the Book of Mormon. He was baptized on April 11, 1830. Prior to the Church conference on September 26, 1830, Hiram came into possession of a small stone that he claimed allowed him to receive revelations—for example, the location of the New Jerusalem. Section 28 constituted a firm rebuke of his claims, which he recanted at the September conference. Hiram and his family later suffered unspeakable abuse in the Missouri persecutions. Having lost his faith in the leadership of the Prophet Joseph, Hiram was eventually excommunicated, though he was ever true to his testimony of the Book of Mormon. He died on his farm near Excelsior Springs, Ray County, Missouri, on August 12, 1852.

D&C 29:9–11—The Second Coming of the Savior will usher in the Millennium. At His first coming, the Savior was born into humble circumstances and cloaked in modesty. By contrast, when He returns at His Second Coming, cloaked in the brilliance of His red robes of judgment (see D&C 133:48) and surrounded by the consuming glory of His presence, He will instill in all the inhabitants of the world in an instant the awe of His majesty. All will proclaim His Saviorhood—either by constraint or by joyful witnessing.

D&C 29:12—The Father has given unto the Son the office of Supreme Judge of all mankind. The Twelve Apostles of the Lord called during His mortal ministry will judge the whole house of Israel. Serving under their direction, the twelve Nephite disciples will judge the Nephite people (1 Ne. 12:9–10; 3 Ne. 27:27; Morm. 3:19). Many others may be called into service to participate in the all-encompassing judgment process under the direction of the Lord. Unto the Savior is left the awesome task of serving as the Almighty Judge over the entire procedure, including the judgments that fall upon the heads of those who have rejected His name and His gospel plan of redemption.

D&C 29:14—The signs that precede the Second Coming are manifold and unmistakable. They have been documented in great detail in the scriptures and the discourses of the prophets. The signs of the times comprise a sequence of milestones that bespeak the ordered consummation of God's design for the earth.

Will the great day of the Lord be one of joy or sorrow? The Prophet Joseph Smith gave this warning: "I will prophesy that the signs of the coming of the Son of Man are already commenced. One pestilence will desolate after another. We shall soon have war and bloodshed. The moon will be turned to blood. I testify of these things, and that the coming of the Son of Man is nigh, even at your doors. If our souls and our bodies are not looking forth for the coming of the Son of Man; and after we are dead, if we are not looking forth, we shall be among those who are calling for the rocks to fall upon them" (HC 3:390).

To avoid this condition, it behooves each of us to be prepared, to come unto Christ and be caught up in the process of being "perfected in him" (Moroni 10:32)—infused with the kind of hope and faith defined by Paul: "For what is our hope, or joy, or crown of rejoicing? Are not even ye in the presence of our Lord Jesus Christ at his coming? For ye are our glory and joy" (1 Thess. 2:19–20). Those who are prepared will rejoice and glorify God with songs of everlasting praise and thanksgiving on the day of the Lord's coming. Those who fail to prepare will bewail their chosen fate, "for behold, my blood shall not cleanse them if they hear me not" (D&C 29:17).

16. And there shall be a great hailstorm sent forth to destroy the crops of the earth;

17. And it shall come to pass, because of the wickedness of the world, that I will take vengeance upon the wicked, for they will not repent; for the cup of mine indignation is full; for behold my blood shall not cleanse them if they hear me not.

18. Wherefore, I the Lord God will send forth flies upon the face of the earth, which shall take hold of the inhabitants thereof, and shall eat their flesh, and shall cause maggots to come in upon them;

19. And their tongues shall be stayed that they shall not utter against me; and their flesh shall fall from off their bones, and their eyes from their sockets:

20. And it shall come to pass that the beasts of the forest, and the fowls of the air shall devour them up;

21. And the great and abominable church, which is the whore of all the earth, shall be cast down by devouring fire, according as it is spoken by the mouth of Ezekiel the prophet, who spoke of these things, which have not come to pass, but surely must, as I live, for abominations shall not reign.

22. And again, verily, verily, I say unto you, that when the thousand years are ended, and men again begin to deny their God, then will I spare the earth but for a little season;

23. And the end shall come, and the heaven and the earth shall be consumed and pass away, and there shall be a new heaven and a new earth,

24. For all old things shall pass away, and all things shall become new, even the heaven and the earth, and all the fulness thereof, both men and beasts, the fowls of the air, and the fishes of the sea;

25. And not one hair, neither mote, shall be lost, for it is the workmanship of mine hand.

26. But, behold, verily I say unto you, before the earth shall pass away, Michael, mine archangel, shall sound his trump, and then shall all the dead awake, for their graves shall be opened, and they shall come forth; yea, even all.

27. And the righteous shall be gathered on my right hand unto eternal life; and the wicked on my left hand will I be ashamed to own before the Father;

28. Wherefore I will say unto them—Depart from me, ye cursed, into

D&C 29:23, 27—An ultimate division will take place at the final judgment. It behooves all of us to be mindful of the great partition at the time of judgment when our thoughts, desires, deeds, and actions will determine on which side of the Savior we will find ourselves. Let us honor our covenants in such a way that the Savior will be pleased to welcome us among the obedient and faithful.

D&C 29:28—The image of the fate of the damned is dreadful and appalling, yet they have exercised their agency to their own condemnation, and the judgments of the Lord are just. How essential it is that the messengers of Zion warn the world against the patterns of evil that will result in such an outcome.

The great judgment of all of God's children will be accomplished through justice and mercy, encompassing all the details of our lives. President John Taylor explains how this will be done: "My understanding of the thing is, that God has made each man a register within himself, and each man can read his own register, so far as he enjoys his perfect faculties. This can be easily comprehended. . . . It is written that Jesus will judge not after the sight of the eye, or after the hearing of the ear, but with righteousness shall he judge the poor, and reprove with equity the meek of the earth. It is not because somebody has seen things, or heard anything by which a man will be judged and condemned, but it is because that record that is written by the man himself in the tablets of his own mind—that record that cannot lie—will in that day be unfolded before God and angels, and those who shall sit as judges" (*JD* 11:77, 79).

The "Stu-Boy" Bridge over the Vermilion River, which got its name from an incident involving Parley P. Pratt. While laboring as one of four missionaries called to teach the Lamanites, Parley was arrested while preaching in the home of Simeon Carter in Amherst, Ohio (see p. 135 for a photo of Carter's home). Parley spent the night in jail, thanked arresting agent Sheriff Elias Peabody for a delicious breakfast, and then started to run to catch up with the other three missionaries. Sheriff Peabody was astonished that Parley began to run, and Parley then challenged him to a race. At that point, Sheriff Peabody ordered his large and ferocious bulldog, "Stu-Boy," to seize Parley P. Pratt. Parley tricked the dog by sending him into the woods, and the sheriff promptly followed the dog. Parley P. Pratt ran along a back road, crossed the Vermilion River over the bridge pictured here, and ran six miles further through mud and rain before he caught up with his companions. That night, he preached a sermon to a capacity crowd.

everlasting fire, prepared for the devil and his angels.

29. And now, behold, I say unto you, never at any time, have I declared from mine own mouth that they should return, for where I am they cannot come, for they have no power;

30. But remember that all my judgments are not given unto men; and as the words have gone forth out of my mouth even so shall they be fulfilled, that the first shall be last, and that the last shall be first in all things whatsoever I have created by the word of my power, which is the power of my Spirit;

31. For by the power of my Spirit created I them; yea, all things both spiritual and temporal:

32. Firstly, spiritual—secondly, temporal, which is the beginning of my work; and again, firstly, temporal—and secondly, spiritual, which is the last of my work:

33. Speaking unto you that you may naturally understand, but unto myself my works have no end, neither beginning; but it is given unto you that ye may understand, because ye have asked it of me and are agreed.

34. Wherefore, verily I say unto you, that all things unto me are spiritual, and not at any time have I given unto you a law which was temporal; neither any man, nor the children of men; neither Adam, your father, whom I created.

35. Behold, I gave unto him that he should be an agent unto himself; and I gave unto him commandment, but no temporal commandment gave I unto him, for my commandments are spiritual; they are not natural nor temporal, neither carnal nor sensual.

36. And it came to pass, that Adam, being tempted of the devil (for, behold, the devil was before Adam, for he rebelled against me, saying, Give me thine honor, which is my power: and also a third part of the hosts of heaven turned he away from me because of their agency;

37. And they were thrust down, and thus came the devil and his angels.

38. And, behold, there is a place prepared for them from the beginning, which place is hell:

39. And it must needs be that the devil should tempt the children of men, or they could not be agents unto themselves, for if they never should have bitter, they could not know the sweet)

40. Wherefore, it came to pass that the devil tempted Adam, and he partook of the forbidden fruit and transgressed the commandment, wherein he became subject to the

D&C 29:34—The design of God is wholly spiritual in its compass and essence. It extends far above and beyond the earthly and the temporal to embrace that which is eternal and everlasting in its nature and purpose. When the Lord declared it His work and glory to "bring to pass the immortality and eternal life of man" (Moses 1:39), He defined the scope and His mission in spiritual terms—for that which is spiritual partakes of the nature of God, His glory and celestial perfection. Through the gospel plan, men and women would have the opportunity to transcend their carnal nature and be "reborn" into a state of redemption and sanctification, eventually to rise once again to an immortal state—spiritual and eternal in nature. Thus, as verse 32 states, the transition is from spiritual to temporal, and then finally from temporal to spiritual. The application for our lives is clear: As His children, we are to transcend the temporal and aspire to the spiritual. God's laws are spiritual laws, for they define our pathway into the realm of spirituality. President Seymour B. Young explains how to discover the spiritual meaning of our lives:

> The all-important thing in life, after all, is to find a place in the universal scheme of things, for all the acts of our lives. There is a spiritual meaning of all human acts and earthly events. The Lord has specifically declared "not at any time have I given unto you a law which was temporal." It is the business of man to find the spiritual meaning of earthly things. I pay my tithing, for many reasons, perhaps, but the one great reason is that by so doing, I am advancing this great cause, this great purpose, this great plan to which I am committed . . . I keep the Word of Wisdom also, because by so doing I make myself an abler co-laborer with God in carrying onward this great work. . . . So, every act of man, the moment it is fitted into the great plan, the plan of salvation, receives spiritual coinage, and passes from hand to hand, from mind to mind, to accomplish the great work of God. (CR, April 1922, 96–91.)

D&C 29:39—The devil and his hosts tempt mankind. There is a power that trumps such temptation, neutralizing it and rendering it ineffectual. That power is Christ. Declared James: "Blessed is the man that endureth temptation: for when he is tried, he shall receive the crown of life, which the Lord hath promised to them that love him" (James 1:12).

will of the devil, because he yielded unto temptation.

41. Wherefore I the Lord God, caused that he should be cast out from the Garden of Eden, from my presence, because of his transgression, wherein he became spiritually dead, which is the first death, even that same death, which is the last death, which is spiritual, which shall be pronounced upon the wicked when I shall say—Depart, ye cursed.

42. But, behold, I say unto you, that I, the Lord God, gave unto Adam and unto his seed, that they should not die as to the temporal death, until I the Lord God should send forth angels to declare unto them repentance and redemption, through faith on the name of mine Only Begotten Son.

43. And thus did I, the Lord God, appoint unto man the days of his probation; that by his natural death he might be raised in immortality unto eternal life, even as many as would believe;

44. And they that believe not unto eternal damnation, for they cannot be redeemed from their spiritual fall, because they repent not;

45. For they will love darkness rather than light, and their deeds are evil, and they receive their wages of whom they list to obey.

46. But behold, I say unto you, that little children are redeemed from the foundation of the world through mine Only Begotten:

47. Wherefore, they cannot sin, for power is not given unto Satan to tempt little children, until they begin to become accountable before me;

48. For it is given unto them even as I will, according to mine own pleasure, that great things may be required at the hand of their fathers.

49. And, again, I say unto you, that whoso having knowledge, have I not commanded to repent?

50. And he that hath no understanding, it remaineth in me to do according as it is written. And now I declare no more unto you at this time. Amen.

D&C 29:43—Each of us has at one time asked, "What is the purpose of life?" All yearn to understand why it is we find ourselves where we are in the circumstances of life and mortality. The gospel of Jesus Christ teaches that this life is but an interim act of a greater drama that began in the premortal realm and will transition to a successive phase that holds out the promise of enduring glory and joy. We have come to receive a body and pass through a probationary state in which our agency allows us to demonstrate allegiance to the King of Heaven and obedience to His laws and commandments. This life is but a brief hour or two as measured by the clock of eternity—but what stakes there are for us in this mortal time!

In the councils of heaven before the foundation of the earth, God declared to those with Him, concerning the spirit children destined to embark on their mortal journey: "And we will prove them herewith, to see if they will do all things whatsoever the Lord their God shall command them; And they who keep their first estate shall be added upon; and they who keep not their first estate shall not have glory in the same kingdom with those who keep their first estate; and they who keep their second estate shall have glory added upon their heads for ever and ever" (Abr. 3:25–26). Now is the time to prepare to meet God. The successful journey through this probationary state is the main purpose of mortality.

D&C 29:46—The Book of Mormon contains the precious epistle of Mormon to his son Moroni elucidating the doctrine that little children, before they reach the age of accountability, are redeemed through the Atonement of Christ. The Prophet Joseph Smith stated: "And I also beheld that all children who die before they arrive at the years of accountability are saved in the celestial kingdom of heaven" (D&C 137:10; see also Matt. 19:14; Mosiah 15:25; D&C 45:58; 68:25; 93:38). Daniel H. Ludlow also confirms: "The Church and its prophets also teach that little children who die in infancy or childhood come forth in the resurrection in the same physical form they possessed at the time of death. Righteous parents of such children will have the privilege in the resurrection of rearing these children to the full state of the spirits" (CYSNT).

D&C 29:50—This verse makes reference to those who can't understand the law because of mental deficiencies. According to Joseph Smith, God will judge us by our means of obtaining intelligence as well as by the laws we have, our facilities for obtaining correct information, and His inscrutable designs in relationship to the human family. We do not know all His ways of judging, but we will all have to confess that He has done right.

SECTION 30

1. Behold, I say unto you, David, that you have feared man and have not relied on me for strength as you ought:

2. But your mind has been on the things of the earth more than on the things of me, your Maker, and the ministry whereunto you have been called; and you have not given heed unto my Spirit, and to those who were set over you, but have been persuaded by those whom I have not commanded:

3. Wherefore, you are left to inquire for yourself, at my hand, and ponder upon the things which you have received.

4. And your home shall be at your father's house, until I give unto you further commandments. And you shall attend to the ministry in the church, and before the world, and in the regions round about. Amen.

5. Behold, I say unto you, Peter, that you shall take your journey with your brother Oliver, for the time has come that it is expedient in me that you shall open your mouth to declare my gospel; therefore, fear not, but give heed unto the words and advice of your brother, which he shall give you.

6. And be you afflicted in all his afflictions, ever lifting up your heart unto me in prayer, and faith, for his and your deliverance: for I have given unto him power to build up my church among the Lamanites:

7. And none have I appointed to be his counselor over him in the church, concerning church matters, except it is his brother, Joseph Smith, jun.

8. Wherefore, give heed unto these things and be diligent in keeping my commandments, and you shall be blessed unto eternal life. Amen.

9. Behold, I say unto you, my servant John, that thou shalt commence from this time forth to proclaim my gospel, as with the voice of a trump.

10. And your labor shall be at your brother Philip Burrough's, and in that region round about; yea, wherever you can be heard, until I command you to go from hence.

11. And your whole labor shall be in Zion, with all your soul, from henceforth; yea, you shall ever open your mouth in my cause, not fearing what man can do, for I am with you. Amen.

Section 30 Background—Given through the Prophet Joseph Smith at Fayette, New York, in September 1830 to David Whitmer, Peter Whitmer, Jr., and John Whitmer, following the three-day conference of the Church, and prior to the dispersal of the attending priesthood leaders (see HC 1:115–116).

D&C 30:2–3—The priorities we follow in life establish our level of worthiness to receive the guidance of the Lord. If we follow the world, we are left to fend for ourselves among the competing and dissonant voices that invoke our allegiance in a godless sphere. On the other hand, if we obediently follow the Lord and depend fully on His strength, then we are lifted up on the wings of the Spirit to a higher view of life's purpose and meaning.

David Whitmer is reminded that the work of the priesthood is guided by a two-fold compass: heeding the whisperings of the Spirit and abiding by the counsel of the Lord's appointed leaders. When we tune out the Spirit and seek alignment with those who operate outside the boundaries of the kingdom of God, we are consigned to struggle on our own. David Whitmer was to learn this painful lesson. Though he fell away from his priesthood duties, however, he never recanted his testimony of the Book of Mormon.

D&C 30:6–7—The work of the Lord among the Lamanites is to commence according to the promises given in the pages of the Book of Mormon, published only six months before this revelation. One thinks of the mandate given to the sons of Mosiah to reach out to their contemporaries among the Lamanites of their day, for "they [the sons of Mosiah] were desirous that salvation should be declared to every creature, for they could not bear that any human soul should perish; yea, even the very thoughts that any soul should endure endless torment did cause them to quake and tremble" (Mosiah 28:3). The Lord gives a blessing to Peter Whitmer, Jr., just as He had done to Oliver Cowdery (D&C 28:8), to follow in the footsteps of the sons of Mosiah and carry the gospel of Jesus Christ to the Native Americans of their day. Moreover, Peter was instructed to follow the lead of Oliver, who answered to no priesthood leader other than the appointed Prophet of the Restoration, Joseph Smith.

D&C 30:11—The counsel to John Whitmer applies to all who are engaged in the work of spreading the good news of the gospel: we are to work with our full devotion to the cause—"all your soul"—holding back nothing of our talents and testimony to invite people to come unto Christ. When we open our mouths in the cause of Zion without fear, the Spirit prompts our message and conveys its truth to the hearts of those who seek after truth (see D&C 100:5–8).

The grave site of David Whitmer near Richmond, Missouri.

SECTION 31

1. Thomas, my son, blessed are you because of your faith in my work.

2. Behold, you have had many afflictions because of your family: nevertheless, I will bless you and your family; yea, your little ones, and the day cometh that they will believe and know the truth and be one with you in my church.

3. Lift up your heart and rejoice, for the hour of your mission is come: and your tongue shall be loosed; and you shall declare glad tidings of great joy unto this generation.

4. You shall declare the things which have been revealed to my servant, Joseph Smith, jun. You shall begin to preach from this time forth; yea, to reap in the field which is white already to be burned:

5. Therefore, thrust in your sickle with all your soul, and your sins are forgiven you, and you shall be laden with sheaves upon your back, for the laborer is worthy of his hire. Wherefore, your family shall live.

6. Behold, verily I say unto you, go from them only for a little time, and declare my word, and I will prepare a place for them;

7. Yea, I will open the hearts of the people, and they will receive you. And I will establish a church by your hand;

8. And you shall strengthen them and prepare them against the time when they shall be gathered.

9. Be patient in afflictions, revile not against those that revile. Govern your house in meekness, and be steadfast.

10. Behold, I say unto you, that you shall be a physician unto the church, but not unto the world, for they will not receive you.

11. Go your way whithersoever I will, and it shall be given you by the Comforter what you shall do, and whither you shall go.

12. Pray always, lest you enter into temptation, and lose your reward.

13. Be faithful unto the end, and lo, I am with you. These words are not of man nor of men, but of me, even Jesus Christ, your Redeemer, by the will of the Father. Amen.

THOMAS B. MARSH

Thomas B. Marsh was born November 1, 1799, in Action, Middlesex County, Massachusetts. Hungry for religious truth that accorded with the scriptures, he felt prompted to move to western New York, where he became acquainted with the mission of Joseph Smith. He was baptized by David Whitmer on September 3, 1830. A few days later he was ordained an elder and called by revelation to preach the gospel. In 1835 he was called as a member of the Quorum of the Twelve and served as president of that quorum. In 1838 an altercation between his wife and the wife of an associate led to a dispute that burgeoned into a defining rift between Thomas and his priesthood brethren. He was excommunicated on March 17, 1839. For years he pursued a career as an itinerant teacher on biblical subjects. He moved to Utah in 1857 and sought fellowship once again in the Church, being rebaptized on July 16 of that year. He passed away in Ogden in poverty and poor health in January of 1866.

Section 31 Background—Given through the Prophet Joseph Smith in September 1830 to Thomas B. Marsh just after the September conference of the Church; this section continues the Lord's instructions to carry on missionary work.

D&C 31:1, 3—To be called by name by the Lord and characterized as "my son" must have been an overwhelming experience for this new convert to the Church. He is inducted into the ranks of the Lord's missionary force without delay. The Lord has declared repentance—the universal theme of the prophets from the beginning of time—to be the central theme of missionary work, as prompted by the Holy Spirit.

D&C 31:5—In the space of but a few words we see conjoined the elements of a divine covenant formulation: When we serve with full devotion, our sins will be forgiven and we will harvest the promised blessings of the Lord for ourselves and our families. Sacrifice in building the kingdom of God brings choice blessings. The mission of the Church has always been the same: to carry the gospel message with devotion and perseverance throughout the world, to labor without cease in the task of strengthening families and perfecting the Saints, and to build and operate the holy temples of the Lord on behalf of the living and the dead.

D&C 31:7—Missionary work is a partnership with the Almighty. It is He who opens the hearts of the people to receive His emissaries. We bring to the table the strength of the word of God through our testimony and discourse as guided by the Spirit. We gather the sheaves (verse 5), and the Lord prepares and empowers the gathering of the Saints.

D&C 31:9–13—These are words one might expect to hear pronounced upon the head of a missionary being set apart for service—except in this case, it is Jesus Christ who speaks.

Thomas B. Marsh headstone in Ogden, Utah. Because the seniority of the quorum was arranged by age, Thomas B. Marsh was the first president of the Quorum of the Twelve—but an apparent error in his birth date meant the office should have gone to David W. Patton.

SECTION 32

1. And now concerning my servant Parley P. Pratt, behold, I say unto him, that as I live I will that he shall declare my gospel and learn of me, and be meek and lowly of heart;

2. And that which I have appointed unto him is that he shall go with my servants Oliver Cowdery and Peter Whitmer, jun., into the wilderness among the Lamanites.

3. And Ziba Peterson, also, shall go with them, and I myself will go with them and be in their midst; and I am their advocate with the Father, and nothing shall prevail against them.

4. And they shall give heed to that which is written and pretend to no other revelation and they shall pray always that I may unfold the same to their understanding.

5. And they shall give heed unto these words and trifle not, and I will bless them. Amen.

SECTION 33

1. Behold, I say unto you, my servants Ezra and Northrop, open ye your ears and hearken to the voice of the Lord your God, whose word is quick and powerful, sharper than a two-edged sword, to the dividing asunder of the joints and marrow, soul and spirit; and is a discerner of

---

PARLEY P. PRATT

Parley P. Pratt was born April 12, 1807, in Burlington, Otsego County, New York. He was baptized by Oliver Cowdery in September 1830 and ordained an elder soon after that. After converting his brother Orson, he was called to serve a mission among the Lamanites in Ohio and Missouri—traveling some 1,500 miles on foot. Parley also participated in Zion's Camp. On February 21, 1835, he was ordained an Apostle and served on many missions for the Church. No stranger to persecution and tribulation, he was imprisoned unjustly for a period of time. His mortal sojourn ended when he was tragically murdered in May 1857 while on a mission in Arkansas. Ever faithful to the cause of Zion, he is considered, like Joseph and Hyrum, a martyr.

Section 32 Background—Given through the Prophet Joseph Smith to Parley P. Pratt and Ziba Peterson in October 1830. Concerning this revelation, the Prophet wrote: "At this time a great desire was manifested by several of the Elders respecting the remnants of the house of Joseph, the Lamanites, residing in the west—knowing that the purposes of God were great respecting that people, and hoping that the time had come when the promises of the Almighty in regard to them were about to be accomplished, and that they would receive the Gospel, and enjoy its blessings" (*HC* 1:118).

D&C 32:1–2—The expression "as I live" is frequently encountered in the scriptures, especially in the Old Testament, as a pronouncement of Deity to solemnize His word in the minds and hearts of His listeners. In this case, Parley P. Pratt is assured of the divine origin of his mission call. He is to learn of Christ and go in meekness and humility.

D&C 32:3—The four missionary companions have a special companion added to their circle—the Lord Himself. He gives assurance of their safety and confirms the invincible nature of their cause. He will accompany His missionaries through His influence and guidance, or, as He would say in a future revelation in 1832: "And whoso receiveth you, there I will be also, for I will go before your face. I will be on your right hand and on your left, and my Spirit shall be in your hearts, and mine angels round about you, to bear you up" (*D&C* 84:88).

D&C 32:4–5—Missionaries are to focus prayerfully on the word of God as revealed through the prophets. They will be blessed with understanding. The canon of scripture reflects a harmony of principles and values, as President John Taylor testified: "There is one thing that has always been satisfactory to my mind in relation to this Gospel—there has never been one principle revealed, at any time, but what has been instructive and in accordance with the Scriptures, which we consider to be of divine origin" (*JD* 13:226).

Section 33 Background—Given through the Prophet Joseph Smith in October 1830 at Fayette, Seneca County, New York, to Ezra Thayre and Northrop Sweet, who had sought the will of the Lord concerning their role in the Restoration. The Prophet Joseph gave this introductory statement: "The Lord, who is ever ready to instruct such as diligently seek in faith, gave the following revelation. . . [Section 33]" (*HC* 1:126).

D&C 33:1—The two recipients of this revelation are taught that the Lord can discern the thoughts and the intents of their hearts. Did the Lord detect the seeds of vacillation and doubt in these two brethren, who ultimately fell away from the faith? Nevertheless, as the Prophet Joseph Smith recorded, the Lord "is ever ready to instruct such as diligently seek in faith" (*HC* 1:126) and He thus provides marvelous instructions for them in the eleventh hour.

the thoughts and intents of the heart.

2. For verily, verily, I say unto you, that ye are called to lift up your voices as with the sound of a trump, to declare my gospel unto a crooked and perverse generation:

3. For behold, the field is white already to harvest: and it is the eleventh hour, and for the last time that I shall call laborers into my vineyard.

4. And my vineyard has become corrupted every whit; and there is none which doeth good save it be a few; and they err in many instances, because of priestcrafts, all having corrupt minds.

5. And verily, verily, I say unto you, that this church have I established and called forth out of the wilderness:

6. And even so will I gather mine elect from the four quarters of the earth, even as many as will believe in me, and hearken unto my voice:

7. Yea, verily, verily, I say unto you, that the field is white already to harvest; wherefore, thrust in your sickles, and reap with all your might, mind, and strength.

8. Open your mouths and they shall be filled, and you shall become even as Nephi of old, who journeyed from Jerusalem in the wilderness:

9. Yea, open your mouths and spare not, and you shall be laden with sheaves upon your backs, for lo, I am with you:

10. Yea, open your mouths and they shall be filled, saying—Repent, repent, and prepare ye the way of the Lord, and make his paths straight; for the kingdom of heaven is at hand;

11. Yea, repent and be baptized, every one of you, for a remission of your sins; yea, be baptized even by water, and then cometh the baptism of fire and of the Holy Ghost.

12. Behold, verily, verily, I say unto you, this is my gospel, and remember that they shall have faith in me, or they can in nowise be saved;

13. And upon this rock I will build my church; yea, upon this rock ye are built, and if ye continue, the gates of hell shall not prevail against you;

14. And ye shall remember the church articles and covenants to keep them;

15. And whoso having faith you shall confirm in my church, by the laying on of the hands, and I will bestow the gift of the Holy Ghost upon them.

16. And the Book of Mormon and the Holy Scriptures, are given of me for your instruction; and the power of my Spirit quickeneth all things:

17. Wherefore, be faithful, praying

D&C 33:3—The term "eleventh hour" is found only in this passage of scripture and in the New Testament (see Matt. 20:6, 9). The reference in the New Testament is in the context of the parable of the workers in the vineyard.

D&C 33:6—The elect of the Lord are those who respond to the gospel message and come unto Christ in obedience to His commandments and in compliance with his ordinances. According to a statement by Hoyt W. Brewster, Jr., "Those who are ultimately 'elected' for exaltation within God's kingdom will be those who righteously use their free agency and cast their ballots in God's favor, choosing to serve him faithfully to the end" (*DCE*, 148).

D&C 33:8–9—When the prepared and the humble teach the gospel, the Spirit prompts them to speak the words of life as the Lord would have this message presented: "Therefore, verily I say unto you, lift up your voices unto this people; speak the thoughts that I shall put into your hearts, and you shall not be confounded before men; For it shall be given you in the very hour, yea, in the very moment, what ye shall say" (D&C 100:5–6).

The act of opening one's mouth in faith to deliver the truths of the gospel results in miracles. The Prophet Joseph's younger brother, Samuel Harrison, became, in effect, the first missionary in the Church in June 1830. He willingly opened his mouth in the service of God, but felt that his missionary service did not measurably increase the harvest of the Lord. Little did he know at the time how much good would come of his service, as Elder Joe J. Christensen, former president of the MTC, reminds us:

> The record indicates that Samuel left a copy of the Book of Mormon with the Reverend John P. Greene who, at first, was not personally interested. As an evidence of his persistence, Samuel didn't give up easily. He called back three times. At the insistence of his wife, Reverend Greene finally read the Book of Mormon. Later both he and his wife were baptized.
>
> Meanwhile Mrs. Greene's brother, Phineas Young, had earlier obtained a copy of the Book of Mormon from Samuel. He gave it to his brother Brigham, who later passed it along to his sister, Mrs. Murray, the mother of the wife of Heber C. Kimball. Thus we see the serial impact of just one copy of the Book of Mormon in bringing into the Church some of its most influential early leaders. (*HR*, 167.)

D&C 33:13—The metaphor of the "rock" is used frequently by the Lord as a means of conveying to us an understanding concerning the permanence, stability, and eternal nature of His design and plan for the salvation and eternal life of His children. The opposite of rock-solid stability is perilously shifting earth or sand (see Luke 6:48–49; 2 Ne. 28:28; 3 Ne. 18:13)—hardly a suitable foundation upon which to build. The rock is revelation, and it is through revelation that the faithful and obedient can learn that Jesus is the Christ (see 1 Cor. 12:3).

always, having your lamps trimmed and burning, and oil with you, that you may be ready at the coming of the bridegroom:

18. For behold, verily, verily, I say unto you, that I come quickly. Even so. Amen.

SECTION 34

1. My son Orson, hearken and hear and behold what I, the Lord God, shall say unto you, even Jesus Christ your Redeemer;

2. The light and the life of the world; a light which shineth in darkness and the darkness comprehendeth it not;

3. Who so loved the world that he gave his own life, that as many as would believe might become the sons of God; wherefore you are my son,

4. And blessed are you because you have believed;

5. And more blessed are you because you are called of me to preach my gospel,

6. To lift up your voice as with the sound of a trump, both long and loud, and cry repentance unto a crooked and perverse generation, preparing the way of the Lord for his second coming;

7. For behold, verily, verily, I say unto you, the time is soon at hand that I shall come in a cloud with power and great glory,

8. And it shall be a great day at the time of my coming, for all nations shall tremble.

9. But before that great day shall come, the sun shall be darkened, and the moon be turned into blood, and the stars shall refuse their shining, and some shall fall, and great destructions await the wicked:

10. Wherefore lift up your voice and spare not, for the Lord God hath spoken; therefore prophesy, and it shall be given by the power of the Holy Ghost;

Ezra Thayre

Ezra Thayre was born October 14, 1791, at Randolph, Windsor County, Vermont. He became a builder of bridges, dams, and mills in the Palmyra area, where he was converted through the teaching of Hyrum Smith. He was baptized by Parley P. Pratt in October 1830 and soon after was called on a mission by the Lord (see Section 33). Many joined the Church through his service. He was ordained a high priest in June 1831, but failed to heed the Lord's directive to go on another mission (see D&C 52:22). Thereafter he was called to repentance by the Lord (see D&C 56:5, 8–10). A subsequent mission call (see D&C 75:31) found him more responsive and obedient. He participated in Zion's Camp, later served on the high council in Adam-ondi-Ahman, and subsequently moved first to Rochester, New York, then to Michigan. He failed to accept the leadership of the Quorum of the Twelve after the martyrdom of the Prophet and joined the ranks of the reorganized church. Northrop Sweet, who was called on a mission along with Ezra Thayre, soon fell away from the Church and attempted unsuccessfully to form a church of his own.

D&C 33:17–18—Contained in these short verses is a powerful mandate on how to prepare for the Second Coming: read the scriptures, pray always, and be obedient, remembering to keep the commandments and endure to the end. The Savior as Bridegroom is referenced frequently in the scriptures. Precisely when the Bridegroom is to come is not revealed to the Saints—only that they are to be prepared.

Section 34 Background—Nineteen-year-old Orson Pratt had been converted to the Church through the guidance of his brother, Parley P. Pratt, in September 1830, and traveled the following month some 200 miles from the eastern part of New York state to visit the Prophet Joseph at Fayette. The revelation was received in the home of Peter Whitmer, Sr.

D&C 34:1–4—This touching and personal salutation from the Savior defines the relationship between a believing individual and the Redeemer as the Author of salvation; such a relationship constitutes a parental bond, since those who believe are on track to become the sons and daughters of Christ. The Savior is our divine source of light and life and love. He is the Father of all whom Elohim gives unto Him through the plan of salvation and exaltation. Orson is therefore "a son" unto Christ, and he is blessed because he has believed.

D&C 34:5–7—It is one thing to believe; it is a higher state of obedience to go forth and preach faith and repentance to a wayward world. Preaching the gospel prepares the way for the Second Coming. Nothing can stand in the way of the Lord's return, and nothing can hinder the work of the ministry in preaching His gospel to the four quarters of the earth (see D&C 1:5). The time is short; the cause is urgent; the outcome is inexorable. The work of the Church will go forward with power and truth. The timing of the Second Coming is surely anticipated by all who are familiar with the scriptures. The signs of the times alert us to the imminence of His coming; however, the wise will focus less on the endpoint and more on personal righteousness day by day—the oil in their lamps—that they might be prepared. As we choose to be faithful and endure to the end, the Lord will nurture and strengthen us at all times until He comes (see Alma 7:11–12).

11. And if you are faithful, behold, I am with you until I come:

12. And verily, verily, I say unto you, I come quickly. I am your Lord and your Redeemer. Even so. Amen.

SECTION 35

1. Listen to the voice of the Lord your God, even Alpha and Omega, the beginning and the end, whose course is one eternal round, the same to-day as yesterday, and for ever.

2. I am Jesus Christ, the Son of God, who was crucified for the sins of the world, even as many as will believe on my name, that they may become the sons of God, even one in me as I am one in the Father, as the Father is one in me, that we may be one.

3. Behold, verily, verily, I say unto my servant Sidney, I have looked upon thee and thy works. I have heard thy prayers, and prepared thee for a greater work.

4. Thou art blessed, for thou shalt do great things. Behold thou wast sent forth, even as John, to prepare the way before me, and before Elijah which should come, and thou knewest it not.

5. Thou didst baptize by water unto repentance, but they received not the Holy Ghost;

6. But now I give unto thee a commandment, that thou shalt baptize by water, and they shall receive the Holy Ghost by the laying on

---

Orson Pratt

Orson Pratt was born September 19, 1811, at Hartford, Washington County, New York. He was baptized on his nineteenth birthday by his brother Parley P. Pratt, with whom he was subsequently called to serve a mission in Missouri. His career in the Church included serving a second mission (see D&C 75:14), participating in Zion's Camp, and filling the office of Apostle in the Quorum of the Twelve. He became proficient at teaching Hebrew. Because of a lapse into apostasy he was excommunicated on August 20, 1842, but he repented and was rebaptized on January 20, 1843, and restored to his priesthood calling. As a participant in the western exodus, he was one of the very first individuals to view the Salt Lake Valley. He crossed the Atlantic no fewer than 16 times as a missionary to the British Isles. He defended the Church and its doctrines with intensity, served in the Quorum of the Twelve in Utah, and filled the position of historian and general Church recorder beginning in 1874. He passed away in a condition of poor health on October 3, 1881, the last surviving member of the original (1835) Council of the Twelve.

D&C 34:10–11—The sons of Mosiah, through study, fasting, and prayer, received "the spirit of prophecy, and the spirit of revelation, and when they taught, they taught with power and authority of God" (Alma 17:3). Orson Pratt receives, in essence, the same promise. Missionaries who declare the truths of the gospel by the Spirit and guide honest seekers to know by the Spirit that salvation and exaltation are accessible to them through the Atonement are teaching by the Spirit of prophecy and revelation. They are conveying the promise of the Lord that great blessings, even eternal life, will come to the obedient through the power of redemption. Such is the nature of prophecy.

Section 35 Background—Given to the Prophet Joseph Smith and Sidney Rigdon at or near Fayette, New York, December 1830, during the time when the Prophet was engaged in the translation of the Bible. The Prophet recorded the following in his journal: "In December Sidney Rigdon came to inquire of the Lord, and with him came Edward Partridge; the latter was a pattern of piety, and one of the Lord's great men. Shortly after the arrival of these two brethren, thus spake the Lord [Section 35]" (HC 1:128).

D&C 35:1—The phrase "one eternal round" refers to the fact that the Lord's course never varies—and that identical results always flow from the same causes.

D&C 35:2—"As many as believe on my name" is equated with receiving Jesus Christ as our Savior, which we demonstrate when we obey His commandments. We become His sons and daughters through the Holy Ghost; in Him dwells unity and faith, and through Him we cannot be divided.

D&C 35:2–4—To be addressed directly and personally by Alpha and Omega, the Redeemer of mankind, as was Sidney Rigdon, is a miraculous and unforgettable experience. The Lord recognizes Sidney's good intentions with his previous ministerial activities, but confirms that his work was without priesthood authority essential for spiritual transformation. Now, having being called to the ranks of service in the restored and authorized Church, Sidney can proceed to bless the lives of converts by guiding them to baptism and the reception of the Holy Ghost by the laying on of hands.

D&C 35:3–4—Sidney Rigdon had been very influential as a Baptist and had already gathered many who were seeking further truth. Many subsequent great Church leaders were some of his original followers.

of the hands, even as the apostles of old.

7. And it shall come to pass that there shall be a great work in the land, among the Gentiles, for their folly and their abominations shall be made manifest in the eyes of all people;

8. For I am God, and mine arm is not shortened; and I will show miracles, signs, and wonders, unto all those who believe on my name.

9. And whoso shall ask it in my name in faith, they shall cast out devils; they shall heal the sick; they shall cause the blind to receive their sight, and the deaf to hear, and the dumb to speak, and the lame to walk;

10. And the time speedily cometh that great things are to be shown forth unto the children of men;

11. But without faith shall not anything be shown forth except desolations upon Babylon, the same which has made all nations drink of the wine of the wrath of her fornication.

12. And there are none that doeth good, except those who are ready to receive the fulness of my gospel which I have sent forth unto this generation.

13. Wherefore I have called upon the weak things of the world, those who are unlearned and despised, to thresh the nations, by the power of my Spirit:

14. And their arm shall be my arm, and I will be their shield and their buckler; and I will gird up their loins, and they shall fight manfully for me; and their enemies shall be under their feet; and I will let fall the sword in their behalf, and by the fire of mine indignation will I preserve them.

15. And the poor and the meek shall have the gospel preached unto them, and they shall be looking forth for the time of my coming, for it is nigh at hand:

16. And they shall learn the parable of the fig-tree, for even now already summer is nigh,

17. And I have sent forth the fulness of my gospel by the hand of my servant Joseph; and in weakness have I blessed him,

18. And I have given unto him the keys of the mystery of those things which have been sealed, even things which were from the foundation of the world, and the things which shall come from this time until the time of my coming, if he abide in me, and if not, another will I plant in his stead.

19. Wherefore, watch over him that

The Campbellite church in Mantua Corners, Ohio, where Sidney Rigdon at one time served as a minister in the Campbellite Church.

D&C 35:8, 11—The Lord works by faith unto the performance of mighty miracles. The mighty change of conversion through the gospel is no less than a miracle. Revelation is a miracle. The coming forth of the Book of Mormon is a miracle. The operation of the priesthood of God is a miracle. All of these things are miracles to those with spiritual understanding. The Lord unfolds to Sidney Rigdon the miraculous nature of His work in the latter days. Scholar Hoyt Brewster, Jr., discusses the character of such miracles in the context of the Restoration:

> Much of what we take for granted in our world today, such as television and space travel, would have been considered miracles by our forefathers. As Orson F. Whitney succinctly said, "Miracles are not contrary to law; they are simply extraordinary results flowing from superior means and methods of doing things" (CR, Oct. 1928, 64–65). One of the signs of the true Church will be the presence of miracles, for the Lord is a "God of miracles" and "he changeth not" (Morm. 9:19). (DCE, 361.)

D&C 35:13–16—Why does the Lord so often call upon those who are weak in worldly learning and power to do His work? Because they are willing to be instruments in the hands of the Almighty to perform heavenly deeds in the context of eternal salvation and exaltation. Those who are weak in mortal spheres were likely among "the noble and great ones" (Abr. 3:22) in the premortal realm who were prepared from the foundation of the earth to do mighty works for good.

In relation to the majesty of the Lord as defined in the opening verses of Section 35, Sidney Rigdon must certainly have felt something of the "nothingness" of men emphasized by King Benjamin (see Mosiah 4:5, 11). But the weakness of the faithful becomes strong as they valiantly proceed to do God's work. The Lord revealed to Moroni that He gives unto men weaknesses to make them humble. He extends this glorious promise to all: ". . . and my grace is sufficient for all men that humble themselves before me; for if they humble themselves before me, and have faith in me, then will I make weak things become strong unto them" (Ether 12:27).

D&C 35:18–19—The Lord defines who He is, who Sidney Rigdon is, and now who Joseph Smith is. Sidney is about to assist Joseph in the work of translating the Bible through the inspiration of the Holy Ghost. Therefore, Sidney needs to have a clear understanding that Joseph is in charge and has been given the keys of bringing forth the word of God. Besides having the keys of bringing forth the word of God, the Prophet Joseph also had the keys of presidency, which entails the directive powers by which the Church is governed.

his faith fail not, and it shall be given by the Comforter, the Holy Ghost, that knoweth all things:

20. And a commandment I give unto thee, that thou shalt write for him; and the scriptures shall be given, even as they are in mine own bosom, to the salvation of mine own elect;

21. For they will hear my voice, and shall see me, and shall not be asleep, and shall abide the day of my coming, for they shall be purified, even as I am pure.

22. And now I say unto you, tarry with him, and he shall journey with you; forsake him not, and surely these things shall be fulfilled.

23. And inasmuch as ye do not write, behold, it shall be given unto him to prophesy: and thou shalt preach my gospel and call on the holy prophets to prove his words, as they shall be given him.

24. Keep all the commandments and covenants by which ye are bound; and I will cause the heavens to shake for your good, and Satan shall tremble and Zion shall rejoice upon the hills and flourish,

25. And Israel shall be saved in mine own due time; and by the keys which I have given shall they be led, and no more be confounded at all.

26. Lift up your hearts and be glad, your redemption draweth nigh.

27. Fear not, little flock, the kingdom is yours until I come. Behold I come quickly. Even so. Amen.

SECTION 36

1. Thus saith the Lord God, the Mighty One of Israel, Behold, I say unto you, my servant Edward, that you are blessed, and your sins are forgiven you, and you are called to

SIDNEY RIGDON

Sidney Rigdon was born February 19, 1793, near St. Clair Township, Allegheny County, Pennsylvania. An accomplished orator, he became a Baptist minister and later one of the founders of the Campbellite movement. Parley P. Pratt introduced him to the restored Church and provided him with a copy of the Book of Mormon. Sidney was baptized on November 14, 1830. His service to the Church included dedicating Independence, Missouri, as the chosen land of Zion, doing scribal work for the Prophet Joseph for the inspired translation of the Bible, participating with Joseph in a number of revelations, and generally being a spokesman and defender for the cause of Zion. He became a member of the First Presidency on March 18, 1833. He suffered greatly during the Missouri persecutions. Following a dispute with the Prophet Joseph, Sidney was severed from the Church on August 13, 1843, but was later reinstated. He moved to Pittsburgh, returning to Nauvoo following the martyrdom in response to a vision he claimed to have had instructing him that he should become the guardian of the Church. Instead, the Church supported the Twelve under Brigham Young. Sidney was disfellowshipped in September 1844. He returned to Pittsburgh and then moved to Friendship, New York, where he passed away in poverty on July 14, 1876.

D&C 35:20–21—This precious phrase, telling us that the the scriptures should be given from the bosom of the Savior, instructs us of the divine nature of His word, which is inherently part of His being. When we take the scriptures into our own bosom, we are in essence inscribing them upon our own being, much as the Apostle Paul expressed it: "not in tables of stone, but in fleshy tables of the heart" (2 Cor. 3:3). Such a transfer of truth from the bosom of the Savior to His followers is directed unto "the salvation of mine own elect." The resulting transformation allows us to awaken our spiritual faculties, discern His voice, and eventually behold His presence on the day of His coming.

D&C 35:23–25—In addition to his calling as scribe, Sidney Rigdon is also commissioned to confirm the words given through Prophet Joseph by substantiating them on the basis of the sayings of the prophets who came before. In this instance, the Lord is appealing to Sidney to make meaningful contributions to the restored Church based on his gift for oratory and his experience as a former minister well-versed in the Bible. The Lord always draws on our talents and abilities to move His work forward.

Section 36 Background—Given through the Prophet Joseph Smith to Edward Partridge, near Fayette, New York, in December 1830.

D&C 36:1–2—Not long before this revelation was given, Edward had been baptized by the Prophet Joseph Smith. The Lord confirms that the new convert's sins have been forgiven. He is to receive the Holy Ghost by the laying on of hands. Though it is Sidney Rigdon who will be voice while laying his hands upon Edward, the Lord makes the remarkable statement, "I will lay my hand upon you by the hand of my servant" (verse 2). The emerging lesson is that all who are blessed or ordained by the laying on of hands can in their hearts and minds envision that the Lord Himself is performing the act by word and deed. He declares: ". . . my word shall not pass away, but shall all be fulfilled, whether by mine own voice or by the voice of my servants, it is the same" (D&C 1:38).

Sidney Rigdon's grave site in Friendship, New York.

preach my gospel as with the voice of a trump;

2. And I will lay my hand upon you by the hand of my servant Sidney Rigdon, and you shall receive my Spirit, the Holy Ghost, even the Comforter, which shall teach you the peaceable things of the kingdom;

3. And you shall declare it with a loud voice, saying, Hosanna, blessed be the name of the most high God.

4. And now this calling and commandment give I unto you concerning all men,

5. That as many as shall come before my servants Sidney Rigdon and Joseph Smith, jun., embracing this calling and commandment, shall be ordained and sent forth to preach the everlasting gospel among the nations,

6. Crying repentance, saying, Save yourselves from this untoward generation, and come forth out of the fire, hating even the garments spotted with the flesh.

7. And this commandment shall be given unto the elders of my church, that every man which will embrace it with singleness of heart, may be ordained and sent forth, even as I have spoken.

8. I am Jesus Christ the Son of God: wherefore, gird up your loins and I will suddenly come to my temple. Even so. Amen.

SECTION 37

1. Behold, I say unto you, that it is not expedient in me that ye should translate any more until ye shall go to the Ohio, and this because of the enemy and for your sakes.

2. And again, I say unto you, that ye shall not go, until ye have preached my gospel in those parts, and have strengthened up the church whithersoever it is found, and more especially in Colesville; for, behold, they pray unto me in much faith.

3. And again, a commandment I give unto the church, that it is expedient in me that they should assemble together at the Ohio, against the time that my servant Oliver Cowdery shall return unto them.

4. Behold, here is wisdom, and let every man choose for himself until I come. Even so. Amen.

A Note on Ohio. The commandment to go to the Ohio area was given in December 1830. The Lord knew what was to unfold in Ohio: He would reveal to the Saints His law and endow them with power from on high when the Kirtland Temple became operational. Hoyt Brewster, Jr., outlines other developments that were to take place in Ohio:

From within her borders, Ohio was to give birth to the fundamental organization that exists within the Church today. The First Presidency of the Church was established in Ohio, as well as the Quorum of the Twelve Apostles, First Quorum of the Seventy, and the first stake of the Church, with its attendant high council. Between February 1831 and April 1836, sixty-four of the revelations recorded in the Doctrine and Covenants were received in Ohio. The towns of Kirtland, Thompson, Hiram, Orange, and Amherst were the host grounds for the revelatory information received (*DCE*, 393.)

Section 37 Background—As a result of this revelation, the process of the ultimate gathering began as an integral part of the Restoration. The persecution against the Church in New York had become bitter, and it was the Lord's design to gather the Saints to Ohio for a season of time where the spirit was more conducive to the unfolding of the infant church. In fact, the principle of gathering is a key ingredient in the gospel plan itself, for "gathering" is analogous to building strength, enhancing security, increasing protection, sharing of knowledge and revealed wisdom, fostering of temple work, and more efficient nurturing of spiritual development through obedience to the commandments of Christ.

D&C 37:2—Concerning the community of Colesville, Hoyt Brewster, Jr., provides the following account:

The town of Colesville, New York . . . was the home of Joseph Knight, Sr., a faithful man for whom Joseph Smith had labored in 1826. . . . It is located about one hundred miles south of Fayette, and these two towns, together with Palmyra, were the focal points of Church activity in New York during its first year of existence.

It was here that the "first miracle" of the Church took place, when an evil spirit was cast out of Newel Knight. This was also the location where the Prophet Joseph suffered his first arrest, following the organization of the Church. . . . About sixty Saints from this location went en masse to Ohio, where they settled at Thompson, sixteen miles northeast of Kirtland. (*DCE*, 90.)

D&C 37:3—This is the first commandment of the Lord in this dispensation concerning the gathering. The gathering is, at its heart, the organizational process that supports the fulfillment of the Lord's design around His covenant relationship with His elect. In effect, the gathering is a covenant activity by means of which Deity accomplishes the eternal mission of bringing about the immortality and eternal life of man (see Moses 1:39). We come together in obedience to gospel principles so that we might enjoy the blessings of priesthood ordinances of salvation and exaltation and the guidance of a living prophet. The Prophet Joseph Smith taught that the gathering of Israel "was the design of the councils of heaven before the world was, that the principles and laws of the priesthood should be predicated upon the gathering of the people in every age of the world" (*HC* 5:423). The Prophet Joseph also made clear that the Lord will empower and direct the gathering.

D&C 37:4—The Lord commands the gathering. It is for the blessing of the Saints. Nevertheless, the principle of agency is confirmed. We can obediently gather to places of refuge and wisdom and thus be found worthy of the consummate blessings that accrue as a result. Alternately, we can choose to be independent and find our own way in the labyrinth of highways and byways meandering through life. If we do the latter, we forfeit the eternal blessings associated with the gathering. The decision is a covenant decision. The consequences are of eternal import.

SECTION 38

1. Thus saith the Lord your God, even Jesus Christ, the Great I AM, Alpha and Omega, the beginning and the end, the same which looked upon the wide expanse of eternity, and all the seraphic hosts of heaven, before the world was made:

2. The same which knoweth all things, for all things are present before mine eyes;

3. I am the same which spake, and the world was made, and all things came by me:

4. I am the same which have taken the Zion of Enoch into mine own bosom; and verily, I say, even as many as have believed in my name, for I am Christ, and in mine own name, by the virtue of the blood which I have spilt, have I pleaded before the Father for them;

5. But behold, the residue of the wicked have I kept in chains of darkness until the judgment of the great day, which shall come at the end of the earth;

6. And even so will I cause the wicked to be kept, that will not hear my voice but harden their hearts, and wo, wo, wo, is their doom.

7. But behold, verily, verily, I say unto you that mine eyes are upon you. I am in your midst and ye cannot see me;

8. But the day soon cometh that ye shall see me, and know that I am; for the veil of darkness shall soon be rent, and he that is not purified shall not abide the day:

9. Wherefore, gird up your loins and be prepared. Behold, the kingdom is yours, and the enemy shall not overcome.

10. Verily, I say unto you, ye are clean, but not all; and there is none else with whom I am well pleased;

EDWARD PARTRIDGE

Edward Partridge was born August 27, 1793, at Pittsfield, Berkshire County, Massachusetts. He was a hatter by trade. At first reluctant to embrace the restored gospel, he was finally persuaded when he went with Sidney Rigdon to visit the Prophet Joseph Smith in 1830. The Prophet baptized him on December 11 of that year. Edward became the first bishop of the Church (see D&C 41:11). Sent to Missouri to assist the Saints, he was subjected to cruel abuse by the mobs. After returning to Kirtland, he spent his time serving the poor and preaching the gospel on various missions. On a subsequent sojourn in Missouri he was again subjected to much persecution, including imprisonment. Throughout all of these experiences, his family also suffered intensely. On May 27, 1840, Edward passed away at the age of 46 in Nauvoo, impoverished and frail. In terms of eternal wealth, however, he had been, by the Lord's own declaration, received "unto myself" (D&C 124:19). Even though Edward was censured by the Lord from time to time for his failings (see D&C 50:39; 64:17; and 85:8), he was able to rise above his weaknesses and make his mark as a loyal disciple. The Prophet Joseph characterized him as "a pattern of piety, and one of the Lord's great men" (HC 1:128).

Section 38 Background—Given on Sunday, January 2, 1831, at a conference of the Church held at the home of Peter Whitmer, Sr. The Saints had just been commanded to assemble in Ohio, and were eager to learn more about the matter. The commandment to gather in Ohio was a considerable test for the Saints, and not all heeded the word of the Lord with full devotion.

D&C 38:2—The Savior beholds all things. Our lives are before Him constantly. The only security in this life, the only sure foundation upon which we can build, the only failsafe strategy for happiness, is to follow the Redeemer. We depend on our Savior to plead for us, that we might gain eternal life. Our gratitude for His gift of grace and love sustains us in keeping the commandments. The Savior received grace for grace until His mission was perfected in God (see D&C 93:6–19). There is joy in following in the Savior's footsteps by progressing, as He did, grace for grace, in fulfilling the will of the Father. As we seek to know Him, we are on the pathway to receive of the Father in due time a fullness of light and joy (see D&C 84:38; Alma 12:10).

D&C 38:4—Christ is our Advocate before the Father by virtue of His having accomplished the work of the atoning sacrifice. As Alma taught, the state of spiritual darkness in which the impenitent are confined by "the chains of hell" (Alma 5:7) can be transformed through the illumination of the gospel for those mortals who believe in Christ and repent of their sins, thus experiencing the "mighty change" in their hearts (Alma 5:14).

D&C 38:8—"The day soon cometh that ye shall see me, and know that I am" are words that resonate with the same hope and promise as those spoken by John the Beloved: "Beloved, now are we the sons of God, and it doth not yet appear what we shall be: but we know that, when he shall appear, we shall be like him; for we shall see him as he is. And every man that hath this hope in him purifieth himself, even as he is pure" (1 John 3:2–3). Referring to these words, Elder Bruce R. McConkie taught that the Lord is often in our midst—in a real, physical sense—but that we do not see Him as often as we should because of our own failure to do so (see PMFCC, 611).

11. For all flesh is corrupted before me; and the powers of darkness prevail upon the earth, among the children of men, in the presence of all the hosts of heaven,

12. Which causeth silence to reign, and all eternity is pained, and the angels are waiting the great command to reap down the earth, to gather the tares that they may be burned; and, behold, the enemy is combined.

13. And now I show unto you a mystery, a thing which is had in secret chambers, to bring to pass even your destruction in process of time, and ye knew it not;

14. But now I tell it unto you, and ye are blessed, not because of your iniquity, neither your hearts of unbelief; for verily some of you are guilty before me, but I will be merciful unto your weakness.

15. Therefore, be ye strong from henceforth; fear not, for the kingdom is yours:

16. And for your salvation I give unto you a commandment, for I have heard your prayers, and the poor have complained before me, and the rich have I made, and all flesh is mine, and I am no respecter of persons.

17. And I have made the earth rich, and behold it is my footstool, wherefore, again I will stand upon it;

18. And I hold forth and design to give unto you greater riches, even a land of promise, a land flowing with milk and honey, upon which there shall be no curse when the Lord cometh:

19. And I will give it unto you for the land of your inheritance, if you seek it with all your hearts:

20. And this shall be my covenant with you, ye shall have it for the land of your inheritance, and for the inheritance of your children forever, while the earth shall stand, and ye shall possess it again in eternity, no more to pass away.

21. But, verily, I say unto you, that in time ye shall have no king nor ruler, for I will be your king and watch over you.

22. Wherefore, hear my voice and follow me, and you shall be a free people, and ye shall have no laws but my laws when I come, for I am your Lawgiver, and what can stay my hand?

23. But, verily, I say unto you, teach one another according to the office wherewith I have appointed you,

24. And let every man esteem his brother as himself, and practice virtue and holiness before me.

D&C 38:11–12—To render His warning more persuasive, the Lord reveals that the powers of darkness prevail on the earth, causing the hosts of heaven to be pained in their grief and anguish. When in his day Enoch perceived the Lord looking upon the inhabitants of the earth and weeping, he inquired how the Almighty could weep in this manner. The Lord explained the nature of His emotion concerning the wicked: "But behold, their sins shall be upon the heads of their fathers; Satan shall be their father, and misery shall be their doom; and the whole heavens shall weep over them, even all the workmanship of mine hands; wherefore should not the heavens weep, seeing these shall suffer?" (Moses 7:37). Thus the phrase "eternity is pained" refers to the consciousness of the terrible suffering that the wicked must needlessly endure.

D&C 38:20–22—The Lord's relationship with His people is based on covenant terms: great promises are given based on obedience to specific laws and obligations. In this case the requirement is to hear the voice of the Lord and follow Him—then will the inheritance of a promised land be granted, in time and in eternity. The laws that prevail in the land of promise are to be the laws of God. In the millennial period, the Savior will govern according to theocratic principles.

D&C 38:23—We are to teach one another the truth and exemplify the principles of virtue and holiness. The essence of the golden rule is to be the defining principle behind our relationships—with each individual esteeming his neighbor as himself.

Grave site of Edward Partridge— first bishop of the Church—at the Old Nauvoo Burial Grounds on Parley Street in Nauvoo.

25. And again I say unto you, let every men esteem his brother as himself;

26. For what man among you having twelve sons, and is no respecter of them, and they serve him obediently, and he saith unto the one, be thou clothed in robes and sit thou here; and to the other, be thou clothed in rags and sit thou there, and looketh upon his sons and saith I am just.

27. Behold, this I have given unto you a parable, and it is even as I am: I say unto you, be one; and if ye are not one, ye are not mine.

28. And again I say unto you, that the enemy in the secret chambers seeketh your lives.

29. Ye hear of wars in far countries, and you say that there will soon be great wars in far countries, but ye know not the hearts of men in your own land.

30. I tell you these things because of your prayers; wherefore treasure up wisdom in your bosoms, lest the wickedness of men reveal these things unto you by their wickedness, in a manner which shall speak in your ears with a voice louder than that which shall shake the earth; but if ye are prepared, ye shall not fear.

31. And that ye might escape the power of the enemy, and be gathered unto me a righteous people, without spot and blameless:

32. Wherefore, for this cause I gave unto you the commandment that ye should go to the Ohio; and there I will give unto you my law; and there you shall be endowed with power from on high;

33. And from thence, whosoever I will, shall go forth among all nations, and it shall be told them what they shall do; for I have a great work laid up in store, for Israel shall be saved, and I will lead them whithersoever I will, and no power shall stay my hand.

34. And now I give unto the church in these parts a commandment, that certain men among them shall be appointed, and they shall be appointed by the voice of the church;

35. And they shall look to the poor and the needy, and administer to their relief, that they shall not suffer; and send them forth to the place which I have commanded them;

36. And this shall be their work, to govern the affairs of the property of this church.

37. And they that have farms that cannot be sold, let them be left or rented as seemeth them good.

38. See that all things are preserved; and when men are endowed with power from on high and sent forth, all these things shall be gathered unto the bosom of the church.

39. And if ye seek the riches which it is the will of the Father to give unto you, ye shall be the richest of all people, for ye shall have the riches of eternity; and it must needs be that the riches of the earth are mine to give; but beware of pride, lest ye become as the Nephites of old.

40. And again, I say unto you,

D&C 38:27—We are to expunge from our hearts and from our midst the darkness of the world and prepare ourselves in righteousness to be welcomed into the promised land where the laws of God will prevail. According to the covenant arrangement, such an inheritance can accrue only in a state where the Saints are unified in the faith and where each individual is able to "esteem his brother as himself and practice virtue and holiness" before the Lord (verses 24–25). Unity is essential for glory to abound.

D&C 38:30–32—At times of turbulence and peril, fear can be subdued and overcome through preparation. And how shall we prepare? By gathering together in secure places appointed of the Lord, and by receiving His law and the endowment of power from on high. There is indeed security in unity and careful preparation. If we are devoted and unified, we are the Lord's children and reflect the virtues of a Zion people. We are to prepare ourselves that we might merit the blessings of the Lord in protection and defense.

Our preparation includes obedience to the commandment of the Lord to institute temple work. It is through the work of the temples that an endowment of power can be given: "Organize yourselves; prepare every needful thing; and establish a house, even a house of prayer, a house of fasting, a house of faith, a house of learning, a house of glory, a house of order, a house of God" (D&C 88:119; see also D&C 109:8). Such a program proceeds under the direction of the one to whom the Lord has given the keys for such work. Thus, in all of our preparation, we are to look to the living prophet for guidance.

D&C 38:35—The Lord in His compassion wants the poor who flock to the Church to be spared suffering as they gather with the Saints to the place designated. He calls for workers to be organized and appointed by the voice of the Church to accomplish shepherding the needy and overseeing the economic transition. The program of the Church to care for the poor (from these early years even to the present) is aligned with the quest to teach principles of self-reliance and industry.

D&C 38:38–39—From the heavenly perspective, the Saints are gathered "unto the bosom of the Church." The imagery describes the Church as a living thing, the repository of the treasured harvest of souls coming unto Christ. The members of the Church are promised wealth as they gather, for they are to have "the riches of eternity." But the riches of eternities are accessible to the Saints only if they keep the commandments and avoid the destructive influence of pride. Less than a year previous to this revelation, the Lord had provided through the Book of Mormon the fullness of His gospel and cogent historical evidence of the catastrophic effects of pride. He would repeatedly warn the Saints against this evil (see D&C 90:17 and 98:19–20 as examples) and counsel them to be humble, as He had said to Martin Harris: "Learn of me, and listen to my words; walk in the meekness of my Spirit, and you shall have peace in me" (D&C 19:23).

I give unto you a commandment, that every man, both elder, priest, teacher, and also member, go to with his might, with the labor of his hands, to prepare and accomplish the things which I have commanded.

41. And let your preaching be the warning voice, every man to his neighbor, in mildness and in meekness.

42. And go ye out from among the wicked. Save yourselves. Be ye clean that bear the vessels of the Lord. Even so. Amen.

SECTION 39

1. Hearken and listen to the voice of him who is from all eternity to all eternity, the Great I AM, even Jesus Christ,

2. The light and the life of the world; a light which shineth in darkness and the darkness comprehendeth it not:

3. The same which came in the meridian of time unto my own, and my own received me not;

4. But to as many as received me, gave I power to become my sons, and even so will I give unto as many as will receive me, power to become my sons.

5. And verily, verily, I say unto you, he that receiveth my gospel, receiveth me; and he that receiveth not my gospel receiveth not me.

6. And this is my gospel: repentance and baptism by water, and then cometh the baptism of fire and the Holy Ghost, even the Comforter, which showeth all things, and teacheth the peaceable things of the kingdom.

7. And now, behold, I say unto you, my servant James, I have looked upon thy works and I know thee:

8. And verily I say unto thee, thine heart is now right before me at this time, and, behold, I have bestowed great blessings upon thy head:

9. Nevertheless thou hast seen great sorrow, for thou hast rejected

D&C 38:41—Every member of God's Church and Kingdom is to be a missionary—but in mildness and meekness. Such deportment can soften the heart of the neighbor through love and caring. Furthermore, such deportment enables the missionary to receive the guidance of the Spirit and know how to present the truths of the gospel effectively.

D&C 38:42—What a powerful and compelling statement this is concerning how we are to conduct our lives: We extract ourselves from the environments of sin. We avail ourselves of the saving principles of the gospel. We sanctify ourselves in order to be faithful servants of the Lord. It is a matter of withdrawal, transformation, and purification.

Section 39 Background—Not long after the January 2 conference closed, James Covill—who had been a Baptist minister for forty years—came to Joseph Smith and covenanted with the Lord that he would obey any command the Lord gave him through Joseph. The Prophet received Section 39 in response. Details of the birth and death of James Covill are not known, and there is no record of any baptism. James Covill failed to establish a covenant relationship with the Lord; he rejected the word of the Lord that was given him and returned to his former people and principles.

D&C 39:4—The Lord opens with a statement about His nature and Being as the Giver of life and the Eternal I AM. His invitation is covenant-centered, for He promises the power of sonship to any who will receive Him.

D&C 39:5–6—How does the Savior define the act of receiving Him? It is consonant with the act of receiving His gospel of faith, repentance, baptism, and the gift of the Holy Ghost. Those who fail to enter into this covenant relationship fail to receive the Christ. It is not a nominal process; obedience to His principles and covenants is to be manifested through sincere and devoted action. The reward of doing so is the blessing of receiving the Spirit.

D&C 39:9—President Spencer W. Kimball taught that pride is a stumbling block that can cause us to lose a rich reward to which we would otherwise be entitled.

me many times because of pride and the cares of the world;

10. But, behold, the days of thy deliverance are come, if thou wilt hearken to my voice, which saith unto thee, arise and be baptized, and wash away your sins, calling on my name, and you shall receive my Spirit, and a blessing so great as you never have known.

11. And if thou do this, I have prepared thee for a greater work. Thou shalt preach the fulness of my gospel which I have sent forth in these last days; the covenant which I have sent forth to recover my people, which are of the house of Israel.

12. And it shall come to pass that power shall rest upon thee; thou shalt have great faith, and I will be with thee and go before thy face.

13. Thou art called to labor in my vineyard,
and to build up my church, and to bring forth Zion, that it may rejoice upon the hills and flourish.

14. Behold, verily, verily, I say unto thee, thou art not called to go into the eastern countries, but thou art called to go to the Ohio.

15. And inasmuch as my people shall assemble themselves to the Ohio, I have kept in store a blessing such as is not known among the children of men, and it shall be poured forth upon their heads. And from thence men shall go forth into all nations.

16. Behold, verily, verily, I say unto you, that the people in Ohio call upon me in much faith, thinking I will stay my hand in judgment upon the nations, but I cannot deny my word:

17. Wherefore lay to with your might and call faithful laborers into my vineyard, that it may be pruned for the last time.

18. And inasmuch as they do repent and receive the fulness of my gospel, and become sanctified, I will stay mine hand in judgment:

19. Wherefore, go forth, crying with a loud voice, saying, the kingdom of heaven is at hand; crying Hosanna! blessed be the name of the most high God.

20. Go forth baptizing with water, preparing the way before my face, for the time of my coming;

21. For the time is at hand; the day nor the hour no man knoweth; but it surely shall come,

22. And he that receiveth these things receiveth me; and they shall be gathered unto me in time and in eternity.

23. And again, it shall come to pass, that on as many as ye shall baptize with water, ye shall lay your hands, and they shall receive the gift of the Holy Ghost, and shall be looking forth for the signs of my coming, and shall know me.

24. Behold, I come quickly. Even so. Amen.

The old Universalist church in Afton, New York.

D&C 39:11—The Lord knows the heart of James Covill and extends to him the sacred privilege of coming into the fold cleansed from sin through the Atonement and the gospel of salvation. He will then receive magnificent spiritual blessings and become enlisted in missionary activity. His calling will be to preach the fullness of the gospel in order to gather the house of Israel in the spirit of faith and rejoicing. It is instructive that the Lord speaks of sending forth "the covenant" to recover His people. Such interesting language characterizes the covenant as an instrument empowered to retrieve and gather the remnant of Israel scattered across the earth. At a moment of meekness, the erstwhile prideful James is invited to join the forces of good and bless the lives of converts as well as his own.

RECEIVING THE SAVIOR

James Covill had given lengthy service as a Baptist minister, and in that role he would have taught and emphasized the importance of coming to the Savior as the basis for salvation. In this section, Covill is assured that such teachings are true—but that receiving the Savior involves much more than simply expressing desire.

To receive the Savior, one must receive His gospel by entering into a covenant relationship with Him. Such a covenant is established through faith, repentance, and baptism by water and the laying on of hands for the gift of the Holy Ghost.

James Covill had made such a covenant, and the Lord commanded him to be baptized—indicating that the Lord was pleased with Covill's attitude at that time. It's interesting to note that the Lord did comment on some improper actions and weaknesses in Covill's past, a warning that he not repeat the same mistakes.

REJECTING THE SAVIOR

The Lord responded to James Covill's righteous desires and gave him the opportunity to establish a covenant relationship. But Covill did not accept and obey the Lord's command. At the critical moment when James Covill might have pursued the path leading to eternal life, the evil one attacked and led him away from the very goal he had desired to achieve.

Everyone faces critical moments of making decisions, setting goals, and establishing commitments pertaining to future behavior. It is at these critical times that Lucifer enters into the battle to persuade us against pursuing courses of righteousness. He knows we are likely to become spiritually stronger as time goes by as we honor and keep our commitments with the Lord (STDC 1:188–190).

SECTION 40

1. Behold, verily I say unto you, that the heart of my servant James Covill was right before me, for he covenanted with me that he would obey my word.
2. And he received the word with gladness, but straightway Satan tempted him; and the fear of persecution, and the cares of the world, caused him to reject the word;
3. Wherefore he broke my covenant, and it remaineth with me to do with him as seemeth me good. Amen.

SECTION 41

1. Hearken and hear, O ye my people, saith the Lord and your God, ye whom I delight to bless with the greatest blessings, ye that hear me; and ye that hear me not will I curse, that have professed my name, with the heaviest of all cursings.
2. Hearken, O ye elders of my church whom I have called: behold I give unto you a commandment, that ye shall assemble yourselves together to agree upon my word,
3. And by the prayer of your faith ye shall receive my law, that ye may know how to govern my church, and have all things right before me.
4. And I will be your ruler when

The Newel K. Whitney home in Kirtland, Ohio—now a visitors' center—where the Prophet Joseph Smith received Section 41, the first revelation given in Ohio. Joseph and Emma Smith arrived in Kirtland by sleigh on February 1, 1831, when the Church was not yet a year old. Even though the home was small for the large Whitney family, new converts Newel and his wife, Elizabeth Ann, invited Joseph and Emma to live with them; Emma was expecting twins within a few months. The first four Kirtland revelations—beginning with Section 41—were received in this home; eventually, 47 percent of the entire Doctrine and Covenants was revealed in the general Kirtland area.

Section 40 Background—After James Covill rejected the word of the Lord (see Section 39), this section was revealed to the Prophet and Sidney Rigdon to explain "why he obeyed not the word" (*HC* 1:145).

D&C 40:2—James Covill at first rejoiced over the restored gospel and promised to heed the counsel of the Lord—given him directly through revelation. But fear and pride intervened. What had been a moment of meekness and humility for James was transformed into a moment of weakness through a lapse in faith and devotion to the cause of the Lord.

Section 41 Background—Given February 4, 1831, at the Newel K. Whitney home (now a visitors' center) in Kirtland, Ohio (see *HC* 1:146–147). The Prophet introduced this revelation, the first given in Ohio, with the following words: "The branch of the Church in this part of the Lord's vineyard, which had increased to nearly one hundred members, were striving to do the will of God, so far as they knew it, though some strange notions and false spirits had crept in among them. With a little caution and some wisdom, I soon assisted the brethren and sisters to overcome them. The plan of 'common stock,' which had existed in what was called 'the family' [a community organization that preceded the preaching of the restored gospel in Kirtland], whose members generally had embraced the everlasting Gospel, was readily abandoned for the more perfect law of the Lord; and the false spirits were easily discerned and rejected by the light of revelation" (*HC* 1:146).

D&C 41:2–3—President Joseph Fielding Smith sheds light on the state of affairs at this time:

> It was the most natural thing in all the world that so many good and loyal men, coming out of the world and endeavoring to free themselves from all its traditions, would have some difficulty in ridding themselves of false practices and traditions, and the assembling of the elders to be taught what the order of heaven is, was necessary. In this manner the Spirit of the Lord would be given them, under the guiding hand of the Prophet so that errors and traditions which they had previously received would be corrected. The Lord had promised the elders that when they assembled in Ohio he would give them his law. Therefore they were to come from all parts to receive this divine instruction. When this law was given they would understand how to receive it by the prayer of faith, and then they would know how to govern the Church. We should remember, as the Church grew and spread there would naturally arise many problems needing interpretation which had not previously been considered. (*CHMR* 1:163–164.)

I come; and behold, I come quickly, and ye shall see that my law is kept.

5. He that receiveth my law and doeth it, the same is my disciple; and he that saith he receiveth it and doeth it not, the same is not my disciple, and shall be cast out from among you:

6. For it is not meet that the things which belong to the children of the kingdom, should be given to them that are not worthy, or to dogs, or the pearls to be cast before swine.

7. And again, it is meet that my servant Joseph Smith, jun., should have a house built, in which to live and translate.

8. And again, it is meet that my servant Sidney Rigdon should live as seemeth him good, inasmuch as he keepeth my commandments.

9. And again, I have called my servant Edward Partridge, and give a commandment, that he should be appointed by the voice of the church, and ordained a bishop unto the church, to leave his merchandise and to spend all his time in the labors of the church:

10. To see to all things as it shall be appointed unto him, in my laws in the day that I shall give them.

11. And this because his heart is pure before me, for he is like unto Nathanael of old, in whom there is no guile.

12. These words are given unto you, and they are pure before me; wherefore beware how you hold them, for they are to be answered upon your souls in the day of judgment. Even so. Amen.

D&C 41:5—The gospel is a plan of action. King Benjamin declared: ". . . and now, if you believe all these things see that ye do them" (Mosiah 4:10).

D&C 41:9–10—Edward Partridge is called on to relinquish his mercantile vocation as a hatter and give all of his time to the Church in the office of bishop, the duties of which would be further revealed in Section 42. The Lord perceives that Edward's heart is pure and without guile, much as His disciple Nathanael, associate of Phillip, in the meridian of time: "Jesus saw Nathanael coming to him, and saith of him, Behold an Israelite indeed, in whom is no guile!" (John 1:47).

Edward was to serve faithfully in the Church in spite of severe persecution. His purity of heart and guileless disposition were to be dramatically confirmed in an episode that occurred on July 20, 1833, when a mob in Missouri subjected Edward to the excruciating fate of being tarred and feathered when he refused to leave his home. "Until after I had spoken, I knew not what they intended to do with me, whether to kill me, to whip me, or what else I knew not. I bore my abuse with so much resignation and meekness, that it appeared to astound the multitude, who permitted me to retire in silence, many looking very solemn, their sympathies having been touched as I thought; and as to myself, I was so filled with the Spirit and love of God, that I had no hatred towards my persecutors or anyone else" (HC 1:391).

The interior of the Newel K. Whitney home in Kirtland, Ohio, where Section 41—the first revelation given in Ohio—was received.

SECTION 42

1. Hearken, O ye elders of my church, who have assembled yourselves together in my name, even Jesus Christ the Son of the living God, the Savior of the world: inasmuch as ye believe on my name and keep my commandments,

2. Again, I say unto you, hearken and hear and obey the law which I shall give unto you;

3. For verily I say, as ye have assembled yourselves together according to the commandment wherewith I commanded you, and are agreed as touching this one thing, and have asked the Father in my name, even so ye shall receive.

4. Behold, verily I say unto you, I give unto you this first commandment, that ye shall go forth in my name, every one of you, excepting my servants Joseph Smith, jun., and Sidney Rigdon.

5. And I give unto them a commandment that they shall go forth for a little season, and it shall be given by the power of my Spirit when they shall return;

6. And ye shall go forth in the power of my Spirit, preaching my gospel, two by two, in my name, lifting up your voices as with the voice of a trump, declaring my word like unto angels of God;

7. And ye shall go forth baptizing with water, saying—Repent ye, repent ye, for the kingdom of heaven is at hand.

8. And from this place ye shall go forth into the regions westward; and inasmuch as ye shall find them that will receive you, ye shall build up my church in every region,

9. Until the time shall come when it shall be revealed unto you from on high, when the city of the New Jerusalem shall be prepared, that ye may be gathered in one, that ye may be my people and I will be your God.

10. And again, I say unto you, that my servant Edward Partridge shall stand in the office wherewith I have appointed him. And it shall come to pass, that if he transgress, another shall be appointed in his stead. Even so. Amen.

11. Again, I say unto you, that it shall not be given to any one to go forth to preach my gospel, or to build up my church, except he be ordained by some one who has authority, and it is known to the church that he has authority, and has been regularly ordained by the heads of the church.

12. And again, the elders, priests, and teachers of this church shall teach the principles of my gospel, which are in the Bible and the Book of Mormon, in the which is the fulness of the gospel;

Section 42 Background—Given in the Newel K. Whitney home (now a visitors' center) in Kirtland, Ohio. The Lord had promised the Saints on January 2, 1831, that He would "give unto you my law" (D&C 38:32), a promise repeated again on February 4, 1831 (D&C 41:3; see *HC* 1:148–154 for details). Consequently, twelve elders met on February 9 in prayer, and seven elders met on February 23 to inquire of the Lord. The answer came in the form of a revelation now known as Section 42—in many ways an extension of the material given in Section 20 on Church organization and government.

D&C 42:3–6—Of the commandments given to the Church by the Lord as His law, the very first one is to do missionary work—declare the gospel, baptize the people, and build up the kingdom of God. The mandate of the Abrahamic covenant was to bring the gospel to every nation on earth (see Abr. 2:6, 9–11). President David O. McKay's dictum, "Every member a missionary," is the modern-day reminder of this covenant obligation to obey the first law of the Lord—namely, from the outset to be committed to, and active in, missionary work. All who are in the Church are directly or indirectly indebted to missionaries for their introduction to the gospel.

D&C 42:11—Order prevails in the kingdom of God. The priesthood operates by divine authorization known to the Church membership and leadership—not in any secretive or clandestine way. The Lord selects those who act for Him, and designates those who will be His authorized servants. Paul put it forcefully: "And no man taketh this honour unto himself, but he that is called of God, as *was* Aaron" (Heb. 5:4).

D&C 42:12—We are enjoined by the Lord to focus our teaching efforts on the basic truths of the gospel as contained in the holy scriptures. If we treasure up the words of the scriptures in our hearts and then speak by the inspiration of the Holy Ghost, we will be speaking the language of power and conversion—just as the angels of the Lord. We do not intermingle the philosophies and sophistries of the world with our teachings, but deal in pure, divine doctrines.

13. And they shall observe the covenants and church articles to do them, and these shall be their teachings, as they shall be directed by the Spirit;

14. And the Spirit shall be given unto you by the prayer of faith, and if ye receive not the Spirit, ye shall not teach.

15. And all this ye shall observe to do as I have commanded concerning your teaching, until the fulness of my scriptures is given.

16. And as ye shall lift up your voices by the Comforter, ye shall speak and prophesy as seemeth me good;

17. For, behold, the Comforter knoweth all things, and beareth record of the Father and of the Son.

18. And now, behold, I speak unto the church. Thou shalt not kill; and he that kills shall not have forgiveness in this world, nor in the world to come.

19. And again, I say, thou shalt not kill; but he that killeth shall die.

20. Thou shalt not steal; and he that stealeth and will not repent, shall be cast out.

21. Thou shalt not lie; he that lieth and will not repent, shall be cast out.

22. Thou shalt love thy wife with all thy heart, and shalt cleave unto her and none else;

23. And he that looketh upon a woman to lust after her, shall deny the faith, and shall not have the Spirit, and if he repents not he shall be cast out.

24. Thou shalt not commit adultery; and he that committeth adultery, and repenteth not, shall be cast out,

25. But he that has committed adultery and repents with all his heart, and forsaketh it, and doeth it no more, thou shalt forgive;

26. But if he doeth it again, he shall not be forgiven, but shall be cast out.

27. Thou shalt not speak evil of thy neighbor, nor do him any harm.

28. Thou knowest my laws concerning these things are given in my scriptures; he that sinneth and repenteth not, shall be cast out.

29. If thou lovest me thou shalt serve me and keep all my commandments.

30. And behold, thou wilt remember the poor, and consecrate of thy properties for their support that which thou hast to impart unto

D&C 42:14—Faith is the key in teaching by the Spirit. It is the Spirit that teaches and testifies of the truth. Truth without the testimony of the Spirit is hollow. To qualify for the Spirit becomes all important in the teaching process (see Mosiah 23:14).

D&C 42:16—How does this grand promise have application for us today? How does one prophesy in the act of performing missionary service? To declare by the Spirit that Jesus is the Christ, the Author of eternal salvation, is prophecy, for "no man can say that Jesus is the Lord, but by the Holy Ghost" (1 Cor. 12:3). To declare that the Atonement of the Savior will bring about a mighty change and a rebirth of the faithful and obedient is prophecy. To declare by the Spirit that families will be together forever through the sealing powers available in the temples of the Lord is prophecy. To declare by the Spirit that great blessings will flow on the basis of covenant faithfulness and valor is prophecy. It is a grand promise and blessing from the Savior that His authorized servants can speak for Him and testify of the truthfulness of the gospel and the efficacy of the eternal laws upon which it is based.

D&C 42:18–20—The law of the Lord with respect to murder is promulgated. "Thou shalt not kill" has resounded through the generations of time from the beginning (see Ex. 20:13). Cain was cursed by God for committing the first of all murders (see Gen. 4:11). The law still stands at the dawn of the Restoration. Similarly, the commandment against stealing is upheld. We must be honest with ourselves, with our fellowmen, and with our God. In this way our relationships can be built and maintained. The alternative is too high a price to pay: "Wo unto the liar, for he shall be thrust down to hell" (see 2 Ne. 9:34).

D&C 42:24—Virtue and purity are indispensable attributes of those who labor in the vineyard of the Lord. As Alma counseled his son, Shiblon: ". . . see that ye bridle all your passions, that ye may be filled with love; . . ." (Alma 38:12). The Spirit can abide only in temples of holiness and purity.

D&C 42:28–29—The Decalogue is among the most familiar sections of the holy scriptures. The Lord expresses His awareness that the Saints are familiar with the Ten Commandments. The Lord summarizes the essence of fidelity to His gospel teachings in one word: *love*. If we love Him, we will keep His commandments.

them, with a covenant and a deed which cannot be broken;

31. And inasmuch as ye impart of your substance unto the poor, ye will do it unto me, and they shall be laid before the bishop of my church and his counselors, two of the elders, or High Priests, such as he shall or has appointed and set apart for that purpose.

32. And it shall come to pass, that after they are laid before the bishop of my church, and after that he has received these testimonies concerning the consecration of the properties of my church, that they cannot be taken from the church agreeable to my commandments; every man shall be made accountable unto me, a steward over his own property, or that which he has received by consecration, as much as is sufficient for himself and family.

33. And again, if there shall be properties in the hands of the church, or any individuals of it, more than is necessary for their support, after this first consecration, which is a residue to be consecrated unto the bishop, it shall be kept to administer to those who have not, from time to time, that every man who has need may be amply supplied, and receive according to his wants.

34. Therefore, the residue shall be kept in my storehouse, to administer to the poor and the needy, as shall be appointed by the High Council of the church, and the bishop and his council,

35. And for the purpose of purchasing lands for the public benefit of the church, and building houses of worship, and building up of the New Jerusalem which is hereafter to be revealed,

36. That my covenant people may be gathered in one in that day when I shall come to my temple. And this I do for the salvation of my people.

37. And it shall come to pass, that he that sinneth and repenteth not shall be cast out of the church, and shall not receive again that which he has consecrated unto the poor and the needy of my church; or in other words, unto me;

38. For inasmuch as ye do it unto the least of these, ye do it unto me;

39. For it shall come to pass, that which I spake by the mouths of my prophets, shall be fulfilled; for I will consecrate of the riches of those who embrace my gospel among the Gentiles, unto the poor of my people who are of the house of Israel.

40. And again, thou shalt not be proud in thy heart; let all thy garments be plain, and their beauty the beauty of the work of thine own hands;

41. And let all things be done in cleanliness before me.

42. Thou shalt not be idle; for he that is idle shall not eat the

D&C 42:30-31, 36—In the years immediately after the organization of the Church, the Lord began to reveal the details of a sacred law of financial governance that pertains to a Zion people. Unity, charity, mutual support, social cohesion, self-sufficiency, spiritual growth, and cultivating an eye single to the glory of God were all factors related to the law of consecration. Even though the founding Saints were not able to live this law to its full extent, the celestial organizing pattern was established in the early stages of the Restoration as an objective toward which to point the Church in preparation for the Second Coming.

D&C 42:38—The Lord emphasizes the principle that serving the needs of the poor is tantamount to serving Him. That principle is the fulcrum for inculcating this doctrine into the hearts of the Saints of the Restoration. Spiritual priorities underlie all of the gospel: "*Wherefore, seek not the things of this world* but seek ye first *to build up* the kingdom of God, and *to establish* his righteousness, and all these things shall be added unto you*" (JST Matt. 6:38).

How do we consecrate our lives today unto the Lord?

1. Remember God's Divine Purpose—our immortality and eternal life, our happiness, our unity and love for others, and our spiritual growth.

2. Remember God's Goodness and Mercy, including the Atonement.

3. Set Worthy Goals. Plan for a full-time mission, take advantage of daily opportunities for consecration, use wisdom and prudence, and prioritize your life so that you can organize every needful thing.

4. Follow a pattern of consecration. Attend the temple often, fast and pray on a regular basis, regularly search the scriptures, remember to give willingly, remember that everything is really the Lord's, and focus on your *needs,* not your wants.

D&C 42:40—There is virtue in simplicity; there is beauty in plainness of adornment. "And they did impart of their substance, every man according to that which he had, to the poor, and the needy, and the sick, and the afflicted; and they did not wear costly apparel, yet they were neat and comely" (Alma 1:27).

D&C 42:41—The Lord's pattern regarding self-sufficiency is simple and pure: be humble in thought and action; be modest in dress; be industrious; be clean; be the Lord's people.

D&C 42:42—Thou shalt not be idle. Central to the law of consecration is the principle of industry and self-reliance. The Lord commanded: "Cease to be idle" (D&C 88:124). Nevertheless, those who remain wanting after striving with all their heart and might to lift themselves from need are fully embraced by the spirit of service and charity on the part of their associates. In great measure, charitable service includes also reaching out to teach principles of self-reliance and self-sufficiency.

bread nor wear the garments of the laborer.

43. And whosoever among you are sick, and have not faith to be healed, but believe, shall be nourished with all tenderness, with herbs and mild food, and that not by the hand of an enemy.

44. And the elders of the church, two or more, shall be called, and shall pray for and lay their hands upon them in my name; and if they die they shall die unto me, and if they live they shall live unto me.

45. Thou shalt live together in love, insomuch that thou shalt weep for the loss of them that die, and more especially for those that have not hope of a glorious resurrection.

46. And it shall come to pass that those that die in me, shall not taste of death, for it shall be sweet unto them;

47. And they that die not in me, wo unto them, for their death is bitter.

48. And again, it shall come to pass that he that hath faith in me to be healed, and is not appointed unto death, shall be healed;

49. He who hath faith to see shall see;

50. He who hath faith to hear shall hear;

51. The lame who hath faith to leap shall leap;

52. And they who have not faith to do these things, but believe in me, have power to become my sons, and inasmuch as they break not my laws, thou shalt bear their infirmities.

53. Thou shalt stand in the place of thy stewardship;

54. Thou shalt not take thy brother's garment; thou shalt pay for that which thou shalt receive of thy brother;

55. And if thou obtainest more than that which would be for thy support, thou shalt give it into my store-house, that all things may be done according to that which I have said.

56. Thou shalt ask, and my Scriptures shall be given as I have appointed, and they shall be preserved in safety;

57. And it is expedient that thou shouldst hold thy peace concerning them, and not teach them until ye have received them in full.

58. And I give unto you a commandment that then ye shall teach them unto all men; for they shall be taught unto all nations, kindreds, tongues and people.

59. Thou shalt take the things which thou hast received, which have been given unto thee in my Scriptures for a law, to be my law to govern my church;

D&C 42:48—The Lord decreed that the priesthood was given to mankind for the blessing of His children. One of the tender and choice aspects of this divine blessing is the charitable use of the priesthood to ameliorate the suffering of those with physical illness. Note that the Lord prescribes also the administering of natural remedies ("herbs and mild foods"; see also D&C 89:10). Within the framework of charity and prudent dietary intake there can be blessings administered under the hands of the priesthood to invoke relief through the Spirit, according to the faith of the individual and the will of the Father.

D&C 42:59–61—The holy canon constitutes the record of the law of the Lord. But the record itself does not constitute sufficiency, since the foundation of Church governance is continual revelation. The canon is continually supplemented by the words of the living prophets under the guidance of the Holy Ghost, who is the agent of the light of Christ to the sons and daughters of God.

LAWS CONCERNING DEATH AND ADMINISTRATIONS TO THE SICK

Section 42 teaches several things about death and illness. Concerning death, we learn:

1. It is appropriate to weep for the loss of a loved one (see D&C 42:45).

2. Death is sweet to those who die in Christ, but it is bitter to those who do not (see D&C 42:46–47).

Both of these concepts are vividly illustrated as Mormon described the conditions in Alma's day (see Alma 28:10–12).

If we can grasp the true concept of life, we can understand that death is not a fearful end, but rather an important step in our advancement to continued life. President Joseph F. Smith said of death, "I have nothing to be sad over, nothing to make me sorrowful.... On the contrary, it is cause for joy unspeakable, and for pure happiness" (CR, Oct. 1899, p. 70).

Pertaining to illness, we learn:

1. The Lord has provided foods and herbs (medicines) for the healing of the sick (see D&C 42:43).

2. The Lord has directed the elders of the Church to administer to the sick by the laying on of hands (see D&C 42:44).

3. Faith is essential to our obtaining the blessings of the Lord (see D&C 42:48–52).

4. There is a time in life when man is appointed unto death (see D&C 42:48).

We have responsibility, too, to do all we can to bring about healing. President Brigham Young said we should "apply every remedy that comes within the range of [our] knowledge.... Many people are unwilling to do one thing for themselves, in case of sickness, but ask God to do it all" (JD 4:24–25) (see STDC 1:203–205).

60. And he that doeth according to these things shall be saved, and he that doeth them not shall be damned, if he continues.

61. If thou shalt ask, thou shalt receive revelation upon revelation, knowledge upon knowledge, that thou mayest know the mysteries and peaceable things—that which bringeth joy, that which bringeth life eternal.

62. Thou shalt ask, and it shall be revealed unto you in mine own due time where the New Jerusalem shall be built.

63. And behold, it shall come to pass that my servants shall be sent forth to the east and to the west, to the north and to the south;

64. And even now, let him that goeth to the east, teach them that shall be converted to flee to the west, and this in consequence of that which is coming on the earth, and of secret combinations.

65. Behold, thou shalt observe all these things, and great shall be thy reward; for unto you it is given to know the mysteries of the kingdom, but unto the world it is not given to know them.

66. Ye shall observe the laws which ye have received and be faithful.

67. And ye shall hereafter receive church covenants, such as shall be sufficient to establish you, both here and in the New Jerusalem.

68. Therefore, he that lacketh wisdom, let him ask of me, and I will give him liberally and upbraid him not.

69. Lift up your hearts and rejoice, for unto you the kingdom, or in other words, the keys of the church have been given. Even so. Amen.

70. The priests and teachers shall have their stewardships, even as the members;

71. And the elders, or High Priests who are appointed to assist the bishop as counselors in all things, are to have their families supported out of the property which is consecrated to the bishop, for the good of the poor, and for other purposes, as before mentioned;

72. Or they are to receive a just remuneration for all their services, either a stewardship or otherwise, as may be thought best or decided by the counselors and bishop.

73. And the bishop, also, shall receive his support, or a just remuneration for all his services in the church.

74. Behold, verily I say unto you, that whatever persons among you, having put away their companions for the cause of fornication, or in other words, if they shall testify before you in all lowliness of heart that this is the case, ye shall not cast them out from among you;

75. But if ye shall find that any persons have left their companions for the sake of adultery, and they themselves are the offenders, and their companions are living, they shall be cast out from among you.

76. And again, I say unto you, that ye shall be watchful and careful, with all inquiry, that ye receive none such among you if they are married;

D&C 42:62—The term "the New Jerusalem" is used four times in Section 42: verses 9, 35, 62, and 67. The risen Lord taught the ancient American Saints: "And behold, this people will I establish in this land, unto the fulfilling of the covenant which I made with your father Jacob; and it shall be a New Jerusalem. And the powers of heaven shall be in the midst of this people; yea, even I will be in the midst of you" (3 Ne. 20:22; see also the words of the Lord to Enoch given in Moses 7:62–64).

D&C 42:68—This language is reminiscent of the very scripture that brought the young Joseph Smith to the cusp of spiritual discovery leading to the Restoration. Joseph was doubtless edified and uplifted to come once again upon these words of the Savior and must have rejoiced in his heart that he had had the courage to act upon his convictions and become an agent for good in the hands of God. The keys of the Church had now been given to God's representatives on the earth—keys of power and hope opening the doorway to salvation, eternal life, and exaltation for all who would come unto Christ in faith and obedience.

D&C 42:72–73—Within the parameters of the law of consecration there was provision made for the support of the families of those who consecrated their time to priesthood leadership duties. The Prophet Joseph was directed by the Lord specifically to give full time to the Kingdom: "For thou shalt devote all thy service in Zion; and in this thou shalt have strength" (D&C 24:7). Scholar Clark V. Johnson elaborates on how the system was to operate:

> According to Joseph Smith, the amount of the inheritance depended upon the properties consecrated and the means provided for the poor. [See *The Personal Writings of Joseph Smith*, ed. Dean C. Jessee (Salt Lake City: Deseret Book Co., 1984), 277.] The more wealth given to the storehouse, the larger the stewardship. Thus the living standard of everyone, including the poor, rose according to the selfless dedication of members of the united order. Every person was accountable to the Lord for his stewardship. The Savior reminded his people that there were two kinds of stewardship—temporal and spiritual. For example, the bishop, who is charged with operating a storehouse, receiving consecrations, and managing the Lord's properties, has a spiritual stewardship; however, because he also draws from the storehouse the goods he needs to provide for himself he enjoys a temporal stewardship. (D&C 42:33, 71.) Thus Church leaders claimed goods from the storehouse for their support or to be reimbursed for their expenses. (D&C 42:71-72; 51:14.) In the Lord's eyes, both temporal and spiritual stewardships serve to build his kingdom (D&C 70:12). (Clark V. Johnson, in Susan Easton Black et al., *DE*, 100.)

77. And if they are not married, they shall repent of all their sins, or ye shall not receive them.

78. And again, every person who belongeth to this church of Christ, shall observe to keep all the commandments and covenants of the church.

79. And it shall come to pass, that if any persons among you shall kill, they shall be delivered up and dealt with according to the laws of the land; for remember that he hath no forgiveness, and it shall be proved according to the laws of the land.

80. And if any man or woman shall commit adultery, he or she shall be tried before two elders of the church, or more, and every word shall be established against him or her by two witnesses of the church, and not of the enemy; but if there are more than two witnesses it is better.

81. But he or she shall be condemned by the mouth of two witnesses, and the elders shall lay the case before the church, and the church shall lift up their hands against him or her, that they may be dealt with according to the law of God.

82. And if it can be, it is necessary that the bishop is present also.

83. And thus ye shall do in all cases which shall come before you.

84. And if a man or woman shall rob, he or she shall be delivered up unto the law of the land.

85. And if he or she shall steal, he or she shall be delivered up unto the law of the land.

86. And if he or she shall lie, he or she shall be delivered up unto the law of the land.

87. And if he or she do any manner of iniquity, he or she shall be delivered up unto the law, even that of God.

88. And if thy brother or sister offend thee, thou shalt take him or her between him or her and thee alone; and if he or she confess, thou shalt be reconciled.

89. And if he or she confess not, thou shalt deliver him or her up unto the church, not to the members, but to the elders. And it shall be done in a meeting, and that not before the world.

90. And if thy brother or sister offend many, he or she shall be chastened before many.

91. And if any one offend openly, he or she shall be rebuked openly, that he or she may be ashamed. And if he or she confess not, he or she shall be delivered up unto the law of God.

92. If any shall offend in secret, he or she shall be rebuked in secret, that he or she may have opportunity to confess in secret to him or her whom he or she has offended, and to God, that the church may not speak reproachfully of him or her.

93. And thus shall ye conduct in all things.

D&C 42:74–93—Latter-day Saints are known as loyal citizens of the countries in which they live. About eighteen months after The Church of Jesus Christ of Latter-day Saints was organized, the Lord commanded his people not to break the law of the land, for if they kept the laws of God there would be no reason for breaking the laws of the land (see D&C 58:21–22). Before this time, instructions were given to the authorities of the Church that in cases of infractions of the moral law, the guilty should "be delivered up unto the law of the land" (D&C 42:84–87). Later, in two revelations, the saints came to know that the Constitution of the United States was an inspired document and that they should uphold it (D&C 98:4–7; 101:76–80) (*Doxey*, 2:428).

LAWS CONCERNING APPROPRIATE ACTION PERTAINING TO TRANSGRESSORS

Transgression occurs in many forms. There are varying degrees of seriousness of sin, and it is impossible for man to comprehend or legislate all courses of action that should appropriately be taken in dealing with transgressors. Consequently, the Lord has described basic principles and established some fundamental laws by which His kingdom should be administered. He has also charged the officers of His Church with the responsibility of seeking the Spirit for guidance that they may deal justly with every case.

Some of these fundamental laws are contained in D&C 42:74–93. One area that deserves special mention is the handling of offenses or differences that arise between the Saints.

When members of the Church are offended, they often alienate themselves from the offender and instead discuss the issue with others who are not party to the offense. Such behavior is not keeping with the Lord's instructions; He has specifically instructed that the offended one should go to the offender for the purpose of being reconciled. If reconciliation is not realized, then the course of action should be to seek the counsel and judgment of presiding officers of the Church. Any rebuking procedures should be limited to those who are necessarily involved in the case (see D&C 42:88–92).

If Saints would obey this counsel, vicious rumors would be eliminated, tender hearts would not be bruised, the spiritual welfare of the individual would be uppermost in the minds and hearts of all, and love for one another would be the supreme influence in our relationships (*STDC* 1:205–206).

SECTION 43

1. O hearken, ye elders of my church, and give an ear to the words which I shall speak unto you;

2. For behold, verily, verily, I say unto you, that ye have received a commandment for a law unto my church, through him whom I have appointed unto you, to receive commandments and revelations from my hand.

3. And this ye shall know assuredly that there is none other appointed unto you to receive commandments and revelations until he be taken, if he abide in me.

4. But verily, verily, I say unto you, that none else shall be appointed unto this gift except it be through him, for if it be taken from him, he shall not have power except to appoint another in his stead;

5. And this shall be a law unto you, that ye receive not the teachings of any that shall come before you as revelations or commandments;

6. And this I give unto you that you may not be deceived, that you may know they are not of me.

7. For verily I say unto you, that he that is ordained of me shall come in at the gate and be ordained as I have told you before, to teach those revelations which you have received, and shall receive through him whom I have appointed.

8. And now, behold, I give unto you a commandment, that when ye are assembled together, ye shall instruct and edify each other, that ye may know how to act and direct my church, how to act upon the points of my law and commandments, which I have given;

9. And thus ye shall become instructed in the law of my church, and be sanctified by that which ye have received, and ye shall bind yourselves to act in all holiness before me,

10. That inasmuch as ye do this, glory shall be added to the kingdom which ye have received. Inasmuch as ye do it not, it shall be taken, even that which ye have received.

11. Purge ye out the iniquity which is among you; sanctify yourselves before me,

12. And if ye desire the glories of the kingdom, appoint ye my servant Joseph Smith, jun., and uphold him before me by the prayer of faith.

13. And again, I say unto you, that if ye desire the mysteries of the kingdom, provide for him food and raiment, and whatsoever thing he needeth to accomplish the work, wherewith I have commanded him;

14. And if ye do it not, he shall remain

Section 43 Background—Given in February 1831 at Kirtland, Ohio (see *HC* 1:154–156). At the time, some members of the Church were concerned about certain individuals claiming to receive revelations. For example, a woman by the name of Hubble came to Kirtland, professing to be a prophetess, and persuaded some members of the Church of her authenticity:

> She professed to be a prophetess of the Lord, and professed to have many revelations, and knew the Book of Mormon was true, and that she should become a teacher in te church of Christ. She appeared to be very sanctimonious and deceived some who were not able to detect her in her hypocrisy; others, however, had the spirit of discernment and her follies and abominations were manifest" (*HC* 1:154, footnote).

Joseph Smith inquired of the Lord and received counsel on how to discern and deflect the influence of such false teachers.

D&C 43:3—We have an essential need for a living prophet who is authorized and commissioned to speak for the Lord. In ancient times, God's servant Amos crystallized the essence of the prophetic office in memorable terms: "Surely the Lord GOD will do nothing, but he revealeth his secret unto his servants the prophets" (Amos 3:7). On one occasion where some members of the Church were discounting the importance of having a living prophet, Brigham Young rose up in majesty and declared, in the presence of Joseph Smith, "that he would not 'give the ashes of a rye straw' for the books [the scriptures] without the accompanying teachings of 'the living oracles of God'" (Ronald W. Walker, "Brigham Young: Student of the Prophet," *Ensign*, Feb. 1998, 51).

D&C 43:5—The Lord makes it abundantly clear that our eyes need to be focused at all times and in all diligence on His appointed prophet as leader and director of the affairs of the kingdom of God upon the earth (see also D&C 21:4–6; 43:3).

D&C 43:7—Here it is emphasized that revelations for the Church must come through proper priesthood channels.

D&C 43:8–11—The pattern for regulating the Kingdom is clear: teach one another the doctrines and laws in unity of spirit and holiness of heart—thus power and glory will be added from on high. When this pattern is followed, the influence of false teachers will be repelled.

D&C 43:9—"That which ye have received" refers to covenants. When we make a covenant, we are bound by our integrity to act a certain way.

D&C 43:13—Joseph Smith's temporal support at this time had been inadequate, and he hadn't been able to finish the translation of the Bible.

unto them that have received him, that I may reserve unto myself a pure people before me.

15. Again I say, hearken ye elders of my church, whom I have appointed; ye are not sent forth to be taught, but to teach the children of men the things which I have put into your hands by the power of my Spirit;

16. And ye are to be taught from on high. Sanctify yourselves and ye shall be endowed with power, that ye may give even as I have spoken.

17. Hearken ye, for, behold, the great day of the Lord is nigh at hand.

18. For the day cometh that the Lord shall utter his voice out of heaven; the heavens shall shake and the earth shall tremble, and the trump of God shall sound both long and loud, and shall say to the sleeping nations, Ye saints arise and live; ye sinners stay and sleep until I shall call again;

19. Wherefore gird up your loins lest ye be found among the wicked.

20. Lift up your voices and spare not. Call upon the nations to repent, both old and young, both bond and free, saying; prepare yourselves for the great day of the Lord;

21. For if I, who am a man, do lift up my voice and call upon you to repent, and ye hate me, what will ye say when the day cometh when the thunders shall utter their voices from the ends of the earth, speaking to the ears of all that live, saying, Repent, and prepare for the great day of the Lord;

22. Yea, and again, when the lightnings shall streak forth from the east unto the west, and shall utter forth their voices unto all that live, and make the ears of all tingle that hear, saying these words, Repent ye, for the great day of the Lord is come.

23. And again, the Lord shall utter his voice out of heaven, saying, Hearken, O ye nations of the earth, and hear the words of that God who made you.

24. O, ye nations of the earth, how often would I have gathered you together as a hen gathereth her chickens under her wings, but ye would not?

25. How oft have I called upon you by the mouth of my servants, and by the ministering of angels, and by mine own voice, and by the voice of thunderings, and by the voice of lightnings, and by the voice of tempests, and by the voice of earthquakes, and great hailstorms, and by the voice of famines and pestilences of every kind, and by the

D&C 43:15—The emissaries of the Lord deliver a message of profound importance: that the Lord has again spoken, that the fullness of His everlasting gospel has been restored to the earth, and that the blessings of salvation and eternal life are again accessible to those with faith to come unto Jesus and follow Him in all diligence. This message supersedes in importance any other message on earth. Missionaries are not to relinquish their commission by yielding to others who would teach them of worldly or misguided philosophies.

D&C 43:17–25—The message of salvation and mercy is sent forth in a sequence of voices: the voice of the Lord Himself, the voice of angels, the voice of the Lord's missionaries, and the more strident and dissonant voices of natural calamities and geological dislocations. The warnings come through the whisperings of the Spirit or, as needed, the thunderings of destructive forces clamoring to capture the attention of a prideful and wayward world. The earlier we respond, the quieter is the message of salvation; the longer we wait, the more shrill and discordant are the sounds. Orson Pratt taught concerning the chronic and persistent hardness of hearts occurring among the nations:

It is true that the Lord has not yet spoken by the voice of thunders, calling upon the people from the ends of the earth, saying, "Repent and prepare for the great day of the Lord," but such an event will come; and when it does come it will not be a mere ordinary, common thunderstorm, such as we experience occasionally, extending only over a small extent of country, but the Lord will cause the thunders to utter their voices from the ends of the earth until they sound in the ears of all that live, and these thunders shall use the very words here predicted—"Repent, O ye inhabitants of the earth, and prepare the way of the Lord, prepare yourselves for the great day of the Lord." These words will be distinctly heard by every soul that lives, whether in America, Asia, Africa, Europe, or upon the islands of the sea. And not only the thunders, but the lightnings will utter forth their voices in the ears of all that live, saying, "Repent, for the great day of the Lord is come." Besides the voices of thunder and lightning, the Lord himself, before he comes in his glory, will speak by his own voice out of heaven in the ears of all that live, commanding them to repent and to prepare for his coming. (JD 15:332–333.)

great sound of a trump, and by the voice of judgment, and by the voice of mercy all the day long, and by the voice of glory, and honor, and the riches of eternal life, and would have saved you with an everlasting salvation, but ye would not?

26. Behold the day has come, when the cup of the wrath of mine indignation is full.

27. Behold, verily I say unto you, that these are the words of the Lord your God;

28. Wherefore labor ye, labor ye in my vineyard for the last time— for the last time call upon the inhabitants of the earth,

29. For in mine own due time will I come upon the earth in judgment, and my people shall be redeemed and shall reign with me on earth;

30. For the great Millennium, of which I have spoken by the mouth of my servants, shall come.

31. For Satan shall be bound, and when he is loosed again he shall only reign for a little season, and then cometh the end of the earth;

32. And he that liveth in righteousness shall be changed in the twinkling of an eye, and the earth shall pass away so as by fire;

33. And the wicked shall go away into unquenchable fire, and their end no man knoweth on earth, nor ever shall know, until they come before me in judgment.

34. Hearken ye to these words; Behold, I am Jesus Christ, the Savior of the world. Treasure these things up in your hearts, and let the solemnities of eternity rest upon your minds.

35. Be sober. Keep all my commandments. Even so. Amen.

SECTION 44

1. Behold, thus saith the Lord unto you my servants, it is expedient in me that the elders of my church should be called together, from the

D&C 43:26—When the day comes that the Lord is constrained to speak with the voice of wrath and indignation, then the words of the revelations on the final days will be fulfilled, as Brigham Young explained in a sermon given on July 15, 1860: "Do you think there is calamity abroad now among the people? Not much. All we have yet heard and all we have experienced is scarcely a preface to the sermon that is going to be preached. When the testimony of the Elders ceases to be given, and the Lord says to them, 'Come home; I will now preach my own sermons to the nations of the earth,' all you now know can scarcely be called a preface to the sermon that will be preached with fire and sword, tempests, earthquakes, hail, rain, thunders and lightnings, and fearful destruction" (JD 8:123).

D&C 43:29–34—The vision of the millennial era awakens feelings of rejoicing in the hearts of the righteous, but the wicked will be removed in ignominy and consigned to their just reward. Jesus Christ will reign. We are to treasure up in our hearts the verity of these revealed truths and let "the solemnities of the eternities" rest upon our minds. Concerning the binding of Satan, George Q. Cannon explained: "Satan will be bound by the power of God; but he will be bound also by the determination of the people of God not to listen to him, not to be governed by him. The Lord will not bind him and take his power from the earth while there are men and women willing to be governed by him. That is contrary to the plan of salvation. . . . There was a time on this continent, of which we have an account, when the people were so righteous that Satan did not have power among them. Nearly four generations passed away in righteousness. They lived in purity, and died without sin. That was through their refusal to yield to Satan [4 Ne. 10–18]" (CR, Oct. 1897, 65).

D&C 43:35—The Lord gives His benedictory counsel to all who receive this revelation: be sober and fully obedient. Those two measures of discipleship lead to unspeakable blessings of glory and spiritual ascendancy.

Section 44 Background—Given in the latter part of February 1831 at Kirtland, Ohio (see HC 1:157). The revelation calls for a conference to be held in Ohio. The conference— the fourth held in the newly organized Church and the first in Ohio—was convened on Friday, June 3, 1831, and lasted through the weekend. Also referenced in the revelation at this early date in the Church's history is the commandment to "visit the poor and the needy and administer to their relief."

east and from the west, and from the north and from the south, by letter or some other way.

2. And it shall come to pass, that inasmuch as they are faithful, and exercise faith in me, I will pour out my Spirit upon them in the day that they assemble themselves together.

3. And it shall come to pass that they shall go forth into the regions round about, and preach repentance unto the people,

4. And many shall be converted, insomuch that ye shall obtain power to organize yourselves, according to the laws of man;

5. That your enemies may not have power over you, that you may be preserved in all things; that you may be enabled to keep my laws, that every bond may be broken wherewith the enemy seeketh to destroy my people.

6. Behold I say unto you, that ye must visit the poor and the needy, and administer to their relief, that they may be kept until all things may be done according to my law which ye have received. Amen.

SECTION 45

1. Hearken, O ye people of my church, to whom the kingdom has been given—hearken ye and give ear to him who laid the foundation of the earth, who made the heavens and all the hosts thereof, and by whom all things were made which live, and move, and have a being.

2. And again I say, hearken unto my voice, lest death shall overtake you; in an hour when ye think not the summer shall be past, and the

The site of the Isaac Morley farm, the gathering place for the Saints as they arrived in Kirtland. Joseph Smith himself lived on this farm for about six months. This farm is where the Prophet received Section 45 and is the site of the fourth general conference of the Church, at which the first high priests were ordained.

D&C 44:2–3—The promise of the Lord is to pour out His Spirit upon the assembled elders if they are "faithful" (having a disposition of faith and trust) and "exercise faith"—actually come forth and do what is commanded. Thus both a spiritual attitude as well as obedient action are requisite to receive the promised blessing. What the Lord asks for is a faithful heart from the beginning and a willingness to obey His commands through action.

D&C 44:4—The laws of the land—in this case the United States of America, with its inspired foundational Constitution—provide a shield and protection for the growing body of Saints. If they are organized according to the principles of democratic rights and liberties, they have a far better chance of sustaining themselves against the lawless incursions of mobs than if they were politically inactive.

D&C 44:6—According to George Q. Cannon, the Prophet Joseph Smith was imbued with an enduring attitude of compassion for the needy:

At no time during the Prophet's career did the care of the poor escape his attention or become a matter of indifference to him. He was a man of large benevolence, and his sympathies were quickly aroused by any tale of sorrow or appeal for relief. In the most busy and trying periods of his life those who went to him for counsel in their troubles, always found him willing to listen, and they were sure to receive encouragement and assistance. To extend comfort to the bruised spirit, and to help the needy and distressed appeared a constant pleasure to him. His hospitality, also, was a marked feature in his character. His house was always open to entertain the stranger. One of the most cherished recollections of many of the old members of the Church is the kindness with which they were treated by "Brother Joseph," and the warm welcome he gave them to his house upon their arrival at Kirtland and other places where he lived. (*LDPDC* 2:72.)

Section 45 Background—Given on March 7, 1831, at the Morley Farm in Kirtland, Ohio (see *HC* 1:158–163). The Prophet recorded in his journal: "At this age of the Church [early in the year of 1831] many false reports, lies, and foolish stories, were published in the newspapers, and circulated in every direction, to prevent people from investigating the work, or embracing the faith. A great earthquake in China, which destroyed from one to two thousand inhabitants, was burlesqued in some papers, as 'Mormonism' in China.' But to the joy of the Saints who had to struggle against every thing that prejudice and wickedness could invent, I received [Section 45]" (*HC* 1:158).

harvest ended, and your souls not saved.

3. Listen to him who is the advocate with the Father, who is pleading your cause before him,

4. Saying, Father, behold the sufferings and death of him who did no sin, in whom thou wast well pleased; behold the blood of thy Son which was shed—the blood of him whom thou gavest that thyself might be glorified;

5. Wherefore, Father, spare these my brethren that believe on my name, that they may come unto me and have everlasting life.

6. Hearken, O ye people of my church, and ye elders listen together, and hear my voice while it is called to-day, and harden not your hearts,

7. For verily I say unto you that I am Alpha and Omega, the beginning and the end, the light and the life of the world—a light that shineth in darkness and the darkness comprehendeth it not.

8. I came unto mine own, and mine own received me not; but unto as many as received me, gave I power to do many miracles, and to become the sons of God, and even unto them that believed on my name gave I power to obtain eternal life.

9. And even so I have sent mine everlasting covenant into the world, to be a light to the world, and to be a standard for my people and for the Gentiles to seek to it, and to be a messenger before my face to prepare the way before me;

10. Wherefore, come ye unto it, and with him that cometh I will reason as with men in days of old, and I will show unto you my strong reasoning.

11. Wherefore hearken ye together and let me show unto you, even my wisdom—the wisdom of him whom ye say is the God of Enoch, and his brethren,

12. Who were separated from the earth, and were received unto myself—a city reserved until a day of righteousness shall come—a day which was sought for by all holy men, and they found it not because of wickedness and abominations;

13. And confessed they were strangers and pilgrims on the earth;

14. But obtained a promise that they should find it and see it in their flesh.

15. Wherefore, hearken and I will reason with you, and I will speak unto you and prophesy, as unto men in days of old;

16. And I will show it plainly as I showed it unto my disciples as I stood before them in the flesh, and spake unto them, saying; as ye have

D&C 45:2–7—As so frequently in the early revelations given to the Church, the Savior provides as an overture the magnificent summation of His divine commission, viewed from the highest eternal perspective, but directed to the attention of His humble followers on earth who depend on His advocacy before the Father for their redemption and ultimate endowment of enduring light and eternal life. The reference in Section 45 provides a particularly poignant insight into the advocacy process of the Son before the Father, the Savior rehearsing His sacrificial Atonement of suffering and love, and then pleading that the Father might spare "these my brethren" so that they can come unto the Savior and have everlasting life (verse 5).

D&C 45:9—The gospel of Jesus Christ is surely the good news of salvation and redemption—but it is more than that, for it contains the covenant powers and keys to seal the elect up unto eternal life as sons and daughters of God. When the Savior says that He has sent "mine everlasting covenant" into the world, He confirms that all requisite truth, knowledge, priesthood powers, ordinances, and blessings are restored to bring about the ultimate consummation of His mission on behalf of those who come unto Him in faith and valor. The Doctrine and Covenants—as a sacred document—confirms the return of His covenant operation to the world, and the fulfillment of His promise to honor His covenant agreement with the fathers of old.

D&C 45:11—Enoch and his people were taken up to the Lord because of their exceeding righteousness in a world of wickedness: The reference to Enoch by the Lord is a reminder that the city of Enoch would return as part of the winding-up scenes of earth's history in connection with the Second Coming.

D&C 45:16—The Lord recounts the teachings He gave to His disciples in the meridian of time concerning the destiny of mankind and the unfolding of His purposes—including the judgments of heaven. The temple in Jerusalem was indeed destroyed in 70 A.D. at the hands of the Romans. Jews in large numbers were killed or scattered. The word of the Lord regarding circumstances in the last days will also be fulfilled in every respect. The Lord teaches these things in the dispensation of the fullness of times with the same degree of clarity and plainness, for He wants people to understand and be warned of the eternal consequences associated with how they prepare for His return.

asked of me concerning the signs of my coming, in the day when I shall come in my glory in the clouds of heaven, to fulfil the promises that I have made unto your fathers,

17. For as ye have looked upon the long absence of your spirits from your bodies to be a bondage, I will show unto you how the day of redemption shall come, and also the restoration of the scattered Israel.

18. And now ye behold this temple which is in Jerusalem, which ye call the house of God, and your enemies say that this house shall never fall.

19. But, verily, I say unto you, that desolation shall come upon this generation as a thief in the night, and this people shall be destroyed and scattered among all nations.

20. And this temple which ye now see shall be thrown down that there shall not be left one stone upon another.

21. And it shall come to pass, that this generation of Jews shall not pass away, until every desolation which I have told you concerning them shall come to pass.

22. Ye say that ye know that the end of the world cometh; ye say also that ye know that the heavens and the earth shall pass away;

23. And in this ye say truly, for so it is; but these things which I have told you shall not pass away until all shall be fulfilled,

24. And this I have told you concerning Jerusalem, and when that day shall come, shall a remnant be scattered among all nations;

25. But they shall be gathered again, but they shall remain until the times of the Gentiles be fulfilled.

26. And in that day shall be heard of wars and rumors of wars, and the whole earth shall be in commotion, and men's hearts shall fail them, and they shall say that Christ delayeth his coming until the end of the earth.

27. And the love of men shall wax cold, and iniquity shall abound;

28. And when the times of the Gentiles is come in, a light shall break forth among them that sit in darkness, and it shall be the fulness of my gospel;

29. But they receive it not, for they perceive not the light, and they turn their hearts from me because of the precepts of men;

30. And in that generation shall the times of the Gentiles be fulfilled;

31. And there shall be men standing in that generation, that shall not pass, until they shall see an overflowing scourge; for a desolating sickness shall cover the land;

32. But my disciples shall stand in

D&C 45:19–21—In verse 19, "this people" refers to the Jews, who were "scattered" when the surviving Jews were sold into slavery. In verse 20, the "temple" was destroyed when it was burned by Roman soldiers. In verse 21, 1.5 million Jews were killed in 70 A.D.

D&C 45:22—According to Elder Bruce R. McConkie, the "end of the world" in this verse refers to the end of worldliness. Once worldliness comes to an end, the Millennium begins, along with the Savior's millennial reign.

D&C 45:25—The "times of the Gentiles" started shortly after Jesus died. Because the Jews had rejected the gospel, it was taken to the Gentiles.

D&C 45:25, 28, 32—The Jewish people will be gathered again in the due time of the Lord. The Restoration will take place during the times of the Gentiles as a light breaking forth, even the fullness of the gospel. When the times of the Gentiles are fulfilled, a period of desolation and sickness will set in, but the righteous will be protected, for they will "stand in holy places." "Stand in holy places" has been an age-old directive from the Lord (see D&C 45:32; 101:22). Those places include the temples of the Lord, the homes of the faithful, and the congregations of Saints assembled in the stakes of Zion to worship in the spirit of unity and truth (see John 4:23–24). There is security in the gatherings of the Saints. There is opportunity there to enjoy the interactive communion of the Saints as they study the gospel and seek to remember their covenant vows. There is a feeling of joy in bearing testimonies together and sharing praise for the Lord.

D&C 45:26–27—Men's hearts will fail them in both a spiritual and a physical sense; the "love of men will wax cold" refers in part to a lack of unity among believers in Christ (the Christian sects).

D&C 45:30—Some of the great signs of the times include that 1) the Jews will be gathered back to Jerusalem; 2) there will be a time of great social turmoil; 3) the Gentiles will reject the gospel; and 4) Jerusalem will no longer be trodden down by the Gentiles. It is interesting to note that in 1917, Jerusalem was freed from Turkish rule, and the United Kingdom declared Palestine a refuge for the Jews. Beginning in 1967, Jerusalem was under Jewish rule for the first time since 70 A.D.

holy places, and shall not be moved; but among the wicked, men shall lift up their voices, and curse God and die.

33. And there shall be earthquakes also in divers places, and many desolations; yet men will harden their hearts against me, and they will take up the sword, one against another, and they will kill one another.

34. And, now, when I the Lord had spoken these words unto my disciples, they were troubled:

35. And I said unto them, be not troubled, for when all these things shall come to pass, ye may know that the promises which have been made unto you shall be fulfilled;

36. And when the light shall begin to break forth, it shall be with them like unto a parable which I will show you:

37. Ye look and behold the fig-trees, and ye see them with your eyes, and ye say when they begin to shoot forth, and their leaves are yet tender, that summer is now nigh at hand;

38. Even so it shall be in that day when they shall see all these things, then shall they know that the hour is nigh.

39. And it shall come to pass that he that feareth me shall be looking forth for the great day of the Lord to come, even for the signs of the coming of the Son of man:

40. And they shall see signs and wonders, for they shall be shown forth in the heavens above, and in the earth beneath;

41. And they shall behold blood, and fire, and vapors of smoke;

42. And before the day of the Lord shall come, the sun shall be darkened, and the moon be turned into blood, and stars fall from heaven;

43. And the remnant shall be gathered unto this place,

44. And then they shall look for me, and, behold, I will come; and they shall see me in the clouds of heaven, clothed with power and great glory, with all the holy angels; and he that watches not for me shall be cut off.

45. But before the arm of the Lord shall fall, an angel shall sound his trump, and the saints that have slept shall come forth to meet me in the cloud;

46. Wherefore, if ye have slept in peace blessed are you, for as you now behold me and know that I am, even so shall ye come unto me and your souls shall live, and your redemption shall be perfected, and the saints shall come forth from the four quarters of the earth.

47. Then shall the arm of the Lord fall upon the nations,

48. And then shall the Lord set his foot upon this mount, and it shall cleave in twain, and the earth shall

D&C 45:35–37—The Lord gives calming counsel for those troubled by the prophecies of impending destruction. The signs of the times alert discerning observers to the calamities lying ahead, but these signs are also evidence that the benevolent promises of the Lord are about to be fulfilled on behalf of the righteous.

D&C 45:44—The signs of the times point to the transcendent event of the Lord's Second Coming. The wise are continually watchful in regard to this consummate event, that they might be prepared to meet the Savior with the spirit of rejoicing. Every day is a day to prepare to meet God (see Alma 34:32), for we never know when we might be called home early to meet our Savior, and no mortal knows the hour of the Savior's return—"no, not the angels of heaven, but my Father only" (Matt. 24:36).

D&C 45:45–46—At this juncture in world history, the gathering takes on a magnified and eternal perspective, for the dead who "have slept in peace" will be gathered to the congregation of Saints through the power of the resurrection, and the Saints on earth will be gathered from all quarters to come unto the Lord.

D&C 45:48–52—The Master's role as Savior takes on a new and urgent meaning for the Jewish nation when He returns to save them from destruction by their encompassing enemies:

Orson Pratt and Charles W. Penrose declared that prior to the glorious coming of the Son of God, the Jews are going to be beleaguered by the nations who threaten the very existence of the Jewish race. Then, according to Zechariah, down through the gates of heaven shall come the Lord Jesus Christ, the Captain and King for whom the Jews have wept and prayed so long, and he shall set his feet upon the Mount of Olives, and the Mount shall cleave asunder, and the Jews shall escape destruction. The God of heaven shall then, with the armies of heaven, have judgment upon the wicked, and the wicked shall be destroyed. When Jesus stands before the Jews, they will see the wounds in his hands and, recognizing their Lord and God, they shall say: ". . . What are these wounds in thine hands?" And then Jesus shall break the hearts of the Jews by saying: "Those with which I was wounded in the house of my friends." (Zechariah 13:6.) And that nation then, and not until then, shall be born in a day. By the authorized servants of God they shall receive the baptism of repentance; they shall receive the gift of the Holy Ghost, and become the children of God their Father and the servants of the great Jehovah. At that time a fountain shall be opened up unto the Jews and the inhabitants of Jerusalem, a fountain for the cleansing of sin and iniquity, and that fountain shall be as it always has been, the Lord Jesus Christ (as reported by Charles A. Callis of the Quorum of the Twelve.) (CR, Oct. 1945, Afternoon Session, 81.)

tremble, and reel to and fro, and the heavens also shall shake,

49. And the Lord shall utter his voice, and all the ends of the earth shall hear it, and the nations of the earth shall mourn, and they that have laughed shall see their folly,

50. And calamity shall cover the mocker, and the scorner shall be consumed, and they that have watched for iniquity shall be hewn down and cast into the fire.

51. And then shall the Jews look upon me and say, What are these wounds in thine hands and in thy feet?

52. Then shall they know that I am the Lord; for I will say unto them, These wounds are the wounds with which I was wounded in the house of my friends. I am he who was lifted up. I am Jesus that was crucified. I am the Son of God.

53. And then shall they weep because of their iniquities; then shall they lament because they persecuted their King.

54. And then shall the heathen nations be redeemed, and they that knew no law shall have part in the first resurrection; and it shall be tolerable for them;

55. And Satan shall be bound that he shall have no place in the hearts of the children of men.

56. And at that day, when I shall come in my glory, shall the parable be fulfilled which I spake concerning the ten virgins;

57. For they that are wise and have received the truth, and have taken the Holy Spirit for their guide, and have not been deceived; verily I say unto you, they shall not be hewn down and cast into the fire, but shall abide the day.

58. And the earth shall be given unto them for an inheritance; and they shall multiply and wax strong, and their children shall grow up without sin unto salvation,

59. For the Lord shall be in their midst, and his glory shall be upon them, and he will be their King and their Lawgiver.

60. And now, behold I say unto you, it shall not be given unto you to know any further concerning this

D&C 45:54–55—The compassion and mercy of the Lord are of infinite scope. The ultimate judgments will take into account the degree of enlightenment that has been provided all peoples, including the heathen nations who have not received the truth. Who are the heathens? Elder Bruce R. McConkie taught that *heathens* are those who worship idols or other false gods and who have no knowledge of the true God as He is described in the scriptures. These are different from people who worship the Lord but who are laboring under false notions of His nature and the kind of being He is (see *MD*, 347).

D&C 45:55—The righteous will participate in the binding of Satan during the millennial period, for they will be endowed through the strength of the Lord with the capacity to withstand Satan's temptations. Even today we have power to bind Satan from our lives by choosing righteousness (see Alma 48:11–13, 17) and exercising our faith, that we might live by the Spirit.

D&C 45:57–59—The parable of the ten virgins (see Matt. 25:1–13) was a parable with a prophetic forward view, for it will be fulfilled as part of the millennial process.

D&C 45:60–62—Speaking about the Prophet's inspired translation of the Bible, scholar Robert J. Matthews reports:

The translation began with the Old Testament. About ten months later [in February 1831] the Lord instructed Joseph Smith to make a translation of the New Testament also, and promised him that in doing so he would learn many great things (see D&C 45:60–62). Until this time the Prophet had translated from Genesis only, but the manuscript of the JST shows that in obedience to this command he began translating the New Testament on 8 March 1831, just one day after being instructed to do so. The promptness of the Prophet in responding to the commandment to translate the New Testament manifests his regard for the work he was engaged in and his desire to do what the Lord expected of him. Through this work great things would be revealed to him and through him be made known to the Church.

From March 1831 until February 1833, the Prophet and his scribes continued to work through the New Testament, making hundreds of corrections and additions, and a few deletions. On 10 January 1832 the Lord encouraged the Brethren to continue the translation "until it be finished" (D&C 73:3–4).

Although there were many interruptions, the work progressed, and on 2 February 1833, in Kirtland, Ohio, the Prophet recorded in his journal: "I completed the translation and review of the New Testament, on the 2nd of February, 1833 and sealed it up, no more to be opened till it arrived in Zion." "Zion" meant Independence, Missouri. . . . (*BB*, 136.)

chapter, until the New Testament be translated, and in it all these things shall be made known;

61. Wherefore I give unto you that ye may now translate it, that ye may be prepared for the things to come;

62. For verily I say unto you, that great things await you;

63. Ye hear of wars in foreign lands, but, behold, I say unto you, they are nigh, even at your doors, and not many years hence ye shall hear of wars in your own lands.

64. Wherefore I, the Lord, have said, gather ye out from the eastern lands, assemble ye yourselves together ye elders of my church; go ye forth into the western countries, call upon the inhabitants to repent, and inasmuch as they do repent, build up churches unto me;

65. And with one heart and with one mind, gather up your riches that ye may purchase an inheritance which shall hereafter be appointed unto you,

66. And it shall be called the New Jerusalem, a land of peace, a city of refuge, a place of safety for the saints of the most High God;

67. And the glory of the Lord shall be there, and the terror of the Lord also shall be there, insomuch that the wicked will not come unto it, and it shall be called Zion.

68. And it shall come to pass, among the wicked, that every man that will not take his sword against his neighbor, must needs flee unto Zion for safety.

69. And there shall be gathered unto it out of every nation under heaven; and it shall be the only people that shall not be at war one with another.

70. And it shall be said among the wicked, Let us not go up to battle against Zion, for the inhabitants of Zion are terrible; wherefore we cannot stand.

71. And it shall come to pass that the righteous shall be gathered out from among all nations, and shall come to Zion singing with songs of everlasting joy.

72. And now I say unto you, keep these things from going abroad unto the world, until it is expedient in me that ye may accomplish this work in the eyes of the people, and in the eyes of your enemies, that they may not know your works until ye have accomplished the thing which I have commanded you;

73. That when they shall know it, that they may consider these things;

74. For when the Lord shall appear he shall be terrible unto them, that fear may seize upon them, and they shall stand afar off and tremble;

75. And all nations shall be afraid because of the terror of the Lord, and the power of his might. Even so. Amen.

D&C 45:66—The Lord concludes His presentation of the last days with a promise that the Saints will gather from among the nations and come to Zion with joy to participate in the building of the city of New Jerusalem—the holy venue designated as the place of safety for the Saints of the Most High God. The glory of the Lord shall be there, which glory shall cause terror and trembling among the wicked.

D&C 45:67—Zion is a place of 1) gathering, 2) preparation, 3) defense, and 4) refuge.

THE SAVIOR'S APPEARANCE AT HIS SECOND COMING

This revelation teaches that the Savior's Second Coming will include at least three general appearances:

1. *To the Saints* (see D&C 45:45–46, 56–57). Referring to the Saints who receive the Savior, these are people who have made and kept covenants with the Lord. They are referred to as "children of light" (D&C 106:5) and are those who have received the truth, received the Holy Ghost, and were not deceived, thus fulfilling the parable that describes the five wise virgins (see D&C 45:56–57).

2. *To the Jews at Jerusalem* (see D&C 45:47–53). The Lord's appearance to the Jews will take place at a time when they will be engaged in a battle for their survival. When the Savior intervenes in their behalf, He will be recognized and acknowledged as the Messiah and Savior of the world.

3. *To the world* (see D&C 45:74–75). The Lord's appearance to the world will not be to a select group of people. This appearance will be of such magnitude that the wicked will be destroyed and the remaining righteous will see, know, and dwell with Him upon the earth for a millennial period (*STDC* 1:219–220).

SECTION 46

1. Hearken, O ye people of my church, for verily I say unto you, that these things were spoken unto you for your profit and learning;

2. But notwithstanding those things which are written, it always has been given to the elders of my church from the beginning and ever shall be to conduct all meetings as they are directed and guided by the Holy Spirit;

3. Nevertheless ye are commanded never to cast any one out from your public meetings, which are held before the world;

4. Ye are also commanded not to cast any one, who belongeth to the church out of your sacrament meetings; nevertheless, if any have trespassed, let him not partake until he makes reconciliation.

5. And again I say unto you, ye shall not cast any out of your sacrament meetings, who are earnestly seeking the kingdom: I speak this concerning those who are not of the church.

6. And again I say unto you, concerning your confirmation meetings, that if there be any that are not of the church, that are earnestly seeking after the kingdom, ye shall not cast them out;

7. But ye are commanded in all things to ask of God, who giveth liberally; and that which the Spirit testifies unto you, even so I would that ye should do in all holiness of heart, walking uprightly before me, considering the end of your salvation, doing all things with prayer and thanksgiving, that ye may not be seduced by evil spirits, or doctrines of devils, or the commandments of men, for some are of men, and others of devils.

8. Wherefore, beware lest ye are deceived; and that ye may not be deceived, seek ye earnestly the best gifts, always remembering for what they are given;

9. For verily I say unto you, they

Section 46 Background—Step by step during the restoration period, the Lord unfolded to His fledgling Church the principles and practices that would bring about the emergence of the kingdom of God from obscurity. A key aspect of spiritual development was the commandment of the Lord to seek and apply spiritual gifts for righteous purposes. The young Church was still cultivating a standard pattern for conducting Church services at this time, including the issue of whether to admit a general audience or limit the services just to members and earnest seekers of the truth. The Lord makes His will known through this revelation that the Church is to be inclusive and charitable to all who attend services.

D&C 46:2—The miracle of inspiration concerning how to proceed to build the kingdom of God comes in two ways: by treasuring up the words of Christ as a compass for life, and by following the promptings of the Holy Ghost (see 2 Ne. 32:3–5).

D&C 46:3–4—This makes clear to the early Saints of the Church that they are not to conduct meetings in the spirit of exclusion and selectivity. The gospel is extended to all in the spirit of charitable welcoming and nurturing. The phrase "confirmation meetings" referred to in verse 6 apparently refers to special meetings—held separately from sacrament meetings in those days—in which baptized individuals were confirmed as members of the Church and given the gift of the Holy Ghost (see *DCE*, 97).

D&C 46:4—President David O. McKay stressed the consequences of partaking of the sacrament unworthily: "To partake of the sacrament unworthily is to take a step toward spiritual death. No man can be dishonest within himself without deadening the susceptibility of his spirit. Sin can stun the conscience as a blow on the head can stun the physical senses. He who promises one thing and deliberately fails to keep his word, adds sin to sin" (*CR*, Oct. 1929, 14–15).

D&C 46:7—This statement is a splendid summary of how to live as a disciple of the Lord by remembering and following the counsel from on high: pray, follow the Spirit, walk uprightly, keep the eternal goal in mind, thank the Lord—and thus resist influences of evil, whether from devils or misguided men ("for some are of men, and others of devils").

D&C 46:8–9—Heavenly Father has endowed His children with one or more gifts of the Spirit to edify and lift them up in preparation for their various commissions in the ongoing enterprise to build up the kingdom of God. Seeking the best gifts and cultivating them for the good of others is one of the sacred privileges of membership in the Lord's Church. To assist in this process of discovery and cultivation, the Lord has outlined in various places in the scriptures what these gifts comprise and how they lead to magnificent blessings for mankind. (Besides the material in Section 46, see also 1 Cor. 12–13, and Moroni 10:8–18.)

are given for the benefit of those who love me and keep all my commandments, and him that seeketh so to do, that all may be benefited that seeketh or that asketh of me, that asketh and not for a sign that he may consume it upon his lusts.

10. And again, verily I say unto you, I would that ye should always remember, and always retain in your minds what those gifts are, that are given unto the church,

11. For all have not every gift given unto them; for there are many gifts, and to every man is given a gift by the Spirit of God:

12. To some is given one, and to some is given another, that all may be profited thereby;

13. To some it is given by the Holy Ghost to know that Jesus Christ is the Son of God, and that he was crucified for the sins of the world;

14. To others it is given to believe on their words, that they also might have eternal life if they continue faithful.

15. And again, to some it is given by the Holy Ghost to know the difference of administration, as it will be pleasing unto the same Lord, according as the Lord will, suiting his mercies according to the conditions of the children of men.

16. And again, it is given by the Holy Ghost to some to know the diversities of operations, whether it be of God, that the manifestations of the Spirit may be given to every man to profit withal.

17. And again, verily I say unto you, to some it is given, by the Spirit of God, the word of wisdom;

18. To another is given the word of knowledge, that all may be taught to be wise and to have knowledge.

19. And again, to some it is given to have faith to be healed,

20. And to others it is given to have faith to heal.

21. And again, to some it is given the working of miracles;

22. And to others it is given to prophesy,

23. And to others the discerning of spirits.

24. And again, it is given to some to speak with tongues,

25. And to another is given the interpretation of tongues:

26. And all these gifts come from God, for the benefit of the children of God.

27. And unto the bishop of the church, and unto such as God shall appoint and ordain to watch over the church, and to be elders unto the church, are to have it given unto them to discern all those gifts, lest there shall be any among you professing and yet be not of God.

28. And it shall come to pass that he that asketh in Spirit shall receive in Spirit;

29. That unto some it may be given to have all those gifts, that there may be a head, in order that every member may be profited thereby:

30. He that asketh in the Spirit, asketh according to the will of God;

D&C 46:12—The community of God is bonded together by acts of service and charity. Through the wisdom of God, the gifts of the Spirit are imparted unto individuals, to each his or her own gift or gifts, in such a way that a synergistic interdependence is made manifest. We share our gifts to bless the lives of others, and receive of their gifts with thanksgiving. The sum is far greater than the individual parts. We cannot prosper and move forward toward optimum spiritual outcomes without uniting together to benefit from the full tapestry of gifts sent from heaven.

D&C 46:13–26—How many such gifts are there? Elder Bruce R. McConkie responds:

> These gifts are infinite in number and endless in their manifestations because God himself is infinite and endless, and because the needs of those who receive them are as numerous, varied, and different as there are people in the kingdom. All saints are commanded to seek earnestly the best gifts. Chief among them are the testimony of Jesus, a believing spirit, divine wisdom, heavenly knowledge, faith in the Lord, the working of miracles, prophecy, the beholding of angels and ministering spirits, the discerning of spirits, tongues and their interpretations, the gift of preaching, administrative ability, and the insight to discern and recognize all of the gifts of God, lest there be confusion or deception in the Church. (*NWAF*, 270–71.)

There is a depth of meaning and purpose associated with each of the gifts of the Spirit. While most of those mentioned in these verses are fairly understandable, several might require additional explanation. For example, the gift to know "the differences of administration" means to understand the distinctive ways people can minister and serve in the Church. A related gift, "to know the diversities of operations, whether they be of God" (verse 16), assists a person to discern through the Spirit whether an influence is from the Holy Spirit or from some other source.

D&C 46:27–29—The Lord's anointed priesthood leaders are blessed with the gift of discernment in order to watch over the regulation of the Church through inspiration, thus guarding against counterfeit or false manifestations.

D&C 46:30–33—These four verses are so abundant in doctrinal wealth that it is difficult to isolate and abbreviate the key phrases. One would do well to memorize these verses in their entirety as a summary of the Lord's counsel on following the Spirit. We ask by the Spirit according to the will of God. We do all things in the name of Christ. We give thanks in the Spirit to our Heavenly Father for His bounteous blessings. Living by the Spirit in virtue and holiness is the key to a righteous life.

wherefore it is done even as he asketh.

31. And again, I say unto you, all things must be done in the name of Christ, whatsoever you do in the Spirit;

32. And ye must give thanks unto God in the Spirit for whatsoever blessings ye are blessed with;

33. And ye must practice virtue and holiness before me continually. Even so. Amen.

SECTION 47

1. Behold, it is expedient in me that my servant John should write and keep a regular history, and assist you, my servant Joseph, in transcribing all things which shall be given you, until he is called to further duties.

2. Again, verily I say unto you, that he can also lift up his voice in meetings, whenever it shall be expedient.

3. And again, I say unto you that it shall be appointed unto him to keep the church record and history continually, for Oliver Cowdery I have appointed to another office.

4. Wherefore it shall be given him, inasmuch as he is faithful, by the Comforter, to write these things. Even so. Amen.

SECTION 48

1. It is necessary that ye should remain for the present time in your places of abode, as it shall be suitable to your circumstances;

2. And inasmuch as ye have lands,

Section 47 Background—Given in Kirtland, Ohio, March 8, 1831. Since the beginning of time, the Lord has commanded His people to keep records. The Prophet provided this statement: "The same day that I received the foregoing revelation [Section 46], I also received the following [Section 47], setting apart John Whitmer as a historian, inasmuch as he is faithful" (HC 1:166). Before this, Oliver Cowdery had acted as historian and recorder, and John Whitmer had acted as secretary to the Prophet in recording a number of the revelations given at Fayette, New York. John Whitmer said he would rather not keep the Church history, but would do it if such was the Lord's will as revealed through Joseph Smith. In response, this revelation was given.

D&C 47:1—Record-keeping is not restricted to those who keep the history of the Church. All members of the Church have been counseled to keep personal histories. We are all responsible to be "historians" in the Church by recording our own history and providing a written record that can serve and benefit others who read it (STDC 1:228).

D&C 47:3—All of the early records and manuscripts are in Oliver Cowdery's handwriting.

D&C 47:4—Faithfulness and the companionship of the Holy Ghost are requisite factors in fulfilling this commission, as in all other commissions given in the Church. John Whitmer was faithful in fulfilling his duties in the early years. Unfortunately, he became embittered later on, in connection with allegations against him concerning financial irregularities in Missouri and was excommunicated on March 10, 1838. Nevertheless, as one of the eight witnesses he remained faithful to his testimony of the Book of Mormon.

Section 48 Background—Given at Kirtland, Ohio, March 1831. The Prophet provides this introduction: "Upon inquiry how the brethren should act in regard to purchasing lands to settle upon, and where they should finally make a permanent location, I received [Section 48]" (HC 1:166). A footnote to this entry adds: "This question was agitating the minds of the brethren in consequence of the expected arrival in the near future, of the Saints from New York, who had been commanded to gather to Ohio, and for whose reception it was necessary to make preparations."

D&C 48:1—Many erroneously believed that Ohio was Zion, the place of gathering. But the phrase "present time" is used three times in this section, indicating that Ohio was to be a temporary center of the Church, not the permanent place of gathering.

ye shall impart to the eastern brethren;

3. And inasmuch as ye have not lands, let them buy for the present time in those regions round about as seemeth them good, for it must needs be necessary that they have places to live for the present time.

4. It must needs be necessary, that ye save all the money that ye can, and that ye obtain all that ye can in righteousness, that in time ye may be enabled to purchase land for an inheritance, even the city.

5. The place is not yet to be revealed, but after your brethren come from the east, there are to be certain men appointed, and to them it shall be given to know the place, or to them it shall be revealed.

6. And they shall be appointed to purchase the lands, and to make a commencement to lay the foundation of the city; and then shall ye begin to be gathered with your families, every man according to his family, according to his circumstances, and as is appointed to him by the Presidency and the bishop of the church according to the laws and commandments which ye have received, and which ye shall hereafter receive. Even so. Amen.

SECTION 49

1. Hearken unto my word, my servants Sidney, and Parley, and

LEMAN COPLEY

Leman Copley was born in 1781 in Connecticut. He was a member of the Shakers (the United Society of Believers in Christ's Second Coming). In 1831 he became a convert of the restored Church. The Prophet Joseph Smith discerned that Leman's conversion was somewhat frail and sought counsel from the Lord, who gave directions for Leman and two colleagues—Sidney Rigdon and Parley P. Pratt—to preach the gospel to the Shakers. The three fulfilled the commission by going to the small Shaker settlement in North Union, Ohio, and presenting the doctrines of the gospel, including a reading of the new revelation [Section 49]. The Shakers rejected the message. Leman's subsequent years were characterized by instability in his Church service and relationships. (He was chastised by the Lord in D&C 54:5 for dishonoring his pledge to assist those gathering to Ohio from the East.) Eventually his apostasy was complete and he took up other religious affiliations. He passed away as a wealthy landowner in Ohio in December 1862.

D&C 48:3—Charity and fellowship are to prevail as principles of the gathering in all ages. In that context, the Saints in Ohio were commanded to share their property with those gathering from the East. Among the early arrivals from New York were the Joseph Smith Sr. family and the Peter Whitmer family. Funds were scarce, and the Saints needed to assist one another. When the Prophet Joseph inquired of the Lord for counsel in this challenging matter, he received the guidance given in Section 48. Doors were opened and opportunities emerged. The stress of the situation was eased when Leman Copley, a former Shaker who lived about twenty miles east of Kirtland, joined the Church and let incoming Saints settle on his large farm. Most of the Saints who moved to Ohio from New York settled on that farm.

D&C 48:4–5—The location of the New Jerusalem was not given at that time, but the Lord promised to reveal it in the future. The counsel for the present moment was to prepare for a future investment in the divine city of refuge. Leaun G. Otten and C. Max Caldwell explain, "There is a lesson for us that can be learned from this revelation. The Lord knows the future, the needs of His people, and how to provide for those needs. Knowing that the Saints would eventually need to purchase lands, He counseled them to save their money that they might be prepared when the time came to purchase. . . . The Lord knows all things from the beginning to the end. When He counsels us to obtain a year's supply of food, participate in welfare projects, stay out of debt, etc. it is in our best interest to heed His counsel" (STDC 1:233).

Section 49 Background—Given through the Prophet Joseph Smith to Sidney Rigdon, Parley P. Pratt, and Leman Copley in March 1831 (some sources indicate May 1831) at Kirtland, Ohio (see HC 1:167–169). The Prophet gave this introduction: "At about this time came Leman Copley, one of the sect called Shaking Quakers, and embraced the fulness of the everlasting Gospel, apparently honest-hearted, but still retaining the idea that the Shakers were right in some particulars of their faith. In order to have more perfect understanding on the subject, I inquired of the Lord, and received the following [Section 49]" (HC 1:167). The Lord gave counsel on how to reach out to the Shakers and disabuse them of their errors, among others the practice of celibacy, abstaining from meat, and professing that the Lord had already returned for His Second Coming (in the form of a woman). In contrast to these errors, the Lord proclaimed true doctrine as revealed through the Restoration of the fullness of the gospel. Unfortunately, the Shakers rejected this word of the Lord when it was presented to them. Nevertheless, Section 49 stands as a warning to all to remain focused on the doctrine of Christ: faith, repentance, baptism, and the gift of the Holy Ghost.

Leman, for behold, verily I say unto you, that I give unto you a commandment that you shall go and preach my gospel which ye have received, even as ye have received it, unto the Shakers.

2. Behold, I say unto you, that they desire to know the truth in part, but not all, for they are not right before me and must needs repent;

3. Wherefore, I send you, my servants Sidney and Parley, to preach the gospel unto them;

4. And my servant Leman shall be ordained unto this work, that he may reason with them, not according to that which he has received of them, but according to that which shall be taught him by you my servants, and by so doing I will bless him, otherwise he shall not prosper.

5. Thus saith the Lord, for I am God, and have sent mine Only Begotten Son into the world for the redemption of the world, and have decreed that he that receiveth him shall be saved, and he that receiveth him not shall be damned.

6. And they have done unto the Son of man even as they listed; and he has taken his power on the right hand of his glory, and now reigneth in the heavens, and will reign till he descends on the earth to put all enemies under his feet, which time is nigh at hand:

7. I, the Lord God, have spoken it, but the hour and the day no man knoweth, neither the angels in heaven, nor shall they know until he comes;

8. Wherefore, I will that all men shall repent, for all are under sin, except them which I have reserved unto myself, holy men that ye know not of;

9. Wherefore I say unto you, that I have sent unto you mine everlasting covenant, even that which was from the beginning,

10. And that which I have promised I have so fulfilled, and the nations of the earth shall bow to it; and, if not of themselves, they shall come down, for that which is now exalted of itself shall be laid low of power;

11. Wherefore I give unto you a commandment that ye go among this people and say unto them, like unto mine apostle of old, whose name was Peter;

12. Believe on the name of the Lord Jesus, who was on the earth, and is to come, the beginning and the end,

13. Repent and be baptized in the name of Jesus Christ, according to the holy commandment, for the remission of sins;

14. And whoso doeth this shall receive the gift of the Holy Ghost, by the laying on of the hands of the elders of this church.

15. And again, I say unto you, that whoso forbiddeth to marry is not ordained of God, for marriage is ordained of God unto man;

D&C 49:5–7—Central to the message commissioned for the Shakers is the Atonement of Christ and His imminent return. This message is to be proclaimed through the revelations of God in the scriptures and through the voice of the living prophet and his elect associates. The Shakers were promulgating the error that the Lord had already returned, but the Lord confirms that no one knows the hour—not even the angels of heaven—nor shall it be known until it occurs. It will be an event of surpassing power and glory in which the Lord will place all enemies under His feet. As Kent P. Jackson explains, "Most people on earth do not know Jesus, and relatively few others believe in his literal Second Coming. Thus, to the world, he will come unexpectedly (D&C 106:4; JS–Matt. 1:41–43). But the Lord's Saints are not of the world. They will expect his coming and will not be surprised when it takes place" (HO, 174).

D&C 49:12–14—The plainness and consistency of the gospel are two of its radiant hallmarks. Cleansing, renewal, rebirth as a new individual, and liberation from the effects of sin are the beautiful and refreshing factors involved in the fundamental ordinances of the gospel—baptism by water and by fire of those who have faith unto repentance. By this gateway we enter into a covenant with the Lord to become His sons and daughters, taking upon ourselves His sacred name forever, and promising to keep His commandments and endure to the end. All are in need of this message, for all are under the influence of sin, except for "holy men that ye know not of"—an apparent reference to translated beings, such as John the Beloved and the three Nephite disciples who desired to stay among mortals in the service of God (see DCC, 283–284).

D&C 49:15—The institution of marriage between a man and a woman was inaugurated by God, beginning with Adam and Eve (Gen. 2:18, 22–24). The Lord taught His disciples: "What therefore God hath joined together, let not man put asunder" (Mark 10:9).

The Leman Copley farm site in Thompson, Ohio. Leman Copley was a brandnew convert when he covenanted under the law of consecration to allow Saints from New York to live on his land. Members of the Colesville (New York) Branch stayed there for a brief period in 1831. Copley became disaffected shortly thereafter and broke his promise about letting the Saints stay on his land. Joseph Smith then sent the Saints who were staying on the Copley farm to Jackson County, Missouri. Though it was not a success, the law of consecration was first implemented here.

16. Wherefore it is lawful that he should have one wife, and they twain shall be one flesh, and all this that the earth might answer the end of its creation,

17. And that it might be filled with the measure of man, according to his creation before the world was made.

18. And whoso forbiddeth to abstain from meats, that man should not eat the same, is not ordained of God;

19. For, behold, the beasts of the field and the fowls of the air, and that which cometh of the earth, is ordained for the use of man for food and for raiment, and that he might have in abundance:

20. But it is not given that one man should possess that which is above another, wherefore the world lieth in sin;

21. And wo be unto man that sheddeth blood or that wasteth flesh and hath no need.

22. And again, verily I say unto you, that the Son of man cometh not in the form of a woman, neither of a man traveling on the earth;

23. Wherefore be not deceived, but continue in steadfastness, looking forth for the heavens to be shaken, and the earth to tremble and to reel to and fro as a drunken man, and for the valleys to be exalted, and for the mountains to be made low, and for the rough places to become smooth; and all this when the angel shall sound his trumpet.

24. But before the great day of the Lord shall come, Jacob shall flourish in the wilderness, and the Lamanites shall blossom as the rose.

25. Zion shall flourish upon the hills and rejoice upon the mountains, and shall be assembled together unto the place which I have appointed.

26. Behold, I say unto you, go forth as I have commanded you—repent of all your sins, ask and ye shall receive, knock and it shall be opened unto you:

27. Behold, I will go before you and be your rearward; and I will be in your midst, and you shall not be confounded;

28. Behold, I am Jesus Christ, and I come quickly. Even so. Amen.

D&C 49:19—A few months later, in August 1831, the Lord would expand on this principle, saying:

> Yea, all things which come of the earth, in the season thereof, are made for the benefit and the use of man, both to please the eye and to gladden the heart;
>
> Yea, for food and for raiment, for taste and for smell, to strengthen the body and to enliven the soul.
>
> And it pleaseth God that he hath given all these things unto man; for unto this end were they made to be used, with judgment, not to excess, neither by extortion.
>
> And in nothing doth man offend God, or against none is his wrath kindled, save those who confess not his hand in all things, and obey not his commandments. (D&C 59:18–21.)

D&C 49:23–27—Great signs will be given of the impending arrival of the millennial Sovereign, including dramatic and earthshaking changes in the structural makeup of the earth. But the soothing and comforting aspects of the final phase will be the unfolding of the kingdom of God in the last days, marked by the joyous gathering of the Saints to the appointed place of refuge. How can we prepare ourselves to participate in this movement of Zion toward the heavenly reunion? Through repentance, prayer, and cultivation of the conviction that the Savior will be in the midst of His hosts, ensuring that His disciples are not confounded but rather illuminated with the light of the gospel—even the light of Christ. The essence of the Lord's message to the Shakers—and to all of us—is given in verse 23; the same word was used by Nephi in his message to his contemporaries and to his future readership: "Wherefore, ye must press forward with a steadfastness in Christ, having a perfect brightness of hope, and a love of God and of all men. Wherefore, if ye shall press forward, feasting upon the word of Christ, and endure to the end, behold, thus saith the Father: Ye shall have eternal life" (2 Ne. 31:20).

Shaker Heights at North Union, Ohio, home of the Center Family North Union Society of Shakers, established in 1822. A Shaker meetinghouse on this site was where Leman Copley attended church. The Shakers did not believe in eating meat or in marriage; men and women were separated. As such, the text of Section 49 challenged their core beliefs. The text was taken to this compound and was read to the Shakers who lived there by missionaries Sidney Rigdon, Parley P. Pratt, and Leman Copley (a new convert at the time). The Shakers formally rejected the text, an event recorded by Ashbel Kitchel, one of the Shaker leaders at the compound.

SECTION 50

1. Hearken, O ye elders of my church, and give ear to the voice of the living God, and attend to the words of wisdom which shall be given unto you, according as ye have asked and are agreed as touching the church, and the spirits which have gone abroad in the earth.

2. Behold, verily I say unto you, that there are many spirits which are false spirits, which have gone forth in the earth, deceiving the world;

3. And also Satan hath sought to deceive you, that he might overthrow you.

4. Behold, I the Lord, have looked upon you, and have seen abominations in the church that profess my name;

5. But blessed are they who are faithful and endure, whether in life or in death, for they shall inherit eternal life.

6. But wo unto them that are deceivers and hypocrites, for, thus saith the Lord, I will bring them to judgment.

7. Behold, verily I say unto you, there are hypocrites among you, who have deceived some, which has given the adversary power, but behold such shall be reclaimed;

8. But the hypocrites shall be detected and shall be cut off, either in life or in death, even as I will; and wo unto them who are cut off from my church, for the same are overcome of the world;

9. Wherefore, let every man beware lest he do that which is not in truth and righteousness before me.

10. And now come, saith the Lord, by the Spirit, unto the elders of his church, and let us reason together, that ye may understand:

11. Let us reason even as a man reasoneth one with another face to face;

12. Now when a man reasoneth he is understood of man because he reasoneth as a man, even so will I,

Section 50 Background—Given in May 1831 at the Morley Farm in Kirtland, Ohio (see *HC* 1:170–173). Strange spiritual manifestations were being reported among some members of the Church, as described by Parley P. Pratt after returning from his assignment to the Shakers:

> Feeling our weakness and inexperience, and lest we should err in judgment concerning these spiritual phenomena, myself, John Murdock, and several other Elders, went to Joseph Smith, and asked him to inquire of the Lord concerning these spirits or manifestations.
>
> After we had joined in prayer in his translating room, he dictated in our presence the following revelation [Section 50]:—(Each sentence was uttered slowly and very distinctly, and with a pause between each, sufficiently long for it to be recorded, by an ordinary writer, in long hand. . . . (*APPP*, 48.)

Both Joseph Wakefield and John Corrill apostatized not long after joining the Church.

D&C 50:2–3—Through prayer, faith, and vigilance we can discern among the influences and "spirits" along the pathway of mortality, and make wise judgments and choices that will ensure our spiritual well-being. Keeping the commandments through obedience will allow us to have the Spirit—and we will not sin when we are acting under the influence of the Holy Ghost.

D&C 50:5–9—In the risen Lord's statement of the Beatitudes among the Saints in the New World, He presented an incredible array of divine promises for His righteous sons and daughters. Here the Lord adds a splendid new promise to the list: ". . . blessed are they who are faithful and endure, whether in life or in death, for they shall inherit eternal life" (verse 5). The class of people who fall outside the beatific circle altogether are the hypocrites—who "shall be detected and shall be cut off."

D&C 50:11–14—The logic put forward by the Lord to the understanding of man is that the Spirit was, is, and always will be given as the primary guide in matters of salvation—particularly as it relates to disseminating the word of God for the building up of the Church and kingdom. If we are humble and easily entreated (see Alma 7:23), then the Holy Ghost will be able to bless us with divine knowledge and teachings.

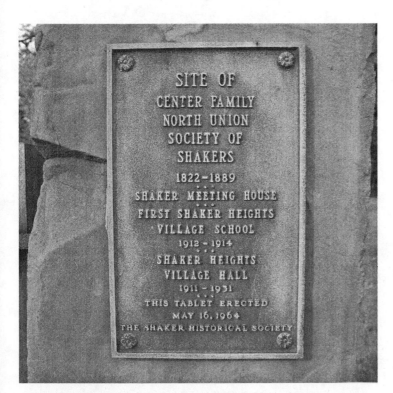

Tablet erected at Shaker Heights, North Union, Ohio, where Leman Copley worshipped before joining the Church.

the Lord, reason with you that you may understand;

13. Wherefore, I the Lord, asketh you this question, unto what were ye ordained?

14. To preach my gospel by the Spirit, even the Comforter which was sent forth to teach the truth;

15. And then received ye spirits which ye could not understand, and received them to be of God; and in this are ye justified?

16. Behold ye shall answer this question yourselves; nevertheless I will be merciful unto you— he that is weak among you hereafter shall be made strong.

17. Verily, I say unto you, he that is ordained of me and sent forth to preach the word of truth by the Comforter, in the Spirit of truth, doth he preach it by the Spirit of truth or some other way?

18. And if it be by some other way, it be not of God.

19. And again, he that receiveth the word of truth, doth he receive it by the Spirit of truth or some other way?

20. If it be some other way it be not of God:

21. Therefore, why is it that ye cannot understand and know that he that receiveth the word by the Spirit of truth, receiveth it as it is preached by the Spirit of truth?

22. Wherefore, he that preacheth and he that receiveth, understandeth one another, and both are edified and rejoice together;

23. And that which doth not edify is not of God, and is darkness;

24. That which is of God is light; and he that receiveth light and continueth in God, receiveth more light, and that light groweth brighter and brighter until the perfect day.

25. And again, verily I say unto you, and I say it that you may know the truth, that you may chase darkness from among you;

26. For he that is ordained of God and sent forth the same is appointed to be the greatest, notwithstanding he is the least and the servant of all:

27. Wherefore he is possessor of all things; for all things are subject unto him, both in heaven and on the earth, the life and the light, the Spirit and the power, sent forth by the will of the Father, through Jesus Christ, his Son;

28. But no man is possessor of all things; except he be purified and cleansed from all sin;

29. And if ye are purified and cleansed from all sin, ye shall ask

D&C 50:17–22—The Lord's blessing to mankind is the ability to communicate and learn through the Spirit. The foundation for all learning is the word of God as recorded in the holy scriptures and given by the voice of living prophets. The Spirit of the Lord confirms the truth of the word of God and brings peace and light into the lives of those who study the gospel and desire to learn more of the Lord and His ways. As such, teaching and learning according to the pattern of heaven is a process involving a collaborative partnership of teacher, student, and the Holy Ghost. When the pattern of the Lord is followed in the teaching environment, then both teacher and learner are touched by the Spirit and "are edified and rejoice together."

D&C 50:23–25—If something is of God, it will *edify*—improve, lift up, enlighten—especially in the spiritual sense. The word *edify* comes from a Latin word meaning "to build," as a house or a temple. Since we are characterized as "the temple of the living God" (2 Cor. 6:16), the word *edify* seems to apply to someone noble or something pure that contributes to the spiritual building up and development of the sons and daughters of God. Paul counseled: ". . . seek that ye may excel to the edifying of the church. . . . Let all things be done unto edifying" (1 Cor. 14:12, 26). When we commit ourselves to this process of edification, we can learn how to "chase darkness" from us—how to be filled with light and truth and pure knowledge.

D&C 50:26–30—These verses contain a covenant promise of extraordinary scope and grandeur. If an individual is ordained of God and sent forth to declare the word, he is "possessor of all things," meaning that all things are subject to him that are provided by the will of the Father and Son—on condition that the individual is purified and cleansed from all sin. The pure and clean who are ordained of God move and act in the power of God to accomplish the divine purposes of the gospel plan. They are fully empowered because they do nothing but the will of God and ask whatever they are prompted to ask, in faith and obedience.

Monuments at Orange, Ohio, located about fifteen miles east of Cleveland. The first settler arrived here in 1815, and the town was named after his Connecticut hometown. Originally an agricultural settlement, Orange was home to one of the four branches of the Church established in Ohio. During 1831, it was a site of missionary activity, and some were ordained to the Melchizedek Priesthood here. A general conference of the Church was held in Orange on October 25–26, 1831, at which Oliver Cowdery and David Whitmer received instructions on selection of the members of the Council of the Twelve.

whatsoever you will in the name of Jesus and it shall be done:

30. But know this, it shall be given you what you shall ask, and as ye are appointed to the head, the spirits shall be subject unto you.

31. Wherefore it shall come to pass, that if you behold a spirit manifested that you cannot understand, and you receive not that spirit, ye shall ask of the Father in the name of Jesus, and if he give not unto you that spirit, then you may know that it is not of God:

32. And it shall be given unto you power over that spirit, and you shall proclaim against that spirit with a loud voice that it is not of God:

33. Not with railing accusation, that ye be not overcome, neither with boasting, nor rejoicing, lest you be seized therewith.

34. He that receiveth of God, let him account it of God, and let him rejoice that he is accounted of God worthy to receive,

35. And by giving heed and doing these things which ye have received and which ye shall hereafter receive: and the kingdom is given you of the Father, and power to overcome all things which are not ordained of him.

36. And behold, verily I say unto you, blessed are you who are now hearing these words of mine from the mouth of my servant, for your sins are forgiven you.

37. Let my servant Joseph Wakefield, in whom I am well pleased, and my servant Parley P. Pratt, go forth among the churches and strengthen them by the word of exhortation;

38. And also my servant John Corrill, or as many of my servants as are ordained unto this office, and let them labor in the vineyard; and let no man hinder them of doing that which I have appointed unto them:

39. Wherefore in this thing my servant Edward Partridge is not justified, nevertheless let him repent and he shall be forgiven.

40. Behold, ye are little children and ye cannot bear all things now, ye must grow in grace and in the knowledge of the truth.

41. Fear not, little children, for you are mine, and I have overcome the world, and you are of them that my Father hath given me;

42. And none of them that my Father hath given me shall be lost:

43. And the Father and I are one: I am in the Father and the Father in me: and inasmuch as ye have received me, ye are in me and I in you;

44. Wherefore I am in your midst, and I am the good Shepherd, and the Stone of Israel. He that buildeth upon this rock shall never fall,

D&C 50:34—The conclusion of the matter is to ask God in faith, nothing wavering, for guidance from the Holy Ghost concerning spiritual manifestations you do not understand. The Lord will provide the answer and give power to thwart that spirit that is not of Him. When we receive enlightenment from God on such matters, it is enough. We account it of God—we recognize and acknowledge with gratitude the divine origin of the light—and we act accordingly, having received power to overcome those things not ordained of God.

D&C 50:38—Specific instructions are given to several of the priesthood brethren concerning their duties and requirements. The nature of the correction needed in the case of Edward Partridge is not mentioned. However, he must have complied in obedience, for his tenure in Church service was praiseworthy, and, by the Lord's own declaration, he was received "unto myself" (D&C 124:19). The Prophet Joseph characterized him as "a pattern of piety, and one of the Lord's great men" (*HC* 1:128). By contrast, Joseph Wakefield and John Corrill did not endure in obedience to the covenant and fell by the wayside of their own choice.

D&C 50:40–45—The Lord closes His message with a poignant and compassionate expression of love—a parental blessing to His children—"the children of the covenant" and the "children of the prophets," as He stated to the Saints in ancient America (3 Ne. 20:25, 26). Just as the Lord Himself "received not of the fulness at the first, but received grace for grace" (D&C 93:12), so He gives us the privilege of following in His footsteps to "grow in grace and in the knowledge of the truth" (verse 40). We can build upon the Savior as the Good Shepherd (see also Hel. 7:18; Alma 5:38–39; John 10:14) and the Stone of Israel (see also Ps. 118:22; Matt. 21:42; Jacob 4:14–16; Hel. 5:12).

45. And the day cometh that you shall hear my voice and see me, and know that I am.

46. Watch, therefore, that ye may be ready. Even so. Amen.

SECTION 51

1. Hearken unto me, saith the Lord your God, and I will speak unto my servant Edward Partridge, and give unto him directions, for it must needs be that he receive directions how to organize this people;

2. For it must needs be that they be organized according to my laws—if otherwise, they will be cut off;

3. Wherefore let my servant Edward Partridge, and those whom he has chosen, in whom I am well pleased, appoint unto this people their portions, every man equal according to their families, according to his circumstances, and their wants and needs.

4. And let my servant Edward Partridge, when he shall appoint a man his portion, give unto him a writing that shall secure unto him his portion, that he shall hold it, even this right and this inheritance in the church, until he transgresses and is not accounted worthy by the voice of the church, according to the laws and covenants of the church, to belong to the church;

5. And if he shall transgress and is not accounted worthy to belong to the church, he shall not have power to claim that portion which he has consecrated unto the bishop for the poor and needy of my church; therefore he shall not retain the gift, but shall only have claim on that portion that is deeded unto him.

6. And thus all things shall be made sure, according to the laws of the land.

7. And let that which belongs to this people be appointed unto this people;

8. And the money which is left unto this people, let there be an agent appointed unto this people, to take the money to provide food and raiment, according to the wants of this people.

9. And let every man deal honestly,

Section 51 Background—Given in May 1831 on the Leman Copley Farm in Thompson, Ohio (see *HC* 1:173–174). The Church was nearing 1,000 members and was struggling with basic necessities. In May there were preparations underway to receive 200 Saints coming in from New York (Lucy Mack Smith, the Colesville Branch, and the "main group" led by Thomas B. Marsh). The Colesville Saints, a group of about 50, settled on Leman Copley's land. Section 51 is directed toward these Saints. The Prophet Joseph Smith gives this introduction: "Not long after [Section 50] was received, the Saints from the State of New York began to come on, and it seemed necessary to settle them; therefore at the solicitation of Bishop Partridge, I inquired, and received [Section 51]" (*HC* 1:173). This revelation introduced for the first time the specifics of the law of consecration.

D&C 51:2–7—The Lord provides fundamental counsel on the operation of the law of consecration—the law according to which a celestial society functions. The law of consecration is a gift to the Saints based on the eternal pattern of governance established by the Lord as the epitome for a Zion people. "The law of consecration was never fully practiced in Ohio but was implemented in Missouri in several forms between 1831 and 1839. In its 1831 form, the law of consecration required all participants, or 'stewards,' to consecrate or convey their possessions to the Church storehouse. The bishop would then give back to each individual or family a 'stewardship' of land, money, and other possessions according to just wants and needs. Surplus profits generated from these stewardships were contributed to the storehouse to assist the poor and serve other general purposes" (*EM*, 314). Being organized under the law of God ensures complete self-sufficiency and organizational integrity for the Saints.

D&C 51:9—Heavenly Father would have a Zion people who are unified in charity and service. "I say unto you, be one; and if ye are not one ye are not mine" (D&C 38:27). We cannot be one in an environment of greed, envy, inequality, and dishonesty. All are as nothing when measured against the majesty of God (see Mosiah 4:5, 11). Thus we are to aspire through integrity and honor to serve our fellowman and practice honesty in all our dealings.

Grave markers at the cemetery in Thompson, Ohio, the town where a group of 50 Saints from Colesville settled and where Saints first practiced the law of consecration.

and be alike among this people, and receive alike, that ye may be one, even as I have commanded you.

10. And let that which belongeth to this people not be taken and given unto that of another church;

11. Wherefore, if another church would receive money of this church, let them pay unto this church again according as they shall agree;

12. And this shall be done through the bishop or the agent, which shall be appointed by the voice of the church.

13. And again, let the bishop appoint a storehouse unto this church, and let all things both in money and in meat, which are more than is needful for the want of this people, be kept in the hands of the bishop.

14. And let him also reserve unto himself for his own wants, and for the wants of his family, as he shall be employed in doing this business.

15. And thus I grant unto this people a privilege of organizing themselves according to my laws;

16. And I consecrate unto them this land for a little season, until I, the Lord, shall provide for them otherwise, and command them to go hence;

17. And the hour and the day is not given unto them, wherefore let them act upon this land as for years, and this shall turn unto them for their good.

18. Behold, this shall be an example unto my servant Edward Partridge, in other places, in all churches.

19. And whoso is found a faithful, a just, and a wise steward, shall enter into the joy of his Lord, and shall inherit eternal life.

20. Verily, I say unto you, I am Jesus Christ, who cometh quickly, in an hour you think not. Even so. Amen.

SECTION 52

1. Behold, thus saith the Lord unto the elders whom he hath called and chosen in these last days, by the voice of his Spirit,

2. Saying, I, the Lord, will make known unto you what I will that ye

D&C 51:13—The earliest reference to "storehouse" in the Doctrine and Covenants was given on February 9, 1831: "Therefore, the residue shall be kept in my storehouse, to administer to the poor and the needy, as shall be appointed by the high council of the church, and the bishop and his council" (D&C 42:34). The principle of the Lord's storehouse, inaugurated early in the restored Church, continues today to help bishops care for the temporally needy among them. The Lord is deeply concerned with the welfare of His people—both in the temporal as well as in the spiritual sense. His hands reach out in mercy to lift and bless, guide and direct. If we listen and obey, the way is opened up for salvation and eternal life.

D&C 51:19—Whatever we are called upon to do, whatever the Lord requires of us—we are granted and promised magnificent blessings if our contribution to the covenant relationship is grounded in righteousness and valor. If joy and eternal life are made of the same fabric—which they truly are—then the threads thereof, according to this scripture, are faith, justice, and wisdom.

Section 52 Background—Given June 1831, on the Isaac Morley Farm at Kirtland, Ohio (see HC 1:175–179). This revelation was given following the three-day conference convened on June 3, 1831—a rather significant conference attended by a large congregation of Saints. Joseph Smith described the conference as follows: ". . . the Lord displayed His power to the most perfect satisfaction of the Saints. The man of sin was revealed [the influence of Satan at one point was repelled], and the authority of the Melchizedek Priesthood was manifested and conferred for the first time [the office of high priest] upon several of the Elders. It was clearly evident that the Lord gave us power in proportion to the work to be done, and strength according to the race set before us, and grace and help as our needs required. Great harmony prevailed; several were ordained; faith was strengthened; and humility, so necessary for the blessing of God to follow prayer, characterized the Saints" (HC 1:175–177).

Section 52 is highly unusual because of the large number of individuals referenced within the revelation. Besides the Prophet Joseph Smith, thirty-four individuals are named and given assignments from the Lord. All of these individuals are recently baptized members of the restored Church—what they do not share in common is a consistently valiant record of service and loyalty to the Lord from that point forward.

shall do from this time until the next conference, which shall be held in Missouri, upon the land which I will consecrate unto my people, which are a remnant of Jacob, and them who are heirs according to the covenant.

3. Wherefore, verily I say unto you, let my servants Joseph Smith, jun., and Sidney Rigdon take their journey as soon as preparations can be made to leave their homes, and journey to the land of Missouri.

4. And inasmuch as they are faithful unto me, it shall be made known unto them what they shall do;

5. And it shall also, inasmuch as they are faithful, be made known unto them the land of your inheritance.

6. And inasmuch as they are not faithful, they shall be cut off, even as I will, as seemeth me good.

7. And again, verily I say unto you, let my servant Lyman Wight, and my servant John Corrill take their journey speedily:

8. And also my servant John Murdock, and my servant Hyrum Smith, take their journey unto the same place by the way of Detroit.

9. And let them journey from thence preaching the word by the way, saying none other things than that which the prophets and apostles have written, and that which is taught them by the Comforter through the prayer of faith.

10. Let them go two by two, and thus let them preach by the way in every congregation, baptizing by water, and the laying on of the hands by the water's side;

11. For thus saith the Lord, I will cut my work short in righteousness, for the days cometh that I will send forth judgment unto victory.

12. And let my servant Lyman Wight beware, for Satan desireth to sift him as chaff.

13. And behold, he that is faithful shall be made ruler over many things.

14. And again, I will give unto you a pattern in all things, that ye may not be deceived, for Satan is abroad in the land, and he goeth forth deceiving the nations;

15. Wherefore he that prayeth whose spirit is contrite, the same is accepted of me if he obey mine ordinances.

16. He that speaketh, whose spirit is contrite, whose language is meek and edifieth, the same is of God if he obey mine ordinances.

17. And again, he that trembleth under my power shall be made strong, and shall bring forth fruits of praise and wisdom, according to the revelations and truths which I have given you.

18. And again, he that is overcome and bringeth not forth fruits, even according to this pattern, is not of me;

19. Wherefore by this pattern ye shall know the spirits in all cases under the whole heavens.

20. And the days have come, according to men's faith it shall be done unto them.

21. Behold, this commandment is

D&C 52:3—The purpose of this revelation was to call missionaries to service; thirty eventually accepted the call and served.

D&C 52:9—In this brief sentence is embedded the essence of the divine mandate for missionary work in the kingdom: Move forward, preaching along the way the words of the prophets and Apostles—plus that which is imparted by the Holy Spirit, the Comforter. Thus the Lord in Section 52 gives counsel to be used as a governing agenda for His emissaries from this point forward until the next conference of the Church is held. This is still the standard for what missionaries and teachers in the Church should teach: we should teach the word of God, not our own opinions. According to Elder Bruce R. McConkie, the truth of all things is measured by what is found in the scriptures. Modern prophets follow the same pattern as they conclude general conference with an appeal for the membership of the Church to follow the inspired counsel given and to look forward to the next general conference for additional light and truth.

D&C 52:14–17—This is the Lord's pattern for the deportment of His missionaries and for helping the Saints avoid deception and discern who is of God. The key dimensions are contrition, meekness, an edifying nature, obedience to the Lord's ordinances (all His commandments and directives), acting in the strength of the Lord, bringing forth good fruits, and alignment with the word of God. The opposites would be pride, arrogance, a deflating and fear-engendering nature, defiance of the Lord's ordinances, egotism, absence of good fruits, and departure from the word of God. Using this kind of filter we can discern and reject the ungodly and welcome the godly. Our language and behavior are a reflection of our character; we should seek to strengthen, uplift, and edify one another (see D&C 108:7; 136:24).

A PATTERN IN ALL THINGS

In the Lord's pattern, He provided a description of a person whose actions and attributes are acceptable to Him. He is one who (see D&C 52:15–21):

1. Prays
2. Is humble or contrite.
3. Receives the Lord's ordinances and obeys the requirements of them.
4. Uses meek and uplifting language.
5. Receives and recognizes the Lord's power.
6. Reflects truth given by relevation from the Lord in all works and teachings (STDC 1:257–258).

given unto all the elders whom I have chosen.

22. And again, verily I say unto you, let my servant Thomas B. Marsh, and my servant Ezra Thayre, take their journey also, preaching the word by the way unto this same land.

23. And again, let my servant Isaac Morley, and my servant Ezra Booth take their journey, also preaching the word by the way unto this same land.

24. And again, let my servants Edward Partridge and Martin Harris take their journey with my servants Sidney Rigdon and Joseph Smith, jun.

25. Let my servants David Whitmer and Harvey Whitlock also take their journey and preach by the way unto this same land.

26. And let my servants Parley P. Pratt and Orson Pratt take their journey and preach by the way, even unto this same land.

27. And let my servants Solomon Hancock and Simeon Carter also take their journey unto this same land, and preach by the way.

28. Let my servants Edson Fuller and Jacob Scott also take their journey.

29. Let my servants Levi W. Hancock and Zebedee Coltrin also take their journey.

30. Let my servants Reynolds Cahoon and Samuel H. Smith also take their journey.

31. Let my servants Wheeler Baldwin and William Carter also take their journey.

32. And let my servants Newel Knight and Selah J. Griffin, both be ordained, and also take their journey;

33. Yea, verily I say, let all these take their journey unto one place, in their several courses, and one man shall not build upon another's foundation, neither journey in another's track.

34. He that is faithful, the same shall be kept and blessed with much fruit.

35. And again, I say unto you, let my servants Joseph Wakefield and Solomon Humphrey take their journey into the eastern lands:

36. Let them labor with their families, declaring none other things than the prophets and apostles, that which they have seen and heard, and most assuredly believe, that the prophecies may be fulfilled.

37. In consequence of transgression, let that which was bestowed upon Heman Basset be taken from him, and placed upon the head of Simonds Ryder.

38. And again, verily I say unto you, let Jared Carter be ordained a priest, and also George James be ordained a priest.

39. Let the residue of the elders watch over the churches, and declare the word in the regions among them: and let them labor with their own hands that there be no idolatry nor wickedness practised.

40. And remember in all things the poor and the needy, the sick and the afflicted, for he that doeth not these things, the same is not my disciple.

41. And again, let my servants Joseph Smith, jun., and Sidney

D&C 52:33—The wording used here makes it clear that the Lord wanted Newel Knight and Selah Griffin to follow different routes in their missionary work.

D&C 52:34—The Lord's revelations consistently reflect a covenant spirit. In this case the promise for those who are faithful is twofold: they shall be "kept" and they shall receive much fruit. *To be kept* is to fall under the canopy of the Lord's parental mercy and protection—to belong to the fold of Christ and benefit from His loving guidance and benevolence. *To receive much fruit* is to be part of the living Church where time, talents, energy, and resources—given willingly and faithfully—blossom into a bounteous harvest of blessings leading to salvation and eternal life.

D&C 52:39—The Lord hoped to prevent those who stayed behind in Ohio from seeking power and prestige to the point where they no longer worshipped God.

D&C 52:40—Christ devoted His ministry and spent His precious blood caring for the "poor and needy"—comprising everyone who has ever lived and who will ever live. "Are we not all beggars?" is the haunting question posed by King Benjamin. "Do we not all depend upon the same Being, even God, for all the substance which we have, for both food and raiment, and for gold, and for silver, and for all the riches which we have of every kind?" (Mosiah 4:19).

By extension of this indisputable logic, we should, in kind, also structure our lives to care for the poor and needy around us—those with less than the needful measure of material substance and support, and those with dwindling supplies of spiritual strength and vitality. Our very discipleship depends on the quality of unconditional charity: "And inasmuch as ye impart of your substance unto the poor, ye will do it unto me" (D&C 42:31). Our devotion to God is expressed in our love and service toward our fellowmen (see Matt. 25:40; Mosiah 2:16–17). Our prayers are in vain if we forget the poor and needy (see Alma 34:28–29). If we are blessed abundantly in temporal things and forget those in need, we are in danger of losing our very souls (see D&C 56:16).

Rigdon, and Edward Partridge, take with them a recommend from the church. And let there be one obtained for my servant Oliver Cowdery also;

42. And thus, even as I have said, if ye are faithful, ye shall assemble yourselves together to rejoice upon the land of Missouri, which is the land of your inheritance, which is now the land of your enemies.

43. But, behold, I the Lord, will hasten the city in its time, and will crown the faithful with joy and with rejoicing.

44. Behold, I am Jesus Christ, the Son of God, and I will lift them up at the last day. Even so. Amen.

SECTION 53

1. Behold, I say unto you, my servant Sidney Gilbert, that I have heard your prayers; and you have called upon me that it should be made known unto you, of the Lord your God, concerning your calling and election in this church, which I, the Lord, have raised up in these last days.

2. Behold, I, the Lord, who was crucified for the sins of the world, give unto you a commandment that you shall forsake the world.

3. Take upon you mine ordination, even that of an elder, to preach faith and repentance and remission of sins, according to my word, and the reception of the Holy Spirit by the laying on of hands;

4. And also to be an agent unto this church in the place which shall be appointed by the bishop, according to commandments which shall be given hereafter.

5. And again, verily I say unto you, you shall take your journey with my servants Joseph Smith, Jun., and Sidney Rigdon.

6. Behold, these are the first ordinances which you shall receive; and the residue shall be made known in a time to come, according to your labor in my vineyard.

7. And again, I would that ye should learn that he only is saved who endureth unto the end. Even so. Amen.

The grocery and dry goods store opened and operated by Algernon Sidney Gilbert—along with Newel K. Whitney—in Independence, Missouri.

D&C 52:43—The Lord controls the agenda according to which the plan of happiness unfolds on behalf of the faithful and obedient. The revelations in the Doctrine and Covenants are footnotes to the covenant of God, once again sent into the world. The Restoration unleashed the powers of heaven and the keys of the priesthood by means of which the Saints are to be gathered to "stand in holy places" (see D&C 45:32). In due time the city of the New Jerusalem will be built and the millennial era will commence. Our mission is to do what the Lord commanded Hyrum Smith to do: "Behold, this is your work, to keep my commandments, yea, with all your might, mind and strength" (D&C 11:20). The promised reward is a crown of joy and rejoicing.

Section 53 Background—Given to Algernon Sidney Gilbert at Kirtland, Ohio, June 1831 (see *HC* 1:179–180). Sidney Gilbert had requested that the Prophet inquire of the Lord concerning his calling and duties in the Church. B. H. Roberts said that "the Lord has had few more devoted servants in this dispensation." He owned a successful mercantile, but closed his store to appease the mobs, sacrificing all his goods and offering himself as a ransom for the Saints. He was so shy and terrified to tract that he said he would "rather die than preach to the Gentiles." Shortly thereafter he contracted cholera and died, prompting Heber C. Kimball to say, "The Lord took him at his word." *See p. 99 for a profile of Algernon Sidney Gilbert.*

D&C 53:1, 7—*Election* in this general sense carries the same meaning as to be called into service in the kingdom of God. As those elected to serve in the kingdom progress in their development, they become more and more established in their unyielding commitment to obey the Lord and faithfully execute their duties in compliance with covenant promises. Their patterns of loyalty and devotion confirm with greater certainty their capacity to endure to the end.

The word *election*, then, covers a range of developmental applications over time, and our adherence to those applications is necessary if we are to gain exaltation. Elder Bruce R. McConkie taught that, based on our choices in the premortal existence, we as righteous spirits were *elected* to participate in mortality and inherit the associated blessings resulting from that choice. We are then *elected* again when we choose to join the Lord's true Church (see D&C 53:1). Finally, through devoted obedience and enduring to the end, our *calling and election are made sure* (see 2 Pet. 1), which seals us "up unto eternal life" (D&C 131:5) (see *MD*, 216–17).

D&C 53:2—Forsaking the world is required of all those who are born again and who enter a covenant relationship with the Lord.

D&C 53:4—Section 57 gives much greater detail about how Algernon Sidney Gilbert was to act as an agent for the Church.

SECTION 54

1. Behold, thus saith the Lord, even Alpha and Omega, the beginning and the end, even he who was crucified for the sins of the world.

2. Behold, verily, verily I say unto you, my servant Newel Knight, you shall stand fast in the office wherewith I have appointed you;

3. And if your brethren desire to escape their enemies, let them repent of all their sins, and become truly humble before me and contrite;

4. And as the covenant which they made unto me has been broken, even so it has become void and of none effect;

5. And wo to him by whom this offence cometh, for it had been better for him that he had been drowned in the depth of the sea;

6. But blessed are they who have kept the covenant and observed the commandment, for they shall obtain mercy.

7. Wherefore, go to now and flee the land, lest your enemies come upon you; and take your journey, and appoint whom you will to be your leader, and to pay moneys for you.

8. And thus you shall take your journey into the regions westward, unto the land of Missouri, unto the borders of the Lamanites.

9. And after you have done journeying, behold, I say unto you, seek ye a living like unto men, until I prepare a place for you.

10. And again, be patient in tribulation until I come; and, behold, I come quickly, and my reward is with me, and they who have sought me early shall find rest to their souls. Even so. Amen.

Algernon Sidney Gilbert

Algernon Sidney Gilbert was born December 28, 1789, at New Haven, New Haven County, Connecticut. He became a merchant and real property entrepreneur in Ohio, establishing in due time a partnership with Newel K. Whitney to operate a store in Kirtland. During this time he and Newel became members of the restored Church. On June 6, 1831, Sidney was ordained an elder and soon thereafter traveled with the Prophet Joseph Smith to Independence, Missouri, where he opened a grocery and dry goods store in obedience to revelation (see D&C 57:8, 10). Although he felt inadequate and self-conscious as a speaker, he did personally make and preserve valuable handwritten copies of many of the early revelations. Sidney subsequently raised eyebrows through insinuations against leaders in Kirtland, and the Lord called Sidney to repentance in March 1833 (see D&C 90:35). Mob action partially destroyed Sidney's store in Independence in 1833, forcing him to move to another location to continue supporting generously the needs of the Saints for goods and services. He also opened his home to members of Zion's Camp, a number of whom were suffering from cholera. Several expired while in Sidney's home, and he also contracted the disease and passed away on June 29, 1834.

Section 54 Background—Given to Newel Knight at Kirtland, Ohio, June 1831 (see *HC* 1:180–181). The Saints coming from Colesville, New York, were in the process of settling in Thompson (near Kirtland) when a disagreement with several local Saints arose. At the heart of the matter was the action by Leman Copley to withdraw from his agreement to make property available according to the law of consecration. Ezra Thayre supported Leman's rebellious stance. Consequently, Newel Knight and other elders asked the Prophet Joseph how to proceed. The Prophet inquired of the Lord and received Section 54 in reply. Section 56 is also related to this matter.

D&C 54:2, 4—The "office whereunto I have appointed you" was to lead the Saints from Colesville, New York. In verse 4, the "covenant" was to provide land for the Saints from Colesville.

D&C 54:2, 6—In times of tribulation and dislocation, the first line of defense for leaders is to stand fast in their offices, showing courage and determination to follow the will of the Lord. In this instance, a covenant had been broken by some of the parties involved. Those who had honored the covenant receive reassurance that they would still harvest the associated blessing of mercy—even though the covenant arrangement was suspended. As the Lord would confirm in the future, they were to continue with a commitment to live lives of obedience and righteousness.

When others raise roadblocks to our obedience, the Lord is understanding and merciful: "The Lord does not regard us as guilty when we are prevented from keeping his commandments through no fault of our own. He knows our hearts—whether or not we really would willingly have been obedient if given the opportunity. He accepted the efforts of the Saints who had been thwarted in their attempts to build a temple in Missouri, but he gave them an opportunity to demonstrate their good faith by building a temple in Nauvoo (see D&C 124:49–55)" (Richard O. Cowan, *AQDC*, 69).

D&C 54:7–9—The Saints would arrive in Missouri before the law of consecration could be fully implemented. This is the Lord's instruction on what they should do in the meantime.

D&C 54:10—How long are we to be patient? Until the Lord comes. Those who have been patient from the beginning will inherit "rest to their souls"—a most desirable and noble blessing.

SECTION 55

1. Behold, thus saith the Lord unto you, my servant William, yea, even the Lord of the whole earth, thou art called and chosen, and after thou hast been baptized by water, which, if you do with an eye single to my glory, you shall have a remission of your sins, and a reception of the Holy Spirit by the laying on of hands;

2. And then thou shalt be ordained by the hand of my servant Joseph Smith, jun., to be an elder unto this church, to preach repentance and remission of sins by way of baptism in the name of Jesus Christ, the Son of the living God;

3. And on whomsoever you shall lay your hands, if they are contrite before me, you shall have power to give the Holy Spirit.

4. And again, you shall be ordained to assist my servant Oliver Cowdery to do the work of printing, and of selecting and writing books for schools in this church, that little children also may receive instruction before me as is pleasing unto me.

5. And again, verily I say unto you, for this cause you shall take your journey with my servants Joseph Smith, jun., and Sidney Rigdon, that you may be planted in the land of your inheritance to do this work.

6. And again, let my servant Joseph Coe also take his journey with them. The residue shall be made known hereafter, even as I will. Amen.

SECTION 56

1. Hearken, O ye people who profess my name, saith the Lord your God, for behold, mine anger is kindled against the rebellious, and they shall know mine arm and mine indignation, in the day of visitation and of wrath upon the nations.

2. And he that will not take up his cross and follow me, and keep my

---

JOSEPH COE

Joseph Coe was born November 12, 1784, in Genoa, Cayuga County, New York. An early convert, Joseph moved to Kirtland in time to participate in the fourth general conference of the Church held in June 1831. He was called shortly thereafter to serve a mission in Missouri, where he was present at the dedication of Missouri as a land of inheritance. Joseph played a role in various financial arrangements for the Church, including contributing funds for purchasing Egyptian mummies. He ended his affiliation with the Church in June 1837, alleging that Joseph Smith was a fallen prophet. Joseph Coe was excommunicated in December 1838. He passed away in Kirtland on October 17, 1854.

Section 55 Background—Given to William W. Phelps at Kirtland, Ohio, June 1831. The Prophet provides this introduction: "About the middle of June, while we were preparing for our journey to Missouri, William W. Phelps and his family arrived among us—'to do the will of the Lord,' he said: so I inquired of the Lord concerning him and received [Section 55]" (HC 1:184–185). *A profile of William W. Phelps is found on p. 102.*

D&C 55:4—As an integral part of the forward motion of the Church in the age of the Restoration, little children are to be included in the program of instruction in gospel principles. By the Lord's holy design, the word of truth is to be imparted to all, regardless of gender or age. As such, the Lord opens up a way, through the service of William W. Phelps, to prepare curriculum for children in the schools of the Church. Said William: "We are preparing to go out from among the people, where we can serve God in righteousness; and the first thing is, to teach our children; for they are as the Israel of old. It is our children who will take the kingdom and bear it off to all the world. . . . We will instruct our children in the paths of righteousness" (*Times and Seasons*, Nov. 1, 1845, 1015).

Section 56 Background—Given in June 1831 at Kirtland, Ohio (see HC 1:186–188). Calls had been issued to a number of brethren to journey to Missouri, preaching as they traveled. But commercial interests got in the way of Ezra Thayre's preparations, and since he had been appointed to be the companion of Thomas B. Marsh, the revelation rescinds the commandment and another is appointed to travel in his stead with Brother Marsh. The framework of the revelation is the establishment of spiritual priorities over material ones, and the Lord issues a stern warning to both rich (who are prideful and selfish) and poor (who are covetous), since both fail to remain humble and grateful for the blessings of heaven.

D&C 56:2—To His disciples in the Holy Land the Savior said: "If any *man* will come after me, let him deny himself, and take up his cross, and follow me" (Matt. 16:24). In the inspired translation of the New Testament, Joseph Smith added: "And now for a man to take up his cross, is to deny himself all ungodliness, and every worldly lust, and keep my commandments" (JST Matt. 16:26).

commandments, the same shall not be saved.

3. Behold, I, the Lord, command, and he that will not obey, shall be cut off in mine own due time, after I have commanded, and the commandment is broken;

4. Wherefore I, the Lord, command and revoke, as it seemeth me good; and all this to be answered upon the heads of the rebellious, saith the Lord;

5. Wherefore, I revoke the commandment which was given unto my servants Thomas B. Marsh and Ezra Thayre, and give a new commandment unto my servant Thomas that he shall take up his journey speedily, to the land of Missouri, and my servant Selah J. Griffin shall also go with him;

6. For behold, I revoke the commandment which was given unto my servants Selah J. Griffin and Newel Knight, in consequence of the stiffneckedness of my people which are in Thompson, and their rebellions;

7. Wherefore, let my servant Newel Knight remain with them, and as many as will go may go, that are contrite before me, and be led by him to the land which I have appointed.

8. And again, verily I say unto you, that my servant Ezra Thayre must repent of his pride, and of his selfishness, and obey the former commandment which I have given him concerning the place upon which he lives;

9. And if he will do this, as there shall be no divisions made upon the land, he shall be appointed still to go to the land of Missouri;

10. Otherwise he shall receive the money which he has paid, and shall leave the place, and shall be cut off out of my church, saith the Lord God of hosts;

11. And though the heaven and the earth pass away, these words shall not pass away, but shall be fulfilled.

12. And if my servant Joseph Smith, jun., must needs pay the money; behold, I, the Lord, will pay it unto him again in the land of Missouri, that those of whom he shall receive may be rewarded again, according to that which they do;

13. For according to that which they do, they shall receive, even in lands for their inheritance.

14. Behold, thus saith the Lord unto my people,you have many things to do and to repent of; for behold, your sins have come up unto me, and are not pardoned, because you seek to counsel in your own ways.

15. And your hearts are not satisfied. And ye obey not the truth, but have pleasure in unrighteousness.

16. Wo unto you rich men, that will not give your substance to the poor, for your riches will canker your souls; and this shall be your lamentation in the day of visitation, and of judgment, and of indignation—The harvest is past, the summer is ended, and my soul is not saved!

17. Wo unto you poor men, whose hearts are not broken, whose spirits are not contrite, and whose bellies are not satisfied, and whose hands are not stayed from laying hold upon

D&C 56:4—Said Joseph Smith:

That which is wrong under one circumstance, may be, and often is, right under another.

God said, "Thou shalt not kill;" at another time He said, "Thou shalt utterly destroy." This is the principle on which the government of heaven is conducted—by revelation adapted to the circumstances in which the children of the kingdom are placed. Whatever God requires is right, no matter what it is, although we may not see the reason thereof till long after the events transpire. If we seek first the kingdom of God, all good things will be added. (*TPJS*, 256.)

Scholars Leaun Otten and C. Max Caldwell raise an appropriate question of conscience from this principle: "What should we learn? The Lord directs His church and all policies and practices will come from Him through His living prophets. Let us not be guilty of resisting changes and rebelling against revelations coming from the Lord, whether they be new commandments or the revocation of previous ones. One of the great evidences of a Latter-day Saint's faith in Jesus Christ is his willingness to accept and render obedience to policies, directions, practices, and commandments that have been given and will yet be given by the Lord as announced by His authorized servants" (*STDC* 1:270–271).

Such a lesson was rejected by Ezra Thayre at the time of this revelation. B. H. Roberts gives the particulars in a footnote to section 56: "The phrase in the ninth verse of the foregoing revelation, '*As there shall be no divisions made upon the land*,' undoubtedly has reference to the land upon which Ezra Thayre was living at Thompson, and which he had covenanted, under some arrangement for compensation, to grant to the Church, and which contract he attempted, at least, to repudiate" (*HC* 1:188).

D&C 56:16–17—The insidious influence of greed is manifest in the lives of the prideful—both rich and poor—whenever the obsession with worldly goods take precedence over a focused desire to acquire heavenly wealth. Greed and possessiveness are anathema to the principle of consecration and sacrifice. In the celestial sphere the vertical orientation (so common in the class-conscious world) is replaced by the horizontal—with all individuals and families prospering on the same plane, being nurtured and blessed according to individual needs and circumstances based on righteous principles. It was this transition to the vertical, accompanied by the abdication of covenant vows, that brought about the eventual extinction of the Nephite nation. In the days of the Restoration of the gospel, the Lord repeatedly warns the people to extinguish their pride and greed, to be industrious, and to cultivate contrition and humility. "And if ye seek the riches which it is the will of the Father to give unto you, ye shall be the richest of all people, for ye shall have the riches of eternity; and it must needs be that the riches of the earth are mine to give; but beware of pride, lest ye become as the Nephites of old" (D&C 38:39).

other men's goods, whose eyes are full of greediness, and who will not labor with your own hands!

18. But blessed are the poor who are pure in heart, whose hearts are broken, and whose spirits are contrite, for they shall see the kingdom of God coming in power and great glory unto their deliverance; for the fatness of the earth shall be theirs.

19. For behold, the Lord shall come, and his recompense shall be with him, and he shall reward every man, and the poor shall rejoice;

20. And their generations shall inherit the earth from generation to generation, forever and ever. And now I make an end of speaking unto you. Even so. Amen.

SECTION 57

1. Hearken, O ye elders of my church, saith the Lord your God, who have assembled yourselves together, according to my commandments, in this land, which is the land of Missouri, which is the land which I have appointed and consecrated for the gathering of the saints:

2. Wherefore this is the land of promise, and the place for the city of Zion.

3. And thus saith the Lord your God, if you will receive wisdom, here is wisdom. Behold, the place which is now called Independence, is the center place, and a spot for the temple is lying westward, upon a lot which is not far from the courthouse.

4. Wherefore it is wisdom that the land should be purchased by the

---

WILLIAM W. PHELPS

William W. Phelps was born February 17, 1792, in Dover, Morris County, New Jersey. He purchased a copy of the Book of Mormon from Parley P. Pratt in April 1830 and was immediately persuaded of its divine authenticity. In June 1831 he moved to Kirtland; he was baptized June 10, 1831. Subsequently he was ordained an elder and journeyed with the Prophet to Missouri, where he set up shop as a printer. In July 1833 a mob attacked his house and destroyed the press on which he was printing the Book of Commandments (the predecessor to the Doctrine and Covenants). Though courageous in standing up against such violence, he was constrained by persecution to return to Kirtland, where he assisted in the preparation of the 1835 edition of the Doctrine and Covenants and the first Church hymnbook. He donated funds to support the building of the Kirtland Temple and composed the celebrated hymn sung at its dedication—"The Spirit of God Like a Fire Is Burning." Upon returning to Missouri he turned his assets over to Bishop Edward Partridge for the building up of the kingdom, but he was chastened and excommunicated. Though embittered, William repented and was forgiven. In Nauvoo he served on the city council, and he loyally stood by the Prophet in the hour of martyrdom. Thereafter he journeyed with the Saints to the Salt Lake Valley, where he spent his final years in civic service and Church service, passing away on March 6, 1872.

D&C 56:18—The Lord would soon declare in a revelation on September 11, 1831: "Behold, the Lord requireth the heart and a willing mind; and the willing and obedient shall eat the good of the land of Zion in these last days" (D&C 64:34). Would this promise not also include the wealthy who were righteous and charitable? Elder Melvin J. Ballard thought so: "I am sure that in perfect harmony with this revelation [Section 56:18–19] I could add 'and blessed are the rich, too, who are pure in heart, whose hearts are, broken, whose spirits are contrite, for they shall see the kingdom of God coming in power and great glory unto their great deliverance.'" (CR, April 1937, Third Day, Morning Session, 89). Both rich and poor can embrace the gospel in virtue and holiness; both rich and poor can esteem others and bring their offerings before the Lord in humility and contrition. The key is to cultivate purity of heart and seek heavenly wealth by advancing the cause of Zion.

Section 57 Background—Given July 20, 1831, at Jackson County, Missouri, identifying Independence, Missouri, as the central gathering place of Zion. Historian Lyndon W. Cook gives the following summary:

> Obedient to the instructions of section 52, numerous pairs of missionaries started for Independence, Missouri. Joseph Smith with seven others (Martin Harris, Sidney Rigdon, Edward Partridge, William W. Phelps, Joseph Coe, A. Sidney Gilbert, and his wife, Elizabeth) left Kirtland for Missouri on 19 June 1831. This group traveled to Cincinnati by wagon, canal boat, and stage, from Cincinnati to Louisville, Kentucky, and from Louisville to St. Louis, Missouri by steamer. At St. Louis Sidney Rigdon and the Gilberts waited for water conveyance while the others went on foot to Independence, where they arrived before 17 July 1831. At Independence the Prophet and his party were greeted by Oliver Cowdery, others of the Lamanite Mission, and a handful of Missouri converts. Joseph Smith declared that this "meeting of our brethren, who had long awaited our arrival, was a glorious one, and moistened with many tears." After "viewing the county [and] seeking diligently at the hand of God," Joseph Smith received section 57, which designated "the very spot upon which [the Lord] designed to commence the work of gathering," and the upbuilding of an 'holy city,' even the New Jerusalem. On 2 August 1831, some twelve miles west of Independence, Sidney Rigdon consecrated and dedicated the land for the gathering of the Saints. (RPJS, 91.)

D&C 57:2–3—In September 1835, the Prophet Joseph Smith looked back on the occasion where the Lord revealed for the first time the specific location for the city of Zion:

> I received, by a heavenly vision, a commandment in June following [1831], to take my journey to the western boundaries of the State of Missouri, and there designate the very spot which was to be the central place for the commencement of the

saints; and also every tract lying westward, even unto the line running directly between Jew and Gentile.

5. And also every tract bordering by the prairies, inasmuch as my disciples are enabled to buy lands. Behold, this is wisdom, that they may obtain it for an everlasting inheritance.

6. And let my servant Sidney Gilbert stand in the office which I have appointed him, to receive moneys, to be an agent unto the church, to buy land in all the regions round about, inasmuch as can be in righteousness, and as wisdom shall direct.

7. And let my servant Edward Partridge, stand in the office which I have appointed him, to divide the saints their inheritance, even as I have commanded; and also those whom he has appointed to assist him.

8. And again, verily I say unto you, let my servant Sidney Gilbert plant himself in this place, and establish a store, that he may sell goods without fraud, that he may obtain money to buy lands for the good of the saints, and that he may obtain whatsoever things the disciples may need to plant them in their inheritance.

9. And also let my servant Sidney Gilbert obtain a license—(behold here is wisdom, and whoso readeth let him understand)—that he may send goods also unto the people, even by whom he will, as clerks employed in his service,

10. And thus provide for my saints, that my gospel may be preached unto those who sit in darkness, and in the region and shadow of death.

11. And again, verily I say unto you, let my servant William W. Phelps be planted in this place, and be established as a printer unto the church;

12. And lo, if the world receiveth his writings—(behold here is wisdom)—let him obtain whatsoever he can obtain in righteousness for the good of the saints.

13. And let my servant Oliver Cowdery, assist him, even as I have commanded, in whatsoever place I shall appoint unto him, to copy, and to correct, and select, that all things may be right before me, as it shall be proved by the Spirit through him.

14. And thus let those of whom I have spoken be planted in the land of Zion, as speedily as can be, with their families, to do those things even as I have spoken.

15. And now concerning the gathering. Let the bishop and the agent make preparations for those families which have been commanded to come to this land as soon as possible, and plant them in their inheritance.

16. And unto the residue of both elders and members, further directions shall be given hereafter. Even so. Amen.

gathering together of those who embrace the fullness of the everlasting Gospel. Accordingly I undertook the journey, with certain ones of my brethren, and after a long and tedious journey, suffering many privations and hardships, arrived in Jackson County, Missouri, and after viewing the country, seeking diligently at the hand of God, He manifested Himself unto us, and designated, to me and others, the very spot upon which He designed to commence the work of the gathering, and the upbuilding of an "holy city," which should be called Zion—Zion, because it is a place of righteousness, and all who build thereon are to worship the true and living God, and all believe in one doctrine, even the doctrine of our Lord and Savior Jesus Christ. "Thy watchmen shall lift up the voice; with the voice together shall they sing: for they shall see eye to eye, when the Lord shall bring again Zion" (Isaiah 52:8). (HC 2:254.)

D&C 57:14—The several organizational dimensions of the gathering are addressed in the divine commissions given of the Lord: real estate acquisition, dividing portions to the settlers according to their needs and circumstance under provisions of the law of consecration, establishment of a store for the distribution of goods, preparation of materials to be published, and the actual publication of the same. The reference to "the line running directly between Jew and Gentile" refers to the frontier between the existing settlers and the Lamanites.

The home of Jones H. Flournoy in Independence, Missouri. One of the first brick homes in Independence, it is also one of the oldest. A prominent man in the 1820s and 1830s, Flournoy oversaw the construction of the first segment of the Oregon Trail. After Joseph Smith visited his home, Flournoy sold a parcel of the land to the Church, including the lot where the temple in Jackson County will one day stand; Joseph purchased the 63 acres for $130. Flournoy later became a staunch anti-Mormon and was one of the leaders who drove more than 1,200 Saints out of Independence and who participated in destroying the printing press, burning homes, and tarring and feathering Edward Partridge.

SECTION 58

1. Hearken, O ye elders of my church, and give ear to my word, and learn of me what I will concerning you, and also concerning this land unto which I have sent you:

2. For verily I say unto you, blessed is he that keepeth my commandments, whether in life or in death; and he that is faithful in tribulation, the reward of the same is greater in the kingdom of heaven.

3. Ye cannot behold with your natural eyes, for the present time, the design of your God concerning those things which shall come hereafter, and the glory which shall follow after much tribulation.

4. For after much tribulation cometh the blessings. Wherefore the day cometh that ye shall be crowned with much glory; the hour is not yet, but is nigh at hand.

5. Remember this, which I tell you before, that you may lay it to heart, and receive that which shall to follow.

6. Behold, verily I say unto you, for this cause I have sent you that you might be obedient, and that your hearts might be prepared to bear testimony of the things which are to come;

7. And also that you might be honored of laying the foundation, and of bearing record of the land upon which the Zion of God shall stand;

8. And also that a feast of fat things might be prepared for the poor; yea, a feast of fat things, of wine on the lees well refined, that the earth may know that the mouths of the prophets shall not fail;

9. Yea a supper of the house of the Lord, well prepared, unto which all nations shall be invited.

10. Firstly, the rich and the learned, the wise and the noble;

11. And after that cometh the day of my power: then shall the poor,

Section 58 Background—Given on August 1, 1831, in Jackson County, Missouri (see HC 1:190–195), shortly after the arrival there of Sidney Rigdon and members of the Colesville Branch. The gathering Saints were eager to know the will of the Lord pertaining to their service and mission in their new surroundings, so the Prophet inquired and received this revelation, which contains powerful doctrine concerning repentance, taking initiative in serving others, and following the laws of the land in the spirit of good citizenship.

D&C 58:4—With these words the Lord characterized the nature of the work of His kingdom—and the blessings that await those who labor with valor, despite the challenges and burdens of mortal travail. It is especially in missionary work that sacrifice is called for. The harvest is not easy, but the rewards are glorious. The pattern of righteousness includes being valiant in the gospel despite persecution. Overcoming tribulation is one of the predicted dimensions of authentic discipleship.

D&C 58:7—There is joy in the knowledge that we are laying the foundation of Zion. Our message is that the gospel of faith and repentance will prepare us to be worthy participants in the glorious winding-up scenes leading to the dawning of the millennial era. The Prophet Joseph Smith described this process in language of eloquence and power:

> The building up of Zion is a cause that has interested the people of God in every age; it is a theme upon which prophets, priests and kings have dwelt with peculiar delight; they have looked forward with joyful anticipation to the day in which we live; and fired with heavenly and joyful anticipations they have sung and written and prophesied of this our day; but they died without the sight; we are the favored people that God has made choice of to bring about the Latter-day glory; it is left for us to see, participate in and help to roll forward the Latter-day glory. . . . The heavenly Priesthood will unite with the earthly, to bring about those great purposes; and whilst we are thus united in the one common cause, to roll forth the kingdom of God, the heavenly Priesthood are not idle spectators, the Spirit of God will be showered down from above, and it will dwell in our midst. The blessings of the Most High will rest upon our tabernacles, and our name will be handed down to future ages; our children will rise up and call us blessed; and generations yet unborn will dwell with delight upon the scenes that we have passed through, the privations that we have endured; the untiring zeal that we have manifested; the all but insurmountable difficulties that we have overcome in laying the foundation of a work that brought about the glory and blessing which they will realize; a work that God and angels have contemplated with delight for generations past; that fired the souls of the ancient patriarchs and prophets; a work that is destined to bring about the destruction of the powers of darkness, the renovation of the earth, the glory of God, and the salvation of the human family. (HC 4:609–10.)

the lame, and the blind, and the deaf, come in unto the marriage of the Lamb, and partake of the supper of the Lord, prepared for the great day to come.

12. Behold, I, the Lord, have spoken it.

13. And that the testimony might go forth from Zion, yea, from the mouth of the city of the heritage of God:

14. Yea, for this cause I have sent you hither, and have selected my servant Edward Partridge, and have appointed unto him his mission in this land;

15. But if he repent not of his sins, which are unbelief and blindness of heart, let him take heed lest he fall.

16. Behold his mission is given unto him, and it shall not be given again.

17. And whoso standeth in his mission is appointed to be a judge in Israel, like as it was in ancient days, to divide the lands of the heritage of God unto his children.

18. And to judge his people by the testimony of the just, and by the assistance of his counselors, according to the laws of the kingdom which are given by the prophets of God;

19. For verily I say unto you, my law shall be kept on this land.

20. Let no man think he is ruler, but let God rule him that judgeth, according to the counsel of his own will; or, in other words, him that counseleth or sitteth upon the judgment seat.

21. Let no man break the laws of the land, for he that keepeth the laws of God hath no need to break the laws of the land:

22. Wherefore, be subject to the powers that be, until He reigns whose right it is to reign, and subdues all enemies under his feet.

23. Behold, the laws which ye have received from my hand are the laws of the church, and in this light ye shall hold them forth. Behold, here is wisdom.

24. And now as I spake concerning my servant Edward Partridge, this land is the land of his residence, and those whom he has appointed for his counselors. And also the land of the residence of him whom I have appointed to keep my store-house;

25. Wherefore let them bring their families to this land, as they shall counsel between themselves and me:

26. For behold, it is not meet that I should command in all things, for he that is compelled in all things, the same is a slothful and not a wise servant; wherefore he receiveth no reward.

27. Verily I say, men should be anxiously engaged in a good cause, and do many things of their own free will, and bring to pass much righteousness;

28. For the power is in them, wherein they are agents unto themselves. And inasmuch as men do good they shall in nowise lose their reward.

D&C 58:17, 20—The bishop in Israel proceeds to fulfill his commission according to the laws and principles given through God's chosen prophets—and with the assistance of his counselors and the testimony of the just. It is according to divine regulation that the bishop renders his service in the kingdom. He does not elevate himself as a ruler among the people, but recognizes the Lord as the ruler and follows His counsel.

D&C 58:21–23—The Lord instructs those gathering to Missouri to remember to operate within the parameters of the laws of the land. Severe persecution lay ahead—but the Saints were to proceed with a commitment to act in lawful ways to obtain and secure their rights and liberties under the Constitution. They were to be proactive responsible citizens devoted to carrying out their civic duty—while at the same time striving to build the kingdom of God in righteousness. It is a tenet of the living Church that the Saints are to obey the laws of the land (see Article of Faith 12). James Talmage counseled:

> It is a fundamental necessity that laws shall be established among men for general governance; and obedience to law is the obvious duty of every member of organized society. Violation of the law, therefore, is not only a secular offense but a transgression of the principles of true religion. This world would be a happier one if men carried more religion into their daily affairs—into business, politics, and statesmanship. Mark you, I say religion, not church. Under existing conditions it is imperative that State and Church be kept separate; and this segregation must be maintained until the inauguration of Christ's personal reign." (VM, 186–87.)

D&C 58:26–28—These now-famous words constitute a grand gesture of acknowledgment given by the Creator to His children as they struggle to perform their labors under a divine mandate to gather together and establish the kingdom and Church on earth. They are endowed with the power of creative choice to bring about much righteousness as agents of the Lord. They are not to look to the Lord for meticulous instruction on every facet of their office and commission, but to operate within the boundaries of revealed gospel principles to do much good of their own free will. The quality of self-reliance is rooted in the reality of agency—and this agency extends to both temporal and spiritual matters, for God's children can prayerfully elect to use their talents, skills, and energy to learn, plan, and act for the improvement of their situation and the unfolding of increased spirituality. Such was a key part of the design of God's plan for the blessing of His children.

29. But he that doeth not anything until he is commanded, and receiveth a commandment with doubtful heart, and keepeth it with slothfulness, the same is damned.

30. Who am I that made man, saith the Lord, that will hold him guiltless that obeys not my commandments?

31. Who am I, saith the Lord, that have promised and have not fulfilled?

32. I command and a man obey not; I revoke and they receive not the blessing;

33. Then they say in their hearts, this is not the work of the Lord, for his promises are not fulfilled. But wo unto such, for their reward lurketh beneath, and not from above.

34. And now I give unto you further directions concerning this land.

35. It is wisdom in me that my servant Martin Harris should be an example unto the church, in laying his moneys before the bishop of the church.

36. And also, this is a law unto every man that cometh unto this land, to receive an inheritance; and he shall do with his moneys according as the law directs.

37. And it is wisdom also, that there should be lands purchased in Independence, for the place of the store-house, and also for the house of the printing.

38. And other directions concerning my servant Martin Harris shall be given him of the Spirit, that he may receive his inheritance as seemeth him good.

39. And let him repent of his sins, for he seeketh the praise of the world.

40. And also let my servant William W. Phelps stand in the office which I have appointed him, and receive his inheritance in the land;

41. And also he hath need to repent, for I, the Lord, am not well pleased with him, for he seeketh to excel, and he is not sufficiently meek before me.

42. Behold, he who has repented of his sins, the same is forgiven, and I, the Lord, remember them no more.

43. By this ye may know if a man repenteth of his sins. Behold, he will confess them and forsake them.

44. And now, verily, I say, concerning the residue of the elders of my church, the time has not yet come, for many years, for them to receive their inheritance in this land, except they desire it through the prayer of faith, only as it shall be appointed unto them of the Lord.

45. For, behold, they shall push the people together from the ends of the earth;

46. Wherefore, assemble yourselves together, and they who are not appointed to stay in this land, let them preach the gospel in the regions round about, and after that let them return to their homes.

47. Let them preach by the way, and bear testimony of the truth in all places, and call upon the rich, the high and the low, and the poor to repent;

48. And let them build up churches inasmuch as the inhabitants of the earth will repent.

49. And let there be an agent

D&C 58:32—The Lord thinks and operates according to covenant processes anchored in the sanctity of His sacred word. We in the world tend to think at times in terms of our wants—the objectives of our desires—and less in terms of the faith and action needed to obtain noble objectives. When we desire eternal blessings of peace and happiness, then we are to conduct our lives according to eternal principles in order to achieve just ends. President Joseph F. Smith elaborates:

> If we do not [keep the commandments], is it not because we think only once in a while of God and of godliness, and all the rest of the time we think of the world and of worldliness? We give our hopes, our time, our talent, our thoughts, our words, our actions, to the temporalities of life, and, once in a while, we think of God. We come before Him in that pitiful form of unworthiness to crave His blessings and His favors. Do you wonder that we are often denied that which we ask for, and fail to receive that which we desire? It is because we do not ask aright. When we approach God in this way, we are not in a condition to ask aright, nor are we in a condition to receive that which we ask for, for God is not likely to bestow upon his children gifts and blessings of which they are not worthy. (CR, Oct. 1913, 7.)

D&C 58:42–43—Through the miracle of the Atonement and the transformation of the old into the new through the "mighty change" of heart (see Mosiah 5:2; Alma 5:14), the Lord promises that He does not remember the confessed and forsaken sins of the penitent and faithful. What peace and holiness flows into the lives of individuals from that sacred process. Said President Gordon B. Hinckley: "Forgiveness is a mark of divinity. There is hope for you. Your lives are ahead, and they can be filled with happiness, even though the past may have been marred by sin. This is a work of saving and assisting people with their problems. This is the purpose of the gospel" (TGBH, 548).

D&C 58:47–58—The gospel of Jesus Christ is not just a concept but a process; not just a nexus of principles but a program of encompassing power leading to outcomes of eternal consequence. The Lord gives the call to action: promulgate the word, bear witness by the Spirit at all times, gather the faithful and penitent into congregations of Zion, acquire property for the Saints to dwell on, do all in an orderly fashion—not in haste nor by flight, but by following the revelations given from on high.

The same process is underway now as in the early days of the Restoration. The same program for blessing the children of God is in force in our day just as from the foundations of the earth. We have a covenant obligation to preach the gospel and help in the building up of the kingdom of God.

In an interesting footnote to verse 57, it was Sidney Rigdon who received the commission to dedicate the temple site in Independence. However, the Prophet Joseph Smith actually served as voice for the ceremony (see HC 1:199).

appointed by the voice of the church, unto the church in Ohio, to receive moneys to purchase lands in Zion.

50. And I give unto my servant, Sidney Rigdon, a commandment that he shall write a description of the land of Zion, and a statement of the will of God, as it shall be made known by the Spirit unto him;

51. And an epistle and subscription, to be presented unto all the churches to obtain moneys, to be put into the hands of the bishop to purchase lands for an inheritance for the children of God, of himself or the agent, as seemeth him good or as he shall direct.

52. For, behold, verily I say unto you, the Lord willeth that the disciples and the children of men should open their hearts, even to purchase this whole region of country, as soon as time will permit.

53. Behold, here is wisdom. Let them do this lest they receive none inheritance, save it be by the shedding of blood.

54. And again, inasmuch as there is land obtained, let there be workmen sent forth of all kinds unto this land, to labor for the saints of God.

55. Let all these things be done in order; and let the privileges of the lands be made known from time to time, by the bishop or the agent of the church;

56. And let the work of the gathering be not in haste, nor by flight, but let it be done as it shall be counseled by the elders of the church at the conferences, according to the knowledge which they receive from time to time.

57. And let my servant Sidney Rigdon consecrate and dedicate this land, and the spot of the temple, unto the Lord.

58. And let a conference meeting be called, and after that let my servants Sidney Rigdon and Joseph Smith, jun., return, and also Oliver Cowdery with them, to accomplish the residue of the work which I have appointed unto them in their own land, and the residue as shall be ruled by the conferences.

59. And let no man return from this land, except he bear record by the way of that which he knows and most assuredly believes.

60. Let that which has been bestowed upon Ziba Peterson be taken from him; and let him stand as a member in the church, and labor with his own hands, with the brethren, until he is sufficiently chastened for all his sins, for he confesseth them not, and he thinketh to hide them.

61. Let the residue of the elders of this church, who are coming to this land, some of whom are exceedingly blessed even above measure, also hold a conference upon this land.

62. And let my servant Edward Partridge direct the conference which shall be held by them.

63. And let them also return, preaching the gospel by the way, bearing record of the things which are revealed unto them;

64. For, verily, the sound must go forth from this place into all the world, and unto the uttermost parts of the earth—the gospel must be preached unto every creature, with signs following them that believe.

65. And behold the Son of man cometh. Amen.

D&C 58:50—There were no photographs available at this time, so the description of the land was critical in giving Saints a visual picture that would encourage them to make monetary donations.

D&C 58:52–53—The Lord wanted absolutely no dispute around the acquisition of lands; the Saints were instructed to purchase the lands so that all transactions would be legal and so that there would be no questions. As alluded to in verse 53, the Saints were to never be the aggressor or cause bloodshed in acquiring lands.

D&C 58:57—Sidney Rigdon dedicated the land for the gathering of the Saints on August 2, 1831. The next day—August 3, 1831—Joseph Smith dedicated the spot for the temple.

D&C 58:64—The resurrected Savior charged His Apostles with the commission: "Go ye therefore, and teach all nations, baptizing them in the name of the Father, and of the Son, and of the Holy Ghost: Teaching them to observe all things whatsoever I have commanded you: and, lo, I am with you alway, *even* unto the end of the world. Amen" (Matt. 28:19–20). This is the mandate to all the Saints under the Abrahamic covenant (see Abr. 2:6, 9–11). We manifest through our works and testimony that the gospel has been restored, that Jesus Christ is our Redeemer, that the Lord again speaks and invites all to come unto Him to receive the blessings of salvation and exaltation through the principles and ordinances of His Church.

From a careful study of Church history in modern times, we gain new insight into, and appreciation for, the profound blessings granted unto those who "gather together, and stand in holy places" (D&C 101:22). From the blossoming of the Church in the desert valleys of Utah, to the unfolding of the kingdom of God in glory around the globe, we deepen our grateful realization of the design of the Father to bless and nurture His children as they rise in the majesty of their potential as sons and daughters of God: "For verily I say unto you, blessed is he that keepeth my commandments, whether in life or in death; and he that is faithful in tribulation, the reward of the same is greater in the kingdom of heaven. Ye cannot behold with your natural eyes, for the present time, the design of your God concerning those things which shall come hereafter, and the glory which shall follow after much tribulation" (D&C 58:2–3).

SECTION 59

1. Behold, blessed, saith the Lord, are they who have come up unto this land with an eye single to my glory, according to my commandments;

2. For them that live shall inherit the earth, and them that die shall rest from all their labors, and their works shall follow them, and they shall receive a crown in the mansions of my Father, which I have prepared for them;

3. Yea, blessed are they whose feet stand upon the land of Zion, who have obeyed my gospel, for they shall receive for their reward the good things of the earth; and it shall bring forth in its strength;

4. And they shall also be crowned with blessings from above, yea, and with commandments not a few; and with revelations in their time: they that are faithful and diligent before me.

5. Wherefore I give unto them a commandment, saying thus: Thou shalt love the Lord thy God with all thy heart, with all thy might, mind, and strength; and in the name of Jesus Christ thou shalt serve him.

6. Thou shalt love thy neighbor as thyself. Thou shalt not steal; neither commit adultery, nor kill, nor do anything like unto it.

7. Thou shalt thank the Lord thy God in all things.

8. Thou shalt offer a sacrifice unto the Lord thy God in righteousness, even that of a broken heart and a contrite spirit.

9. And that thou mayest more fully keep thyself unspotted from the

Section 59 Background—As part of the Restoration, the Lord provided special guidance on keeping the Sabbath day holy—especially the material in Section 59, given on August 7, 1831, in Jackson County, Missouri (see *HC* 1:196–201). The Colesville Saints (some sixty in number) had been evicted from Leman Copley's land in Thompson, Ohio, and had arrived in Jackson County about two weeks before this revelation was received. Polly Knight, wife of Joseph Knight, Sr., lived long enough to reach Zion and then passed away on August 6. She was buried the following day, the date of this revelation, which honors those who pass away in the labor of Zion.

Concerning the events of August 7, 1831, Joseph Smith relates: "On the 7th, I attended the funeral of Sister Polly Knight, wife of Joseph Knight, Sen. This was the first death in the Church in this land, and I can say, a worthy member sleeps in Jesus till the resurrection" (*HC* 1:199). The Knight family was loyal to Joseph and his cause even prior to his receiving the golden plates. On the family's journey to Missouri from Kirtland, Polly Knight's health worsened. "Yet," relates her son Newel, "she would not consent to stop traveling; her only, or her greatest desire was to set her feet upon the land of Zion, and to have her body interred in that land. I went on shore and bought lumber to make a coffin in case she should die before we arrived at our place of destination—so fast did she fail. But the Lord gave her the desire of her heart, and she lived to stand upon that land" (*HC* 1:199, note 13).

D&C 59:2–4—It is exceedingly refreshing to be enabled to view things from the heavenly perspective. We discern from that point of view that all will be well—that the Lord in His infinite mercy and compassion will care for those who pass away in His service and bless the faithful and diligent who remain below. Elder Rudger Clawson said: "There are two things connected with these words that impress me deeply and that is this, blessed are those who have obeyed the gospel and, secondly, who have come up to the land of Zion. . . . It mattered little whether they lived or they died. If they died, they were to be blessed and were to enter into the mansions that were prepared for them, and if they lived, the earth was to be blessed for their sake, and it was to give forth in its strength; and, moreover, and what is of far greater importance, they were to receive the revelations of the Lord not a few" (*CR*, Oct. 1916, Second Day, Morning Session, 35).

D&C 59:5–8—The Lord had reviewed for His Saints in Ohio the agenda of the Ten Commandments (see D&C 42:18–28). Now He provides again the essence of these divine commandments as the Saints arrive in the place designated as the land of Zion, the place where the central headquarters of the coming millennial kingdom would be located.

world, thou shalt go to the house of prayer and offer up thy sacraments upon my holy day;

10. For verily this is a day appointed unto you to rest from your labors, and to pay thy devotions unto the Most High;

11. Nevertheless thy vows shall be offered up in righteousness on all days and at all times;

12. But remember that on this the Lord's day, thou shalt offer thine oblations and thy sacraments unto the Most High, confessing thy sins unto thy brethren, and before the Lord.

13. And on this day thou shalt do none other thing, only let thy food be prepared with singleness of heart that thy fasting may be perfect, or, in other words, that thy joy may be full.

14. Verily, this is fasting and prayer; or in other words, rejoicing and prayer.

15. And inasmuch as ye do these things with thanksgiving, with cheerful hearts and countenances; not with much laughter, for this is sin, but with a glad heart and a cheerful countenance;

16. Verily I say, that inasmuch as ye do this, the fulness of the earth is yours: the beasts of the field and the fowls of the air, and that which climbeth upon the trees and walketh upon the earth;

17. Yea, and the herb, and the good things which cometh of the earth, whether for food or for raiment, or for houses, or for barns, or for orchards, or for gardens, or for vineyards;

18. Yea, all things which come of the earth, in the season thereof, are made for the benefit and the use of man, both to please the eye and to gladden the heart;

19. Yea, for food and for raiment, for taste and for smell, to strengthen the body and to enliven the soul.

20. And it pleaseth God that he hath given all these things unto man; for unto this end were they made to be used with judgment, not to excess, neither by extortion:

21. And in nothing doth man offend God, or against none is his wrath kindled, save those who confess not his hand in all things, and obey not his commandments.

22. Behold, this is according to the law and the prophets: wherefore, trouble me no more concerning this matter,

23. But learn that he who doeth the works of righteousness shall receive his reward, even peace in this world, and eternal life in the world to come.

24. I, the Lord, have spoken it, and the Spirit beareth record. Amen.

D&C 59:8—The requisite sacrifice unto the Lord is that of a "broken heart and a contrite spirit." Elder Joseph Fielding Smith explains: "What is a broken heart? One that is humble, one that is touched by the Spirit of the Lord, and which is willing to abide in all the covenants and the obligations which the Gospel entails . . . " (*CR*, Oct. 1941, Second Day, Afternoon Session, 93).

D&C 59:12—The Sabbath day is a day of rest. Man's rest implies, in large measure, a respite from workday involvements; however, the Lord's "rest" is defined as "the fulness of his glory" (D&C 84:24). In that sense, the Sabbath is a unique day on which we continue our prayerful quest—our penitent rehearsal—in preparation for entering the Lord's rest when that hour arrives for each of us, individually, to join the ranks of those who are "taken home to that God who gave them life" (Alma 40:11).

The Sabbath is a day on which earthly cares are set aside in deference to the cares of the spirit, a day on which we can focus our whole might, mind, and soul on the affairs of the kingdom, on communal worship, on the renewing of our covenants by partaking of the sacrament, on scripture study, on paying our tithes and offerings, and on service to our fellow beings. Only those distracted by earthly entanglements would consider the Sabbath a burden or a trial; the righteous and faithful look forward to it as the gateway to God's glory, a more sure way to step forward toward communion with the Spirit, and a milestone that marks, each week, the passage of yet another unit of mortal experience leading back home.

D&C 59:14—To fast with joy and humility is to remember things spiritual and to confirm our willingness to subsume our own desires and needs beneath the will of the Father.

D&C 59:15–16—When we enter into the Sabbath, we enter into a holy time frame—one in which rich blessings lie in store for those who serve the Lord in righteousness and bring Him gifts of devotion and prayerful worship. The blessings of the Sabbath include peace, spirituality, unity with family and friends, enhanced understanding of the plan of salvation, humility, spiritual awakenings, escape from the fetters of earthly constraints and pressures, and the satisfaction of knowing that one is abiding by the will of the Lord.

D&C 59:23—Honoring the Sabbath and doing the works of righteousness lead to blessings of profound consequence: "peace in this world, and eternal life in the world to come" (verse 23). This is the word of the Lord as confirmed by His Holy Spirit. Salvation and celestial exaltation are thus brought within the reach of the faithful and obedient:

These precious promises—made available through the atoning blood of Jesus our Lord—give focus and direction to our actions. *Salvation, eternal life, eternal lives, exaltation*—all expressions connoting the glories of the celestial kingdom and a life which is similar to God's own life—repre-

SECTION 60

1. Behold, thus saith the Lord unto the elders of his church, who are to return speedily to the land from whence they came. Behold, it pleaseth me, that you have come up hither;

2. But with some I am not well pleased, for they will not open their mouths, but hide the talent which I have given unto them, because of the fear of man. Wo unto such, for mine anger is kindled against them.

3. And it shall come to pass, if they are not more faithful unto me, it shall be taken away, even that which they have;

4. For I, the Lord, rule in the heavens above, and among the armies of the earth; and in the day when I shall make up my jewels, all men shall know what it is that bespeaketh the power of God.

5. But verily, I will speak unto you concerning your journey unto the land from whence you came. Let there be a craft made, or bought, as seemeth you good, it mattereth not unto me, and take your journey speedily for the place which is called St. Louis.

6. And from thence let my servant Sidney Rigdon, and Joseph Smith, jr., and Oliver Cowdery, take their journey for Cincinnati;

7. And in this place let them lift up their voice and declare my word with loud voices, without wrath or doubting, lifting up holy hands upon them. For I am able to make you holy, and your sins are forgiven you.

8. And let the residue take their journey from St. Louis, two by two, and preach the word, not in haste, among the congregations of the wicked, until they return to the churches from whence they came.

9. And all this for the good of the churches; for this intent have I sent them.

10. And let my servant Edward Partridge impart of the money which I have given him, a portion unto mine elders who are commanded to return;

11. And he that is able, let him return it by the way of the agent, and he that is not, of him it is not required.

12. And now I speak of the residue who are to come unto this land.

13. Behold, they have been sent to preach my gospel among the congregations

sent the grand ends to our myriad means, the reason we do what we do in the Church and in the home. To those who have developed "like precious faith" [2 Pet. 1:1] with the ancients come the blessings enjoyed by the ancients: the fulness of the glory of the Father and a continuation of the seeds forever and ever. We exult, "How glorious is the voice we hear from heaven, proclaiming in our ears, glory, and salvation, and honor, and immortality, and eternal life; kingdoms, principalities, and powers!" (D&C 128:23). (Robert L. Millet and Joseph Fielding McConkie, *LB*, 143.)

Section 60 Background—Given on August 8, 1831, in Jackson County, Missouri (see *HC* 1:201–202). Following the dedication of Jackson County, Missouri, as the site of the New Jerusalem, a conference for the Ohio missionaries was convened on August 4, 1831. The missionaries wanted to know how they should proceed with respect to their return to Ohio; the Prophet inquired of the Lord and received Section 60 in response.

D&C 60:2, 7—Those who give themselves over to the Lord in faith as His emissaries are transformed by His power and made holy. Their talent is magnified in the capacity to proclaim the word of God without fear and without doubt. But those who refuse to open their mouths because of the fear of man anger the Lord and stand in peril of losing their commission and their capacity to speak by the Spirit.

D&C 60:13—Idleness, refusing to apply one's gifts and talents in the work of the Lord, and turning away His invitation to strengthen and empower those who come forward with faith are serious infractions of covenant obligations that can lead to no less a consequence than damnation.

The site of the future Jackson County temple. The two-acre lot was dedicated by the Prophet Joseph Smith in 1831 as the site of the New Jerusalem. The lot itself is currently owned by the Church of Christ; the Community of Christ (formerly the RLDS Church) owns most of the rest of the original 63-acre parcel sold to the Church by Jones H. Flournoy. The LDS Church currently operates a visitors' center one block east of the temple lot.

of the wicked; wherefore, I give unto them a commandment thus: Thou shalt not idle away thy time, neither shalt thou bury thy talent that it may not be known.

14. And after thou hast come up unto the land of Zion, and hast proclaimed my word, thou shalt speedily return, proclaiming my word among the congregations of the wicked, not in haste, neither in wrath nor with strife;

15. And shake off the dust of thy feet against those who receive thee not; not in their presence, lest thou provoke them, but in secret, and wash thy feet, as a testimony against them in the day of judgment.

16. Behold, this is sufficient for you, and the will of him who hath sent you.

17. And by the mouth of my servant Joseph Smith, jun., it shall be made known concerning Sidney Rigdon and Oliver Cowdery. The residue hereafter. Even so. Amen.

SECTION 61

1. Behold, and hearken unto the voice of him who has all power, who is from everlasting to everlasting, even Alpha and Omega, the beginning and the end.

2. Behold, verily thus saith the Lord unto you, O ye elders of my church, who are assembled upon this spot, whose sins are now forgiven you, for I, the Lord, forgive sins, and am merciful unto those who confess their sins with humble hearts;

3. But verily I say unto you, that it is not needful for this whole company of mine elders to be moving swiftly upon the waters, whilst the inhabitants on either side are perishing in unbelief;

4. Nevertheless, I suffered it that ye might bear record; behold, there are many dangers upon the waters, and more especially hereafter;

5. For I, the Lord, have decreed in mine anger, many destructions upon the waters; yea, and especially upon these waters.

6. Nevertheless, all flesh is in mine hand, and he that is faithful among you shall not perish by the waters.

7. Wherefore it is expedient that

D&C 60:15–16—The missionaries of the Lord will doubtless play a solemn role as participants in the final judgment process, for their witness will be called forth in the case of those who had the opportunity to hear and receive the gospel but refused to do so (see D&C 75:21). Their testimony is ceremoniously solemnized by the act of cleansing their feet as a confirmation of their having completed their duty to God as commanded—even though the word was rejected.

Section 61 Background—Given on the bank of the Missouri River at McIlwaine's Bend, August 12, 1831 (see HC 1:202–205). The Prophet provided this introduction: "On the 9th, in company with ten Elders, I left Independence landing for Kirtland. We started down the river in canoes, and went the first day as far as Fort Osage, where we had an excellent wild turkey for supper. Nothing very important occurred till the third day, when many of the dangers so common upon the western waters, manifested themselves; and after we had encamped upon the bank of the river, at McIlwaine's Bend, Brother Phelps, in open vision by daylight, saw the destroyer in his most horrible power, ride upon the face of the waters; others heard the noise, but saw not the vision. The next morning after prayer, I received [Section 61]" (HC 1:202–203).

The banks of McIlwaine's Bend, on the Missouri River, where Joseph Smith and a group of ten elders camped on their return trip to Kirtland after visiting Independence. On the third day of the journey, Elder William W. Phelps saw in daytime vision the destroyer riding on the face of the waters.

my servant Sidney Gilbert and my servant William W. Phelps be in haste upon their errand and mission;

8. Nevertheless, I would not suffer that ye should part until you were chastened for all your sins, that you might be one, and you might not perish in wickedness;

9. But now, verily I say, it behooveth me that ye should part, wherefore let my servants Sidney Gilbert and William W. Phelps take their former company, and let them take their journey in haste that they may fill their mission, and through faith they shall overcome;

10. And inasmuch as they are faithful they shall be preserved, and I, the Lord, will be with them.

11. And let the residue take that which is needful for clothing.

12. Let my servant Sidney Gilbert take that which is not needful with him, as you shall agree.

13. And now, behold, for your good I gave unto you a commandment concerning these things; and I, the Lord, will reason with you as with men in days of old.

14. Behold, I, the Lord, in the beginning blessed the waters, but in the last days, by the mouth of my servant John, I cursed the waters;

15. Wherefore, the days will come that no flesh shall be safe upon the waters,

16. And it shall be said in days to come that none is able to go up to the land of Zion upon the waters, but he that is upright in heart.

17. And, as I, the Lord, in the beginning cursed the land, even so in the last days have I blessed it, in its time, for the use of my saints, that they may partake the fatness thereof.

18. And now I give unto you a commandment that what I say unto one I say unto all, that you shall forewarn your brethren concerning these waters, that they come not in journeying upon them, lest their faith fail and they are caught her snares;

19. I, the Lord, have decreed, and the destroyer rideth upon the face thereof, and I revoke not the decree;

20. I, the Lord, was angry with you yesterday, but to-day mine anger is turned away.

21. Wherefore, let those concerning whom I have spoken, that should take their journey in haste,

22. And it mattereth not unto me, after a little, if it so be that they fill their mission, whether they go by water or by land; let this be as it is made known unto them according to their judgments hereafter.

23. And now, concerning my servants Sidney Rigdon, and Joseph Smith, jun., and Oliver Cowdery, let them come not again upon the waters, save it be upon the canal, while journeying unto their homes, or in other words, they shall not come upon the waters to journey, save upon the canal.

24. Behold, I, the Lord, have appointed a way for the journeying of my saints, and behold, this is the way—that after they leave the canal, they shall journey by land, inasmuch as they are commanded to journey and go up into the land of Zion;

25. And they shall do like unto the children of Israel, pitching their tents by the way.

26. And, behold, this commandment you shall give unto all your brethren;

27. Nevertheless unto whom is given power to command the

D&C 61:15–29—In the last days the Lord has blessed the land for the sake of His gathering Saints, but issued warnings concerning the water. John the Beloved reported: "And the second angel poured out his vial upon the sea; and it became as the blood of a dead *man*: and every living soul died in the sea. And the third angel poured out his vial upon the rivers and fountains of waters; and they became blood" (Rev. 16:3–4). The geophysical upheavals that will attend the final stages of earth's history in conjunction with the dawning of the millennial reign will doubtless enhance the dangers of travel upon the waters. Nevertheless, those who are "upright in heart" will be able to gather to the land of Zion upon the waters. And those with power to command the waters can know through the Spirit how to proceed, "whether upon the land or upon the waters."

THE WATERS AND THE LAND

In this revelation, the Lord provided information pertaining to the waters and the land. He indicated that the land was originally cursed, but has been blessed in the latter days. While the water was originally blessed, that blessing has been withdrawn in the latter days (see D&C 61:14–17).

President Joseph Fielding Smith provided the following insights:

In the early millenniums of this earth's history, men did not understand the composition of the soils, and how they needed building up when crops were taken from them . . . the manner of cultivation did not lend itself to the abundant production which we are receiving today . . . in those early days of world history, there could not be the production, nor the varities of fruits coming from the earth, and the Lord can very properly speak of this as a curse, or the lack of blessing, upon the land. In those early periods we have every reason to believe that the torrents, floods, and the dangers upon the waters were not as great as they are today, and by no means as great as what the Lord has promised us. . . . we have seen the dangers upon the waters increase until the hearts of men failed them and only the brave, and those who were compelled to travel the seas, ventured out upon them. In regard to the Missouri–Mississippi waters, we hae seen year by year great destruction upon them, and coming from them (CHMR 1:206–207) (STDC 1:299–300).

waters, unto him it is given by the Spirit to know all his ways;

28. Wherefore let him do as the Spirit of the living God commandeth him, whether upon the land or upon the waters, as it remaineth with me to do hereafter;

29. And unto you is given the course for the saints, or the way for the saints of the camp of the Lord, to journey.

30. And again, verily I say unto you, my servants Sidney Rigdon, and Joseph Smith, jun., and Oliver Cowdery, shall not open their mouths in the congregations of the wicked, until they arrive at Cincinnati;

31. And in that place they shall lift up their voices unto God against that people; yea unto him whose anger is kindled against their wickedness; a people who are well-nigh ripened for destruction;

32. And from thence let them journey for the congregations of their brethren, for their labors even now are wanted more abundantly among them, than among the congregations of the wicked.

33. And now concerning the residue, let them journey and declare the word among the congregations of the wicked, inasmuch as it is given;

34. And inasmuch as they do this, they shall rid their garments, and they shall be spotless before me;

35. And let them journey together, or two by two, as seemeth them good, only let my servant Reynolds Cahoon, and my servant Samuel H. Smith, with whom I am well pleased, be not separated until they return to their homes, and this for a wise purpose in me.

36. And now, verily I say unto you, and what I say unto one I say unto all, be of good cheer little children, for I am in your midst, and I have not forsaken you;

37. And inasmuch as you have humbled yourselves before me, the blessings of the kingdom are yours.

38. Gird up your loins and be watchful and be sober, looking forth for the coming of the Son of Man, for he cometh in an hour you think not.

39. Pray always that you enter not into temptation, that you may abide the day of his coming, whether in life or in death. Even so. Amen.

SECTION 62

1. Behold, and hearken O ye elders of my church, saith the Lord your God, even Jesus Christ, your advocate, who knoweth the weakness of

D&C 61:35—The missionaries travel in pairs for security, protection from temptation, and to magnify their testimonies in unison by the Spirit. President Joseph Fielding Smith discusses this principle:

> The Lord called upon these brethren to travel two by two. This is how he sent his disciples out in the days of his ministry. When they traveled two by two they had protection. They were not as likely to fall into sin and they were not as likely to be attacked. . . . Although they were to travel in pairs, yet the Lord cautioned them against temptation while on the way. Satan is always alert and it requires extreme diligence, humility and prayer to keep the guidance of the Spirit of the Lord and be able to overcome." (CHMR 1:208.)

D&C 61:36–39—Our commission in life is to prepare in all soberness and conviction to meet the Savior and enter into His rest. The ancient prophet Micah encapsulated the entire process in a single sentence: "He hath shewed thee, O man, what is good; and what doth the LORD require of thee, but to do justly, and to love mercy, and to walk humbly with thy God?" (Micah 6:8). This philosophy of righteous living is reflected again and again in plainness in the Doctrine and Covenants and in the other holy scriptures. It is for us to read and savor the words of life and bring them with clarity before our families, that we might be of good cheer and together endure the rapture of the Second Coming with joy and thanksgiving.

Section 62 Background—Given on the bank of the Missouri River at Chariton, Missouri, August 13, 1831, as Joseph Smith and his group were making their way from Independence to Kirtland (see HC 1:205–206). The Prophet gave this introduction: "On the 13th [of August] I met several of the Elders on their way to the land of Zion, and after the joyful salutations with which brethren meet each other, who are actually contending for the faith once delivered to the Saints [see Jude 1:3] I received [Section 62]" (HC 1:205).

The Missouri River near Miami, Missouri. A few of those evicted from Jackson County, Missouri, moved into this area, including Jacob Haun. In December 1836, the Missouri General Assembly created Caldwell County, which was dedicated to the Mormons. Far West was designated as the county seat.

man and how to succor them who are tempted;

2. And verily mine eyes are upon those who have not as yet gone up unto the land of Zion; wherefore your mission is not yet full;

3. Nevertheless ye are blessed, for the testimony which ye have borne, is recorded in heaven for the angels to look upon, and they rejoice over you, and your sins are forgiven you.

4. And now continue your journey. Assemble yourselves upon the land of Zion, and hold a meeting and rejoice together, and offer a sacrament unto the Most High;

5. And then you may return to bear record, yea, even altogether, or two by two, as seemeth you good, it mattereth not unto me, only be faithful, and declare glad tidings unto the inhabitants of the earth, or among the congregations of the wicked.

6. Behold, I, the Lord, have brought you together that the promise might be fulfilled, that the faithful among you should be preserved and rejoice together in the land of Missouri. I, the Lord, promise the faithful and cannot lie.

7. I, the Lord, am willing, if any among you desireth to ride upon horses, or upon mules, or in chariots, he shall receive this blessing, if he receive it from the hand of the Lord, with a thankful heart in all things.

8. These things remain with you to do according to judgment and the directions of the Spirit.

9. Behold, the kingdom is yours. And behold, and lo, I am with the faithful always. Even so. Amen.

TITUS BILLINGS

Titus Billings was born March 1793 at Greenfield, Franklin County, Massachusetts. He was a stonemason and one of the first to be baptized in Kirtland. By revelation he was commanded to dispose of his land and journey to Missouri (see D&C 63:39). Titus obeyed and moved to Zion, where he consecrated his holdings and received an inheritance. In 1833 he was called as a counselor to Bishop Edward Partridge but was driven out of Jackson County by a mob before beginning his service. He moved to Clay County for a time and then to Far West, where he was able to serve as a counselor to Edward Partridge. He participated in the Battle of Crooked River and suffered starvation and frostbite in the flight that followed. His family joined him in Illinois, where they had respite for a time until the mobs forced them to flee to Nauvoo and then onward to Iowa to join the westward migration. Titus was ever helpful to the Saints in their travels and settlements. He passed away in Provo on February 6, 1866.

D&C 62:3—This statement is remarkable in its scope and implication—that our earthly witness for the truth is recorded in heaven and brings joy to the angels above. Further, we learn that righteous service in the missionary fold of Christ facilitates repentance and forgiveness for the missionary. Said James: "Brethren, if any of you do err from the truth, and one convert him; Let him know, that he which converteth the sinner from the error of his way shall save a soul from death, and shall hide a multitude of sins" (Jas. 5:19–20). In addition, the Lord declared in 1832: "For I will forgive you of your sins with this commandment—that you remain steadfast in your minds in solemnity and the spirit of prayer, in bearing testimony to all the world of those things which are communicated unto you" (D&C 84:61).

D&C 62:5–9—We are to receive all blessings with a thankful heart, especially the blessing of the companionship of the Savior, our Lord, and the guidance of His Holy Spirit. President Joseph F. Smith enjoined us: ". . . let the spirit of wisdom, of good judgment, of intelligence govern and direct all the acts and labors, and all the thoughts and desires of the Latter-day Saints" (CR, Oct. 1911, First Day, Morning Session, 2–3). President Joseph Fielding Smith, the firstborn son of Joseph F. Smith, later provided this concurring observation: *"The man who is guided by the Holy Spirit and who keeps the commandments of God, who abides in God, will have the clearest understanding and the better judgment always, because he is directed by the Spirit of truth. And the man who relies upon himself, or the knowledge of other men, will not have as clear a vision as will the man who abides in the truth and is directed by the Holy Spirit"* (DS 1:299).

NEWEL K. WHITNEY

Newel K. Whitney was born February 5, 1795, in Marlborough, Windham County, Vermont. He settled in Ohio as a merchandiser and worked with Algernon Sidney Gilbert in the capacity of clerk and bookkeeper. Newel and his wife, Elizabeth, had spiritual promptings about receiving the word of the Lord. Soon thereafter the missionaries taught them the gospel and they were baptized in November 1830. In a vision, the Prophet Joseph Smith saw Newel pleading with the Lord that the Prophet would come to Kirtland. In response, the Prophet showed up at the Whitney store around February 1, 1831, much to the joy of the young couple. On December 4, 1831, Newel was called by revelation to serve as a bishop (see D&C 72:1–8). Ever beloved of the Prophet, Newel was called as presiding bishop following the martyrdom. He and his family joined the westward trek in 1848. He passed away of severe chest pains on September 23, 1850, at his home in Salt Lake City.

SECTION 63

1. Hearken, O ye people, and open your hearts and give ear from afar; and listen, you that call yourselves the people of the Lord, and hear the word of the Lord and his will concerning you:

2. Yea, verily, I say, hear the word of him whose anger is kindled against the wicked and rebellious;

3. Who willeth to take even them whom he will take, and preserveth in life them whom he will preserve;

4. Who buildeth up at his own will and pleasure; and destroyeth when he pleases, and is able to cast the soul down to hell.

5. Behold, I, the Lord, utter my voice, and it shall be obeyed.

6. Wherefore, verily I say, let the wicked take heed, and let the rebellious fear and tremble; and let the unbelieving hold their lips, for the day of wrath shall come upon them as a whirlwind, and all flesh shall know that I am God.

7. And he that seeketh signs shall see signs, but not unto salvation.

8. Verily, I say unto you, there are those among you who seek signs, and there have been such even from the beginning;

9. But, behold, faith cometh not by signs, but signs follow those that believe.

10. Yea, signs come by faith, not by the will of men, nor as they please, but by the will of God.

11. Yea, signs come by faith, unto mighty works, for without faith no man pleaseth God: and with whom God is angry he is not well pleased; wherefore, unto such he showeth no signs, only in wrath unto their condemnation.

12. Wherefore, I, the Lord, am not pleased with those among you who have sought after signs and wonders for faith, and not for the good of men unto my glory;

13. Nevertheless, I give commandments, and many have turned away from my commandments and have not kept them.

14. There were among you adulterers and adulteresses; some of whom have turned away from you, and others remain with you, that hereafter shall be revealed.

15. Let such beware and repent speedily, lest judgment shall come upon them as a snare, and their folly shall be made manifest, and their works shall follow them in the eyes of the people.

16. And, verily, I say unto you, as I have said before, he that looketh on a woman to lust after her, or if any shall commit adultery in their hearts, they shall not have the Spirit, but shall deny the faith and shall fear:

17. Wherefore, I, the Lord, have said that the fearful, and the unbelieving, and all liars, and whosoever

Section 63 Background—Given in August 1831 at the Isaac Morley Farm in Kirtland, Ohio (see *HC* 1:206–211). Joseph Smith returned from his trip to Missouri on August 27, 1831, to find that apostasy was on the rise. At the same time, there was intense interest in the concept and land of Zion. Joseph describes how he "enquired" of the Lord concerning the situation at hand: "In these infant days of the Church, there was a great anxiety to obtain the word of the Lord upon every subject that in any way concerned our salvation; and as the land of Zion was now the most important temporal object in view, I enquired of the Lord for further information upon the gathering of the Saints, and the purchase of the land, and other matters, and received [Section 63]" (see *HC* 1:207).

D&C 63:1, 6—The universal commandment of the Lord is that we hear His word and listen with reverence and humility to learn His will concerning us. In this particular case, the Lord reminds the listeners that the wicked, rebellious, and unbelieving are ripe for the "wrath" of judgment. "The 'wrath of God' is usually a term indicating the Father's disapproval of the deeds of the wicked and justifying the inevitable punishments that will occur if they do not repent.

D&C 63:11—Signs—manifestations of the power of the Spirit—follow those who believe (D&C 58:64), rather than the other way around. Those who demand signs as proof of divine authenticity have inverted the designs of God, who blesses the humble and contrite with a strengthening of their faith unto the performance of wondrous acts. Said the Prophet Joseph Smith: "FAITH comes by hearing the word of God, through the testimony of the servants of God; that testimony is always attended by the Spirit of prophecy and revelation" (*HC* 3:379).

D&C 63:16—Our heart is the place of our affections and the center of our soul, the place where decisions are made. Thoughts precede actions. Lusting is caused by impure thoughts. We are commanded to seek the love of God that we might have pure hearts, pure thoughts, and righteous actions—thus putting ourselves in the right place doing the right thing, being even as the people of Nephi following Christ's appearance and teachings (see 4 Ne. 1:15–16). Joseph Smith made the connection between fault-finding sign-seekers and the lustful: "I will give you one of the *Keys* of the mysteries of the Kingdom. It is an eternal principle, that has existed with God from all eternity: That man who rises up to condemn others, finding fault with the Church, saying that they are out of the way, while he himself is righteous, then know assuredly, that that man is in the high road to apostasy; and if he does not repent, will apostatize, as God lives. The principle is as correct as the one that Jesus put forth in saying that he who seeketh a sign is an adulterous person; and that principle is eternal, undeviating, and firm as the pillars of heaven; for whenever you see a man seeking after a sign, you may set it down that he is an adulterous man" (*HC* 3:385).

loveth and maketh a lie, and the whoremonger, and the sorcerer, shall have their part in that lake which burneth with fire and brimstone which is the second death.

18. Verily I say, that they shall not have part in the first resurrection.

19. And now, behold, I, the Lord, say unto you, that ye are not justified because these things are among you;

20. Nevertheless, he that endureth in faith and doeth my will, the same shall overcome, and shall receive an inheritance upon the earth when the day of transfiguration shall come;

21. When the earth shall be transfigured, even according to the pattern which was shown unto mine apostles upon the mount; of which account the fulness ye have not received.

22. And now, verily I say unto you, that as I said that I would make known my will unto you, behold I will make it known unto you, not by the way of commandment, for there are many who observe not to keep my commandments;

23. But unto him that keepeth my commandments, I will give the mysteries of my kingdom, and the same shall be in him a well of living water, springing up unto everlasting life.

24. And now, behold, this is the will of the Lord your God concerning his saints, that they should assemble themselves together unto the land of Zion, not in haste, lest there should be confusion, which bringeth pestilence.

25. Behold, the land of Zion, I, the Lord, hold it in mine own hands;

26. Nevertheless, I, the Lord, render unto Caesar the things which are Caesar's:

27. Wherefore I the Lord, will that you should purchase the lands that you may have advantage of the world, that you may have claim on the world, that they may not be stirred up unto anger.

28. For Satan putteth it into their hearts to anger; against you, and to the shedding of blood;

29. Wherefore the land of Zion shall not be obtained but by purchase or by blood, otherwise there is none inheritance for you.

30. And if by purchase, behold you are blessed;

31. And if by blood, as you are forbidden to shed blood, lo, your enemies are upon you, and ye shall be scourged from city to city, and from synagogue to synagogue, and but few shall stand to receive an inheritance.

32. I, the Lord, am angry with the wicked; I am holding my Spirit from the inhabitants of the earth.

33. I have sworn in my wrath, and decreed wars upon the face of the earth, and the wicked shall slay the wicked, and fear shall come upon every man,

D&C 63:17–18—Among the condemned in this statement—the fearful, the unbelieving, liars, whoremongers, sorcerers—there is a common characteristic: to deny God with unremitting pridefulness. Even the "fearful" turn their backs on God in order to appease men and seek worldly honors. In that sense, all of these categories of wickedness reflect the central and defining quality of lying, or bearing false witness. Such are excluded from taking part in the first resurrection. Referring to this passage, Joseph Fielding McConkie and Robert L. Millet have written: "There will be no liars in the celestial kingdom. Unrepentant liars shall be ushered into hell (outer darkness) at the time of death and shall come forth in the resurrection to inherit the telestial kingdom" (*DCBM* 1:256).

D&C 63:20–23—The Spirit conveys the "living water" to quench the thirst for saving truth and pure knowledge. Elder Bruce R. McConkie defined *living water* as the words of eternal life and the message of salvation—in other words, the doctrines of the gospel (see Bruce R. McConkie, *DNTC* 1:151).

D&C 63:24—The gathering is to be a process of managed order. All things are to be done in wisdom and order, prepared and organized with respect to "every needful thing" (see D&C 88:119). Rushing, scurrying, confusion, disarray—these are not characteristics of a Zion people.

D&C 63:29–30—The Saints, as a group, did not follow the counsel of the Lord to "purchase" the land of Zion by applying the law of consecration in obedience to divine directives. President Lorenzo Snow provides this instructive analysis of the historical lesson:

> We learn from these verses [D&C 63:25–31] that the Lord determined that the Latter-day Saints could secure the land of Zion only by two ways: One by purchase, the other by the shedding of blood. The Lord also [be] determined that possession of that country should not he gained except by the purchase of the land. It should be bought and paid for by the means furnished by the Latter-day Saints, whether rich or poor. It should be bought as other people buy land. The Lord would not permit them to take possession of the land by force, or by antagonizing the people's interests. . . . And if you and I ever get any possession upon the land of Zion, it will be by purchase, not by force. This has been the will of the Lord from the beginning. (*CR*, Oct. 1899, Second Day, Morning Session, 23–24.)

D&C 63:33—The prophet/historian Mormon included this confirming statement in his record: "But, behold, the judgments of God will overtake the wicked; and it is by the wicked that the wicked are punished; for it is the wicked that stir up the hearts of the children of men unto bloodD&C shed" (Mormon 4:5).

34. And the saints also shall hardly escape; nevertheless, I, the Lord, am with them, and will come down in heaven from the presence of my Father and consume the wicked with unquenchable fire,

35. And behold, this is not yet, but by and by;

36. Wherefore, seeing that I, the Lord, have decreed all these things upon the face of the earth, I will that my saints should be assembled upon the land of Zion;

37. And that every man should take righteousness in his hands and faithfulness upon his loins, and lift a warning voice unto the inhabitants of the earth; and declare both by word and by flight that desolation shall come upon the wicked.

38. Wherefore let my disciples in Kirtland arrange their temporal concerns, who dwell upon this farm.

39. Let my servant Titus Billings, who has the care thereof, dispose of the land, that he may be prepared in the coming spring to take his journey up unto the land of Zion, with those that dwell upon the face thereof, excepting those whom I shall reserve unto myself, that shall not go until I shall command them.

40. And let all the monies which can be spared, it mattereth not unto me whether it be little or much, be sent up unto the land of Zion, unto them whom I have appointed to receive.

41. Behold, I, the Lord, will give unto my servant Joseph Smith, jun., power that he shall be enabled to discern by the Spirit those who shall go up unto the land of Zion, and those of my disciples who shall tarry.

42. Let my servant Newel K. Whitney retain his store, or in other words, the store, yet for a little season.

43. Nevertheless, let him impart all the money which he can impart, to be sent up unto the land of Zion.

44. Behold, these things are in his own hands, let him do according to wisdom.

45. Verily I say, let him be ordained as an agent unto the disciples that shall tarry, and let him be ordained unto this power;

46. And now speedily visit the churches, expounding these things unto them, with my servant Oliver Cowdery. Behold, this is my will, obtaining monies even as I have directed.

47. He that is faithful and endureth shall overcome the world.

48. He that sendeth up treasures unto the land of Zion, shall receive an inheritance in this world, and his works shall follow him, and also a reward in the world to come:

49. Yea, and blessed are the dead that die in the Lord from henceforth, when the Lord shall come, and old things shall pass away, and all things become new, they shall rise from the dead and shall not die after, and shall receive an inheritance before the Lord, in the holy city.

50. And he that liveth when the Lord shall come, and has kept the

D&C 63:34—All flesh is subject to death, and some righteous will suffer in the flesh because of that reality. The difference is that the righteous will be saved in the kingdom of God.

D&C 63:36, 48—The gathering is accomplished in unity of purpose and through coordinated economics. The Saints consecrate their means to the building up of the kingdom of God, thereby ensuring themselves of an inheritance in this world and treasures in the world to come. What the Lord required of early Saints such as Titus Billings and Newel K. Whitney (*profiles of Newel K. Whitney and Titus Billings are on p. 114*), He requires of us today, each in his or her own way and calling, according to the word of the Lord proclaimed by the voice of His living prophets. Declared President Heber J. Grant: "I say, what doth it profit to go to the ends of the earth and proclaim the Gospel of Jesus Christ, and yet fail to do your duty here in laboring for the advancement of God's kingdom? I say to the Latter-day Saints, be honest with God, pay your tithes and your offerings, support every institution of Zion, build up the Church of Christ, pray for the authorities of the Church, and then sustain them in every labor and in all that they undertake to do" (*CR*, April 1900, Morning Session, 24).

FAITH OF THE SAINTS IN ZION

The Saints in Ohio were anxious to be part of the establishment of Zion. In this revelation, the Lord gave a warning to those who had not sufficient faith and were unbelieving, calling them the wicked and rebellious (see D&C 63:2, 6).

One cannot live in Zion without faith in the Lord Jesus Christ. Without such faith, one cannot live the celestial laws on which Zion will be built.

What is faith? First, it is not a perfect knowledge. Second, one who has faith trusts in the Lord, even though the individual may not understand or see the purpose or end result of exercising faith. Third, one who has faith has a hope in things to come that are not yet seen but are true (see Alma 32:21).

The Lord warned that some of these Saints were seeking evidence or signs as proof that things pertaining to the Lord's work in Zion were really true. They wanted to know before they were willing to exercise faith (see D&C 63:1, 7–11).

There were others among these Saints who were not capable of having the Spirit in their lives because they lacked faith in the Lord's standards of morality. They were also warned that they must repent and exercise faith in Him and His teachings. Otherwise, they would live in a state of fear of the judgments that would come upon them, and such conditions were not compatible with the requirements for people to live in Zion (*STDC* 1:306–307).

faith, blessed is he; nevertheless it is appointed to him to die at the age of man.

51. Wherefore, children shall grow up until they become old, old men shall die; but they shall not sleep in the dust, but they shall be changed in the twinkling of an eye;

52. Wherefore, for this cause preached the apostles unto the world the resurrection of the dead;

53. These things are the things that ye must look for, and speaking after the manner of the Lord, they are now nigh at hand; and in time to come, even in the day of the coming of the Son of Man.

54. And until that hour there will be foolish virgins among the wise, and at that hour cometh an entire separation of the righteous and the wicked, and in that day will I send mine angels to pluck out the wicked and cast them into unquenchable fire.

55. And now, behold, verily I say unto you, I the Lord, am not pleased with my servant Sidney Rigdon, he exalted himself in his heart, and received not counsel but grieved the Spirit;

56. Wherefore his writing is not acceptable unto the Lord and he shall make another, and if the Lord receive it not, behold he standeth no longer in the office which I have appointed him.

57. And again, verily I say unto you, those who desire in their hearts, in meekness, to warn sinners to repentance, let them be ordained unto this power;

58. For this is a day of warning, and not a day of many words. For I, the Lord, am not to be mocked in the last days.

59. Behold, I am from above, and my power lieth beneath. I am over all, and in all, and through all, and search all things, and the day cometh that all things shall be subject unto me.

60. Behold, I am Alpha and Omega, even Jesus Christ.

61. Wherefore let all men beware how they take my name in their lips;

62. For, behold, verily I say, that many there be who are under this condemnation, who use the name of the Lord, and use it in vain, having not authority.

63. Wherefore, let the church repent of their sins, and I, the Lord, will own them, otherwise they shall be cut off.

64. Remember that that which cometh from above is sacred, and must be spoken with care, and by constraint of the Spirit, and in this there is no condemnation, and ye receive the Spirit through prayer; wherefore, without this there remaineth condemnation.

65. Let my servants Joseph Smith, jun., and Sidney Rigdon, seek them a home, as they are taught through prayer by the Spirit.

66. These things remain to overcome through patience, that such may receive a more exceeding and eternal weight of glory, otherwise, a greater condemnation. Amen.

D&C 63:51—The physical processes and conditions during the Millennium will be different from our current experience. Elder Bruce R. McConkie taught that there will be no graves during the Millennium; those who have reached the "age of a tree" (generally considered to be one hundred) will instead be "changed in the twinkling of an eye, and shall be caught up, and his rest shall be glorious" (D&C 101:30-31).

D&C 63:53—The "foolish virgins" refer to the New Testament parable of the ten virgins (see Matt. 25).

D&C 63:55–56—Sidney Rigdon had been commanded to write a description of the land of Zion (see D&C 58:50). While his first effort had failed, this second effort was accepted by the Lord.

D&C 63:57–58—In a previous revelation, the Lord declared: "Behold, the day has come, when the cup of the wrath of mine indignation is full" (D&C 43:26). The time was short back then; it is even shorter today. There is urgency to warn the world of the Savior's imminent return. If we are to come before "the pleasing bar of the great Jehovah" (Moroni 10:34)—that is, if we are to find our circumstances in that hour "pleasing" rather than devastatingly burdensome under the crushing weight of sin—then we are to prepare ourselves through faith and obedience, and warn our neighbors to do the same. Our attitude and deportment in warning sinners is to be one of meekness and dependence upon the Spirit. The Spirit will confirm the truth of our witness if we are humble and obedient: "He that speaketh, whose spirit is contrite, whose language is meek and edifieth, the same is of God if he obey mine ordinances" (D&C 52:16).

D&C 63:62—Using the name of the Lord in vain is an egregious sin. Elder James E. Talmage enumerates the points:

    1. We may take the name of God in vain by profane speech.

    2. We take it in vain when we swear falsely, not being true to our oaths and promises.

    3. We take it in vain in a blasphemous sense when we presume to speak in that name without authority.

    4. And we take His name in vain whenever we willfully do aught that is in defiance of His commandments, since we have taken His name upon ourselves. (See CR, Oct. 1931, Second Day, Morning Session, 53.)

SECTION 64

1. Behold, thus saith the Lord your God unto you, O ye elders of my church, hearken ye and hear, and receive my will concerning you;

2. For verily I say unto you, I will that ye should overcome the world; wherefore I will have compassion upon you.

3. There are those among you who have sinned; but verily I say, for this once, for mine own glory, and for the salvation of souls, I have forgiven you your sins.

4. I will be merciful unto you, for I have given unto you the kingdom:

5. And the keys of the mysteries of the kingdom shall not be taken from my servant Joseph Smith, jun., through the means I have appointed, while he liveth, inasmuch as he obeyeth mine ordinances.

6. There are those who have sought occasion against him without cause;

7. Nevertheless he has sinned, but verily I say unto you, I, the Lord, forgive sins unto those who confess their sins before me and ask forgiveness, who have not sinned unto death.

8. My disciples, in days of old, sought occasion against one another and forgave not one another in their hearts, and for this evil they were afflicted and sorely chastened:

9. Wherefore I say unto you, that ye ought to forgive one another, for he that forgiveth not his brother his trespasses, standeth condemned before the Lord, for there remaineth in him the greater sin.

10. I, the Lord, will forgive whom I will forgive, but of you it is required to forgive all men;

11. And ye ought to say in your hearts, let God judge between me

---

FREDERICK G. WILLIAMS

Frederick G. Williams was born October 28, 1787, at Suffield, Hartford County, Connecticut. A self-trained medical practitioner, he found his way to Kirtland, where he and his wife were converted by the missionaries. He was baptized in October 1830 and was then ordained an elder. In March 1832 he was called by revelation to be a counselor to Joseph Smith (see D&C 81:1–3, 6). The Prophet placed a great deal of trust in him. In May 1834 Frederick deeded his farm to the Prophet and then subsequently participated in Zion's Camp as paymaster. He continued his devoted service in Kirtland, but by 1837 he had stumbled in his position and lost his counselorship and his membership, though he was rebaptized the following year prior to joining the Saints in Missouri (see HC 3:55). In Missouri the process of stumbling and being received again into fellowship took place once more for Frederick, but he maintained his association with the Prophet and passed away in poor health in Quincy, Illinois, in October 1842, faithful to the cause of the kingdom.

Section 64 Background—Given to the elders of the Church on September 11, 1831, at the Isaac Morley Farm in Kirtland, Ohio (see HC 1:211–214). This section was given one day before the Prophet and his family, along with Sidney Rigdon, moved to Hiram, Ohio, to live with the Johnson family. The Prophet was planning to once again take up the process of translating the Bible, which had been interrupted while he was in Missouri. In his journal the Prophet wrote: "The early part of September was spent in making preparations to remove to the town of Hiram, and renew our work on the translation of the Bible. The brethren who were commanded to go up to Zion were earnestly engaged in getting ready to start in the coming October. On the 11th of September I received [Section 64]" (HC 1:211).

D&C 64:2—When we put aside the things of the world, the commandments become easy.

D&C 64:7—Those who have sinned unto death are the sons of perdition—those who, according to Elder Bruce R. McConkie, have turned from the light, given themselves up to Satan, enlisted in his cause, support and sustained that cause, and have therefore become Satan's children. For these there is no repentance or forgiveness.

D&C 64:10—This statement is among the most compelling of all revelatory pronouncements concerning forgiveness. It comes in the context of a discussion of several associated divine principles relating to forgiveness: (1) The Lord, in His glory, forgives out of mercy and compassion and for the salvation of the forgiven. (2) His leaders will remain empowered and forgiven, provided they obey His ordinances. (3) Forgiveness comes to those who confess their sins and ask for forgiveness—provided they have not "sinned unto death"—that is, turned willfully away from the divine light and enlisted fully and incorrigibly in the service of Satan (see Alma 5:41–42; Matt. 12:31–32; Heb. 10:26–27). (4) The Saints are to forgive one another and not seek cause against one another, lest there remain in them the greater sin. (5) They are to let God be the judge.

and thee, and reward thee according to thy deeds.

12. And he that repenteth not of his sins, and confesseth them not, then ye shall bring him before the church, and do with him as the Scripture saith unto you, either by commandment or by revelation.

13. And this ye shall do that God may be glorified, not because ye forgive not, having not compassion, but that ye may be justified in the eyes of the law, that ye may not offend him who is your Law-giver.

14. Verily I say, for this cause ye shall do these things.

15. Behold, I, the Lord, was angry with him who was my servant Ezra Booth, and also my servant Isaac Morley, for they kept not the law, neither the commandment;

16. They sought evil in their hearts, and I, the Lord, withheld my Spirit. They condemned for evil that thing in which there was no evil; nevertheless I have forgiven my servant Isaac Morley.

17. And also my servant Edward Partridge, behold, he hath sinned, and Satan seeketh to destroy his soul; but when these things are made known unto them, and they repent of the evil, they shall be forgiven.

18. And now, verily I say, that it is expedient in me that my servant Sidney Gilbert, after a few weeks, should return upon his business, and to his agency in the land of Zion;

19. And that which he hath seen and heard may be made known unto my disciples, that they perish not. And for this cause have I spoken these things.

20. And again, I say unto you, that my servant Isaac Morley may not be tempted above that which he is able to bear, and counsel wrongfully to your hurt, I gave commandment that his farm should be sold.

21. I will not that my servant Frederick G. Williams should sell his farm, for I, the Lord, will to retain a strong hold in the land of Kirtland, for the space of five years, in the which I will not overthrow the wicked, that thereby I may save some;

22. And after that day, I, the Lord, will not hold any guilty that shall go with an open heart up to the land of Zion; for I the Lord, require the hearts of the children of men.

23. Behold, now it is called to-day (until the coming of the Son of man), and verily it is a day of sacrifice, and a day for the tithing of my people; for he that is tithed shall not be burned (at his coming);

24. For after to-day cometh the burning: this is speaking after the manner of the Lord; for verily I say, to-morrow all the proud and they that do wickedly shall be as stubble; and I will burn them up, for I am the Lord of hosts: and I will not spare any that remain in Babylon.

25. Wherefore, if ye believe me, ye will labor while it is called today.

D&C 64:12—How to deal with those who refuse to repent is given through the word of God by revelation—either in the scriptural canon or through the Spirit, according to the laws of God.

D&C 64:21—Without this commandment, and obedience to it, the temple could not have been built.

D&C 64:22—In scripture, the heart represents three things: 1) the center of physical life and power; 2) the center of emotions and rational thought; and 3) the center of mortal life. When we understand the significance of the heart, it is obvious why the Lord requires it: the heart represents love, hate, thought, knowledge, feelings, affections, joy, pain, ill will, despair, fear, and reverence. It is the center of spiritual growth and the dwelling place of either the Lord or Satan. Basically, the heart is the center of the entire person.

D&C 64:23—The law of tithing was not formally instituted in the Church until July 1838 (see Section 119). At this early phase of the Restoration the word *tithing* in Section 64 seems to imply offerings in general—based on the principle of sacrifice and generous giving in support of the building up of the kingdom of God and the establishment of Zion.

Heavenly Father provides all things for mankind, including the earth and everything therein. With the subsequent institution of the law of tithing, He would ask us to give a tenth of our "interest" annually. We are stewards. Paying our tithes and offerings is a key part of our responsibility to build up the kingdom of God here upon the earth. The Lord's method for handling the temporal affairs of His Church is currently the law of tithing—as well as the paying of fast offerings. It is also the Lord's method for enriching His Saints with the spiritual blessings that attend the cultivation of a charitable and giving nature. By paying an honest tithe, we can help sanctify and purify ourselves and show our devotion to the Lord.

26. And it is not meet that my servants, Newel K. Whitney and Sidney Gilbert, should sell their store and their possessions here, for this is not wisdom, until the residue of the church, which remaineth in this place, shall go up unto the land of Zion.
27. Behold, it is said in my laws, or forbidden, to get in debt to thine enemies;
28. But behold, it is not said at any time that the Lord should not take when he please, and pay as seemeth him good:
29. Wherefore as ye are agents, and ye are on the Lord's errand; and whatever ye do according to the will of the Lord is the Lord's business,
30. And he hath set you to provide for his saints in these last days, that they may obtain an inheritance in the land of Zion:
31. And behold, I, the Lord, declare unto you, and my words are sure and shall not fail, that they shall obtain it;
32. But all things must come to pass in their time;
33. Wherefore, be not weary in well-doing, for ye are laying the foundation of a great work. And out of small things proceedeth that which is great.
34. Behold, the Lord requireth the heart and a willing mind; and the willing and obedient shall eat the good of the land of Zion in these last days;
35. And the rebellious shall be cut off out of the land of Zion, and shall be sent away, and shall not inherit the land:
36. For, verily I say that the rebellious are not of the blood of Ephraim, wherefore they shall be plucked out.
37. Behold, I, the Lord, have made my church in these last days like unto a judge sitting on a hill, or in a high place, to judge the nations;
38. For it shall come to pass that the inhabitants of Zion shall judge all things pertaining to Zion;
39. And liars and hypocrites shall be proved by them, and they who are not apostles and prophets shall be known.
40. And even the bishop, who is a judge, and his counselors, if they are not faithful in their stewardships, shall be condemned, and others shall be planted in their stead;
41. For, behold, I say unto you that Zion shall flourish, and the glory of the Lord shall be upon her,
42. And she shall be an ensign unto the people, and there shall come

D&C 64:27–29—The burden of debt is an oppressive form of bondage. The spirit of the gospel is the spirit of liberation and independence: "That through my providence, notwithstanding the tribulation which shall descend upon you, that the church may stand independent above all other creatures beneath the celestial world" (D&C 78:14).

D&C 64:33–34—This celebrated statement enjoins the Saints to use their God-given talents and resources to help build Zion. The Lord has made clear that His word is extended to the Saints through the mouths of His chosen servants: "What I the Lord have spoken, I have spoken, and I excuse not myself; and though the heavens and the earth pass away, my word shall not pass away, but shall all be fulfilled, whether by mine own voice or by the voice of my servants, it is the same" (D&C 1:38).

Beneath the glory of the canopy of heaven, the light of one individual may not seem to emit illumination of any consequence; however, the Lord promises that out of small contributions—proceeding from the heart and a willing mind—great outcomes can emerge.

D&C 64:36—The Lord is the Exemplar of obedience, for He "suffered the will of the Father in all things from the beginning" (3 Ne. 11:11). In Ephraim is anchored the birthright of Israel (see Gen. 48:5–22; 1 Chr. 5:1; Jer. 31:9). Those of the "royal priesthood" (1 Peter 2:9) who rebel abdicate their place in the covenant domain. Obedience and enduring to the end ensure fellowship in the kingdom and access to the promised blessings of heaven.

D&C 64:37—In the "true and living church" (D&C 1:30) are enshrined the standards of righteousness commanded of God. The Church is an ensign to the nations, the means of conveying the word of God to the four quarters of the world. The word of God is the standard for divine judgment. How great is the responsibility placed upon members of the Church to uphold and proclaim this standard with complete devotion.

D&C 64:41—To the assembled elders of the infant Church in August 1831 the Lord gave a magnificent promise: that Zion would in due course flourish and reflect the glory of the Lord, that people would flock to her from every nation, and that she should instill fear in those who would behold her magnificence and power. To this small handful of eager and courageous Saints, the vision of such a panoramic unfolding of Zion must have seemed a distant possibility. Even today the Church constitutes but a small segment of the world's billions. Yet the signs of the emergence of God's grand kingdom are becoming more and more visible as the stone cut from the mountain without hands rolls forth on its inexorable course to fill the entire world with the power of truth and light (see Dan. 2:34–35, 45; D&C 65:2). That is the ultimate destiny of Zion and her people.

unto her out of every nation under heaven.

43. And the day shall come when the nations of the earth shall tremble because of her, and shall fear because of her terrible ones. The Lord hath spoken it. Amen.

SECTION 65

1. Hearken, and lo, a voice as of one from on high, who is mighty and powerful, whose going forth is unto the ends of the earth, yea, whose voice is unto men—Prepare ye the way of the Lord, make his paths straight.

2. The keys of the kingdom of God are committed unto man on the earth, and from thence shall the gospel roll forth unto the ends of the earth, as the stone which is cut out of the mountain without hands shall roll forth, until it has filled the whole earth;

3. Yea, a voice crying—Prepare ye the way of the Lord, prepare ye the supper of the Lamb, make ready for the Bridegroom;

4. Pray unto the Lord, call upon his holy name, make known his wonderful works among the people;

5. Call upon the Lord, that his kingdom may go forth upon the earth, that the inhabitants thereof may receive it, and be prepared for the days to come, in the which the Son of man shall come down in heaven, clothed in the brightness of his glory, to meet the kingdom of God which is set up on the earth;

6. Wherefore may the kingdom of God go forth, that the kingdom of heaven may come, that thou, O God, mayest be glorified in heaven so on earth, that thy enemies may be subdued; for thine is the honor, power and glory, for ever and ever. Amen.

Section 65 Background—Given in October 1831 at Hiram, Ohio (see *HC* 1:218). According to the *Evening and Morning Star* and the "Kirtland Revelation Book" (p. 87), this revelation was given on October 30, though the Prophet states in his journal, "In the fore part of October, I received the following prayer through revelation" (*HC* 1:218). This section is an inspiring and edifying prayer on behalf of missionary work, a theme that is pervasive in the Doctrine and Covenants (salient passages also occur in sections 1, 3, 88, 109, 115, and 123). Verse two is a vivid echoing of the words of Daniel (compare Daniel 2:34–35, 45; see also D&C 109:72–73).

D&C 65:1–2—The Lord has spoken. The gospel will roll forth by divine mandate. Nothing can stop its forward motion toward the fulfillment of its destiny. We as a people and as a Church are to bring this about. We are preaching the gospel on every continent. The Book of Mormon has been translated into a multitude of languages, with in excess of 50,000 full-time missionaries active in the vineyard at any given time. We can do our part as member missionaries and full-time missionaries—this can be our glory and joy (Alma 29:9–10).

What is the kingdom of God that we are helping to establish? The Prophet Joseph Smith explained it thus: "I say, in the name of the Lord, that the kingdom of God was set up upon the earth in the days of Adam to the present time, whenever there has been a righteous man on earth unto whom God revealed His word and gave power and authority to administer in His name. And where there is a priest of God . . . to administer in the ordinances of the gospel, and officiate in the priesthood of God—there is the kingdom of God. . . . Where there is a prophet, a priest, or a righteous man unto whom God gives His oracles, there is the kingdom of God; and where the oracles of God are not, there the kingdom of God is not" (*TPJS*, 271–272).

D&C 65:6—In the consummation of the divine plan for this earth and its inhabitants there will be a grand confluence of the two spheres of divine glory: the kingdom of God upon the earth and the kingdom of heaven descending from on high. It will be a celestial family reunion in scope and majesty without precedent. James E. Talmage explained: "The kingdom of God is the Church of Christ; the kingdom of heaven is that system of government and administration which is operative in heaven, and which we pray may some day prevail on earth. The kingdom of heaven will be established when the King shall come, as come He shall, in power and might and glory, to take dominion in and over and throughout the earth. . . . The kingdom of heaven shall come, and then shall justice rule in the earth" (*CR*, April 1917, 65–66).

SECTION 66

1. Behold, thus saith the Lord unto my servant William E. McLellin, Blessed are you, inasmuch as you have turned away from your iniquities, and have received my truths, saith the Lord your Redeemer, the Savior of the world, even of as many as believe on my name.

2. Verily I say unto you, blessed are you for receiving mine everlasting covenant, even the fulness of my gospel, sent forth unto the children of men, that they might have life and be made partakers of the glories which are to be revealed in the last days, as it was written by the prophets and apostles in days of old.

3. Verily I say unto you, my servant William, that you are clean, but not all; repent, therefore of those things which are not pleasing in my sight, saith the Lord, for the Lord will show them unto you.

4. And now, verily, I, the Lord, will show unto you what I will concerning you, or what is my will concerning you;

5. Behold, verily I say unto you, that it is my will that you should proclaim my gospel from land to land, and from city to city; yea, in those regions round about where it has not been proclaimed.

6. Tarry not many days in this place; go not up unto the land of Zion as yet; but inasmuch as you can send, send; otherwise, think not of thy property.

7. Go unto the eastern lands, bear testimony in every place, unto every people, and in their synagogues, reasoning with the people.

8. Let my servant Samuel H. Smith go with you, and forsake him not, and give him thine instructions; and he that is faithful shall be made strong in every place, and I, the Lord, will go with you.

9. Lay your hands upon the sick, and they shall recover. Return not till I the Lord shall send you. Be patient in affliction. Ask and ye shall receive. Knock and it shall be opened unto you.

10. Seek not to be cumbered. Forsake all unrighteousness. Commit not adultery, a temptation with which thou hast been troubled.

11. Keep these sayings, for they are true and faithful, and thou shalt magnify thine office, and push many people to Zion with songs of everlasting joy upon their heads.

12. Continue in these things even unto the end, and you shall have a

Section 66 Background—Given at Orange, Ohio, October 25, 1831 (see *HC* 1:219–221). This was the first day of an important two-day conference involving some three dozen priesthood holders and a large congregation. The Prophet gives this introduction: "At the request of William E. McLellin, I inquired of the Lord, and received [Section 66]." An interesting aspect of this conference was the report, included in the minutes as published in the *Far West Record*, concerning the Prophet's account of the coming forth of the Book of Mormon:

> Brother Hyrum Smith said that he thought best that the information of the coming forth of the Book of Mormon be related by Joseph himself to the Elders present, that all might know for themselves. .   .   .
>
> Brother Joseph Smith, Jun., said that it was not intended to tell the world all the particulars of the coming forth of the Book of Mormon; and also said that it was not expedient for him to relate these things (p. 13). Editor B. H. Roberts concludes: "This will account for the Prophet confining himself to the merest generalities in all his statements concerning the coming forth of the Book of Mormon." (*HC* 1:220, footnote 18.)

D&C 66:9–12—For William McLellin (see profile on p. 124), as for all of us, counsel from the Lord is formulated in terms of covenant requirements and promises. If we do the will of the Lord—through our patience, obedience, purity, and actions in magnifying our callings—then the Lord blesses us with a harvest of righteous outcomes and the ultimate bestowal of eternal life in the presence of Deity. In all of this, the individual is to aspire to spiritual freedom—not being encumbered with sin and worldliness. In a previous revelation, the Lord defined explicitly what would lead to the state of "not to be cumbered":

> He that is ordained of God and sent forth, the same is appointed to be the greatest, notwithstanding he is the least and the servant of all.
>
> Wherefore, he is possessor of all things; for all things are subject unto him, both in heaven and on the earth, the life and the light, the Spirit and the power, sent forth by the will of the Father through Jesus Christ, his Son.
>
> But no man is possessor of all things except he be purified and cleansed from all sin.
>
> And if ye are purified and cleansed from all sin, ye shall ask whatsoever you will in the name of Jesus and it shall be done. (D&C 50:26–29.)

crown of eternal life at the right hand of my Father, who is full of grace and truth.

13. Verily, thus saith the Lord your God, your Redeemer, even Jesus Christ. Amen.

SECTION 67

1. Behold and hearken, O ye elders of my church, who have assembled yourselves together, whose prayers I have heard, and whose hearts I know, and whose desires have come up before me.

2. Behold and lo, mine eyes are upon you, and the heavens and the earth are in mine hands, and the riches of eternity are mine to give.

3. Ye endeavored to believe that ye should receive the blessing which was offered unto you; but behold, verily, I say unto you, there were fears in your hearts, and verily this is the reason that ye did not receive.

4. And now I, the Lord, give unto you a testimony of the truth of these commandments which are lying before you;

5. Your eyes have been upon my servant Joseph Smith, jun., and his language you have known, and his imperfections you have known; and you have sought in your hearts knowledge that you might express beyond his language, this you also know.

6. Now seek ye out of the book of Command-ments, even the least that is among them, and appoint him that is the most wise among you;

7. Or, if there be any among you, that shall make one like unto it, then ye are justified in saying that ye do not know that they are true;

8. But if ye cannot make one like unto it, ye are under condemnation

---

WILLIAM E. MCLELLIN

William E. McLellin was born January 18, 1806, in Smith County, Tennessee. He learned of the restored Church in the summer of 1831 and was baptized August 20, 1831, by Hyrum Smith. He traveled to Ohio, where he stayed several weeks with the Prophet Joseph and received counsel from the Lord by revelation (see Section 66). At first receptive to the revelation, William soon thereafter criticized the language and fell under the challenge of the Lord to anyone who felt so inclined to try to come up with revelations equal to what had been given (see D&C 68:6–7). William soon learned that such was impossible. He went on to hold positions of responsibility in the Church and became a member of the Quorum of the Twelve on February 15, 1835. The following year he apostatized, claiming that he had lost confidence in the leadership of the Church. His actions led to his excommunication in 1838. Subsequently he joined the mobbers in persecuting the Saints and driving them from Missouri. After dabbling with various other religious organizations, he eventually abandoned his religious interests and passed away in obscurity on April 24, 1883. Of significance is the fact that he remained true to his witness of the Book of Mormon.

Section 67 Background—Given at Hiram, Ohio, November 1831 (see *HC* 1:224–225). The occasion for this revelation was a special conference where the publication of the already received revelations was considered and acted upon. Plans were made to publish the Book of Commandments, as the collection was to be titled, in Independence, Missouri. Just prior to this revelation the Lord had given His preface to the opus of doctrines, commandments, and covenants pertaining to the Restoration (see Section 1 Background). Following the reception of the preface, the Prophet Joseph indicated that "some conversation was had concerning revelations and language" (*HC* 1:225), meaning that some were raising questions about the nature of the language being used in the revelations. Section 67 was then received, which gives the Lord's perspective on the sanctity of His word as given through His ordained and chosen prophet.

D&C 67:2–3—The Lord hears our prayers and knows our thoughts and the desires of our hearts. What is it on our part that suppresses the flow of eternal blessings into our lives? Fear is the inhibiting element in this case, followed by the influence of pride, impatience, carnality, and jealousy (as indicated in the verses that follow). The Lord loves us and wants to fill our lives with His blessings, but He requires "the heart and a willing mind" (D&C 64:34)—with faith unto ultimate perfection.

D&C 67:4–9—In response to the murmuring and discontent among some of the priesthood associates of the Prophet, the Lord put forth a challenge that they should attempt, on their own initiative, to produce a revelation of equal stature and power. Such was destined to fail. Man can indeed produce language of merit and elegance, but it takes the Spirit of God to endow expression with eternal power and make it conform to divine principles. The reason is that such truth emanates from "the Father of lights"—an expression that occurs in only one other passage of scripture: "Every good gift and every perfect gift is from above, and cometh down from the Father of lights, with whom is no variableness, neither shadow of turning" (James 1:17). One of the doubters on this occasion was William E. McLellin, concerning whom the Prophet said:

> After the foregoing was received, William E. M'Lellin, as the wisest man, in his own estimation, having more learning than sense, endeavored to write a commandment like unto one of the least of the Lord's, but failed; it was an awful responsibility to write in the name of the Lord. The Elders and all present that witnessed this vain attempt of a man to imitate the language of Jesus Christ, renewed their faith in the fulness of the Gospel, and in the truth of the commandments and revelations which the Lord had given to the Church through my instrumentality; and the Elders signified a willingness to bear testimony of their truth to all the world. (*HC* 1:226.)

if ye do not bear record that they are true;

9. For ye know that there is no unrighteousness in them, and that which is righteous cometh down from above, from the Father of lights.

10. And again, verily I say unto you, that it is your privilege, and a promise I give unto you that have been ordained unto this ministry, that inasmuch as you strip yourselves from jealousies and fears, and humble yourselves before me, for ye are not sufficiently humble, the vail shall be rent and you shall see me and know that I AM; not with the carnal, neither natural mind, but with the spiritual;

11. For no man has seen God at any time in the flesh, except quickened by the Spirit of God;

12. Neither can any natural man abide in the presence of God; neither after the carnal mind;

13. Ye are not able to abide the presence of God now, neither the ministering of angels; wherefore continue in patience until ye are perfected.

14. Let not your minds turn back, and when ye are worthy, in mine own due time, ye shall see and know that which was conferred upon you by the hands of my servant Joseph Smith, jun. Amen.

SECTION 68

1. My servant, Orson Hyde, was called by his ordination to proclaim the everlasting gospel, by the Spirit of the living God, from people to people, and from land to land, in the congregations of the wicked, in their synagogues, reasoning with and expounding all Scriptures unto them.

ORSON HYDE

Orson Hyde was born January 8, 1805, at Oxford, New Haven County, Connecticut. An orphan in his early years, he moved to Ohio as a teenager and eventually got a job at the Gilbert and Whitney Store in Kirtland. He became convinced of the truthfulness of the Book of Mormon and was baptized by Sidney Rigdon on October 30, 1831. He was called by revelation to preach the restored gospel and subsequently went on a mission with Samuel Smith. He knew the Bible by heart in three languages: English, German, and Hebrew. As a clerk for the First Presidency he recorded many of the early revelations and historical minutes of the Church. After participating in Zion's Camp, he returned to Kirtland and received a call to the Council of the Twelve in 1835. Thereafter he served a mission in Great Britain with Heber C. Kimball. In 1838 he and others brought cause against the Prophet Joseph. Orson consequently lost his fellowship in the Church. After repenting, Orson was reinstated and received a promise from the Prophet Joseph Smith that he would be called upon to dedicate the Holy Land—a commission he fulfilled on October 24, 1841. Following the martyrdom, he migrated with the Saints to the Salt Lake Valley in 1852 and served with distinction in public office and as a member of the Quorum of the Twelve. He passed away on November 28, 1878.

D&C 67:10–13—In a revelation given through the Prophet Joseph Smith on December 16, 1833, the Lord declared the ultimate challenge for His disciples: "And seek the face of the Lord always, that in patience ye may possess your souls, and ye shall have eternal life" (D&C 101:38). To seek the face of the Lord is to set one's course for a celestial destination—a goal that will admit the faithful and the righteous into the presence of Deity.

Section 68 Background—Given in November 1831 in connection with a conference at Hiram, Portage County, Ohio, at the request of Orson Hyde, Luke S. Johnson, Lyman E. Johnson, and William E. McLellin (see *HC* 1:227–229). The four received the revelation with varying levels of acceptance; two eventually left the Church.

LYMAN E. JOHNSON

Lyman E. Johnson, younger brother of Luke S. Johnson, was born October 24, 1811, at Pomfret, Windsor County, Vermont. Following his baptism into the Church, Lyman was called by revelation in November 1831 to preach the gospel. He received a second mission call the following year to serve with Orson Pratt. After his participation in Zion's Camp, Lyman was chosen on February 14, 1835, to serve as a member of the Quorum of the Twelve—the first Apostle so chosen in the dispensation of the fullness of times. He was disfellowshipped in 1837 over specious charges against the Prophet Joseph Smith, was reinstated, but was excommunicated for apostate actions, though he remained friendly toward the Saints and lamented his own downfall. He passed away in a sleighing accident in 1856.

LUKE S. JOHNSON

Luke S. Johnson was born November 3, 1807, at Pomfret, Windsor County, Vermont. The conversion of his parents laid the groundwork for his own baptism into the restored Church on May 10, 1831, by the Prophet Joseph. He was called into missionary service by revelation and later participated in Zion's Camp as a scout. When he returned to Kirtland he was called to serve on the first high council of the Church and later became a member of the Quorum of the Twelve. Over the next period of time his faith and resolve weakened to the extent that he was excommunicated in Far West in 1838. He was rebaptized in March 1846. The following year he journeyed to the Salt Lake Valley with the original company of pioneers. In Utah he served in various Church leadership capacities and made his mark as a person of charity. Luke died on December 9, 1861.

2. And behold, and lo, this is an ensample unto all those who were ordained unto this Priesthood, whose mission is appointed unto them to go forth;

3. And this is the ensample unto them, that they shall speak as they are moved upon by the Holy Ghost,

4. And whatsoever they shall speak when moved upon by the Holy Ghost, shall be scripture, shall be the will of the Lord, shall be the mind of the Lord, shall be the word of the Lord, shall be the voice of the Lord, and the power of God unto salvation:

5. Behold this is the promise of the Lord unto you, O ye my servants;

6. Wherefore be of good cheer, and do not fear, for I the Lord am with you, and will stand by you; and ye shall bear record of me, even Jesus Christ, that I am the Son of the living God, that I was, that I am, and that I am to come.

7. This is the word of the Lord unto you my servant, Orson Hyde, and also unto my servant Luke Johnson, and unto my servant Lyman Johnson, and unto my servant William E. McLellin, and unto all the faithful elders of my church.

8. Go ye into all the world, preach the gospel to every creature, acting in the authority which I have given you, baptizing in the name of the Father, and of the Son, and of the Holy Ghost;

9. And he that believeth and is baptized shall be saved, and he that believeth not shall be damned;

10. And he that believeth shall be blest with signs following, even as it is written;

11. And unto you it shall be given to know the signs of the times, and the signs of the coming of the Son of man;

12. And of as many as the Father shall bear record, to you shall be given power to seal them up unto eternal life. Amen.

13. And now concerning the items in addition to the covenants and commandments, they are these:—

14. There remaineth hereafter, in the due time of the Lord, other bishops to be set apart unto the church, to minister even according to the first;

15. Wherefore they shall be High Priests who are worthy, and they shall be appointed by the First Presidency of the Melchisedek priesthood, except they be literal descendants of Aaron,

16. And if they be literal descendants of Aaron, they have a legal right to the bishopric, if they are the firstborn among the sons of Aaron;

17. For the firstborn holds the right of the presidency over this priesthood, and the keys of authority of the same.

18. No man has a legal right to this office to hold the keys of this priesthood, except he be a literal

D&C 68:3–4—To speak when one is "moved upon by the Holy Ghost" is to speak the words of Christ—and the words of Christ constitute scripture. Nephi taught that those who become baptized and receive the Holy Ghost can "speak with a new tongue, yea, even with the tongue of angels" (2 Ne. 31:14). The implication is that all those who are called to proclaim the gospel—and do so under inspiration from the Spirit—give forth a message that is equivalent to scripture. They have treasured up in their hearts the words of Christ and are prompted by the Spirit "in the very hour, yea, in the very moment" what they are to say (D&C 100:6).

D&C 68:6—The Lord has frequently given the commandment to "be of good cheer" (among them Matt. 14:27; Mark 6:50; John 16:33; Acts 23:11; 27:22, 25; Alma 17:31; 3 Ne. 1:13; and D&C 61:36; 68:6; 78:18; 112:4). Thus the Lord makes clear that He wants His children to experience joy and to cultivate a walk in life based on hope and a positive, edifying attitude that is anchored in righteousness and obedience.

D&C 68:8–10—From verse 7 it is clear that the Lord is speaking here of "all" the elders who proceed by faith to go into the world to perform their labors for the Lord. A great harvest awaits them. What is the nature of the "signs" that follow as a blessing to those baptized into the Church? The Prophet Joseph Smith commented on this issue in an editorial on "The Gift of the Holy Ghost" dated June 15, 1842:

> . . . it not infrequently occurs, that when Elders of this Church preach to the inhabitants of the world, that if they obey the Gospel they shall receive the gift of the Holy Ghost, that the people expect to see some wonderful manifestation, some great display of power, or some extraordinary miracle performed; and it is often the case that young members of this Church for want of better information, carry along with them their old notions of things, and sometimes fall into egregious errors." (HC 5:26–27.)

He then proceeded to enumerate the rational and consistent manifestations of the signs of the Spirit in terms of power to organize and regulate the Church through the operation of the priesthood, the granting of revelations and inspired discourse, the comforting influence and witness of the Holy Ghost, healing of the sick, and so forth.

descendant and the first born of Aaron.

19. But as a High Priest of the Melchisedek Priesthood has authority to officiate in all the lesser offices, he may officiate in the office of bishop when no literal descendant of Aaron can be found, provided he is called, and set apart and ordained unto this power under the hands of the First Presidency of the Melchisedek Priesthood.

20. And a literal descendant of Aaron, also, must be designated by this Presidency, and found worthy, and anointed, and ordained under the hands of this Presidency, otherwise they are not legally authorized to officiate in their priesthood;

21. But by virtue of the decree concerning their right of the priesthood descending from father to son, they may claim their anointing, if at any time they can prove their lineage, or do ascertain it by revelation from the Lord under the hands of the above named Presidency.

22. And again, no bishop or High Priest who shall be set apart for this ministry, shall be tried or condemned for any crime, save it be before the First Presidency of the church;

23. And inasmuch as he is found guilty before this Presidency, by testimony that cannot be impeached, he shall be condemned;

24. And if he repents he shall be forgiven, according to the covenants and commandments of the church.

25. And again, inasmuch as parents have children in Zion, or in any of her Stakes which are organized, that teach them not to understand the doctrine of repentance, faith in Christ the son of the living God, and of baptism and the gift of the Holy Ghost by the laying on of the hands when eight years old, the sin be upon the heads of the parents;

26. For this shall be a law unto the inhabitants of Zion, or in any of her Stakes which are organized;

27. And their children shall be baptized for the remission of their sins when eight years old, and receive the laying on of the hands;

28. And they shall also teach their children to pray and to walk uprightly before the Lord.

29. And the inhabitants of Zion shall, also, observe the Sabbath day to keep it holy.

30. And the inhabitants of Zion, also, shall remember their labors, inasmuch as they are appointed to labor, in all faithfulness; for the idler shall be had in remembrance before the Lord.

31. Now, I the Lord, am not well pleased with the inhabitants of Zion, for there are idlers among them; and their children are also growing up in wickedness; they also seek not earnestly the riches of eternity, but their eyes are full of greediness.

D&C 68:19—Concerning the regulations of the Church in calling bishops, President John Taylor gave this statement, reflecting the information in D&C 68:18–21:

> If we had among us a literal descendant of Aaron, who was the firstborn, he would have a right to the keys, or presiding authority of the Bishopric. But then he would have to be set apart and directed by the First Presidency, no matter what his or their claims might be, or how clear their proofs. The same would have to be acknowledged by the First Presidency. These claims of descent from Aaron would have to be acknowledged by the First Presidency, and, further, the claimant would have to be set apart to his Bishopric by them, the same as in the case of a High Priest of the Melchisedek Priesthood called to fill the same office. Thus, in either case, as a literal descendant of Aaron, or as a High Priest, the right to officiate is held first by authority of the Priesthood, and by appointment and ordination as above stated." (*JD* 21:361.)

D&C 68:25—The primary responsibility to teach children the gospel of Jesus Christ lies with the parents. To love and teach children the principles of salvation is the most sacred duty of parenthood. President Brigham Young gave this stirring advice concerning the accountability of parents to teach the gospel to their children:

> Bring up your children in the love and fear of the Lord; study their dispositions and their temperaments, and deal with them accordingly, never allowing yourself to correct them in the heat of passion; teach them to love you rather than to fear you, and let it be your constant care that the children that God has so kindly given you are taught in their early youth the importance of the oracles of God, and the beauty of the principles of our holy religion, that when they grow to the years of man and womanhood they may always cherish a tender regard for them and never forsake the truth. . . . Parents, teach your children by precept and example, the importance of addressing the Throne of grace; teach them how to live, how to draw from the elements the necessaries of life, and teach them the laws of life that they may know how to preserve themselves in health and be able to minister to others. And when instructing them in the principles of the Gospel, teach them that they are true, truth sent down from heaven for our salvation, and that the Gospel incorporates every truth whether in heaven, in earth, or in hell; and teach them, too, that we hold the keys of eternal life, and that they must obey and observe the ordinances and laws pertaining to this holy Priesthood, which God has revealed and restored for the exaltation of the children of men. . . . If the law of Christ becomes the tradition of this people, the children will be brought up according to the law of the celestial kingdom, else they are not brought up in the way they should go. (*DBY*, 207.)

32. These things ought not to be, and must be done away from among them: wherefore let my servant Oliver Cowdery carry these sayings unto the land of Zion.

33. And a commandment I give unto them, that he that observeth not his prayers before the Lord in the season thereof, let him be had in remembrance before the judge of my people.

34. These sayings are true and faithful; wherefore transgress them not neither take therefrom.

35. Behold, I am Alpha and Omega, and I come quickly. Amen.

SECTION 69

1. Hearken unto me, saith the Lord your God, for my servant Oliver Cowdery's sake. It is not wisdom in me that he should be entrusted with the commandments and the monies which he shall carry unto the land of Zion, except one go with him who will be true and faithful;

2. Wherefore, I the Lord will that my servant, John Whitmer, should go with my servant Oliver Cowdery;

3. And also that he shall continue in writing and making a history of all the important things which he shall observe and know concerning my church:

4. And also that he receive counsel and assistance from my servant Oliver Cowdery and others.

5. And also my servants who are abroad in the earth, should send forth the accounts of their stewardships to the land of Zion;

6. For the land of Zion shall be a seat and a place to receive and do all these things;

7. Nevertheless, let my servant, John Whitmer, travel many times from place to place, and from church to church, that he may the more easily obtain knowledge;

8. Preaching and expounding, writing, copying, selecting, and obtaining all things which shall be for the good of the church, and for the rising generations, that shall grow up on the land of Zion, to possess it from generation to generation, for ever and ever. Amen.

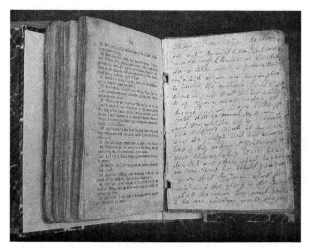

An 1833 edition of the Book of Commandments.

Section 69 Background—Given at Hiram, Ohio, November 1831 (see *HC* 1:234–235). The publication of a compilation of the revelations received to that point in time was approved. On November 3, the Lord provided an epilogue or appendix (now known as Section 133) for the collection. The Prophet Joseph provided this introductory statement concerning Section 69: "The Book of Commandments and Revelations was to be dedicated by prayer to the service of Almighty God by me; and after I had done this, I inquired of the Lord concerning these things, and received [Section 69]" (*HC* 1:234).

D&C 69:2—Oliver was conveying the priceless manuscript of the Lord's revelations, plus financial resources to accomplish the task of publication—hence the wisdom in providing a companion for him, especially since the route of about a thousand miles passed through sparsely populated terrain with a myriad of dangers.

D&C 69:3, 8—John Whitmer had been commissioned on March 8, 1831, to succeed Oliver Cowdery as Church historian (see Section 47). The importance of the work of preserving the particulars of the unfolding of the restored kingdom of God is accentuated by the Lord in Section 69, for it is to be "for the good of the church, and for the rising generations." Elder Orson Pratt declared:

> If every elder had . . . kept a faithful record of all that he had seen, heard, and felt of the goodness, wisdom, and power of God, the Church would now have been in possession of many thousand volumes, containing much important and useful information. How many have been miraculously healed in this Church, and yet no one has recorded the circumstances. Is this right? Should these miraculous manifestations of the power of God be forgotten and pass into oblivion? Should the knowledge of these things slumber in the hearts of those who witnessed them? . . . We should keep a record because Jesus has commanded it. We should keep a record because the same will benefit us and the generations of our children after us. We should keep a record because it will furnish many important items for the general history of the Church which would otherwise be lost. (*Millennial Star*, May 15, 1849, 11:152.)

The Prophet Joseph Smith confirms one of the key reasons for keeping careful records: "If you assemble from time to time, and proceed to discuss important questions, and pass decisions upon the same, and fail to note them down, by and by you will be driven to straits from which you will not be able to extricate yourselves, because you may be in a situation not to bring your faith to bear with sufficient perfection or power to obtain the desired information; or, perhaps, for neglecting to write these things when God had revealed them, not esteeming them of sufficient worth, the Spirit may withdraw and God may be angry; and there is, or was, a vast knowledge, of infinite importance, which is now lost" (*HC* 2:199).

SECTION 70

1. Behold, and hearken, O ye inhabitants of Zion, and all ye people of my church, who are far off, and hear the word of the Lord which I give unto my servant Joseph Smith, jun., and also unto my servant Martin Harris, and also unto my servant Oliver Cowdery, and also unto my servant John Whitmer, and also unto my servant Sidney Rigdon, and also unto my servant William W. Phelps, by the way of commandment unto them;

2. For I give unto them a commandment; wherefore hearken and hear, for thus saith the Lord unto them—

3. I, the Lord, have appointed them, and ordained them to be stewards over the revelations and commandments which I have given unto them, and which I shall hereafter give unto them;

4. And an account of this stewardship will I require of them in the day of judgment:

5. Wherefore I have appointed unto them, and this is their business in the church of God, to manage them and the concerns thereof; yea, the benefits thereof.

6. Wherefore a commandment I give unto them, that they shall not give these things unto the church, neither unto the world:

7. Nevertheless, inasmuch as they receive more than is needful for their necessities and their wants, it shall be given into my storehouse,

8. And the benefits shall be consecrated unto the inhabitants of Zion, and unto their generations, inasmuch as they become heirs according to the laws of the kingdom.

9. Behold, this is what the Lord requires of every man in his stewardship, even as I, the Lord, have appointed, or shall hereafter appoint unto any man.

10. And, behold none are exempt from this law who belong to the church of the living God;

11. Yea, neither the bishop, neither the agent who keepeth the Lord's storehouse, neither he who is appointed in a stewardship over temporal things;

12. He who is appointed to administer spiritual things, the same is worthy of his hire, even as those

Section 70 Background—Given at Kirtland, Ohio, November 12, 1831. The Prophet gave this introduction in his history: "My time was occupied closely in reviewing the commandments and sitting in conference, for nearly two weeks; for from the first to the twelfth of November we held four special conferences. In the last which was held at Brother Johnson's, in Hiram, after deliberate consideration, in consequence of the book of revelations, now to be printed, being the foundation of the Church in these last days, and a benefit to the world, showing that the keys of the mysteries of the kingdom of our Savior are again entrusted to man; and the riches of eternity within the compass of those who are willing to live by every word that proceedeth out of the mouth of God—therefore the conference voted that they prize the revelations to be worth to the Church the riches of the whole earth, speaking temporally. The great benefits to the world which result from the Book of Mormon and the revelations which the Lord has seen fit in His infinite wisdom to grant unto us for our salvation, and for the salvation of all that will believe, were duly appreciated; and in answer to an inquiry, I received [Section 70]" (*HC* 1:235). The Saints were instructed that proceeds from the sale of the Book of Commandments were to be used first for their temporal needs, then for the needs of the Church, and that they were strictly accountable for how the money was used.

D&C 70:3—Stewardship includes management, responsibility, and accountability to the owner or master.

D&C 70:3, 5—The brethren named in verse 1 were assigned a stewardship as their "business" in the Church, meaning their divine commission under the law of consecration. They were to manage the publication and sale of the Book of Commandments and account for the proceeds. This assignment was a matter of great significance, since the revelations that had been given, and that would subsequently be given, constituted "the foundation of the Church in these last days."

D&C 70:7–8—The surplus funds went to the storehouse to care for the poor, widows, orphans, and full-time ministering elders who needed the support.

D&C 70:12—Of those who labor in spiritual matters and missionary service, the Savior has said, ". . . the labourer is worthy of his hire" (Luke 10:7; compare D&C 31:5, 70:12, 84:79, and 106:3). When the servants of the Lord are called upon to give their all to the Church (see, for example, D&C 24:7), the Lord is prepared to provide for them an inheritance to care for their needs. Beyond that, the blessings of the Spirit are made manifest in their lives in abundance.

who are appointed to a stewardship, to administer in temporal things;

13. Yea, even more abundantly, which abundance is multiplied unto them through the manifestations of the Spirit;

14. Nevertheless, in your temporal things you shall be equal, and this not grudgingly, otherwise the abundance of the manifestations of the Spirit shall be withheld.

15. Now this commandment I give unto my servants for their benefit while they remain, for a manifestation of my blessings upon their heads, and for a reward of their diligence and for their security;

16. For food and for raiment; for an inheritance; for houses and for lands, in whatsoever circumstances I, the Lord, shall place them, and whithersoever I, the Lord, shall send them;

17. For they have been faithful over many things, and have done well inasmuch as they have not sinned.

18. Behold, I, the Lord, am merciful and will bless them, and they shall enter into the joy of these things. Even so. Amen.

SECTION 71

1. Behold, thus saith the Lord unto you my servants Joseph Smith, jun., and Sidney Rigdon, that the time has verily come, that it is necessary and expedient in me that you should open your mouths in proclaiming my gospel, the things of the kingdom, expounding the mysteries thereof out of the scriptures, according to that portion of Spirit and power which shall be given unto you, even as I will.

2. Verily, I say unto you, proclaim unto the world in the regions round about, and in the church also, for the space of a season, even until it shall be made known unto you.

3. Verily this is a mission for a season, which I give unto you.

4. Wherefore, labor ye in my vineyard. Call upon the inhabitants of the earth, and bear record, and prepare the way for the commandments and revelations which are to come.

5. Now, behold this is wisdom; whoso readeth, let him understand and receive also;

6. For unto him that receiveth it

D&C 70:14, 18—The term *equal* as used by the Lord in this and similar statements doesn't mean that each person receives the same compensation, but that each receives according to his needs. The law of consecration, as with all commandments of the Lord, operates according to covenant principles. There is a *quid pro quo*. The servants of the Lord participate faithfully, diligently, and willingly—"not grudgingly" (verse 14)—and keep themselves free of sin. In response, the Lord pours out an abundance of spiritual and temporal blessings.

Section 71 Background—Given at Hiram, Ohio, December 1, 1831. The Prophet gave this introduction: "After Oliver Cowdery and John Whitmer had departed for Jackson county, Missouri [to see to the publication of the Book of Commandments], I resumed the translation of the Scriptures [the Bible], and continued to labor in this branch of my calling with Elder Sidney Rigdon as my scribe, until I received [Section 71]" (*HC* 1:238). The Lord redirected the Prophet's efforts away from translating for a time so that he and Sidney Rigdon could redress the negative influence of anti-Church literature being disseminated by the apostate Ezra Booth (see D&C 64:15). Booth had written nine letters that were highly critical of the Church and that had been published in the *Ohio Star* in Ravenna, Ohio. The Prophet found himself in a situation where it was necessary to meet the attacks fearlessly and with ability.

D&C 71:1—The most powerful countermeasure against false doctrine is the word of God as given in the scriptures and through the voice of the living prophets. Alma declared the following on the eve of his departure to reclaim the apostate Zoramites (a mission not unlike the one Joseph and Sidney were being sent to accomplish): "And now, as the preaching of the word had a great tendency to lead the people to do that which was just—yea, it had had more powerful effect upon the minds of the people than the sword, or anything else, which had happened unto them—therefore Alma thought it was expedient that they should try the virtue of the word of God" (Alma 31:5).

D&C 71:1—A "mystery" is a truth that can't be known except through divine relevation. Examples of mysteries are the reestablishment of the Church, the restoration of the priesthood, and temple work for the dead, all of which required divine revelation.

D&C 71:5–6, 9—A key principle of the gospel is that power and spiritual abundance is bestowed upon those who receive with an open heart the truths of heaven. Alma taught the dissenter Zeezrom: "And therefore, he that will harden his heart, the same receiveth the lesser portion of the word; and he that will not harden his heart, to him is given the greater portion of the word, until it is given unto him to know the mysteries of God until he know them in full" (Alma 12:10).

shall be given more abundantly, even power;

7. Wherefore, confound your enemies; call upon them to meet you both in public and in private; and inasmuch as ye are faithful, their shame shall be made manifest.

8. Wherefore, let them bring forth their strong reasons against the Lord.

9. Verily, thus saith the Lord unto you, there is no weapon that is formed against you shall prosper;

10. And if any man lift his voice against you, he shall be confounded in mine own due time;

11. Wherefore, keep my commandments, they are true and faithful. Even so. Amen.

SECTION 72

1. Hearken and listen to the voice of the Lord, O ye who have assembled yourselves together, who are the High Priests of my church, to whom the kingdom and power have been given.

2. For verily thus saith the Lord, it is expedient in me for a bishop to be appointed unto you, or of you, unto the church in this part of the Lord's vineyard;

3. And verily in this thing ye have done wisely, for it is required of the Lord, at the hand of every steward, to render an account of his stewardship, both in time and in eternity.

4. For he who is faithful and wise in time, is accounted worthy to inherit the mansions prepared for him of my Father.

5. Verily I say unto you, the elders of the church in this part of my vineyard, shall render an account of their stewardship unto the bishop which shall be appointed of me, in this part of my vineyard.

6. These things shall be had on record, to be handed over unto the bishop in Zion;

7. And the duty of the bishop shall be made known by the commandments which have been given, and the voice of the conference.

8. And now, verily I say unto you, my servant Newel K. Whitney is

D&C 71:7—This verse did not give Joseph and Sidney permission to *debate*, but rather instructed that they directly refute any falsehoods and lies without arguing. As it turned out, the enemies of the Church were surprised by the sudden, bold challenge to the falsehoods that were being published.

Section 72 Background—Given at Kirtland, Ohio, December 4, 1831 (see *HC* 1:239–241). The Prophet gave this introduction: "Knowing now the mind of the Lord, that the time had come that the Gospel should be proclaimed in power and demonstration to the world, from the Scriptures, reasoning with men as in days of old, I took a journey to Kirtland, in company with Elder Sidney Rigdon on the 3rd day of December, to fulfil the above revelation [Section 71]. On the 4th, several of the Elders and members assembled together to learn their duty, and for edification, and after some time had been spent in conversing about our temporal and spiritual welfare, I received [Section 72]" (*HC* 1:239). The revelation came in two parts: verses 1 through 8 concerning the calling of Newel K. Whitney as a bishop, and the remainder (following his ordination) providing additional information on the duties of a bishop.

D&C 72:3—James E. Talmage expressed concern that sometimes we don't work as hard to develop spiritual wealth as we work to amass temporal wealth, often in preparation for our retirement. While it is important to be able to meet our temporal needs, he said, the day in which we can use earthly riches will soon pass, and we will be completely dependent on our spiritual reserves. We should use zeal and forethought in preparing for our spiritual future.

D&C 72:3—At first, the presiding bishop of the Church was the only bishop. This section makes known the calling of Newel K. Whitney as a bishop, and he is tasked with receiving an accounting of all stewardships.

D&C 72:3–4—This covenant declaration gives a memorable formula for understanding and living the universal law of stewardship. To each mortal is given a stewardship—both spiritual and temporal—for which he or she will be expected to render an accounting before the Lord and His appointed servants. The exercise of one's stewardship is based on that individual's faith and wisdom. The blessing for an acceptable and worthy management of the stewardship obligation during mortality is an inheritance in the eternal mansions of the Father. That is the covenant arrangement given from on high according to which stewardships are judged and rewarded.

In section 72, the specific references are to stewardships of consecration (the United Order); however, the principle applies to all that the Lord requires at our hands. In the parable of the talents, the outcome for the wise steward was stated thus: "Well done, good and faithful servant; thou hast been faithful over a few things, I will make thee ruler over many things: enter thou into the joy of thy lord" (Matt. 25:23; see also D&C 124:113, 132:53).

the man who shall be appointed and ordained unto this power. This is the will of the Lord your God, your Redeemer. Even so. Amen.

9. The word of the Lord, in addition to the law which has been given, making known the duty of the bishop which has been ordained unto the church in this part of the vineyard, which is verily this—

10. To keep the Lord's storehouse; to receive the funds of the church in this part of the vineyard;

11. To take an account of the elders as before has been commanded; and to administer to their wants, who shall pay for that which they receive, inasmuch as they have wherewith to pay;

12. That this also may be consecrated to the good of the church, to the poor and needy.

13. And he who hath not wherewith to pay, an account shall be taken and handed over to the bishop of Zion, who shall pay the debt out of that which the Lord shall put into his hands;

14. And the labors of the faithful who labor in spiritual things, in administering the gospel and the things of the kingdom unto the church, and unto the world, shall answer the debt unto the bishop in Zion;

15. Thus it cometh out of the church, for according to the law every man that cometh up to Zion, must lay all things before the bishop in Zion.

16. And now, verily I say unto you, that as every elder in this part of the vineyard must give an account of his stewardship unto the bishop in this part of the vineyard,

17. A certificate from the judge or bishop in this part of the vineyard, unto the bishop in Zion, rendereth every man acceptable, and answereth all things, for an inheritance, and to be received as a wise steward, and as a faithful laborer;

18. Otherwise he shall not be accepted of the bishop of Zion.

19. And now, verily I say unto you, let every elder who shall give an account unto the bishop of the church, in this part of the vineyard be recommended by the church or churches, in which he labors, that he may render himself and his accounts approved in all things.

20. And again, let my servants who are appointed as stewards over the literary concerns of my church have claim for assistance upon the bishop or bishops, in all things,

21. That the revelations may be published, and go forth unto the ends of the earth, that they also may obtain funds which shall benefit the church in all things,

22. That they also may render themselves approved in all things, and be accounted as wise stewards.

23. And now, behold, this shall be an ensample for all the extensive branches of my church, in whatsoever land they shall be established. And now I make an end of my sayings. Amen.

24. A few words in addition to the laws of the kingdom, respecting the members of the church; they that are appointed by the Holy Spirit to go up unto Zion, and they who are privileged to go up unto Zion;

25. Let them carry up unto the bishop a certificate from three elders of the church, or a certificate from the bishop,

26. Otherwise he who shall go up unto the land of Zion, shall not be accounted as a wise steward. This is also an ensample. Amen.

D&C 72:9–11—It is a manifestation of the Lord's compassion and mercy that multiple references in the revelations of the Restoration instruct Church leaders to organize and operate a storehouse system for the poor and needy (see D&C 42:34, 55, 71–73; 51:1–8, 13; 58:24; and 70:7, 11). The storehouse is the Lord's design for the independence and self-sufficiency of His servants. The bishop's storehouse is not intended to sustain the entire membership of the Church in times of duress but is principally a resource for those in special need from time to time.

D&C 72:17, 25—In 1831, Bishop Whitney was to act under the jurisdiction of Bishop Edward Partridge in Missouri—the first of the bishops (see D&C 41:9–11)—and report to him concerning the certification of the elders in Kirtland. Bishop Partridge therefore became the equivalent of the presiding bishop of the Church. When he passed away on May 27, 1840, Bishop Whitney then assumed the presiding bishopric duties. It has always been the case in the kingdom of God that members are to be certified or recommended as to their worthiness to enjoy fellowship in the family of God. This early revelation confirms the principle of ecclesiastical leaders serving as judges in Zion to facilitate maintaining order and authentic fellowship. Temple recommends, membership certificates, and documentation concerning the completion of personal ordinances and priesthood ordinations are manifestations of this principle today.

The United States Post Office at Ravenna, Ohio; Joseph Smith and Sidney Rigdon were forced to temporarily halt the translation of the Bible so they could travel to several areas—among them Ravenna—and proselyte in an attempt to reestablih friendly feelings toward the Church following publication of a series of newspaper articles by apostate Ezra Booth.

SECTION 73

1. For verily, thus saith the Lord, it is expedient in me, that they should continue preaching the gospel, and in exhortation to the churches in the regions round about, until conference;

2. And then, behold, it shall be made known unto them, by the voice of the conference, their several missions.

3. Now, verily, I say unto you my servants, Joseph Smith, jun., and Sidney Rigdon, saith the Lord, it is expedient to translate again,

4. And, inasmuch as it is practicable, to preach in the regions round about until conference; and after that it is expedient to continue the work of translation until it be finished.

5. And let this be a pattern unto the elders until further knowledge, even as it is written.

6. Now I give no more unto you at this time. Gird up your loins and be sober. Even so. Amen.

SECTION 74

1. For the unbelieving husband is sanctified by the wife, and the unbelieving wife is sanctified by the husband, else were your children unclean, but now are they holy.

2. Now in the days of the apostles the law of circumcision was had among all the Jews who believed not the gospel of Jesus Christ.

3. And it came to pass that there arose a great contention among the

Section 73 Background—Given at Hiram, Ohio, January 10, 1832. (See *HC* 1:241–242.) The Prophet gave this introduction: "From this time [December 4, 1831] until the 8th or 10th of January, 1832, myself and Elder Rigdon continued to preach in Shalersville, Ravenna, and other places, setting forth the truth, vindicating the cause of our Redeemer; showing that the day of vengeance was coming upon this generation like a thief in the night; that prejudice, blindness and darkness filled the minds of many, and caused them to persecute the true Church, and reject the true light; by which means we did much towards allaying the excited feelings which were growing out of the scandalous letters then being published in the *Ohio Star*, at Ravenna, by the before-mentioned apostate, Ezra Booth. On the 10th of January, I received the following revelation [Section 73], making known the will of the Lord concerning the Elders of the Church until the convening of the next conference [scheduled for January 25, 1832]" (*HC* 1:241).

D&C 73:1–2—In many respects, the general conferences of the Church serve as milestones along the pathway to salvation and exaltation. We are to continue our labors in devotion and valiant service from one conference to the next, being edified and instructed at each new conference through the voice of the Lord's appointed servants. We do not wait in idleness for the next conference to convene, but carry on our labors with diligence, being "anxiously engaged in a good cause" (D&C 58:27) to accomplish much righteousness.

Section 74 Background—Given at Hiram, Ohio, January 1832. The Prophet gave this introduction: "Upon the reception of the foregoing word of the Lord [Section 73], I recommended the translation of the Scriptures, and labored diligently until just before the conference, which was to convene on the 25th of January. During this period I also received the following [Section 74], as an explanation of the First Epistle to the Corinthians, 7th chapter, 14th verse" (*HC* 1:242).

D&C 74:1—How should families prosper spiritually in the situation of a marriage where only one partner is a member of the Church? The essence of the counsel—which addresses the challenge of a mixed marriage at the time of Paul's ministry (where one partner is committed to the law of Moses and the other to the Lord's Church)—is that there can be a sanctifying influence in the home through the spirit of the gospel of Jesus Christ, provided the parents understand that the children are "whole" through the Atonement (see Moroni 8:8) and do not need rejuvenating ordinances because they "are alive in Christ, even from the foundation of the world" (Moroni 8:12).

Little children do not need the saving ordinance of baptism until they reach the age of accountability (D&C 68:25). Thus it is a matter of mercy and love that the children not be subjected to imperatives from a religious philosophy contrary to the doctrine of children being innocent and whole before the Lord.

people concerning the law of circumcision, for the unbelieving husband was desirous that his children should be circumcised and become subject to the law of Moses, which law was fulfilled.

4. And it came to pass that the children, being brought up in subjection to the law of Moses, gave heed to the traditions of their fathers and believed not the gospel of Christ, wherein they became unholy;

5. Wherefore, for this cause the apostle wrote unto the church, giving unto them a commandment, not of the Lord, but of himself, that a believer should not be united to an unbeliever, except the law of Moses should be done away among them,

6. That their children might remain without circumcision; and that the tradition might be done away, which saith that little children are unholy; for it was had among the Jews,

7. But little children are holy, being sanctified through the atonement of Jesus Christ; and this is what the scriptures mean

SECTION 75

1. Verily, verily, I say unto you, I who speak even by the voice of my Spirit; even Alpha and Omega, your Lord and your God;

2. Hearken, O ye who have given your names to go forth to proclaim my gospel, and to prune my vineyard.

3. Behold, I say unto you, that it is my will that you should go forth and not tarry, neither be idle, but labor with your mights,

4. Lifting up your voices as with the sound of a trump, proclaiming the truth according to the revelations and commandments which I have given you.

5. And thus if ye are faithful ye shall be laden with many sheaves, and crowned with honor, and glory, and immortality, and eternal life.

Commentators Hyrum M. Smith and Janne M. Sjodahl explain:

> St. Paul says, in substance, that the conversion of one of the partners has brought a sanctifying influence into the family. As Meyer puts it, "The non-believing partner in a marriage becomes partaker—as if by sacred contagion—of the higher, divinely consecrated character of his consort." "Else," the Apostle argues, "were your children unclean." If the wife—this is the argument—must abandon a husband because he is not a Church member, she would also be obliged to abandon her children. But this is not required.
>
> . . .
>
> The consecration of the believing parent includes the children. (*DCC*, 432.)

Section 75 Background—Given on January 25, 1832, at Amherst, Lorain County, Ohio (see *HC* 1:242–245). The occasion was a special conference of the Church at which Joseph Smith was sustained and ordained President of the High Priesthood. The assembled elders (including Orson Hyde, Hyrum Smith, Samuel H. Smith, Luke Johnson, and others) received counsel of the Lord in respect to their stewardships as emissaries in proclaiming His gospel.

Some twenty-four priesthood holders were called by revelation to serve as missionaries for the Lord. Of those mentioned for the first time in this section, some (such as Seymour Brunson, Gideon Carter, Emer Harris, Eden Smith, Daniel Stanton, Micah B. Welton, and Calves Wilson) kept the faith in the years that followed. Others (such as Major N. Ashley, Stephen Burnett, Ruggles Eames, Burr Riggs, and Sylvester Smith) slipped and abdicated their place of honor and fellowship—despite the grand opportunity given to them.

D&C 75:3–4—In the space of not many words, key principles of missionary work—then as now—are revealed: immediate action, full and energetic commitment, boldness of discourse, conveying the revealed word of God, and having an eye focused on eternal consequences and blessings. From President Brigham Young we have a contemporary view of someone embarking in the service of God in alignment with these principles and values:

> With regard to preaching, let a man present himself before the Saints, or go into the world before the nobles and great men of the earth, and let him stand up full of the Holy Ghost, full of the power of God, and though he may use words and sentences in an awkward style, he will convince and convert more, of the truth, than can the most polished orator destitute of the Holy Ghost; for that Spirit will prepare the minds of the people to receive the truth, and the spirit of the speaker will influence the hearers so that they will feel it. (*JD* 4:21.)

6. Therefore, verily I say unto my servant William E. McLellin, I revoke the commission which I gave unto him to go unto the eastern countries,

7. And I gave him a new commission and a new commandment, in the which I, the Lord, chasten him for the murmurings of his heart;

8. And he sinned, nevertheless I forgive him, and say unto him again, go ye into the south countries,

9. And let my servant Luke Johnson go with him, and proclaim the things which I have commanded them,

10. Calling on the name of the Lord for the Comforter, which shall teach them all things that are expedient for them,

11. Praying always that they faint not, and inasmuch as they do this, I will be with them even unto the end.

12. Behold, this is the will of the Lord your God concerning you. Even so. Amen.

13. And again, verily thus saith the Lord, let my servant Orson Hyde, and my servant Samuel H. Smith, take their journey into the eastern countries, and proclaim the things which I have commanded them; and inasmuch as they are faithful, lo, I will be with them even unto the end.

14. And again, verily I say unto my servant Lyman Johnson, and unto my servant Orson Pratt, they shall also take their journey into the eastern countries; and behold, and lo, I am with them also even unto the end.

15. And again, I say unto my servant Asa Dodds, and unto my servant Calves Wilson, that they also shall take their journey unto the western countries, and proclaim my gospel, even as I have commanded them.

16. And he who is faithful shall overcome all things, and shall be lifted up at the last day.

17. And again, I say unto my servant Major N. Ashley, and my servant Burr Riggs, let them take their journey also into the south country;

18. Yea, let all those take their journey as I have commanded them, going from house to house, and from village to village, and from city to city;

19. And in whatsoever house ye enter, and they receive you, leave your blessing upon that house;

20. And in whatsoever house ye enter, and they receive you not, ye shall depart speedily from that house, and shake off the dust of your feet as a testimony against them;

21. And you shall be filled with joy and gladness; and know this, that in the day of judgment you shall be judges of that house, and condemn them;

22. And it shall be more tolerable for the heathen in the day of judgment, than for that house; therefore gird up your loins and be faithful, and ye shall overcome all things, and be lifted up at the last day. Even so. Amen.

23. And again, thus saith the Lord unto you, O ye elders of my church, who have given your names that you might know his will concerning you;

24. Behold, I say unto you, that it is the duty of the church to assist in supporting the families of

D&C 75:9–10—The confirmation of the truths of the gospel is given through the Holy Ghost, the agent-administrator of the Light of Christ—the "light which is in all things, which giveth life to all things, which is the law by which all things are governed, even the power of God who sitteth upon his throne, who is in the bosom of eternity, who is in the midst of all things" (D&C 88:13). The Light of Christ empowers the saving and exalting designs of heaven and illuminates and transforms the honest at heart who aspire to be made "perfect in Christ" (Moroni 10:32) through His grace and mercy. The Holy Ghost guides the missionaries in their labors (see 2 Ne. 32:5; D&C 75:27).

D&C 75:21—Missionary work, despite its challenges and reversals, is a work of joy and gladness (see D&C 18:15–16). Even in those cases where the word of the Lord is rejected, there is satisfaction on the part of the missionaries to know that they have fulfilled their commission with honor in bearing witness of the truth. They can rejoice in the knowledge that their actions are recognized in the higher world: ". . . ye are blessed, for the testimony which ye have borne is recorded in heaven for the angels to look upon; and they rejoice over you, and your sins are forgiven you" (D&C 62:3).

The Simeon Carter home in Amherst, Ohio, where Parley P. Pratt was arrested for preaching. Parley P. Pratt spent the night in jail, thanked Sheriff Elias Peabody for breakfast, and then ran to catch up with the other three missionaries who had been called with him on a mission to the Lamanites (see Section 32).

those, and also to support the families of those who are called and must needs be sent unto the world to proclaim the gospel unto the world;

25. Wherefore, I, the Lord, give unto you this commandment, that ye obtain places for your families, inasmuch as your brethren are willing to open their hearts;

26. And let all such as can obtain places for their families, and support of the church for them, not fail to go into the world, whether to the east or to the west, or to the north, or to the south;

27. Let them ask and they shall receive, knock and it shall be opened unto them, and made known from on high, even by the Comforter, whither they shall go.

28. And again, verily I say unto you, that every man who is obliged to provide for his own family, let him provide, and he shall in no wise lose his crown; and let him labor in the church.

29. Let every man be diligent in all things. And the idler shall not have place in the church, except he repents and mends his ways.

30. Wherefore, let my servant Simeon Carter, and my servant Emer Harris, be united in the ministry;

31. And also my servant Ezra Thayre, and my servant Thomas B. Marsh;

32. Also my servant Hyrum Smith, and my servant Reynolds Cahoon;

33. And also my servant Daniel Stanton, and my servant Seymour Brunson;

34. And also my servant Sylvester Smith, and my servant Gideon Carter;

35. And also my servant Ruggles Eames, and my servant Stephen Burnett;

36. And also my servant Micah B. Welton, and also my servant Eden Smith. Even so. Amen.

D&C 75:24, 29—It is truly our duty to strengthen and nurture everyone (see Moroni 6:4–5; D&C 81:5)—and by so doing to strengthen the family unit. When we teach compassion and live with charity in our hearts, we will truly seek to bless and serve one another: "Therefore, strengthen your brethren in all your conversation, in all your prayers, in all your exhortations, and in all your doings" (D&C 108:7).

Within the Doctrine and Covenants there is a corpus of interrelated sections that constitute a powerful missionary guidebook. A prayerful pondering of Sections 4, 11, 12, 14, 15, 16, 18, 31, 33, and 75 (together with many other similar passages in holy writ) will provide a substantial framework for successful missionary work in keeping with the Lord's principles and guidelines—whether for the extended commission to labor as a full-time missionary or for the day-by-day harvest in which all the Saints are enlisted as part of their obligations under the Abrahamic covenant.

Truly the harvest is at hand, and God's laborers are called to serve with all of their "heart, might, mind and strength" (D&C 4:2). We can rejoice that "the worth of souls is great in the sight of God" (D&C 18:10). We can cry repentance unto the world and know the joy of bringing one or many back into the fold: "And now, if your joy will be great with one soul that you have brought unto me into the kingdom of my Father, how great will be your joy if you should bring many souls unto me!" (D&C 18:16).

D&C 75:29—President David O. McKay taught that the privilege to work is a gift; the power to work is a blessing; and the love of work is success.

LABOR WITH YOUR MIGHT

Before the Church was even organized in this dispensation, the Lord made it clear that to labor with Him in the ministry included a commitment to labor with all one's heart, might, mind, and strength (see D&C 4:2). To elders who are engaged in the work of the Savior, the Lord gave counsel: ". . . neither be idle but labor with your might . . ." (D&C 75:3). Saving souls requires great labor. Missionaries who please the Lord use their time in diligent and productive efforts to assist others to come to an understanding of the gospel plan of salvation.

President Henry D. Moyle said, "I shall go to my grave saying that missionaries . . . never rise in their entire life above the stature they carve out for themselves in the mission field. . . . [Later in their lives, they should] get down on their knees, pray, and work a little harder and seek to overcome that tremendous handicap they placed upon themselves by their lack of application, lack of appreciation, and lack of dedication to the mission field" (address to California Mission, June 2, 1962).

It pleases the Lord when His missionaries lift up their voices "as with the sound of a trump, proclaiming the truth according to the revelations and commandments . . ." (D&C 75:4). A trump symbolizes a clear, far-reaching, penetrating message of truth. The message of the missionary will be in harmony with the sound of a trump when he proclaims the truth " . . . according to the revelations and commandments . . ." (D&C 75:4; see also D&C 42:12 and D&C 52:9, 36).

In 1839, the Quorum of the Twelve Apostles wrote a letter addressed to the elders and members of the Church throughout the world. In the letter they counseled:

> Be careful that you teach not for the word of God the commandments of men, nor the doctrines of men, nor the ordinances of men, inasmuch as you are God's messengers. Study the word of God, and preach it and not your opinions, for no man's opinion is worth a straw. Advance no principles but what you can prove, for one scriptural proof is worth ten thousand opinions. . . . (HC 3:395–396.) (STDC 2:21–23.)

SECTION 76

1. Hear O ye heavens, and give ear O earth, and rejoice ye inhabitants thereof, for the Lord is God, and beside him there is no Savior:

2. Great is his wisdom, marvelous are his ways, and the extent of his doings none can find out;

3. His purposes fail not, neither are there any who can stay his hand;

4. From eternity to eternity he is the same, and his years never fail.

5. For thus saith the Lord, I, the Lord, am merciful and gracious unto those who fear me, and delight to honor those who serve me in righteousness and in truth unto the end;

6. Great shall be their reward and eternal shall be their glory;

7. And to them will I reveal all mysteries, yea, all the hidden mysteries of my kingdom from days of old, and for ages to come will I make known unto them the good pleasure of my will concerning all things pertaining to my kingdom;

8. Yea, even the wonders of eternity shall they know, and things to come will I show them, even the things of many generations;

9. And their wisdom shall be great, and their understanding reach to heaven: and before them the wisdom of the wise shall perish, and the understanding of the prudent shall come to naught;

10. For by my Spirit will I enlighten them, and by my power will I make known unto them the secrets of my will; yea, even those things which eye has not seen, nor ear heard, nor yet entered into the heart of man.

11. We, Joseph Smith, jun., and Sidney Rigdon, being in the Spirit on the sixteenth of February, in the year of our Lord, one thousand eight hundred and thirty-two,

12. By the power of the Spirit our eyes were opened and our understandings were enlightened, so as to see and understand the things of God—

13. Even those things which were from the beginning before the world was, which were ordained of the Father, through his Only Begotten Son, who was in the bosom of the Father, even from the beginning,

14. Of whom we bear record; and

AN EYEWITNESS TO THE VISION

Philo Dibble—an eyewitness to the vision of Joseph Smith and Sidney Rigdon—wrote: ". . . during the time that Joseph and Sidney were in the spirit and saw the heavens open there were other men in the room, perhaps twelve, among whom I was one during a part of the time—probably two-thirds of the time,—I saw the glory and felt the power, but did not see the vision.

"Joseph would, at intervals, say: 'What do I see?' as one might say while looking out the window and beholding what all in the room could not see. Then he would relate what he had seen or what he was looking at. Then Sidney replied, 'I see the same.' Presently Sidney would say, 'what do I see?' and would repeat what he had seen or was seeing, and Joseph would reply, 'I see the same' . . . During the whole time, not a word was spoken by any other person ("Recollections of Joseph Smith," *Instructor* 27, 1892, 303–304).

Section 76 Background—Given on February 16, 1832, at the John Johnson home in Hiram, Ohio (see *HC* 1:245–252). This vision, with its profound impact on the canon of Church doctrine, resulted from the Prophet's diligent inquiries of the Lord while translating the Bible. This revelation is one of the greatest statements in all of the scriptures about the post-mortal phase of existence, with its several domains of glory to which all mankind (save only the sons of perdition) will be assigned according to individual obedience and compliance with the Lord's commandments. In this vision, Joseph Smith and Sidney Rigdon viewed the glory of the throne of God and had their understanding expanded concerning death, the resurrection, the judgments of God, the different heavens in the post-mortal realm, and the characteristics of those who will inhabit those heavens. Significant is that they saw and conversed with the Savior (see D&C 76:14) while a dozen men were in the room.

Joseph Smith gave this description: "Nothing could be more pleasing to the Saints upon the order of the kingdom of the Lord, than the light which burst upon the world through the foregoing vision. Every law, every commandment, every promise, every truth, and every point touching the destiny of man, from Genesis to Revelation, where the purity of the scriptures remains unsullied by the folly of men, go to show the perfection of the theory [of different degrees of glory in the future life] and witnesses the fact that that document is a transcript from the records of the eternal world. . . . every honest man is constrained to exclaim: 'It came from God'" (*HC* 1:252).

There are actually six main visions described in Section 76:

1. The Savior and the Father—verses 20–24
2. Lucifer rebelling and being thrust down—verses 25–28
3. The sons of perdition and their fate—verses 29–38, 43–49
4. The celestial glory—verses 50–70, 92–96
5. The terrestrial glory—verses 71–80, 91, 97
6. The telestial glory—verses 81–90, 98–106, 109–113

There are also two recurring aspects: (1) The Lord commanded them to write the vision while still in the Spirit, and (2) there is a recurring affirmation of the vision and testimony of Christ.

D&C 76:1—Many of the revelations contained in this canon begin with the witness of the Lord Himself concerning His Being and His design for the salvation and exaltation of mankind. Section 76 is no exception. Elder Bruce R. McConkie said:

No tongue can tell, no pen can write, no man can utter, no human mind can conceive of the glory, majesty, might, power, and dominion that is Christ's. He is the Lord God Almighty, the Creator of heaven and earth and all that in them is, the Eternal Jehovah, the Holy One of Israel, the Savior and Redeemer. He made the earth; salvation comes by him; his atoning sacrifice is infinite and eternal. (*DNTC*, 2:533.)

the record which we bear is the fulness of the gospel of Jesus Christ, who is the Son, whom we saw and with whom we conversed in the heavenly vision;

15. For while we were doing the work of translation, which the Lord had appointed unto us, we came to the twenty-ninth verse of the fifth chapter of John, which was given unto us as follows.

16. Speaking of the resurrection of the dead, concerning those who shall hear the voice of the Son of Man,

17. And shall come forth; they who have done good in the resurrection of the just, and they who have done evil in the resurrection of the unjust.

18. Now this caused us to marvel, for it was given unto us of the Spirit.

19. And while we meditated upon these things, the Lord touched the eyes of our understandings and they were opened, and the glory of the Lord shone round about;

20. And we beheld the glory of the Son, on the right hand of the Father, and received of his fulness;

21. And saw the holy angels, and they who are sanctified before his throne, worshiping God, and the Lamb, who worship him forever and ever.

22. And now, after the many testimonies which have been given of him, this is the testimony last of all, which we give of him, that he lives;

23. For we saw him, even on the right hand of God, and we heard the voice bearing record that he is the Only Begotten of the Father—

24. That by him and through him, and of him the worlds are and were created, and the inhabitants thereof are begotten sons and daughters unto God.

25. And this we saw also, and bear record, that an angel of God who was in authority in the presence of God, who rebelled against the Only Begotten Son, whom the Father loved, and who was in the bosom of the Father—was thrust down from the presence of God and the Son,

26. And was called Perdition, for the heavens wept over him—he was Lucifer, a son of the morning.

27. And we beheld, and lo, he is fallen! is fallen! even a son of the morning.

D&C 76:14–17—The credentials of those who are voice to these sayings (Joseph Smith and Sidney Rigdon) are unassailable and incontrovertible, for they are being taught by the Lord personally and directly. Thus the word of the Lord concerning these eternal matters comes to us unfiltered.

D&C 76:19—President Marion G. Romney said that meditation is a form of prayer—an effective approach to the Spirit of the Lord. In a similar sentiment, President David O. McKay said that meditation is a form of devotion, one of the most secret, sacred doors through which we can pass into the presence of the Lord.

D&C 76:22–23—This oft-cited witness is one of the most celebrated prophetic testimonies in the scriptures. Christ, "the resurrection, and the life" (John 11:25), was the firstfruits of the resurrection (see 1 Cor. 15:23). The risen Lord was seen and touched by His Apostles (see Luke 24:39), and many were resurrected at this time (see Matt. 27:52). The Saints at Bountiful in the New World witnessed firsthand the reality of the Lord (see 3 Ne. 11:15–17). Now the Prophet of the Restoration and his companion solemnly confirm the fact that Christ lives. This knowledge fills us with hope and with the desire to come forth in the morning of the first resurrection.

D&C 76:24—Jesus created worlds without number (see Gen 1:1; John 1:3; Rom. 11:36; Heb. 1:2; Mosiah 4:2; Morm. 9:11; and D&C 14:9).

D&C 76:25–26—In this segment of the revelation no fewer than seven names are given for the personality opposing God in the premortal existence: fallen angel, Perdition, Lucifer, son of the morning, Satan, old serpent, and devil. The word *perdition* in English usage comes from the Latin verb *perdere*, meaning "to lose." The word "Lucifer" means literally "the shining one" or "the lightbringer" (see Bible Dictionary, 726). This name, which derives from the Latin word for "light" (compare the related word *lucid*), is the equivalent of the appellation "son of the morning." The word *Satan* in its Greek, Latin, and Hebrew sources means "adversary." The word "devil" in its Latin and Greek etymological derivation means "slanderer."

The case of Lucifer is the most fundamental example of irony in the scriptures, for how could a being of light (son of the morning) transform himself into the arch-representative of darkness? Section 76 reveals with great power the contrast between this benighted personality and the grandeur of the eternal source of light and truth, even the Father and the Son.

The heavens wept over Lucifer, for he was an angel "in authority in the presence of God" (verse 25). He held high office. It was this tragic transformation, this total abdication of godly potential in one of the leading sons of God in the spirit realm, that caused the heavens to so weep (verse 26).

According to George Q. Cannon, Satan is only one of many sons of perdition.

28. And while we were yet in the Spirit, the Lord commanded us that we should write the vision, for we beheld Satan, that old serpent—even the devil—who rebelled against God, and sought to take the kingdom of our God, and his Christ,

29. Wherefore he maketh war with the saints of God, and encompasses them round about.

30. And we saw a vision of the sufferings of those with whom he made war and overcame, for thus came the voice of the Lord unto us.

31. Thus saith the Lord, concerning all those who know my power, and have been made partakers thereof, and suffered themselves, through the power of the devil, to be overcome, and to deny the truth and defy my power—

32. They are they who are the sons of perdition, of whom I say that it had been better for them never to have been born,

33. For they are vessels of wrath, doomed to suffer the wrath of God, with the devil and his angels in eternity;

34. Concerning whom I have said there is no forgiveness in this world nor in the world to come,

35. Having denied the Holy Spirit after having received it, and having denied the Only Begotten Son of the Father—having crucified him unto themselves and put him to an open shame.

36. These are they who shall go away into the lake of fire and brimstone, with the devil and his angels,

37. And the only ones on whom the second death shall have any power;

38. Yea, verily, the only ones who shall not be redeemed in the due time of the Lord, after the sufferings of his wrath;

39. For all the rest shall be brought forth by the resurrection of the dead, through the triumph and the glory of the Lamb, who was slain, who was in the bosom of the Father before the worlds were made.

40. And this is the gospel, the glad tidings which the voice out of the heavens bore record unto us,

41. That he came into the world, even Jesus, to be crucified for the world, and to bear the sins of the world, and to sanctify the world, and to cleanse it from all unrighteousness;

42. That through him all might be saved whom the Father had put into his power and made by him;

D&C 76:32, 36–38—In the vision of Perdition and the ungodly we see a stark confirmation of the words of Lehi: "For it must needs be, that there is an opposition in all things" (2 Ne. 2:11). The most tragic and awful demonstration of this inevitability is the nature and final status of those who know the light intimately and nevertheless declare it to be darkness and "defy" the power of God through rebellion—unto their utter doom and destruction.

D&C 76:39–43—The Atonement is central to all aspects of the gospel. It is the empowering crux of the plan of salvation and the pillar of God's design for "the immortality and eternal life of man" (Moses 1:39). Every member of the Church, even the very young, have these words on the tongue: "We believe that through the Atonement of Christ, all mankind may be saved, by obedience to the laws and ordinances of the Gospel" (Articles of Faith: 3). Because the Son accommodated Himself meticulously and graciously to the will of the Father, the Atonement, in all of its glory, unfolded as a magnificent gift to all mankind through the resurrection (even to those mortals, like Cain, who became sons of perdition), and an eternal opportunity for the faithful and obedient to gain access once again to the presence of God: "But, behold, my Beloved Son, which was my Beloved and Chosen from the beginning, said unto me—Father, thy will be done, and the glory be thine forever" (Moses 4:2).

From the triumph of the Redeemer over death springs hope eternal. The Atonement of our Savior is the center of the plan of happiness and the foundation of the Church and kingdom of God here upon the earth. All things point to Christ. For that reason, we are all invited through the word of Christ to come unto Him, that we may be "perfected in him" (Moroni 10:32). Counseled the Prophet Joseph Smith:

> The great plan of salvation is a theme which ought to occupy our strict attention, and be regarded as one of heaven's best gifts to mankind. No consideration whatever ought to deter us from showing ourselves approved in the sight of God, according to His divine requirement. Men not unfrequently forget that they are dependent upon heaven for every blessing which they are permitted to enjoy, and that for every opportunity granted them they are to give an account. You know, brethren, that when the Master in the Savior's parable of the stewards called his servants before him he gave them several talents to improve on while he should tarry abroad for a little season, and when he returned he called for an accounting. So it is now. Our Master is absent only for a little season, and at the end of it He will call each to render an account; and where the five talents were bestowed, ten will be required; and he that has made no improvement will be cast out as an unprofitable servant, while the faithful will enjoy everlasting honors. Therefore we earnestly implore the grace of our Father to rest upon you, through Jesus Christ His Son, that you may not faint in the hour of temptation, nor be overcome in the time of persecution." (*HC* 2:23–24.)

43. Who glorifies the Father, and saves all the works of his hands, except those sons of perdition, who deny the Son after the Father has revealed him;

44. Wherefore, he saves all except them: they shall go away into everlasting punishment, which is endless punishment, which is eternal punishment, to reign with the devil and his angels in eternity, where their worm dieth not, and the fire is not quenched, which is their torment;

45. And the end thereof, neither the place thereof, nor their torment, no man knows,

46. Neither was it revealed, neither is, neither will be revealed unto man, except to them who are made partakers thereof:

47. Nevertheless, I, the Lord, show it by vision unto many, but straightway shut it up again;

48. Wherefore the end, the width, the height, the depth, and the misery thereof, they understand not, neither any man except them who are ordained unto this condemnation.

49. And we heard the voice, saying, Write the vision, for lo! this is the end of the vision of the sufferings of the ungodly!

50. And again, we bear record, for we saw and heard, and this is the testimony of the gospel of Christ concerning them who shall come forth in the resurrection of the just;

51. They are they who received the testimony of Jesus, and believed on his name and were baptized after the manner of his burial, being buried in the water in his name, and this according to the commandment which he has given,

52. That by keeping the commandments they might be washed and cleansed from all their sins, and receive the Holy Spirit by the laying on of the hands of him who is ordained and sealed unto this power,

53. And who overcome by faith, and are sealed by the Holy Spirit of promise, which the Father sheds forth upon all those who are just and true.

54. They are they who are the church of the first born.

55. They are they into whose hands the Father has given all things—

56. They are they who are Priests and Kings, who have received of his fulness, and of his glory,

57. And are Priests of the Most High, after the order of Melchisedek,

D&C 76:42—The Lord cited for Moses the petition of Satan in the premortal existence: "Behold, here am I, send me, I will be thy son, and I will redeem all mankind, that one soul shall not be lost, and surely I will do it; wherefore give me thine honor" (Moses 4:1). Satan promulgated a program that would allegedly reclaim every mortal soul—on the basis of the suspension of moral agency, the abandonment of eternal principles, and the usurpation of the glory and honor of God. By contrast, the Savior, who was the "Beloved and Chosen from the beginning," declared: "Father, thy will be done, and the glory be thine forever" (Moses 4:2). As it turned out, the Savior would indeed save every soul given unto Him: "Fear not, little children, for you are mine, and I have overcome the world, and you are of them that my Father hath given me; And none of them that my Father hath given me shall be lost" (D&C 50:41-42). Of mortal beings, only the sons of perdition would be lost. The Prophet Joseph Smith wrote:

> All sins shall be forgiven, except the sin against the Holy Ghost; for Jesus will save all except the sons of perdition. What must a man do to commit the unpardonable sin? He must receive the Holy Ghost, have the heavens opened unto him, and know God, and then sin against Him. After a man has sinned against the Holy Ghost, there is no repentance for him. He has got to say that the sun does not shine while he sees it; he has got to deny Jesus Christ when the heavens have been opened unto him, and to deny the plan of salvation with his eyes open to the truth of it; and from that time he begins to be an enemy. This is the case with many apostates of the Church of Jesus Christ of Latter-day Saints. (*TPJS*, 358; see also Heb. 6:4–6; 2 Thess. 2:3; John 17:12.)

The John Johnson home in Hiram, Ohio, where the Prophet Joseph Smith received the vision that was to become Section 76. During the vision, both Joseph Smith and Sidney Rigdon viewed the glory of the throne of God and had their understanding expanded concerning death, the resurrection, the judgments of God, the different heavens in the post-mortal realm, and the characteristics of those who would inhabit those heavens.

which was after the order of Enoch, which was after the order of the Only Begotten Son;

58. Wherefore, as it is written, they are Gods, even the sons of God—

59. Wherefore all things are theirs, whether life or death, or things present, or things to come, all are theirs and they are Christ's and Christ is God's;

60. And they shall overcome all things;

61. Wherefore let no man glory in man, but rather let him glory in God, who shall subdue all enemies under his feet—

62. These shall dwell in the presence of God and his Christ for ever and ever.

63. These are they whom he shall bring with him, when he shall come in the clouds of heaven, to reign on the earth over his people.

64. These are they who shall have part in the first resurrection.

65. These are they who shall come forth in the resurrection of the just.

66. These are they who are come unto Mount Zion, and unto the city of the living God, the heavenly place, the holiest of all.

67. These are they who have come to an innumerable company of angels, to the general assembly and church of Enoch, and of the first born.

68. These are they whose names are written in heaven, where God and Christ are the judge of all.

69. These are they who are just men made perfect through Jesus the mediator of the new covenant, who wrought out this perfect atonement through the shedding of his own blood.

70. These are they whose bodies are celestial, whose glory is that of the sun, even the glory of God, the highest of all, whose glory the sun of the firmament is written of as being typical.

71. And again, we saw the terrestrial world, and behold and lo, these are they who are of the terrestrial, whose glory differs from that of the church of the first born who have received the fulness of the Father, even as that of the moon differs from the sun in the firmament.

D&C 76:54–70—The vision of the celestial kingdom—in this revelation the highest degree of the celestial kingdom—is singular in its transcendent language and depiction and in inspiring the faithful with the hope of dwelling in the presence of God. This is the purpose for the gospel of Jesus Christ and the plan of salvation—to guide mankind to a level of righteousness that they might have confidence in the presence of the Lord, having established themselves as valiant in the testimony of Jesus Christ, having put all enemies beneath their feet, not the least of which is pride, worldliness, and (through the grace of the Atonement) death and sin. Such are destined to inherit the celestial kingdom, even the highest degree thereof, to live forever in the house of the Father and the Son.

How does one gain the right to pass through the eternal gates and proceed into the presence of God? Section 76 outlines the key requirements: those who receive the testimony of Jesus and become reborn through the power of the gospel and its ordinances; those who overcome by faith and are sealed by the Holy Spirit of promise; those who remain just and true in their callings within the Church and kingdom of God; and those who are made perfect through Christ and His infinite Atonement. Such are endowed with magnificent blessings: the capacity of being gods, even the sons and daughters of God; possession of all things eternal; overcoming all things; residing forever in the presence of the Father and the Son; joining with the Savior at the Second Coming; participating in the first resurrection as celestial beings of glory; and enjoying the everlasting communion of celestial beings in the assemblies of heaven.

We are blessed when we always retain in our mind's eye the unspeakably joyful image of being among those whom the Lord is able to bring home into His presence. We are blessed when we prayerfully seek a place for ourselves and our families among those who are acceptable before the throne of the Lord. We are blessed when we live in such a way that our confidence can "wax strong in the presence of God" (D&C 121:45). We are blessed when we strive with all diligence to become just men and women—righteous in all things—who live and act according to our faith in Jesus Christ (see Rom. 1:17; Heb. 10:38).

Interior of the John Johnson home in Hiram, Ohio.

72. Behold, these are they who died without law,

73. And also they who are the spirits of men kept in prison, whom the Son visited, and preached the gospel unto them, that they might be judged according to men in the flesh,

74. Who received not the testimony of Jesus in the flesh, but afterwards received it.

75. These are they who are honorable men of the earth, who were blinded by the craftiness of men.

76. These are they who receive of his glory, but not of his fulness.

77. These are they who receive of the presence of the Son, but not of the fulness of the Father;

78. Wherefore they are bodies terrestrial, and not bodies celestial, and differ in glory as the moon differs from the sun.

79. These are they who are not valiant in the testimony of Jesus; wherefore they obtain not the crown over the kingdom of our God.

80. And now this is the end of the vision which we saw of the terrestrial, that the Lord commanded us to write while we were yet in the Spirit.

81. And again, we saw the glory of the telestial, which glory is that of the lesser, even as the glory of the stars differs from that of the glory of the moon in the firmament.

82. These are they who received not the gospel of Christ, neither the testimony of Jesus.

83. These are they who deny not the Holy Spirit.

84. These are they who are thrust down to hell.

85. These are they who shall not be redeemed from the devil, until the last resurrection, until the Lord, even Christ the Lamb shall have finished his work.

86. These are they who receive not of his fulness in the eternal world, but of the Holy Spirit through the ministration of the terrestrial;

87. And the terrestrial through the ministration of the celestial.

88. And also the telestial receive it of the administering of angels who are appointed to minister for them, or who are appointed to be ministering spirits for them, for they shall be heirs of salvation.

89. And thus we saw, in the heavenly vision, the glory of the telestial, which surpasses all understanding,

90. And no man knows it except him to whom God has revealed it.

91. And thus we saw the glory of the terrestrial, which excels in all things the glory of the telestial, even in glory, and in power, and in might, and in dominion.

92. And thus we saw the glory of the celestial, which excels in all

D&C 76:71–79—According to the vision of the terrestrial kingdom, those of the terrestrial glory (compared to the glory of the moon) include those who died without law, those who rejected Christ in the flesh but accepted Him in the spirit world, and those who were "honorable men of the earth" (verse 75) but were blinded by worldly influences—in other words, not valiant in the testimony of the Savior. Such receive not a fullness of glory. A similar disposition awaits those members of the Church who are not valiant, but who are instead lukewarm in their devotion to righteousness.

When this section was given ("they who died without law"), the doctrine of work for the dead in the spirit realm had not yet been fully revealed. After Section 137 was given (January 21, 1836) and the principles of baptism for the dead were established through Sections 127 and 128 (both given in September 1842), it would have become clear to the Saints that "they who died without law" implied those who did not have an opportunity to hear the gospel in the mortal realm and then later, upon hearing it in the spirit realm, failed to repent and embrace the gospel.

Bottom line for those of a terrestrial glory: "These are they who are not valiant in the testimony of Jesus" (D&C 76:79). These are they who will have the privilege of beholding the presence of the Son, but "not of the fulness of the Father" (verse 77). Though refulgent and blazing, the glory of the terrestrial kingdom is no equal of the celestial. To rise above the terrestrial level and cross upward and into the celestial realm requires the kind of deportment and endurance described so eloquently by Nephi: "Wherefore, ye must press forward with a steadfastness in Christ, having a perfect brightness of hope, and a love of God and of all men. Wherefore, if ye shall press forward, feasting upon the word of Christ, and endure to the end, behold, thus saith the Father: Ye shall have eternal life" (2 Ne. 31:20).

D&C 76:81, 86—Those of the telestial glory (as of the stars) rejected the gospel and the testimony of Christ and persisted in gross wickedness. They must therefore suffer the wrath of the Almighty God and wait until the last resurrection for their redemption. Nevertheless, the vision of the telestial kingdom "surpasses all understanding" in its glory. Even the most wicked—short of being sons of perdition—inherit this degree of glory through the beneficence and mercy of God. Still, they are isolated by their chosen natures, and, tragically, "where God and Christ dwell they cannot come, worlds without end" (D&C 76:112).

The term *telestial* is unique to Mormon theology, as scholar Hoyt Brewster, Jr., explains: "The Apostle Paul described the bodies to be possessed by the inhabitants of the three kingdoms of glory in the hereafter, but our present King James Bible only refers to two of them by name—the celestial, or glory of the sun, and the terrestrial, or glory of the moon (1 Cor. 15:39–42). Nevertheless, Paul spoke of the glory of the stars, which glory is that of a telestial order (D&C 76:81, 98). The Prophet Joseph Smith, in his inspired version of the Bible, used the term *telestial* to identify the glory of those resurrected bodies who inhabit such a kingdom (JST, 1 Cor. 15:40)" (DCE, 580).

things—where God, even the Father, reigns upon his throne for ever and ever;

93. Before whose throne all things bow in humble reverence and give him glory for ever and ever.

94. They who dwell in his presence are the church of the first born; and they see as they are seen, and know as they are known, having received of his fulness and of his grace;

95. And he makes them equal in power, and in might, and in dominion.

96. And the glory of the celestial is one, even as the glory of the sun is one.

97. And the glory of the terrestrial is one, even as the glory of the moon is one.

98. And the glory of the telestial is one, even as the glory of the stars is one, for as one star differs from another star in glory, even so differs one from another in glory in the telestial world;

99. For these are they who are of Paul, and of Apollos, and of Cephas.

100. These are they who say they are some of one and some of another—some of Christ and some of John, and some of Moses, and some of Elias, and some of Esaias, and some of Isaiah, and some of Enoch;

101. But received not the gospel, neither the testimony of Jesus, neither the prophets, neither the everlasting covenant.

102. Last of all, these all are they who will not be gathered with the saints, to be caught up unto the church of the first born, and received into the cloud.

103. These are they who are liars, and sorcerers, and adulterers, and whoremongers, and whosoever loves and makes a lie.

104. These are they who suffer the wrath of God on the earth.

105. These are they who suffer the vengeance of eternal fire.

106. These are they who are cast down to hell and suffer the wrath of Almighty God, until the fulness of times when Christ shall have subdued all enemies under his feet, and shall have perfected his work,

107. When he shall deliver up the kingdom, and present it unto the Father spotless, saying—I have overcome and have trodden the wine-press alone, even the wine-press of the fierceness of the wrath of Almighty God.

108. Then shall he be crowned with the crown of his glory, to sit on the throne of his power to reign for ever and ever.

109. But behold, and lo, we saw the glory and the inhabitants of the telestial world, that they were as innumerable as the stars in the

D&C 76:96–98—The Prophet Joseph articulates in these verses a summary of the three kingdoms and their relative levels of glory. It is instructive that the celestial kingdom comprises three distinct levels, or "heavens or degrees" (D&C 131:1), and that the telestial kingdom comprises myriad gradations of glory, just as the panoply of the heavens includes many stars of differing magnitudes. Is there any upward migration into a higher kingdom? President Spencer W. Kimball wrote: "After a person has been assigned his place in the kingdom, either in the telestial, the terrestrial or the celestial, or to his exaltation, he will never advance from his assigned glory to another glory. That is eternal! That is why we must make our decisions early in life and why it is imperative that such decisions be right" (MF, 243–244).

D&C 76:106–109—In this epilogue treatment of the telestial realm we have an enumeration of the qualities of life that determine telestial citizenship. All such are to await the consummation of their redemption by dwelling for a time in a realm described as "hell" (verse 106). Thereafter, their ultimate disposition is deliverance into the telestial glory, where their status is to be "servants of the Most High; but where God and Christ dwell they cannot come, worlds without end" (verse 112)—thus there is no advancement from this kingdom of glory upward to a higher kingdom.

D&C 76:107—There is great symbolism in the winepress. The act of stomping grapes stains one's clothing a deep red color. When the Savior comes again in glory, He will be dressed in red, suggesting blood from working out the Atonement (saying that He trod the winepress alone means He atoned by Himself) and the blood of vengeance on the wicked at the Second Coming.

D&C 76:108—The Prophet Joseph Smith and Sidney Rigdon were permitted to view the final episode in the glorious completion of the Savior's work—when He would be crowned with glory and assume His ultimate everlasting regency as Lord of all and Father of the sons and daughters given to Him by Elohim. Our responsibility is crystal clear: to prepare ourselves to be found clean and pure on the day of judgment, that we might have a place in the celestial kingdom with Jesus Christ and the Father.

firmament of heaven, or as the sand upon the sea shore,

110. And heard the voice of the Lord, saying— these all shall bow the knee, and every tongue shall confess to him who sits upon the throne for ever and ever;

111. For they shall be judged according to their works, and every man shall receive according to his own works, his own dominion, in the mansions which are prepared,

112. And they shall be servants of the Most High, but where God and Christ dwell they cannot come, worlds without end.

113. This is the end of the vision which we saw, which we were commanded to write while we were yet in the Spirit.

114. But great and marvelous are the works of the Lord, and the mysteries of his kingdom which he showed unto us, which surpasses all understanding in glory, and in might, and in dominion,

115. Which he commanded us we should not write while we were yet in the Spirit, and are not lawful for man to utter;

116. Neither is man capable to make them known, for they are only to be seen and understood by the power of the Holy Spirit, which God bestows on those who love him, and purify themselves before him;

117. To whom he grants this privilege of seeing and knowing for themselves;

118. That through the power and manifestation of the Spirit, while in the flesh, they may be able to bear his presence in the world of glory.

119. And to God and the Lamb be glory, and honor, and dominion for ever and ever. Amen.

SECTION 77

1.   Q.—What is the sea of glass spoken of by John, 4th chapter, and 6th verse of the Revelations?

A.—It is the earth, in its sanctified, immortal, and eternal state.

2.   Q.—What are we to understand by the four beasts, spoken of in the same verse?

A.—They are figurative expressions, used by the Revelator John,

The John Johnson home in Hiram, Ohio, where Joseph Smith did the translation of the Bible; it was in this home that Section 77, regarding the book of Revelation, was received.

D&C 76:113, 116—Those individual who are pure and righteous, with an abiding love for the Lord, can hope to learn these grand "mysteries" through the power of the Holy Ghost. The Apostle Paul declared: "God hath revealed them unto us by his Spirit: for the Spirit searcheth all things, yea, the deep things of God. . . . even so the things of God knoweth no man, except he has the Spirit of God. . . . But the natural man receiveth not the things of the Spirit of God: for they are foolishness unto him: neither can he know them, because they are spiritually discerned." (JST, 1 Cor. 2:10, 11, 14.)

Section 77 Background—Given at Hiram, Ohio, March 1832. (See *HC* 1:253–255.) The Prophet gave this introduction: "About the first of March, In connection with the translation of the Scriptures, I received the following explanation of the Revelation of St. John [Section 77]" (*HC* 1:253).

D&C 77:1—Brigham Young explained: "This Earth will become a celestial body—be like a sea of glass, or like a urim and thummim; and when you wish to know anything, you can look in this Earth and see all the eternities of God. We shall make our home here, and go on our missions as we do now" (Brigham Young, *JD* 8:200). Scholars Hyrum M. Smith and Janne M. Sjodahl give this commentary: "In the Temple of Solomon there was an immense basin called 'a molten sea' (1 Kings 7:23). In the Temple in heaven, of which the temples on Earth are feeble representations, there is a *glassy* sea, calm, transparent, and solid, and here we are informed that this 'sea' is 'the Earth in its sanctified, immortal, and eternal state.' The 'sea' connected with the temples of God is a baptismal font. It represents the Earth. All who desire access to the Church of Jesus Christ must come through the baptismal font, and be buried with Christ" (*DCC*, 472).

D&C 77:2—Concerning these passages, President Joseph Fielding Smith stated:

> . . . every creature has a spirit, and . . . it existed in the spirit before it was on the earth; the spirit of every creature is in the form of its temporal, or mortal, body. Since this is true . . . therefore they are entitled to the resurrection and shall live again.
>
> We are to understand that there will be beasts of various kinds, after the resurrection, in each of the kingdoms, telestial, terrestrial and celestial. . . . They are the creations of the Almighty and therefore they will be perfect in their own sphere, for the Lord creates no imperfections and it is his purpose, according to the divine plan, to make all of his creatures as happy as it is possible for them to be . . . .
>
> We also learn from this revelation and the word of the Lord in other revelations that in the eternities the animals and all living creatures shall be given knowledge, and enjoy happiness, each in its own sphere, in "their eternal felicity" [D&C 77:3]. These creatures will not then be the dumb creatures that we suppose them to be while in this mortal life. (*CHMR*, 2:67–69.)

in describing heaven, the Paradise of God, the happiness of man, and of beasts, and of creeping things, and of the fowls of the air; that, which is spiritual being in the likeness of that which is temporal; and that which is temporal, is in the likeness of that which is spiritual; the spirit of man in the likeness of his person, as also the spirit of the beast, and every other creature which God has created.

3.　Q.—Are the four beasts limited to individual beasts, or do they represent classes or orders?

A.—They are limited to four individual beasts, which were shown to John, to represent the glory of the classes of beings, in their destined order or sphere of creation, in the enjoyment of their eternal felicity.

4.　Q.—What are we to understand by the eyes, and wings, which the beasts had?

A.—Their eyes are a representation of light and knowledge; that is, they are full of knowledge; and their wings are a representation of power, to move, to act, &c.

5.　Q.—What are we to understand by the four and twenty elders, spoken of by John?

A.—We are to understand that these elders whom John saw, were elders who had been faithful in the work of the ministry, and were dead; who belonged to the seven churches,—and were then in the Paradise of God.

6.　Q.—What are we to understand by the book which John saw, which was sealed on the back with seven seals?

A.—We are to understand that it contains the revealed will, mysteries, and the works of God; the hidden things of his economy concerning this earth during the seven thousand years of its continuance, or its temporal existence.

7.　Q.—What are we to understand by the seven seals with which it was sealed?

A.—We are to understand that the first seal contains the things of the first thousand years, and the second also of the second thousand years, and so on until the seventh.

8.　Q.—What are we to understand by the four angels, spoken of in the 7th chap. and 1st verse of Revelations?

A.—We are to understand that they are four angels sent forth from God, to whom is given power over the four parts of the earth, to save life and to destroy; these are they who have the everlasting gospel to commit to every nation, kindred, tongue, and people; having power to shut up the heavens, to seal up unto life, or to cast down to the regions of darkness.

9.　Q.—What are we to understand by the angel ascending from the east, Revelations 7th chap. and 2nd verse?

A.—We are to understand that the angel ascending from the east, is he to whom is given the seal of the living God, over the twelve tribes of Israel; wherefore he crieth unto

D&C 77:5—President Joseph Fielding Smith provides this commentary: "It will be recalled that the forepart of John's Revelation contains a charge to the seven churches, or branches of the Church, in Asia Minor. [Rev. 1–3.] We may judge from what is written that these seven branches were all that were considered worthy of a standing in the Church at that time, indicating that the apostasy had at that day become extensive, and each of these branches received a deserved rebuke" (CHMR, 2:69).

D&C 77:5—This was an assurance to the persecuted Saints of John's day that faithfully enduring trials results in exaltation.

D&C 77:6—President Joseph Fielding Smith wrote that the seven seals represent the seven thousand years of temporal existence—the earth's existence from the fall of Adam to the end of time, which will come after the Millennium and "a little season" to follow (see D&C 29:22–23 and 88:111). Everything on the earth, including the earth itself, was in a spiritual condition before the Fall, since mortality had not yet caused a temporal state. "The book" is the actual history of the world; Christ is the only one who can open a seal and reveal its contents.

D&C 77:8—President Joseph Fielding Smith taught that these angels have power over the four parts of the earth and have the power to commit the gospel to all on the earth. He pointed out that no one messenger restored the fullness of the gospel to the earth, but that all the ancient prophets who held keys came to restore those keys and had a hand in the Restoration. We learn from this revelation that four angels have power to shut up the heavens and to open them—and, according to President Smith, these four angels are now performing their sacred mission on the earth (see CHMR, 2:70–71). President Wilford Woodruff said that the angels have left the portals of heaven and stand over us now, hovering over the earth waiting to pour out judgments.

D&C 77:9—The Prophet Joseph Smith taught that since so many ancient prophets participated in the Restoration, the "Elias" who was to come and restore all things is actually a composite of several difference individuals instead of a single person. In this verse, the angel who has the seal instructs the four angels who hold the destiny of the earth in their hands that they are not to destroy the earth until the servants of the Lord have been sealed. Obviously, this couldn't be done until the gospel had been restored and preached to all the nations of the world. Elder Bruce R. McConkie said that the phrase "angel ascending from the east" refers to a composite personage of all who participated in restoring the gospel, including John the Revelator.

the four angels having the everlasting gospel, saying, hurt not the earth, neither the sea, nor the trees, till we have sealed the servants of our God in their foreheads; and if you will receive it, this is Elias which was to come to gather together the tribes of Israel and restore all things.

10.　　Q.—What time are the things spoken of in this chapter to be accomplished?

　　　　A.—They are to be accomplished in the sixth thousandth year, or the opening of the sixth seal.

11.　　Q.—What are we to understand by sealing the one hundred and forty-four thousand, out of all the tribes of Israel; twelve thousand out of every tribe?

　　　　A.—We are to understand that those who are sealed are High Priests, ordained unto the holy order of God, to administer the everlasting gospel; for they are they who are ordained out of every nation, kindred, tongue, and people, by the angels to whom is given power over the nations of the earth, to bring as many as will come to the church of the first born.

12.　　Q.—What are we to understand by the sounding of the trumpets, mentioned in the 8th chapter of Revelations?

　　　　A.—We are to understand that as God made the world in six days and on the seventh day he finished his work, and sanctified it, and also formed man out of the dust of the earth even so, in the beginning of the seventh thousand years will the Lord God sanctify the earth, and complete the salvation of man, and judge all things, and shall redeem all things, except that which he hath not put into his power, when he shall have sealed all things, unto the end of all things; and the sounding of the trumpets of the seven angels, are the preparing and finishing of his work, in the beginning of the seventh thousand years; the preparing of the way before the time of his coming.

13.　　Q.—When are the things to be accomplished, which are written in the 9th chapter of Revelations?

　　　　A.—They are to be accomplished after the opening of the seventh seal, before the coming of Christ.

14.　　Q.—What are we to understand by the little book which was eaten by John, as mentioned in the 10th chapter of Revelations?

　　　　A.—We are to understand that it was a mission, and an ordinance, for him to gather the tribes of Israel; behold, this is Elias; who, as it is written, must come and restore all things.

15.　　Q.—What is to be understood by the two witnesses, in the eleventh chapter of Revelations?

　　　　A.—They are two prophets that are to be raised up to the Jewish nation in the last days, at the time of the restoration, and to prophesy to the Jews, after they are gathered, and build the city of Jerusalem, in the land of their fathers.

D&C 77:11—Victor Ludlow wrote:

> John foretells of 144,000 righteous high priests, all of whom have honored the law of chastity, who will receive a special ordinance. (See Rev. 7:3–4; 14:3–4; D&C 77:11.) These 144,000 will be organized into groups or quorums of twelve thousand each according to the twelve tribes of Israel. (See Rev. 7:48.). . . . Depending upon the earth's population when the Millennium is established, each of these 144,000 high priests could have responsibility for many thousands of people. . . . to help the Messiah govern his kingdom on earth. (See D&C 133:18)." (*PPRG*, 612.)

D&C 77:12—It's helpful to have some chronology here. In this case, the Lord refers to thousand-year periods as a day. At the beginning of the seventh thousand–year period after the Fall, the earth (and all on it) will change from a telestial condition to a terrestrial one, a condition of peace and order. At that point, the earth will be renewed and will receive the paradisiacal glory referred to in the Tenth Article of Faith. Right now we are experiencing the restoration of all things, and the earth will eventually be as it was before the Fall. Orson F. Whitney wrote:

> According to received chronology—admittedly imperfect, yet approximately correct—four thousand years, or four of the seven great days given to this planet as the period of its "temporal existence," had passed before Christ was crucified; while nearly two thousand years have gone by since. Consequently, Earth's long week is now drawing to a close, and we stand at the present moment in the Saturday Evening of Time, at or near the end of the sixth day of human history. Is it not a time for thought, a season for solemn meditation? Morning will break upon the Millennium, the thousand years of peace, the Sabbath of the World! (*SNT*, 12.)

D&C 77:14—Scholars Hyrum M. Smith and Janne M. Sjodahl comment as follows:

> In this vision John sees another mighty angel, or messenger, coming from heaven. This angel had a "little book" open, and he cried out his message with a loud voice, declaring solemnly that there would be "time no longer,"—no more delay—but that when the seventh angel begins to sound, the mystery of God—God's plan of salvation—will be completed. This is a vision of the restoration of the Church through the instrumentality of the Prophet Joseph, who came as a messenger from God and declared that the Church was to be restored, preparatory to the second coming of Christ. The coming forth of the "little book" was the beginning of a new prophetic era, for John was told (Rev. 10:11): "Thou must prophesy again before many peoples, and nations, and tongues, and kings." The establishment of the Church in our day is foretold in this chapter of the Revelation. . . . (*DCC*, 477.)

SECTION 78

1. The Lord spake unto Enoch, (Joseph Smith, jr.,) saying, Hearken unto me, saith the Lord your God, who are ordained unto the high priesthood of my church, who have assembled yourselves together;

2. And listen to the counsel of him who has ordained you from on high, who shall speak in your ears the words of wisdom, that salvation may be unto you in that thing which you have presented before me, saith the Lord God;

3. For verily I say unto you, the time has come, and is now at hand; and behold, and lo, it must needs be that there be an organization of my people, in regulating and establishing the affairs of the storehouse for the poor of my people, both in this place and in the land of Zion,

4. Or in other words, the city of Enoch, (Joseph) for a permanent and everlasting establishment and order unto my church, to advance the cause, which ye have espoused, to the salvation of man, and to the glory of your Father who is in heaven;

5. That you may be equal in the bands of heavenly things; yea, and earthly things also, for the obtaining of heavenly things;

6. For if ye are not equal in earthly things, ye cannot be equal in obtaining heavenly things;

7. For if you will that I give unto you a place in the celestial world, you must prepare yourselves by doing the things which I have commanded you and required of you.

8. And now, verily thus saith the Lord, it is expedient that all things be done unto my glory, by you who are joined together in this order;

9. Or in other words, let my servant Ahashdah [Newel K. Whitney] and my servant Gazelam, or Enoch [Joseph Smith, Jun.,] and my

Section 78 Background—Given in March 1832 at Hiram, Ohio, for the purpose of establishing a storehouse for the poor (see *HC* 1:255–257) and taking other steps to assure that the Church could be independent. The United Firm, more commonly known as the United Order, operated for about two years in Kirtland, with a branch in Missouri. This initiative failed when loan payments could not be made due to the destruction of the Missouri printing operation by a mob, the forced closure of the storehouse in Missouri, and other unforeseen expenses. Those included in this order are thought to have been Joseph Smith, Sidney Rigdon, Jesse Gause, Oliver Cowdery, Martin Harris, Sidney Gilbert, Newel K. Whitney, Edward Partridge, William W. Phelps, John Whitmer, Frederick G. Williams, and John Johnson. For a time, the real names of those addressed in the revelation were replaced by code names to protect their identity. In modern editions, the real names are used, as in the original manuscripts.

D&C 78:3–4—The fundamental principles of the law of consecration were given by revelation on February 9, 1831, as part of the "law of the Lord" (see D&C 42:2). Those participating in this covenant arrangement would consecrate their goods and property to the Church and receive back a stewardship sufficient to sustain their families through self-reliance and industry. The surplus from the stewardships would be placed in the bishop's storehouse for distribution to the poor and needy among the Saints.

D&C 78:6—The Lord's law of consecration operates on the principles of faith, obedience, and unity—faith that the Lord will bless us in sufficient measure with the abundance of His creation if we, in turn, are obedient to His commandment to consecrate our time, effort, and earthly goods to the building up of His Kingdom.

George Q. Cannon explained the word *equal* as "to have an equal claim on the blessings of our Heavenly Father—on the properties of the Lord's treasury, and the influences and gifts of His Holy Spirit. This is the equality meant in the revelations, and until we attain to this equality we cannot be equal in spiritual things, and the blessings of God cannot be bestowed upon us until we attain to this as they otherwise would" (*JD* 13:99).

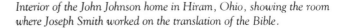

Interior of the John Johnson home in Hiram, Ohio, showing the room where Joseph Smith worked on the translation of the Bible.

servant Peloagoram [Sidney Rigdon,] sit in council with the saints which are in Zion;

10. Otherwise Satan seeketh to turn their hearts away from the truth, that they become blinded and understand not the things which are prepared for them.

11. Wherefore, a commandment I give unto you, to prepare and organize yourselves by a bond or everlasting covenant that cannot be broken.

12. And he who breaketh it shall lose his office and standing in the church, and shall be delivered over to the buffetings of Satan until the day of redemption.

13. Behold, this is the preparation wherewith I prepare you, and the foundation, and the ensample which I give unto you, whereby you may accomplish the commandments which are given you,

14. That through my providence, notwithstanding the tribulation which shall descend upon you, that the church may stand independent above all other creatures beneath the celestial world,

15. That you may come up unto the crown prepared for you, and be made rulers over many kingdoms, saith the Lord God, the Holy One of Zion, who hath established the foundations of Adam-ondi-Ahman;

16. Who hath appointed Michael your prince, and established his feet, and set him upon high, and given unto him the keys of salvation under the counsel and direction of the Holy One, who is without beginning of days or end of life.

17. Verily, verily I say unto you, ye are little children, and ye have not as yet understood how great blessings the Father hath in his own hands and prepared for you;

18. And ye cannot bear all things now, nevertheless, be of good cheer, for I will lead you along: The kingdom is yours and the blessings thereof are yours; and the riches of eternity are yours;

19. And he who receiveth all things with thankfulness shall be made glorious; and the things of this earth shall be added unto him, even an hundred fold, yea, more;

20. Wherefore, do the things which I have commanded you, saith your Redeemer, even the Son Ahman, who prepareth all things before he taketh you;

21. For ye are the church of the first born, and he will take you up in a cloud, and appoint every man his portion.

22. And he that is a faithful and wise steward shall inherit all things. Amen.

D&C 78:8–11—The canopy arching over these principles is the glory of the Lord: the eternal destiny of His children through the plan of happiness. There is nothing solely temporal about the law of consecration. It is a spiritual law, for it facilitates the ongoing development of the children of God in their quest to comply with celestial law and attain celestial objectives. Consecration is a covenant relationship—embracing a covenant and promise of obedience to the commandments of God and a covenant bond with fellow Saints. The nature of the covenant was to be everlasting and irrevocable, lest the participants slip and fall into the grasp of the evil one and become blinded to the truth. "For he who is not able to abide the law of a celestial kingdom cannot abide a celestial glory" (D&C 88:22).

D&C 78:14—Consecration is the covenant formula by means of which the Church—as an organized assembly of unified Saints, acting under priesthood guidance in the name of Jesus Christ and through the providence of God—can be self-sufficient and independent, despite all tribulation and hardship. We can take steps toward the future when the law of consecration will be reinstated: we can be unified in the payment of a more honest tithe and a more generous fast offering, in supporting the welfare system of the Church in greater measure, in facilitating a higher degree of self-reliance and promoting a more wholesome work ethic among our members, in caring for the poor and needy with more devotion and charity in the application of our heaven-sent gifts and talents with more generosity for the building up and expansion of the kingdom of God, and in teaching the principles of sacrifice and consecration with more clarity and consistency in our families.

D&C 78:16—The Prophet Joseph Smith taught that Michael, spoken of in the Bible (see Dan. 10:13; Jude 1:9; Rev. 12:7), is Adam.

D&C 78:18—In all of our trials and tribulations we can live with hope and trust in the Lord Jesus Christ. He will nurture and bless us. This is why we should be of "good cheer." Be glad, for He is in our midst (see D&C 29:5).

D&C 78:19–22—Consecration, just as all covenant arrangements, operates on a specific basis: We are asked to receive all things—all commandments, blessings, obligations, gifts, opportunities, duties, offices, relationships—with the spirit of thankfulness, obedience, faithfulness, and wisdom; then, in turn, the Lord provides an inheritance consisting of "all things"—an extraordinarily good arrangement for the Saints! The Lord knows our hearts, minds, desires, and intentions. He knows our every deed. He is the Judge of all—and the supreme Benefactor who has all power, glory, and dominion necessary to recompense those who consecrate their lives to Him and His Church.

SECTION 79

1. Verily I say unto you, that it is my will that my servant Jared Carter should go again into the eastern countries, from place to place, and from city to city, in the power of the ordination wherewith he has been ordained, proclaiming glad tidings of great joy, even the everlasting gospel;
2. And I will send upon him the Comforter, which shall teach him the truth and the way whither he shall go;
3. And inasmuch as he is faithful, I will crown him again with sheaves;
4. Wherefore, let your heart be glad, my servant Jared Carter, and fear not, saith your Lord, even Jesus Christ. Amen.

SECTION 80

1. Verily, thus saith the Lord, unto you my servant Stephen Burnett, go ye, go ye into the world and preach the gospel to every creature that cometh under the sound of your voice;
2. And inasmuch as you desire a companion, I will give unto you my servant Eden Smith;
3. Wherefore go ye and preach my gospel, whether to the north or to the south, to the east or to the west, it mattereth not, for ye cannot go amiss;
4. Therefore, declare the things which ye have heard and verily believe, and know to be true.
5. Behold, this is the will of him who hath called you, your Redeemer, even Jesus Christ. Amen.

STEPHEN BURNETT

Stephen Burnett was born in 1814. He learned of the gospel in Ohio, where he joined the Church. Soon thereafter he was called as a missionary by revelation (see D&C 75:3; see also D&C 80:1–2 for a subsequent calling). Unfortunately, upon his return to Kirtland, Stephen apostatized and denounced the Prophet and the Church.

EDEN SMITH

Eden Smith was born in 1806 in Indiana. After joining the Church, he was called by revelation in January 1832 as a missionary (see D&C 75:36). A second missionary call was received in March of that year (see D&C 80:1–2). In light of his somewhat contentious nature, he was disfellowshipped on July 2, 1833, but he repented and came back into fellowship in the Church. He joined the Saints in Missouri and later moved to Nauvoo, where he served in the Nauvoo Legion. He passed away in Iowa on December 7, 1851.

Section 79 Background—Given at Hiram, Ohio, March 1832 (see HC 1:257).

D&C 79:1–4—This is a precious missionary call, blending key elements of an authentic priesthood commission: power, authority, gladness, joy in the message of everlasting truth, confirmation and guidance from the Holy Ghost, faithfulness, and courage. Every emissary of the Lord can rejoice in these gifts and endowments from on high. To embark in this manner—"in the strength of the Lord" (Alma 20:4; see also Alma 26:12)—is to go forward with an invincible mindset of service and an unconquerable spirit of charity toward those who "are only kept from the truth because they know not where to find it" (D&C 123:12).

D&C 79:3—The celestial rest is glorious beyond anything we have the capacity to imagine with our finite understanding. We need to undergo a period of preparation before we can enter in and enjoy its blessings.

Section 80 Background—Given at Hiram, Ohio, March 1832 (see HC 1:257).

D&C 80:1–4—Every child of God needs to hear the word of truth. Those called to proclaim the gospel have a divine mandate to speak the truth as they have learned it and bear witness of that which the Holy Ghost confirms to them as having come from God. If they do this, they "cannot go amiss" (verse 3), for the gospel has universal applicability—no matter where it is preached. "And he gathereth his children from the four quarters of the earth; and he numbereth his sheep, and they know him; and there shall be one fold and one shepherd; and he shall feed his sheep, and in him they shall find pasture" (1 Ne. 22:25).

D&C 80:4—This verse underscores the need for missionaries to prepare carefully and thoroughly. President John Taylor said that both the Lord and the missionary have responsbilities and promises in the missionary effort. The Lord promises that He will sustain and sanction the missionary. The missionary promises to be a herald of salvation and legate of the skies. He is commissioned of Christ to bear a great message, and is to call upon men to believe in Christ, to repent of their sins, to be baptized, and to receive the gift of the Holy Ghost. A missionary can come forth with confidence and authority from the Lord, because the Lord is with His missionaries.

SECTION 81

1. Verily, verily I say unto you my servant Frederick G. Williams, listen to the voice of him who speaketh, to the word of the Lord your God, and hearken to the calling wherewith you are called, even to be a High Priest in my church, and a counselor unto my servant Joseph Smith, jun.

2. Unto whom I have given the keys of the kingdom, which belongeth always unto the Presidency of the High Priesthood:

3. Therefore, verily I acknowledge him and will bless him, and also thee, inasmuch as thou art faithful in counsel, in the office which I have appointed unto you, in prayer always vocally and in thy heart, in public and in private, also in thy ministry in proclaiming the gospel in the land of the living, and among thy brethren:

4. And in doing these things thou wilt do the greatest good unto thy fellow beings, and wilt promote the glory of him who is your Lord;

5. Wherefore, be faithful, stand in the office which I have appointed unto you, succor the weak, lift up the hands which hang down, and strengthen the feeble knees;

6. And if thou art faithful unto the end, thou shalt have a crown of immortality and eternal life in the mansions which I have prepared in the house of my Father.

7. Behold, and lo, these are the words of Alpha and Omega, even Jesus Christ. Amen.

SECTION 82

1. Verily, verily I say unto you, my servants, that inasmuch as you have forgiven one another your trespasses, even so I, the Lord, forgive you;

2. Nevertheless there are those among you who have sinned exceedingly;

Section 81 Background—Given in March 1832 at Hiram, Ohio (see *HC* 1:257–258). This section was originally intended for the benefit of Jesse Gause, a former Quaker and one of the original counselors to Joseph Smith. Jesse Gause and Sidney Rigdon had been called and ordained as counselors to Joseph Smith one week before this revelation was given. Jesse served as a counselor to the Prophet for five months before he faded away and apostatized; no further mention is made of him in Church history. The call to serve as a counselor in the First Presidency was subsequently transferred to Frederick G. Williams.

D&C 81:5—The divine commission to rescue and save souls is pervasive throughout the scriptures. Our mortal experience opens up myriad opportunities for charitable and devoted service to others—in our families, our congregations, our communities, and our nation.

D&C 81:6—In the scriptures and the history of the Restoration we find a dependable pattern concerning the process of "rescuing." We gladly follow the guidance of the prophets of God. We willingly follow the Spirit in discerning where succor needs to be administered. We faithfully cultivate qualities of humility, obedience, and gratitude in order to ensure our own rescue. We humbly share the good news of the gospel and bear witness with courage about the truth of its saving principle. We obediently show the straight and narrow way to those who despair of redemptive answers. Above all, we consistently emulate the Savior, the Master of charity.

Section 82 Background—Given on April 26, 1832, in Independence, Jackson County, Missouri (see *HC* 1:267–269). Pursuant to Section 78—which instructed Joseph Smith, Sidney Rigdon, and Newel K. Whitney to "sit in council" with the members of the Church in Missouri (D&C 78:9)—they left Hiram on April 1 with Jesse Gause to make the long trip. They were pursued by mobbers even as far as Cincinnati and Louisville via the Ohio River. Their fear of leaving their families behind can be seen in an excerpt of a letter Joseph wrote to W. W. Phelps:

> [We left] our families in affliction amidst of death [and] upon the mercy of mobs & of brethren who you know sometimes are found to be unstable, unbelieving, unmerciful and, in this trying situation, to keep the commandment of God we took our lives in our hands and traveled through every combination of wickedness to your country for your salvation. (Joseph Smith to William W. Phelps, 31 July 1832, Joseph Smith Collection, Church Archives; spelling and punctuation modernized.)

On his return to Kirtland, Joseph wrote Emma of his commitment to the work: "I will try to be contented with my lot. . . . God is my friend. In him I shall find comfort. I have given my life into His hands. I am prepared to go at his call. I desire to be with Christ. I count not my life dear to me, only to do his will" (Joseph to Emma, Greenville, Indiana, June 6, 1832).

yea, even all of you have sinned, but verily I say unto you, beware from henceforth, and refrain from sin, lest sore judgments fall upon your heads;

3. For unto whom much is given much is required; and he who sins against the greater light shall receive the greater condemnation.

4. Ye call upon my name for revelations, and I give them unto you; and inasmuch as ye keep not my sayings, which I give unto you, ye become transgressors, and justice and judgment are the penalty which is affixed unto my law;

5. Therefore, what I say unto one I say unto all, Watch, for the adversary spreadeth his dominions and darkness reigneth;

6. And the anger of God kindleth against the inhabitants of the earth; and none doeth good, for all have gone out of the way.

7. And now, verily I say unto you, I, the Lord, will not lay any sin to your charge; go your ways and sin no more; but unto that soul who sinneth shall the former sins return, saith the Lord your God.

8. And again, I say unto you, I give unto you a new commandment, that you may understand my will concerning you.

9. Or, in other words, I give unto you directions how you may act before me, that it may turn to you for your salvation.

10. I, the Lord, am bound when ye do what I say, but when ye do not what I say, ye have no promise.

11. Therefore, verily I say unto you, that it is expedient for my servant Alam, and Ahashdah, (Newel K. Whitney,) Mahalaleel, and Pelagoram, (Sidney Rigdon,) and my servant Gazelam, (Joseph Smith,) and Horah, and Olihah, (Oliver Cowdery,) and Shalemanasseh, and Mahemson, (Martin Harris,) to be bound together by a bond and covenant that cannot be broken by transgression, (except judgment shall immediately follow,) in your several stewardships,

12. To manage the affairs of the poor, and all things pertaining to the bishopric both in the land of Zion and in the land of Shinehah, (Kirtland,)

13. For I have consecrated the land of Shinehah, (Kirtland,) in mine own due time for the benefit of the saints of the Most High, and for a Stake to Zion.

14. For Zion must increase in beauty, and in holiness; her borders must be enlarged; her Stakes must be strengthened; yea, verily I say

D&C 82:2–3—All of the light that we have comes from one source—even the light of Christ. When we act contrary to that sacred light—the light of life and the light of truth—we commit sin. All are sinners, as verse 2 confirms. No one accommodates the law of God to perfection. We can be justified only through the power and mercy of the Redeemer, imparted to us through the plan of salvation. The more light we admit into our lives, the greater our momentum along the pathway to perfection—whereby we may become "perfect in Christ" (Moroni 10:32).

D&C 82:7—Repentance means the total forsaking of sins; if we fail to overcome our sins, and allow them to recur, then our former sins return, to our condemnation.

D&C 82:10—Covenant promises are contractual by nature, with specified requirements leading to the fulfillment of sacred promises. When we are obedient in honoring our covenants, then the Lord pours out blessings without measure. When we fall short in keeping our part of the eternal bargain, then we forfeit the promises given.

D&C 82:11—In this verse, the word *bond* refers to the law of consecration. The men named in this verse were members of the United Order and needed to set an example for the Saints. The penalty for breaking the law of consecration was severe.

D&C 82:14—President Harold B. Lee taught that the Church is to the Lord as a bride is to her husband, and a bride would adorn herself in her most beautiful garments for her husband.

D&C 82:14–17—How shall Zion be enlarged and beautified through priesthood power and the abundance of heavenly blessings? What system is there according to which each individual and each family can thrive and progress according to just needs and in keeping with the principles of self-reliance and equality? How can poverty be overcome and dignity upheld? The Lord's system for accomplishing such goals is the law of consecration. Given the conditions of the times, and the shortcomings of many, the early founders of the Restoration were unable to manifest in full measure the glories and practical benefits of this celestial system. It remains a future goal on the horizon of the designs of heaven. Zion will be strengthened, enlarged, and beautified even more than is presently manifested. The Prophet Joseph Smith was given to understand, concerning the strengthening of Zion in the last days: ". . . to put on her strength is to put on the authority of the priesthood, which she, Zion, has a right to by lineage; also to return to that power which she had lost" (D&C 113:8).

unto you: Zion must arise and put on her beautiful garments.

15. Therefore, I give unto you this commandment, that ye bind yourselves by this covenant, and it shall be done according to the laws of the Lord.

16. Behold, here is wisdom also in me for your good.

17. And you are to be equal, or in other words, you are to have equal claims on the properties, for the benefit of managing the concerns of your stewardships, every man according to his wants and his needs, inasmuch as his wants are just;

18. And all this for the benefit of the church of the living God, that every man may improve upon his talent, that every man may gain other talents, yea, even an hundred fold, to be cast into the Lord's storehouse, to become the common property of the whole church.

19. Every man seeking the interest of his neighbor, and doing all things with an eye single to the glory of God.

20. This order I have appointed to be an everlasting order unto you, and unto your successors, inasmuch as you sin not;

21. And the soul that sins against this covenant, and hardeneth his heart against it, shall be dealt with according to the laws of my church, and shall be delivered over to the buffetings of Satan until the day of redemption.

22. And now, verily I say unto you, and this is wisdom, make unto yourselves friends with the mammon of unrighteousness, and they will not destroy you.

23. Leave judgment alone with me, for it is mine and I will repay. Peace be with you; my blessings continue with you,

24. For even yet the kingdom is yours, and shall be for ever, if you fall not from your steadfastness. Even so. Amen.

SECTION 83

1. Verily, thus saith the Lord, in addition to the laws of the church concerning women and children, those who belong to the church, who have lost their husbands or fathers.

D&C 82:19—To take time from a busy schedule and ponder the enormous blessings bestowed upon us by the Lord yields food for thought: We are blessed beyond all understanding; thus we need to cultivate an attitude of full devotion to things spiritual, a full commitment to do all that is asked of us in the name of building the Church and kingdom of God, and an unswerving steadfastness in serving the needs of our fellow beings, forever and ever. The more we practice this kind of lifestyle, the more prepared we will be for the time when the law of consecration emerges as the universal way of life for all who aspire to be a Zion people—with an eye single to the glory of God.

D&C 82:21—The phrase "buffetings of Satan" means to be given over to Satan.

D&C 82:22—We are reminded that we are to treat the enemies of the Church with kindness and respect, without lowering ourselves to their level by participating in sin with them. Adopting an attitude of respect may help to allay prejudice and ease bitterness among enemies of the Church.

D&C 82:23–24—Living a celestial law, including the law of consecration, is possible for the pure in heart who honor their covenants and set aside pride, avarice, and worldly entanglements. One can have peaceable and amicable relationships with others not of the faith (even "the mammon of unrighteousness") and thus preserve order and a spirit of kindliness, provided judgment is left in the hands of God. President Joseph Fielding Smith taught that before we can enter the celestial kingdom, we have to learn to live in unity with our neighbors—with love of them in our heart, desiring their good as well as our own, and not preferring ourselves before them. The promise of the Lord to the obedient is that peace will be theirs, and the blessings of heaven will continue to flow—if steadfastness is preserved.

Section 83 Background—Given at Independence, Missouri, April 30, 1832 (see HC 1:269–270.) The Prophet provides this introduction: "On the 28th and 29th, I visited the brethren above Big Blue river, in Kaw township, a few miles west of Independence, and received a welcome only known by brethren and sisters united as one in the same faith, and by the same baptism, and supported by the same Lord. The Colesville branch, in particular, rejoiced as the ancient Saints did with Paul. It is good to rejoice with the people of God. On the 30th, I returned to Independence, and again sat in council with the brethren, and received [Section 83]" (HC 1:269).

2. Women have claim on their husbands for their maintenance, until their husbands are taken, and if they are not found transgressors they shall have fellowship in the church;

3. And if they are not faithful, they shall not have fellowship in the church; yet they may remain upon their inheritances according to the laws of the land.

4. All children have claim upon their parents for their maintenance until they are of age.

5. And after that they have claim upon the church, or in other words upon the Lord's storehouse, if their parents have not wherewith to give them inheritances.

6. And the storehouse shall be kept by the consecrations of the church, and widows and orphans shall be provided for, as also the poor. Amen.

SECTION 84

1. A revelation of Jesus Christ unto his servant Joseph Smith, jun., and six elders, as they united their hearts and lifted their voices on high.

2. Yea, the word of the Lord concerning his church, established in the last days for the restoration of his people, as he has spoken by the mouth of his prophets, and for the gathering of his saints to stand upon Mount Zion, which shall be the city of New Jerusalem,

D&C 83:2, 4—This passage accords with other scriptures that sustain the same principle. Adam was commanded "to eat his bread by the sweat of his brow" (Moses 5:1). Paul confirmed: "But if any provide not for his own, and specially for those of his own house, he hath denied the faith, and is worse than an infidel" (1 Tim. 5:8). From "The Family: A Proclamation to the World," issued in 1995 by the First Presidency and the Council of the Twelve Apostles, we read: "By divine design, fathers are to preside over their families in love and righteousness and are responsible to provide the necessities of life and protection for their families. Mothers are primarily responsible for the nurture of their children. In these sacred responsibilities, fathers and mothers are obligated to help one another as equal partners."

D&C 83:3, 5—The reference to "inheritances" in these two verses refers to the law of consecration.

D&C 83:5—According to President Spencer W. Kimball, our support should come from, in this order, self, then family, and then the Church (if we are faithful members in good standing).

Section 84 Background—Given on September 22 and 23, 1832, at the Whitney Store in Kirtland, Ohio (see HC 1:286–295). This is the first revelation received after Joseph and Emma and young Julia moved from Hiram on September 12 into their new quarters above the Whitney Store. Three upper rooms in the Whitney Store had distinctive uses. The bedroom in the northwest upper corner was the bedroom for Joseph and Emma. The two other consistent room designations were (1) the "school room" (upper northeast corner, located over Emma's kitchen), and (2) the translating room. It appears that the Prophet pursued his translation and received most of his revelations in this upper southeast corner room in the Whitney Store.

This is yet another revelation that came as an answer to prayer. The Prophet gave this background: "The Elders during the month of September began to return from their missions to the Eastern States, and present the histories of their several stewardships in the Lord's vineyard; and while together in these seasons of joy, I inquired of the Lord, and received on the 22nd and 23rd of September [Section 84]" (HC 1:286).

There were apparently six elders (later referred to as high priests in verse 63) present on September 22 and ten on September 23. Verses 1–41 were apparently given the first day and verses 42–120 on the following (note the shift from third to first person beginning with verse 42). This important section contains significant doctrine, promises, prophecy, and direction, including material on the oath and covenant of the priesthood in verses 33–41.

D&C 84:2—During the Millennium, there will be two capital cities for the kingdom of God: one in the land of Zion (Jackson County, Missouri) and one in Palestine (Jerusalem). In preparation, the Saints are now gathering in the valleys of the mountains in Utah.

3. Which city shall be built, beginning at the temple lot, which is appointed by the finger of the Lord, in the western boundaries of the state of Missouri, and dedicated by the hand of Joseph Smith, jun., and others with whom the Lord was well pleased.

4. Verily this is the word of the Lord, that the city New Jerusalem shall be built by the gathering of the saints beginning at this place, even the place of the temple, which temple shall be reared in this generation;

5. For verily, this generation shall not all pass away until an house shall be built unto the Lord, and a cloud shall rest upon it, which cloud shall be even the glory of the Lord, which shall fill the house.

6. And the sons of Moses, according to the Holy Priesthood which he received under the hand of his father-in-law, Jethro;

7. And Jethro received it under the hand of Caleb;

8. And Caleb received it under the hand of Elihu;

9. And Elihu under the hand of Jeremy;

10. And Jeremy under the hand of Gad;

11. And Gad under the hand of Esaias;

12. And Esaias received it under the hand of God.

13. Esaias also lived in the days of Abraham, and was blessed of him—

14. Which Abraham received the Priesthood from Melchisedek, who received it through the lineage of his fathers, even till Noah;

15. And from Noah till Enoch, through the lineage of their fathers;

16. And from Enoch to Abel, who was slain by the conspiracy of his brother, who received the Priesthood by the commandments of God, by the hand of his father Adam, who was the first man—

17. Which Priesthood continueth in the church of God in all generations, and is without beginning of days or end of years.

18. And the Lord confirmed a priesthood also upon Aaron and his seed, throughout all their generations—which priesthood also continueth and abideth forever with the Priesthood which is after the holiest order of God.

19. And this greater Priesthood administereth the gospel and holdeth the key of the mysteries of

D&C 84:4—Elder Bruce R. McConkie taught that the "gathering" consists of receiving the truth, gaining a testimony of the Savior, and coming back to the true fold. The word *temple* in this verse refers to the temple in Jackson County, Missouri, and the word *generation* refers to this dispensation.

D&C 84:4–5—Independence , Missouri, was identified by revelation as the center place for the New Jerusalem (see D&C 57:3). Enoch had foreseen this future development (see Moses 7:62–64), as had Ether (see Ether 13:2–6). The risen Lord renewed the prophetic pronouncement about the building of the New Jerusalem when He spoke with the Saints in the New World (see 3 Ne. 21:12–23), and Joseph Smith was to memorialize the principle in the Tenth Article of Faith. In Section 84, the Lord confirms that this monumental development, including the temple, would be accomplished "in this generation" (verse 4). President Joseph Fielding Smith explains the meaning of the word *generation* as meaning the time of this present dispensation (see CHMR 2:102).

D&C 84:5—The "cloud" will be a visible sign of God's protecting care over his people, just as happened anciently.

D&C 84:6—This verse outlines lineage from Adam to Moses and begins a sentence that is concluded in verse 31. All the verses in between make up a parenthetical expression that details the lineage. Jethro, a Midianite, and his family were Hebrew descendants of Abraham and were entitled to the blessings of Abraham.

D&C 84:17–20—The priesthood of God spans the generations of time and eternity. It has no beginning and no end because it is an everlasting power that underlies all of creation and all of God's design for the salvation and exaltation of His children. It is impossible to know God and the mysteries without the priesthood. The higher, or Melchizedek, priesthood allows mankind the privilege of receiving the gospel, understanding the mysteries—the pure knowledge that brings joy and eternal life (see D&C 42:61)—and receiving the associated ordinances (such as the reception of the Holy Ghost and all the temple blessings) that manifest the power of godliness and the keys to the knowledge of God. Realizing this, we can see the goodness of God in allowing His children the privilege of exercising His power and authority here upon the earth. These verses inspire reverence for the priesthood and instill in us a commitment never to defile it and always, above all, to live worthy to exercise it and participate in its divine blessings.

the kingdom even the key of the knowledge of God;

20. Therefore, in the ordinances thereof, the power of godliness is manifest;

21. And without the ordinances thereof, and the authority of the priesthood, the power of godliness is not manifest unto men in the flesh;

22. For without this no man can see the face of God, even the Father, and live.

23. Now this Moses plainly taught to the children of Israel in the wilderness, and sought diligently to sanctify his people that they might behold the face of God;

24. But they hardened their hearts and could not endure his presence; therefore the Lord in his wrath (for his anger was kindled against them) swore that they should not enter into his rest while in the wilderness, which rest is the fulness of his glory.

25. Therefore he took Moses out of their midst, and the Holy Priesthood also;

26. And the lesser priesthood continued, which priesthood holdeth the key of the ministering of angels and the preparatory gospel;

27. Which gospel is the gospel of repentance and of baptism, and the remission of sins, and the law of carnal commandments, which the Lord in his wrath, caused to continue with the house of Aaron among the children of Israel until John, whom God raised up, being filled with the Holy Ghost from his mother's womb;

28. For he was baptized while he was yet in his childhood, and was ordained by the angel of God at the time he was eight days old unto this power, to overthrow the kingdom of the Jews, and to make straight the way of the Lord before the face of his people, to prepare them for the coming of the Lord, in whose hand is given all power.

29. And again, the offices of elder and bishop are necessary appendages belonging unto the High Priesthood.

30. And again, the offices of teacher and deacon are necessary appendages belonging to the lesser priesthood, which priesthood was confirmed upon Aaron and his sons.

31. Therefore, as I said concerning the sons of Moses—for the sons of Moses, and also the sons of Aaron shall offer an acceptable offering

D&C 84:22—A simple statement of ultimate truth—profound in its prophetic implications: Our purpose in mortality is to prepare to return to the presence of the Father and the Son, worthy of Their acceptance. Without the higher priesthood, this homecoming would be impossible; with it, we have hope in the transformative process, through the Atonement of Jesus Christ, of being "perfected in him" (Moroni 10:32) and thus prepared to enter the rest of the Lord, "which rest is the fulness of his glory" (D&C 84:24). Just as the Prophet Joseph Smith was privileged to see the face of God, beginning with the First Vision, so can the Lord's righteous children eventually have this same sacred honor and privilege through the gift and power of the Melchizedek Priesthood of God, by means of which the "power of godliness is manifest" (D&C 84:20). The galvanizing force behind this principle enables us to strive with all our might, mind, and strength to become worthy of this destiny through obedience to the principles and ordinances of the gospel of Jesus Christ as restored through the Prophet Joseph Smith.

D&C 84:26—When the children of Israel recoiled in fear from the Lord's invitation to prepare for the transcendent blessing of beholding His face, He was angered and denied them the privilege of entering into His rest—or "the fulness of his glory." This behavior of the people, known as the "first provocation" (see Alma 12:36; see also Psalms 95:8; Heb. 3:8, 15; Jacob 1:7), caused the Lord to withdraw Moses and the higher priesthood from their midst. However, the preparatory gospel and the lower priesthood remained as a blessing to the people. In the meridian of time, the Savior, the "great high priest" (Heb. 4:14), returned with the fulness of His gospel plan.

Though it is "the lesser priesthood" (D&C 84:26), the Aaronic Priesthood nevertheless remains a glorious commission, with power to assist in the building up of the kingdom of God.

D&C 84:31–32—It is according to the design of the Almighty that those who hold the priesthood of God shall rise in majesty to honor, sustain, and uphold their covenant callings, making their "offering and sacrifice in the house of the Lord" acceptable before the Lord (see also D&C 13). By way of blessing, they will be filled with the glory of the Lord. From this promise we can derive hope and faith to carry out our priesthood responsibilities with all diligence and courage, making righteousness our objective and doing the will of the Lord our defining and governing spirit.

and sacrifice in the house of the Lord, which house shall be built unto the Lord in this generation, upon the consecrated spot as I have appointed,

32. And the sons of Moses and of Aaron shall be filled with the glory of the Lord, upon Mount Zion in the Lord's house, whose sons are ye; and also many whom I have called and sent forth to build up my church;

33. For whoso is faithful unto the obtaining these two priesthoods of which I have spoken, and the magnifying their calling, are sanctified by the Spirit unto the renewing of their bodies;

34. They become the sons of Moses and of Aaron and the seed of Abraham, and the church and kingdom, and the elect of God;

35. And also all they who receive this priesthood receive me, saith the Lord;

36. For he that receiveth my servants receiveth me;

37. And he that receiveth me receiveth my Father;

38. And he that receiveth my Father receiveth my Father's kingdom; therefore all that my Father hath shall be given unto him;

39. And this is according to the oath and covenant which belongeth to the Priesthood.

40. Therefore, all those who receive the Priesthood, receive this oath and covenant of my Father, which he cannot break, neither can it be moved;

41. But whoso breaketh this covenant after he hath received it, and altogether turneth therefrom, shall not have forgiveness of sins in this world nor in the world to come.

42. And all those who come not unto this Priesthood which ye have received, which I now confirm upon you who are present this day, by mine own voice out of the heavens, and even I have given the heavenly hosts and mine angels charge concerning you.

43. And I now give unto you a commandment to beware concerning yourselves, to give diligent heed to the words of eternal life:

44. For you shall live by every word that proceedeth forth from the mouth of God.

45. For the word of the Lord is truth, and whatsoever is truth is light, and whatsoever is light is Spirit, even the Spirit of Jesus Christ;

46. And the Spirit giveth light to

D&C 84:38–40—In the oath and covenant of the priesthood, revealed through the Prophet Joseph Smith, the true program of wealth acquisition is outlined with unmistakable clarity. The quest is for *eternal* wealth—the riches of eternity. The protocol is solemnly clear: Receive the priesthood in full faith. Magnify your calling. Receive the servants of the Lord. Receive the Lord. Receive the Father. Give diligent heed to the words of eternal life and live thereby. Hearken to the voice of the Spirit. Learn of and honor the covenant. Then "all that my Father hath" will be given to you. In a celebrated variant of this doctrine, we hear the Savior declare: "But seek ye first the kingdom of God, and his righteousness; and all these things shall be added unto you" (Matt. 6:33; see also 3 Ne. 13:33).

The oath and covenant of the priesthood carries with it eternal blessings—if we are true and faithful. The promises are glorious: sanctification, renewal of our bodies, becoming the seed of Abraham and elect of God, and receiving all that the Father has. When one is given such a magnificent opportunity to serve, it is wise to remember the injunction: "For of him unto whom much is given much is required; and he who sins against the greater light shall receive the greater condemnation" (D&C 82:3).

D&C 84:44—This familiar injunction is an eternal principle (see Deut. 8:3, Matt. 4:4, Luke 4:4, and D&C 98:11). The act of receiving every word from God and conducting our lives accordingly is evidence that one is following the counsel of the Savior to do the will of the Father.

D&C 84:45–51—The wonderful process of conversion is an intimate experience with the light of heaven. The light of heaven, in the form of the Spirit of Jesus Christ, is given as an endowment to every individual who is born into mortality. By this light he or she knows how to discern good from evil (see Moroni 7:16) and see clearly the pathway of righteousness that lies ahead.

When that individual perceives the word of God—through the preaching of the gospel by the Lord's appointed servants (see Romans 10:13–17)—or in the form of the scriptural record and discerns that it is good and true, then he or she is prepared to receive more truth and light through the agency of the Holy Ghost, who confirms and authenticates divine principles and truths (see John 14:26 and 15:26). The individual who receives that higher enlightenment and then acts with faith and courage leaves the world of spiritual bondage as a new person and comes unto the Father. The Father teaches him or her of the covenant of salvation and exaltation empowered through the Atonement of the Son. By means of this covenant, the riches of eternity are made accessible, based on obedience to the principles of the gospel and enduring to the end.

Those who fail to respond to the word, the truth, the light, and the Spirit—and thus come not unto the Father—remain under the bondage of sin.

every man that cometh into the world; and the Spirit enlighteneth every man through the world, that hearkeneth to the voice of the Spirit;

47. And every one that hearkeneth to the voice of the Spirit cometh unto God, even the Father;

48. And the Father teacheth him of the covenant which he has renewed and confirmed upon you, which is confirmed upon you for your sakes, and not for your sakes only, but for the sake of the whole world;

49. And the whole world lieth in sin, and groaneth under darkness and under the bondage of sin;

50. And by this you may know they are under the bondage of sin, because they come not unto me.

51. For whoso cometh not unto me is under the bondage of sin;

52. And whoso receiveth not my voice is not acquainted with my voice, and is not of me;

53. And by this you may know the righteous from the wicked, and that the whole world groaneth under sin and darkness even now.

54. And your minds in times past have been darkened because of unbelief, and because you have treated lightly the things you have received,

55. Which vanity and unbelief have brought the whole church under condemnation.

56. And this condemnation resteth upon the children of Zion, even all:

57. And they shall remain under this condemnation until they repent and remember the new covenant, even the Book of Mormon and the former commandments which I have given them, not only to say, but to do according to that which I have written,

58. That they may bring forth fruit meet for their Father's kingdom, otherwise there remaineth a scourge and judgment to be poured out upon the children of Zion:

59. For shall the children of the kingdom pollute my holy land? Verily, I say unto you, Nay.

60. Verily, verily, I say unto you who now hear my words, which are my voice, blessed are ye inasmuch as you receive these things;

61. For I will forgive you of your sins with this commandment, that you remain steadfast in your minds in solemnity and the spirit of prayer, in bearing testimony to all the world of those things which are communicated unto you.

62. Therefore go ye into all the world, and unto whatsoever place ye cannot go ye shall send, that the testimony may go from you into all the world unto every creature.

63. And as I said unto mine apostles, even so I say unto you, for you are mine apostles, even God's High

D&C 84:55—President Ezra Taft Benson said that we will be condemned if we take the Book of Mormon lightly; our minds will be darkened, we will be under grave consequences, and our souls will be in jeopardy.

D&C 84:57—What is our personal responsibility with regard to the Book of Mormon? To Joseph of old the Lord confirmed: "But a seer will I raise up out of the fruit of thy loins; and unto him will I give power to bring forth my word unto the seed of thy loins—and not to the bringing forth my word only, saith the Lord, but to the convincing them of my word, which shall have already gone forth among them" (2 Ne. 3:11). That seer foretold was Joseph Smith. The Prophet Joseph is indeed this very man, raised up to provide for the world the word of God. We cannot take it lightly lest we stand in condemnation (see D&C 84:57).

D&C 84:60—Nephi opened his account in the Book of Mormon with the statement that he was "highly favored of the Lord in all my days; yea, having had a great knowledge of the goodness and the mysteries of God" (1 Ne. 1:1). What does it mean to be favored of the Lord? It means being blessed with the saving truths of the gospel of Jesus Christ—and then receiving these truths obediently. Obedience brings the favor of the Lord. When we keep the commandments and submit to the will of our Heavenly Father, we will enjoy the extraordinary blessing of having His Spirit with us always (see D&C 20:77, 79). Through obedience in heeding the promptings of the Spirit and honoring the covenant principles, we will be "favored of the Lord" (see also 1 Ne. 3:16, Mosiah 10:13, Alma 48:20, and Ether 1:34). That is one of the most pervasive and overarching themes of the Book of Mormon, and it is also confirmed in the Doctrine and Covenants consistently, for "blessed are ye inasmuch as you receive these things" (D&C 84:60).

D&C 84:61—Forgiveness of sins is conditioned on lasting repentance *and* a willingness to do missionary work. We are to bear witness to the world of the truths we have received in taking upon ourselves the name of Jesus Christ. Through the bearing of solemn testimony we cause the angels in heaven to rejoice and we enable the power of forgiveness to be active in our own lives (see D&C 62:3).

D&C 84:62, 74—The Saints are to deliver the word of God by their witness throughout all the world—either in person or by sending the word into those places where they cannot travel. Those who reject the word cannot be admitted back into the presence of the Father and the Son.

D&C 84:63—The term *apostles* does not necessarily refer to those who are ordained to an office; it is also used to describe the missionaries who first evangelize a nation or to describe a person who is a zealous advocate of a cause.

Priests; ye are they whom my Father hath given me—ye are my friends;

64. Therefore, as I said unto mine apostles I say unto you again, that every soul who believeth on your words, and is baptized by water for the remission of sins, shall receive the Holy Ghost;

65. And these signs shall follow them that believe.

66. In my name they shall do many wonderful works;

67. In my name they shall cast out devils;

68. In my name they shall heal the sick;

69. In my name they shall open the eyes of the blind, and unstop the ears of the deaf;

70. And the tongue of the dumb shall speak;

71. And if any man shall administer poison unto them it shall not hurt them;

72. And the poison of a serpent shall not have power to harm them.

73. But a commandment I give unto them, that they shall not boast themselves of these things, neither speak them before the world, for these things are given unto you for your profit and for salvation.

74. Verily, verily, I say unto you they who believe not on your words, and are not baptized in water, in my name, for the remission of their sins, that they may receive the Holy Ghost, shall be damned, and shall not come into my Father's kingdom, where my Father and I am.

75. And this revelation unto you, and commandment, is in force from this very hour upon all the world, and the gospel is unto all who have not received it.

76. But, verily, I say unto all those to whom the kingdom has been given, from you it must be preached unto them, that they shall repent of their former evil works, for they are to be upbraided for their evil hearts of unbelief; and your brethren in Zion for their rebellion against you at the time I sent you.

77. And again I say unto you, my friends, (for from henceforth I shall call you friends,) it is expedient that I give unto you this commandment, that ye become even as my friends in days when I was with them traveling to preach the gospel in my power,

78. For I suffered them not to have purse or scrip, neither two coats;

79. Behold I send you out to prove the world, and the laborer is worthy of his hire.

80. And any man that shall go and preach this gospel of the kingdom, and fail not to continue faithful in all things shall not be weary in

D&C 84:62–102—Every Melchizedek Priesthood holder is responsible to the Lord for the preaching of the gospel of Jesus Christ to all the world (see D&C 50:13–14). In this revelation, te Lord emphasized the need and responsibility to perform this phase of priesthood work. He identified many ways in which this work could be done more effectively and promised many blessings to the faithful priesthood laborer. Any priesthood holder who accepts the counsel given by the Lord in this section will be responsive and willing to perform any call when it comes from the authorized representatives of the Lord.

D&C 84:79, 84, 88—This remarkable promise to the missionaries of the Lord confirms that they go not alone. They are nurtured, fed, and accompanied by the Savior and His angels (see Matt. 6:24–34). The Father knows of their needs at every moment (see Matt. 6:8). Preaching the gospel is a covenant commission—with sacred obligations and divine promises. The missionaries are to go in faith, preaching the word of truth continually. In return, the Lord will bless them with strength and protection from the elements. They are to treasure up in their minds continually the word of God, and He will reveal to them "in the very hour" (see also D&C 100:5–8) what they are to say. He will go with them, as will His Spirit and His holy angels. It is a companionship of power and light. The Lord will open doors and hearts so that his disciples may be instructed by the servants of God.

THE GREATER AND LESSER PRIESTHOODS

In this revelation, the Lord revealed four functions of the greater (Melchizedek) priesthood. That priesthood:

a. Administers the gospel

b. Holds the keys of the mysteries of the kingdom and the knowledge of God

c. Manifests through its ordinances the power of godliness

d. Allows man to be in the presence of God

Some of the ordinances of the greater priesthood, in which these keys and powers are manifested, are administered only in the temples of the Lord.

Some of the functions of the lesser (Aaronic) priesthood are:

a. It holds the keys of the administering of angels

b. It holds the key of the preparatory gospel

The lesser priesthood provides us with the teachings and ordinances necessary to prepare us for the receiving of that which is administered by the greater priesthood, including the ordinances and teachings of the temple (*STDC* 2:72).

mind, neither darkened, neither in body, limb, nor joint: and an hair of his head shall not fall to the ground unnoticed. And they shall not go hungry, neither athirst.

81. Therefore, take no thought for the morrow, for what ye shall eat, or what ye shall drink, or wherewithal ye shall be clothed;

82. For consider the lilies of the field, how they grow, they toil not, neither do they spin; and the kingdoms of the world, in all their glory, are not arrayed like one of these;

83. For your Father who art in heaven, knoweth that you have need of all these things.

84. Therefore, let the morrow take thought for the things of itself.

85. Neither take ye thought beforehand what ye shall say, but treasure up in your minds continually the words of life, and it shall be given you in the very hour that portion that shall be meted unto every man.

86. Therefore let no man among you, (for this commandment is unto all the faithful who are called of God in the church unto the ministry,) from this hour take purse or scrip, that goeth forth to proclaim this gospel of the kingdom.

87. Behold, I send you out to reprove the world of all their unrighteous deeds, and to teach them of a judgment which is to come.

88. And whoso receiveth you, there I will be also, for I will go before your face: I will be on your right hand and on your left, and my Spirit shall be in your hearts, and mine angels round about you, to bear you up.

89. Whoso receiveth you receiveth me; and the same will feed you, and clothe you, and give you money.

90. And he who feeds you, or clothes you, or gives you money, shall in nowise lose his reward:

91. And he that doeth not these things is not my disciple; by this you may know my disciples.

92. He that receiveth you not, go away from him alone by yourselves, and cleanse your feet even with water, pure water, whether in heat or in cold, and bear testimony of it unto your Father which is in heaven, and return not again unto that man.

93. And in whatsoever village or city ye enter, do likewise.

94. Nevertheless, search diligently and spare not; and wo unto that house, or that village or city that rejecteth you, or your words, or your testimony concerning me.

95. Wo, I say again, unto that house, or that village or city that rejecteth you, or your words, or your testimony of me;

96. For I, the Almighty, have laid my hands upon the nations, to scourge them for their wickedness:

97. And plagues shall go forth, and they shall not be taken from the earth until I have completed my work which shall be cut short in righteousness,

98. Until all shall know me, who remain, even from the least unto the greatest, and shall be filled with

D&C 84:92–94—The emissaries of the Lord participate in the ultimate judgment process. They are to bear witness to the Father concerning those who reject the word. They will be called forth on the Day of Judgment to confirm their witness. The feeling of joy and gladness among the missionaries does not flow from the experience of being rejected, but from the knowledge that they have been faithful in their duties. Even in the case of those who reject the word, the missionaries can rejoice at having represented the truth of the gospel with honor and dignity.

D&C 84:98—The Lord reveals the text of a new song of redemption that will be sung by those who remain after the judgments of God have gone forth in the final phase of the world's history. It is a magnificent anthem of redemption, grace, covenant fulfillment, the bringing together of all things in one, strength, truth, glory, honor, power, might, mercy—all the transcendent themes and principles that pertain to the celestial state of Zion within the millennial kingdom of God.

THE OATH AND COVENANT OF THE PRIESTHOOD

An oath, as it pertains to Deity, is a sworn statement or promise of the Lord describing that which will be or will come to pass. When the Melchizedek Priesthood is conferred upon a man, he receives the oath and covenant of the Father (see D&C 84:40).

The oath that the Father makes is that the faithful Melchizedek Priesthood holder will be given all that the Father hath (see D&C 84:38).

The covenant into which the priesthood holder enters is two-fold (see D&C 84:33):

a. He promises to be faithful

b. He promises to magnify his calling

Those who enter into the oath and covenant of the priesthood and "breaketh this covenant after he hath received it, and altogether turneth therefrom, shall not have forgiveness of sins in this world nor in the world to come" (D&C 84:41). This penalty means they will lose the privilege of bearing the priesthood in eternity. President Joseph Fielding Smith taught:

That does *not* mean that man is going to become a son of perdition, but the meaning is that *he will never again have the opportunity of exercising the priesthood and reaching exaltation*. That is where his forgiveness ends. He will not again have the priesthood conferred upon him, because he has trampled it under his feet; but as far as other things are concerned, he may be forgiven. (*DS* 3:141–142.) (*STDC* 2:73–76.)

the knowledge of the Lord, and shall see eye to eye, and shall lift up their voice, and with the voice together sing this new song, saying—

99.   The Lord hath brought again Zion
     The Lord hath redeemed his people, Israel,
     According to the election of grace,
     Which was brought to pass by the faith
     And covenant of their fathers.

100.   The Lord hath redeemed his people,
     And Satan is bound and time is no longer:
     The Lord hath gathered all things in one:
     The Lord hath brought down Zion from
         above.
     The Lord hath brought up Zion from beneath.

101.   The earth hath travailed and brought forth
         her strength:
     And truth is established in her bowels:
     And the heavens have smiled upon her:
     And she is clothed with the glory of her God:
     For he stands in the midst of his people:

102.   Glory, and honor, and power, and might,
     Be ascribed to our God; for he is full of mercy,
     Justice, grace and truth, and peace,
     Forever and ever, Amen.

103. And again, verily, verily, I say unto you, it is expedient that every man who goes forth to proclaim mine everlasting gospel, that inasmuch as they have families and receive money by gift, that they should send it unto them or make use of it for their benefit, as the Lord shall direct them, for thus it seemeth me good.

104. And let all those who have not families, who receive monies, send it up unto the Bishop in Zion, or unto the Bishop in Ohio, that it may be consecrated for the bringing forth of the revelations and the printing thereof, and for establishing Zion.

105. And if any man shall give unto any of you a coat, or a suit, take the old and cast it unto the poor, and go your way rejoicing.

106. And if any man among you be strong in the Spirit, let him take with him him that is weak, that he may be edified in all meekness, that he may become strong also.

107. Therefore, take with you those who are ordained unto the lesser priesthood, and send them before you to make appointments, and to prepare the way, and to fill appointments that you yourselves are not able to fill.

108. Behold, this is the way that mine apostles, in ancient days, built up my church unto me.

109. Therefore, let every man stand in his own office, and labor in his own calling; and let not the head say unto the feet, it hath no need of the feet, for without the feet how shall the body be able to stand?

D&C 84:106, 109–110—The Lord looks on the process of building the kingdom of God through the eyes of mercy and compassion. He loves His children and includes in the design of heaven a plan for caring for them, nurturing them, providing for their needs through the principle of sacrifice and consecration. The strong are to succor the weak and lift them up. The Lord gives strength and talents to His followers so that the body of Christ might be unified and edified.

PRIESTHOOD LINEAGE

Any authorized servant of the Lord can trace his priesthood lineage back to the Master. The Lord revealed in this section that Moses did not simply assume his authority; instead, the authority of the priesthood was given to him by one having that authority. This process is revealed by the Lord as having extended back to Adam (see D&C 84:6–16).

As it was in ancient times, so it is today. Priesthood holders in the Lord's church can identify the source of their authority. The Lord sent messengers from heaven in this dispensation to confer priesthood authority upon the Lord's designated representatives. These men, in turn, bestowed that authority upon other righteous men according to the Lord's pattern, and this process continues in the Church today. Every official and authorized act or ordinance performed by a priesthood holder has the same efficacy as if the Lord performed it. Therefore, those who perform as well as those who receive ordinances and blessings under the authority of the priesthood realize that such experiences are appropriately done by the authority of the Master.

The Lord informs us that there was no man to bestow the priesthood upon Adam, since he was first. He received his priesthood from the Lord.

110. Also the body hath need of every member, that all may be edified together, that the system may be kept perfect.

111. And behold the High Priests should travel, and also the elders, and also the lesser priests; but the deacons and teachers should be appointed to watch over the church, to be standing ministers unto the church.

112. And the bishop, Newel K. Whitney, also should travel round about and among all the churches, searching after the poor to administer to their wants by humbling the rich and the proud;

113. He should also employ an agent to take charge and to do his secular business as he shall direct;

114. Nevertheless, let the bishop go unto the city of New York, also to the city of Albany, and also to the city of Boston, and warn the people of those cities with the sound of the gospel, with a loud voice, of the desolation and utter abolishment which await them if they do reject these things;

115. For if they do reject these things the hour of their judgment is nigh, and their house shall be left unto them desolate.

116. Let him trust in me and he shall not be confounded; and an hair of his head shall not fall to the ground unnoticed.

117. And verily I say unto you, the rest of my servants, go ye forth as your circumstances shall permit, in your several callings unto the great and notable cities and villages, reproving the world in righteousness of all their unrighteous and ungodly deeds, setting forth clearly and understandingly the desolation of abomination in the last days;

118. For, with you saith the Lord Almighty, I will rend their kingdoms: I will not only shake the earth, but the starry heavens shall tremble;

119. For I, the Lord, have put forth my hand to exert the powers of heaven; ye cannot see it now, yet a little while and ye shall see it, and know that I am, and that I will come and reign with my people.

120. I am Alpha and Omega, the beginning and the end. Amen.

D&C 84:117—Clearly the message of the servants of the Lord is twofold: joy and hope in the gospel of Jesus Christ, but also the warning voice concerning the judgments of God that lie ahead. Author Hoyt Brewster, Jr., explains the term *desolation of abomination* used in this verse:

> The phrase *desolation of abomination* appears twice in the Doctrine and Covenants (84:117; 88:85) and is similar to the terms *abomination of desolation* (Matt. 24:15; JS–M 1:12, 32) and *the abomination that maketh desolate* (Dan 9:27; 12:11). . . . Therefore, in what is known as the desolation of abomination, the Lord will destroy those things which are hateful, wicked, or vile.
>
> The LDS Bible Dictionary indicates that "conditions of desolation, born of abomination and wickedness, were to occur *twice* in fulfillment of Daniel's words" (LDSBD, 601). The first of these was when Jerusalem was destroyed in A.D. 70, and the second is when the city will once again be besieged in the last days. It further states that "in a general sense, abomination of desolation also describes the latter-day judgments to be poured out upon the wicked wherever they may be." (DCE, 131.)

THE ORIGIN OF MAN

Adam was not a descendant of some other form of lower life. He did not evolve. He was born as a son of God, the first man of all men upon this earth (see D&C 84:16; Moses 1:34; Luke 3:38).

Speaking of Adam, President Marion G. Romney said:

> It would please me immensely if . . . we could get away from using the language of those who do not believe in the mission of Adam. I have reference to words and phrases such as "primitive man," "prehistoric man," "before man learned to write," and the like. We sometimes use these terms in a way that offends my feelings. . . . There were no pre-Adamic men in the line of Adam. The Lord said that Adam was the first man. (Moses 1:34, 3:7; D&C 84:16.) It is hard for me to get the idea of a man ahead of Adam, before the first man. The Lord also said that Adam was the first flesh (Moses 3:7) which, as I understand it, means the first mortal on the earth. . . . I am not a scientist. I do not profess to know anything but Jesus Christ, and him crucified, and the principles of his gospel. If, however, there are some things in the strata of the earth indicating there were men before Adam, they were not the ancestors of Adam. (CR, April 1953, 123–124.) (STDC 2:70–71.)

SECTION 85

1. It is the duty of the Lord's clerk, whom he has appointed, to keep a history, and a General Church Record of all things that transpire in Zion, and of all those who consecrate properties, and receive inheritances legally from the bishop;

2. And also their manner of life, their faith, and works; and also of the apostates who apostatize after receiving their inheritances.

3. It is contrary to the will and commandment of God, that those who receive not their inheritance by consecration, agreeable to his law, which he has given, that he may tithe his people, to prepare them against the day of vengeance and burning, should have their names enrolled with the people of God;

4. Neither is their genealogy to be kept, or to be had where it may be found on any of the records or history of the church;

5. Their names shall not be found, neither the names of the fathers, nor the names of the children written in the book of the law of God, saith the Lord of Hosts.

6. Yea, thus saith the still small voice, which whispereth through and pierceth all things, and often times it maketh my bones to quake while it maketh manifest, saying:

7. And it shall come to pass that I, the Lord God, will send one mighty and strong, holding the scepter of power in his hand, clothed with light for a covering, whose mouth shall utter words, eternal words; while his bowels shall be a fountain of truth, to set in order the house of God, and to arrange by lot the inheritances of the saints, whose names are found, and the names of their fathers, and of their children, enrolled in the book of the law of God:

8. While that man, who was called of God and appointed, that putteth forth his hand to steady the ark of God, shall fall by the shaft of death, like as a tree that is smitten by the vivid shaft of lightning;

9. And all they who are not found written in the book of remembrance shall find none inheritance in that day, but they shall be cut asunder, and their portion shall be appointed them among unbelievers, where are wailing and gnashing of teeth.

10. These things I say not of myself; therefore, as the Lord speaketh, he will also fulfil.

11. And they who are of the High Priesthood, whose names are not found written in the book of the law, or that are found to have apostatized, or to have been cut off from the church; as well as the lesser priesthood, or the members, in that day, shall not find an inheritance among the saints of the Most High;

Section 85 Background—Given November 27, 1832, in the Newel K. Whitney Store at Kirtland, Ohio (see *HC* 1:298–299). This section of the Doctrine and Covenants is an excerpt from a letter written by the Prophet to W. W. Phelps, who was then living in Independence, Missouri. Much of it is instruction for John Whitmer, the Church historian. It was given in response to questions about those Saints who had moved to Missouri (Zion), but who had not received their inheritances according to the pattern established by the Church. This section is evidence of the strict record-keeping procedures that the Prophet was directed to implement in order to ensure order and continuity within the kingdom of God.

D&C 85:1–5—The Lord knows our every thought, word, and deed. Covenant doctrine calls for accountability. The record of our manner of life, faith, and works substantiates our alignment with the word of God—or our departure therefrom. On the basis of our obedience and covenant valor we can expect to receive our reward. In the case of the word of the Lord to His Saints of the early Restoration, it is clear that those who did not act "agreeable to His law" (verse 3) were not to be a part of the record of the Church—in other words, were not written in "the book of the law of the God." The Lord knew that there would be some among them who would falter; some who would come to Zion not willing to enroll themselves and consecrate themselves and their property to the welfare of Zion, and therefore could not be given stewardships in the covenant that the Lord had made with the Saints. He, therefore, commanded that all those who came to Zion and who were not willing to receive an inheritance should not be numbered among the faithful.

D&C 85:6–9—An article published in 1907 by the First Presidency (Joseph F. Smith, John R. Winder, and Anthon H. Lund) sheds light on the substance of these verses. The man "who was called of God and appointed" was Bishop Edward Partridge, who at the time of the revelation in 1832 was not embracing his office with full devotion and hence was guilty of "putting forth his hand to steady the ark of God." The reference is to the incident in the Old Testament where David, having defeated the Philistines, was overseeing the return of the ark of the covenant on a cart bound for Jerusalem. When at one point the motion of the oxen was causing the ark to shake, a man named Uzzah reached out to steady the ark and was struck down by the Lord (see 2 Sam. 6:1–7). Bishop Partridge was instructed in no uncertain terms to withdraw any initiative that would be contrary to the revealed principles for regulating the consecrations in Zion, for the Lord did not need him to "steady the ark." Failing to carry on his calling with honor would cause him to "fall by the shaft of death."

Bishop Partridge, in fact, did take steps to reform his ways. He endured vicious persecution in Missouri and stepped forward with great courage in 1833 to offer himself as a sacrifice for the Saints.

12. Therefore it shall be done unto them as unto the children of the priest, as will be found recorded in the second chapter and sixty-first and second verses of Ezra.

SECTION 86

1. Verily, thus saith the Lord unto you my servants, concerning the parable of the wheat and of the tares.
2. Behold, verily I say, the field was the world, and the apostles were the sowers of the seed;
3. And after they have fallen asleep the great persecutor of the church, the apostate, the whore, even Babylon, that maketh all nations to drink of her cup, in whose hearts the enemy, even Satan, sitteth to reign, behold he soweth the tares, wherefore the tares choke the wheat and drive the church into the wilderness.
4. But behold, in the last days, even now while the Lord is beginning to bring forth the word, and the blade is springing up and is yet tender.
5. Behold, verily I say unto you, the angels are crying unto the Lord day and night, who are ready and waiting to be sent forth to reap down the fields;
6. But the Lord saith unto them, pluck not up the tares while the blade is yet tender, (for verily your faith is weak,) lest you destroy the wheat also.
7. Therefore, let the wheat and the tares grow together until the harvest is fully ripe, then ye shall first gather out the wheat from among the tares, and after the gathering of the wheat, behold and lo! the tares are bound in bundles, and the field remaineth to be burned.
8. Therefore, thus saith the Lord unto you, with whom the Priesthood hath continued through the lineage of your fathers,
9. For ye are lawful heirs, according to the flesh, and have been hid from the world with Christ in God;
10. Therefore your life and the priesthood haveth remained, and must needs remain through you and your lineage, until the restoration of all things spoken by the mouths of all the holy prophets since the world began.

Section 86 Background—Given at Kirtland, Ohio, December 6, 1832, while the Prophet Joseph Smith was reviewing and refining the draft of the inspired translation of the Bible. The Prophet wrote this introductory statement: "On the 6th of December, 1832, I received the following revelation [Section 86] explaining the parable of the wheat and tares" (HC 1:300). A parable is a short story that illustrates a spiritual truth. By way of explanation, tares have been identified with the darnel weed, which grows in Palestine; it resembles wheat when young, but is bitter and poisonous when mature.

D&C 86:3—The phrase "fallen asleep" refers to the death of the apostles. "Tares" refers to evil doctrine. And Babylon is a symbol of worldliness and evil, representing the devil's power. The phrase "drive the church into the wilderness" refers to the Great Apostasy.

D&C 86:5—In 1894, during the dedication of the Salt Lake Temple, President Wilford Woodruff said that the angels have left the portals of heaven and are hovering over us; those who will reap are anxiously waiting for permission to do so. It is those angels who are causing calamities and troubles; for example, the indexed number of wars rose from 2.678 in the 12th century to 13,735.98 in the first 25 years of the 20th century. (The index number is calculated using five factors: the duration of the war, the size of the armies, the number of casualties, the number of countries involved, and the proportion of the army to the total population.) In referring to these calamities, President Joseph Fielding Smith said that there is still to be a conflict more horrible than any the world has ever seen.

D&C 86:9—Regarding the concept of being "lawful heirs," one's right to the priesthood comes as a result of being of the House of Israel through lineage.

SOWING AND REAPING

The parable of the wheat and the tares represents the teaching of the gospel of Jesus Christ to the people of the world. That teaching effort is symbolized by the sowing of the good seed (wheat). In the midst of this effort, Satan teaches his false doctrine in opposition to truth, efforts that are symbolized by the sowing of the tares.

There have been two sowings of the good seed. The first sowing was the teaching of the gospel during the Savior's mortal ministry (see D&C 86:2). Because of Satan's false teachings, an apostasy occurred, symbolized by the tares choking the wheat and the church being driving into the wilderness (see D&C 86:3).

The second sowing is the restoration of the gospel to the earth in the last days, the dispensation of the fullness of times (see D&C 86:4). Once again, Lucifer has sowed his false doctrine (tares) in opposition to the Lord's work. Because this apostate influence is among the Lord's people, the angels of heaven are desirous of cleansing the earth of evil doctrines and practices (see D&C 86:5).

After the sowing of the seed and before the time of the harvest, there is a time for growing. The Savior warned against an attempt to harvest before the crop is mature (see D&C 86:6–7). In other words, we are warned against judging or categorizing the individual as to his spiritual worth before there has been adequate time for the distinction to be completely evident. No man is capable of determining the ultimate destiny of a human soul. Many changes may take place during the growing process that will affect the quality of the harvest, and it is a mistake to pre-judge or give up hope for anyone before the Lord's judgment is complete (STDC 2:86–87).

11. Therefore, blessed are ye if ye continue in my goodness, a light unto the Gentiles, and through this Priesthood, a savior unto my people Israel. The Lord hath said it. Amen.

SECTION 87

1. Verily, thus saith the Lord, concerning the wars that will shortly come to pass, beginning at the rebellion of South Carolina, which will eventually terminate in the death and misery of many souls.

2. The days will come that war will be poured out upon all nations, beginning at that place.

3. For behold, the Southern States shall be divided against the Northern States, and the Southern States will call on other nations, even the nation of Great Britain, as it is called, and they shall also call upon other nations, in order to defend themselves against other nations; and then war shall be poured out upon all nations.

4. And it shall come to pass, after many days, slaves shall rise up against their masters, who shall be marshalled and disciplined for war:

5. And it shall come to pass also, that the remnants who are left of the land will marshall themselves, and shall become exceedingly angry, and shall vex the Gentiles with a sore vexation;

6. And thus, with the sword, and by bloodshed, the inhabitants of the earth shall mourn; and with famine, and plague, and earthquake, and the thunder of heaven, and the fierce and vivid lightning also, shall the inhabitants of the earth be made to feel the wrath, and indignation and chastening hand of an Almighty God, until the consumption decreed, hath made a full end of all nations;

7. That the cry of the saints, and of the blood of the saints, shall cease to come up into the ears of the Lord of Sabaoth, from the earth, to be avenged of their enemies.

8. Wherefore, stand ye in holy places, and be not moved, until the day of the Lord come; for behold it cometh quickly, saith the Lord. Amen.

D&C 86:11—Elder Melvin J. Ballard explains the implications of these passages of scripture:

> How great and wonderful is this promise, that through this Church and this Priesthood shall be restored ultimately all that has been predicted and prophesied of concerning the great things God would do for men: and that these things are to be fulfilled and realized in our time. The Latter-day Saints are a people with a mission and a destiny. . . . . We did not aspire to it, the Lord appointed it unto us, and the fulfillment of these promises surely can be and shall be realized in the Lord's own due time, and through his providing. (*CR*, Oct. 1924, 27–28.)

We are saviors as a result of both our missionary work and our work for the dead in the temples of the Lord.

Section 87 Background—Given on December 25, 1832 (see *HC* 1:301–302). The Prophet provided this introduction: "The people of South Carolina, in convention assembled (in November), passed ordinances, declaring their state a free and independent nation; and appointed Thursday, the 31st day of January, 1833, as a day of humiliation and prayer, to implore Almighty God to vouchsafe His blessings, and restore liberty and happiness within their borders. President Jackson issued his proclamation against this rebellion, called out a force sufficient to quell it, and implored the blessings of God to assist the nation to extricate itself from the horrors of the approaching and solemn crisis. On Christmas day [1832], I received the following revelation and prophecy on war" (*HC* 1:301).

D&C 87:1—South Carolina took the initiative by wanting to withdraw from the United States over the issue of tariffs, and the first shots of the Civil War were fired at Fort Sumter on April 12, 1861. This began an era of war that will last until the Second Coming of the Savior.

D&C 87:2—On November 10, 1860, South Carolina recalled her representatives in the U.S. Senate and then passed an ordinance of secession in the State Legislature on November 17. Before newly elected President Abraham Lincoln took office in 1861, seven southern states had seceded. On April 12, 1861, the first shots of the war were fired when Confederate forces attacked a military base at Fort Sumter, South Carolina. The prophecy concerning the Civil War, given on December 25, 1832, had become reality.

D&C 87:4—According to Elder Joseph B. Wirthlin, this verse refers to slaves all over the world, especially in areas where freedom is extremely restricted.

D&C 87:5–8—How can the Saints prepare themselves for the calamities that are to come? By obedience to the Lord's commandment to stand in holy places and be not moved (verse 8; see also D&C 45:32; 101:22).

SECTION 88

1. Verily, thus saith the Lord unto you who have assembled yourselves together to receive his will concerning you.

2. Behold, this is pleasing unto your Lord, and the angels rejoice over you; the alms of your prayers have come up into the ears of the Lord of Sabaoth, and are recorded in the book of the names of the sanctified: even them of the celestial world.

3. Wherefore, I now send upon you another Comforter, even upon you my friends, that it may abide in your hearts, even the Holy Spirit of promise; which other Comforter is the same that I promised unto my disciples, as is recorded in the testimony of John.

4. This Comforter is the promise which I give unto you of eternal life; even the glory of the celestial kingdom:

5. Which glory is that of the church of the first born, even of God, the holiest of all, through Jesus Christ his Son.

6. He that ascended up on high, as also he descended below all things; in that he comprehended all things, that he might be in all and through all things, the light of truth;

7. Which truth shineth. This is the light of Christ. As also he is in the

Section 88 Background—Given on December 27–28, 1832 (verses 1–126), and January 3, 1833 (verses 127–141), in the translating room at the Whitney Store in Kirtland, Ohio (see HC 1:302–312). Ten brethren (Joseph Smith Jr., Joseph Smith Sr., Sidney Rigdon, Orson Hyde, Hyrum Smith, Samuel H. Smith, Newel K. Whitney, Frederick G. Williams, Ezra Thayer, and John Murdock) attended this conference of high priests. One of the best-known of all revelations, it contains sublime doctrine on many key topics and gives new commandments to the Saints, such as to call a solemn assembly, build the Kirtland Temple, establish the School of the Prophets, and institute the ordinance of washing of feet.

That it was a key revelation is evident from the tone and content of the Prophet's personal correspondence and letters to the brethren in Missouri following this event. Joseph wrote to W. W. Phelps in Missouri on January 14, 1833, and described this revelation as follows: "I send you the 'olive leaf' which we have plucked from the Tree of Paradise, the Lord's message of peace to us. . . ; we have the satisfaction of knowing that the Lord approves of us, and has accepted us and established His name in Kirtland for the salvation of the nations; for the Lord will have a place whence His word will go forth, in these last days, in purity" (HC 1:316).

D&C 88:3—In a manner of speaking, this supreme gift of truth is the culmination of a divine sequence that forms a spectrum of blessings leading to salvation and eternal life—all manifestations of the light of Christ, who is the eternal King of glory. The power of the elements constituting this remarkable spectrum of light and truth lifts the obedient—those who are "holy and without blame" (Eph. 1:4)—even to the footstool of Deity, where they are privileged to receive an even higher blessing of comfort. This higher manifestation of comfort comes in the person of the Savior Himself, the Advocate with the Father who can unfold ultimate visions of light and truth for those who are joint-heirs with Him in the celestial realm (see Rom. 8:17). It is Jesus Christ personally who is the "Second Comforter."

D&C 88:7–13—This glorious revelation of truth gives us an inkling of the how the universe and all intelligence in it is governed and illuminated by the power of God in the form of divine light, even the light of Christ. This light sustains the physical operation of the universe and the vitality of all living forms therein; it also empowers our reasoning and understanding and underlies and informs the process of spiritual unfolding for all of God's children.

How humbling and enthralling is the commission given to mankind to receive this light, life, and truth with openness of heart and willingness of mind, that we may learn God's will and act in accordance with it. The Atonement of Jesus Christ was and is an act of light, life, and truth. It is available to all. We are immersed in the heavenly illumination of that eternal blessing and need only receive it with full devotion to make it instantly part of our lives.

The immediate availability of divine light and blessings in our lives is a breathtaking phenomenon. In a simple analogy, we might think of the everyday practice in

sun, and the light of the sun, and the power thereof by which it was made.

8. As also he is in the moon and is the light of the moon, and the power thereof by which it was made.

9. As also the light of the stars, and the power thereof by which they were made.

10. And the earth also, and the power thereof; even the earth upon which you stand.

11. And the light which now shineth, which giveth you light, is through him who enlighteneth your eyes, which is the same light that quickeneth your understandings;

12. Which light proceedeth forth from the presence of God to fill the immensity of space.

13. The light which is in all things; which giveth life to all things: which is the law by which all things are governed: even the power of God who sitteth upon his throne, who is in the bosom of eternity, who is in the midst of all things.

14. Now, verily I say unto you, that through the redemption which is made for you is brought to pass the resurrection from the dead.

15. And the spirit and the body is the soul of man.

16. And the resurrection from the dead is the redemption of the soul;

17. And the redemption of the soul is through him that quickeneth all things, in whose bosom it is decreed that the poor and the meek of the earth shall inherit it.

18. Therefore it must needs be sanctified from all unrighteousness, that it may be prepared for the celestial glory;

19. For after it hath filled the measure of its creation, it shall be crowned with glory, even with the presence of God the Father;

20. That bodies who are of the celestial kingdom may possess it for ever and ever; for, for this intent was it made and created, and for this intent are they sanctified.

21. And they who are not sanctified through the law which I have given unto you, even the law of Christ, must inherit another kingdom, even that of a terrestrial kingdom, or that of a telestial kingdom.

22. For he who is not able to abide the law of a celestial kingdom, cannot abide a celestial glory.

23. And he who cannot abide the law of a terrestrial kingdom, cannot abide a terrestrial glory:

24. And he who cannot abide the law of a telestial kingdom, cannot abide a telestial glory; therefore he is not meet for a kingdom of glory. Therefore he must abide a kingdom which is not a kingdom of glory.

25. And again, verily I say unto

modern life of "tuning in" to the radio waves pervasive all around us and receiving information with the flip of a switch. Is the light of Christ any less accessible? All He asks is that we turn to Him in faith and devotion—and He will immediately enlighten our lives with blessings of glory. "And behold, all that he requires of you is to keep his commandments; and he has promised you that if ye would keep his commandments ye should prosper in the land; and he never doth vary from that which he hath said; therefore, if ye do keep his commandments he doth bless you and prosper you" (Mosiah 2:22).

D&C 88:10—The earth will become pure and will become the dwelling place of gods.

D&C 88:14–15—The light of Christ—which all men receive and by which all men are guided—empowers the resurrection, the essential step forward in the life of every human being whereby the body is restored and reunited with the spirit to form "the soul of man" (verse 15), and thus enabled to receive a fullness of joy (see D&C 93:34). The resurrection of the body is the gateway to a state of liberation from the ills and infirmities of the mortal realm, a great emancipation from disease, deformity, and decay.

D&C 88:17–19—Just as the children of God are to be sanctified and prepared for a celestial inheritance, the earth, too, is to be sanctified and prepared as the abode for celestial beings who merit an inheritance in the glory of God. This parallel process unfolds under the governing Kingship of the Lord Jesus Christ—the preparation of the ultimate Promised Land and the purification and sanctification of the citizens thereof according to celestial principles and laws. The supreme objective is to achieve "the presence of God the Father" (verse 19) in a state of everlasting glory.

D&C 88:22, 28—Individuals will be assigned to a kingdom according to their level of righteousness and valor— whether to a celestial glory, a terrestrial glory, a telestial glory, or (for the sons of perdition—D&C 76:32, 43) to a kingdom not of glory. Those assigned to a kingdom of glory will be resurrected with bodies that are quickened by the glory of that kingdom. James E. Talmage says that if we can't meet celestial requirements, we will not be able to live comfortably in the celestial kingdom (and so on). Those of the celestial kingdom "are gods, even the sons of God—Wherefore, all things are theirs, whether life or death, or things present, or things to come, all are theirs and they are Christ's, and Christ is God's. And they shall overcome all things" (D&C 76:58–60). These concepts open up a rich view of the promised destiny of the faithful and remind us of the ultimate promise given of the Father to allow His children to gain admittance into His presence and that of the Son, "through the merits, and mercy, and grace of the Holy Messiah" (2 Ne. 2:8).

you, the earth abideth the law of a celestial kingdom, for it filleth the measure of its creation, and transgresseth not the law.

26. Wherefore it shall be sanctified; yea, notwithstanding it shall die, it shall be quickened again, and shall abide the power by which it is quickened, and the righteous shall inherit it:

27. For notwithstanding they die, they also shall rise again a spiritual body:

28. They who are of a celestial spirit shall receive the same body which was a natural body; even ye shall receive your bodies, and your glory shall be that glory by which your bodies are quickened.

29. Ye who are quickened by a portion of the celestial glory shall then receive of the same, even a fulness;

30. And they who are quickened by a portion of the terrestrial glory, shall then receive of the same, even a fulness:

31. And also they who are quickened by a portion of the telestial glory shall then receive of the same, even a fulness;

32. And they who remain shall also be quickened; nevertheless they shall return again to their own place, to enjoy that which they are willing to receive, because they were not willing to enjoy that which they might have received.

33. For what doth it profit a man if a gift is bestowed upon him, and he receiveth not the gift? Behold, he rejoices not in that which is given unto him, neither rejoices in him who is the giver of the gift.

34. And again, verily I say unto you, that which is governed by law is also preserved by law, and perfected and sanctified by the same.

35. That which breaketh a law, and abideth not by law, but seeketh to become a law unto itself, and willeth to abide in sin, and altogether abideth in sin, cannot be sanctified by law, neither by mercy, justice, nor judgment. Therefore they must remain filthy still.

36. All kingdoms have a law given:

37. And there are many kingdoms; for there is no space in the which there is no kingdom; and there is no kingdom in which there is no space, either a greater or a lesser kingdom.

38. And unto every kingdom is given a law; and unto every law there are certain bounds also and conditions.

39. All beings who abide not in those conditions are not justified;

40. For intelligence cleaveth unto intelligence; wisdom receiveth wisdom; truth embraceth truth; virtue loveth virtue; light cleaveth unto light; mercy hath compassion on mercy, and claimeth her own; justice continueth its course, and

D&C 88:34–35—To be "perfect in Christ" (Moroni 10:32) is possible through enduring adherence to divine law; to be damned is the result of the willful and persistent violation of divine law. The individual who rejects the opportunity to rise to a state of glory will be denied such a state and forfeit the joy that might have been his through obedience and the beneficence of God. Author Truman Madsen explains the implications:

> In the realm of the good, as elsewhere, light is the "bound and condition" of all preferred ways of life. And these bounds and conditions are inexorable and exceptionless, not because they tell us what our choices must be but because they tell us what the *results* of our choices will be. Of course, one can attempt to "become a law unto [himself]" (D&C 88:35), but only at the cost of diminishing the light. Every minute of every day we are increasing or decreasing in our receptivity to light, and there is no way to escape the inevitability of that consequence in our thoughts, our acts, our very breath. One can look upon the law of light either as the enemy of freedom or as freedom's guarantee, which "is preserved by law and sanctified by the same" (D&C 88:34). One can abide the law only as one can abide the light, and vice versa.
>
> . . . Christ is the true light that is in us, even when we turn our backs on Him. He himself became God by abiding in the light. And even God is bound by the law. (*RL*, 25–26.)

D&C 88:38–41—Our environment of existence operates on the basis of laws given by the Almighty. We do not live in an environment of chance and accident. Our forward motion is within the "bounds and conditions" of the laws that apply to our "kingdom." We are "justified" by abiding by the laws that pertain to us. Bonds and affinities emerge on the basis of laws: intelligence, wisdom, truth, virtue, light, mercy, and justice are attracted, each to its own kind, just as with magnetic attraction in the physical world or the power of gravitational pull. The kingdom of God is to be a unifying force as the Saints abide by the laws that pertain to it, for "if ye are not one ye are not mine" (D&C 38:27). Concerning laws, the Prophet Joseph Smith taught:

> If, then, we admit that God is the source of all wisdom and understanding, we must admit that by His direct inspiration He has taught man that law is necessary in order to govern and regulate His own immediate interest and welfare; for this reason, that law is beneficial to promote peace and happiness among men. And as before remarked, God is the source from whence proceeds all good; and if man is benefited by law, then certainly, law is good; and if law is good, then law, or the principle of it emanated from God; for God is the source of all good; consequently, then, he was the first Author of law, or the principle of it, to mankind. (*TPJS*, 55–56.)

claimeth its own; judgment goeth before the face of him who sitteth upon the throne, and governeth and executeth all things;

41. He comprehendeth all things, and all things are before him, and all things are round about him: and he is above all things, and in all things, and is through all things, and is round about all things; and all things are by him, and of him, even God, for ever and ever.

42. And again, verily I say unto you, he hath given a law unto all things by which they move in their times and their seasons;

43. And their courses are fixed, even the courses of the heavens and the earth, which comprehend the earth and all the planets;

44. And they give light to each other in their times and in their seasons, in their minutes, in their hours, in their days, in their weeks, in their months, in their years: all these are one year with God, but not with man.

45. The earth rolls upon her wings, and the sun giveth his light by day, and the moon giveth her light by night, and the stars also giveth their light, as they roll upon their wings in their glory, in the midst of the power of God.

46. Unto what shall I liken these kingdoms, that ye may understand?

47. Behold, all these are kingdoms, and any man who hath seen any or the least of these, hath seen God moving in his majesty and power.

48. I say unto you, he hath seen him; nevertheless, he who came unto his own was not comprehended.

49. The light shineth in darkness, and the darkness comprehendeth it not; nevertheless, the day shall come when you shall comprehend even God; being quickened in him and by him.

50. Then shall ye know that ye have seen me, that I am, and that I am the true light that is in you, and that you are in me, otherwise ye could not abound.

51. Behold, I will liken these kingdoms unto a man having a field, and he sent forth his servants into the field to dig in the field;

52. And he said unto the first, go ye and labor in the field, and in the first hour I will come unto you, and ye shall behold the joy of my countenance;

53. And he said unto the second, go ye also into the field, and in the second hour I will visit you with the joy of my countenance;

54. And also unto the third saying, I will visit you;

55. And unto the fourth, and so on unto the twelfth.

56. And the lord of the field went unto the first in the first hour, and tarried with him all that hour, and he was made glad with the light of the countenance of his lord;

57. And then he withdrew from the first that he might visit the second also, and the third, and the fourth, and so on unto the twelfth;

58. And thus they all received the light of the countenance of their lord; every man in his hour, and in his time, and in his season;

59. Beginning at the first, and so on unto the last, and from the last unto the first, and from the first unto the last;

60. Every man in his own order,

D&C 88:42–47—In truth, the miraculous operation of the universe in accordance with divine law is another testament of Jesus Christ—just as the word of God given in the holy scriptures and by the voice of living prophets confirms the reality of the Redeemer and Savior.

To see the evidence of universal laws in operation is a confirmation of our faith in the orderly process of spiritual development. We have faith that the Lord can redeem us through the Atonement, for we discern, line upon line and precept upon precept, the operation of divine principles of perfection at work in our own lives—just as in the physical universe around us. It is all from the same eternal hand; it is all a unified blending of eternal principles. We are not adrift on a sea of chaos. We are in the hands of the Master of order and purpose, glory and eternal joy. But we have a solemn obligation to abide by the laws laid down for the achievement of our divine potential as sons and daughters of God and "joint-heirs with Christ" (Rom. 8:17). In this way we are "justified" by abiding by given laws through the grace and merits of the Savior—and we can thus look forward to "the riches of eternity" (D&C 38:39; 78:18).

D&C 88:49–50—Here is a supernal promise from the Lord—that we will one day be quickened in Him and by Him so as to comprehend Him as the "true light" (verse 50) that is in us, and that we are in Him—enabling and empowering us to "abound." The word *abound* comes from the Latin word "abundare," meaning to "overflow." The implication is to be abundant, or fully and completely filled, hence capable of unfolding to the full extent of our potential.

THE RESURRECTION OF THE EARTH

A unique doctrine contained in this section pertains to the earth as a living entity that will eventually die and be resurrected (see D&C 88:25–26). From the earth comes life for all things that grow thereon. President Heber C. Kimball taught:

> [The earth] has a spirit as much as any body has a spirit. How can anything live, except it has a living spirit? How can the earth produce vegetation, fruits, trees, and every kind of production, if there is no life in it? It could not, any more than a woman could produce children when she is dead. . . . (*JD* 5:172.)

In its resurrected state, the earth will be a celestial dwelling place for celestial beings (see D&C 88:17–26). During the flood, it was baptized with water; at the Second Coming, it will be baptized with fire and with the power of the Holy Ghost. As President Joseph Fielding Smith taught, the earth will die, be dissolved, pass away, and then it will be renewed, or raised with a resurrection (see *DS* 1:87–88) (*STDC* 2:108–109).

until his hour was finished, even according as his lord had commanded him, that his lord might be glorified in him, and he in him, that they all might be glorified.

61. Therefore, unto this parable I will liken all these kingdoms, and the inhabitants thereof; every kingdom in its hour, and in its time, and in its season; even according to the decree which God hath made.

62. And again, verily I say unto you, my friends, I leave these sayings with you, to ponder in your hearts, with this commandment which I give unto you, that ye shall call upon me while I am near;

63. Draw near unto me and I will draw near unto you: seek me diligently and ye shall find me; ask and ye shall receive; knock and it shall be opened unto you;

64. Whatsoever ye ask the Father in my name it shall be given unto you, that is expedient for you;

65. And if ye ask anything that is not expedient for you, it shall turn unto your condemnation.

66. Behold, that which you hear is as the voice of one crying in the wilderness—in the wilderness, because you cannot see him—my voice, because my voice is Spirit; my Spirit is truth; truth abideth and hath no end; and if it be in you it shall abound.

67. And if your eye be single to my glory, your whole bodies shall be filled with light, and there shall be no darkness in you, and that body which is filled with light comprehendeth all things.

68. Therefore sanctify yourselves that your minds become single to God, and the days will come that you shall see him; for he will unvail his face unto you, and it shall be in his own time, and in his own way, and according to his own will.

69. Remember the great and last promise which I have made unto you; cast away your idle thoughts and your excess of laughter far from you;

70. Tarry ye, tarry ye in this place, and call a solemn assembly even of those who are the first laborers in this last kingdom;

71. And let those whom they have warned in their traveling, call on the Lord, and ponder the warning in their hearts which they have received for a little season.

72. Behold, and lo! I will take care of your flocks, and will raise up elders and send unto them.

73. Behold, I will hasten my work in its time;

D&C 88:62–65—As we draw near to the Lord, He gives us answers to our prayers in the form of personal revelation. Such a gift of guidance through the Holy Spirit is conditioned on our faith and comes in accordance with our spiritual preparation and worthiness. We are to ask in harmony with the will of the Lord. Asking for things that are "not expedient" will turn to our condemnation.

In his dedicatory prayer in the Kirtland Temple, the Prophet Joseph Smith implored: "But thy word must be fulfilled. Help thy servants to say, with thy grace assisting them: Thy will be done, O Lord, and not ours" (D&C 109:44). As we seek to be directed by the Spirit in our prayers, we will always desire that the Lord's will be done—in His own way and in His own due time (see D&C 67:14; 136:18). Then He will respond with blessings in abundance. This is a universal promise.

D&C 88:66—To take the word of the Lord into our heart is to plant the seed of faith, as Alma counseled (Alma 32). The Spirit is the nurturing force of divine influence that causes the word of God to swell within us and grow, by stages, into a tree of life whose fruit is eternal life.

D&C 88:67–68—Section 88 is a continuous array of divine promises and prophecies of unspeakable glory—almost unfathomable in their implications and eternal consequences for mankind. These promises are formulated consistently as covenant arrangements: divine blessings predicated upon our obedience—with our thoughts, desires, and deeds fully aligned with the will of God. In the verses just cited, we are to sanctify ourselves, with our minds and eyes being single to the glory of God; then we shall be filled with light and hence enabled to comprehend all things and see the face of God in His own due time. Scholars Joseph Fielding McConkie and Robert L. Millet explain this principle:

> If our eye or mind or soul is single to the glory of God; if our desires, our ambitions, our hopes and dreams are centered in the things of righteousness; if our greatest reason for serving is to build up the kingdom of God and establish in the earth the righteousness of God—if we are thus centered, then we will be spiritually transparent, the light of the Spirit of Almighty God will shine through us and we shall be a light to the world. If our will is subject to the will of heaven, then there is in us no hindrance to the power and glory, the light, of the Father; others will see him in our countenances. Those who have and maintain an eye single to the glory of God are on that path which allows them now to see and understand things that are mysterious to the worldly and that will lead them, in the Lord's due time, to that highest of spiritual rewards—the privilege of seeing him face to face. (*DCBM* 4:87.)

74. And I give unto you, who are the first laborers in this last kingdom, a commandment that you assemble yourselves together, and organize yourselves, and prepare yourselves, and sanctify yourselves; yea, purify your hearts, and cleanse your hands and your feet before me, that I may make you clean;

75. That I may testify unto your Father, and your God, and my God, that you are clean from the blood of this wicked generation: that I may fulfil this promise, this great and last promise, which I have made unto you, when I will.

76. Also, I give unto you a commandment, that ye shall continue in prayer and fasting from this time forth.

77. And I give unto you a commandment, that you shall teach one another the doctrine of the kingdom;

78. Teach ye diligently and my grace shall attend you, that you may be instructed more perfectly in theory, in principle, in doctrine, in the law of the gospel, in all things that pertain unto the kingdom of God, that are expedient for you to understand;

79. Of things both in heaven and in the earth, and under the earth; things which have been, things which are, things which must shortly come to pass; things which are at home, things which are abroad; the wars and the perplexities of the nations, and the judgments which are on the land, and a knowledge also of countries and of kingdoms,

80. That ye may be prepared in all things when I shall send you again to magnify the calling whereunto I have called you, and the mission with which I have commissioned you.

81. Behold, I sent you out to testify and warn the people, and it becometh every man who hath been warned, to warn his neighbor.

82. Therefore, they are left without excuse, and their sins are upon their own heads.

83. He that seeketh me early shall find me, and shall not be forsaken.

84. Therefore, tarry ye, and labor diligently, that you may be perfected in your ministry to go forth among the Gentiles for the last time, as many as the mouth of the Lord shall name, to bind up the law and seal up the testimony, and to prepare the saints for the hour of judgment which is to come;

85. That their souls may escape the wrath of God, the desolation of abomination which awaits the wicked, both in this world and in the world to come. Verily, I say unto you, let those who are not the first

D&C 88:76—Fasting and prayer is important because there is some evil that cannot be overcome except through self-denial (fasting) and communication with God (prayer).

D&C 88:77–80—An important dimension of the Restoration was the establishment of an institutionalized process for systematic learning. The School of the Prophets in Kirtland was the earliest model of such a process, and continues to be an inspiration to devoted students of truth even today. The curriculum was centrally "the law of the gospel, in all things that pertain unto the kingdom of God, that are expedient for you to understand" (verse 78). The elders going forth on their missionary assignments were to be imbued with the spirit of the word of God. Their message was the message of the Restoration of the gospel of Jesus Christ for a world lying in sin and ill-prepared for the Second Coming.

D&C 88:79—In this verse, "in heaven" refers to astonomy; "under the earth" refers to geology and minerology; and "things which have been" refers to history. Both religious and secular knowledge are important if we are to be effective as ambassadors to the world.

D&C 88:81—This well-known maxim reminds us that we are all member missionaries—agents for salvation in the Lord's hands (see Alma 29:9–10). As members of the Church and as disciples of Jesus Christ, we have an obligation to stand as witnesses of Christ at all times and thus be approved of the Lord (see D&C 60:2–3).

D&C 88:84—Perfection can seem to be a remote and unattainable objective, but the Lord solemnly declares that the elders are to be "perfected" in their ministry—which is to commence without delay and continue without interruption. If the Lord will have it so, then it can be fulfilled according to His word. To "bind up the law and seal up the testimony" implies that the witness of the elders concerning the reception of their message of salvation among the people will stand as a binding testimony in the Day of Judgment. Concerning the house that rejects the Lord's word He had already said to the elders: ". . . and know this, that in the day of judgment you shall be judges of that house, and condemn them" (D&C 75:21). The Prophet Joseph Smith expanded on this theme:

> But when you are endowed and prepared to preach the Gospel to all nations, kindred, and tongues, in their own languages, you must faithfully warn all, and bind up the testimony, and seal up the law, and the destroying angel will follow close at your heels, and exercise his tremendous mission upon the children of disobedience; and destroy the workers of iniquity, while the Saints will be gathered out from among them, and stand in holy places ready to meet the Bridegroom when he comes. (HC 2:309.)

elders continue in the vineyard until the mouth of the Lord shall call them, for their time is not yet come; their garments are not clean from the blood of this generation.

86. Abide ye in the liberty wherewith ye are made free; entangle not yourselves in sin, but let your hands be clean, until the Lord comes;

87. For not many days hence and the earth shall tremble and reel to and fro as a drunken man, and the sun shall hide his face, and shall refuse to give light, and the moon shall be bathed in blood, and the stars shall become exceeding angry, and shall cast themselves down as a fig that falleth from off a fig tree.

88. And after your testimony cometh wrath and indignation upon the people;

89. For after your testimony cometh the testimony of earthquakes, that shall cause groanings in the midst of her, and men shall fall upon the ground, and shall not be able to stand.

90. And also cometh the testimony of the voice of thunderings, and the voice of lightnings, and the voice of tempests, and the voice of the waves of the sea, heaving themselves beyond their bounds.

91. And all things shall be in commotion; and surely, men's hearts shall fail them; for fear shall come upon all people;

92. And angels shall fly through the midst of heaven, crying with a loud voice, sounding the trump of God, saying, Prepare ye, prepare ye, O inhabitants of the earth; for the judgment of our God is come: behold, and lo! the Bridegroom cometh, go ye out to meet him.

93. And immediately there shall appear a great sign in heaven, and all people shall see it together.

94. And another angel shall sound his trump, saying, That great church, the mother of abominations, that made all nations drink of the wine of the wrath of her fornication, that persecuteth the saints of God, that shed their blood; she who sitteth upon many waters, and upon the islands of the sea; behold, she is the tares of the earth, she is bound in bundles, her bands are made strong, no man can loose them; therefore, she is ready to be burned. And he shall sound his trump both long and loud, and all nations shall hear it.

95. And there shall be silence in heaven for the space of half an hour, and immediately after shall the curtain of heaven be unfolded, as a scroll is unfolded after it is rolled up, and the face of the Lord shall be unvailed;

96. And the saints that are upon

D&C 88:87–94—Even the voice of warning is a mild and loving invitation to come unto the Lord: "And let your preaching be the warning voice, every man to his neighbor, in mildness and in meekness" (D&C 38:41). When the hour of preaching with boldness—yet with mildness, meekness, and love—is past, then comes the hour of wrath where the testimony of heaven resounds in the form of earthquakes, thunderings, lightnings, tempests, and violent commotion. The elders are to gather in the honest in heart to spare them this wrenching torment and devastating ordeal. Those who reject the word of God from His mortal agents will experience His unrestrained indignation as the angels of heaven proclaim the inexorable milestones—one after another—that will prepare the earth for its sanctification on the eve of the Second Coming. The Prophet Joseph Smith explained:

> Judah must return, Jerusalem must be rebuilt, and the temple, and water come out from under the temple, and the waters of the Dead Sea be healed. It will take some time to rebuild the walls of the city and the temple, &c.; and all this must be done before the Son of Man will make His appearance. There will be wars and rumors of wars, signs in the heavens above and on the earth beneath, the sun turned into darkness and the moon to blood, earthquakes in divers places, the seas heaving beyond their bounds; then will appear one grand sign of the Son of Man in heaven. But what will the world do? They will say it is a planet, a comet, &c. But the Son of Man will come as the sign of the coming of the Son of Man, which will be as the light of the morning cometh out of the east. (*HC* 5:337.)

D&C 88:92—A trump is traditionally used to call attention to something or to announce someone or something.

D&C 88:93—Joseph Smith said that the sign in heaven will be as bright and obvious as the sun; some will call it a planet or a comet, but Christ will come out of its midst.

D&C 88:95—According to Orson Pratt, we don't know if this verse means our reckoning of time (30 minutes) or that of the Lord (about 21 years).

D&C 88:95–116—In the space of a few verses of scripture, the consummating agenda of the world is laid before our eyes as a sequence of seven angelic commissions calling forth the winding-up scenes leading to the establishment of the millennial reign of the Lord. As a crowning manifestation of the divine plan of salvation and exaltation, the history of each of the seven millennia will then be unfolded in panoramic view—a sequence of confirmations of the truth, glory, and dominion of the Almighty. Ultimately the Saints will receive their inheritances of glory, and Satan and his minions, "loosed for a little season," will be expelled by Michael and his army to the place prepared for them.

the earth, who are alive, shall be quickened, and be caught up to meet him.

97. And they who have slept in their graves shall come forth; for their graves shall be opened, and they also shall be caught up to meet him in the midst of the pillar of heaven:

98. They are Christ's, the first fruits, they who shall descend with him first, and they who are on the earth and in their graves, who are first caught up to meet him: and all this by the voice of the sounding of the trump of the angel of God.

99. And after this another angel shall sound, which is the second trump; and then cometh the redemption of those who are Christ's at his coming; who have received their part in that prison which is prepared for them, that they might receive the gospel, and be judged according to men in the flesh.

100. And again, another trump shall sound, which is the third trump; and then come the spirits of men who are to be judged, and are found under condemnation:

101. And these are the rest of the dead, and they live not again until the thousand years are ended, neither again, until the end of the earth.

102. And another trump shall sound, which is the fourth trump, saying, There are found among those who are to remain until that great and last day, even the end, who shall remain filthy still.

103. And another trump shall sound, which is the fifth trump, which is the fifth angel who committeth the everlasting gospel, flying through the midst of heaven, unto all nations, kindreds, tongues, and people;

104. And this shall be the sound of his trump, saying, to all people, both in heaven and in earth, and that are under the earth; for every ear shall hear it, and every knee shall bow, and every tongue shall confess, while they hear the sound of the trump, saying, Fear God, and give glory to him who sitteth upon the throne, for ever and ever: for the hour of his judgment is come.

105. And again, another angel shall sound his trump, which is the sixth angel, saying, She is fallen who made all nations drink of the wine of the wrath of her fornication: she is fallen! is fallen!

106. And again, another angel shall sound his trump, which is the seventh angel, saying, It is finished! It is finished! The Lamb of God hath overcome and trodden the wine-press alone, even the winepress of the fierceness of the wrath of Almighty God;

107. And then shall the angels be crowned with the glory of his might, and the saints shall be filled with his glory, and receive their inheritance and be made equal with him.

108. And then shall the first angel

D&C 88:96—Mortals must remain on the earth until after the 1,000-year period of the Millennium has ended. The word "quickening" in this verse does *not* refer to resurrection; instead, it is a process by which our bodies are prepared to live on the earth during the Savior's millennial reign.

D&C 88:97–101—These verses describe the three resurrections: the celestial resurrection (verses 97–98), the terrestrial resurrection (verse 99), and the telestial resurrection (verses 100–101), which will not occur until the end of the 1,000 years of the millennial period. In the meantime, those who are telestial will be thrust down to hell, where they will remain until they are resurrected.

D&C 88:102—The sons of perdition, who will have been thrust down to hell with the wicked for 1,000 years, will be the very last to be resurrected. Following their resurrection, they will be cast into outer darkness forever.

D&C 88:105—With this declaration, the sixth angel verifies that at the end, Satan and his evil forces will lose, and the Lord and His righteousness will be victorious.

D&C 88:106—This verse, with its reference to the Lamb of God and the winepress, refers to the Atonement and Christ's victory over sin and death. This verse is another evidence that Satan will be unsuccessful in his attempt to overthrow righteousness on the earth.

THE SEQUENCE OF THE RESURRECTION

The revelation that became Section 88 teaches that there are four phases of the resurrection: celestial, terrestrial, telestial, and sons of perdition.

These four phases are known scripturally as the first and second resurrections, or the resurrection of the just and the unjust (see D&C 45:45, 54; 76:15–17, 50, 64–65, 85). The first resurrection (that of the just) includes the celestial and terrestrial people. The second resurrection (that of the unjust) includes the telestial people and the sons of perdition.

Occasionally reference is made to "the morning of the first resurrection." This terms applies to the first phase (the celestial phase) of the first resurrection, a phase that is depicted by the sounding of the first trump at the time of the Savior's Second Coming (see D&C 88:92–98). This sounding of the trump pertains to the Saints of God who have died since the Savior's resurrection.

The second resurrection consists of two groups. The telestial is first, and will occur at the conclusion of the thousand-year period of millennial peace (see D&C 88:100–101). It will be followed by the resurrection of the sons of perdition (*STDC* 2:107–108).

again sound his trump in the ears of all living, and reveal the secret acts of men, and the mighty works of God in the first thousandth year.

109. And then shall the second angel sound his trump, and reveal the secret acts of men, and the thoughts and intents of their hearts, and the mighty works of God in the second thousandth year:

110. And so on, until the seventh angel shall sound his trump: and he shall stand forth upon the land and upon the sea, and swear in the name of him who sitteth upon the throne, that there shall be time no longer; and Satan shall be bound, that old serpent, who is called the devil, and shall not be loosed for the space of a thousand years.

111. And then he shall be loosed for a little season, that he may gather together his armies;

112. And Michael, the seventh angel, even the archangel, shall gather together his armies, even the hosts of heaven.

113. And the devil shall gather together his armies; even the hosts of hell, and shall come up to battle against Michael and his armies:

114. And then cometh the battle of the great God; and the devil and his armies shall be cast away into their own place, that they shall not have power over the saints any more at all;

115. For Michael shall fight their battles, and shall overcome him who seeketh the throne of him who sitteth upon the throne, even the Lamb.

116. This is the glory of God, and the sanctified; and they shall not any more see death.

117. Therefore, verily I say unto you, my friends, call your solemn assembly, as I have commanded you;

118. And as all have not faith, seek ye diligently and teach one another words of wisdom; yea, seek ye out of the best books words of wisdom: seek learning, even by study and also by faith.

119. Organize yourselves, prepare every needful thing, and establish a house, even a house of prayer, a house of fasting, a house of faith, a house of learning, a house of glory, a house of order, a house of God;

120. That your incomings may be in the name of the Lord; that your outgoings may be in the name of the Lord; that all your salutations may be in the name of the Lord, with uplifted hands unto the Most High.

121. Therefore, cease from all your light speeches; from all laughter; from all your lustful desires; from all your pride and light-mindedness, and from all your wicked doings.

122. Appoint among yourselves a teacher, and let not all be spokesmen at once; but let one speak at a

D&C 88:109—This is a period of time during which all will be made known. It will be a dreadful time for the evil, but a time of great joy for the righteous.

D&C 88:110—At this time, Satan will be bound in two ways: first, he will not be allowed to tempt, and second, the people will be so righteous that they would not yield to temptation.

D&C 88:111–115—The "battle of the great god" refers to the battle against Gog and Magog. Those who fight for Satan will not dwindle in unbelief or rebel in ignorance; instead, they will rebel willfully against the law of heaven.

D&C 88:117–118—Concerning our duty to learn and progress through faith and study, Brigham Young said:

> The Lord has revealed a great many precious principles to this people, and knowledge which cannot be obtained by the study of the learned of the world, "who are ever learning and never come to the knowledge of the truth." One of the greatest blessings that can be bestowed upon the children of men is to have true knowledge concerning themselves, concerning the human family and the designs of Heaven concerning them. It is also a great blessing to have wisdom to use this knowledge in a way to produce the greatest good to ourselves and all men. All the power of earthly wealth cannot give this knowledge and this wisdom. (JD 10:209.)

D&C 88:119—The ultimate "house of God" is the holy temple. Other institutions of Zion—her homes and other places for learning and gathering—partake of the holiness and sanctity befitting a house of God; but the temple is the consummate edifice of the divine presence and as such draws our awe and inspires our obedience. The blessings of the temple pertain to eternal life. We are endowed there from on high and make covenants in regard to our exaltation. The building of temples and the blessings associated with them bring joy to Heavenly Father and constitute the unfolding of His work for blessing His children.

D&C 88:120–126—This array of counsel and wisdom establishes an environment of spiritual learning and edification appropriate to any gospel setting. Follow the word of God—be your very best and do your very best. Be clean in body and mind. Think good thoughts and see the good in others. Gain adequate rest, which is absolutely imperative to good health and well-being. Be full of charity and pray always. An atmosphere of charity and love is an important ingredient in the process of learning through the Spirit about the things of God. As we call down the powers of heaven through prayer, we can all be edified and learn together by the Spirit of truth (see D&C 50:17–22). Such is the appropriate demeanor within the School of the Prophets—then as now.

time, and let all listen unto his sayings, that when all have spoken, that all may be edified of all, and that every man may have an equal privilege.

123. See that ye love one another; cease to be covetous, learn to impart one to another as the gospel requires;

124. Cease to be idle; cease to be unclean; cease to find fault one with another; cease to sleep longer than is needful; retire to thy bed early, that ye may not be weary; arise early, that your bodies and your minds may be invigorated;

125. And above all things, clothe yourselves with the bond of charity, as with a mantle, which is the bond of perfectness and peace;

126. Pray always, that ye may not faint until I come, behold, and lo, I will come quickly, and receive you unto myself. Amen.

127. And again, the order of the house prepared for the presidency of the school of the prophets, established for their instruction in all things that are expedient for them, even for all the officers of the church, or in other words, those who are called to the ministry in the church, beginning at the High Priests, even down to the deacons:

128. And this shall be the order of the house of the presidency of the school: He that is appointed to be president, or teacher, shall be found standing in his place, in the house which shall be prepared for him.

129. Therefore he shall be first in the house of God, in a place that the congregation in the house may hear his words carefully and distinctly, not with loud speech.

130. And when he cometh into the house of God, (for he should be first in the house, behold, this is beautiful, that he may be an example).

131. Let him offer himself in prayer upon his knees before God, in token or remembrance of the everlasting covenant.

132. And when any shall come in after him, let the teacher arise, and, with uplifted hands to heaven; yea, even directly, salute his brother or brethren with these words:

133. Art thou a brother or brethren? I salute you in the name of the Lord Jesus Christ, in token or remembrance of the everlasting covenant, in which covenant I receive you to fellowship, in a determination that is fixed, immovable, and unchangeable, to be your friend and brother through the grace of God in the bonds of love, to walk in all the commandments of God blameless, in thanksgiving, for ever and ever. Amen.

134. And he that is found unworthy of this salutation shall not have place among you: for ye shall not suffer that mine house shall be polluted by him.

135. And he that cometh in and is faithful before me, and is a brother, or if they be brethren, they shall salute the president or teacher with uplifted hands to heaven, with this same prayer and covenant, or by saying Amen, in token of the same.

136. Behold, verily, I say unto you, this is a sample unto you for a salutation to one another in the

D&C 88:127–140—The Prophet Joseph Smith made this entry in his journal: "This winter [1832–33] was spent in translating the Scriptures; in the School of the Prophets; and sitting in conferences. I had many glorious seasons of refreshing" (HC 1:322). Truly the work of the ministry in building the kingdom of God is a blend of "many glorious seasons of refreshing." The pattern established for gospel learning in the framework of the School of the Prophets set an example that was carried on in similar educational settings in Kirtland and Missouri until 1836, and thereafter for a number of years in Utah following the exodus (see Steven R. Sorensen, "School of the Prophets," in EM, 1269–1270).

The innovative pattern of learning established in the School of the Prophets set a standard for future educational programs. The spirit and close-knit fellowship that characterized that vanguard enterprise is worthy of emulation in all the circles of learning in the Church today. *Lectures on Faith* developed as part of the original curriculum (and given its final editorial stamp by the Prophet Joseph Smith) continues to resonate with clarity and authority for modern readers.

THE SCHOOL OF THE PROPHETS

The school of the prophets consisted of a group of the early Church leaders who came together to be taught and instructed by and under the direction of the Prophet Joseph Smith. According to Elder Bruce R. McConkie, they were to learn all things pertaining to the gospel and to the kingdom of God that it was "expedient for them to know"—but they also studied things pertaining to the arts and sciences and learned about other kingdoms and nations.

As part of the school of the prophets, the brethren were instructed to build the Kirtland Temple, which was, among other things, to be "a house of learning" (D&C 88:119) (STDC 2:112).

house of God, in the school of the prophets.

137. And ye are called to do this by prayer and thanksgiving, as the Spirit shall give utterance in all your doings in the house of the Lord, in the school of the prophets, that it may become a sanctuary, a tabernacle of the Holy Spirit to your edification.

138. And ye shall not receive any among you into this school save he is clean from the blood of this generation:

139. And he shall be received by the ordinance of the washing of feet, for unto this end was the ordinance of the washing of feet instituted.

140. And again, the ordinance of washing feet is to be administered by the President, or Presiding elder of the church.

141. It is to be commenced with prayer, and after partaking of bread and wine, he is to gird himself according to the pattern given in the thirteenth chapter of John's testimony concerning me. Amen.

SECTION 89

1. A Word of Wisdom, for the benefit of the Council of High Priests, assembled in Kirtland, and the church; and also the saints in Zion.

2. To be sent greeting—not by commandment or constraint, but by revelation and the word of wisdom, showing forth the order and will of God in the temporal salvation of all saints in the last days.

3. Given for a principle with promise, adapted to the capacity of the weak and the weakest of all saints, who are or can be called saints.

4. Behold, verily, thus saith the Lord unto you, in consequence of evils and designs which do and will exist in the hearts of conspiring men in the last days, I have warned you, and forewarn you, by giving unto you this word of wisdom by revelation,

5. That inasmuch as any man drinketh wine or strong drink

D&C 88:140–141—At the time of the Last Supper, the Lord performed the gospel ordinance of washing of feet. . . .

This ordinance of the gospel has been restored in this dispensation. When the School of the Prophets was organized, the Lord indicated that the members should "be received by the ordinance of the washing of feet, for unto this end [that ye might be clean from the blood of this generation] was the ordinance of the washing of feet instituted" (D&C 88:139). . . .

The ordinance of washing of feet should not be confused with the instructions that elders serving as missionaries might cleanse their feet as a testimony against those who reject their testimony. (*Ludlow* 2:322–323.)

Section 89 Background—Given on February 27, 1833, in the translating room at the Whitney Store in Kirtland, Ohio (see *HC* 1:327–329). Brigham Young gives this background: "The first school of the prophets was held in a small room situated over the Prophet Joseph's kitchen, in a house which belonged to Bishop Whitney, and which was attached to his store. . . . In the rear of this building was a kitchen, probably ten by fourteen feet, containing rooms and pantries. Over this kitchen was situated the room in which the Prophet received revelations and in which he instructed his brethren. . . . When they assembled together in this room after breakfast, the first thing they did was to light their pipes, and, while smoking, talk about the great things of the kingdom, and spit all over the room, and as soon as the pipe was out of their [mouths] a large chew of tobacco would then be taken. Often when the Prophet entered the room to give the school instructions he would find himself in a cloud of tobacco smoke. This, and the complaints of his wife at having to clean so filthy a floor, made the Prophet [inquire] of the Lord relating to the conduct of the Elders in using tobacco, and the revelation known as the Word of Wisdom was the result of his inquiry" (*JD* 12:157).

Room that housed the first school of the prophets, located in the Newel K. Whitney home directly over the kitchen used by Joseph and Emma Smith.

among you, behold it is not good, neither meet in the sight of your Father, only in assembling yourselves together to offer up your sacraments before him.

6. And, behold, this should be wine, yea, pure wine of the grape of the vine, of your own make.

7. And, again, strong drinks are not for the belly, but for the washing of your bodies.

8. And again, tobacco is not for the body, neither for the belly, and is not good for man, but is an herb for bruises and all sick cattle, to be used with judgment and skill.

9. And again, hot drinks are not for the body or belly.

10. And again, verily I say unto you, all wholesome herbs God hath ordained for the constitution, nature, and use of man.

11. Every herb in the season thereof, and every fruit in the season thereof; all these to be used with prudence and thanksgiving.

12. Yea, flesh also of beasts and of the fowls of the air, I, the Lord, have ordained for the use of man with thanksgiving; nevertheless they are to be used sparingly;

13. And it is pleasing unto me that they should not be used only in times of winter, or of cold, or famine.

14. All grain is ordained for the use of man and of beasts, to be the staff of life, not only for man but for the beasts of the field, and the fowls of heaven, and all wild animals that run or creep on the earth;

15. And these hath God made for the use of man only in times of famine and excess of hunger.

16. All grain is good for the food of man, as also the fruit of the vine, that which yieldeth fruit, whether in the ground or above the ground.

17. Nevertheless, wheat for man, and corn for the ox, and oats for the horse, and rye for the fowls and for swine, and for all beasts of the field, and barley for all useful animals, and for mild drinks, as also other grain.

18. And all saints who remember to keep and do these sayings, walking in obedience to the commandments, shall receive health in their navel, and marrow to their bones,

19. And shall find wisdom and great treasures of knowledge, even hidden treasures;

20. And shall run and not be weary, and shall walk and not faint;

21. And I, the Lord, give unto them a promise, that the destroying angel shall pass by them, as the children of Israel, and not slay them. Amen.

Joseph Smith's kitchen, just below the room where the first school of the prophets was held in the Newel K. Whitney home (attached to the Whitney Store).

D&C 89:5–9—The blessings of the Spirit can be ours if we are pure and clean (see 1 Cor. 6:19–20), and the Spirit is the key to most all things in our lives. The Prophet Joseph Smith stated:

> I am surprised that any human being should think of using it [tobacco]—for an elder especially to eat, or smoke it, is a disgrace to him;—he is not fit for the office, he ought first to learn to keep the word of wisdom, and then to teach others. God will not prosper the man who uses it. And again "hot drinks are not for the body, or belly;" there are many who wonder what this can mean; whether it refers to tea, or coffee, or not. I say it does refer to tea, and coffee. Why is it that we are frequently so dull and languid? It is because we break the word of wisdom, disease preys upon our system, our understandings are darkened, and we do not comprehend the things of God; the devil takes advantage of us, and we fall into temptation. Not only are they injurious in their tendency, and baneful in their effects, but the importation of foreign products might be the means of thousands of our people being poisoned at a future time, through the advantage that an enemy might take of us, if we made use of these things that are thus spoken of as being evil; and be it remembered—that this instruction is given "in consequence of evils that do and will exist in the hearts of conspiring men." (*Times and Seasons*, Vol. 3, No. 15, April 1842, 800–801.)

D&C 89:10–17—The riches of the earth, given through the grace and blessing of God, offer grand opportunities for mankind to follow divine counsel in choosing that which will have the most beneficial impact on health and well-being. Concerning the use of wisdom and prudence in applying the counsel in the Word of Wisdom, President Harold B. Lee taught that we should avoid "*speculative interpretations of the Word of Wisdom*" (THBL, 203).

Commenting on the phrase "in the season thereof," President Joseph Fielding Smith said that it does not refer to the season of growth or the point at which fruits and vegetables have ripened. Instead, he said, any grain or fruit is "out of season" if it is spoiled or otherwise unfit for use (see CHMR, 2:148).

D&C 89:18–21—This section of the Doctrine and Covenants might well be called the "Covenant of Wisdom," for our faithful adherence to these divine principles brings about the fulfillment on our behalf of great promises made by the Lord—health and vitality, wisdom and knowledge, strength and protection. John A. Widtsoe summarizes: ". . . the reward for keeping the Word of Wisdom is four-fold. 1. Self-control is developed. That is implied in verse 3 of the revelation, which states that the Word of Wisdom is 'adapted to the capacity of the weak and the weakest of all Saints, who are or can be called Saints.' 2. Strength of body, including resistance to contagion, is a result of wise living. 3. Clearness of mind is the gift of those whose bodies are in a healthy condition. 4. Spiritual power comes to all who conquer their appetites, live normally and look upward to God" (PC, 39–40).

SECTION 90

1. Thus saith the Lord, verily, verily I say unto you my son, thy sins are forgiven thee, according to thy petition, for thy prayers and the prayers of thy brethren, have come up into my ears;

2. Therefore thou art blessed from henceforth that bear the keys of the kingdom given unto you; which kingdom is coming forth for the last time.

3. Verily, I say unto you the keys of this kingdom shall never be taken from you, while thou art in the world, neither in the world to come;

4. Nevertheless, through you shall the oracles be given to another; yea, even unto the church.

5. And all they who receive the oracles of God, let them beware how they hold them, lest they are accounted as a light thing, and are brought under condemnation thereby; and stumble and fall when the storms descend, and the winds blow, and the rains descend, and beat upon their house.

6. And again, verily I say unto thy brethren, Sidney Rigdon and Frederick G. Williams, their sins are forgiven them also, and they are accounted as equal with thee in holding the keys of this last kingdom;

7. As also through your administration the keys of the school of the prophets, which I have commanded to be organized,

8. That thereby they may be perfected in their ministry for the salvation of Zion, and of the nations of Israel, and of the Gentiles, as many as will believe,

9. That through your administration they may receive the word, and through their administration the word may go forth unto the ends of the earth, unto the Gentiles first, and then, behold, and lo, they shall turn unto the Jews;

10. And then cometh the day when the arm of the Lord shall be revealed in power in convincing the nations, the heathen nations, the house of Joseph, of the gospel of their salvation.

11. For it shall come to pass in that day, that every man shall hear the fulness of the gospel in his own tongue, and in his own language, through those who are ordained unto this power, by the administration of the Comforter, shed forth upon them, for the revelation of Jesus Christ.

12. And now, verily I say unto you, I give unto you a commandment, that you continue in the ministry and Presidency,

Section 90 Background—Given on March 8, 1833, in Kirtland, Ohio (see *HC* 1:329–331). This section signaled an important further step in the organization of the First Presidency. The Prophet wrote of a later meeting of the School of the Prophets on March 18, 1833: "... Elder Rigdon expressed a desire that himself and Brother Frederick G. Williams should be ordained to the offices to which they had been called, viz., those of Presidents of the High Priesthood, and to be equal in holding the keys of the kingdom with Brother Joseph Smith, Jun. . . . Accordingly I laid my hands on Brothers Sidney and Frederick, and ordained them to take part with me in holding the keys of this last kingdom, and to assist in the Presidency of the High Priesthood, as my Counselors. . . . Many of the brethren saw a heavenly vision of the Savior, and concourses of angels, and many other things, of which each one has a record of what he saw" (*HC* 1:334–335).

D&C 90:5—The power of heaven will preserve and sanctify the channel of revelation flowing unto the Church. Joseph and his successors holding the keys of presidency will carry out the will of the Lord—or they will be removed from office. President Joseph F. Smith bears witness to this principle:

I testify in the name of Israel's God that He will not suffer the head of the Church, him whom He has chosen to stand at the head, to transgress His laws and apostatize; the moment he should take a course that would in time lead to it, God would take him away. Why? Because to suffer a wicked man to occupy that position, would be to allow, as it were, the fountain to become corrupted, which is something He will never permit. And why will He not suffer it? Because it is not the work of Joseph Smith; it is not the work of Brigham Young or of John Taylor. It is not the work of man but of God Almighty; and it is His business to see that the men who occupy this position are men after His own heart, men that will receive instructions from Him, and that will carry out the same according to the counsels of His will. (*JD* 24:193–194.)

D&C 90:6–11—In these verses we find a succinct and authoritative formulation of the vision of missionary work in the latter days. The First Presidency presides over the process of declaring the gospel message of salvation unto the world. All nations are to receive the fullness of the gospel, beginning with the Jews (who heard it from the Messiah Himself before rejecting it) and then going to the Gentiles during the age of the Restoration, and finally once again to the Jews. Furthermore, every man is to have the privilege of hearing the fullness of the gospel in his own language and tongue.

It is through this means that Jesus Christ is to be revealed to the world in the last days—first to the Gentiles, and then again to the Jews.

13. And when you have finished the translation of the prophets, you shall from thenceforth preside over the affairs of the church and the school;

14. And from time to time as shall be manifested by the Comforter, receive revelations to unfold the mysteries of the kingdom,

15. And set in order the churches, and study and learn, and become acquainted with all good books, and with languages, tongues, and people.

16. And this shall be your business and mission in all your lives, to preside in council, and set in order all the affairs of this church and kingdom.

17. Be not ashamed, neither confounded; but be admonished in all your high-mindedness and pride, for it bringeth a snare upon your souls.

18. Set in order your houses; keep slothfulness and uncleanness far from you.

19. Now, verily I say unto you, let there be a place provided as soon as it is possible, for the family of thy counselor and scribe, even Frederick G. Williams:

20. And let mine aged servant, Joseph Smith, sen., continue with his family upon the place where he now lives, and let it not be sold until the mouth of the Lord shall name.

21. And let my counselor, even Sidney Rigdon, remain where he now resides, until the mouth of the Lord shall name.

22. And let the bishop search diligently to obtain an agent, and let it be a man who has got riches in store—a man of God, and of strong faith;

23. That thereby he may be enabled to discharge every debt; that the storehouse of the Lord may not be brought into disrepute before the eyes of the people.

24. Search diligently, pray always, and be believing, and all things shall work together for your good, if ye walk uprightly and remember the covenant wherewith ye have covenanted one with another.

25. Let your families be small, especially mine aged servant Joseph Smith, sen., as pertaining to those who do not belong to your families;

26. That those things that are provided for you, to bring to pass my work, are not taken from you and given to those that are not worthy,

27. And thereby you be hindered in accomplishing those things which I have commanded you.

28. And again, verily I say unto you, it is my will that my handmaid, Vienna Jaques should receive money to bear her expenses, and go up unto the land of Zion;

29. And the residue of the money may be consecrated unto me, and she be rewarded in mine own due time.

30. Verily I say unto you, that it is meet in mine eyes that she should go up unto the land of Zion, and receive an inheritance from the hand of the bishop,

31. That she may settle down in peace inasmuch as she is faithful,

D&C 90:13–18—These verses outline the tasks of the First Presidency, which included Joseph Smith, Sidney Rigdon, and Frederick G. Williams. In verse 13, "the translation of the prophets" refers to the Joseph Smith translation of the Bible. The admonition against pride in verse 17 is applicable to all of us, but was especially important for Sidney Rigdon and Frederick G. Williams, both of whom eventually left the Church and opposed Joseph Smith.

D&C 90:15–18—Herein is a humbling admonition against pride and a reminder to "set in order your houses." How can the Church be set in order? By setting in order the homes of Zion. Christ is the Exemplar; the Spirit sheds forth light and truth; the Lord's ordained leaders raise the banner of obedience and honor; and the Saints at large respond with "works and faith agreeable to the holy scriptures—walking in holiness before the Lord" (D&C 20:69). President J. Reuben Clark taught: "Now, brethren, do not put off putting yourself in order, if you are not in order, yielding obedience to the commandments of the Lord, so that when the time comes, if it comes, and I pray that it will not come to any of you, but when the time comes, you will be able to go to the Lord with a pure heart, and invoke his blessings upon you" (CR, Oct. 1952, 84).

D&C 90:19–37—In these verses, specific instructions are given by revelation to various individuals, each according to his or her circumstances, so that the work of the kingdom might go forward. The central theme is formulated in the now-famous maxim beginning with the words, "Search diligently, pray always, and be believing" (verse 24). This is a covenant formulation, with grand blessings flowing to those who perform specific actions and commandments. We are to search for truth with diligence, pray always, exercise our faith, walk uprightly, and remember the covenants that unite us within the fold of Christ. In response, the Lord pronounces a promissory blessing that all things will work together for our good.

All aspects of covenant service in the kingdom of God reflect the bonding of us as chidren of God. The sacred sealing covenants of the temple are anchored in the abiding love of God and the unifying love of others. Work for the dead is a constant reminder that covenants before God always imply a melding of interests with our brothers and sisters, even those who have passed beyond the veil: "For we without them cannot be made perfect; neither can they without us be made perfect" (D&C 128:18). Under the law of consecration, goods are consecrated for the well-being of the poor "with a covenant and a deed which cannot be broken" (D&C 42:30).

D&C 90:25—The injunction to "let your families be small" did not apply to the size of the immediate family, but to extended family and other visitors who often took advantage of the open homes and open hearts of members of the Church who were already living in the area.

and not be idle in her days from thenceforth.

32. And behold, verily I say unto you, that ye shall write this commandment, and say unto your brethren in Zion, in love greeting, that I have called you also to preside over Zion in mine own due time:

33. Therefore, let them cease wearying me concerning this matter.

34. Behold, I say unto you that your brethren in Zion begin to repent, and the angels rejoice over them;

35. Nevertheless, I am not well pleased with many things, and I am not well pleased with my servant William E. McLellin, neither with my servant Sidney Gilbert; and the bishop also, and others have many things to repent of;

36. But verily I say unto you, that I, the Lord, will contend with Zion, and plead with her strong ones, and chasten her until she overcomes and is clean before me:

37. For she shall not be removed out of her place. I the Lord, have spoken it. Amen.

SECTION 91

1. Verily, thus saith the Lord unto you concerning the Apocrypha, there are many things contained therein that are true, and it is mostly translated correctly;

2. There are many things contained therein that are not true, which are interpolations by the hands of men.

3. Verily, I say unto you, that it is not needful that the Apocrypha should be translated.

4. Therefore, whoso readeth it, let him understand, for the Spirit manifesteth truth;

5. And whoso is enlightened by the Spirit shall obtain benefit therefrom;

6. And whoso receiveth not by the Spirit, cannot be benefited, therefore it is not needful that it should be translated. Amen.

VIENNA JAQUES

Vienna Jaques was born June 10, 1787, in Beverly, Essex County, Massachusetts. The Book of Mormon so moved her that she journeyed alone to Kirtland to meet with, and be instructed by, the Prophet Joseph Smith. Following her baptism, she returned again to the Boston area, shared the gospel with her family, and then came back to Kirtland with her valuables, including $1,400 in savings. On March 8, 1833, she was instructed of the Lord to consecrate her wealth to the Church and then journey to Missouri to receive a promised inheritance (see D&C 90:28–31). This she did; however, the mounting persecution there forced her to abandon her holdings and flee to northern Missouri, where she used her nursing skills to relieve the suffering of the Saints. Eventually she crossed the plains to the Salt Lake Valley, driving her own wagon. Faithful and self-reliant to the end, she passed away at 96 on February 7, 1884.

Section 91 Background—Given at Kirtland, Ohio, March 9, 1833 (see *HC* 1:331–332), when the Prophet came to that portion of the ancient writings called the Apocrypha (see *HC* 1:331). James E. Talmage gives this summary:

> The Apocrypha embrace a number of books of doubtful authenticity, though such have been at times highly esteemed. Thus, they were added to the Septuagint, and for a time were accorded recognition among the Alexandrine Jews. However, they have never been generally admitted, being of uncertain origin. They are not quoted in the New Testament. (*AF*, 222.)

D&C 91:1–5—The Spirit "manifesteth truth" and can bless seekers of truth to discover those aspects of the Apocrypha that are helpful and beneficial. However, the Lord declined to include the Apocrypha in His canon for the blessing of the Saints. The fullness of the gospel comes forth in the authorized scriptural texts.

Modern research has shed much light on the Apocryphal texts since the time of Joseph Smith, as C. Wilford Griggs explains:

> Since the nineteenth century, increased understanding . . . has shown the Apocrypha to be historically important and religiously valuable. These writings display a belief in resurrection, eternal life, and eschatological teachings concerning the last days. . . .
>
> Additionally, during the past two centuries many writings have been discovered that were purportedly written by ancient prophets or apostles, or were otherwise related to biblical texts. . . . Many of these writings were considered sacred to certain groups of Jews or Christians, but were rejected in the long process of biblical canonization. . . .
>
> One important aspect of the expanded collection of the Apocrypha has to do with the canon itself. Centuries after it was determined which books were to be included in the Bible, people began to believe and teach that the Bible was both complete (containing all that God had given through ancient prophets and apostles) and infallible (having been transmitted without any errors). Joseph Smith received correctives to both ideas, being given additional scripture originally written by ancient prophets and being inspired to make corrections in the texts of the Bible. Among the ancient writings he restored are the book of Abraham and the writings of Moses (canonized as the book of Moses, itself including a restoration to Moses of an older Enoch writing; see Moses 6–7); quotations from ancient biblical prophets in the Book of Mormon (such as Joseph of Egypt and four otherwise unknown writers named Zenos, Zenock, Neum, and Ezias); and writings from the New Testament apostle John (see D&C 7 and 93). Corrections to the biblical text include an expanded version of Matthew 24 and alternate readings in Isaiah. (C. Wilford Griggs, "Apocrypha and Pseudepigrapha," in *EM*, 55–56.)

SECTION 92

1. Verily, thus saith the Lord, I give unto the united order, organized agreeable to the commandment previously given, a revelation and commandment concerning my servant Shederlaomach, (Frederick G. Williams,) that ye shall receive him into the order. What I say unto one, I say unto all.

2. And again, I say unto you my servant Shederlaomach, (Frederick G. Williams,) you shall be a lively member in this order, and inasmuch as you are faithful in keeping all former commandments, you shall be blessed for ever. Amen.

SECTION 93

1. Verily, thus saith the Lord, it shall come to pass that every soul who forsaketh their sins and cometh unto me, and calleth on my name, and obeyeth my voice, and keepeth my commandments, shall see my face and know that I am,

2. And that I am the true light that lighteth every man that cometh into the world;

3. And that I am in the Father, and the Father in me, and the Father and I are one:

4. The Father because he gave me of his fulness, and the Son because I was in the world and made flesh my tabernacle, and dwelt among the sons of men.

5. I was in the world and received of my Father, and the works of him were plainly manifest;

6. And John saw and bore record of the fulness of my glory, and the fulness of John's record is hereafter to be revealed:

7. And he bore record, saying, I saw his glory that he was in the beginning before the world was;

Section 92 Background—Given at Kirtland, Ohio, March 15, 1833 (see *HC* 1:333). The revelation is directed to Frederick G. Williams, who on March 8 of that year had been appointed a counselor in the First Presidency.

D&C 92:1–2—The admonition "what I say unto one I say unto all" is used five times in the Doctrine and Covenants (see D&C 61:18, 36; 82:5; 92:1; 93:49). This pattern was established by the Savior during His earthly ministry (see JS–Matt. 1:46). The word of truth is often given to one individual, but the principle behind it often has universal application. That is what makes the scriptural record so appealing: the story of real individuals is recounted and we then discern the application to our own personal lives. In Section 92 the general principles are to receive a servant of God into the circle of fellowship without discrimination and without condition.

Section 93 Background—Given on May 6, 1833, in Kirtland, Ohio, at the Newel K. Whitney Store (probably in the translating room). At the time, the Prophet was engaged in the inspired translation of the Bible and was attending to important developments in building the Kingdom as mob violence was raising its ugly head. This choice section of significant doctrine was evidently given in partial fulfillment of D&C 90:14: "And from time to time, as shall be manifested by the Comforter, receive revelations to unfold the mysteries of the kingdom." A portion of this section is attributed to the record of John (see verses 7–17). Section 93 gives a resounding witness of Christ's mission as the empowering force behind the plan of salvation.

D&C 93:1–3—The transcendent blessing of seeing the face of the Lord and knowing of His divinity is the fulfillment of the sacred quest to return home to the presence of God. "And seek ye the face of the Lord always," is the admonition in a later revelation, "that in patience ye may possess your souls, and ye shall have eternal life" (D&C 101:38).

D&C 93:6—The John referred to in this verse is John the Beloved, Apostle of the Lord. Some have taken a different position—for example, both John Taylor and Orson Pratt believed the record to be that of John the Baptist. Author Richard O. Cowan shows how both positions can be harmonized: "In verses 7–17, the Lord refers to the testimony of John the Baptist as quoted in the gospel written by the apostle John; the Baptist had the privilege of beholding and bearing witness to Christ's glory" (*DCOMS*, 145).

According to this last position, both Johns are involved—John the Baptist, whose testimony is being cited, and John the Beloved, whose record is the source for this testimony. If this is correct, we have before us an edifying blending of two noble and righteous voices upholding the divinity of the mission of Christ and the saving power of the gospel.

8. Therefore in the beginning the Word was, for he was the Word, even the messenger of salvation,

9. The light and the Redeemer of the world; the Spirit of truth, who came into the world, because the world was made by him, and in him was the life of men and the light of men.

10. The worlds were made by him; men were made by him; all things were made by him, and through him, and of him.

11. And I, John, bear record that I beheld his glory, as the glory of the Only Begotten of the Father, full of grace and truth, even the Spirit of truth, which came and dwelt in the flesh, and dwelt among us.

12. And I, John, saw that he received not of the fulness at the first, but received grace for grace:

13. And he received not of the fulness at first, but continued from grace to grace, until he received a fulness;

14. And thus he was called the Son of God, because he received not of the fulness at the first.

15. And I, John, bear record, and lo, the heavens were opened, and the Holy Ghost descended upon him in the form of a dove, and sat upon him, and there came a voice out of heaven
saying, This is my beloved Son.

16. And I, John, bear record that he received a fulness of the glory of the Father;

17. And he received all power, both in heaven and on earth, and the glory of the Father was with him, for he dwelt in him.

18. And it shall come to pass, that if you are faithful you shall receive the fulness of the record of John.

19. I give unto you these sayings that you may understand and know how to worship, and know what you worship, that you may come unto the Father in my name, and in due time receive of his fulness.

20. For if you keep my commandments you shall receive of his fulness, and be glorified in me as I am in the Father; therefore, I say unto you, you shall receive grace for grace.

21. And now, verily I say unto you, I was in the beginning with the Father, and am the first-born;

22. And all those who are begotten through me are partakers of the glory of the same, and are the church of the first-born.

23. Ye were also in the beginning with the Father; that which is Spirit, even the Spirit of truth,

D&C 93:8–17—This consummate and celestial portrait of the Savior derives from John, who beheld in real life and in vision the grand scope and majesty of the Master's role in bringing about the immortality and eternal life of man. Section 93 provides the most complete explanation of the principle of "grace for grace." The model is the Savior, who did not receive a fullness of glory at first, "but continued from grace to grace, until he received a fulness" (verse 13). B. H. Roberts provides the background for the opening stages of this inaugural process in the meridian of time:

Of his youth, we know but little; but the little we know reveals a shining quality, either for God or man to possess. You must remember, in all our consideration of the life of Messiah, one truth, which comes to us from the scriptures in an incidental way, viz., that "In his humiliation his judgment was taken from him." [Acts 8:33.] As the veil is drawn over our minds when our pre-existent spirits come into this world, and we forget the Father and Mother of the spirit world, and the positions we occupied there, so, too, with Jesus; in his humiliation his judgment was taken from him; he knew not at first whence he came, nor the dignity of his station in heaven. It was only by degrees that he felt the Spirit working within him and gradually unfolding the sublime idea that he was peculiarly and pre-eminently the Son of God in very deed. [At the age of twelve] he began to understand his mission. The spirit promptings were at work in his soul. And while ultimately the spirit was given without measure unto him, it was not so at first, for "He received not of the fullness at the first, but received grace for grace." [D&C 93:12.] The child Jesus "grew, and waxed strong in spirit, filled with wisdom: and the grace of God was upon him. . . . . And Jesus increased in wisdom and stature, and in favor with God and man." (B. H. Roberts, "Jesus Christ: the Revelation of God," *IE*, Vol. V, Oct. 1902, No. 12, 970–971.)

D&C 93:19–20—We worship the Father in the name of Jesus Christ. By obedience to the gospel plan, we can become sons and daughters of Christ through the atoning sacrifice (Mosiah 5:7); in that sense He becomes our Father and we become His "seed" (see Isa. 53:10; Mosiah 14:10; 15:10). This process of regeneration for the obedient proceeds "grace for grace"—just as in the mission of Jesus Christ—so that they can "receive of his fulness" (verse 20).

24. And truth is knowledge of things as they are, and as they were, and as they are to come;

25. And whatsoever is more or less than this is the spirit of that wicked one who was a liar from the beginning.

26. The Spirit of truth is of God. I am the Spirit of truth, and John bore record of me, saying—He received a fulness of truth, yea, even of all truth;

27. And no man receiveth a fulness unless he keepeth his commandments.

28. He that keepeth his commandments receiveth truth and light, until he is glorified in truth and knoweth all things.

29. Man was also in the beginning with God. Intelligence, or the light of truth, was not created or made, neither indeed can be.

30. All truth is independent in that sphere in which God has placed it, to act for itself, as all intelligence also, otherwise there is no existence.

31. Behold, here is the agency of man, and here is the condemnation of man, because that which was from the beginning is plainly manifest unto them, and they receive not the light.

32. And every man whose spirit receiveth not the light is under condemnation.

33. For man is spirit. The elements are eternal, and spirit and element, inseparably connected, receive a fulness of joy;

34. And when separated, man cannot receive a fulness of joy.

35. The elements are the tabernacle of God; yea, man is the tabernacle of God, even temples; and whatsoever temple is defiled, God shall destroy that temple.

36. The glory of God is intelligence, or, in other words, light and truth;

37. Light and truth forsaketh that evil one.

38. Every spirit of man was innocent in the beginning, and God having redeemed man from the fall, men became again in their infant state, innocent before God.

39. And that wicked one cometh and taketh away light and truth,

D&C 93:24–27—Truth is manifested in the eternal patterns of things; to perceive and begin to understand such never-changing patterns and principles is to know the truth. Scholar Victor Ludlow suggests this approach:

> Studying spiritual truths is eternally important because our perception of them teaches us eternal values about the purpose of existence and includes an understanding of the glory, nature, and purpose of God. These truths are revealed through visions and revelations recorded by ancient prophets in the Holy Scriptures, are taught through the teachings of modern-day prophets, and, finally, are received through personal enlightenment by the Holy Ghost. Sometimes, enlightenment into spiritual truths comes to us directly and profoundly. Usually, however, we receive spiritual insights indirectly and subtly through gentle spiritual whisperings. (*PPRG*, 12.)

D&C 93:29—Just as the Prophet Joseph Smith restored once again our knowledge of the true nature of the Godhead, so did he also shed inspired light on the true nature of man as the offspring of Deity and thus of premortal provenance—with a destiny, through the process of perfection and sanctification, to become even as God is. We are children of the Most High with a potential to rise in spirituality and take on more and more of His divine nature. In many, perhaps most, hearts is the intimation of the antiquity of man and his eternal, premortal relationship with the Creator; however, it is only through the restored gospel that we have a clear vision of our spiritual roots, reaching back to the presence of the Father and the Son.

D&C 93:36—This oft-quoted statement has become an enduring maxim from the record of latter-day revelation. B. H. Roberts gives this perspective:

> Looked at from any standpoint one cannot see how it could be otherwise than that "intelligence," par-excellent, must be the glory of God. For intelligence is the attribute in God that perceives and knows truth; which both cognizes truth and applies it to needful ends. Thence comes knowledge which brings forth wisdom, and from wisdom the demonstration of intelligence: thence follows justice, judgment, mercy—these said to be the habitation of God's throne—and love. The circle of excellences is completed; but the source of these is intelligence; and hence intelligence in God the moving and the regulating force in all these things—the eternal birth-spring of his glory. (*CHC* 1:309.)

through disobedience, from the children of men, and because of the tradition of their fathers.

40. But I have commanded you to bring up your children in light and truth;

41. But verily I say unto you, my servant Frederick G. Williams, you have continued under this condemnation;

42. You have not taught your children light and truth, according to the commandments, and that wicked one hath power, as yet, over you, and this is the cause of your affliction.

43. And now a commandment I give unto you, if you will be delivered, you shall set in order your own house, for there are many things that are not right in your house.

44. Verily, I say unto my servant Sidney Rigdon, that in some things he hath not kept the commandments concerning his children; therefore, firstly set in order thy house.

45. Verily, I say unto my servant Joseph Smith, jun., or, in other words, I will call you friends, for you are my friends, and ye shall have an inheritance with me.

46. I called you servants for the world's sake, and ye are their servants for my sake;

47. And now, verily, I say unto Joseph Smith, jun., you have not kept the commandments, and must needs stand rebuked before the Lord.

48. Your family must needs repent and forsake some things, and give more earnest heed unto your sayings, or be removed out of their place.

49. What I say unto one I say unto all; pray always lest that wicked one have power in you, and remove you out of your place.

50. My servant Newel K. Whitney, also a bishop of my church, hath need to be chastened, and set in order his family, and see that they are more diligent and concerned at home, and pray always, or they shall be removed out of their place.

51. Now, I say unto you, my friends, let my servant Sidney Rigdon go on his journey, and make haste, and also proclaim the acceptable year of the Lord, and the gospel of salvation, as I shall give him utterance, and by your prayer of faith with one consent, I will uphold him.

52. And let my servant Joseph Smith, jun., and Frederick G. Williams, make haste also, and it shall be given them even according to the prayer of faith, and inasmuch as you keep my sayings, you shall not be confounded in this world, nor in the world to come.

53. And verily, I say unto you, that it is my will that you should hasten to translate my scriptures, and to obtain a knowledge of history, and of countries, and of kingdoms, of laws of God and man, and all this for the salvation of Zion. Amen.

D&C 93:38–40—The burden of what some have labeled "original sin" was lifted forever by Christ through the redeeming power of the Atonement. The arrogant strategy of the evil one is to "take away light and truth" by inducing disobedience among mortals and helping to perpetuate false traditions down through the generations. God has delegated to parents much of the responsibility to preserve righteous principles by bringing up their children "in light and truth" (verse 40), thus countering Satan's insidious plots.

D&C 93:43–52—The Lord of the universe, the Great I Am, the Creator, the Redeemer, the Lamb of God—this eternal Being was aware in minute detail of what was going on in the family circles and homes of Frederick G. Williams, Sidney Rigdon, Joseph Smith Jr., and Newel K. Whitney. The Lord knows us all personally and by name. He is familiar with our struggles, our problems, our challenges, our strengths, our weaknesses, our yearnings and desires. His counsel is direct and specific. What He says to one He says to all. He calls us "friends." He reminds us to "pray always." He encourages us to complete our assignments in building the Kingdom. He wants to pour blessings down upon our heads on the basis of our purity, obedience, and charity—"and all this for the salvation of Zion."

HOW AND WHAT TO WORSHIP

In order to attain a level of appropriate worship, it is essential that we properly prepare ourselves. The Lord describes that preparation in five steps:

1. Forsake sins
2. Come unto the Lord
3. Pray to the Lord
4. Obey the voice of the Lord
5. Keep the Lord's commandments

Not only did the Lord stress the need for each individual to sanctify and prepare himself for worship, He also taught us another way by which we are able to strengthen our worship experience. He called our attention to the content of scripture that teaches us more about Him and that helps us come closer to Him by searching for and receiving scriptural witnesses (see D&C 93:6–18).

That which we are to worship are God our Father and His Son, Jesus Christ. The Savior personified the Father in two ways:

1. The Father gave His fullness to Jesus Christ; this included all power in heaven and on earth, including the glory of the Father (see D&C 93:4, 17).

2. Jesus Christ was the Only Begotten of the Father in the flesh; the Eternal Father in Heaven is the father of the Savior's physical body (*STDC* 2:140–141).

SECTION 94

1. And again, verily I say unto you, my friends, a commandment I give unto you, that ye shall commence a work of laying out and preparing a beginning and foundation of the city of the Stake of Zion, here in the land of Kirtland, beginning at my house.

2. And behold it must be done according to the pattern which I have given unto you.

3. And let the first lot on the south, be consecrated unto me for the building of an house, for the Presidency, for the work of the Presidency, in obtaining revelations; and for the work of the ministry of the Presidency, in all things pertaining to the church and kingdom.

4. Verily I say unto you, that it shall be built fifty-five by sixty-five feet in the width thereof and in the length thereof, in the inner court;

5. And there shall be a lower court and a higher court, according to the pattern which shall be given unto you hereafter;

6. And it shall be dedicated unto the Lord from the foundation thereof, according to the order of the Priesthood, according to the pattern which shall be given unto you hereafter.

7. And it shall be wholly dedicated unto the Lord for the work of the Presidency.

8. And ye shall not suffer any unclean thing to come in unto it; and my glory shall be there, and my presence shall be there;

9. But if there shall come into it any unclean thing, my glory shall not be there; and my presence shall not come into it.

10. And again, verily I say unto you, the second lot on the south shall be dedicated unto me for the building of a house unto me, for the work of the printing of the translation of my scriptures, and all things whatsoever I shall command you;

11. And it shall be fifty-five by sixty-five feet in the width thereof and the length thereof, in the inner court; and there shall be a lower and a higher court;

12. And this house shall be wholly dedicated unto the Lord from the foundation thereof, for the work of the printing, in all things whatsoever I shall command you, to be holy, undefiled, according to the pattern in all things, as it shall be given unto you.

13. And on the third lot shall my servant Hyrum Smith receive his inheritance,

14. And on the first and second lots

The Stannard Quarry in Chapin Forest, near Kirtland, that yielded some of the stone for the Kirtland Temple. After being rebuked by the Lord in Section 95, members of the temple committee rushed to the quarry and started digging with their hands, because they had no tools. Joseph Smith Jr. himself worked in the quarry at times. While three different quarries were used for the Kirtland Temple, this is the best known of the three. (The drilling marks seen here were likely created during work on a later project.)

Section 94 Background—Given at Kirtland, Ohio, May 6, 1833 (see *HC* 1:346–347).

D&C 94:7–12—The buildings to be erected for the administration of Church affairs and the preparation and printing of the scriptures are to be dedicated to the Lord and rendered holy—in other words, kept free from unclean influences. Virtually the same atmosphere of cleanliness and holiness that one expects to find in the temples of the Lord is also appropriate for the other edifices that belong to the kingdom of God—the buildings that serve as centers for the management of the affairs of the Kingdom, plus the chapels, stake centers, and homes of Zion. Parents especially can contribute to the common good of Zion in this regard by ensuring that their homes are kept neat and orderly, and that no unrighteous influence be admitted in the form of profane language, questionable literature, degrading television programs, or immoral Internet communications. The blessing that comes from maintaining a pure and wholesome environment in our homes is that the glory and presence of the Lord can be there through the influence of His Holy Spirit.

The Prophet Isaiah foresaw the time when the glory and influence of the Lord would rest visibly upon every home in Zion—just as it did in the case of the tabernacle in the wilderness following the exodus from Egypt:

> And the Lord will create upon every dwelling place of mount Zion, and upon her assemblies, a cloud and smoke by day, and the shining of a flaming fire by night: for upon all the glory *shall be* a defence.
>
> And there shall be a tabernacle for a shadow in the daytime from the heat, and for a place of refuge, and for a covert from storm and from rain. (Isa. 4:5–6; see also 2 Ne. 14:5–6.)

on the north shall my servants Reynolds Cahoon and Jared Carter receive their inheritances.

15. That they may do the work which I have appointed unto them, to be a committee to build mine houses, according to the commandment, which I, the Lord God, have given unto you.

16. These two houses are not to be built until I give unto you a commandment concerning them.

17. And now I give unto you no more at this time. Amen.

SECTION 95

1. Verily, thus saith the Lord unto you, whom I love, and whom I love I also chasten, that their sins may be forgiven, for with the chastisement I prepare a way for their deliverance in all things out of temptation, and I have loved you.

2. Wherefore ye must needs be chastened and stand rebuked before my face

3. For ye have sinned against me a very grievous sin, in that ye have not considered the great commandment in all things, that I have given unto you concerning the building of mine house,

4. For the preparation wherewith I design to prepare mine apostles to prune my vineyard for the last time, that I may bring to pass my strange act, that I may pour out my Spirit upon all flesh.

5. But behold, verily I say unto you, that there are many who have been ordained among you, whom I have called, but few of them are chosen;

6. They who are not chosen have sinned a very grievous sin, in that they are walking in darkness at noon-day;

7. And for this cause I gave unto you a commandment that you should call your solemn assembly, that your fastings and your mourning might come up into the ears of the Lord of Sabaoth, which is by interpretation, the Creator of the first day, the beginning and the end.

8. Yea, verily I say unto you, I gave

D&C 94:15—In verse 15 we have reference to "a committee to build mine houses." This is the first instance where the word "committee" is used in the scriptures. What at first glance is an instance of a basic, rudimentary construction enterprise is—upon further investigation—a microcosm of the greater Kingdom, with its unfolding vision of thousands and tens of thousands of chapels and temples and millions upon millions of homes of Zion worldwide. The small bricks and stones that would go to make up the future structures of the Church (including the Kirtland Temple) are types and shadows of the stone in Nebuchadnezzar's dream, interpreted by Daniel as "the stone . . . cut out of the mountain without hands" (Dan. 2:45) that "became a great mountain, and filled the whole earth" (Dan. 2:35).

Section 95 Background—Given on June 1, 1833, at Kirtland, Ohio, in the Newel K. Whitney Store (most likely in the translating room). The Lord had commanded Joseph Smith to erect the Kirtland Temple in the revelation given December 28, 1832 (see D&C 88:119–136). In the intervening five months, except for acquiring land, no effort had been made to start building the temple. The Church was in dire circumstances, essentially lacking all resources needed to build the temple—money, materials, tools, and experienced manpower. No architectural or engineering plans existed. The Prophet Joseph had been occupied with the completion of the inspired translation of the Bible (see D&C 93:53). Priesthood leaders were busily engaged in establishing the United Order or "Firm" and purchasing properties such as the Tannery, the Johnson Inn, and the Peter French Farm to become part of that enterprise. Persecution against the Church was escalating in Ohio and Missouri. The Lord now gets Joseph's attention in D&C Section 95 and addresses the urgency of building the Kirtland Temple in order to endow the Saints with "power from on high."

D&C 95:1–6—Love and chastening are never incompatible. They are inseparable aspects of the divine nature. Love without essential chastening is passive and not forward reaching; chastening without love is a form of unrighteous dominion. The Lord balances the two—love and correction—with perfectness. Pride, worldly ambition, sin, and unrighteous dominion referred to in Section 95 all constituted a "grievous sin" and a serious distraction from the urgent need to build a temple to the Lord.

The question for us is this: Is there any commandment of the Lord we need to hasten to obey? Are we procrastinating our salvation and exaltation by allowing worldly distractions to interfere with the fulfilling of our covenant obligations to the Lord? If so, then the chastening of the Lord may enter into the picture as we seek to redress the situation and pray for a way to find "deliverance in all things."

unto you a commandment that you should build an house, in the which house I design to endow those whom I have chosen with power from on high;

9. For this is the promise of the Father unto you; therefore I command you to tarry, even as mine apostles at Jerusalem;

10. Nevertheless my servants sinned a very grievous sin, and contentions arose in the school of the prophets, which was very grievous unto me, saith your Lord; therefore I sent them forth to be chastened.

11. Verily I say unto you, it is my will that you should build a house. If you keep my commandments, you shall have power to build it;

12. If you keep not my commandments, the love of the Father shall not continue with you, therefore you shall walk in darkness.

13. Now here is wisdom, and the mind of the Lord; let the house be built, not after the manner of the world, for I give not unto you that ye shall live after the manner of the world;

14. Therefore let it be built after the manner which I shall show unto three of you, whom ye shall appoint and ordain unto this power.

15. And the size thereof shall be fifty and five feet in width, and let it be sixty-five feet in length, in the inner court thereof;

16. And let the lower part of the inner court be dedicated unto me for your sacrament offering, and for your preaching, and your fasting, and your praying, and the offering up your most holy desires unto me, saith your Lord.

17. And let the higher part of the inner court be dedicated unto me, for the school of mine apostles, saith Son Ahman; or, in other words, Alphus; or, in other words, Omegus; even Jesus Christ your Lord. Amen.

SECTION 96

1. Behold, I say unto you, Here is wisdom, whereby ye may know how to act concerning this matter, for it is expedient in me that this Stake that I have set for the strength of Zion should be made strong;

JOHN JOHNSON

John Johnson was born April 11, 1778, at Chesterfield, Cheshire County, New Hampshire. Eventually he moved to Hiram, Ohio, and became a prosperous farmer. While visiting the Prophet Joseph Smith in Kirtland, John witnessed the miraculous healing of his rheumatic wife under the hands of the Prophet. The couple was converted and subsequently baptized. In September 1831 they opened their home in Hiram to the Prophet and his family. The Johnsons later moved to Kirtland, where John was ordained an elder and subsequently a high priest. John became a member of the Kirtland high council on February 17, 1834. Among other things, he displayed the Michael Chandler mummies and papyri in his inn at Kirtland on July 3, 1835 (see *HC* 2:235–236) and contributed resources and service toward the building of the Kirtland Temple. Thereafter, financial and legal difficulties, together with his loss of commitment to gospel truths, led to his falling away from the Church. He died in Kirtland on July 30, 1843.

D&C 95:8—It is in the nature of Deity to want to give His children light, truth, and power of a saving and exalting kind. To "endow" is to give—to bestow a divine blessing. In this case, the reference is to the kind of endowment given in a sanctuary prepared of the Lord for this purpose. The endowment intended for the Saints in the Kirtland Temple was of a partial nature, and not the same as today's temple endowment. The first complete endowments in this dispensation were given in Nauvoo on May 4, 1842, but were not given in a temple.

D&C 95:11–17—The eternal Architect works on covenant principles: If you keep the commandments, then power will be given to build this temple. And so it was. The Kirtland Temple, erected through the power of God and the sacrifice and obedience of His Saints, was to be dedicated fewer than three years later, on March 27, 1836. It was to be a house acceptable to the Lord and dedicated for spiritual worship, the training of the leadership and emissaries of the Church, and the granting of a partial endowment of sacred truth and power by the Lord. It was in this house that the Lord Himself would appear on April 3, 1836, in a glorious manifestation to accept the offering of His Saints and inaugurate the process whereby the keys of temple work and the gathering of the Saints might again be activated in the dispensation of the fullness of times.

Section 96 Background—Given on June 4, 1833, at Kirtland, Ohio (see *HC* 1:352–353). The Prophet gives this introduction: "A similar conference [to the one held on June 3] assembled at the same place [in the translating room in Kirtland] and took into consideration how the [recently purchased] French farm should be disposed of. The conference could not agree who should take charge of it, but all agreed to inquire of the Lord; accordingly we received [Section 96]" (*HC* 1:352).

D&C 96:1, 5—Some two and a half millennia earlier, the Lord had inspired Isaiah to proclaim: "Enlarge the place of thy tent, and let them stretch forth the curtains of thine habitations: spare not, lengthen thy cords, and strengthen thy stakes" (Isa. 54:2). Now, in 1833, the Lord again calls for the emergence of a stake of strength—the first in the new and final dispensation—to begin the process of supporting the canopy of gospel truth being restored and disseminated to the world. Central to the process of establishing the Church throughout the world would be the temple—the sanctuary of holy truth that would transcend the boundaries of mortality and open the gates of heaven to the blessing of mankind. It would be only three years later in the completed temple at Kirtland that Elijah would return to convey the keys of the sealing powers by means of which the hearts of the fathers and the children would be united (see D&C 110:13–15).

2. Therefore let my servant Ahashdah [Newel K. Whitney] take charge of the place which is named among you, upon which I design to build mine holy house;

3. And again, let it be divided into lots according to wisdom, for the benefit of those who seek inheritances, as it shall be determined in council among you.

4. Therefore, take heed that ye see to this matter, and that portion that is necessary to benefit mine order, for the purpose of bringing forth my word to the children of men;

5. For behold, verily I say unto you, this is the most expedient in me, that my word should go forth unto the children of men, for the purpose of subduing the hearts of the children of men for your good. Even so. Amen.

6. And again, verily I say unto you, it is wisdom and expedient in me, that my servant Zombre [John Johnson] whose offering I have accepted, and whose prayers I have heard, unto whom I give a promise of eternal life inasmuch as he keepeth my commandments from henceforth,

7. For he is a descendant of Seth, [Joseph,] and a partaker of the blessings of the promise made unto his fathers.

8. Verily I say unto you, it is expedient in me that he should become a member of the order, that he may assist in bringing forth my word unto the children of men;

9. Therefore ye shall ordain him unto this blessing, and he shall seek diligently to take away incumbrances that are upon the house named among you, that he may dwell therein. Even so. Amen.

SECTION 97

1. Verily I say unto you my friends, I speak unto you with my voice, even the voice of my Spirit, that I may show unto you my will concerning your brethren in the land of Zion, many of whom are truly humble and are seeking diligently to learn wisdom and to find truth.

2. Verily, verily I say unto you, blessed are such, for they shall obtain, for I, the Lord, show mercy unto all the meek, and upon all whomsoever I will, that I may be justified when I shall bring them into judgment.

3. Behold, I say unto you, concerning

D&C 96:6–8—John Johnson contributed much support to the work of the Prophet Joseph Smith, having opened his home to the Prophet and his family. This was the venue for many conferences of the priesthood and the reception of glorious revelations, including Section 76. Johnson became a member of the United Order and consecrated his surplus property and business profit to the Church. The large frame home he sold along with his farm for the benefit of the Church is still standing today and is used as a visitors' center for the Church. The money from that sale was combined with the funds in the United Order to pay the mortgage on the Peter French Farm, where the Kirtland Temple was eventually built. The long-awaited restoration of priesthood keys was made possible in part by John Johnson's offering—a prime example of what one person can do.

Section 97 Background—Given on June 4, 1833, in the Newel K. Whitney Store at Kirtland, Ohio (see *HC* 1:400–402). Although unknown to Joseph Smith at the time, the Saints in Missouri were experiencing insurmountable problems. Thirteen days before this revelation was given, a mob destroyed the printing office along with most of the almost-completed Book of Commandments. The mob then ransacked the Church store and partially stripped Bishop Edward Partridge and Charles Allen of their clothes and tarred and feathered them in the public square, surrounded by hundreds. The mob demanded that the Saints leave Jackson County.

It should be noted that on the very day that Joseph and his brethren laid the cornerstones for the Kirtland Temple, Church leaders in Missouri signed a formal agreement to leave Jackson County by January 1, 1834. Considering this coincidence, Brigham Young's statement comes to mind, "We never began to build a Temple without the bells of hell beginning to ring. . . . We completed a temple in Kirtland and in Nauvoo; and did not the bells of hell toll all the time we were building them? They did, every week and every day" (*JD* 8:355–356).

D&C 97:1–2—The first answer to a query by the Latter-day Saint as to why he should be humble is that God has commanded men to be humble. The benefits of being humble must also give the answer to the need for this virtue (Mosiah 3:18–19). . . . The Lord blesses the person of humility. In what ways? (1) He "shall lead thee by the hand, and give thee answer to thy prayers." (D&C 112:10.) (2) The Lord's spirit enlightens the humble. (*Ibid.*, 136:33.) (3) "Let him that is ignorant learn wisdom by humbling himself." (*Ibid.*, v. 32.) (4) The promise of seeing and knowing the Lord is made to the humble. (*Ibid.*, 67:10.) (5) His arm of mercy is extended to the humble in freeing them of bondage. (Mosiah 29:18–20.) (6) The weak are made strong and are thus able to fulfill other commandments. (Ether 12:26–27.) (7) The humble receive knowledge. (D&C 1:28.) (8) The blessing of assisting the Lord in his work comes to the humble (*Ibid.*, 12:8) (*Doxey*, 336–337).

the school in Zion, I, the Lord, am well pleased that there should be a school in Zion, and also with my servant Parley P. Pratt, for he abideth in me;

4. And inasmuch as he continueth to abide in me; he shall continue to preside over the school in the land of Zion, until I shall give unto him other commandments;

5. And I will bless him with a multiplicity of blessings, in expounding all scriptures and mysteries to the edification of the school, and of the church in Zion;

6. And to the residue of the school, I, the Lord, am willing to show mercy, nevertheless there are those that must needs be chastened, and their works shall be made known.

7. The ax is laid at the root of the trees, and every tree that bringeth not forth good fruit, shall be hewn down and cast into the fire: I, the Lord, have spoken it.

8. Verily I say unto you, all among them who know their hearts are honest, and are broken, and their spirits contrite, and are willing to observe their covenants by sacrifice; yea, every sacrifice which I, the Lord, shall command, they are accepted of me,

9. For I, the Lord, will cause them to bring forth as a very fruitful tree which is planted in a goodly land, by a pure stream, that yieldeth much precious fruit.

10. Verily, I say unto you, that it is my will that an house should be built unto me in the land of Zion, like unto the pattern which I have given you;

11. Yea, let it be built speedily, by the tithing of my people:

12. Behold, this is the tithing and the sacrifice which I, the Lord, require at their hands, that there may be an house built unto me for the salvation of Zion,

13. For a place of thanksgiving for all saints, and for a place of instruction for all those who are called to the work of the ministry in all their several callings and offices,

14. That they may be perfected in the understanding of their ministry—in theory, in principle, and in doctrine—in all things pertaining to the kingdom of God on the earth, the keys of which kingdom have been conferred upon you.

15. And inasmuch as my people build an house unto me in the name of the Lord, and do not suffer any unclean thing to come into it that it be not defiled, my glory shall rest upon it;

16. Yea, and my presence shall be there, for I will come into it, and all the pure in heart that shall come into it shall see God;

17. But if it be defiled I will not come into it, and my glory shall not be there, for I will not come into unholy temples.

D&C 97:3–5—In his autobiography, Parley P. Pratt gives this report:

> In the latter part of summer and in the autumn, I devoted almost my entire time in ministering among the churches; holding meetings; visiting the sick; comforting the afflicted, and giving counsel. A school of Elders was also organized, over which I was called to preside. This class, to the number of about sixty, met for instruction once a week. The place of meeting was in the open air, under some tall trees, in a retired place in the wilderness, where we prayed, preached and prophesied, and exercised ourselves in the gifts of the Holy Spirit. Here great blessings were poured out, and many great and marvelous things were manifested and taught. . . . To attend this school I had to travel on foot, and sometimes with bare feet at that, about six miles. This I did once a week, besides visiting and preaching in five or six branches a week.

> While thus engaged, and in answer to our correspondence with the Prophet, Joseph Smith, at Kirtland, Ohio, [Section 97] was sent to us by him, dated August, 1833. (*APPP*, 75–76.)

D&C 97:8—Those who desire to be accepted of the Lord have in this verse a succinct statement of divine origin as to how they should proceed. Beyond the requirement of spiritual meekness and contrition, the Lord states that sacrifice in keeping one's covenants is essential to being accepted of Him. How much sacrifice? Every sacrifice that the Lord will command. There is no limit. Some, like the Prophet Joseph Smith and his brother Hyrum, were required to give their lives as martyrs for the cause of Zion. Everyone—all members of the Church—are required to give their lives in service for the building up of the Kingdom.

D&C 97:17—The Lord often teaches by contrast. Having unfolded the majestic vision and promise of beholding God in His holy house, The Lord gives the somber warning that He will not enter into a defiled environment. The pure in heart, however, have the transcendent opportunity to be immersed in the wonders of heaven, as John A. Widtsoe declared:

> Temple work . . . gives a wonderful opportunity for keeping alive our spiritual knowledge and strength. . . . The mighty perspective of eternity is unraveled before us in the holy temples; we see time from its infinite beginning to its endless end; and the drama of eternal life is unfolded before us. Then I see more clearly my place amidst the things of the universe, my place among the purposes of God; I am better able to place myself where I belong, and I am better able to value and to weigh, to separate and to organize the common, ordinary duties of my life so that the little things shall not oppress me or take away my vision of the greater things that God has given us. (*CR*, April 1922, 97–98.)

18. And, now, behold, if Zion do these things she shall prosper, and spread herself and become very glorious, very great, and very terrible,

19. And the nations of the earth shall honor her, and shall say, surely Zion is the city of our God, and surely Zion cannot fall, neither be moved out of her place, for God is there, and the hand of the Lord is there,

20. And he hath sworn by the power of his might, to be her salvation and her high tower;

21. Therefore, verily, thus saith the Lord, let Zion rejoice, for this is Zion—the pure in heart; therefore, let Zion rejoice, while all the wicked shall mourn;

22. For behold, and lo, vengeance cometh speedily upon the ungodly as the whirlwind, and who shall escape it;

23. The Lord's scourge shall pass over by night and by day, and the report thereof shall vex all people; yet, it shall not be stayed until the Lord come;

24. For the indignation of the Lord is kindled against their abominations and all their wicked works;

25. Nevertheless Zion shall escape if she observe to do all things whatsoever I have commanded her,

26. But if she observe not to do whatsoever I have commanded her, I will visit her according to all her works, with sore affliction, with pestilence, with plague, with sword, with vengeance, with devouring fire;

27. Nevertheless, let it be read this once in their ears, that I, the Lord, have accepted of her offering, and if she sin no more, none of these things shall come upon her,

28. And I will bless her with blessings, and multiply a multiplicity of blessings upon her, and upon her generations forever and ever, saith the Lord your God. Amen.

THE SCHOOL OF THE ELDERS

In order to help the priesthood holders better understand their callings and responsibilities, a school was organized for the elders in Missouri; Parley P. Pratt was called to preside over and teach the elders. (This was different from the school of the prophets, which was presided over by the Prophet Joseph Smith.) Parley P. Pratt described his labors and sacrifices in conducting the school of the elders:

In the latter part of summer and in the autumn, I devoted almost my entire time in ministering among the churches; holding meetings; visiting the sick; comforting the afflicted, and giving counsel. A school of Elders was also organized, over which I was called to preside. This class, to the number of about sixty, met for instruction once a week. The place of meeting was in the open air, under some tall trees, in a retired place in the wilderness, where we prayed, preached, and prophesied, and exercised ourselves in the gifts of the Holy Spirit. . . . To attend this school I had to travel on foot, and sometimes with bare feet at that, about six miles. This I did once a week, besides visiting and preaching in five or six branches a week (APPP, 93–94) (STDC 2:159–160).

D&C 97:21—The pure people—"the pure in heart"—constitute Zion, upon which the Lord bestows marvelous blessings. The Saints are to cultivate, through faith and sacrifice, the nature and qualities of a Zion people: "And Zion cannot be built up unless it is by the principles of the law of the celestial kingdom; otherwise I cannot receive her unto myself. And my people must needs be chastened until they learn obedience, if it must needs be, by the things which they suffer" (D&C 105:5–6). Similarly, Zion consists of a people unified in the discipleship of the Redeemer, like unto the people of Enoch.

The term *Zion* is perhaps the closest thing to a freestanding linguistic emblem or ensign among all the vocabulary words of the gospel. "Zion" draws the mind heavenward toward God, the spirit inward toward a state of worthiness and gratitude, the heart outward in service toward others, and the feet onward toward "a place of refuge, and for a covert from storm and from rain" (Isa. 4:6). Zion is a place, an institution, a state of mind, a noble destination, a people, a vision of perfection, an abode of God, an encapsulating summary of everything that is "honest, true, chaste, benevolent, virtuous. . . lovely, or of good report or praiseworthy" (Article of Faith 13).

Zion is not a utopia ever nestled beyond mortal access: it is a reality that has already been manifested at times upon the earth among mortals who have risen to such a noble level of covenant righteousness that their exemplary level of peace, unity, and spiritual attainment have evoked upon them the highest blessings of our Father in Heaven.

D&C 97:22—Joseph Smith said that they who will not hear the Savior's voice must expect to feel His wrath.

D&C 97:25, 28—The judgments of God will descend upon the nations with divine vengeance in the final chapters of the earth's history. How will Zion be protected during this period of monumental upheaval? We as a people, even a Zion people, can and will be blessed as we keep the commandments. We will enjoy the Spirit of the Lord, which will show us all things that we are to do (see 2 Nephi 32:5). We will be pure in heart, a righteous people, and enjoy happiness and the protection of the Almighty.

D&C 97:26—The Saints didn't fully heed this warning, and devastation came in November 1833 when mobs drove Saints from their homes in Jackson County. That situation included threats of death against many individuals. Many lost all their personal property, and most of the crops that had been planted were destroyed.

SECTION 98

1. Verily I say unto you my friends, fear not, let your hearts be comforted; yea, rejoice evermore, and in everything give thanks,

2. Waiting patiently on the Lord, for your prayers have entered into the ears of the Lord of Sabaoth, and are recorded with this seal and testament; the Lord hath sworn and decreed that they shall be granted;

3. Therefore he giveth this promise unto you, with an immutable covenant that they shall be fulfilled and all things wherewith you have been afflicted, shall work together for your good, and to my name's glory, saith the Lord.

4. And now, verily I say unto you concerning the laws of the land, it is my will that my people should observe to do all things whatsoever I command them;

5. And that law of the land which is constitutional, supporting that principle of freedom in maintaining rights and privileges, belongs to all mankind, and is justifiable before me;

6. Therefore, I, the Lord, justify you, and your brethren of my church, in befriending that law which is the constitutional law of the land;

7. And as pertaining to law of man, whatsoever is more or less than these, cometh of evil.

8. I, the Lord God, make you free, therefore ye are free indeed; and the law also maketh you free;

9. Nevertheless, when the wicked rule the people mourn;

10. Wherefore, honest men, and wise men should be sought for diligently, and good men and wise men ye should observe to uphold; otherwise whatsoever is less than these cometh of evil.

11. And I give unto you a commandment, that ye shall forsake all evil and cleave unto all good, that ye shall live by every word which proceedeth forth out of the mouth of God;

12. For he will give unto the faithful line upon line, precept upon precept; and I will try you and prove you herewith;

13. And whoso layeth down his life in my cause, for my name's sake, shall find it again, even life eternal:

14. Therefore be not afraid of your enemies, for I have decreed in my heart, saith the Lord, that I will prove you in all things, whether you will abide in my covenant, even

Section 98 Background—Given on August 6, 1833, at Kirtland, Ohio (see *HC* 1:403–406). Much persecution was being heaped on the Saints in Missouri at this time—though the scope and intensity of the persecution taking place some 900 miles away was unknown to the Prophet, except as word might come through revelation. This revelation is a reminder to view things from a higher perspective. Without perspective, the Lord's message to the beleaguered Saints in this revelation might have been a bitter pill to swallow—because it involved the application of patience and peace, while extending an olive leaf to their abusive and hateful neighbors.

D&C 98:3—In the revelation given through Brigham Young on the eve of the exodus to the West, the Lord confirmed an eternal principle: "My people must be tried in all things, that they may be prepared to receive the glory that I have for them, even the glory of Zion; and he that will not bear chastisement is not worthy of my kingdom" (D&C 136:31). In the words of C. S. Lewis, "Suffering is the megaphone God uses to get our attention."

D&C 98:9— The Book of Mormon is replete with evidence of the destructive forces of tyrannizing rulers acting on their own out of pride and greed or being complicit with secret combinations bent on the extinction of liberty and rights.

D&C 98:10—James E. Talmage stated: "Our religion should purify our politics, and make us honest, tolerant, and bold, to do that which is required of citizens, and to exercise our rights at the polls. Our religion should make us honest in business, truthful in all our doings. To be so is to be in line with the keeping of the commandments of the Lord. I pray that this may continue to be a characteristic of the Latter-day Saints, in the name of Jesus Christ" (*CR*, Oct. 1920, 66).

D&C 98:11–14—To "live" by every word of God is to harvest the blessing of eternal life. To abide in the covenant of God—regardless of the sacrifices we are called on to make—is to be assured of immortality and exaltation. Elder Orson Pratt made a remarkable personal declaration concerning this principle:

> These revelations, these books are more precious than the riches, and kingdoms, and glories, and honors of this present life, so far as I am concerned. Do I esteem them more than I do my own life? I would be unworthy of my Father and my God in the eternal worlds if I would refuse to lay down my life, if it were required of me of the Lord. . . . I do not wish to be thus tried, I do not covet this trial, I do not pray for it; but if ever I should be brought to this condition, with my present feelings, with the feelings I have had for a great many years, I would say: "Come martyrdom, come burnings at the stake, come any calamity and affliction of the body that may be devised by wicked and ungodly men—let me choose that, and have life eternal beyond the grave; but let me not deny the work of God." (*JD* 21:173.)

unto death, that you may be found worthy;

15. For if ye will not abide in my covenant, ye are not worthy of me;

16. Therefore renounce war and proclaim peace, and seek diligently to turn the hearts of their children to their fathers, and the hearts of the fathers to the children;

17. And again, the hearts of the Jews unto the prophets, and the prophets unto the Jews, lest I come and smite the whole earth with a curse, and all flesh be consumed before me.

18. Let not your hearts be troubled, for in my Father's house are many mansions, and I have prepared a place for you, and where my Father and I am, there ye shall be also.

19. Behold, I, the Lord, am not well pleased with many who are in the church at Kirtland,

20. For they do not forsake their sins, and their wicked ways, the pride of their hearts, and their covetousness, and all their detestable things, and observe the words of wisdom and eternal life which I have given unto them.

21. Verily I say unto you, that I, the Lord, will chasten them, and will do whatsoever I list, if they do not repent and observe all things whatsoever I have said unto them.

22. And again I say unto you, if ye observe to do whatsoever I command you, I, the Lord, will turn away all wrath and indignation from you, and the gates of hell shall not prevail against you.

23. Now I speak unto you concerning your families; if men will smite you, or your families, once, and ye bear it patiently and revile not against them, neither seek revenge, ye shall be rewarded;

24. But if ye bear it not patiently, it shall be accounted unto you as being meted out a just measure unto you.

25. And again, if your enemy shall smite you the second time, and you revile not against your enemy, and bear it patiently, your reward shall be an hundred fold.

26. And again, if he shall smite you the third time, and ye bear it patiently, your reward shall be doubled unto you four fold;

27. And these three testimonies shall stand against your enemy if he repent not, and shall not be blotted out.

28. And now verily I say unto you, if that enemy shall escape my vengeance, that he be not brought into judgment before me, then ye shall see to it that ye warn him in my name, that he come no more upon you, neither upon your family, even your childrenchildren unto the third and fourth generation;

29. And then if he shall come upon you, or your children, or your children's children unto the third and fourth generation; I have delivered thine enemy into thine hands,

30. And then if thou wilt spare him, thou shalt be rewarded for thy righteousness; and also thy children and thy children's children unto the third and fourth generation;

31. Nevertheless thine enemy is in thine hands, and if thou rewardest him according to his works, thou art justified, if he has sought thy life, and thy life is endangered by him,

D&C 98:16–18—The nature of our "heart" determines our ultimate destiny. Hearts filled with the spirit of peace and the desire to promote unity and oneness within family generations will have more "confidence" (D&C 121:45) in the presence of God. Hearts that are full of hope and faith—not "troubled" with doubt and spiritual anxiety—will more surely merit admission into the presence of the Father and Son.

D&C 98:16–48—These verses outline the laws by which the Saints are governed in times of adversity: the Law of Retaliation (verses 23–32), the Law of War (verses 33–38), and the Law of Forgiveness (verses 39–48). Elder Bruce R. McConkie prophesied in warning that great times of tribulation are yet coming when the Saints will need to look to these three laws.

THE PURPOSE OF LAW

All promises of the Lord are contingent upon compliance with the conditions upon which the promises were made. The Lord revealed certain principles that must be understood and practiced before His Saints could expect the blessings and promises previously mentioned. In order to teach the purpose of the law, the Lord said, "I, the Lord God, made you free, therefore you are free indeed; and the law also maketh you free" (D&C 98:8).

This statement specifically referred to the inspired constitutional law of the land (see D&C 101:79–80). The principle, however, is universally applicable to all of God's laws.

The purpose of each of God's laws is to make men free. Obedience to the law provides freedom from sorrow, regret, tyranny, and all unrighteousness in all of its many forms. Obedience to law is the way by which men obtain happiness and peace.

As to the laws of the land, how does one know whether any given law is constitutional and justifiable before the Lord? The revelation of the Lord provides the answer. Any law that supports the principle of freedom in maintaining the rights and privileges of mankind is constitutional in the eyes of the Lord (see D&C 98:5–6). Any law that restricts or diminishes the right of free agency of an individual is not constitutional.

We not only must support constitutional laws, but we are enjoined by the Lord to seek for and uphold honest men to administer righteous laws (see D&C 98:10). The Lord expects His people to be righteously involved in the political process.

As we reflect on the counsel of the Lord pertaining to the purpose of law, a fundamental principle is apparent. Our righteous attitude and obedience to laws inspired of the Lord are prerequisite to our righteous relationship with Him (*STDC* 2:165–167).

thine enemy is in thine hands and thou art justified.

32. Behold, this is the law I gave unto my servant Nephi, and thy fathers Joseph, and Jacob, and Isaac, and Abraham, and all mine ancient prophets and apostles.

33. And again, his is the law that I gave unto mine ancients, that they should not go out unto battle against any nation, kindred, tongue, or people, save I, the Lord, commanded them.

34. And if any nation, tongue, or people, should proclaim war against them, they should first lift a standard of peace unto that people, nation, or tongue;

35. And if that people did not accept the offering of peace neither the second nor the third time, they should bring these testimonies before the Lord;

36. Then I, the Lord, would give unto them a commandment, and justify them in going out to battle against that nation, tongue, or people,

37. And I, the Lord, would fight their battles, and their children's battles, and their children's children's, until they had avenged themselves on all their enemies, to the third and fourth generation.

38. Behold, this is an ensample unto all people, saith the Lord your God, for justification before me.

39. And again, verily I say unto you, if after thine enemy has come upon thee the first time, he repent and come unto thee praying thy forgiveness, thou shalt forgive him, and shall hold it no more as a testimony against thine enemy,

40. And so on unto the second and third time; and as oft as thine enemy repenteth of the trespass wherewith he has trespassed against thee, thou shalt forgive him, until seventy times seven:

41. And if he trespass against thee and repent not the first time, nevertheless thou shalt forgive him;

42. And if he trespass against thee the second time, and repent not, nevertheless thou shalt forgive him;

43. And if he trespass against thee the third time, and repent not, thou shalt also forgive him;

44. But if he trespass against thee the fourth time, thou shalt not forgive him, but shalt bring these testimonies before the Lord, and they shall not be blotted out until he repent and reward thee four fold in all things wherewith he has trespassed against thee;

45. And if he do this, thou shalt forgive him with all thine heart, and if he do not this, I the Lord, will avenge thee of thine enemy an hundred fold;

46. And upon his children, and upon his children's children of all them that hate me, unto the third and fourth generation;

47. But if the children shall repent, or the children's children, and turn to the Lord their God, with all their hearts, and with all their might, mind, and strength, and restore four fold for all their trespasses, wherewith they have trespassed, or wherewith their fathers have trespassed, or their father's fathers, then thine indignation shall be turned away,

48. And vengeance shall no more come upon them, saith the Lord thy God, and their trespasses shall never be brought any more as a testimony before the Lord against them. Amen.

D&C 98:33—Amidst the persecutions and violence heaped on the Saints in the early years of the Restoration unfolds this dawning light of wisdom from the Lord in answer to the question: How should we protect our families when they are attacked? Central to the revealed response are three principles: (1) We are to do all we can to protect our families and secure their safety and well-being; (2) we are to infuse our strategies for response with genuine forgiveness and forbearance when the enemy repents and desists; and (3) we are to await the command of God when the hour for justified proactive retribution arrives.

Forgiving those who come against our families with violence and destruction is a challenging principle. "That seems very difficult indeed for us mortals," said President Spencer W. Kimball, "and yet there are still harder things to do. When they have repented and come on their knees to ask forgiveness, most of us can forgive, but the Lord has required that we shall forgive even if they do not repent nor ask forgiveness of us. . . .

It must be very clear to us, then, that we must still forgive without retaliation or vengeance, for the Lord will do for us such as is necessary (*FPM*, 191–192).

D&C 98:38—An "ensample" is a model of conduct, a precedent that can be followed.

THE LAW OF FORGIVENESS AND RETRIBUTION

To teach the Saints how to dispel their feelings of hate and revenge toward their persecutors, the Lord counseled them to seek redress, not revenge (see D&C 98:23–24). If they did not obtain justice under the laws of the land, they were to bear their afflictions patiently before the Lord. Even if their enemies were to come upon them a second and a third time, they still were not to revile. Instead, the Saints were to warn their enemy. The Lord further stated that after the third time, the Lord would give the Saints power over their enemy (see D&C 98:25–29).

In 1833, the Saints were driven from Jackson County, Missouri. In 1838, they were driven from the state of Missouri. In 1845, they were driven from Illinois. On each of these three occasions, the Saints collectively followed the counsel of the Lord in this revelation. They did not retaliate. Thus, the blessings promised in this revelation have literally been fulfilled for the benefit of the Church. There are many third- and fourth-generation descendants who are now reaping the blessings of the obedience of their forefathers (see D&C 98:30).

The Lord also instructed the Saints regarding forgiveness; feelings of forgiveness toward a person who has wronged us ought to be in our hearts continually and unconditionally. The Lord has admonished us not to limit the number of times we are willing to work with a wrongdoer who is seeking forgiveness (see D&C 98:39–40) (*STDC* 2:167–168).

SECTION 99

1. Behold, thus saith the Lord unto my servant John Murdock, thou art called to go into the eastern countries from house to house, from village to village, and from city to city, to proclaim mine everlasting gospel unto the inhabitants thereof, in the midst of persecution and wickedness;

2. And who receiveth you receiveth me, and you shall have power to declare my word in the demonstration of my Holy Spirit;

3. And who receiveth you as a little child, receiveth my kingdom, and blessed are they, for they shall obtain mercy;

4. And whoso rejecteth you shall be rejected of my Father and his house; and you shall cleanse your feet in the secret places by the way for a testimony against them.

5. And behold, and lo, I come quickly to judgment, to convince all of their ungodly deeds which they have committed against me, as it is written of me in the volume of the book.

6. And now, verily I say unto you, that it is not expedient that you should go until your children are provided for, and kindly sent up unto the bishop in Zion;

7. And after a few years, if thou desirest of me, thou mayest go up also unto the goodly land, to possess thine inheritance:

8. Otherwise thou shalt continue proclaiming my gospel until thou be taken. Amen.

SECTION 100

1. Verily, thus saith the Lord unto you, my friends Sidney, and Joseph, your families are well; they are in

---

JOHN GOULD

John Gould was born in Ontario, Canada. While serving as a Baptist minister in New York in 1831, he was converted to the restored gospel and brought a large segment of his congregation into the Church. In 1833 he and Orson Hyde were sent by the Prophet Joseph Smith to Missouri to give counsel and assistance to the beleaguered Saints there. The Lord subsequently gave assurances to the concerned Prophet that these agents would be protected (see D&C 100:14). Such was the case, as they returned from their assignment unharmed. John helped the Prophet recruit participants for Zion's Camp in 1834, and was also active in doing missionary work. He later became for a time one of the seven presidents of the seventies. He passed away in Iowa on May 9, 1851.

Section 99 Background—Given through the Prophet Joseph Smith to John Murdock, August 1832, at Hiram, Ohio, as confirmed by earlier editions of the revelations and other historical records. John Murdock had joined the Church in Kirtland during Oliver Cowdery's first mission to the Lamanites. When his wife died shortly after delivering their twin son and daughter, John gave the twins to Joseph and Emma to raise as their own—within days of Joseph and Emma losing their own newborn twins. John Murdock was a great support to the Prophet and stayed faithful until the end.

D&C 99:2–8—The commission to be an emissary for the Lord comes with a promise that the Holy Ghost will confirm the truth of the word (see also D&C 100:8). Such service has extraterrestrial implications, for the Father and the Son are intimately engaged in the work at the same time to record the process and outcomes—blessing those who receive the message willingly and bringing judgment on those who reject the message. Thus the work of faithful missionaries has binding power, just as if the Lord were acting directly in the role. "Until thou be taken" (verse 8) is an explicit measure for the tenure for missionary work as it applies to all members of the Church, for we are to labor in the service until the end of our days—and then even beyond that in the spirit realm (see D&C 138:57).

D&C 99:4—George Q. Cannon said that "whoso rejecteth you" included the indifferent, those who wouldn't take time to investigate the gospel, those who wouldn't ask God, those who thought it was beneath them, and those who were too proud, too rich, and too well situated.

Section 100 Background. Given on October 12, 1933, at Perrysburg, New York (see HC 1:419–421). On October 5, 1833, Joseph Smith, Sidney Rigdon, and Freeman Nickerson left Kirtland on a one-month mission to Canada. One week later they stopped at Freeman Nickerson's home in Perrysburg, New York. Joseph had a number of concerns at this time, but was told not to worry about the enemies of the Church. In August, Oliver Cowdery had come to Kirtland to inform Joseph and the Church of the mob actions in Missouri on July 20–23. Joseph's heart was no doubt burdened for the Saints in Missouri. Joseph sent Orson Hyde and John Gould as messengers to assure the Saints in Missouri that the Church knew of their plight and to advise them in their actions; in sending them, Joseph must have been concerned for their safety. He and Sidney were also concerned about their own families; in fact, Joseph recorded the following in his journal on October 11, 1833: "I feel very well in my mind. The Lord is with us, but have much anxiety about my family" (HC 1:419). They went as far as Canada, calm and full of hope and faith.

When Joseph arrived back in Kirtland on November 4, he wrote, "I . . . found my family well, according to the promise of the Lord in the revelation of October 12th, for which I felt to thank my Heavenly Father" (HC 1:423).

mine hands, and I will do with them as seemeth me good; for in me there is all power;

2. Therefore, follow me, and listen to the counsel which I shall give unto you.

3. Behold, and lo, I have much people in this place, in the regions round about, and an effectual door shall be opened in the regions round about in this eastern land.

4. Therefore, I, the Lord, have suffered you to come unto this place; for thus it was expedient in me for the salvation of souls;

5. Therefore, verily, I say unto you, lift up your voices unto this people, speak the thoughts that I shall put into your hearts, and you shall not be confounded before men;

6. For it shall be given you in the very hour, yea, in the very moment, what ye shall say.

7. But a commandment I give unto you, that ye shall declare whatsoever things ye declare in my name, in solemnity of heart, in the spirit of meekness, in all things.

8. And I give unto you this promise, that inasmuch as ye do this, the Holy Ghost shall be shed forth in bearing record unto all things whatsoever ye shall say.

9. And it is expedient in me that you, my servant Sidney, should be a spokesman unto this people; yea, verily, I will ordain you unto this calling, even to be a spokesman unto my servant Joseph;

10. And I will give unto him power to be mighty in testimony;

11. And I will give unto thee power to be mighty in expounding all scriptures, that thou mayest be a spokesman unto him, and he shall be a revelator unto thee, that thou mayest know the certainty of all things pertaining to the things of my kingdom on the earth.

12. Therefore, continue your journey and let your hearts rejoice; for behold, and lo, I am with you even unto the end.

13. And now I give unto you a word concerning Zion. Zion shall be redeemed, although she is chastened for a little season.

14. Thy brethren, my servants Orson Hyde, and John Gould, are in my hands, and inasmuch as they keep my commandments, they shall be saved.

15. Therefore let your hearts be comforted, for all things shall work together for good to them that walk uprightly, and to the sanctification of the church;

16. For I will raise up unto myself a pure people, that will serve me in righteousness;

17. And all that call on the name of the Lord, and keep his commandments, shall be saved. Even so. Amen.

D&C 100:1–3—The early missionaries often had to leave their families entirely in the care of the Lord. From His infinite perspective, the Lord can declare that "your families are well; they are in mine hands." He knows all things. He knows where "an effectual door" awaits opening—where the honest in heart are looking for the truth and where the testimony of the righteous will resonate with spiritual efficacy. Thus the Lord knows where to send His servants for optimum outcomes.

D&C 100:6–8—This counsel is among the most celebrated of all the scriptural passages given in support of the doctrines associated with missionary work. A similar statement had been made in an earlier revelation: "Neither take ye thought beforehand what ye shall say; but treasure up in your minds continually the words of life, and it shall be given you in the very hour that portion that shall be meted unto every man" (D&C 84:85). The Lord gave the same directive to His disciples in the Holy Land (see Matt. 10:19–20) and through Nephi (see 2 Ne. 32:3, 5). The Lord blesses His servants through the Spirit to deliver the words of truth through "the effectual door" of salvation unto those waiting for deliverance and exaltation.

D&C 100:9, 11—Sidney Rigdon's call to be a spokesman for Joseph Smith was prophesied in 2 Nephi 3:18. Sadly, that call led him to believe he should lead the Church when Joseph Smith died.

D&C 100:15–16—In our anguish and concern over the course of events in our lives from time to time, we are blessed with the illumination of hope that comes into our hearts from above, giving the gentle command: "be comforted." How we need that assurance! This process has validity and authenticity in the context of the divine covenant: walk uprightly, be pure, and be righteous—and "all things shall work together for good" (verse 15). Our blessing in this regard extends beyond the limits of our personal lives, for if we as individuals are faithful and devoted, then the Church as a whole, collectively, is sanctified and made pure. We then begin to realize our potential as "children of the prophets" and "children of the covenant" (3 Ne. 20:25, 26).

A street in Perrysburg, New York, where Joseph Smith, Sidney Rigdon, and Freeman Nickerson stopped on the way to their mission to Canada. The three stopped here at Freeman Nickerson's home, where the Prophet received Section 100.

SECTION 101

1. Verily I say unto you, concerning your brethren who have been afflicted, and persecuted, and cast out from the land of their inheritance,

2. I, the Lord, have suffered the affliction to come upon them, wherewith they have been afflicted, in consequence of their transgressions;

3. Yet I will own them, and they shall be mine in that day when I shall come to make up my jewels.

4. Therefore, they must needs be chastened and tried, even as Abraham, who was commanded to offer up his only son,

5. For all those who will not endure chastening, but deny me, cannot be sanctified.

6. Behold, I say unto you, there were jarrings, and contentions, and envyings, and strifes, and lustful and covetous desires among them; therefore by these things they polluted their inheritances.

7. They were slow to hearken unto the voice of the Lord their God, therefore the Lord their God is slow to hearken unto their prayers, to answer them in the day of their trouble.

8. In the day of their peace they esteemed lightly my counsel; but, in the day of their trouble, of necessity they feel after me.

9. Verily I say unto you, notwithstanding their sins, my bowels are filled with compassion towards them: I will not utterly cast them off; and in the day of wrath I will remember mercy.

10. I have sworn, and the decree hath gone forth by a former commandment which I have given unto

View looking into Clay County, Missouri, where the Saints were suffering intense persecution when Section 101 was received.

Section 101 Background—Given at Kirtland, Ohio, December 16, 1833 (see *HC* 1:458–464). The Saints in Missouri were suffering intense persecution at the time, having been forced to flee from Jackson County. The record states: "The destruction of crops, household furniture, and clothing, is very great, and much of their stock is lost. The main body of the Church is now in Clay county, where the people are as kind and accommodating as could reasonably be expected. The continued threats of death to individuals of the Church, if they make their appearance in Jackson County, prevent the most of them, even at this day, from returning to that county, to secure personal property, which they were obliged to leave in their flight" (*HC* 1:457). In a letter to the Prophet dated December 15, 1833, William W. Phelps reported:

> The condition of the scattered Saints is lamentable, and affords a gloomy prospect. . . . I am sensible that we shall not be able to live again in Zion, till God or the President rules out the mob.
>
> . . .
>
> If, from what has been done in Zion, we, or the most of us, have got to be persecuted from city to city, and from synagogue to synagogue, we want to know it; for there are those among us that would rather earn eternal life on such conditions than lose it; but we hope for better things and shall wait patiently for the word of the Lord." (*HC* 1:457–458.)

In this deplorable state of affairs, Joseph received the revelation known as Section 101, in which the Lord explains why the Saints had been driven from Jackson County

Chastening cleanses us, can lead to forgiveness of sins, teaches us obedience, and refines us as pure gold. President Harold B. Lee taught that in the midst of our trials, angels may minister to us (see Matt. 4:11).

D&C 101:1—The "land of inheritance" mentioned here refers to the fact that Church members will receive the inheritance promised to Abraham (if they are not literal descendants, they are grafted in at baptism). One promised land is in America, with its "center place" in Missouri.

D&C 101:2–5, 9—The Saints, in their imperfection, fell short of the celestial standard assigned by the Lord to those who would be citizens of Zion. As a result, they suffered intensely at the hands of their enemies. Since none are perfect in this life, all partake of the chastening of the Lord to one degree or another until the soul-felt lesson is learned: only those who endure chastening without denying the Lord have the capacity to be sanctified. Since Zion consists of "the pure in heart" (D&C 97:21), we can assume that all who qualify for that appellation will have passed through the chastening trials of mortality and risen on the wings of God's compassion and mercy to a higher state of spiritual preparation.

you, that I would let fall the sword of mine indignation in behalf of my people; and even as I have said, it shall come to pass.

11. Mine indignation is soon to be poured out without measure upon all nations, and this will I do when the cup of their iniquity is full.

12. And in that day all who are found upon the watch tower, or in other words, all mine Israel shall be saved.

13. And they that have been scattered shall be gathered;

14. And all they who have mourned shall be comforted;

15. And all they who have given their lives for my name shall be crowned.

16. Therefore, let your hearts be comforted concerning Zion; for all flesh is in mine hands: be still and know that I am God.

17. Zion shall not be moved out of her place, notwithstanding her children are scattered.

18. They that remain, and are pure in heart, shall return, and come to their inheritances, they and their children, with songs of everlasting joy, to build up the waste places of Zion;

19. And all these things that the prophets might be fulfilled.

20. And, behold, there is none other place appointed than that which I have appointed; neither shall there be any other place appointed than that which I have appointed, for the work of the gathering of my saints,

21. Until the day cometh when there is found no more room for them; and then I have other places which I will appoint unto them, and they shall be called Stakes, for the curtains, or the strength of Zion.

22. Behold, it is my will, that all they who call on my name, and worship me according to mine everlasting gospel, should gather together, and stand in holy places,

23. And prepare for the revelation which is to come, when the vail of the covering of my temple, in my tabernacle, which hideth the earth, shall be taken off, and all flesh shall see me together.

24. And every corruptible thing, both of man, or of the beasts of the field, or of the fowls of the heavens, or of the fish of the sea, that dwell upon all the face of the earth, shall be consumed;

25. And also that of element shall melt with fervent heat; and all things shall become new, that my knowledge and glory may dwell upon all the earth.

26. And in that day the enmity of man, and the enmity of beasts, yea, the enmity of all flesh, shall cease from before my face.

27. And in that day whatsoever any

D&C 101:11–16—In the face of vicious persecution the Saints at the time were anguishing over their fate and wondering about the intercession of the Almighty on their behalf. The Lord assures them that His response would be poured out "without measure" upon the nations—as soon as "the cup of their iniquity is full." The timetable is the Lord's; He acts in His "own due time" as it states repeatedly in the scriptures. At the same time, the promise of relief is extended to the Saints: blessings of being saved, gathered, comforted, and crowned are forthcoming. The bottom line is the exquisite counsel to "be still and know that I am God" (verse 16).

D&C 101:19–21—Elder George Q. Cannon spoke of the return to the center stake of Zion:

> We talk about going back to build up the centre stake of Zion; it is the burden of our daily prayers. The aspirations of thousands of the people ascend in the ears of the Lord of Sabaoth in behalf of the redemption of Zion, and that the purposes of God may be forwarded, and that the time may soon come when the centre stake of Zion shall be built up and the people be prepared to go back and inhabit that land. . . . We expect when that day shall come that we will be a very different people to what we are today. We will be prepared to commune with heavenly beings. . . . (JD 11:336–37.)

D&C 101:22—From a careful study of the Doctrine and Covenants, we gain valuable and uplifting insight into the Lord's design in gathering Israel—whether in specific designated places of historic refuge and spiritual germination such as Kirtland or Missouri, or, as the gathering proceeds today, in the myriad "holy places" that constitute the homes of the righteous, the congregations of the Saints assembled in the stakes and missions of the Church throughout the world, or in the sacred temples of the Lord across the earth. The Lord uses the gathering to bless His sons and daughters of the covenant: "Yea the hearts of thousands and tens of thousands shall greatly rejoice in consequence of the blessings which shall be poured out, and the endowment with which my servants have been endowed in this house" (D&C 110:9).

D&C 101:23–26—We think of the revealed word of God as "revelation" in a specific sense; however, the grand revelation, the ultimate revelation is the moment when the Lord Himself will be revealed and "all flesh shall see me together" (verse 23). The earth will be transformed and rendered capable of being a site where the knowledge and glory of the Lord "may dwell" (verse 25). United under the leadership of the Holy One of Israel, the Saints from all quarters of the earth will press forward in the sacred work of salvation unimpeded by Lucifer and his accomplices until the final hour has come at the end of the thousand years, and the celestialization of the earth is complete.

man shall ask, it shall be given unto him.

28. And in that day Satan shall not have power to tempt any man.

29. And there shall be no sorrow because there is no death.

30. In that day an infant shall not die until he is old, and his life shall be as the age of a tree,

31. And when he dies he shall not sleep, (that is to say in the earth,) but shall be changed in the twinkling of an eye, and shall be caught up, and his rest shall be glorious.

32. Yea, verily I say unto you, in that day when the Lord shall come, he shall reveal all things—

33. Things which have passed, and hidden things which no man knew—things of the earth, by which it was made, and the purpose and the end thereof—

34. Things most precious—things that are above, and things that are beneath—things that are in the earth, and upon the earth, and in heaven.

35. And all they who suffer persecution for my name, and endure in faith, though they are called to lay down their lives for my sake, yet shall they partake of all this glory.

36. Wherefore, fear not even unto death; for in this world your joy is not full, but in me your joy is full.

37. Therefore, care not for the body, neither the life of the body; but care for the soul, and for the life of the soul;

38. And seek the face of the Lord always, that in patience ye may possess your souls, and ye shall have eternal life.

39. When men are called unto mine everlasting gospel, and covenant with an everlasting covenant, they are accounted as the salt of the earth, and the savor of men;

40. They are called to be the savor of men. Therefore, if that salt of the earth lose its savor, behold, it is thenceforth good for nothing, only to be cast out, and trodden under the feet of men.

41. Behold, here is wisdom concerning the children of Zion, even many, but not all; they were found transgressors, therefore they must needs be chastened:

42. He that exalteth himself shall be abased, and he that abaseth himself shall be exalted.

43. And now, I will show unto you a parable, that you may know my will concerning the redemption of Zion.

44. A certain nobleman had a spot of land, very choice; and he said unto his servants, Go ye unto my vineyard, even upon this very choice piece of land, and plant twelve olive trees,

45. And set watchmen round about

D&C 101:30–31—Loss of loved ones to death, and the division and separation of families when the curtain of mortality falls, haunt our thoughts and worry our hearts. How glorious is the impending millennial change when death is no longer supreme. No children will pass away in infancy. All will grow to maturity until a higher form of death transpires and they are transformed "in the twinkling of an eye"—caught up to a glorious rest.

D&C 101:32–35—During the millennium, the Lord will reveal all light and truth concerning the earth, its creation, and its relationship with the purposes of God. It will be a time of the unfolding of knowledge to an unprecedented degree. Learning will proceed in panoramic scope in an environment of light and glory. The persecuted who endure in faith—even though they may have suffered a martyr's death—will be brought into a state of existence where they shall "partake of all this glory."

D&C 101:36–38—To seek the face of the Lord is to aspire to a fullness of joy and glory through the patient fulfillment of the heavenly commission to become sons and daughters of God through the atoning sacrifice of Jesus Christ. Doing so, one receives the ultimate blessing of eternal life—"which gift is the greatest of all the gifts of God" (D&C 14:7).

D&C 101:41–42—Chastening is a part of true and ultimate love. It is the way the Lord assists us in getting back on the straight and narrow path and in remaining spiritually productive and useful as "the salt of the earth." James E. Talmage explains the significance of the metaphor of salt:

> Salt is the great preservative; as such it has had practical use since very ancient times. Salt was prescribed as an essential addition to every meat offering under the Mosaic law. Long before the time of Christ, the use of salt had been accorded a symbolism of fidelity, hospitality, and covenant. To be of use salt must be pure; to be of any saving virtue as salt, it must be salt indeed, and not the product of chemical alteration or of earthy admixture, whereby its saltiness or "savor" would be lost. . . . Against such change of faith . . . the disciples were especially warned. (JC, 217.)

D&C 101:43–62—Hyrum M. Smith and Janne M. Sjodahl provide this explanation of the various dimensions of the Lord's parable:

> *The vineyard*] In this Revelation, the vineyard is regarded as separate from the olive grove, for the nobleman planted olive trees in his vineyard, doubling its value.
> *Build a tower*] The safety of the settlement of the Saints depends on the Temple, or rather on the power of God manifest in His holy House.
> *While they were at variance * * * slothful*] This never fails. Strife always engenders slothfulness and neglect of duty.

them, and build a tower, that one may overlook the land round about, to be a watchman upon the tower, that mine olive trees may not be broken down, when the enemy shall come to spoil and take upon themselves the fruit of my vineyard.

46. Now, the servants of the nobleman went and did as their lord commanded them; and planted the olive trees, and built a hedge round about, and set watchmen, and began to build a tower.

47. And while they were yet laying the foundation thereof, they began to say among themselves, And what need hath my lord of this tower?

48. And consulted for a long time, saying among themselves, What need hath my lord of this tower, seeing this is a time of peace?

49. Might not this money be given to the exchangers? for there is no need of these things!

50. And while they were at variance one with another they became very slothful, and they hearkened not unto the commandments of their lord,

51. And the enemy came by night, and broke down the hedge, and the servants of the nobleman arose and were affrighted, and fled; and the enemy destroyed their works, and broke down the olive trees.

52. Now, behold, the nobleman, the lord of the vineyard, called upon his servants, and said unto them, Why! what is the cause of this great evil?

53. Ought ye not to have done even as I commanded you? and after ye had planted the vineyard, and built the hedge round about, and set watchmen upon the walls thereof, built the tower also, and set a watchman upon the tower, and watched for my vineyard, and not have fallen asleep, lest the enemy should come upon you?

54. And behold, the watchman upon the tower would have seen the enemy while he was yet afar off, and then ye could have made ready and kept the enemy from breaking down the hedge thereof, and saved my vineyard from the hands of the destroyer.

55. And the lord of the vineyard said unto one of his servants, Go and gather together the residue of my servants, and take all the strength of mine house, which are my warriors, my young men, and they that are of middle age also among all my servants, who are the strength of mine house, save those only whom I have appointed to tarry;

56. And go ye straightway unto the land of my vineyard, and redeem my vineyard, for it is mine, I have bought it with money.

57. Therefore, get ye straightway unto my land; break down the walls of mine enemies; throw down their tower, and scatter their watchmen:

58. And inasmuch as they gather together against you, avenge me of mine enemies, that by and by I may come with the residue of mine house, and possess the land.

59. And the servant said unto his lord, When shall these things be?

60. And he said unto his servant, When I will, go ye straightway, and do all things whatsoever I have commanded you;

61. And this shall be my seal and blessing upon you—a faithful and wise steward in the midst of mine house, a ruler in my kingdom.

62. And his servant went straightway, and did all things whatsoever his lord commanded him, and after many days all things were fulfilled.

63. Again, verily I say unto you, I will show unto you wisdom in me concerning all the churches, inasmuch

Watchmen upon the walls] Watchmen upon the tower or walls, has reference to those who are appointed to positions of responsibility. The watchman on the tower is the presiding officer in the stake, ward or community.

Unto one of his servants] The Prophet Joseph (See Section 103:21).

Redeem my vineyard] The Prophet Joseph is commanded to gather up a company of men, faithful and true, and proceed to Zion and scatter the enemies; but he was not to make war upon them, but redeem the land by purchase (See Sec. 103:23).

After many days] The Prophet did as directed by Revelation, and in due time "all things were fulfilled" (DCC, 648).

D&C 101:45—The "tower" mentioned in this verse refers to the temple.

D&C 101:47–50—The people became at variance with each other and failed to build the temple, as they had been commanded to do. The temple would have been a spiritual refuge that would have allowed Church leaders to discern the movements of the enemy.

D&C 101:51—This verse refers to the Missouri persecutions.

D&C 101:56, 62—Joseph Smith organized Zion's Camp to try to redeem Zion. While the effort did not succeed at that time, Zion will still be redeemed in the Lord's due time and as He wills it. Verse 62 indicates that a long period of time—possibly many years—would elapse before the success would occur.

D&C 101:60—The phrase "when I will" indicates that it will occur in the Lord's due time. When we desire something, even a righteous desire, it can be a test of patience to wait with faith until the time for the desired blessing has arrived according to the Lord's timetable. It is up to us, then, to remember that the Lord's plan—and timing—is perfect.

D&C 101:63—The principles of wisdom in governance enunciated by the Lord at this early stage in the Restoration continue to inform the practices and patterns of Church administration today. A prominent example is the Church Correlation program established in our day.

as they are willing to be guided in a right and proper way for their salvation,

64. That the work of the gathering together of my saints may continue, that I may build them up unto my name upon holy places; for the time of harvest is come, and my word must needs be fulfilled.

65. Therefore, I must gather together my people, according to the parable of the wheat and the tares, that the wheat may be secured in the garners to possess eternal life, and be crowned with celestial glory when I shall come in the kingdom of my Father, to reward every man according as his work shall be,

66. While the tares shall be bound in bundles, and their bands made strong, that they may be burned with unquenchable fire.

67. Therefore, a commandment I give unto all the churches, that they shall continue to gather together unto the places which I have appointed.

68. Nevertheless, as I have said unto you in a former commandment, let not your gathering be in haste, nor by flight; but let all things be prepared before you:

69. And in order that all things be prepared before you, observe the commandment which I have given concerning these things,

70. Which saith, or teacheth, to purchase all the lands by money, which can be purchased for money, in the region round about the land which I have appointed to be the land of Zion, for the beginning of the gathering of my saints;

71. All the land which can be purchased in Jackson county, and the counties round about, and leave the residue in mine hand.

72. Now, verily I say unto you, let all the churches gather together all their monies; let these things be done in their time, but not in haste, and observe to have all things prepared before you.

73. And let honorable men be appointed, even wise men and send them to purchase these lands;

74. And the churches in the eastern countries, when they are built up, if they will hearken unto this counsel, they may buy lands and gather together upon them, and in this way they may establish Zion.

75. There is even now already in store a sufficient, yea, even abundance, to redeem Zion, and establish her waste places, no more to be thrown down, were the churches, who call themselves after my name, willing to hearken to my voice.

76. And again I say unto you, those who have been scattered by their enemies, it is my will that they should continue to importune for redress, and redemption, by the hands of those who are placed as rulers and are in authority over you,

77. According to the laws and constitution of the people, which I have suffered to be established, and should be maintained for the rights and protection of all flesh, according to just and holy principles,

78. That every man may act in doctrine and principle pertaining to futurity, according to the moral agency which I have given unto him, that every man may be accountable for his own sins in the day of judgment.

79. Therefore, it is not right that

D&C 101:65–77—The principle of the wheat and the tares provides that the wheat (the righteous) and the tares (the worldly and unrighteous) should "grow together until the harvest is fully ripe" (D&C 86:7)—when the time has come for a grand sifting of the yield to garner the precious crop and discard the tares. It is in the design of the Almighty that the Saints should prosper and grow in, but not of, the world—using the light of the gospel to preserve and magnify their callings as servants of God and law-abiding citizens of their lands of residence. The Saints are to continue to gather in an orderly and circumspect manner, acquiring lands by wise purchases. Those scattered by their enemies are to seek redress according to the laws of the land.

D&C 101:68—Here the Lord cautions the Saints against haste. Many of the problems that had already occurred were due to the fact that the Saints had come to Missouri ill-prepared, thinking that the Lord would take care of them despite their failure to appropriately prepare.

D&C 101:75—Zion could have already been redeemed (see D&C 105:1–10). It is not the Lord who causes delays in bringing forth Zion; the rate at which His promises are fulfilled is determined by our willingness to respond to His counsel.

D&C 101:79–80—Ezra Taft Benson, as a member of the Quorum of the Twelve Apostles, reminded us that the Constitution of the United States is a glorious standard:

> It is no wonder that the Prophet Joseph said—even though he knew he would suffer martyrdom in this land—"The Constitution of the United States is a glorious standard; it is founded in the wisdom of God. It is a heavenly banner."
>
> Yet, according to his contemporaries, he foresaw the time when the destiny of the nation would be in danger and would hang as by a thread. Thank God he did not see the thread break. He also indicated the important part that this people should yet play in standing for the principles embodied in these sacred documents—the Declaration of Independence and the Constitution. (CR, *April 1948*, Second Day, Morning Session, 85.)

President Charles W. Penrose said that the principles of the United States Constitution are to go forth to all nations, and the time will come when those principles will prevail as surely as the sun shines.

any man should be in bondage one to another.

80. And for this purpose have I established the constitution of this land, by the hands of wise men whom I raised up unto this very purpose, and redeemed the land by the shedding of blood.

81. Now, unto what shall I liken the children of Zion? I will liken them unto the parable of the woman and the unjust judge (for men ought always to pray and not to faint) which saith,

82. There was in a city a judge which feared not God, neither regarded man.

83. And there was a widow in that city, and she came unto him saying, Avenge me of mine adversary.

84. And he would not for a while, but afterward he said within himself, Though I fear not God, nor regard man, yet because this widow troubleth me I will avenge her, lest by her continual coming she weary me.

85. Thus will I liken the children of Zion.

86. Let them importune at the feet of the judge;

87. And if he heed them not, let them importune at the feet of the Governor;

88. And if the Governor heed them not, let them importune at the feet of the President;

89. And if the President heed them not, then will the Lord arise and come forth out of his hiding place, and in his fury vex the nation,

90. And in his hot displeasure, and in his fierce anger, in his time, will cut off those wicked, unfaithful, and unjust stewards, and appoint them their portion among hypocrites, and unbelievers;

91. Even in outer darkness, where there is weeping, and wailing, and gnashing of teeth.

92. Pray ye, therefore, that their ears may be opened unto your cries, that I may be merciful unto them, that these things may not come upon them.

93. What I have said unto you, must needs be, that all men may be left without excuse;

94. That wise men and rulers may hear and know that which they have never considered;

95. That I may proceed to bring to pass my act, my strange act, and perform my work, my strange work, that men may discern between the righteous and the wicked, saith your God.

96. And again, I say unto you, it is contrary to my commandment and my will that my servant Sidney Gilbert should sell my storehouse, which I have appointed unto my people, into the hands of mine enemies.

97. Let not that which I have appointed be polluted by mine enemies, by the consent of those who call themselves after my name;

98. For this is a very sore and grievous sin against me, and against my people, in consequence of those things which I have decreed and are soon to befall the nations.

99. Therefore, it is my will that my people should claim, and hold claim upon that which I have appointed unto them, though they should not be permitted to dwell thereon;

D&C 101:80—This often-referred-to verse tells us that the Lord Himself established the United States Constitution. The "wise men" mentioned in this verse refer to those who resisted Great Britain and led the Revolutionary War.

D&C 101:81–100—The Lord invokes the spirit of the parable of the woman and unjust judge (see Luke 18:1–8). Elder Bruce R. McConkie explained that this parable teaches that when our cause is just, we are to continue in determined and unceasing prayer—as long as we live, if needs be—a process that strengthens our faith and leads to attainment of the blessing for which we seek (see *DNTC* 1:542). This parable allowed the Lord to provide a spiritual framework in which the beleaguered Saints could proceed to seek redress from the unconstitutional attacks being leveled against them.

D&C 101:85–88—The Lord wanted the Saints to seek redress through every possible legal channel. If they were denied, the officials would have no excuse, and the Lord's judgments on them would be justified.

D&C 101:95—"My strange act" refers to the restoration of the gospel.

D&C 101:98—The "grievous sin" referred to here is that the Lord did not want the Church's properties—His properties, in essence—to be sold to the enemies of the Church.

D&C 101:99—Joseph Smith promised the Saints that even if they were driven off their lands, that they would be able to stand upon their lands and, with Job, see God in their flesh. Even if they couldn't live on their land, he told them, they were not to sell it.

100. Nevertheless, I do not say they shall not dwell thereon; for inasmuch as they bring forth fruit and works meet for my kingdom, they shall dwell thereon;

101. They shall build, and another shall not inherit it; they shall plant vineyards, and they shall eat the fruit thereof. Even so. Amen.

SECTION 102

1. This day a general council of twenty-four High Priests assembled at the house of Joseph Smith, Jun., by revelation, and proceeded to organize the High Council of the Church of Christ, which was to consist of twelve High Priests, and one or three Presidents as the case might require.

2. The High Council was appointed by revelation for the purpose of settling important difficulties which might arise in the church, which could not be settled by the church or the bishop's council to the satisfaction of the parties.

3. Joseph Smith, jun., Sidney Rigdon and Frederick G. Williams were acknowledged Presidents by the voice of the council; and Joseph Smith, sen., John Smith, Joseph Coe, John Johnson, Martin Harris, John S. Carter, Jared Carter, Oliver Cowdery, Samuel H. Smith, Orson Hyde, Sylvester Smith, and Luke Johnson, Hgh Priests, were chosen to be a standing Council for the church, by the unanimous voice of the Council.

4. The above-named councilors were then asked whether they accepted their appointments and whether they would act in that office according to the law of heaven; to which they all answered that they accepted their appointments, and would fill their offices according to the grace of God bestowed upon them.

5. The number composing the council, who voted in the name and for the church, in appointing the above-named councilors were forty-three, as follows—Nine High Priests, seventeen elders, four priests, and thirteen members.

6. Voted: that the High Council cannot have power to act without seven of the above-named councilors, or their regularly appointed successors are present.

7. These seven shall have power to appoint other High Priests, whom they may consider worthy and capable to act in the place of absent councilors.

8. Voted: that whenever any vacancy shall occur by the death, removal from office for transgression,

JOHN S. CARTER

John S. Carter was born in 1796 at Killingworth, Middlesex County, Connecticut, the son of Gideon Carter. He was baptized a member of the Church in 1832 and ordained an elder and a high priest that same year. Shortly thereafter he completed a mission in Vermont with his brother Jared. On February 17, 1834, he was called to serve on the newly organized Kirtland high council, a position cut short by a second mission call to the East. He succumbed to cholera on June 26, 1834, while serving in Zion's Camp.

Section 102 Background—The minutes of the organization of the first high council of the Church, occurring at a conference in Joseph Smith's home at Kirtland, Ohio, February 17, 1834 (see *HC* 2:28–31). Twenty-four high priests were in attendance. Although the high council was to have many responsibilities, this section deals with only one of them—that of acting as a Church court. Stake high councils acting as disciplinary councils still use Section 102 today.

The Lord established the high council before directing the organization of the Quorum of the Twelve (which took place in February 1935). Since there was only one stake in the Church at that time, the high council served as the highest authority under the First Presidency. The president of the Church also served as stake president. As more stakes were added, Joseph relinquished this office and stake presidents were chosen over each stake. Verses 30–32, concerning the Council of the Twelve Apostles, were added by the Prophet in 1835.

JOHN SMITH

John Smith, brother of Joseph Smith Sr., was born on July 16, 1781, at Derryfield, Rockingham County, New Hampshire. Receiving a copy of the Book of Mormon from his brother, he joined the Church on January 9, 1832. He moved to Kirtland in May 1833 and was called to the Kirtland high council on February 17, 1834. He suffered persecution by mobs in Kirtland and later at Adam-ondi-Ahman while serving as president of the local stake. He served faithfully in many additional capacities in the Church, including that of fifth Patriarch of the Church following his move to the West with the Saints. He died on May 23, 1854.

SYLVESTER SMITH

Sylvester Smith was born in 1805. He was ordained a high priest on October 25, 1831, by Oliver Cowdery and was called by revelation in January 1832 to serve as a missionary (see D&C 75:34). As a participant in Zion's Camp, he was distinguished by the notoriety of his recalcitrant and quarrelsome nature, evoking the reproach of the Prophet Joseph Smith. Upon his return to Kirtland, Sylvester vilified the Prophet with false accusations, but repented when a court verdict exonerated Joseph Smith. Sylvester later served on the Kirtland high council and was for a time president of the seventies. By 1838 he had withdrawn his affiliation with the Church.

or removal from the bounds of this church government, of any one of the above-named councilors, it shall be filled by the nomination of the President or Presidents, and sanctioned by the voice of a general council of High Priests, convened for that purpose, to act in the name of the church.

9. The President of the church, who is also the President of the council, is appointed by revelation, and acknowledged in his administration, by the voice of the church;

10. And it is according to the dignity of his office that he should preside over the Council of the church; and it is his privilege to be assisted by two other Presidents, appointed after the same manner that he himself was appointed;

11. And in case of the absence of one or both of those who are appointed to assist him, he has power to preside over the Council without an assistant: and in case he himself is absent, the other Presidents have power to preside in his stead, both or either of them.

12. Whenever an High Council of the church of Christ is regularly organized, according to the foregoing pattern, it shall be the duty of the twelve councilors to cast lots by numbers, and thereby ascertain, who of the twelve shall speak first, commencing with number one, and so in succession to number twelve.

13. Whenever this Council convenes to act upon any case, the twelve councilors shall consider whether it is a difficult one or not; if it is not, two only of the councilors shall speak upon it, according to the form above written.

14. But if it is thought to be difficult, four shall be appointed; and if more difficult, six; but in no case shall more than six be appointed to speak.

15. The accused, in all cases, has a right to one half of the Council, to prevent insult or injustice;

16. And the councilors appointed to speak before the Council are to present the case, after the evidence is examined, in its true light before the Council, and every man is to speak according to equity and justice.

17. Those councilors who draw even numbers, that is 2, 4, 6, 8, 10, and 12, are the individuals who are to stand up in behalf of the accused, and prevent insult or injustice.

18. In all cases the accuser and the accused shall have a privilege of speaking for themselves before the Council, after the evidences are heard, and the councilors who are appointed to speak on the case, have finished their remarks.

19. After the evidences are heard, the councilors, accuser and accused have spoken, the President shall give a decision according to the understanding which he shall have of the case, and call upon the twelve councilors to sanction the same by their vote.

20. But should the remaining councilors, who have not spoken, or any one of them, after hearing the evidences and pleadings impartially, discover an error in the decision of the President, they can manifest it, and the case shall have a re-hearing;

21. And if, after a careful re-hearing, any additional light is shown upon the case, the decision shall be altered accordingly;

22. But in case no additional light is given, the first decision shall stand, the majority of the Council having power to determine the same.

23. In case of difficulty respecting doctrine or principle, (if there is not a sufficiency written to make the

D&C 102:12–22—These verses outline the principles governing disciplinary councils. Anciently, no one was allowed to whisper, fall asleep, or leave the room until the voice of the Lord was heard by revelation.

D&C 102:19—Joseph Smith said that no one is capable of judging another unless his own heart is pure; he must rely on prayer and the Spirit of the Lord in making judgment.

D&C 102:19–23—The principles for the operation of the high council provide for the application of equity and justice in all cases. Both accuser and accused have the right to speak after the evidence is presented "in its true light" and after members of the council have spoken—half of which are always to stand up for the accused to prevent insult and injustice. The decision of the high council is made by the president, then sanctioned by the vote of the council. Revelation is the central operating principle involved, since the president may "inquire and obtain the mind of the Lord" in cases where additional truth and light are needed concerning doctrine or principle. This section of the Doctrine and Covenants confirms the design of the Lord to uphold the sanctity of the Kingdom and ensure that accused persons have the privilege of receiving just and equitable treatment before the priesthood leadership. The prevailing tone and spirit of such disciplinary councils is charity and the desire to facilitate the process of sincere repentance by those who are found errant in their spiritual well-being.

THE UNIQUE NATURE OF A HIGH COUNCIL COURT

When a high council functions as a Church court, the members are equally divided into two groups. One group represents the interests of the Church, and the other group represents the interests of the accused. This court is unique in that neither of these two groups constitute a prosecution, defense, or jury element. Instead, their function is to prevent insult and injustice to either the Church or the accused. Members of the council who are assigned to speak are to carry out this function for and in behalf of the respective parties (see D&C 102:12–18).

After the high council members have spoken, the responsibility for giving a decision rests with the president, assisted by his two counselors. The high council members are then called upon to sustain the decision (see D&C 102:19).

The decision of the president is final unless:

1. An error is discovered in the decision (in this case, a rehearing is scheduled and the error is corrected)

2. An appeal is made (in this case, the appeal goes to the First Presidency, whose decision is final and cannot be appealed) (STDC 2:195).

case clear to the minds of the council,) the President may inquire and obtain the mind of the Lord by revelation.

24. The High Priests, when abroad, have power to Call and Organize a council after the manner of the foregoing, to settle difficulties, when the parties, or either of them shall request it.

25. And the said council of High Priests shall have power to appoint one of their own number, to preside over such council for the time being.

26. It shall be the duty of said council to transmit, immediately, a copy of their proceedings, with a full statement of the testimony accompanying their decision, to the High Council of the seat of the First Presidency of the Church.

27. Should the parties, or either of them be dissatisfied with the decision of said council, they may appeal to the High Council of the seat of the First Presidency of the church, and have a re-hearing, which case shall there be conducted, according to the former pattern written, as though no such decision had been made.

28. This council of High Priests abroad is only to be called on the most difficult cases of church matters; and no common or ordinary case is to be sufficient to call such council.

29. The traveling or located High Priests abroad, have power to say whether it is necessary to call such a council or not.

30. There is a distinction between the High Council or traveling High Priests abroad, and the traveling High Council composed of the Twelve apostles, in their decisions.

31. From the decision of the former there can be an appeal, but from the decision of the latter there cannot.

32. The latter can only be called in question by the general authorities of the church in case of transgression.

33. Resolved, that the President or Presidents of the seat of the First Presidency of the church, shall have power to determine whether any such case, as may be appealed, is justly entitled to a re-hearing, after examining the appeal and the evidences and statements accompanying it.

34. The twelve councilors then proceeded to cast lots or ballot, to ascertain who should speak first, and the following was the result, namely: 1, Oliver Cowdery; 2, Joseph Coe; 3, Samuel H. Smith; 4, Luke Johnson; 5, John S. Carter; 6, Sylvester Smith; 7, John Johnson; 8, Orson Hyde; 9, Jared Carter; 10, Joseph Smith, Sen.; 11, John Smith; 12, Martin Harris.

After prayer, the conference adjourned.

OLIVER COWDERY,
ORSON HYDE,
Clerks.

THE PURPOSE OF CHURCH COURTS

The Prophet Joseph Smith wrote:

At a council of the High Priests and Elders, (Orson Hyde, clerk,) at my house in Kirtland, on the evening of the 12th of February, I remarked that I should endeavor to set before the council the dignity of the office which had been conferred on me by the ministering of the angel of God, by His own voice, and by the voice of this Church; that I had never set before any council in all the order in which it ought to be conducted, which, perhaps, has deprived the councils of some or many blessings.

And I continued and said, no man is capable of judging a matter, in council, unless his own heart is pure; and that we are frequently so filled with prejudice, or have a beam in our own eye, that we are not capable of passing right decisions.

Our acts are recorded, and at a future day they will be laid before us, and if we should fail to judge right and injure our fellow-beings, they may there, perhaps, condemn us; there they are of great consequence, and to me the consequence appears to be of force, beyond anything which I am able to express. Ask yourselves, brethren, how much you have exercised yourselves in prayer since you heard of this council; and if you are now prepared to sit in council upon the soul of your brother. (HC 2:31.)

A few days later, the Prophet reviewed the minutes; they were read three times and unanimously adopted with the provision "that if the President should hereafter discover anything lacking in the same, he should be privileged to supply it" (HC 2:31).

Church courts are courts of love, and there is a need to be sensitive to the feelings of the accused. Emphasis is given to the need to provide equity and fairness and protect the accused, as well as the Church, from insult and injustice (see D&C 102:16–17). When a Church court functions within the framework of these guidelines, they are fulfilling their purpose as courts of love.

SECTION 103

1. Verily I say unto you, my friends, behold I will give unto you a revelation and commandment, that you may know how to act in the discharge of your duties concerning the salvation and redemption of your brethren, who have been scattered on the land of Zion;

2. Being driven and smitten by the hands of mine enemies, on whom I will pour out my wrath without measure in mine own time;

3. For I have suffered them thus far, that they might fill up the measure of their iniquities, that their cup might be full;

4. And that those who call themselves after my name might be chastened for a little season with a sore and grievous chastisement, because they did not hearken altogether unto the precepts and commandments which I gave unto them.

5. But verily I say unto you, that I have decreed a decree which my people shall realize, inasmuch as they hearken from this very hour, unto the counsel which I, the Lord their God, shall give unto them.

6. Behold they shall, for I have decreed it, begin to prevail against mine enemies from this very hour,

7. And by hearkening to observe all the words which I, the Lord their God, shall speak unto them, they shall never cease to prevail until the kingdoms of the world are subdued under my feet, and the earth is given unto the saints, to possess it for ever and ever.

8. But inasmuch as they keep not my commandments, and hearken not to observe all my words, the kingdoms of the world shall prevail against them,

9. For they were set to be a light unto the world, and to be the saviors of men;

10. And inasmuch as they are not the saviors of men, they are as salt that has lost its savor, and is thenceforth good for nothing but to be cast out and trodden under foot of men.

11. But verily I say unto you, I have decreed that your brethren which have been scattered shall return to the land of their inheritances, and build up the waste places of Zion;

12. For after much tribulation, as I have said unto you in a former commandment, cometh the blessing.

13. Behold, this is the blessing which I have promised after your tribulations, and the tribulations of your brethren; your redemption, and the redemption of your

Section 103 Background—Given on February 24, 1834, in Joseph Smith's home at Kirtland, Ohio (see *HC* 2:36–39). The Lord's instruction to form Zion's Camp and go to Missouri arose as a result of the arrival of Lyman Wight and Parley P. Pratt in Kirtland from Missouri on February 22, 1834. It appears that after they reported to Joseph Smith on the conditions of the Saints in Missouri, he received the revelation. Parley P. Pratt described his desperate journey from Jackson County to Kirtland:

> I was at this time entirely destitute of proper clothing for the journey; and I had neither horse, saddle, bridle, money nor provisions to take with me; or to leave with my wife, who lay sick and helpless most of the time.
>
> Under the circumstances I knew not what to do. Nearly all had been robbed and plundered, and all were poor." A man named Higbee, "moved by the Spirit," gave him a horse and saddle. Sidney A. Gilbert gave him some material, which some women made into a suit, and Brother Gilbert furnished a coat.
>
> Faith and the blessings of God had cleared up our way to accomplish what seemed impossible," he continued. "We were soon ready, and on the first of February we mounted our horses, and started in good cheer to ride one thousand or fifteen hundred miles through a wilderness country.
>
> We had not one cent of money in our pockets on starting. We travelled every day, whether through storm or sunshine, mud, rain or snow. (Parley P. Pratt, *APPP*, 87–89.)

Lyman Wight, Parley's companion on this mission, also placed his faith in the Lord. Before he left, it was reported, "his wife lay by the side of a log in the woods, with a child three days old and he had three days' provisions on hand" (Lyman Wight, "History," *Millennial Star* 27 [July 22, 1865], 455).

D&C 103:4—The enemies of the Church were perpetrating atrocities against the Saints, who were suffering intensely at this time. This was being permitted by the Lord so the cup of iniquity of the enemies might become full (thus shifting the eternal balance of justice against them in the due time of the Lord)—and so that Saints might learn to repent of their own iniquities through the operation of divine chastening.

D&C 103:9—In the midst of travail and adversity, we can lose sight of the light of promise within us, the divine potential to rise to the stature of sons and daughters of God with infinite capacity to participate in the process of redemption as "saviors of men" unto the world. Declared Orson Pratt:

> We are willing to go the earth over to save the living; we are willing to build temples and administer in ordinances to save the dead; we are willing to enter the eternal worlds and preach to every creature who has not placed himself beyond the reach of mercy. We are willing to labour both in this world and in the next to save men. (*JD* 7:91.)

brethren, even their restoration to the land of Zion, to be established no more to be thrown down;

14. Nevertheless, if they pollute their inheritances, they shall be thrown down, for I will not spare them if they pollute their inheritances.

15. Behold, I say unto you, the redemption of Zion must needs come by power;

16. Therefore, I will raise up unto my people a man, who shall lead them like as Moses led the children of Israel,

17. For ye are the children of Israel, and of the seed of Abraham, and ye must needs be led out of bondage by power, and with a stretched out arm:

18. And as your fathers were led at the first, even so shall the redemption of Zion be.

19. Therefore let not your hearts faint, for I say not unto you as I said unto your fathers, mine angel shall go up before you, but not my presence,

20. But I say unto you, mine angels shall go up before you, and also my presence, and in time ye shall possess the goodly land.

21. Verily, verily I say unto you, that my servant Baurak Ale [Joseph Smith, jr.] is the man to whom I likened the servant to whom the Lord of the vineyard spake in the parable which I have given unto you.

22. Therefore let my servant Baurak Ale [Joseph Smith, jr.] say unto the strength of my house, my young men and the middle aged, gather yourselves together unto the land of Zion, upon the land which I have bought with money that has been consecrated unto me;

23. And let all the churches send up wise men with their moneys, and purchase lands even as I have commanded them;

24. And inasmuch as mine enemies come against you to drive you from my goodly land, which I have consecrated to be the land of Zion; even from your own lands after these testimonies, which ye have brought before me, against them, ye shall curse them;

25. And whomsoever ye curse, I will curse, and ye shall avenge me of mine enemies;

26. And my presence shall be with you even in avenging me of mine enemies, unto the third and fourth generation of them that hate me.

27. Let no man be afraid to lay down his life for my sake, for whoso layeth down his life for my sake shall find it again.

28. And whoso is not willing to lay down his life for my sake, is not my disciple.

29. It is my will that my servant Sidney Rigdon shall lift up his voice in the congregations in the eastern countries, in preparing the churches to keep the commandments which I have given unto them, concerning the restoration and redemption of Zion.

30. It is my will that my servant Parley P. Pratt and my servant Lyman Wight should not return to the land of their brethren, until they

D&C 103:12-20—The Lord had declared earlier, on August 1, 1831: "For after much tribulation come the blessings. Wherefore the day cometh that ye shall be crowned with much glory; the hour is not yet, but is nigh at hand" (D&C 58:4). The Lord knew that the "hour is not yet" but would come in due time through power—the power of heaven acting to advance the inexorable cause of Zion, plus the power of faithful leadership in the mode of Moses of old.

There has been some confusion about the identity of the "man . . . like as Moses." John Taylor wrote, "The president [of the Church] stands in the same relationship to the Church as Moses did to the Children of Israel" (*Times and Seasons* 6:922). And Elder John A Widtsoe stated, "The man like unto Moses in the Church is the President of the Church." (*Evidences and Reconciliations* 1:197.)

D&C 103:16—The phrase "a man" in this verse refers to the president of the Church; he will lead the Saints as did Moses, when the Lord's power was apparent and visible.

D&C 103:20—The Saints are promised that the Lord's angels will go up before them because the people who go to redeem Jackson County will be living a celestial law; they will be purified and will be able to be brought back into the presence of God. Those who go on this errand must be sanctified. Because of this, the Lord may have to use drastic measures to cleanse the Church for this event. The redemption of Jackson County will resemble the deliverance of ancient Israel from Egypt.

D&C 103:21-27—From these words we learn that the Lord's parable of the watchtower and the vineyard given in Section 101 was in prophetic anticipation of the formation of Zion's Camp under the direction of Joseph Smith (see D&C 101:44, 55). As such, Joseph Smith would prefigure the man—"like as Moses" (D&C 103:16)—who would rise up in the last days to reclaim and redeem Zion. In all of this, the Lord gives the promise that His presence will be with the faithful Saints, and that individuals who would lay down their lives for the cause would "find it again" as His true disciples.

D&C 103:22—Zion's Camp was instructed that they were not to go to Zion until they had at least 100 men, and Joseph Smith was to personally preside. Eventually Zion's Camp had 207 men, 11 women, and 11 children; a smaller group was sent ahead to raise money.

have obtained companies to go up unto the land of Zion, by tens, or by twenties, or by fifties, or by an hundred, until they have obtained to the number of five hundred of the strength of my house.

31. Behold this is my will; ask and ye shall receive, but men do not always do my will;

32. Therefore, if you cannot obtain five hundred, seek diligently, that peradventure you may obtain three hundred;

33. And if ye cannot obtain three hundred, seek diligently, that peradventure ye may obtain one hundred.

34. But verily I say unto you, a commandment I give unto you, that ye shall not go up unto the land of Zion, until you have obtained a hundred of the strength of my house, to go up with you unto the land of Zion.

35. Therefore as I said unto you, ask and ye shall receive; pray earnestly that peradventure my servant Baurak Ale (Joseph Smith, jr.) may go with you, and preside in the midst of my people, and organize my kingdom upon the consecrated land, and establish the children of Zion upon the laws and commandments which have been, and which shall be given unto you.

36. All victory and glory is brought to pass unto you through your diligence, faithfulness and prayers of faith.

37. Let my servant Parley P. Pratt journey with my servant Joseph Smith, jr.

38. Let my servant Lyman Wight journey with my servant Sidney Rigdon.

39. Let my servant Hyrum Smith journey with my servant Frederick G. Williams.

40. Let my servant Orson Hyde journey with my servant Orson Pratt, whithersoever my servant Joseph Smith, jr., shall counsel them, in obtaining the fulfilment of these commandments which I have given unto you, and leave the residue in my hands. Even so. Amen.

D&C 103:34, 36—The Lord gives directives and assignments concerning the empowerment and deployment of Zion's Camp and other activities on behalf of the Saints. As with all activities related to the building of God's Kingdom, this one calls for diligence, faith, and prayers. Hoyt Brewster, Jr., gives this summary of the work of Zion's Camp:

The camp included contingents from Ohio and Michigan and eventually had a strength of 205 men and 25 wagons. The first group left Kirtland on May 1, 1834, and the camp was ultimately disbanded on June 25, near Rush Creek in Missouri. (HC 2:64–114.)

Some of their experiences included the following: the discovery of the skeletal remains of a "white Lamanite" named "Zelph"; an outbreak of cholera that afflicted sixty-eight persons and claimed fourteen lives, partly due to the rebellious spirit shown by some members of the camp; and the divine protection afforded the men when the elements preserved them from mobocracy.

Upon arriving in Missouri, the Lord informed the Prophet Joseph, who was commander-in-chief of the expedition, that in consequence of transgression, the time for Zion's redemption was not yet at hand (D&C 105). Though many were disappointed, and some even looked upon the march as a failure, it had served a providential purpose. (DCE, 658.)

D&C 103:37–40—The assignments in these verses were to raise money for Zion's Camp.

THE CONDITIONAL PROMISE OF REDEMPTION

In the beginning of this revelation, the Lord reviewed the reasons for the persecutions of the Saints in Jackson County and their subsequent expulsion (see D&C 103:1–4). He then decreed that Zion could yet be redeemed on conditions of strict obedience of the Saints in both Missouri and Ohio.

The Saints in Missouri were promised a reinstatement to their lands provided they hearkened to the Lord from that very hour. But if they failed to hearken, their enemies would continue to prevail against them (see D&C 103:5–11).

The Saints in Ohio were to assist in the redemption of their brethren in Zion by sending a relief expedition. Ideally, this expedition was to consist of 500 men with sufficient funds to purchase land as previously commanded by the Lord (see D&C 103:22–23, 30–34). (Note: Revelation had been previously given instructing the Saints to save money in order to purchase land in Missouri; see D&C 48, 57, 58, and 101.)

This relief expedition, which consisted of approximately 200 men, was subsequently known as Zion's Camp. It was led by the Prophet Joseph Smith, who is referred to in this revelation as ". . . a man, who shall lead them like as Moses led the children of Israel" (D&C 103:16). When the Prophet Joseph Smith led Zion's Camp to Missouri, he did so in fulfillment of the parable of the redemption of Zion (see D&C 101:55–56; 103:21) (STDC 2:201).

SECTION 104

1. Verily I say unto you, my friends, I give unto you counsel, and a commandment, concerning all the properties which belong to the order which I commanded to be organized and established, to be an united order, and an everlasting order for the benefit of my church, and for the salvation of men until I come,

2. With promise immutable and unchangeable, that inasmuch as those whom I commanded were faithful they should be blessed with a multiplicity of blessings;

3. But inasmuch as they were not faithful they were nigh unto cursing.

4. Therefore, inasmuch as some of my servants have not kept the commandment, but have broken the covenant through covetousness, and with feigned words, I have cursed them with a very sore and grievous curse;

5. For I, the Lord, have decreed in my heart, that inasmuch as any man belonging to the order, shall be found a transgressor, or, in other words, shall break the covenant with which ye are bound, he shall be cursed in his life, and shall be trodden down by whom I will,

6. For I, the Lord, am not to be mocked in these things;

7. And all this that the innocent among you may not be condemned with the unjust, and that the guilty among you may not escape, because I, the Lord, have promised unto you a crown of glory at my right hand.

8. Therefore inasmuch as you are found transgressors, you cannot escape my wrath in your lives;

9. Inasmuch as ye are cut off for transgression, ye cannot escape the buffetings of Satan, until the day of redemption.

10. And I now give unto you power from this very hour, that if any man among you, of the order, is found a transgressor, and repenteth not of the evil, that ye shall deliver him over unto the buffetings of Satan, and he shall not have power to bring evil upon you.

11. It is wisdom in me: therefore, a commandment I give unto you, that ye shall organize yourselves and appoint every man his stewardship,

12. That every man may give an account unto me of the stewardship which is appointed unto him;

13. For it is expedient that I, the Lord, should make every man accountable, as stewards over earthly blessings, which I have made and prepared for my creatures.

14. I, the Lord, stretched out the heavens, and built the earth as a very handiwork, and all things therein are mine:

15. And it is my purpose to provide for my saints, for all things are mine;

16. But it must needs be done in mine own way; and behold this is the way that I, the Lord, have decreed to provide for my saints, that the poor shall be exalted, in that the rich are made low;

17. For the earth is full, and there is enough and to spare; yea, I prepared all things, and have given unto the children of men to be agents unto themselves.

18. Therefore, if any man shall take

Section 104 Background—Given on April 23, 1834, in Kirtland, Ohio (see *HC* 2:54–60). In the Prophet's journal we learn that he "Assembled in Council with Elders Sidney Rigdon, Frederick G. Williams, Newel K. Whitney, John Johnson, and Oliver Cowdery." These men, with the addition of Martin Harris, comprised the members of the United Order (or "Firm") in Kirtland. Their debts were apparently staggering, and Joseph needed $2,000 immediately to pay off debts incurred by the Kirtland Firm. On March 31, Orson wrote to Joseph that they were not likely to succeed and not to expect the money. Joseph wrote Orson a pleading response on April 7 asking him to solicit other Saints in New York for the money. Joseph indicated that if the money could not be raised, then he could not go on Zion's Camp. Joseph then recorded that he, Bishop Whitney, and Frederick G. Williams "bowed down before the Lord, and prayed that He would furnish the means to deliver the Firm from debt" (*HC* 2:47).

Still without the money, the members of the Firm met on April 10 and "agreed that the Order should be dissolved, and each one have his stewardship set off to him" (*HC* 2:49). Thirteen days later Joseph dispatched Zebedee Coltrin on a mission to borrow money from Church member Jacob Myres.

D&C 104:1, 11–16—The Lord responds to the petition and supplication of His financially troubled servants by unfolding to their view a program by which they could manage and control their temporal affairs with prudence, abundance, and thanksgiving—rather than in a state of turmoil and indebtedness occasioned by the covetousness, disloyalty, and/or misjudgment of some. The restructured order is to be operated in the manner prescribed by the Lord and based on these eternal principles:

(1) The abundance of the earth belongs to the Creator—not to man.

(2) The abundance of the earth is sufficient to provide for the needs of all mankind.

(3) The Lord is willing, of His abundance, to impart individual stewardships to His faithful servants.

(4) Each steward is to render an accounting of his stewardship.

(5) The poor are to be "exalted."

(6) The rich are to be "made low."

As an outgrowth to this model, today's Church Welfare Program is a magnificent manifestation of the spirit of charity and the wise application of the principles of industry and self-reliance. The Lord makes us responsible to care for the poor and needy, and we are accountable to the Lord for the bounties of the earth that He has given to us.

of the abundance which I have made, and impart not his portion, according to the law of my gospel, unto the poor and the needy, he shall, with the wicked, lift up his eyes in hell, being in torment.

19. And now, verily I say unto you, concerning the properties of the order.

20. Let my servant Pelagoram [Sidney Rigdon] have appointed unto him the place where he now resides and the lot of Tahhannes [the tannery] for his stewardship, for his support while he is laboring in my vineyard, even as I will when I shall command him;

21. And let all things be done according to the counsel of the order, and united consent or voice of the order, which dwell in the land of Shinehah [Kirtland].

22. And this stewardship and blessing, I, the Lord, confer upon my servant Pelagoram, [Sidney Rigdon,] for a blessing upon him, and his seed after him;

23. And I will multiply blessings upon him, inasmuch as he shall be humble before me.

24. And again, let my servant Mahemson [Martin Harris] have appointed unto him, for his stewardship, the lot of land which my servant Zombre [John Johnson] obtained in exchange for his former inheritance, for him and his seed after him;

25. And inasmuch as he is faithful, I will multiply blessings upon him, and his seed after him.

26. And let my servant Mahemson [Martin Harris] devote his moneys for the proclaiming of my words, according as my servant Gazelam [Joseph Smith, jr.] shall direct.

27. And again, let my servant Shederlaomach [Frederick G. Williams] have the place upon which he now dwells.

28. And let my servant Olihah [Oliver Cowdery] have the lot which is set off joining the house, which is to be for the Laneshine-house [printing office] which is lot number one, and also the lot upon which his father resides.

29. And let my servants Shederlaomach [Frederick G. Williams] and Olihah [Oliver Cowdery] have the Laneshine-house, [printing office,] and all things that pertain unto it;

30. And this shall be their stewardship which shall be appointed unto them:

31. And inasmuch as they are faithful, behold I will bless, and multiply blessings upon them,

32. And this is the beginning of the stewardship which I have appointed them, for them and their seed after them;

33. And, inasmuch as they are faithful, I will multiply blessings upon them, and their seed after them, even a multiplicity of blessings.

34. And again, let my servant Zombre [John Johnson] have the house in which he lives, and the inheritance—all, save the ground which has been reserved for the building of my houses, which pertains to that inheritance, and those lots which have been named for my servant Olihah [Oliver Cowdery].

35. And, inasmuch as he is faithful, I will multiply blessings upon him.

36. And it is my will that he should sell the lots that are laid off for the building up of the city of my saints, inasmuch as it shall be made known to him by the voice of the Spirit, and according to the counsel of the order, and by the voice of the order.

37. And this is the beginning of the stewardship which I have appointed unto him, for a blessing unto him, and his seed after him;

38. And, inasmuch as he is faithful, I will multiply a multiplicity of blessings upon him.

39. And again, let my servant Ahashdah [Newel K. Whitney] have appointed unto him the houses and lot where he now resides, and the lot and building on which the Ozondah [mercantile establishment] stands, and also the lot which

D&C 104:19–46—In these verses, specific instructions fare given for stewardships under the United Order. It is instructive to note that the Lord chose people with a variety of skills to participate and utilized them appropriately:

• Sidney Rigdon (verse 22), a tanner, was given a tannery

• Martin Harris (verse 24), a farmer, was given land and was told to give the resulting money for the "proclaiming of my words" (a publication business)

• Frederick G. Williams and Oliver Cowdery (verses 27–28), printers, were put in charge of the printing office

• John Johnson (verse 34), a real estate agent, was put in chage of selling building lots (verse 36)

• Newel K. Whitney (verse 39), a merchant, was given a merchantile business

D&C 104:21, 22, 57, 78–80—In granting to these individuals their several stewardships, the Lord put into effect additional principles of the United Order:

(1) A multiplicity of talents and experiences was combined to enhance the good of the community: tanning, farming, preaching, printing, real estate development, retail sales and merchandising, elder care, accounting, management, and the like. It was to be a community of Saints unified in the conducting of temporal and spiritual affairs.

(2) The organization was to be local in nature (with Kirtland having one order and Missouri another) for purposes of operational efficiency and equity.

(3) Blessings would flow based on faithfulness, diligence, humility, and prayerfulness.

(4) Two central treasuries (one for Church revenues, as from printing, and the other for the proceeds from individual stewardships) were to be established and operated according to the principle of common consent.

(5) Revenues from the stewardship treasury were to be distributed to individuals based on their justifiable needs in developing their stewardships.

(6) Those belonging to the Order were to pay their debts.

(7) In responding to the supplications of the members, the Lord would soften the hearts of the creditors or benefactors in order to bring relief to the Saints.

is on the corner south of the Ozondah [mercantile establishment], and also the lot on which the Shule [ashery] is situated.

40. And all this I have appointed unto my servant Ahashdah, [Newel K. Whitney,] for his stewardship, for a blessing upon him and his seed after him, for the benefit of the Ozondah [mercantile establishment] of my order which I have established for my Stake in the land of Shinehah; [Kirtland;]

41. Yea, verily, this is the stewardship which I have appointed unto my servant Ahashdah, [N. K. Whitney,] even this whole Ozondah, [mercantile establishment,] him and his agent, and his seed after him;

42. And, inasmuch as he is faithful in keeping my commandments which I have given unto him, I will multiply blessings upon him, and his seed after him, even a multiplicity of blessings.

43. And again, let my servant Gazelam [Joseph Smith, jr.] have appointed unto him the lot which is laid off for the building of my house, which is forty rods long and twelve wide, and also the inheritance upon which his father resides;

44. And this is the beginning of the stewardship which I have appointed unto him, for a blessing upon him, and upon his father;

45. For, behold, I have reserved an inheritance for his father, for his support; therefore he shall be reckoned in the house of my servant Gazelam, [Joseph Smith, jr.,]

46. And I will multiply blessings upon the house of my servant Gazelam, [Joseph Smith, jr.,] inasmuch as he is faithful, even a multiplicity of blessings.

47. And now, a commandment I give unto you concerning Zion, that you shall no longer be bound as an United Order to your brethren of Zion, only on this wise.

48. After you are organized, you shall be called the United Order of the Stake of Zion, the city of Shinehah. [Kirtland.] And your brethren, after they are organized, shall be called the United Order of the City of Zion;

49. And they shall be organized in their own names, and in their own name; and they shall do their business in their own name, and in their own names;

50. And you shall do your business in your own name, and in your own names.

51. And this I have commanded to be done for your salvation, and also for their salvation, in consequence of their being driven out, and that which is to come.

52. The covenants being broken through transgression, by covetousness and feigned words;

53. Therefore, you are dissolved as a United Order with your brethren, that you are not bound only up to this hour unto them, only on this wise, as I said, by loan as shall be agreed by this order in council, as your circumstances will admit and the voice of the council direct.

54. And again, a commandment I give unto you concerning your stewardship which I have appointed unto you.

55. Behold, all these properties are mine, or else your faith is vain, and ye are found hypocrites, and the covenants which ye have made unto me are broken;

56. And if the properties are mine, then ye are stewards, otherwise ye are no stewards.

57. But, verily I say unto you, I have appointed unto you to be stewards over mine house, even stewards indeed;

58. And for this purpose I have commanded you to organize yourselves,

D&C 104:43, 45—In these verses, we see that Joseph Smith is given two responsibilities: one for the temple lot (verse 43) and one to care for his aging father (verse 45).

D&C 104:48—Two separate United Orders were formed—one in Kirtland and one in Missouri—because the geographic distance between the two was too great for them to function as a single order.

D&C 104:52–53—These two verses provide a simple and clear explanation of the basic principle of the United Order.

THE LORD PROVIDES—HIS WAY

Perhaps the most fundamental principle pertaining to our temporal salvation was revealed by the Lord as follows: "I, the Lord, stretched out the heavens, and built the earth, my very handiwork; and all things therein are mine" (D&C 104:14).

Inasmuch as all things are the Lord's, then it is His prerogative to determine the way in which the resources of the earth are used. To the Latter-day Saints, the Lord said it is His purpose to provide for His Saints with the following stipulation: It must be accomplished in His own way (see D&C 104:15–16).

And what is His way?

. . . behold, this is the way that I, the Lord have decreed to provide for my saints, that the poor shall be exalted, in that the rich are made low.

For the earth is full, and there is enough and to spare; yea, I prepared all things, and have given unto the children of men to be agents unto themselves (D&C 104:16–17).

President Joseph Fielding Smith pointed out that it is not the Lord's intention to take from the rich and give to the poor; but that all humanity would be rich from the abundance that was gathered into the Lord's storehouse, and that all would have according to their needs (see CHMR 3:24–25). And President Harold B. Lee taught that the rich would be "made low" (humbled and willing to give of their substance) while the poor would be "exalted" (uplifted because the rich were willing to share) (see CR, Oct. 1941, 113).

The organizational vehicle to accomplish these purposes is at the discretion of the Lord. When this revelation (Section 104) was given, the concepts were to be applied within the framework of the United Order. The Lord ordered that it be restructured at that time to benefit the Saints in both Missouri and Ohio. In our day, the Church Welfare Program is the vehicle designed by the Lord to provide for His Saints (STDC 2:205–206).

even to Shinelah [print] my words, the fulness of my scriptures, the revelations which I have given unto you, and which I shall, hereafter, from time to time give unto you—

59. For the purpose of building up my church and kingdom on the earth, and to prepare my people for the time when I shall dwell with them, which is nigh at hand.

60. And ye shall prepare for yourselves a treasury, and consecrate it unto my name;

61. And ye shall appoint one among you to keep the treasury, and he shall be ordained unto this blessing;

62. And there shall be a seal upon the treasury, and all the sacred things shall be delivered into the treasury, and no man among you shall call it his own, or any part of it, for it shall belong to you all with one accord;

63. And I give it unto you from this very hour :and now see to it, that ye go to and make use of the stewardship which I have appointed unto you, exclusive of the sacred things, for the purpose of Shinelane [printing] these sacred things as I have said;

64. And the avails of the sacred things shall be had in the treasury, and a seal shall be upon it, and it shall not be used or taken out of the treasury by any one, neither shall the seal be loosed which shall be placed upon it only by the voice of the order, or by commandment.

65. And thus shall ye preserve the avails of the sacred things in the treasury, for sacred and holy purposes:

66. And this shall be called the sacred treasury of the Lord; and a seal shall be kept upon it that it may be holy and consecrated unto the Lord.

67. And again, there shall be another treasury prepared, and a treasurer appointed to keep the treasury, and a seal shall be placed upon it;

68. And all moneys that you receive in your stewardships, by improving upon the properties which I have appointed unto you, in houses, or in lands, or in cattle, or in all things save it be the holy and sacred writings, which I have reserved unto myself for holy and sacred purposes, shall be cast into the treasury as fast as you receive moneys, by hundreds, or by fifties, or by twenties, or by tens, or by fives;

69. Or in other words, if any man among you obtain five talents, (dollars,) let him cast them into the treasury; or if he obtain ten, or twenty, or fifty, or an hundred, let him do likewise;

70. And let not any man among you say that it is his own, for it shall not be called his, nor any part of it,

71. And there shall not any part of it be used, or taken out of the treasury, only by the voice and common consent of the order.

72. And this shall be the voice and common consent of the order; that any man among you say to the treasurer; I have need of this to help me in my stewardship—

73. If it be five talents, (dollars,) or if it be ten talents, (dollars,) or twenty, or fifty, or an hundred, the treasurer shall give unto him the sum which he requires, to help him in his stewardship,

74. Until he be found a transgressor, and it is manifest before the council of the order plainly, that he is an unfaithful and an unwise steward;

75. But so long as he is in full fellowship, and is faithful, and wise in his stewardship, this shall be his token unto the treasurer, that the treasurer shall not withhold.

76. But in case of transgression, the

D&C 104:67—According to President J. Reuben Clark, the treasury referred to in this verse is a sacred treasury that was for the proceed from the sale of the Book of Mormon and the Doctrine and Covenants. The other treasury was for the proceeds from the improvement of various stewardships (the general funds the Church).

D&C 104:71–77—These verses provide instructions for administering the sacred funds in the treasury.

DEBT: THE LORD'S COUNSEL

A fundamental principle of temporal salvation concerns financial indebtedness. The Lord's counsel to His church was given: ". . . it is my will that you shall pay all your debts" (D&C 104:78). Meeting one's financial obligations is a matter of honesty and integrity with one's fellow men in order to stand approved of the Lord. President N. Eldon Tanner said that "a man's good name is worth more than any material thing he could have" (see CR, Oct. 1966, 100).

Under certain economic circumstances, there are some justifiable debts. However, one should realize there are undesirable financial burdens connected with indebtedness. One of those is interest—something that, according to President J. Reuben Clark, "never sleeps nor sickens nor dies; it never goes to the hospital; it works on Sundays and holidays; it never takes a vacation; it never visits nor travels; it takes no pleasure; it is never laid off work nor discharged from employment; it never works on reduced hours; it never has short crops nor droughts; it never pays taxes; it buys no food; it wears no clothes; it is unhoused and without home and so has no repairs, no replacements, no shingling, plumbing, painting, or whitewashing . . . it has no love, no sympathy; it is as hard and soulless as a granite cliff. Once in debt, interest is your companion every minute of the day and night; you cannot shun it or slip away from it; you cannot dismiss it; it yields neither to entreaties, demands, or orders; and whenever you get in its way or cross its course or fail to meet its demands, it crushes you" (CR, April 1938, 102–103).

treasurer shall be subject unto the council and voice of the order.

77. And in case the treasurer is found an unfaithful, and an unwise steward, he shall be subject to the council and voice of the order, and shall be removed out of his place, and another shall be appointed in his stead.

78. And again, verily I say unto you, concerning your debts, behold it is my will that you shall pay all your debts;

79. And it is my will that you shall humble yourselves before me, and obtain this blessing by your diligence and humility, and the prayer of faith;

80. And inasmuch as you are diligent and humble, and exercise the prayer of faith, behold, I will soften the hearts of those to whom you are in debt, until I shall send means unto you for your deliverance.

81. Therefore write speedily unto Cainhannoch, (New York), and write according to that which shall be dictated by my Spirit, and I will soften the hearts of those to whom you are in debt, that it shall be taken away out of their minds to bring affliction upon you.

82. And inasmuch as ye are humble and faithful, and call upon my name, behold, I will give you the victory.

83. I give unto you a promise, that you shall be delivered this once out of your bondage;

84. Inasmuch as you obtain a chance to loan money by hundreds, or thousands, even until you shall loan enough to deliver yourselves from bondage, it is your privilege;

85. And pledge the properties which I have put into your hands, this once, by giving your names by common consent or otherwise, as it shall seem good unto you.

86. I give unto you this privilege, this once, and behold, if you proceed to do the things which I have laid before you, according to my commandments, all these things are mine, and ye are my stewards, and the master will not suffer his house to be broken up. Even so. Amen.

SECTION 105

1. Verily I say unto you who have assembled yourselves together that you may learn my will concerning

Section 105 Background—Given on June 22, 1834, on Fishing River, Clay County, Missouri (*HC* 2:108–11). Historian Lyndon W. Cook gives the following summary:

"Zion's Camp marched out of Kirtland on 5 May 1834. The plight of the Missouri Saints engaged the attention of the approximately two hundred Mormons who joined the camp to defend the rights of their brethren. With a pledge from the Missouri governor to give the homeless Mormons a military escort back to their lands in Jackson County, members of Zion's Camp traveled one thousand miles to protect and defend the Missouri Saints from local harassment after their return. . . .

"The Mormon army crossed the Mississippi River in early June, arriving at the Salt River Branch of the Church in Monroe County, Missouri, on 7 June 1834. After a short respite the camp resumed its march on 12 June. Three days later Orson Hyde and Parley P. Pratt returned to the camp from Jefferson City with news that Governor Daniel Dunklin had 'refused to fulfill his promise of reinstating' the Mormons on their lands in Jackson County. Dunklin apparently made his earlier promise in good faith; however, in the intervening six months, as Mormon-non-Mormon conditions worsened, he perceived that an armed conflict would inevitably ensue if the Mormons returned to their lands, and 'pragmatically withdrew his promise in order to avert a civil war.'

"Inasmuch as the camp intended only to work in concert with state authorities and under state protection, the governor's refusal insured that Zion's Camp would not enter Jackson County. With its primary objective out of reach, all that remained for the camp was to move into Clay County, where the body of the Church was residing, and discuss possible compromises. (*RPJS*, 211–213.)

Two days after this revelation was received, Zion's Camp was disbanded without reaching its goal. Zion's Camp did, however, accomplish several important things: it furnished the experience that allowed the Church to assist 20,000 people in traveling to the Rocky Mountains, and it provided a proving ground for future Church leaders (the Quorum of the Twelve and the First Quorum of the Seventy were all members of Zion's Camp).

the redemption of mine afflicted people—

2. Behold, I say unto you, were it not for the transgressions of my people, speaking concerning the church and not individuals, they might have been redeemed even now;

3. But behold, they have not learned to be obedient to the things which I required at their hands, but are full of all manner of evil, and do not impart of their substance, as becometh saints, to the poor and afflicted among them,

4. And are not united according to the union required by the law of the celestial kingdom;

5. And Zion cannot be built up unless it is by the principles of the law of the celestial kingdom, otherwise I cannot receive her unto myself.

6. And my people must needs be chastened until they learn obedience, if it must needs be, by the things which they suffer.

7. I speak not concerning those who are appointed to lead my people, who are the first elders of my church, for they are not all under this condemnation;

8. But I speak concerning my churches abroad—there are many who will say, Where is their God? Behold, he will deliver them in time of trouble, otherwise we will not go up unto Zion, and will keep our moneys.

9. Therefore, in consequence of the transgressions of my people, it is expedient in me that mine elders should wait for a little season for the redemption of Zion—

10. That they themselves may be prepared, and that my people may be taught more perfectly, and have experience, and know more perfectly concerning their duty, and the things which I require at their hands.

11. And this cannot be brought to pass until mine elders are endowed with power from on high;

12. For behold, I have prepared a great endowment and blessing to be poured out upon them, inasmuch as they are faithful and continue in humility before me;

13. Therefore it is expedient in me that mine elders should wait for a little season, for the redemption of Zion;

14. For behold, I do not require at their hands to fight the battles of Zion; for, as I said in a former commandment, even so will I fulfil. I will fight your battles.

15. Behold, the destroyer I have sent forth to destroy and lay waste mine enemies: and not many years hence they shall not be left to pollute mine heritage, and to blaspheme my name upon the lands which I have consecrated for the gathering together of my saints.

16. Behold, I have commanded my servant Baurak Ale [Joseph Smith, jr.] to say unto the strength of my house, even my warriors, my young men, and middle-aged, to gather together for the redemption of my

D&C 105:4–5—We must obey a celestial law if we are to inherit the celestial kingdom. The law of consecration requires us to control our heart; therefore, Zion is the pure in heart. President Lorenzo Snow said that we will not be allowed to build Jackson County until our hearts are prepared to live the law of consecration.

D&C 105:5—In our mortal existence we live in a telestial realm. Line upon line and precept upon precept—through the benevolence of God—we learn the principles of a higher calling. We are destined by invitation and covenant arrangement to become part of a celestial family, unified in the spirit of charity and love for all, given over to enduring obedience to divine commandments. It is a process of following the Spirit and being made "perfect in Christ" (Moroni 10:32) through the power of the Atonement.

D&C 105:6—Zion is a unique place—her only tenants are those who have learned to be celestial in nature, often being instructed and enlightened in the throes of adversity and suffering. *Chastening*, according to Elder Bruce R. McConkie, is the process by which the Lord prepares us for salvation and is one way in which He leads us back to paths of righteousness. Depending on the circumstances, such chastening may consist of chastisement (corporal punishment), rebukes, or trials and affliction (see *MD*, 122).

D&C 105:9–12—The redemption of Zion comes through the orderly application of divine power and the operation of the Spirit in the lives of faithful and valiant sons and daughters of God. This process is one of gradual and consistent growth, promoted through the compassionate and chastening hand of God, crowned ultimately with glory through the transformational renewal ushered in at the dawning of the millennial era. We can all be part of the process of establishing Zion and helping the Lord perform His redeeming acts of mercy, grace, and love—but we are called on to repent and learn more perfectly our duty as required by the Master.

D&C 105:11—The endowment was to prepare the elders for their missions. It is an ordinance that serves as a protection, saving us now and exalting us later. While some endowments were performed in Nauvoo before the temple was completed, the endowment was generally first available in this dispensation in the Nauvoo Temple.

D&C 105:14, 19—In a previous revelation the Lord commanded the people to practice forgiveness in dealing with their enemies and to leave judgment to God. The Lord again confirms His design to fight the battles of Zion and protect His divine heritage from being polluted by those who blaspheme His name. He has heard the prayers of the faithful, sent heavenward from the valley of persecution, and will bless them with an endowment of truth. Their suffering has contributed to a maturing and confirmation of their faith.

people, and throw down the towers of mine enemies, and scatter their watchmen;

17. But the strength of mine house have not hearkened unto my words;

18. But inasmuch as there are those who have hearkened unto my words, I have prepared a blessing and an endowment for them, if they continue faithful.

19. I have heard their prayers, and will accept their offering; and it is expedient in me, that they should be brought thus far for a trial of their faith.

20. And now, verily I say unto you, a commandment I give unto you, that as many as have come up hither, that can stay in the region round about, let them stay;

21. And those that cannot stay, who have families in the east, let them tarry for a little season, inasmuch as my servant Joseph shall appoint unto them;

22. For I will counsel him concerning this matter, and all things whatsoever he shall appoint unto them shall be fulfilled.

23. And let all my people who dwell in the regions round about be very faithful, and prayerful, and humble before me, and reveal not the things which I have revealed unto them, until it is wisdom in me that they should be revealed.

24. Talk not of judgments, neither boast of faith nor of mighty works, but carefully gather together, as much in one region as can be consistently with the feelings of the people;

25. And behold, I will give unto you favor and grace in their eyes, that you may rest in peace and safety, while you are saying unto the people, Execute judgment and justice for us according to law, and redress us of our wrongs.

26. Now, behold, I say unto you, my friends, in this way you may find favor in the eyes of the people, until the army of Israel becomes very great;

27. And I will soften the hearts of the people, as I did the heart of Pharaoh, from time to time, until my servant Baurak Ale, (Joseph Smith, jr.,) and Baneemy, (mine elders,) whom I have appointed, shall have time to gather up the strength of my house,

28. And to have sent wise men, to fulfil that which I have commanded concerning the purchasing of all the lands in Jackson county that can be purchased, and in the adjoining counties round about;

29. For it is my will that these lands should be purchased, and after they are purchased that my saints should possess them according to the laws of consecration which I have given;

30. And after these lands are purchased, I will hold the armies of Israel guiltless in taking possession of their own lands, which they have previously purchased with their moneys, and of throwing down the towers of mine enemies that may be upon them, and scattering their watchmen, and avenging me of mine enemies unto the third and fourth generation of them that hate me.

31. But firstly let my army become very great, and let it be sanctified before me, that it may become fair as the sun, and clear as the moon, and that her banners may be terrible unto all nations;

32. That the kingdoms of this world may be constrained to acknowledge, that the kingdom of Zion is in very deed the kingdom of our God and

D&C 105:24, 27, 31—The strategy of the Lord is to nurture and cultivate His people in the midst of their fellow citizens in such a way that the kingdom of God might unfold in safety and glory. But such requires wisdom and prudence on the part of the Saints, that they might not invoke an unpleasant response from their neighbors through talk of impending judgment or claims of superior faith and works. Instead, the Saints are enjoined to radiate a spirit of humility, faith, and prayerfulness. The Lord will then soften the hearts of their countrymen so that peace and safety will prevail—until such time as the army of God should become very great and sanctified, capable of inducing respect and compliance on the part of the kingdoms of the world. Meanwhile, the Saints are to acquire lands in the appointed region—not by conquest, but through a process of wise and lawful purchase. Again, the redemption of Zion comes according to the timetable of the Lord, and in keeping with the preparations of His people to live the celestial law.

REQUIREMENTS FOR THE EVENTUAL REDEMPTION OF ZION

The Lord said that Zion would have to wait for a little season before it could be redeemed (see D&C 105:9). He also said that His people must be prepared in order to accomplish this great mission (see D&C 105:10). Some of the requirements that must be met by the Lord's Church and His people before they are prepared to redeem Zion include the following:

• The Saints must learn obedience (verses 3, 6). In order to learn obedience, an individual must confront opposition and have the freedom of choice.

• The Saints must be united (verses 4–5). Unity—being one with the leaders, teachings, and practices of the Church—is a celestial law and can only be achieved when we are obedient.

• The Saints must be taught more perfectly (verse 10). Knowledge must be obtained before perfection can be achieved; teaching occurs in priesthood quorums, auxiliary classes, seminaries, institutes, lectures, and workshops, to name but a few sources of learning.

• The Saints need experience and to know more perfectly concerning their duty (verse 10). Part of the effectiveness of the Church is the opportunity for members to participate in so many of its programs.

• The Saints need to be endowed with power (verses 11–12). The Lord has endowed His Church with power in many ways since this revelation was given, among them the restoration of the Twelve, temple ordinances, welfare programs, and keys of the priesthood.

• The Saints must be sanctified (verse 31). Sanctification, to be clean before the Lord, is accomplished first by knowing, and then abiding by the law of the Lord (STDC 2:212–214).

his Christ; therefore, let us become subject unto her laws.

33. Verily I say unto you, it is expedient in me that the first elders of my church should receive their endowment from on high in my house which I have commanded to be built unto my name in the land of Kirtland;

34. And let those commandments which I have given concerning Zion and her law be executed, and fulfilled, after her redemption.

35. There has been a day of calling, but the time has come for a day of choosing, and let those be chosen that are worthy;

36. And it shall be manifest unto my servant, by the voice of the Spirit, those that are chosen, and they shall be sanctified;

37. And inasmuch as they follow the counsel which they receive, they shall have power after many days to accomplish all things pertaining to Zion.

38. And again I say unto you, sue for peace, not only to the people that have smitten you, but also to all people;

39. And lift up an ensign of peace, and make a proclamation of peace unto the ends of the earth;

40. And make proposals for peace unto those who have smitten you, according to the voice of the Spirit which is in you, and all things shall work together for your good;

41. Therefore, be faithful, and behold, and lo, I am with you even unto the end. Even so. Amen.

SECTION 106

1. It is my will that my servant Warren A. Cowdery should be appointed and ordained a presiding High Priest over my church, in the land of Freedom and the regions round about;

2. And should preach my everlasting gospel, and lift up his voice and warn the people, not only in his own place, but in the adjoining countries,

3. And devote his whole time in this high and holy calling which I now give unto him, seeking diligently the kingdom of heaven and its righteousness, and all things necessary shall be added thereunto, for the laborer is worthy of his hire.

4. And again, verily I say unto you the coming of the Lord draweth nigh, and it overtaketh the world as a thief in the night:

5. Therefore, gird up your loins, that

WARREN A. COWDERY

Warren A. Cowdery was born in October 1788 at Poultney, Rutland County, Vermont. He became a successful farmer and medical practitioner in Freedom, New York. Introduced to the Book of Mormon by his brother Oliver, he joined the Church in 1831 and was called in 1834 as a priesthood leader in his community. He was censured for a prideful repudiation of the Twelve Apostles, but repented in moving to Kirtland in 1836. He served in various capacities as a scribe, recorder, editor, and agent for the Church and was also a member of the Kirtland high council for a period of time. He left the Church after 1838 as a result of his disaffection with Church leaders. Warren passed away on February 23, 1851.

D&C 105:33–41—The unfolding of the kingdom of God in the early days of the Restoration was a dynamic process—changing from day to day according to the expanding canon of new revelations being given and the shifting circumstances in which the Saints found themselves. But the purpose, the design, the objective, the ultimate outcome—these were eternal and fixed according to the master plan laid down in the premortal realm for the salvation and exaltation of God's children. Even while Zion's Camp was being deployed, the Lord had His eye on the coming endowment of essential truth and light that would soon be available in the temple at Kirtland, the dedication of which was fewer than two years away.

D&C 105:34—The "law" refers to the law of consecration. The United Order won't be lived again until Jackson County is redeemed. The Lord rarely mentions it after this section; the Saints had been given the opportunity to live it, but had failed. The Lord subsequently gave His Saints the law of tithing.

Section 106 Background—Given at Kirtland, Ohio, November 25, 1834, on behalf of Warren A. Cowdery (see HC 2:170–171). Of the eight children in the Cowdery family, Warren was the oldest, and Oliver was the youngest. At the time this revelation was received, Joseph was staying at Warren's house.

D&C 106:1—At this time there were Saints in small towns scattered all over western New York, including Perrysburg, Palmersville, Westfield, Villanova, Genese, Avon, and Livonia in the counties of Cattaraugus, Chataurua, and Livingston.

D&C 106:4—The designation "children of light" conveys the essence of the covenant promise, for it expresses the objective of the divine plan to open the gateway to salvation and exaltation in the realms of glory for those who respond to the light of the gospel. The scriptures use various positive appellations for the Saints in connection with the word "children"—the Savior called His followers "children of the prophets," "children of the covenant," "children of the most high," "children of God," "children of the living God," "children of your Father which is in heaven," "children of the Highest," "children of the resurrection," "children of Abraham," "children of the promise," "children of the day," "children of the kingdom," and "children of Zion," among others.

These expressions convey the comforting spirit of belonging—a kinship with the Creator and with things divine—plus an affinity with the eternal light "which proceedeth forth from the presence of God to fill the immensity of space" (D&C 88:12). As "children of light" we are capable of receiving that light and enjoying the spiritual power it brings into our lives. Thus the Lord's admonition to Warren A. Cowdery—and all other members of the restored Church—was to "gird up your loins, that you may be the children of light" (D&C 106:5).

you may be the children of light, and that day shall not overtake you as a thief.

6. And again, verily I say unto you, there was joy in heaven when my servant Warren bowed to my scepter, and separated himself from the crafts of men:

7. Therefore, blessed is my servant Warren, for I will have mercy on him, and notwithstanding the vanity of his heart, I will lift him up, inasmuch as he will humble himself before me;

8. And I will give him grace and assurance wherewith he may stand, and if he continue to be a faithful witness and a light unto the church, I have prepared a crown for him in the mansions of my Father. Even so. Amen.

SECTION 107

1. There are, in the church, two Priesthoods, namely, the Melchisedek and Aaronic, including the Levitical priesthood.

2. Why the first is called the Melchisedek Priesthood is because Melchisedek was such a great High Priest.

3. Before his day it was called the Holy Priesthood, after the order of the Son of God;

4. But out of respect or reverence to the name of the Supreme Being, to avoid the too frequent repetition

D&C 106:8—The Lord confirms a covenant contract with Warren Cowdery: If he continues in humility, being a faithful witness of the gospel and a light to the Church, then his reward will be mercy, grace, assurance, and a crown in the eternal realm. Warren A. Cowdery did not honor his covenant with the Lord, but slipped into the by-ways and shadows of pride and self-conceit. He apostasized in 1837 and openly rebelled against the Prophet.

Section 107 Background—"Revelation on Priesthood" given at Kirtland, Ohio, dated March 28, 1835 (see HC 2:209–217). At a special conference in Kirtland on February 14–15, 1835, members of the Quorum of Twelve Apostles were chosen by the three witnesses to the Book of Mormon under commission of the First Presidency. The Twelve met in council to confess their individual shortcomings; they had been light-minded and vain, and had not realized the importance of their callings, something that had wounded the feelings of the First Presidency. After this historic organization, the Prophet met from time to time with the newly called Apostles and gave instructions to them. On one such occasion (March 12, 1835), it was decided that the Twelve should "take [their] first mission through the Eastern States, to the Atlantic Ocean, and hold conferences in the vicinity of the several branches of the Church for the purpose of regulating all things necessary for their welfare" (HC 2:209). Later, on March 28, in the late afternoon, members of the quorum confessed their sins, committed themselves to greater service, and received instruction from Joseph Smith. Knowing that they would soon depart for the East, members of the quorum requested that the Prophet "inquire of God for us, and obtain a revelation, (if consistent) that we may look upon it when we are separated, that our hearts may be comforted" (HC 2:210). "Our worthiness has not inspired us to make this request, but our unworthiness," they said. The resulting instruction, Section 107, apparently combines various interrelated revelations received during this period of time and provides important doctrine and policy on the operation of the priesthood.

D&C 107:1—Elder Bruce R. McConkie explained that everything on earth is subject to the power and authority of the Melchizedek Priesthood, and that it is designed to enable men to attain salvation in the highest degree of the celestial kingdom. It is the priesthood, he says, that enables men to become joint heirs with Christ in gaining all that the Father has (see MD, 476–480).

The lesser priesthood was instituted by the Lord to administer the preparatory gospel. From the time of Aaron until that of John the Baptist, the lesser priesthood was given only to worthy members of a certin lineage that had been chosen to receive the priesthood. Because he was a descendant of Aaron, John the Baptist held the keys of the Aaronic priesthood. This priesthood did not exist among the Nephites before the Savior appeared to them, because no one from the tribe of Levi had gone with the Nephites to the promised land.

of his name, they, the church, in ancient days, called that Priesthood after Melchisedek, or the Melchisedek Priesthood.

5. All other authorities or offices in the church are appendages to this Priesthood;

6. But there are two divisions or grand heads—one is the Melchisedek Priesthood, and the other is the Aaronic, or Levitical priesthood.

7. The office of an elder comes under the Priesthood of Melchisedek.

8. The Melchisedek Priesthood holds the right of Presidency, and has power and authority over all the offices in the church in all ages of the world, to administer in spiritual things.

9. The Presidency of the High Priesthood, after the order of Melchisedek, have a right to officiate in all the offices in the church.

10. High Priests after the order of the Melchisedek Priesthood have a right to officiate in their own standing, under the direction of the Presidency, in administering spiritual things; and also in the office of an elder, priest, (of the Levitical order,), teacher, deacon, and member.

11. An elder has a right to officiate in his stead when the High Priest is not present.

12. The High Priest and elder are to administer in spiritual things, agreeable to the covenants and commandments of the church; and they have a right to officiate in all these offices of the church when there are no higher authorities present.

13. The second priesthood is called the priesthood of Aaron, because it was conferred upon Aaron and his seed, throughout all their generations.

14. Why it is called the lesser priesthood, is because it is an appendage to the greater or the Melchisedek Priesthood, and has power in administering outward ordinances.

15. The bishopric is the presidency of this priesthood and holds the keys or authority of the same.

16. No man has a legal right to this office, to hold the keys of this priesthood, except he be a literal descendant of Aaron.

17. But as a High Priest of the Melchisedek Priesthood has authority to officiate in all the lesser offices, he may officiate in the office of bishop when no literal descendant of Aaron can be found, provided he is called and set apart and ordained unto this power by the hands of the Presidency of the Melchisedek Priesthood.

18. The power and authority of the Higher, or Melchisedek Priesthood, is to hold the keys of all the spiritual blessings of the church—

19. To have the privilege of receiving the mysteries of the kingdom of heaven—to have the heavens opened unto them—to commune with the general assembly and church of the first born, and to enjoy the communion and presence of God the

D&C 107:8—President John Taylor stated:

> . . . there is a difference between the general authority of the Melchizedek priesthood and the one that is designated, which presides over them all: and that which presides over the whole has the right to administer in all things. The Aaronic priesthood is an appendage unto the Melchizedek priesthood, and is under its direction. (GK, 196–197.)

D&C 107:13–15—Elder Orson Pratt elaborates on this principle of priesthood governance:

> . . . if we have literal descendants of Aaron, they have the birthright, through their obedience to the Gospel of the Son of God, to the bishoprick, which pertains to the lesser Priesthood, they have the right to claim it, and to all the keys and powers pertaining to it, they have the right to be ordained and set apart to that calling and to officiate therein, and that too without the aid of two counsellors. . . . But as we have none at present, to our knowledge, that belong to the seed of Aaron, . . . the Lord has pointed out that those who are ordained to the higher Priesthood have the right, by virtue of this higher authority, to administer, when set apart by the First Presidency, or under their direction and according to their instruction as Bishops to officiate in the Presidency of the lower Priesthood. . . . A Bishop must be ordained to the high Priesthood, and by authority of that Priesthood, he may be set apart as a Bishop to preside over the lesser Priesthood, to exercise the functions thereof . . . he must have two counsellors ordained from among the high Priests of the Church. These three persons must officiate in relation to all the ordinances that pertain to the lesser Priesthood, and to administer in temporal things, having a knowledge of them by the inspiration of the Holy Ghost, as we are taught in the Book of Doctrine and Covenants. (JD 18:364.)

D&C 107:18–20—Whereas the lesser priesthood grants the keys to the ministering of angels (a blessing of no small scope and magnitude), the higher priesthood is the instrumentality for the faithful and sanctified to gain access to the very presence of the Father and the Son. Through the restoration of the gospel of Jesus Christ in the latter days, the powers, purposes, and blessings of the priesthood of God have again been made manifest in the world for the redemption and edification of God's children. By divinely commissioned stages, priesthood doctrines, keys, and administrative policies were revealed in an orderly process through the Prophet Joseph Smith and his colleagues as the kingdom of God was once again established in its glory and fullness. Ultimately all of the keys—including the sealing powers—were restored for the consummation of the "marvellous work and a wonder" (Isa. 29:14) foretold by prophets of old and confirmed by Apostles in the meridian of time (see Acts 3:19–21).

Father, and Jesus the Mediator of the new covenant.

20. The power and authority of the lesser, or Aaronic priesthood, is to hold the keys of the ministering of angels, and to administer in outward ordinances, the letter of the gospel—the baptism of repentance for the remission of sins, agreeable to the covenants and commandments.

21. Of necessity there are presidents, or presiding offices growing out of, or appointed of or from among those who are ordained to the several offices in these two priesthoods.

22. Of the Melchisedek Priesthood, three Presiding High Priests, chosen by the body, appointed and ordained to that office, and upheld by the confidence, faith, and prayer of the church, form a quorum of the Presidency of the church.

23. The Twelve traveling councilors are called to be the Twelve apostles, or special witnesses of the name of Christ in all the world; thus differing from other officers in the church in the duties of their calling.

24. And they form a quorum, equal in authority and power to the three Presidents previously mentioned.

25. The seventy are also called to preach the gospel, and to be especial witnesses unto the Gentiles and in all the world. Thus differing from other officers in the church in the duties of their calling;

26. And they form a quorum, equal in authority to that of the Twelve special witnesses or apostles just named.

27. And every decision made by either of these quorums, must be by the unanimous voice of the same; that is, every member in each quorum must be agreed to its decisions, in order to make their decisions of the same power or validity one with the other.

28. (A majority may form a quorum, when circumstances render it impossible to be otherwise.)

29. Unless this is the case, their decisions are not entitled to the same blessings which the decisions of a quorum of three Presidents were anciently, who were ordained after the order of Melchisedek, and were righteous and holy men.

30. The decisions of these quorums, or either of them, are to be made in all righteousness, in holiness, and lowliness of heart, meekness and long suffering, and in faith, and virtue, and knowledge, temperance, patience, godliness, brotherly kindness and charity;

31. Because the promise is, if these things abound in them, they shall not be unfruitful in the knowledge of the Lord.

32. And in case that any decision of these quorums is made in unrighteousness, it may be brought before a general assembly of the several quorums, which constitute the spiritual authorities of the church, otherwise there can be no appeal from their decision.

D&C 107:19—Among the spiritual blessings of the Church available to the righteous are to personally behold the face of God, to personally see the ministrations of angels, and to be crowned with glory in the celestial kingdom.

D&C 107:22–24—In the meaning of these few words is anchored the principle of orderly succession in the highest leadership of the Church. Less than a decade after this revelation was received, the mission of the Prophet Joseph Smith would be completed and sealed with a martyr's death. Brigham Young of the Twelve would receive the mantle of leadership. Where the scriptures recount the moments of succession in the prophetic office, there emerge inevitably principles and qualities that characterize the spiritual nature of the transition of leadership in the kingdom of God. Following the death of Moses, the mantle of authority fell on Joshua to lead the Israelites into the Promised Land. When Elisha succeeded Elijah as prophet, the men of Israel testified: "The spirit of Elijah doth rest on Elisha. And they came to meet him, and bowed themselves to the ground before him" (2 Kings 2:15). Upon the death of Lehi, his son Nephi succeeded to the station of leadership and prepared the way for a future transition. Upon the passing of Nephi, Jacob and Joseph assumed the reigns of leadership.

From such passages we gain an understanding of the nature of succession in priesthood leadership: the Lord provides the direction, the Holy Spirit illuminates the transition, the new leadership acts with courage and strength, and the successor leaders act in all diligence to magnify their office. Upon the passing of the Prophet Joseph Smith, the same principles and qualities of succession were to prevail as Brigham Young assumed the mantle of leadership. The Lord had prepared the way by revealing the nature and powers of authority vested in the several quorums and offices of the priesthood, including the First Presidency and the Quorum of the Twelve.

D&C 107:24, 26—While these verses refer to a quorum "equal in authority," it is important to note that there can never be two or three quorums equal in authority at the same time. This condition of authority applies only when the ranking quorum no longer exists.

D&C 107:32—The First Presidency, the Quorum of the Twelve, and the First Quorum of the Seventy in combined assembly is the only body that can hear an appeal from a leading quorum.

33. The Twelve are a traveling presiding High Council, to officiate in the name of the Lord, under the direction of the Presidency of the church, agreeable to the institution of heaven; to build up the church, and regulate all the affairs of the same in all nations; first unto the Gentiles, and secondly unto the Jews.

34. The seventy are to act in the name of the Lord, under the direction of the Twelve or the traveling High Council, in building up the church and regulating all the affairs of the same in all nations—first unto the Gentiles and then to the Jews;

35. The Twelve being sent out, holding the keys, to open the door by the proclamation of the gospel of Jesus Christ—and first unto the Gentiles and then unto the Jews.

36. The standing High Councils, at the Stakes of Zion, form a quorum equal in authority, in the affairs of the church, in all their decisions, to the quorum of the Presidency, or to the traveling High Council.

37. The High Council in Zion form a quorum equal in authority, in the affairs of the church, in all their decisions, to the Councils of the Twelve at the Stakes of Zion.

38. It is the duty of the traveling High Council to call upon the seventy, when they need assistance, to fill the several calls for preaching and administering the gospel, instead of any others.

39. It is the duty of the Twelve, in all large branches of the church, to ordain evangelical ministers, as they shall be designated unto them by revelation.

40. The order of this Priesthood was confirmed to be handed down from father to son, and rightly belongs to the literal descendants of the chosen seed, to whom the promises were made.

41. This order was instituted in the days of Adam, and came down by lineage in the following manner—

42. From Adam to Seth, who was ordained by Adam at the age of 69 years, and was blessed by him three years previous to his (Adam's) death, and received the promise of God by his father, that his posterity should be the chosen of the Lord, and that they should be preserved unto the end of the earth,

43. Because he (Seth) was a perfect man, and his likeness was the express likeness of his father's, insomuch that he seemed to be like unto his father in all things, and could be distinguished from him only by his age.

44. Enos was ordained at the age of 134 years and four months, by the hand of Adam.

45. God called upon Cainan in the wilderness, in the fortieth year of his age, and he met Adam in journeying to the place Shedolamak. He was 87 years old when he received his ordination.

46. Mahalaleel was 496 years and seven days old when he was ordained by the hand of Adam, who also blessed him.

47. Jared was 200 years old when he was ordained under the hand of Adam, who also blessed him.

48. Enoch was 25 years old when he was ordained under the hand of Adam, and he was 65 and Adam blessed him.

D&C 107:33–34—We witness today in the growth of the Area Presidencies throughout the earth a fulfillment of this passage. They, along with the Area Authority Seventies assigned to their area, regulate the affairs of the Church under the direction of the Quorum of the Twelve Apostles. The Quorum of the Twelve provide leadership and administration and are responsible for teaching all nations; the Seventy supervise administrative details.

D&C 107:35—Consider what marvelous truths and principles the Lord has seen fit to reveal through the prophet of the Restoration: the authority, operational principles, and ordinances of the holy priesthood of God—including the foundational offices of prophets and Apostles; knowledge of the premortal existence and the ultimate venues of glory for mankind; the exalting principles and sealing purposes of the temple (including baptism for the dead, the endowment, and eternal marriage); the expanding archive of the word of God (Book of Mormon, Pearl of Great Price, Doctrine and Covenants, Inspired Translation of the Bible); and the true nature and character of the Godhead, among many others.

D&C 107:36–37—There were two standing high councils at the time: one at Kirtland, Ohio, and one at Clay County, Missouri. The high council "equal in authority" means that all stake high councils in the Church have the same authority; that authority is simply limited to the boundaries of the stakes in which they preside.

D&C 107:39—Besides calling the Seventy to preach and administer the gospel as needed, the Twelve also ordain patriarchs. Joseph Smith declared: "An Evangelist is a Patriarch, even the oldest man of the blood of Joseph or of the seed of Abraham. Wherever the Church of Christ is established in the earth, there should be a Patriarch for the benefit of the posterity of the Saints, as it was with Jacob in giving his patriarchal blessing unto his sons" (HC 3:381).

D&C 107:40—The priesthood referred to in this verse is the patriarchal priesthood; after Noah (see verse 52) the priesthood was given to Abraham and was passed in turn to Isaac, Jacob, Joseph, Ephraim, Joseph Smith Sr., and Hyrum Smith. The patriarchal priesthood will once again be the order in the celestial kingdom.

49. And he saw the Lord, and he walked with him, and was before his face continually; and he walked with God 365 years, making him 430 years old when he was translated.

50. Methuselah was 100 years old when he was ordained under the hand of Adam.

51. Lamech was 32 years old when he was ordained under the hand of Seth.

52. Noah was 10 years old when he was ordained under the hand of Methuselah.

53. Three years previous to the death of Adam, he called Seth, Enos, Cainan, Mahalaleel, Jared, Enoch, and Methuselah, who were all High Priests, with the residue of his posterity who were righteous, into the valley of Adam-ondi-Ahman, and there bestowed upon them his last blessing.

54. And the Lord appeared unto them, and they rose up and blessed Adam, and called him Michael, the Prince, the Archangel.

55. And the Lord administered comfort unto Adam, and said unto him; I have set thee to be at the head—a multitude of nations shall come of thee, and thou art a prince over them for ever.

56. And Adam stood up in the midst of the congregation, and notwithstanding he was bowed down with age, being full of the Holy Ghost, predicted whatsoever should befall his posterity unto the latest generation.

57. These things were all written in the book of Enoch, and are to be testified of in due time.

58. It is the duty of the Twelve, also, to ordain and set in order all the other officers of the church, agreeable to the revelation which says:

59. To the church of Christ in the land of Zion, in addition to the church laws respecting church business—

60. Verily, I say unto you, says the Lord of Hosts, there must needs be presiding elders to preside over those who are of the office of an elder;

61. And also priests to preside over those who are of the office of a priest;

62. And also teachers to preside over those who are of the office of a teacher; in like manner, and also the deacons;

63. Wherefore, from deacon to teacher, and from teacher to priest, and from priest to elder, severally as they are appointed, according to the covenants and commandments of the church.

64. Then comes the High Priesthood, which is the greatest of all;

65. Wherefore it must needs be that one be appointed of the High Priesthood to preside over the priesthood, and he shall be called President of the High Priesthood of the church;

66. Or, in other words, the Presiding High Priest over the High Priesthood of the church.

67. From the same comes the administering of ordinances and blessings upon the church, by the laying on of the hands.

68. Wherefore the office of a bishop

D&C 107:53–55—Said Joseph Smith: "I saw Adam in the valley of Adam-ondi-Ahman. He called together his children and blessed them with a patriarchal blessing. The Lord appeared in their midst, and he (Adam) blessed them all, and foretold what should befall them to the latest generation. This is why Adam blessed his posterity; he wanted to bring them into the presence of God" (HC 3:388). President John Taylor provides the following commanding view of this extraordinary meeting:

Adam, before he left the earth, gathered his people together in the Valley of Adam-ondi-Ahman, and the curtain of eternity was unfolded before him, and he gazed upon all events pertaining to his descendants, which should transpire in every subsequent period of time, and he prophesied to them. He saw the flood and its desolating influence; he saw the introduction again of a people in the days of Noah; he saw their departure from the right path. He saw Abraham, Moses, and the prophets make their appearance and witnessed the results of their acts; he saw nations rise and fall; he saw the time when Jesus would come and restore the Gospel and when he would preach that Gospel to those who perished in the days of Noah; and in fact, he saw everything that should transpire upon the earth, until the winding up scene. He was acquainted with the day in which we live and the circumstances with which we are surrounded. (JD 17:372.)

Sometime prior to the Second Coming, a similar meeting will be held again at Adam-ondi-Ahman.

D&C 107:53–57—These verses form a blessing that Joseph Smith Jr. gave his father on December 18, 1833.

D&C 107:58–65—James E. Talmage comments on the authority vested in the Twelve Apostles: "Though an Apostle is thus seen to be essentially an envoy or ambassador, his authority is great, as is also the responsibility associated therewith, for he speaks in the name of a power greater than his own,—the name of Him whose special witness he is. When one of the Twelve is sent to minister in any stake, mission or other division of the Church, or to labor in regions where no Church organization has been effected, he acts as the representative of the First Presidency, and has the right to use his authority in doing whatever is requisite for the furtherance of the work of God" (Liahona, or Elders' Journal 11:581).

D&C 107:65—The Church president is the president of the priesthood on the earth; all are subject to him, and only he can receive revelation for the Church. President John Taylor taught that this calling depends on order and seniority, not on genealogy.

is not equal unto it; for the office of a bishop is in administering all temporal things;

69. Nevertheless a bishop must be chosen from the High Priesthood, unless he is a literal descendant of Aaron;

70. For unless he is a literal descendant of Aaron he cannot hold the keys of that priesthood.

71. Nevertheless, a High Priest, that is, after the order of Melchisedek, may be set apart unto the ministering of temporal things, having a knowledge of them by the spirit of truth,

72. And also to be a judge in Israel, to do the business of the church, to sit in judgment upon transgressors upon testimony as it shall be laid before him according to the laws, by the assistance of his counselors, whom he has chosen, or will choose among the elders of the church.

73. This is the duty of a bishop who is not a literal descendant of Aaron, but has been ordained to the High Priesthood after the order of Melchisedek.

74. Thus shall he be a judge, even a common judge among the inhabitants of Zion, or in a Stake of Zion, or in any branch of the church where he shall be set apart unto this ministry, until the borders of Zion are enlarged, and it becomes necessary to have other bishops or judges in Zion, or elsewhere;

75. And inasmuch as there are other bishops appointed they shall act in the same office.

76. But a literal descendant of Aaron has a legal right to the presidency of this priesthood, to the keys of this ministry, to act in the office of bishop independently, without counselors, except in a case where a president of the High Priesthood, after the order of Melchisedek, is tried, to sit as a judge in Israel.

77. And the decision of either of these councils, agreeable to the commandment which says,

78. Again, verily, I say unto you, the most important business of the church, and the most difficult cases of the church, inasmuch as there is not satisfaction upon the decision of the bishop or judges, it shall be handed over and carried up unto the Council of the church, before the Presidency of the High Priesthood;

79. And the Presidency of the Council of the High Priesthood shall have power to call other High Priests, even twelve, to assist as counselors; and thus the Presidency of the High Priesthood and its counselors shall have power to decide upon testimony according to the laws of the church.

80. And after this decision it shall be had in remembrance no more before the Lord; for this is the highest Council of the church of God, and a final decision upon controversies in spiritual matters.

81. There is not any person belonging to the church who is exempt from this Council of the church.

82. And inasmuch as a President of the High Priesthood shall transgress, he shall be had in remembrance before the common council of the church, who shall be assisted by twelve counselors of the High Priesthood;

83. And their decision upon his head shall be an end of controversy concerning him.

84. Thus, none shall be exempted from the justice and the laws of God, that all things may be done in

D&C 107:68–74—Author Hoyt Brewster, Jr., summarized the office and calling of a bishop by saying that the title *bishop* is applied to several categories of men in the Church. First were those "general bishops" who served in the early days of the Church when members were few in number and scattered broadly; these included men like Newel K. Whitney and Edward Partridge. Second is the Presiding Bishop of the Church and his counselors (who are general authorities). Third are men who previously served as bishop. And fourth are men who are currently serving as bishops (see *DCE*, 46).

D&C 107:69–74—President Spencer W. Kimball said that the bishop makes decisions for people that affect their progress and development in this life; he gives opportunities for growth, judges accomplishments, and holds the keys to the temple for his members. President Marion G. Romney outlined a bishop's responsibilities as receiving consecrations, judging temporal and spiritual matters, succoring the poor, and serving as an agent for the Church's temporal business.

D&C 107:76—If a member of the First Presidency is tried, a special council is called consisting of the presiding bishop, his two counselors, and twelve high priests; this body makes the decision, and no appeal of their decision is permitted.

D&C 107:79–84—As the supreme priesthood authority acting under the direction of the Lord Jesus Christ, the First Presidency of the Church directs the regulation and building up of the kingdom of God on earth and the administration of all the keys of priesthood authority among mortals. President Joseph Fielding Smith commented on this majestic commission as follows:

> The First Presidency preside over all councils, all quorums, and all organizations of the Church, with supreme appointing power and power of nomination. These powers of appointment, nomination, and presiding may be delegated by the First Presidency to others whom they may choose and whom the people sustain to represent the presidency in the government of the Church.
>
> The First Presidency are the living oracles of God and the supreme adjudicators and interpreters of the law of the Church. They supervise the work of the entire Church in all matters of policy, organization, and administration. No part of the work of the Church is beyond their authority. (*IE*, November 1966, 978.)

D&C 107:80–81—No member of the Church, even its president, is exempt from the decision of the "highest council of the church," meaning the First Presidency. Even Joseph Smith was tried before this council on charges related to Zion's Camp.

order and in solemnity before him, according to truth and righteousness.

85. And again, verily I say unto you, the duty of a president over the office of a deacon is to preside over twelve deacons, to sit in council with them, and to teach them their duty—edifying one another, as it is given according to the covenants.

86. And also the duty of the president over the office of the teachers is to preside over twenty- four of the teachers, and to sit in council with them, teaching them the duties of their office, as given in the covenants.

87. Also the duty of the president over the priesthood of Aaron is to preside over forty-eight priests, and sit in council with them, to teach them the duties of their office, as is given in the covenants.

88. This president is to be a bishop; for this is one of the duties of this priesthood.

89. Again, the duty of the president over the office of elders is to preside over ninety-six elders, and to sit in council with them, and to teach them according to the covenants.

90. This presidency is a distinct one from that of the seventy, and is designed for those who do not travel into all the world.

91. And again, the duty of the President of the office of the High Priesthood is to preside over the whole church, and to be like unto Moses.

92. Behold, here is wisdom; yea, to be a seer, a revelator, a translator, and a prophet, having all the gifts of God which he bestows upon the head of the church.

93. And it is according to the vision, showing the order of the seventy, that they should have seven presidents to preside over them, chosen out of the number of the seventy;

94. And the seventh president of these presidents is to preside over the six;

95. And these seven presidents are to choose other seventy besides the first seventy, to whom they belong, and are to preside over them;

96. And also other seventy, until seven times seventy, if the labor in the vineyard of necessity requires it.

97. And these seventy are to be traveling ministers unto the Gentiles first, and also unto the Jews;

98. Whereas other officers of the church, who belong not unto the Twelve, neither to the Seventy, are not under the responsibility to travel among all nations, but are to travel as their circumstances shall allow, notwithstanding they may hold as high and responsible offices in the church.

99. Wherefore now let every man learn his duty, and to act in the office in which he is appointed, in all diligence.

100. He that is slothful shall not be counted worthy to stand, and he that learns not his duty and shows himself not approved, shall not be counted worthy to stand. Even so. Amen.

D&C 107:93—The first Quorum of the Seventy was organized by Joseph Smith, but it did not function after the Saints settled in Utah. After the exodus to Utah, the Seventy as a quorum was not organized again until it was organized by President Spencer W. Kimball in October 1975.

D&C 107:98—This verse provides for additional officers to be called as needed. Examples of these include the Assistants to the Twelve, which were organized as a body from 1941 to 1976, and the Regional Representatives, which were part of the Church's organizational structure from 1967 to 1995.

D&C 107:100—This verse points out that "he that is slothful shall not be counted worthy to stand," which means that those who neglect their priesthood responsibilities will not be worthy to stand in God's presence.

THE POWER AND AUTHORITY OF THE MELCHIZEDEK AND AARONIC PRIESTHOODS

There are at least two primary functions of the Melchizedek Priesthood:

The right of presidency (see D&C 107:8–12). All organizations of the Church are subject to the presiding authority of the priesthood leaders in the wards and stakes, and these local leaders are likewise responsible to the power and authority of the general priesthood leaders and officers of the Church.

The keys to spiritual blessings (see D&C 107:18–19). The gift of the Holy Ghost and all subsequent blessings are conferred upon the Lord's people by the power and authority of the Melchizedek Priesthood.

The Aaronic Priesthood is the right or authority to represent our Father in Heaven in His service among the people of the earth. To represent Him is a sacred obligation, and all official acts of the Aaronic Priesthood ought to be seen and treated as sacred moments in the lives of the participants. The Aaronic Priesthood, which includes the office of Bishop, has the authority "to administer in outward ordinances, the letter of the gospel . . ." (D&C 107:20).

Some of the duties of the Aaronic Priesthood include baptizing, administering the sacrament, attending to the tithing, buying lands, looking after the poor, taking care of the properties of the Church, attending generally to temporal affairs, and assisting the Melchizedek Priesthood. The Aaronic Priesthood holds the keys of the ministering of angels, and they administer in the outward ordinances of the gospel (*STDC* 2:223–225).

SECTION 108

1. Verily, thus saith the Lord unto you, my servant Lyman, your sins are forgiven you, because you have obeyed my voice in coming up hither this morning to receive counsel of him whom I have appointed.

2. Therefore, let your soul be at rest concerning your spiritual standing, and resist no more my voice;

3. And arise up and be more careful henceforth, in observing your vows which you have made, and do make, and you shall be blessed with exceeding great blessings.

4. Wait patiently until the solemn assembly shall be called of my servants, then you shall be remembered with the first of mine elders, and receive right by ordination with the rest of mine elders, whom I have chosen.

5. Behold, this is the promise of the Father unto you if you continue faithful;

6. And it shall be fulfilled upon you in that day that you shall have right to preach my gospel wheresoever I shall send you, from henceforth from that time.

7. Therefore, strengthen your brethren in all your conversation, in all your prayers, and in all your exhortations, and in all your doings.

8. And behold! and lo! I am with you to bless you and deliver you for ever. Amen.

LYMAN SHERMAN

Lyman was born May 22, 1804, at Monkton, Addison County, Vermont. Through his interest in the Book of Mormon he became a member of the Church and was ordained a high priest. He was also ordained a seventy on February 28, 1835, and served for a time as a president of the Seventies. Later that year he sought counsel from the Prophet for clarification concerning his duty. The resulting revelation on his behalf (Section 108) defined his "spiritual standing." Lyman participated in the dedication of the Kirtland Temple in 1836 and was called to be a member of the Kirtland high council. He defended the Church and its leaders with courage. Lyman moved to Missouri in 1838 and became a member of the Far West high council. From Liberty Jail, the Prophet sent a letter dated January 16, 1839, calling Lyman to the Apostleship to replace Orson Hyde. But Lyman passed away a few days later, on January 27.

Section 108 Background—Given at Kirtland, Ohio, December 26, 1835 (see *HC* 2:345), at the request of Lyman Sherman, who had served faithfully in Zion's Camp. The Prophet writes in his journal: "Commenced again studying the Hebrew language, in company with Brothers [Warren] Parrish and [Frederick G.] Williams. In the meantime, Brother Lyman Sherman came in, and requested to have the word of the Lord through me; 'for,' said he, 'I have been wrought upon to make known to you my feelings and desires, and was promised that I should have a revelation which should make known my duty'"(*HC* 2:345).

D&C 108:1—The "sins" referred to in this verse are those of resisting the voice of the Lord. Lyman Sherman had been struggling with whether to go forward or to turn back; he eventually decided to continue in the faith.

D&C 108:2–3, 7—How can we be "at rest" concerning our "spiritual standing"? The answer is explicit from this example: be obedient, heed the word of the Lord, observe your covenants consistently, wait in patience for callings from the Lord, continue faithful, and strengthen others in all you do. As Brigham Young taught, all the Lord asks is strict obedience to covenants, serving Him with an undivided heart. Is this advice restricted to Lyman Sherman? The Lord said: "And what I say unto you I say unto all, Watch" (Mark 13:37; see also Alma 12:5; D&C 61:18, 36; 82:5; 92:1; 93:49; 112:14; JS–Matt. 1:46). As often happens in the Doctrine and Covenants, counsel is given to specific individuals and then extended, by principle, to all.

D&C 108:4—The solemn assembly mentioned in this verse refers to a sacred meeting for the priesthood held in the Kirtland Temple.

D&C 108:7—The sentiments expressed in this verse underscore the fact that we can all help each other resist temptation and bear up under opposition.

SECTION 109

1. Thanks be to thy name O Lord God of Israel, who keepest covenant and showest mercy unto thy servants who walk uprightly before thee, with all their hearts.

2. Thou who hast commanded thy servants to build a house to thy name in this place. (Kirtland.)

3. And now thou beholdest, O Lord, that thy servants have done according to thy commandment,

4. And now we ask thee, Holy Father, in the name of Jesus Christ, the Son of thy bosom, in whose name alone, salvation can be administered to the children of men, we ask thee, O Lord, to accept of this house, the workmanship of the hands of us, thy servants, which thou didst command us to build;

5. For thou knowest that we have done this work through great tribulation; and out of our poverty we have given of our substance, to build a house to thy name, that the Son of man might have a place to manifest himself to his people.

6. And as thou hast said in a revelation, given to us, calling us thy friends, saying, "Call your solemn assembly, as I have commanded you;

7. And as all have not faith, seek ye diligently, and teach one another words of wisdom; yea, seek ye out of the best books, words of wisdom, seek learning even by study, and also by faith.

8. Organize yourselves; prepare every needful thing, and establish a house, even a house of prayer, a house of fasting, a house of faith, a house of learning, a house of glory, a house of order, a house of God,

9. That your incomings may be in the name of the Lord, that your outgoings may be in the name of the Lord, that all your salutations may be in the name of the Lord, with uplifted hands unto the Most High."

10. And now, Holy Father, we ask thee to assist us, thy people, with thy grace, in calling our solemn assembly, that it may be done to thy honor and to thy divine acceptance,

11. And in a manner that we may be found worthy, in thy sight, to secure a fulfilment of the promises which thou hast made unto us, thy people, in the revelations given unto us;

12. That thy glory may rest down upon thy people, and upon this thy house, which we now dedicate to thee, that it may be sanctified and consecrated to be holy, and that thy holy presence may be continually in this house,

13. And that all people who shall enter upon the threshold of the Lord's house, may feel thy power, and feel constrained to acknowledge that thou hast sanctified it, and that it is thy house, a place of thy holiness.

14. And do thou grant, Holy Father, that all those who shall worship in this house, may be taught words of wisdom out of the best books, and that they may seek learning even by study, and also by faith, as thou hast said;

15. And that they may grow up in thee, and receive a fulness of the Holy Ghost, and be organized according to thy laws, and be prepared to obtain every needful thing;

16. And that this house may be a house of prayer, a house of fasting, a house of faith, a house of glory and of God, even thy house;

Section 109 Background—Given by revelation through the Prophet Joseph Smith and offered as the dedicatory prayer on the occasion of the dedication of the Kirtland Temple on March 27, 1836, at Kirtland, Ohio (see *HC* 2:420–426). Oliver Cowdery records that he, Joseph Smith, Sidney Rigdon, and scribes Warren Parrish and Warren Cowdery assisted in writing the prayer (see *RPJS*, 218). This prayer is often used, even today, as a pattern for dedications of all types.

The weeks surrounding the dedication of the Kirtland Temple represented the high point in the seven-year Kirtland period and one of the greatest occasions for rejoicing and spiritual outpouring in Church history. On March 27 the long-awaited day of dedication burst upon a city bulging with visitors. Not even a seven-hour dedication service would deter Saints who had labored and sacrificed all they possessed for this heaven-inspired temple. Personal comforts were discarded as they sat on each other's laps and otherwise occupied any possible space. One thousand Saints squeezed together into a space that accommodates barely four hundred today.

D&C 109:1–2—The pinnacle of the Lord's design for His children, under the plan of salvation and Atonement, is the holy temple, with its sealing ordinances, its washings and anointings, and its sacred endowments. The Kirtland Temple, first in the dispensation of the fullness of times, holds a singularly important place in the history of the Restoration because it inaugurated the unfolding of temple work in the latter days.

D&C 109:4–5—It is difficult to imagine today the extraordinary sacrifice of the early Saints in fulfilling this commandment. From their poverty arose a magnificent venue for heavenly visitation, the bestowal of eternal keys, the presentation and learning of truth, and the inauguration of an era of glory that still continues with even more urgency today.

D&C 109:8–12—The Saints presented before the Lord a most excellent product of toil and sacrifice. He blessed them with a Pentecostal experience and a grand measure of glory, to be followed soon thereafter with His presence and that of many of His servants, prophets holding keys essential for the restored Church to operate and expand.

D&C 109:14–16—The expressions "to grow up in thee" and receive "a fulness of the Holy Ghost" are apt summaries of the blessings invoked on the occasion of the dedication of the Kirtland Temple. Ultimately, this temple would be the site where sacred keys would be restored leading to the inauguration of a fullness of temple ordinances as the Lord opened the way to empower the Saints to advance line upon line, and precept upon precept, in their quest for spiritual development.

17. That all the incomings of thy people, into this house, may be in the name of the Lord;

18. That all their outgoings from this house may be in the name of the Lord;

19. And that all their salutations may be in the name of the Lord, with holy hands, uplifted to the Most High;

20. And that no unclean thing shall be permitted to come into thy house to pollute it;

21. And when thy people transgress, any of them, they may speedily repent, and return unto thee, and find favor in thy sight, and be restored to the blessings which thou hast ordained to be poured out upon those who shall reverence thee in thy house.

22. And we ask thee, Holy Father, that thy servants may go forth from this house, armed with thy power, and that thy name may be upon them, and thy glory be round about them, and thine angels have charge over them;

23. And from this place they may bear exceedingly great and glorious tidings, in truth, unto the ends of the earth, that they may know that this is thy work, and that thou hast put forth thy hand, to fulfil that which thou hast spoken by the mouths of the prophets, concerning the last days.

24. We ask thee, Holy Father, to establish the people that shall worship, and honorably hold a name and standing in this thy house, to all generations, and for eternity;

25. That no weapon formed against them shall prosper; that he who diggeth a pit for them shall fall into the same himself;

26. That no combination of wickedness shall have power to rise up and prevail over thy people upon whom thy name shall be put in this house;

27. And if any people shall rise against this people, that thine anger be kindled against them,

28. And if they shall smite this people, thou wilt smite them, thou wilt fight for thy people as thou didst in the day of battle, that they may be delivered from the hands of all their enemies.

29. We ask thee, Holy Father, to confound, and astonish, and bring to shame and confusion, all those who have spread lying reports, abroad, over the world, against thy servant, or servants, if they will not repent, when the everlasting gospel shall be proclaimed in their ears,

30. And that all their works may be brought to naught, and be swept away by the hail, and by the judgments which thou wilt send upon them in thine anger, that there may be an end to lyings and slanders against thy people;

31. For thou knowest, O Lord, that thy servants have been innocent before thee in bearing record of thy name, for which they have suffered these things;

32. Therefore we plead before thee a full and complete deliverance from under this yoke;

33. Break it off, O Lord; break it off from the necks of thy servants, by thy power, that we may rise up in the midst of this generation and do thy work.

34. O Jehovah, have mercy upon

D&C 109:22–23—Those who were instructed in the ways of the Lord within the walls of the Kirtland Temple were indeed "armed with power" to carry on the work of building up the kingdom of God, having received an endowment of blessings of glory. Their witness of the truths of the gospel of Jesus Christ was immeasurably strengthened. As to the angels mentioned in this verse, Brigham Young said that angels are all around us, and that through them the Lord is cognizant of our every action.

D&C 109:24, 32–33—Persecution against the Saints had been severe—and would become even greater. The dedicatory prayer supplicates the Lord for deliverance and protection—not for the sake of ease, but to unleash the power of service, "that we may rise up . . . and do thy work." This significant formulation inspires us to rethink our prayers asking for deliverance and relief from tribulation and suffering. Is our motivation for such prayers to receive relief on behalf of self, or for the purpose of increasing our capacity to serve the Lord and further the cause of Zion?

D&C 109:25—The promises of protection made in this verse also apply to and include any future opposition and persecution that might be heaped upon the Church and its members.

The Kirtland Temple. Section 109 was offered as the dedicatory prayer in the temple on March 27, 1836. Four others helped Joseph Smith Jr. write the dedicatory prayer.

all men sin, forgive the transgressions of thy peo-
be blotted out forever.

ting of thy ministers be sealed upon them with

ed upon them, as upon those on the day of Pen-
of tongues be poured out upon thy people, even
of fire, and the interpretation thereof,

use be filled, as with a rushing mighty wind, with

rvants the testimony of the covenant, that when
oclaim thy word, they may seal up the law, and
of thy saints for all those judgments thou art
hy wrath, upon the inhabitants of the earth, be-
gressions, that thy people may not faint in the day

r city thy servants shall enter, and the people of
eir testimony, let thy peace and thy salvation be
they may gather out of that city the righteous,
e forth to Zion, or to her Stakes, the places of
, with songs of everlasting joy;

e accomplished, let not thy judgments fall upon

r city thy servants shall enter, and the people of
the testimony of thy servants, and thy servants
hemselves from this untoward generation, let it
cording to that which thou hast spoken by the
ets;

, O Jehovah, we beseech thee, thy servants from
anse them from their blood.

ght not in the destruction of our fellow men!
their souls are precious before thee;

44. But thy word must be fulfilled; help thy servants to say, with thy grace assisting them, thy will be done, O Lord, and not ours.

45. We know that thou hast spoken by the mouth of thy prophets terrible things concerning the wicked, in the last days—that thou wilt pour out thy judgments, without measure;

46. Therefore, O Lord, deliver thy people from the calamity of the wicked; enable thy servants to seal up the law, and bind up the testimony, that they may be prepared against the day of burning.

47. We ask thee, Holy Father, to remember those who have been driven (by the inhabitants of Jackson County, Missouri) from the lands of their inheritance, and break off, O Lord, this yoke of affliction that has been put upon them.

48. Thou knowest, O Lord, that they have been greatly oppressed and afflicted by wicked men, and our hearts flow out with sorrow, because of their grievous burdens.

49. O Lord, how long wilt thou suffer this people to bear this affliction, and the cries of their innocent ones to ascend up in thine ears, and

D&C 109:38, 44—Leaun Otten and Max Caldwell concluded, "It is little wonder that the missionaries of the Lord's church are given an opportunity to participate in temple ordinances before embarking upon their missionary service as servants of the Lord. Nor is it difficult to see why the Lord's people are continually encouraged to attend regularly and be faithful participants in the sacred activities and ordinances of temple worship" (*STDC* 2:242).

BLESSINGS PROMISED TO THE SAINTS

In Section 109, the dedicatory prayer offered at the Kirtland Temple, fourteen specific blessings were promised to the Saints:

1. The glory of the Lord would rest upon the people and the temple (see verse 12).
2. All who worship in the temple would be taught words of wisdom (see verse 14).
3. All who worship in the temple would grow up in the Lord and receive a fullness of the Holy Ghost (see verse 15).
4. The temple would be a house of prayer, a house of fasting, a house of faith, a house of glory, and a house of God (see verse 16).
5. No unclean thing would be permitted to come into the temple to pollute it (see verse 20).
6. Those who transgressed would speedily repent and return to the Lord (see verse 21).
7. The servants of the Lord would go forth from the temple armed with power, and the Lord's angels would have charge over them (see verse 22).
8. No weapon formed against the Saints would prosper (see verse 25).
9. The Lord would forgive the transgressions of the Saints (see verse 34).
10. The anointing of the Lord would be fulfilled upon the Saints as it was on the day of Pentecost (see verse 36).
11. The testimony of the covenant would be put upon the Lord's servants, preparing them to be powerful and effective missionaries (see verse 38).
12. The Saints would be delivered from the calamity of the wicked (see verse 46).
13. The Lord would have mercy on all the nations of the earth, so that their hearts would be softened in preparation for receiving the gospel (see verses 54, 56).
14. Additional stakes would be organized and appointed (see verse 59).

In asking that the Saints receive the blessings, Joseph asked "that we may be found worthy, in thy sight, to secure a fulfillment of the promises which thou hast made unto us, thy people . . ." (D&C 109:11).

their blood come up in testimony before thee, and not make a display of thy testimony in their behalf?

50. Have mercy, O Lord, upon that wicked mob, who have driven thy people, that they may cease to spoil, that they may repent of their sins, if repentance is to be found;

51. But if they will not, make bare thine arm, O Lord, and redeem that which thou didst appoint a Zion unto thy people!

52. And if it cannot be otherwise, that the cause of thy people may not fail before thee, may thine anger be kindled, and thine indignation fall upon them, that they may be wasted away, both root and branch, from under heaven;

53. But inasmuch as they will repent, thou art gracious and merciful, and wilt turn away thy wrath, when thou lookest upon the face of thine anointed.

54. Have mercy, O Lord, upon all the nations of the earth, have mercy upon the rulers of our land; may those principles which were so honorably and nobly defended, viz., the Constitution of our land, by our fathers, be established for ever;

55. Remember the kings, the princes, the nobles, and the great ones of the earth, and all people, and the churches, all the poor, the needy, and afflicted ones of the earth,

56. That their hearts may be softened, when thy servants shall go out from thy house, O Jehovah, to bear testimony of thy name, that their prejudices may give way before the truth, and thy people may obtain favor in the sight of all,

57. That all the ends of the earth may know that we thy servants have heard thy voice, and that thou hast sent us,

58. That from among all these, thy servants the sons of Jacob may gather out the righteous to build a holy city to thy name, as thou hast commanded them.

59. We ask thee to appoint upon Zion other Stakes besides this one which thou hast appointed, that the gathering of thy people may roll on in great power and majesty, that thy work may be cut short in righteousness.

60. Now these words, O Lord, we have spoken before thee, concerning the revelations and commandments which thou hast given unto us, who are identified with the Gentiles;

61. But thou knowest that thou hast a great love for the children of Jacob, who have been scattered upon the mountains, for a long time, in a cloudy and dark day;

62. We therefore ask thee to have mercy upon the children of Jacob, that Jerusalem, from this hour, may begin to be redeemed,

63. And the yoke of bondage may begin to be broken off from the house of David,

64. And the children of Judah may begin to return to the lands which thou didst give to Abraham, their father;

65. And cause that the remnants

D&C 109:50–52—The Prophet pleads for relief on behalf of the persecuted Saints, that they may be delivered from "the calamity of the wicked" foretold by the prophets of God. At the same time, remarkably, the Prophet pleads for mercy on behalf of the mobs—provided they will repent. Otherwise, to preserve the "cause of thy people," he asked that the Lord might bring judgments upon the enemies of the Church "that they may be wasted away."

D&C 109:54–57—These words are further evidence that the dedicatory prayer of the Kirtland Temple was, in effect, a missionary prayer. The Prophet invokes a blessing of mercy from the Lord upon all the nations of the earth—including the princes and the poor, the nobles and the needy—that hearts might be softened toward the truths of the gospel and the gathering of Israel might be facilitated.

D&C 109:62, 67—These blessings on behalf of scattered Israel, including the "children of Judah" and the "remnants of Jacob," are being fulfilled in our day and constitute one of the signs of the times. The dedicatory prayer also included a blessing for the Lamanite people and their restoration to the truth—reminiscent of the references from an earlier revelation in 1828:

> And this testimony shall come to the knowledge of the Lamanites, and the Lemuelites, and the Ishmaelites, who dwindled in unbelief because of the iniquity of their fathers, whom the Lord has suffered to destroy their brethren the Nephites, because of their iniquities and their abominations.
>
> And for this very purpose are these plates preserved, which contain these records—that the promises of the Lord might be fulfilled, which he made to his people;
>
> And that the Lamanites might come to the knowledge of their fathers, and that they might know the promises of the Lord, and that they may believe the gospel and rely upon the merits of Jesus Christ, and be glorified through faith in his name, and that through their repentance they might be saved. Amen. (D&C 3:18–20.)

The resulting outcome, prior to the Second Coming, would be that "Jacob shall flourish in the wilderness, and the Lamanites shall blossom as the rose. Zion shall flourish upon the hills and rejoice upon the mountains, and shall be assembled together unto the place which I have appointed" (D&C 49:24–25).

of Jacob, who have been cursed and smitten, because of their transgression, be converted from their wild and savage condition, to the fulness of the everlasting gospel,

66. That they may lay down their weapons of bloodshed, and cease their rebellions,

67. And may all the scattered remnants of Israel, who have been driven to the ends of the earth, come to a knowledge of the truth, believe in the Messiah, and be redeemed from oppression, and rejoice before thee.

68. O Lord, remember thy servant, Joseph Smith, junior, and all his afflictions and persecutions, how he has covenanted with Jehovah, and vowed to thee, O mighty God of Jacob, and the commandments which thou hast given unto him, and that he hath sincerely striven to do thy will.

69. Have mercy, O Lord, upon his wife and children, that they may be exalted in thy presence, and preserved by thy fostering hand;

70. Have mercy upon all their immediate connexions, that their prejudices may be broken up, and swept away as with a flood, that they may be converted and redeemed with Israel, and know that thou art God.

71. Remember, O Lord, the presidents, even all the presidents of thy church, that thy right hand may exalt them, with all their families, and their immediate connexions, that their names may be perpetuated, and had in everlasting remembrance, from generation to generation.

72. Remember all thy church, O Lord, with all their families, and all their immediate connexions, with all their sick and afflicted ones, with all the poor and meek of the earth, that the kingdom which thou hast set up without hands, may become a great mountain, and fill the whole earth;

73. That thy church may come forth out of the wilderness of darkness, and shine forth fair as the moon, clear as the sun, and terrible as an army with banners,

74. And be adorned as a bride for that day when thou shalt unvail the heavens, and cause the mountains to flow down at thy presence, and the valleys to be exalted, the rough places made smooth; that thy glory may fill the earth,

75. That when the trump shall sound for the dead we shall be caught up in the cloud to meet thee, that we may ever be with the Lord,

76. That our garments may be pure, that we may be clothed upon with robes of righteousness, with palms in our hands, and crowns of glory upon our heads, and reap eternal joy for all our sufferings.

77. O Lord God Almighty, hear us in these our petitions, and answer us from heaven, thy holy habitation, where thou sittest enthroned, with glory, honor, power, majesty, might, dominion, truth, justice, judgment, mercy, and an infinity of fulness, from everlasting to everlasting.

78. O hear, O hear, O hear us, O Lord, and answer these petitions, and accept the dedication of this

D&C 109:72—The Prophet is inspired to pray for himself and his family, and for all the Church leaders and their families, and, indeed, for the entire Church and "all the poor and meek of the earth." Why? That the prophetic utterance of Daniel might be fulfilled concerning the stone cut out of the mountain without hands that would roll forth until it should become a great mountain and fill the entire world (see Dan. 2:34–35).

D&C 109:73–80—These final pronouncements of triumph and adulation conclude the prayer of dedication. It is a prayer of dedication not only for the edifice itself, but also for those who occupy it—for all of God's children are the temple of God (see 1 Cor. 3:16–17) preparing to receive blessings of sanctification and glory. Scholar Hoyt Brewster, Jr., gives these insights:

> The Prophet petitioned the Lord to remember the Saints, that on the day of resurrection they might come forth with "palms in [their] hands" (D&C 109:76). John the Revelator saw "a great multitude, which . . . stood before the Lamb, clothed with white robes, and palms in their hands" (Rev. 7:9). The palms in the hands of these celestial Saints are "the antitype to Christ's entry into Jerusalem amidst the palm-bearing multitude. . . . The palm branch is the symbol of joy and triumph." (DNTC 3:495.) Surely, the joy of being in the eternal presence of the Father and Son is the ultimate triumph. . . .
>
> During the dedicatory prayer of the Kirtland Temple, the Prophet pleaded that on the day of resurrection the Saints would be "clothed upon with robes of righteousness" (D&C 109:76). These robes are also mentioned as the apparel to be worn by the Twelve Apostles who will stand at the right hand of the Savior upon his return (D&C 29:12). . . .
>
> Robes of righteousness are those white robes given celestial Saints, whose names are to be found in the book of life (Rev. 3:5), symbolizing their purity before God. . . . The whiteness of these robes testifies to the complete sanctification and purification of the Saints wearing them. (DCE, 409, 476.)

D&C 109:74—According to Parley P. Pratt, the events described in this verse will occur during the resurrection and change of the earth.

D&C 109:75—This event will occur during the first resurrection.

house unto thee, the work of our hands, which we have built unto thy name!

79. And also this church, to put upon it thy name; and help us by the power of thy Spirit, that we may mingle our voices with those bright, shining seraphs around thy throne, with acclamations of praise, singing, Hosanna to God and the Lamb;

80. And let these thine anointed ones be clothed with salvation, and thy saints shout aloud for joy. Amen, and Amen.

SECTION 110

1. The vail was taken from our minds, and the eyes of our understanding were opened.

2. We saw the Lord standing upon the breast work of the pulpit, before us, and under his feet was a paved work of pure gold in color like amber.

3. His eyes were as a flame of fire, the hair of his head was white like the pure snow, his countenance shone above the brightness of the sun, and his voice was as the sound of the rushing of great waters, even the voice of Jehovah, saying—

4. I am the first and the last, I am he who liveth, I am he who was slain, I am your advocate with the Father.

5. Behold, your sins are forgiven

The Kirtland Temple.

D&C 109:79—The final words of the dedicatory prayer call forth the expression of joy and glory associated with the "Hosanna Shout." While standing and waving white handkerchiefs with each word or phrase of praise, all in the congregation repeat three times, "Hosanna, Hosanna, Hosanna, To God and the Lamb" sealed by the words, "Amen, Amen, Amen!" Following the dedication of the Conference Center in Salt Lake City, President Gordon B. Hinckley encouraged us from time to time to silently repeat what he called "those beautiful words of worship" (Gordon B. Hinckley, "'An Humble and a Contrite Heart'," *Ensign*, November 2000, 88–89).

Section 110 Background—A record of the visions manifested to the Prophet Joseph Smith and to Oliver Cowdery in the Kirtland Temple on April 3, 1836 (see *HC* 2:435–436). The Prophet writes the following in his journal: "Attended meeting in the Lord's House, and assisted the other Presidents of the Church in seating the congregation, and then became an attentive listener to the preaching from the stand. Thomas B. Marsh and David W. Patten spoke in the forenoon to an attentive audience of about one thousand persons. In the afternoon, I assisted the other Presidents in distributing the Lord's Supper to the Church. . . . I retired to the pulpit, the veils being dropped, and bowed myself, with Oliver Cowdery, in solemn and silent prayer. After rising from prayer, the following vision was opened to both of us—[Section 110]" (*HC* 2:434–435). The calendar date was significant, for it was Easter Sunday.

D&C 110:2–3, 7—This was an event of unspeakable transcendence, one that defies all description. The words used in these opening passages of the revelation are consistent with those used by John the Beloved in the wake of his vision of the Savior: "His head and his hairs were white like wool, as white as snow; and his eyes *were* as a flame of fire; And his feet like unto fine brass, as if they burned in a furnace; and his voice as the sound of many waters" (Rev. 1:14–15; see also Rev. 19:12). Truly the holy temple is a place of visitation. What grandeur is associated with the heavenly events that took place at the Kirtland Temple during its few years of service in the Restoration. That the Lord should have come to His house to honor His people with extraordinary, divine manifestations and bestow upon them truth of immeasurable power is a miracle of singular proportions. We can remember in gratitude the circumstances surrounding the presentation of the Lord's gifts brought to this house to His Saints, and the implication of these gifts for salvation and exaltation through the power of the Atonement.

you, you are clean before me, therefore lift up your heads and rejoice,

6. Let the hearts of your brethren rejoice, and let the hearts of all my people rejoice, who have, with their might, built this house to my name,

7. For behold, I have accepted this house, and my name shall be here, and I will manifest myself to my people in mercy in this house,

8. Yea, I will appear unto my servants, and speak unto them with mine own voice, if my people will keep my commandments, and do not pollute this holy house,

9. Yea the hearts of thousands and tens of thousands shall greatly rejoice in consequence of the blessings which shall be poured out, and the endowment with which my servants have been endowed in this house;

10. And the fame of this house shall spread to foreign lands, and this is the beginning of the blessing which shall be poured out upon the heads of my people. Even so. Amen.

11. After this vision closed, the heavens were again opened unto us, and Moses appeared before us, and committed unto us the keys of the gathering of Israel from the four parts of the earth, and the leading of the ten tribes from the land of the north.

12. After this, Elias appeared, and committed the dispensation of the gospel of Abraham, saying, that in us, and our seed, all generations after us should be blessed.

13. After this vision had closed, another great and glorious vision burst upon us, for Elijah the prophet, who was taken to heaven without tasting death, stood before us, and said—

14. Behold, the time has fully come, which was spoken of by the mouth of Malachi, testifying that he (Elijah) should be sent before the great and dreadful day of the Lord come,

15. To turn the hearts of the fathers to the children, and the children to the fathers, lest the whole earth be smitten with a curse.

16. Therefore the keys of this dispensation are committed into your hands, and by this ye may know that the great and dreadful day of the Lord is near, even at the doors.

The Kirtland Temple.

D&C 110:11—Why do the Saints needs to be gathered? The revelations are clear: In order to "prepare their hearts and be prepared in all things against the day when tribulation and desolation are sent forth upon the wicked" (D&C 29:8). Furthermore, the Saints are gathered in order that they might "stand in holy places" (D&C 101:22), be instructed in the ways of the Lord (see Isa. 2:2–3), and be endowed with "power from on high" (D&C 95:8). And again: "Verily I say unto you all: Arise and shine forth, that thy light may be a standard for the nations; And that the gathering together upon the land of Zion, and upon her stakes, may be for a defense, and for a refuge from the storm, and from wrath when it shall be poured out without mixture upon the whole earth" (D&C 115:5–6). Thus the gathering is for safety, instruction, receiving an endowment of power from on high, and to facilitate missionary work by sending forth a light or "a standard for the nations."

D&C 110:12—The Elias referred to in this verse is in fact Noah, who is also the angel Gabriel (see Joseph Fielding Smith, *AGQ* 3:138–141). It is of interest that the ancient prophet Noah may have still been alive, in his very senior years, during the time of Abraham (see Gen. 9:28–29).

D&C 110:13–16—Concerning the mission of Elijah, the Prophet Joseph Smith declared:

> Elijah was the last Prophet that held the keys of the Priesthood, and who will, before the last dispensation, restore the authority and deliver the keys of the Priesthood, in order that all the ordinances may be attended to in righteousness. . . . Why send Elijah? Because he holds the keys of the authority to administer in all the ordinances of the Priesthood; and without the authority . . . , the ordinances could not be administered in righteousness. (*TPJS*, 172.)

Through Elijah the sealing powers were restored. But the mission of Elijah accomplished more than that: as scholar Kent Jackson confirms, ". . . they seal and validate *all* ordinances of the priesthood so that ordinances performed on earth are binding in heaven as well. . . . The appearance of Moses, Elias, and Elijah in the Kirtland Temple repeated in many ways the similar event that the ancient apostles Peter, James, and John experienced, as recorded in the New Testament (Matt. 17:1–9). At that time, as in 1836, the Lord was beginning a new dispensation of his Church, and ancient holders of priesthood power came to pass on the keys of their ministry to enable the Lord's work to be carried forward. In the latter days, this transmittal of keys was an indispensable step in the process of the Restoration" (Kent P. Jackson, *FAR*, 222–223).

SECTION 111

1. I, the Lord your God, am not displeased with your coming this journey, notwithstanding your follies;

2. I have much treasure in this city for you, for the benefit of Zion; and many people in this city whom I will gather out in due time for the benefit of Zion, through your instrumentality!

3. Therefore it is expedient that you should form acquaintance with men in this city, as you shall be led, and as it shall be given you;

4. And it shall come to pass in due time, that I will give this city into your hands, that you shall have power over it, insomuch that they shall not discover your secret parts; and its wealth pertaining to gold and silver shall be yours.

5. Concern not yourselves about your debts, for I will give you power to pay them.

6. Concern not yourselves about Zion, for I will deal mercifully with her.

7. Tarry in this place, and in the regions round about;

8. And the place where it is my will that you should tarry, for the main, shall be signalized unto you by the peace and power of my Spirit, that shall flow unto you.

9. This place you may obtain by hire, &c. And inquire diligently concerning the more ancient inhabitants and founders of this city;

10. For there are more treasures than one for you in this city;

11. Therefore be ye as wise as serpents and yet without sin, and I will order all things for your good, as fast as ye are able to receive them. Amen.

Section 111 Background—Given at Salem, Massachusetts, August 6, 1836 (see *HC* 2:465–466). The construction of the Kirtland Temple had left the Church and many of its Saints in considerable debt, and the problems in Missouri had taxed the physical and spiritual resources of the Church. Word had come to Church leaders that a significant amount of money might be made available in Salem that could relieve financial pressures on the Church: a man named William Burgess had told Church leaders that a widow had died and left money in her cellar. For this reason, and to preach the gospel, the Prophet Joseph, Sidney Rigdon, Hyrum Smith, and Oliver Cowdery traveled to Salem from Kirtland, Ohio (see *CHC* 1:411). Burgess met the four Church leaders in Salem, but then said he could not recognize the house. When they determined that the claim of a money source in Salem could not be substantiated, they returned to Kirtland, but not before this revelation (Section 111) was given through the Prophet (*HC* 2:465). The "folly" referred to in verse 1 was not the trip to Salem, but the continued indebtedness of the Church.

D&C 111:1–3—The Prophet and his associates had traveled to Salem in a well-intentioned quest to find a solution to the Church's indebtedness; however, the Lord had in mind a "treasure" of another sort—the treasure of souls: "Remember the worth of souls is great in the sight of God" (D&C 18:10). It is instructive that in 1841 Erastus Snow was inspired by the words in Section 111 to travel to Salem for the purpose of doing missionary work. His journal confirms that he baptized more than one hundred people in that community (see *DCSM*, 170–171).

D&C 111:4–6—From such words as these we find confirmation that the Lord will care for His people—temporally and spiritually. Through faith and obedience, the early Saints would experience the blessings of the Lord in helping them overcome their financial obligations—notwithstanding their failure as a Church to follow with full devotion the divine counsel for temporal welfare through the law of consecration.

D&C 111:9–11—By "ancient inhabitants" the Lord apparently had reference to the importance of history—and particularly to family history—and its role in missionary work. Such research helps uncover the "treasures" harvested through the gospel ministry.

D&C 111:10—One of the treasures in the city were genealogical records, which eventually led to the salvation of men.

D&C 111:11—This is the general counsel of the Lord to His servants: be prudent and righteous, sensible and sinless. Similar counsel was given by the Savior to His Apostles in the meridian of time: "Behold, I send you forth as sheep in the midst of wolves: be ye therefore wise as serpents, and harmless as doves" (Matt. 10:16).

SECTION 112

1. Verily, thus saith the Lord unto you my servant Thomas, I have heard thy prayers and thine alms have come up as a memorial before me, in behalf of those thy brethren who were chosen to bear testimony of my name, and to send it abroad among all nations, kindreds, tongues, and people, and ordained through the instrumentality of my servants.

2. Verily I say unto you, there have been some few things in thine heart and with thee with which I, the Lord, was not well pleased;

3. Nevertheless, inasmuch as thou hast abased thyself thou shalt be exalted; therefore all thy sins are forgiven thee.

4. Let thy heart be of good cheer before my face, and thou shalt bear record of my name, not only unto the Gentiles, but also unto the Jews; and thou shalt send forth my word unto the ends of the earth.

5. Contend thou, therefore, morning by morning, and day after day let thy warning voice go forth, and when the night cometh, let not the inhabitants of the earth slumber because of thy speech.

6. Let thy habitation be known in Zion, and remove not thy house, for I, the Lord, have a great work for thee to do, in publishing my name among the children of men;

7. Therefore, gird up thy loins for the work. Let thy feet be shod also, for thou art chosen, and thy path lieth among the mountains, and among many nations;

8. And by thy word many high ones shall be brought low, and by thy word many low ones shall be exalted.

9. Thy voice shall be a rebuke unto the transgressor, and at thy rebuke let the tongue of the slanderer cease its perverseness.

10. Be thou humble, and the Lord thy God shall lead thee by the hand, and give thee answer to thy prayers.

11. I know thy heart, and have heard thy prayers concerning thy brethren. Be not partial towards them in love above many others, but let thy love be for them as for thyself; and let thy love abound unto all men, and unto all who love my name.

12. And pray for thy brethren of the Twelve. Admonish them sharply for my name's sake, and let them be admonished for all their sins, and be ye faithful before me unto my name.

13. And after their temptations,

Section 112 Background—Given through Joseph Smith to Thomas B. Marsh on July 23, 1837, at Kirtland, Ohio (see *HC* 2:499–501). The Prophet characterized this revelation as being "The word of the Lord unto Thomas B. Marsh, concerning the Twelve Apostles of the Lamb" (*HC* 2:499). It was given one day before a meeting of the Twelve that had been called by Thomas B. Marsh, at the time President of the Quorum of Twelve. Thomas apparently desired to unify the quorum and take leadership in directing assignments of the Twelve.

Joseph described the situation in 1837 as follows:

> ...evil surmisings, fault-finding, disunion, dissension, and apostasy followed in quick succession, and it seemed as though all the powers of earth and hell were combining their influence in an especial manner to overthrow the Church at once, and make a final end. . . . [M]any became disaffected toward me as though I were the sole cause of those very evils I was most strenuously striving against, and which were actually brought upon us by the brethren not giving heed to my counsel. No quorum in the Church was entirely exempt from the influence of those false spirits who are striving against me for the mastery; even some of the Twelve were so far lost to their high and responsible calling, as to begin to take sides, secretly, with the enemy." (*HC* 2:487–488.)

This period was therefore a test for the Twelve as well as for the Church as a whole. John Taylor explained, "Some people have wondered why so many of the Twelve fell away. God tries people according to the position they occupy." He related that Joseph told the Twelve, "You will have all kinds of trials to pass through. And it is quite as necessary for you to be tried as it was for Abraham and other men of God, and (said he) God will feel after you, and He will take hold of you and wrench your very heart strings, and if you cannot stand it you will not be fit for an inheritance in the Celestial Kingdom of God" (*JD* 24:197–198).

D&C 112:5–11—What exceptional advice for any agent of the Lord who has been called to proclaim the gospel! The time commitment is total, in conformity with the counsel the Lord gave to the Prophet Joseph Smith: "For thou shalt devote all thy service in Zion; and in this thou shalt have strength" (D&C 24:7). Thomas is assured that the Lord has a "great work" for him to accomplish—a phrase that the Lord used on several other occasions in speaking of His consummating design for the latter days (see D&C 35:7; 38:33; 64:33). It was to Thomas that the Lord expressed the memorable counsel: "Be thou humble; and the Lord thy God shall lead thee by the hand, and give thee answer to thy prayers." And the word *abound* in verse 11 is a dynamic action word that places charity in the mode of rendering service in a vigorous, vibrant, forceful, and committed way—not passive or reactive, but filled with the spirit of joyful outreach and abundant harvest.

and much tribulation, behold, I, the Lord, will feel after them, and if they harden not their hearts, and stiffen not their necks against me, they shall be converted, and I will heal them.

14. Now, I say unto you, and what I say unto you, I say unto all the Twelve, Arise and gird up your loins, take up your cross, follow me, and feed my sheep.

15. Exalt not yourselves; rebel not against my servant Joseph, for verily I say unto you, I am with him and my hand shall be over him; and the keys which I have given unto him, and also to youward, shall not be taken from him till I come.

16. Verily I say unto you, my servant Thomas, Thou art the man whom I have chosen to hold the keys of my kingdom (as pertaining to the Twelve) abroad among all nations,

17. That thou mayest be my servant to unlock the door of the kingdom in all places where my servant Joseph, and my servant Sidney, and my servant Hyrum, cannot come;

18. For on them have I laid the burden of all the churches for a little season;

19. Wherefore, whithersoever they shall send you, go ye, and I will be with you; and in whatsoever place ye shall proclaim my name, an effectual door shall be opened unto you, that they may receive my word;

20. Whosoever receiveth my word receiveth me, and whosoever receiveth me, receiveth those (the First Presidency) whom I have sent, whom I have made counselors for my name's sake unto you.

21. And again, I say unto you, That whosoever ye shall send in my name, by the voice of your brethren, the Twelve, duly recommended and authorized by you, shall have power to open the door of my kingdom unto any nation whithersoever ye shall send them,

22. Inasmuch as they shall humble themselves before me, and abide in my word, and hearken to the voice of my Spirit.

23. Verily, verily I say unto you, Darkness covereth the earth, and gross darkness the minds of the people, and all flesh has become corrupt before my face.

24. Behold, vengeance cometh speedily upon the inhabitants of the earth, a day of wrath, a day of burning, a day of desolation, of weeping, of mourning, and of lamentation, and as a whirlwind it shall come upon all the face of the earth, saith the Lord.

25. And upon my house shall it begin, and from my house shall it go forth, saith the Lord.

26. First among those among you, saith the Lord, who have professed to know my name and have not known me, and have blasphemed

D&C 112:12–14— Everyone called to a position of leadership in the kingdom—whether parents, teachers, or administrators at all levels—can discern in the counsel given to Thomas Marsh words of wisdom that they can apply in their own service. We pray for those with whom we are yoked together in our callings; we encourage humility and receptivity to the Spirit; we express our commitment to take up the cross and follow the Savior along the pathway of salvation and eternal life.

D&C 112:19–20—We are to go where bidden; we are to serve where called. The counsel to Thomas B. Marsh applies to us all as a covenant commission, with the promise that the Lord will open the doors before us and bless us as His agents and representatives. We are reminded of the words of Ruth, which express poignantly her commitment to follow Naomi: "Intreat me not to leave thee, or to return from following after thee: for whither thou goest, I will go; and where thou lodgest, I will lodge: thy people shall be my people, and thy God my God" (Ruth 1:16). It is that same attitude that is inherent in our commitment to do the will of the Lord, no matter what the sacrifice, and no matter where He might send us.

D&C 112:24–28—The Lord will prepare the earth for the millennial reign by cleansing the nations and rooting out the wicked. The process of purification begins within His own circle of followers, where many confess His name in veiled hypocrisy and therefore have need of chastening. The process of sifting and searching for the honest at heart is accomplished by agents of purity through whom the Holy Ghost can operate. Thus the admonition "purify your hearts" before embarking on the errand of the Lord is the fundamental dimension of missionary preparation. Conveyed and witnessed in purity and faith, the testimony of the Saints is a powerful tool for witnessing the truth of the gospel of Jesus Christ.

Monument at Far West, Missouri, listing—among other things—revelations dealing with the official name of the Church, the law of tithing, and missionary work to take the gospel to the world. Far West is the county seat of Caldwell County, which was created by the Missouri General Assembly for the Mormons and which was dedicated to the Saints.

against me in the midst of my house, saith the Lord.

27. Therefore, see to it that ye trouble not yourselves concerning the affairs of my church in this place, saith the Lord;

28. But purify your hearts before me, and then go ye into all the world, and preach my gospel unto every creature who has not received it,

29. And he that believeth and is baptized shall be saved, and he that believeth not, and is not baptized, shall be damned.

30. For unto you, (the Twelve,) and those (the First Presidency) who are appointed with you, to be your counselors and your leaders, is the power of this priesthood given, for the last days and for the last time, in the which is the dispensation of the fulness of times.

31. Which power you hold in connection with all those who have received a dispensation at any time from the beginning of the creation;

32. For verily I say unto you, the keys of the dispensation which ye have received, have come down from the fathers; and last of all, being sent down from heaven unto you.

33. Verily I say unto you, Behold how great is your calling. Cleanse your hearts and your garments, lest the blood of this generation be required at your hands.

34. Be faithful until I come, for I come quickly, and my reward is with me to recompense every man according as his work shall be. I am Alpha and Omega. Amen.

SECTION 113

1. Who is the Stem of Jesse spoken of in the 1st, 2nd, 3rd, 4th, and 5th verses of the 11th chapter of Isaiah?

2. Verily thus saith the Lord, it is Christ.

3. What is the rod spoken of in the first verse of the 11th chapter of Isaiah that should come of the Stem of Jesse?

4. Behold thus saith the Lord, it is a servant in the hands of Christ, who is partly a descendant of Jesse as well as of Ephraim, or of the house of Joseph, on whom there is laid much power.

5. What is the root of Jesse spoken of in the 10th verse of the 11th chapter?

6. Behold thus saith the Lord, it is a descendant of Jesse, as well as of

Country road in present-day Far West, Missouri.

Section 113 Background—In the Prophet's journal for March 1838 is this entry: "The Prophet's Answers to Questions on Scripture" (*HC* 3:9). The material that follows is now known as Section 113 (see *HC* 3:9–10).

D&C 113:3–5—Author Richard O. Cowan writes:

Comparing what the Lord said about the "rod" and "root of Jesse" (D&C 113:4, 6), suggests that both refer to the same person. Unto him, declared the Lord, "rightly belongs the priesthood" (D&C 113:6). Who better fits this promise than does the Prophet Joseph Smith? reasoned Dr. Sidney B. Sperry. As the "'servant in the hands of Christ,' . . . Joseph Smith fits naturally into Isaiah's prophecy, and it is easy to understand why Moroni quoted and explained Isaiah 11 to him" (*Improvement Era,* Oct. 1966, 869, 914). When Moroni appeared to Joseph Smith in 1823, he said that the prophecies in Isaiah 11 were "about to be fulfilled" (Joseph Smith–History 1:40). "That fulfillment began," suggested Dr. Kent Jackson of Brigham Young University, "at that very moment, when the Prophet began to receive the instruction and training that led to the restoration of all things. It will culminate in a glorious fulfillment—in the millennial reign of the Lord Jesus Christ" ("Revelations Concerning Isaiah," 333). (*AQDC,* 131–132.)

ELIAS HIGBEE

Elias Higbee was born October 23, 1795, at Galloway, Gloucester County, New Jersey. He joined the Church in Ohio and moved his family to Missouri, where he held various Church positions and was elected as judge in Caldwell County. As judge he ordered the militia to disperse the mobs of terror that were acting against the Saints. The Battle of Crooked River ensued. In March of 1838 he asked the Prophet Joseph Smith to explain certain passages in Isaiah (see D&C 113:7–10). Having been forced to leave Missouri by the mobs, Elias moved to Illinois and continued his ecclesiastical and civic duties. In Nauvoo, Elias, who had earned the friendship and respect of the Prophet Joseph, served on the temple committee, but not without some chastening from the Prophet on one occasion. Elias passed away of ill health on June 7, 1843. The Prophet eulogized him in appreciative and laudatory terms.

Joseph, unto whom rightly belongs the Priesthood, and the keys of the Kingdom, for an ensign, and for the gathering of my people in the last days.

7. Questions by Elias Higbee, as follows—"What is meant by the command in Isaiah, 52d chapter, 1st verse, which saith, put on thy strength, O Zion? And what people had Isaiah reference to?"

8. He had reference to those whom God should call in the last days, who should hold the power of Priesthood to bring again Zion, and the redemption of Israel; and to put on her strength is to put on the authority of the Priesthood, which she (Zion) has a right to by lineage; also to return to that power which she had lost.

9. "What are we to understand by Zion loosing herself from the bands of her neck, 2d verse?"

10. We are to understand that the scattered remnants are exhorted to return to the Lord from whence they have fallen, which if they do, the promise of the Lord is that he will speak to them, or give them revelation. See the 6th, 7th, and 8th verses. The bands of her neck are the curses of God upon her, or the remnants of Israel in their scattered condition among the Gentiles.

SECTION 114

1. Verily thus saith the Lord, it is wisdom in my servant David W. Patten, that he settle up all his business as soon as he possibly can, and make a disposition of his merchandise, that he may perform a mission unto me next spring, in company with others, even Twelve including himself, to testify of my name, and bear glad tidings unto all the world;

2. For verily thus saith the Lord, that inasmuch as there are those among you who deny my name, others shall be planted in their stead, and receive their bishopric. Amen.

DAVID W. PATTEN

David W. Patten was born November 14, 1799, near Indian River Falls, New York. He was introduced to the restored gospel by his brother John. David was baptized and subsequently ordained an elder on June 19, 1832. He served several missions for the Church before the Prophet Joseph Smith sent him to aid the Saints in Missouri in 1834, where he blessed many with his gift of healing. He also journeyed to the southern states to preach the gospel before being called as a member of the Quorum of the Twelve Apostles on February 15, 1835. Thereafter he served missions in the eastern states and the southern states—but not without intense persecution from enemies of the Church. At the Battle of Crooked River, Missouri, in October 1838, David courageously led a charge against the mob in the defense of the Saints. He received a severe gunshot wound and passed away on October 25, 1838. In a revelation dated January 19, 1841, the Lord declared: "David Patten . . . is with me at this time" (D&C 124:19). And also: "David Patten I have taken unto myself; behold, his priesthood no man taketh from him; but, verily I say unto you, another may be appointed unto the same calling" (D&C 124:130).

D&C 113:7—In the metaphorical language of the revelation, "put on thy strength" (as with a mantle or garment) is a tactile and understandable way of expressing the bestowal of priesthood authority upon the leaders of the chosen lineage in the latter days.

D&C 113:9—This reference, according to the revelation, is a metaphorical treatment of the process of the gathering of Israel in the latter days. The gathering brings the blessings of protection, security, access to the word of the Lord as it is revealed, and the opportunity to participate in the saving ordinances of the priesthood, including the higher ordinances of the temple.

Section 114 Background—Given at Far West, Missouri, April 17, 1838 (see *HC* 3:23). The revelation was received on behalf of David W. Patten, one of the original members of the Quorum of the Twelve. At Joseph Smith's direction, David Patten had led a group of seventy-five volunteers against a mob of thirty or forty, hoping to free three prisoners who were being held. During what became known as the Battle of Crooked River, he was shot in the stomach and died on October 25, 1838. Joseph Smith said of David Patten, "He died as he had lived, a man of God, and strong in the faith of a glorious resurrection, in a world where mobs will have no power or place."

D&C 114:1–2—Few of the early leaders of the Church served with valor and loyalty to exceed that of David Patten. He died willingly as a martyr to the cause of Zion. All who receive the priesthood of God have a covenant obligation to magnify their callings with devotion and faith.

In contrast to the valiant service of David W. Patten at that time were the disappointing examples of leaders such as David Whitmer, John Whitmer, W. W. Phelps, Oliver Cowdery, Luke Johnson, Lyman E. Johnson, John F. Boynton, and William E. McLellin (see *LJSP*, 237–238). All of these brethren (the last four of whom were members of the original Quorum of the Twelve Apostles) lost their standing in the Church through pride and disobedience, a stark reminder that "inasmuch as there are those among you who deny my name, others shall be planted in their stead." Six of the original Twelve were eventually excommunicated.

The word "bishopric" means any office or position of importance in the Church, and is not limited to a position in the bishopric.

SECTION 115

1. Verily thus saith the Lord unto you, my servant Joseph Smith, jr., and also my servant Sidney Rigdon, and also my servant Hyrum Smith, and your counselors who are and shall be appointed hereafter;

2. And also unto you my servant Edward Partridge, and his counselors;

3. And also unto my faithful servants, who are of the High Council of my church in Zion (for thus it shall be called) and unto all the elders and people of my Church of Jesus Christ of Latter-day Saints, scattered abroad in all the world;

4. For thus shall my church be called in the last days, even The Church of Jesus Christ of Latter-day Saints.

5. Verily I say unto you all, Arise and shine forth, that thy light may be a standard for the nations,

6. And that the gathering together upon the land of Zion, and upon her Stakes, may be for a defense, and for a refuge from the storm, and from wrath when it shall be poured out without mixture upon the whole earth.

7. Let the city, Far West, be a holy and consecrated land unto me, and it shall be called most holy, for the ground upon which thou standest is holy;

8. Therefore I command you to build a house unto me, for the gathering together of my saints, that they may worship me;

9. And let there be a beginning of this work, and a foundation, and a preparatory work, this following summer;

10. And let the beginning be made on the 4th day of July next; and from that time forth let my people labor diligently to build a house unto my name,

11. And in one year from this day let them re-commence laying the foundation of my house:

12. Thus let them from that time forth labor diligently until it shall be finished, from the corner stone thereof unto the top thereof, until there shall not anything remain that is not finished.

13. Verily I say unto you, let not my servant Joseph, neither my servant Sidney, neither my servant Hyrum, get in debt any more for the building of an house unto my name;

14. But let a house be built unto my name according to the pattern which I will show unto them.

15. And if my people build it not according to the pattern which I shall show unto their Presidency, I will not accept it at their hands;

16. But if my people do build it according to the pattern which I shall show unto their Presidency, even my servant Joseph and his

Section 115 Background—Given on April 26, 1838, at Far West, Caldwell County, Missouri. The Prophet gave this introductory statement: *"Revelation Given at Far West making known the will of God concerning the building up of that place, and of the Lord's House"* (HC 3:23). This is the best-known revelation that gives the name of the Church, which had previously been known as the "Church of Christ" and the "Church of the Latter Day Saints." The name given in this revelation remains to this day. At the time of this revelation, there were 150 houses, a school house, several stores, and a number of hotels in Far West; all stood deserted because of the mobs.

D&C 115:1—The "counselors" in this verse included Joseph Smith Sr. and John Smith, who were assistant counselors to the Prophet. Later, in Nauvoo, additional counselors included John C. Bennett, William Law, and Amasa Lyman.

D&C 115:4—By the most fundamental application of logic and reason, the Church bears the name of its Founder and Celestial Administrator, even Jesus Christ the Redeemer. The Lord confirms that while the Church is *His* Church, it is also *our* Church, for He adds the wondrous words "of Latter-day Saints." Elder B. H. Roberts said that the name shows the beautiful relationship between the Savior and His Saints—He owns the Church, but the Saints have a conjoint ownership with Him.

D&C 115:5–6—Just as a lighthouse sends forth life-saving beams to guide a ship past treacherous cliffs in perilous seas, the Church is a beacon of glory that guides the faithful safely through the tempests of life and into holy harbors of truth and security. In the Kingdom of the Father, the ultimate illumination will be experienced, as John the Beloved foresaw: "And the city had no need of the sun, neither of the moon, to shine in it: for the glory of God did lighten it, and the Lamb is the light thereof" (Rev. 21:23).

A "standard," as used in verse 5, is an individual responsibility as well as a responsibility for the entire Church to serve as a standard for those seeking safety, peace, and happiness. Being a standard to the nations is a mission of the Church.

D&C 115:6—The stakes are designed to provide a defense for their members, but members are not to gather in this way until instructed by the First Presidency.

D&C 115:8—The cornerstones for a temple were laid on July 4, 1838; the foundation, which measured 120 feet by 80 feet and which was 5 feet deep, was dug in half a day by 500 men. Nothing else was done on the temple because the Saints were driven out by intense persecution.

counselors, then I will accept it at the hands of my people.

17. And again, verily I say unto you, it is my will that the city of Far West should be built up speedily by the gathering of my saints,

18. And also that other places should be appointed for Stakes in the regions round about, as they shall be manifested unto my servant Joseph, from time to time;

19. For behold, I will be with him, and I will sanctify him before the people, for unto him have I given the keys of this kingdom and ministry. Even so. Amen.

SECTION 116

1. Adam-ondi-Ahman, because, said he, it is the place where Adam shall come to visit his people, or the Ancient of days shall sit, as spoken of by Daniel the prophet.

SECTION 117

1. Verily thus saith the Lord unto my servant William Marks, and also unto my servant N. K. Whitney, let them settle up their business speedily and journey from the land of Kirtland, before I, the Lord, send again the snows upon the earth;

2. Let them awake, and arise, and come forth, and not tarry, for I, the Lord, command it;

3. Therefore if they tarry it shall not be well with them.

4. Let them repent of all their sins, and of all their covetous desires, before me, saith the Lord, for what is property unto me saith the Lord?

5. Let the properties of Kirtland be turned out for debts, saith the Lord. Let them go, saith the Lord, and whatsoever remaineth, let it remain in your hands, saith the Lord;

6. For have I not the fowls of heaven, and also the fish of the sea, and the beasts of the mountains? Have I not made the earth? Do I not hold the destinies of all the armies of the nations of the earth?

D&C 115:18–19—The president of the Church, who holds "the keys of this kingdom and ministry," determines the means and pace for the unfolding of the kingdom of God under the direction of Jesus Christ.

Section 116 Background—Given at Spring Hill, Daviess County, Missouri, on May 19, 1838. The Prophet gives this context: "In the afternoon I went up the river about half a mile to Wight's Ferry, accompanied by President Rigdon, and my clerk, George W. Robinson, for the purpose of selecting and laying claim to a city plat near said ferry . . . which the brethren called 'Spring Hill,' but by the mouth of the Lord it was named Adam-ondi-Ahman . . ." (HC 3:35).

D&C 116:1—Adam-ondi-Ahman had been used earlier in a revelation given to the priesthood brethren (see D&C 78:15) and in a revelation in relation to the line of priesthood descent during the time of Adam (see D&C 107:53). Orson Pratt said: "'Adam-Ondi-Ahman' . . . means the place where Adam dwelt. 'Ahman' signifies God. The whole term means Valley of God where Adam dwelt. It is the original language spoken by Adam, as revealed to the Prophet Joseph" (JD 18:343).

It is at Adam-ondi-Ahman that a special convocation will take place where those who received and exercised keys over the various dispensations will again congregate under the auspices of Adam and return those keys to him. He, in turn, will return the keys to the Savior at the inauguration of His personal millennial reign.

Section 117 Background—Given at Far West, Missouri, July 8, 1838, concerning the duties of three brethren: William Marks, Newel K. Whitney, and Oliver Granger (see HC 3:45–46).

OLIVER GRANGER

Oliver Granger was born February 7, 1794, at Phelps, Ontario County, New York. A sheriff and militia officer in New York, Oliver obtained a copy of the Book of Mormon in 1830 and became converted. He was baptized and ordained an elder by Brigham Young and Brigham's brother Joseph. Oliver moved to Kirtland in 1833, where he served on the high council and worked on the temple before mob violence forced him to leave and go to Missouri. On July 8, 1838, Oliver was called by revelation to help settle the financial affairs of the Church (see D&C 117:12–15)—a mission he performed with distinction, earning him the respect and appreciation of the Prophet and the eternal commendation of the Savior. Oliver continued his service for the Church as a land agent in Illinois and Iowa until passing away on August 25, 1841.

WILLIAM MARKS

William Marks was born November 15, 1792, in Rutland, Rutland County, Virginia. He joined the Church in New York and moved his family to Kirtland, where he opened a bookstore. He was called to serve on the high council, and soon became an agent working with Bishop Newel K. Whitney. On July 8, 1838, William was called by revelation to move to Missouri and preside among the people at Far West. Mob violence in Missouri forced the Saints to leave before William could fulfill his calling there. He made his way to Commerce (later Nauvoo) and filled a number of Church and civic callings before his testimony began to waver in 1844. He allied himself with the enemies of the Church after the martyrdom, but recanted and returned to fellowship for a time. Later he left the Church and became associated with other religious groups, including the RLDS church. William died on May 22, 1872.

7. Therefore will I not make solitary places to bud and to blossom, and to bring forth in abundance, saith the Lord.

8. Is there not room enough on the mountains of Adam-ondi-Ahman, and upon the plains of Olaha Shinehah, or the land where Adam dwelt, that you should covet that which is but the drop, and neglect the more weighty matters?

9. Therefore come up hither unto the land of my people, even Zion.

10. Let my servant William Marks be faithful over a few things, and he shall be a ruler over many. Let him preside in the midst of my people in the city of Far West, and let him be blessed with the blessings of my people.

11. Let my servant N. K. Whitney be ashamed of the Nicholatine band and of all their secret abominations, and of all his littleness of soul before me, saith the Lord, and come up to the land of Adam-ondi-Ahman, and be a bishop unto my people, saith the Lord, not in name but in deed, saith the Lord.

12. And again, I say unto you, I remember my servant Oliver Granger, behold, verily I say unto him, that his name shall be had in sacred remembrance from generation to generation, for ever and ever, saith the Lord.

13. Therefore let him contend earnestly for the redemption of the First Presidency of my church, saith the Lord, and when he falls he shall rise again, for his sacrifice shall be more sacred unto me than his increase, saith the Lord:

14. Therefore let him come up hither speedily, unto the land of Zion, and in the due time he shall be made a merchant unto my name, saith the Lord, for the benefit of my people;

15. Therefore let no man despise my servant Oliver Granger, but let the blessings of my people be on him for ever and ever.

16. And again, verily I say unto you, let all my servants in the land of Kirtland remember the Lord their God, and mine house also, to keep and preserve it holy, and to overthrow the money changers in mine own due time, saith the Lord. Even so. Amen.

SECTION 118

1. Verily, thus saith the Lord, let a conference be held immediately, let the Twelve be organized, and let men be appointed to supply the place of those who are fallen.

2. Let my servant Thomas remain for a season in the land of Zion, to publish my word.

3. Let the residue continue to preach from that hour, and if they will do this in all lowliness of heart, in meekness and humility, and long-suffering, I, the Lord, give unto them a promise that I will

D&C 117:4–8—The Lord had commanded the Saints at Kirtland to gather to Far West "speedily" (D&C 115:17). Unbeknown to the Prophet Joseph Smith, a party of more than 500 Saints left Kirtland for Missouri on July 6, 1838, two days before the revelation in Section 117 was received. None of the three individuals named in the revelation was part of this party, the residue of which was to arrive at Adam-ondi-Ahman on October 4 (see *DCC*, 744). The Lord was aware of the situation, however, and revealed to the Prophet a commandment for William Marks and Newel K. Whitney to repent, as they had fallen under the spirit of speculation so prevalent in Kirtland.

Hyrum M. Smith and Janne M. Sjodahl give the following footnote to this revelation from the Lord:

> *Shinehah* means "sun" . . . and *Olaha* is, possibly a variant of the word *Olea*, which is "the moon". . . . If so, the Plains of Olaha Shinehah would be the Plains of the Moon and the Sun, so called, perhaps because of astronomical observations there made. . . . That the study of astronomy dates back to our first ancestor, there is no reason to doubt. (*DCC*, 745.)

D&C 117:10–11—Despite His firm chastening, the Lord shows mercy in giving William Marks and Newell K. Whitney the chance to repent and go forward in righteousness to fulfill their callings. The reference to "Nicolaitane band" seems to relate to an unrighteous syndrome practiced by a group referred to in the book of Revelation (see Rev. 2:6, 15)—Church members who were trying to maintain their standing in the Church while living after the manner of the world. Newel K. Whitney humbly and penitently turned from his "Nicolaitane" ways. However, William Marks did not endure to the end, but ultimately left the Church for other religious pursuits, and thus lost his covenant blessings.

Section 118 Background—Given at Far West, Missouri, July 8, 1838, in response to the supplication: "*Show unto us thy will O Lord concerning the Twelve*" (HC 3:46).

D&C 118:1–4—Continuity of leadership in the Church is assured and secured through revelation. Elders William E. McLellin, Luke S. Johnson, John F. Boynton, and Lyman E. Johnson (all members of the original Twelve) had defected and lost their positions (see HC 2:509; 3:31–32). John E. Page, one of the four replacements, also later apostatized. But the other three remained ever faithful, two of them (John Taylor and Wilford Woodruff) later serving as president of the Church. The European mission campaign called for in this revelation proved to be a fruitful and productive era in Church development, with thousands of converts joining the Church.

Concerning the prophetic announcement that the Twelve would take their leave overseas beginning April 26, 1839, it is instructive how this was fulfilled, in light of the severe persecution being inflicted upon the Saints during

provide for their families, and an effectual door shall be opened for them, from henceforth;

4. And next spring let them depart to go over the great waters, and there promulgate my gospel, the fulness thereof, and bear record of my name.

5. Let them take leave of my saints in the city Far West, on the 26 day of April next, on the building spot of my house, saith the Lord.

6. Let my servant John Taylor, and also my servant John E. Page, and also my servant Wilford Woodruff, and also my servant Willard Richards, be appointed to fill the places of those who have fallen, and be officially notified of their appointment.

SECTION 119

1. Verily, thus saith the Lord, I require all their surplus property to be put into the hands of the bishop of my church in Zion,

2. For the building of mine house, and for the laying of the foundation of Zion and for the Priesthood, and for the debts of the Presidency of my church;

3. And this shall be the beginning of the tithing of my people;

4. And after that, those who have thus been tithed, shall pay one-tenth of all their interest annually; and this shall be a standing law unto them for ever, for my holy Priesthood, saith the Lord.

5. Verily I say unto you, it shall come to pass, that all those who gather unto the land of Zion shall be tithed of their surplus properties, and shall observe this law or they shall not be found worthy to abide among you.

JOHN E. PAGE

John E. Page was born February 25, 1799, in Trenton Township, Oneida County, New York. He was baptized in 1833 and served two productive missions in Canada, guiding many of his converts to Missouri in 1838. Tragically, John's wife and two children were killed by mob violence that year. Still grieving, John was called by revelation to be a member of the Quorum of the Twelve Apostles on July 8, 1838. He did not comply with a call to serve a mission in England, nor with a subsequent call in 1840 to accompany Orson Hyde on a mission to dedicate the Holy Land for the return of the Jews. Over the next several years he professed repentance for his behavior and a desire to return to activity, but eventually he formed an allegiance with James J. Strang, who claimed to be the rightful successor to the martyred Prophet Joseph Smith. John lost his Apostleship and was excommunicated on June 26, 1846. He took up affiliation with several other upstart groups thereafter, and eventually helped the Hedrickites to secure the temple lot in Independence. John died on October 14, 1867.

this period: A few minutes after midnight on Friday, April 26, 1839, a number of the Twelve Apostles gathered with a few other Saints at the temple site in Far West, Missouri, for an unusual meeting. Among those present were Brigham Young, Heber C. Kimball, Orson Pratt, John E. Page, and John Taylor. These brethren ordained Wilford Woodruff and George A. Smith Apostles (as provided in D&C 118:6 and D&C 124:129) and then two others as Seventies. After prayers and a hymn ("Adam-ondi-Ahman" *Hymns,* No. 49), the Twelve departed into the night.

Why this clandestine midnight meeting? Because the angry mobs that had driven the Saints away the previous Fall had sworn that no such meeting would take place. They were well aware of the revelation given by the Lord through the Prophet Joseph Smith on July 8, 1838, announcing that the Twelve would ". . . take leave of my saints in the city of Far West, on the twenty-sixth day of April next, on the building-spot of my house, saith the Lord" (D&C 118:5) to perform missionary duties in Europe. What better way to prove "Joe Smith" a false prophet than to prevent the gathering from taking place on that date? Imagine their shock when they learned later the same day that the event had already occurred just as the Lord had commanded (see *HC* 3:336–340).

Section 119 Background—Given on July 8, 1838, in Far West, Missouri, in response to his inquiry: "O Lord! Show unto thy servant how much thou requirest of the properties of the people for a tithing" (*HC* 3:44). The law of tithing as we understand it today had not been given to the Church previous to this revelation. Before this revelation, the word *tithing* meant all free-will offerings or contributions to Church funds of any amount. Elder Melvin J. Ballard said, "No man may hope or expect to have an inheritance on this celestial globe who has failed to pay his tithing. By the payment of his honest tithing he is establishing a right and a title to this inheritance, and he cannot secure it upon any other terms." The law of tithing is actually a lesser law that serves as a schoolmaster to prepare us to live the law of consecration, which requires that we do away with selfishness, greed, pride, envy, and poverty. According to Elder Orson F. Whitney, those who obey the law of tithing will be able to live the law of consecration.

D&C 119:1—In this verse, "surplus property" is anything left over after providing a comfortable and necessary subsistence—generally considered to be shelter, food, and clothing. Such is not required of us today.

D&C 119:4—The law of tithing is an opportunity for faithful Saints to understand and experience the process of being edified and blessed through humble and charitable giving. After all, everything in this world belongs to the Lord, and when He blesses us with a measure of temporal increase, the paying of tithing is but an act of returning a portion of that which was borrowed in the first place.

6. And I say unto you, if my people observe not this law, to keep it holy, and by this law sanctify the land of Zion unto me, that my statutes and my judgments may be kept thereon, that it may be most holy, behold, verily I say unto you, it shall not be a land of Zion unto you;

7. And this shall be an ensample unto all the Stakes of Zion. Even so. Amen.

SECTION 120

1. Verily, thus saith the Lord, the time is now come, that it shall be disposed of by a Council, composed of the First Presidency of my church, and of the bishop and his council, and by my High Council; and by mine own voice unto them, saith the Lord. Even so. Amen.

SECTION 121

1. O God, where art thou? And where is the pavilion that covereth thy hiding place?

2. How long shall thy hand be stayed, and thine eye, yea thy pure eye, behold from the eternal heavens the wrongs of thy people and of thy servants, and thine ear be penetrated with their cries?

3. Yea, O Lord, how long shall they suffer these wrongs and unlawful oppressions, before thine heart shall be softened towards them, and thy bowels be moved with compassion towards them?

4. O Lord God Almighty, maker of heaven, earth, and seas, and of all things that in them are and who controllest and subjectest the devil, and the dark and benighted dominion of Sheole! Stretch forth thy hand; let thine eye pierce; let thy pavilion be taken up; let thy hiding place no longer be covered; let thine ear be

WILLARD RICHARDS

Willard Richards was born June 24, 1804, at Hopkinton, Middlesex County, Massachusetts. He established a medical practice in Boston. When he acquired a copy of the Book of Mormon he soon became convinced of its truth and journeyed to Kirtland in 1836 to continue his investigation of the Church. His cousin Brigham Young baptized him on December 31 of that year. Willard served a mission in the British Isles the following year and married one of his converts, Jennetta Richards, in 1838. While still in England, he learned of his call to the Quorum of the Twelve (see D&C 118:6) and was ordained by visiting members of the Twelve on April 14, 1840. Upon his return to America, he was appointed private secretary to the Prophet Joseph in Nauvoo. On June 27, 1844, he was a witness to the martyrdom in Carthage Jail (see D&C 135:2). Thereafter he gave the same dedicated service to Brigham Young, whom he accompanied to the Salt Lake Valley in 1847. He served as second counselor to President Young from 1847 until his death on March 11, 1854.

D&C 119:6—The law of tithing is a sanctifying law. Those who participate with full devotion will be sanctified and rendered more holy by virtue of their obedience. Elder James E. Talmage said: "Tithing is the Lord's revenue system, and He requires it of the people, not because He is lacking in gold or silver, but because [we] need to pay it. . . . The prime . . . purpose behind the establishment of the law of the tithe is the development of the soul of the tithe-payer, rather than the providing of revenue" (*AF*, 472–473).

Section 120 Background—Given on July 8, 1838, at Far West, Missouri, on the same day as Section 119 was received (see *HC* 3:44).

D&C 120:1—The Lord's Church is a church of order and accountability. Donations are meticulously managed and expended for the building up of the kingdom of God on the earth.

Section 121 Background—Given in the form of an epistle dated March 20, 1839, while Joseph Smith was imprisoned in Liberty Jail, Missouri (see *HC* 3:289–300). On October 27, 1838, Governor Lilburn W. Boggs issued an order to Major–General John B. Clark, giving him command of an overwhelming force of militia, with instructions to proceed at once against the Mormons. "Their outrages are beyond all description," said the Governor, "They must be exterminated or driven from the State" (*HC* 3:175). Other generals were ordered to take part, under Clark, in the military campaign. The resulting dislocations and persecutions soon led to the imprisonment of the Prophet Joseph Smith and several of his colleagues for a number of months in the decrepit darkness of Liberty Jail. The complete epistle is given in the *History of the Church* (3:298–305); while Section 121 consists of selected excerpts, the entire epistle is most instructive to read and contemplate.

It is instructive and poignant that the Prophet Joseph wanted his wife Emma to be the first to read the epistle from which Section 121 is taken. In a letter to her dated March 21, 1839, he writes (in part):

Affectionate Wife

I have sent an Epistle to the church directed to you because I wanted you to have the first reading of it and then I want Father and Mother to have a copy of it. Keep the original yourself as I dictated the matter myself and shall send another as soon as possible. I want to be with you very much but the powers of mobocracy are too many for me at present. . . . Dear Emma, I very well know your toils and sympathize with you. If God will spare my life once more to have the privilege of taking care of you I will ease your care and endeavor to comfort your heart (*PWJS*, 408; grammatically updated).

inclined; let thine heart be softened, and thy bowels moved with compassion toward us;

5. Let thine anger be kindled against our enemies; and in the fury of thine heart, with thy sword avenge us of our wrongs;

6. Remember thy suffering saints, O our God! and thy servants will rejoice in thy name forever.

7. My son, peace be unto thy soul; thine adversity and thine afflictions shall be but a small moment;

8. And then, if thou endure it well, God shall exalt thee on high; thou shalt triumph over all thy foes;

9. Thy friends do stand by thee, and they shall hail thee again, with warm hearts and friendly hands;

10. Thou art not yet as Job; thy friends do not contend against thee, neither charge thee with transgression, as they did Job;

11. And they who do charge thee with transgression, their hope shall be blasted, and their prospects shall melt away as the hoar frost melteth before the burning rays of the rising sun;

12. And also that God hath set his hand and seal, to change the times and seasons, and to blind their minds, that they may not understand his marvelous workings; that he may prove them also and take them in their own craftiness;

13. Also because their hearts are corrupted, and the things which they are willing to bring upon others, and love to have others suffer, may come upon themselves, to the very uttermost;

14. That they may be disappointed also, and their hopes may be cut off;

15. And not many years hence, that they and their posterity shall be swept from under heaven, saith God, that not one of them is left to stand by the wall:

16. Cursed are all those that shall lift up the heel against mine anointed, saith the Lord, and cry they have sinned when they have not sinned before me, saith the Lord, but have done that which was meet in mine eyes, and which I commanded them;

17. But those who cry transgression do it because they are the servants of sin, and are the children of disobedience themselves;

18. And those who swear falsely against my servants, that they might bring them into bondage and death:

19. Wo unto them; because they have offended my little ones, they shall be severed from the ordinances of mine house;

20. Their basket shall not be full, their houses and their barns shall perish, and they themselves shall be despised by those that flattered them;

The Historic Liberty Jail site in Independence, Missouri, now a visitors' center.

D&C 121:1, 6—The Lord knows of our sufferings and afflictions. In His mortal experience in the meridian of time, He walked the pathways of tribulation more trying and severe than any of us can imagine: "Surely he hath borne our griefs, and carried our sorrows: yet we did esteem him stricken, smitten of God, and afflicted. But he was wounded for our transgressions, he was bruised for our iniquities: the chastisement of our peace was upon him; and with his stripes we are healed" (Isa. 53:4–5). His condescension imparted to Him lessons in understanding and beneficence that resonate with effectual compassion in all that He does as Redeemer and Savior. His mercy was infused with first-hand experience by virtue of His willingness to see, hear, and feel with mortal perspective: "And he shall go forth, suffering pains and afflictions and temptations of every kind; and this that the word might be fulfilled which saith he will take upon him the pains and the sicknesses of his people. And he will take upon him death, that he may loose the bands of death which bind his people; and he will take upon him their infirmities, that his bowels may be filled with mercy, according to the flesh, that he may know according to the flesh how to succor his people according to their infirmities" (Alma 7:11–12).

D&C 121:7–9—There is opposition in all things (see 2 Ne. 2:11); adversity is part of this opposition and is necessary for our growth and development. This is the test of mortality. We are counseled to endure all things, that we might be worthy of the blessings from our Heavenly Father. Out of one of the darkest periods in Church history—the confinement in a jail ironically called "Liberty"—came a revelation that brings us strength to endure any hardship we may encounter.

D&C 121:16—What is not always apparent to the embattled Saints is known to the Lord: His designs will be fulfilled in His own due time in justice and judgment on those who seek to destroy His work. Nothing will stand in the way of the advancement of the Lord's designs. No force can impede the inexorable forward motion of the kingdom of God. President Heber J. Grant confirmed this truth:

> Our enemies have never done anything that has injured this work of God, and they never will. I look around, I read, I reflect, and I ask the question, Where are the men of influence, of power and prestige, who have worked against the Latter-day Saints? . . . Where are the men who have assailed this work? Where is their influence? They have faded away like dew before the sun. We need have no fears, we Latter-day Saints. God will continue to sustain this work; He will sustain the right. If we are loyal, if we are true, if we are worthy of this Gospel, of which God has given us a testimony, there is no danger that the world can ever injure us. We can never be injured . . . by any mortals, except ourselves. (CR, April 1909, Third Day, Morning Session.)

21. They shall not have right to the Priesthood, nor their posterity after them, from generation to generation;

22. It had been better for them that a millstone had been hanged about their necks, and they drowned in the depth of the sea.

23. Wo unto all those that discomfort my people, and drive, and murder, and testify against them, saith the Lord of Hosts; a generation of vipers shall not escape the damnation of hell.

24. Behold, mine eyes see and know all their works, and I have in reserve a swift judgment in the season thereof, for them all;

25. For there is a time appointed for every man, according as his works shall be.

26. God shall give unto you (the saints) knowledge by his Holy Spirit, yea by the unspeakable gift of the Holy Ghost, that has not been revealed since the world was until now;

27. Which our forefathers have awaited with anxious expectation to be revealed in the last times, which their minds were pointed to, by the angels, as held in reserve for the fulness of their glory:

28. A time to come in the which nothing shall be withheld, whether there be one God or many Gods, they shall be manifest;

29. All thrones and dominions, principalities and powers, shall be revealed and set forth upon all who have endured valiantly for the gospel of Jesus Christ;

30. And also if there be bounds set to the heavens or to the seas, or to the dry land, or to the sun, moon, or stars;

31. All the times of their revolutions, all the appointed days, months, and years, and all the days of their days, months, and years, and all their glories, laws and set times, shall be revealed, in the days of the dispensation of the fulness of times,

32. According to that which was ordained in the midst of the Council of the Eternal God of all other Gods, before this world was, that should be reserved unto the finishing and the end thereof, when every man shall enter into his eternal presence, and into his immortal rest.

33. How long can rolling waters remain impure? What power shall stay the heavens? As well might man stretch forth his puny arm to stop the Missouri river in its decreed course, or to turn it up stream, as to hinder the Almighty from pouring down knowledge from heaven,

D&C 121:26–28—The following passages from the Prophet's epistle from Liberty Jail preceded the passage now known as D&C 121:26–32:

A fanciful and flowery and heated imagination beware of; because the things of God are of deep import; and time, and experience, and careful and ponderous and solemn thoughts can only find them out. Thy mind, O man! if thou wilt lead a soul unto salvation, must stretch as high as the utmost heavens, and search into and contemplate the darkest abyss, and the broad expanse of eternity—thou must commune with God. How much more dignified and noble are the thoughts of God, than the vain imaginations of the human heart! None but fools will trifle with the souls of men.

How vain and trifling have been our spirits, our conferences, our councils, our meetings, our private as well as public conversations—too low, too mean, too vulgar, too condescending for the dignified characters of the called and chosen of God, according to the purposes of His will, from before the foundation of the world! We are called to hold the keys of the mysteries of those things that have been kept hid from the foundation of the world until now. Some have tasted a little of these things, many of which are to be poured down from heaven upon the heads of babes; yea, upon the weak, obscure and despised ones of the earth. Therefore we beseech of you, brethren, that you bear with those who do not feel themselves more worthy than yourselves, while we exhort one another to a reformation with one and all, both old and young, teachers and taught, both high and low, rich and poor, bond and free, male and female; let honesty, and sobriety, and candor, and solemnity, and virtue, and pureness, and meekness, and simplicity crown our heads in every place; and in fine, become as little children, without malice, guile or hypocrisy.

And now, brethren, after your tribulations, if you do these things, and exercise fervent prayer and faith in the sight of God always, "He shall give unto you knowledge by His Holy Spirit, yea by the unspeakable gift of the Holy Ghost, that has not been revealed since the world was until now." (HC 3:295–296; D&C 121:26 shown within quotation marks.)

A mill stone from Haun's Mill, where a group of mobbers killed seventeen Saints and one nonmember, and where thirteen more were wounded at a small Mormon settlement at Jacob Haun's mill in Caldwell County, Missouri. The massacre involved sixty to seventy armed men who rode into the settlement on horseback and attacked the unarmed Saints; the men sought refuge in the blacksmith shop, while the women and children ran into the nearby woods. Stone currently located at Breckenridge, Missouri.

upon the heads of the Latter-day Saints.

34. Behold, there are many called, but few are chosen. And why are they not chosen?

35. Because their hearts are set so much upon the things of this world, and aspire to the honors of men, that they do not learn this one lesson—

36. That the rights of the priesthood are inseparably connected with the powers of heaven, and that the powers of heaven cannot be controlled nor handled only upon the principles of righteousness.

37. That they may be conferred upon us, it is true; but when we undertake to cover our sins, or to gratify our pride, our vain ambition, or to exercise control, or dominion, or compulsion upon the souls of the children of men, in any degree of unrighteousness, behold, the heavens withdraw themselves; the Spirit of the Lord is grieved; and when it is withdrawn, Amen to the Priesthood, or the authority of that man.

38. Behold! ere he is aware, he is left unto himself, to kick against the pricks; to persecute the saints, and to fight against God.

39. We have learned, by sad experience, that it is the nature and disposition of almost all men, as soon as they get a little authority, as they suppose, they will immediately begin to exercise unrighteous dominion.

40. Hence many are called, but few are chosen.

41. No power or influence can or ought to be maintained by virtue of the Priesthood, only by persuasion, by long-suffering, by gentleness, and meekness, and by love unfeigned;

42. By kindness, and pure knowledge, which shall greatly enlarge the soul without hypocrisy, and without guile,

43. Reproving betimes with sharpness, when moved upon by the Holy Ghost, and then showing forth afterwards an increase of love toward him whom thou hast reproved, lest he esteem thee to be his enemy;

44. That he may know that thy faithfulness is stronger than the cords of death;

45. Let thy bowels also be full of charity towards all men, and to the

D&C 121:36—True power, eternal power, is operative only on principles of righteousness. God, in His mercy and benevolence, allows men of the priesthood to act on His behalf for the salvation of mankind, but only within the bounds of the divine nature: faith, virtue, knowledge, temperance, patience, godliness, brotherly kindness, and charity—all aspects and dimensions of righteousness (see 2 Pet. 1:4–7). To exercise the authority of the priesthood "in any degree of unrighteousness" causes the Spirit to withdraw and the priesthood or authority of that man to be suspended.

D&C 121:41–46—Within these six verses is contained a full agenda of principles upon which all righteous priesthood service is defined and exercised: persuasion, long-suffering, gentleness, meekness, genuine love, kindness, pure knowledge (knowledge of a saving and exalting kind), the capacity to follow the prompting of the Holy Ghost without delay ("betimes"), faithfulness, charity, and virtue. These principles underlie the covenant of the priesthood (see D&C 84:33–40).

Divine covenants always involve a promise for the obedient and faithful. In this case the promise is transcendent and unspeakably glorious: that our confidence will grow strong in the presence of God, that the doctrine of the priesthood will infuse our very being, that the Holy Ghost will be our constant companion, that our authority and stewardship will be one of righteousness and truth, and that our dominion within the household of God will be everlasting. All of these celestial blessings constitute, in their totality, the fulfillment of the promise to the righteous priesthood holder: ". . . all that my Father hath shall be given unto him" (D&C 84:38).

A cutaway view of Liberty Jail in Independence, Missouri, where the Prophet Joseph Smith and five others—Hyrum Smith, Sidney Rigdon, Lyman Wight, Alexander McRae, and Caleb Baldwin—were detained from December 1838 to April 1839 on charges of treason. The prisoners were allowed to "escape" while being moved to a facility in another county.

household of faith, and let virtue garnish thy thoughts unceasingly, then shall thy confidence wax strong in the presence of God, and the doctrine of the Priesthood shall distil upon thy soul as the dews from heaven.

46. The Holy Ghost shall be thy constant companion, and thy sceptre an unchanging sceptre of righteousness and truth, and thy dominion shall be an everlasting dominion, and without compulsory means it shall flow unto thee for ever and ever.

SECTION 122

1. The ends of the earth shall enquire after thy name, and fools shall have thee in derision, and hell shall rage against thee,

2. While the pure in heart, and the wise, and the noble, and the virtuous, shall seek counsel, and authority, and blessings constantly from under thy hand,

3. And thy people shall never be turned against thee by the testimony of traitors;

4. And although their influence shall cast thee into trouble, and into bars and walls, thou shalt be had in honor, and but for a small moment and thy voice shall be more terrible in the midst of thine enemies, than the fierce lion, because of thy righteousness; and thy God shall stand by thee for ever and ever.

5. If thou art called to pass through tribulation; if thou art in perils among false brethren; if thou art in perils among robbers; if thou art in perils by land or by sea;

6. If thou art accused with all manner of false accusations; if thine enemies fall upon thee; if they tear thee from the society of thy father and mother and brethren and sisters; and if with a drawn sword thine enemies tear thee from the bosom of thy wife, and of thine offspring, and thine elder son, although but six years of age, shall cling to thy garments, and shall say, My father, my father, why can't you stay with us? O, my father, what are the men going to do with you? and if then he shall be thrust from thee by the sword, and thou be dragged to prison, and thine enemies prowl around thee like wolves for the blood of the lamb;

7. And if thou shouldst be cast into the pit, or into the hands of murderers, and the sentence of death passed upon thee; if thou be cast

Site of the Haun's Mill Massacre in Caldwell County, Missouri, a landmark of suffering in the history of the Church.

Section 122 Background—Given in March 1839 at Liberty Jail in Liberty, Clay County, Missouri (see *HC* 3:300–301). This section is an additional excerpt from the inspired epistle the Prophet wrote dated March 20, 1839 (see Section 121 Background). Few passages of scripture provide a more moving and memorable testimony to the purity and truth of spiritual courage in the face of adversity than Sections 121 and 122. As the Prophet Joseph Smith—falsely accused and cruelly abused by the civil authorities—languished in the squalor and filth of Liberty Jail, he experienced an epiphany of spiritual ascendancy as the Lord opened his vision to greater views of the cause of Zion and buoyed his spirits beyond the suffering of life's tribulations.

D&C 122:1, 4—These words are reminiscent of the initial message delivered to Joseph Smith by the Angel Moroni on the night of September 21, 1823: "He called me by name, and said unto me . . . that my name should be had for good and evil among all nations, kindreds, and tongues, or that it should be both good and evil spoken of among all people" (JS–H 1:33). Now, in Liberty Jail, Joseph hears the words of the Lord to the effect that those who spoke evil of him would face a voice more terrible than that of a lion; furthermore, Joseph's friends would seek "counsel, and authority, and blessings" from his hand.

D&C 122:5–6—Lyman Wight describes the traumatic event in the Prophet's life to which this verse alludes as follows: "About the hour the prisoners were to have been shot on the public square in Far West, they were exhibited in a wagon in the town, all of them having families there, but myself; and it would have broken the heart of any person possessing an ordinary share of humanity, to have seen the separation. The aged father and mother of Joseph Smith were not permitted to see his face, but to reach their hands through the curtains of the wagon, and thus take leave of him. When passing his own house, he was taken out of the wagon and permitted to go into the house, but not without a strong guard, and not permitted to speak with his family but in the presence of his guard and his eldest son, Joseph, about six or eight years old, hanging to the tail of his coat, crying father, is the mob going to kill you? The guard said to him, 'you d—d little brat, go back, you will see your father no more'" (cited in *RPJS*, 240; compare the account by the Prophet Joseph Smith in *HC* 3:193).

D&C 122:7—What do the scriptures reveal concerning the value or blessing of tribulations? One of the major purposes of this life is to prove ourselves that we may be worthy of the greatest measure of salvation. . . .

Calamities mentioned in sacred history have ultimately been blessings. The fall of Adam and Eve brought forth opportunities for God's spirit children to receive bodies and to prove themselves. The great suffering of Christ and his crucifixion were calamities, but man was redeemed from death and hell by that atoning sacrifice. The scattering of Israel throughout the world sprinkled the blood that believes—

into the deep; if the billowing surge conspire against thee; if fierce winds become thine enemy; if the heavens gather blackness, and all the elements combine to hedge up the way; and above all, if the very jaws of hell shall gape open the mouth wide after thee, know thou, my son, that all these things shall give thee experience, and shall be for thy good.

8. The Son of Man hath descended below them all; art thou greater than he?

9. Therefore, hold on thy way, and the Priesthood shall remain with thee, for their bounds are set, they cannot pass. Thy days are known, and thy years shall not be numbered less; therefore, fear not what man can do, for God shall be with you for ever and ever.

SECTION 123

1. And again, we would suggest for your consideration the propriety of all the saints gathering up a knowledge of all the facts, and sufferings and abuses put upon them by the people of this State,

2. And also of all the property and amount of damages which they have sustained, both of character and personal injuries, as well as real property;

3. And also the names of all persons that have had a hand in their oppressions, as far as they can get hold of them and find them out;

4. And perhaps a committee can be appointed to find out these things, and to take statements, and affidavits, and also to gather up the libelous publications that are afloat,

5. And all that are in the magazines, and in the encyclopedias, and all the libelous histories that are published, and are writing, and by whom, and present the whole concatenation of diabolical rascality, and nefarious and murderous impositions that have been practised upon this people,

6. That we may not only publish to all the world, but present them to the heads of government in all their dark and hellish hue, as the last effort which is enjoined on us by our Heavenly Father, before we can fully and completely claim that promise which shall call him forth from his hiding place, and also that the whole nation may be left without excuse before he can

that many nations might partake of the gospel plan. The history of the Nephites is one of trials, calamities, and sufferings, but through it all the experiences gained brought strength and development (*Doxey* 2:372).

D&C 122:7—Clearly, Jesus Christ, the Savior of all mankind, surpassed any suffering that any of us will ever be called on to bear. As a result, He is uniquely positioned to succor us in our afflictions. And also as a result of His suffering, no one will ever be able to stand before the Savior and suggest that too much is being asked. As Elder Orson F. Whiney said, "We will be all the stronger and better when we have swum the flood and stand on the farther shore."

D&C 122:8—We are not alone. What the Lord said by way of comfort to Joseph Smith in his deep hour of tribulation applies likewise to each of us as we honor our covenants and uphold all principles of righteousness: "Thy days are known, and thy years shall not be numbered less; therefore, fear not what man can do, for God shall be with you forever and ever" (verse 9). Faith in God's redeeming power and hope in His everlasting charity and kindness—these are two of the essential keys for transcending adversity. Beyond tribulation beckon the blessings; beyond adversity lies glory.

Section 123 Background—Given in March 1839 at Liberty, Missouri (see *HC* 3:302–303). While he was confined in Liberty Jail on false and spurious charges, the Prophet set forth the duties of the Saints concerning the actions of their persecutors. This material is a further excerpt from the epistle written by the Prophet dated March 25, 1839, from which Sections 121 and 122 were also taken.

D&C 123:1—Having the Saints make a record of these wrongdoings made it possible for records to be kept in heaven and on earth and for appropriate punishment to be meted out. We must bear in mind that the greater part of such punishment is usually reserved for a future day.

D&C 123:6—The law of witnesses applies also to the actions of those who rise up to destroy the work of God. As the cup of evil becomes full, the voices of the victims rise in volume and breadth to confirm the evidence against the perpetrators of malevolence and wickedness. In the due time of the Lord, divine justice will prevail and the guilty will be called on to pay their debt. President Joseph Fielding Smith comments:

> The law of retribution is often slow, but it is sure. The Lord promised to punish his enemies and mete out to them suitable reward for all the evil they had heaped upon his servants. Punishment for sin does not always follow in this mortal life; the greater part of it quite generally is held in reserve for a future day. (*CHMR* 3:203–4.)

send forth the power of his mighty arm.

7. It is an imperious duty that we owe to God, to angels, with whom we shall be brought to stand, and also to ourselves, to our wives and children, who have been made to bow down with grief, sorrow, and care, under the most damning hand of murder, tyranny, and oppression, supported, and urged on, and upheld by the influence of that spirit which hath so strongly riveted the creeds of the fathers, who have inherited lies, upon the hearts of the children, and filled the world with confusion, and has been growing stronger and stronger, and is now the very main-spring of all corruption, and the whole earth groans under the weight of its iniquity.

8. It is an iron yoke, it is a strong band; they are the very handcuffs, and chains, and shackles, and fetters of hell.

9. Therefore, it is an imperious duty that we owe, not only to our own wives and children, but to the widows and fatherless, whose husbands and fathers have been murdered under its iron hand;

10. Which dark and blackening deeds are enough to make hell itself shudder, and to stand aghast and pale, and the hands of the very devil to tremble and palsy.

11. And also it is an imperious duty that we owe to all the rising generation, and to all the pure in heart;

12. (For there are many yet on the earth among all sects, parties, and denominations, who are blinded by the subtle craftiness of men, whereby they lie in wait to deceive, and who are only kept from the truth because they know not where to find it;)

13. Therefore, that we should waste and wear out our lives in bringing to light all the hidden things of darkness, wherein we know them; and they are truly manifest from heaven.

14. These should then be attended to with great earnestness.

15. Let no man count them as small things; for there is much which lieth in futurity, pertaining to the saints, which depends upon these things.

16. You know, brethren, that a very large ship is benefited very much by a very small helm in the time of a storm, by being kept workways with the wind and the waves.

17. Therefore, dearly beloved brethren, let us cheerfully do all things that lie in our power, and then may we stand still with the utmost assurance, to see the salvation of God, and for his arm to be revealed.

D&C 123:12—This oft-cited passage serves to encourage the missionaries of the Lord and galvanize them into concerted action on behalf of the gospel. Their noble calling is to show the world where the truth can be found. In many cases the missionaries, through their spirit of love and righteousness, serve to penetrate the veil of darkness placed against Zion by the enemies of the Church with their lies and deceits.

D&C 123:15, 17—The Prophet counsels his associates not to consider as a small thing the commission to make a record of the sufferings of the Saints. There is divine leverage at work in the assignment—for eventually great benefit will come from obeying the commandment to serve as witnesses of the events associated with the coming forth of the Church, even though it be amidst trial and tribulation. The justice of God will prevail in the Lord's due time. At the appointed hour, the Saints can stand back in silence as the salvation of God is revealed and justice is served.

The expression "see the salvation of God" is reminiscent of the words of Abinadi: "The time shall come when all shall see the salvation of the Lord; when every nation, kindred, tongue, and people shall see eye to eye and shall confess before God that his judgments are just" (Mosiah 16:1).

The Prophet Joseph Smith gave an inspired reference to this phrase in connection with an event that occurred on June 19, 1834, when members of Zion's Camp were protected by divine intervention in the form of a severe thunderstorm at Fishing River in Clay County, Missouri. A mob of nearly 400 men who had vowed "to kill Joe Smith and his army" (HC 2:104) were converging on the Saints' location. Five scouts from the mob visited the Camp of Zion threatening that the Mormons will "see hell before morning" (HC 2:103). Some of the brethren desired to load their weapons and fight, but Joseph tells them, "Stand still and see the salvation of God" (CHFT, 148).

Elder Wilford Woodruff records what appeared in the hitherto cloudless heavens moments after the scouts' departure: "… a small cloud like a black spot appeared in the north west, and it began to unroll itself like a scroll, and in a few minutes the whole heavens were covered with a pall as black as ink" (HC 2:104). The ensuing storm, of unprecedented violence, entirely frustrated the schemes of the scattering mob. Joseph declared: "God is in this storm" (HC 2:104). The surviving mobocrats decided that "when Jehovah fights they would rather be absent" (HC 2:104).

Divine justice was served without delay at Fishing River. In the designs of the Lord, the ultimate action of justice in resolving the vast accumulation of misdeeds heaped on the Latter-day Saints will come at a time deemed appropriate by the Lord. If we meanwhile cheerfully execute our duties with faith and endurance, we may at that time "stand still, with the utmost assurance, to see the salvation of God, and for his arm to be revealed" (verse 17).

SECTION 124

1. Verily, thus saith the Lord unto you, my servant Joseph Smith, I am well pleased with your offering and acknowledgments, which you have made, for unto this end have I raised you up, that I might show forth my wisdom through the weak things of the earth.

2. Your prayers are acceptable before me, and in answer to them I say unto you, that you are now called immediately to make a solemn proclamation of my gospel, and of this Stake which I have planted to be a corner stone of Zion, which shall be polished with the refinement which is after the similitude of a palace.

3. This proclamation shall be made to all the kings of the world—to the four corners thereof—to the honorable President elect, and the high minded Governors of the nation in which you live, and to all the nations of the earth scattered abroad.

4. Let it be written in the spirit of meekness and by the power of the Holy Ghost, which shall be in you at the time of the writing of the same;

5. For it shall be given you by the Holy Ghost to know my will concerning those kings and authorities, even what shall befall them in a time to come.

6. For, behold! I am about to call upon them to give heed to the light and glory of Zion, for the set time has come to favor her.

7. Call ye, therefore, upon them with loud proclamation, and with your testimony, fearing them not, for they are as grass, and all their glory as the flower thereof which soon falleth, that they may be left also without excuse,

8. And that I may visit them in the day of visitation, when I shall unvail the face of my covering, to

---

Heber C. Kimball

Heber C. Kimball was born June 14, 1801, at Sheldon, Franklin County, Vermont. In Kirtland he joined with the Prophet Joseph Smith as a faithful and loyal member of the restored Church. In February 1835 he was called as one of the original Apostles in the Quorum of the Twelve and two years later journeyed to England to proclaim the gospel. Following a period of intense persecution in Missouri, Heber served a second mission in England with Brigham Young as his companion. After the Nauvoo period, he completed the trek west to the Salt Lake Valley and was called in December 1847 as first counselor to Brigham Young in the First Presidency. During the remainder of his life he served with honor in Church and civic functions and was universally respected and admired. He passed away on June 22, 1868, having suffered a fall from a wagon. Heber is mentioned only one time in the Doctrine and Covenants (see D&C 124:129). However, his life and service are indelibly impressed upon the history and annals of the restored Church. Joseph Smith once remarked, concerning the loyalty and devotion of Heber C. Kimball and Brigham Young, that of the original Twelve Apostles chosen in Kirtland, they were the only two who had not "lifted their heel against me" (HC 5:412).

Section 124 Background—Given on January 19, 1841, at Nauvoo, Illinois (see HC 4:274–286). Historian Lyndon W. Cook summarizes the background to this section as follows:

> After the Prophet was freed from his Missouri imprisonment (16 April 1839), immediate plans were made to locate the Saints at another gathering place. Upon viewing properties in Lee County, Iowa, and Hancock County, Illinois, Church land agents purchased thousands of acres of unimproved land in these two counties, and soon Nauvoo (Commerce) became the headquarters of the Church.
>
> With the land problem temporarily solved, Joseph Smith turned his attention to balancing accounts for wrongs suffered in Missouri. With others, the Prophet traveled to Washington, D.C., November 1839–March 1840, where he held audience with President Martin Van Buren, presented Congress with claims against the State of Missouri, and lobbied for redress of Missouri grievances. After achieving little or no success in the East, Joseph Smith returned to Nauvoo, where he began to build up and strengthen the Church. Section 124, the first known revelation since July 1838, was received about four weeks after the governor of Illinois had signed charters for the city of Nauvoo, the University of Nauvoo, the Nauvoo House Association, the Nauvoo Agricultural and Mechanical Association, and the Nauvoo Legion. The revelation had monumental importance to the Prophet and his associates because its fulfillment engaged nearly every waking moment of the Prophet's time until his death. (RPJS, 242–243.)

Section 124 is unique in that it includes the names of no fewer than sixty individuals—more than any other section of the Doctrine and Covenants.

D&C 124:1–4—Surely the Prophet Joseph Smith is one of the greatest examples of how one of the "weak things of the earth" can be sublimated and emerge in the stature of a spiritual giant in keeping with the pattern of strength and endless capacity for good he must have displayed in the premortal realm. The Lord has the wisdom and power to transform His sons and daughters, in their humility and meekness, into mighty forces for salvation (see 1 Cor. 1:27; Ether 12:27; D&C 1:19; 35:13; 133:59). Then as now, the leaders of the Church are under a solemn obligation to proclaim throughout the world the good news of the restored gospel of Jesus Christ and warn the nations that the judgments of God await all who reject that message. How was this proclamation received by national leaders in the highest circles at the time of the Prophet Joseph Smith? They paid no heed.

appoint the portion of the oppressor among hypocrites, where there is gnashing of teeth, if they reject my servants and my testimony which I have revealed unto them.

9. And again, I will visit and soften their hearts, many of them for your good, that ye may find grace in their eyes, that they may come to the light of truth, and the Gentiles to the exaltation or lifting up of Zion.

10. For the day of my visitation cometh speedily, in an hour when ye think not of, and where shall be the safety of my people, and refuge for those who shall be left of them?

11. Awake! O kings of the earth! Come ye, O come ye, with your gold and your silver, to the help of my people, to the house of the daughters of Zion.

12. And again, verily I say unto you, Let my servant Robert B. Thompson help you to write this proclamation, for I am well pleased with him, and that he should be with you;

13. Let him, therefore, hearken to your counsel, and I will bless him with a multiplicity of blessings; let him be faithful and true in all things from henceforth, and he shall be great in mine eyes;

14. But let him remember that his stewardship will I require at his hands.

15. And again, verily I say unto you, Blessed is my servant Hyrum Smith, for I, the Lord, love him because of the integrity of his heart, and because he loveth that which is right before me, saith the Lord.

16. Again let my servant John C. Bennett, help you in your labor in sending my word to the kings and people of the earth, and stand by you, even you my servant Joseph Smith, in the hour of affliction, and his reward shall not fail if he receive counsel.

17. And for his love he shall be great, for he shall be mine if he do this, saith the Lord. I have seen the work which he hath done, which I accept, if he continue, and will crown him with blessings and great glory.

18. And again, I say unto you, that it is my will that my servant Lyman Wight should continue in preaching for Zion, in the spirit of meekness, confessing me before the world, and I will bear him up as on eagles' wings, and he shall beget glory and honor to himself and unto my name.

19. That when he shall finish his work, that I may receive him unto myself, even as I did my servant David Patten, who is with me at this time, and also my servant Edward Partridge, and also my aged servant Joseph Smith, sen., who sitteth with Abraham at his right hand, and blessed and holy is he, for he is mine.

20. And again, verily I say unto you, my servant George Miller is without guile; he may be trusted because of the integrity of his heart; and for the love which he has to my testimony I, the Lord, love him;

21. I therefore say unto you, I seal upon his head the office of a bishopric, like unto my servant Edward Partridge, that he may receive the consecrations of mine house, that he may administer blessings upon the heads of the poor of my people, saith the Lord. Let no man despise my servant George, for he shall honor me.

22. Let my servant George, and my servant Lyman, and my servant John Snider, and others, build a house unto my name, such an one as my servant Joseph shall show unto

D&C 124:15, 19—The work of the Restoration is a divine enterprise involving forces for good on both sides of the veil—righteous leadership on the earth and eternal guidance from the heavens. The Lord smiles down lovingly on Hyrum, the Prophet's brother, because of his integrity and because "he loveth that which is right before me." President Heber J. Grant said: "No mortal man who ever lived in this Church desired more to do good than did Hyrum Smith, the patriarch. I have it from the lips of my own sainted mother, that of all the men she was acquainted with in her girlhood days in Nauvoo, she admired Hyrum Smith most for his absolute integrity and devotion to God, and his loyalty to the prophet of God" (CR, Oct. 1920, 84).

Two different views of the Joseph Smith Homestead in Nauvoo, the home where the Prophet Joseph, Emma, and their children lived during the tumultuous Nauvoo period of the Church. The Prophet moved to the log house, located on the east shores of the Mississippi River, after he escaped the severe persecution in Missouri in April 1839. The Homestead served as Church headquarters for two years; Joseph received the doctrine of baptism for the dead here, as well as instructions to build the Nauvoo Temple. The Prophet enlarged the home in 1840, three years before he, Emma, and their family moved across the street to the Mansion House (the place where Joseph and Hyrum were brought and their bodies viewed after the martyrdom). The Joseph Smith Family Cemetery is located adjacent to the Homestead. The Community of Christ (formerly the RLDS Church) now owns the Homestead.

them, upon the place which he shall show unto them also.

23. And it shall be for a house for boarding, a house that strangers may come from afar to lodge therein: therefore let it be a good house, worthy of all acceptation, that the weary traveler may find health and safety while he shall contemplate the word of the Lord; and the corner stone I have appointed for Zion.

24. This house shall be a healthful habitation if it be built unto my name, and if the governor which shall be appointed unto it shall not suffer any pollution to come upon it. It shall be holy, or the Lord your God will not dwell therein.

25. And again, verily I say unto you, Let all my saints come from afar;

26. And send ye swift messengers, yea, chosen messengers, and say unto them; come ye, with all your gold, and your silver, and your precious stones, and with all your antiquities; and with all who have knowledge of antiquities, that will come, may come, and bring the box tree, and the fir tree, and the pine tree, together with all the precious trees of the earth;

27. And with iron, with copper, and with brass, and with zinc, and with all your precious things of the earth, and build a house to my name, for the Most High to dwell therein;

28. For there is not a place found on earth that he may come to and restore again that which was lost unto you, or which he hath taken away, even the fulness of the Priesthood;

29. For a baptismal font there is not upon the earth, that they, my saints, may be baptized for those who are dead;

30. For this ordinance belongeth to my house, and cannot be acceptable to me, only in the days of your poverty, wherein ye are not able to build a house unto me.

31. But I command you, all ye my saints, to build a house unto me; and I grant unto you a sufficient time to build a house unto me; and during this time your baptisms shall be acceptable unto me.

32. But behold, at the end of this appointment, your baptisms for your dead shall not be acceptable unto me; and if you do not these things at the end of the appointment, ye shall be rejected as a church, with your dead, saith the Lord your God.

33. For verily I say unto you, that after you have had sufficient time to build a house to me, wherein the ordinance of baptizing for the dead belongeth, and for which the same was instituted from before the foundation of the world, your baptisms for your dead cannot be acceptable unto me,

34. For therein are the keys of the holy priesthood ordained, that you may receive honor and glory.

35. And after this time, your baptisms for the dead, by those who are scattered abroad, are not acceptable unto me, saith the Lord;

36. For it is ordained that in Zion, and in her stakes, and in Jerusalem, those places which I have appointed for refuge, shall be the places for your baptisms for your dead.

37. And again, verily I say unto

D&C 124:23—The Lord is ever aware of the ensign raised by the Church and kingdom of God on earth. Visitors and inquirers would come from all sectors of the globe to learn more of the restored gospel, as Isaiah foresaw (see Isa. 2:2–3). The "Nauvoo House," as it was to be called (see verse 60), was intended to become a platform for introducing the principles of salvation and exaltation to the honest in heart—just as the Church's modern array of information centers do today. The house was never finished—both because of the intense persecution and because of the need to devote all energies to the building of the temple.

D&C 124:27–28—The blessings of the "fulness of the priesthood" are essential for the faithful to return to the presence of God:

> And this greater priesthood administereth the gospel and holdeth the key of the mysteries of the kingdom, even the key of the knowledge of God.
>
> Therefore, in the ordinances thereof, the power of godliness is manifest.
>
> And without the ordinances thereof, and the authority of the priesthood, the power of godliness is not manifest unto men in the flesh;
>
> For without this no man can see the face of God, even the Father, and live. (D&C 84:19–22.)

The fullness of priesthood ordinances can be received only in the temples of the Lord.

D&C 124:29–30—The Lord gives a commission of joy: to build again a House of the Lord. With this order to build the Nauvoo Temple, the Saints were commissioned to prepare themselves to receive the unspeakable endowment of truth and glory attached to the "ordinance of my holy house" (D&C 124:39). In an epistle to the Twelve in October 1840, the Prophet Joseph Smith had previously explained the ordinance of baptism for the dead:

> I presume the doctrine of "baptism for the dead" has ere this reached your ears [the Twelve in England], and may have raised some inquiries in your minds respecting the same. . . .
>
> I first mentioned the doctrine in public when preaching the funeral sermon of Brother Seymour Brunson; and have since then given general instructions in the Church on the subject. The Saints have the privilege of being baptized for those of their relatives who are dead, whom they believe would have embraced the Gospel, if they had been privileged with hearing it, and who have received the Gospel in the spirit, through the instrumentality of those who have been commissioned to preach to them while in prison.
>
> Without enlarging on the subject, you will undoubtedly see its consistency and reasonableness; and it presents the Gospel of Christ in probably a more enlarged scale than some have imagined it. (HC 4:231.)

you, How shall your washings be acceptable unto me, except ye perform them in a house which you have built to my name?

38. For, for this cause I commanded Moses that he should build a tabernacle, that they should bear it with them in the wilderness, and to build a house in the land of promise, that those ordinances might be revealed which had been hid from before the world was;

39. Therefore, verily I say unto you, that your anointings, and your washings, and your baptisms for the dead, and your solemn assemblies, and your memorials for your sacrifices, by the sons of Levi, and for your oracles in your most holy places, wherein you receive conversations, and your statutes and judgments, for the beginning of the revelations and foundation of Zion, and for the glory, honor, and endowment of all her municipals, are ordained by the ordinance of my holy house which my people are always commanded to build unto my holy name.

40. And verily I say unto you, Let this house be built unto my name, that I may reveal mine ordinances therein, unto my people;

41. For I deign to reveal unto my church, things which have been kept hid from before the foundation of the world, things that pertain to the dispensation of the fulness of times;

42. And I will show unto my servant Joseph all things pertaining to this house, and the priesthood thereof, and the place whereon it shall be built;

43. And ye shall build it on the place where you have contemplated building it, for that is the spot which I have chosen for you to build it;

44. If ye labor with all your might, I will consecrate that spot that it shall be made holy;

45. And if my people will hearken unto my voice, and unto the voice of my servants whom I have appointed to lead my people, behold, verily I say unto you, they shall not be moved out of their place.

46. But if they will not hearken to my voice, nor unto the voice of these men whom I have appointed, they shall not be blest, because they pollute mine holy grounds, and mine holy ordinances, and charters, and my holy words which I give unto them.

47. And it shall come to pass, That if you build a house unto my name, and do not do the things that I say, I will not perform the oath which I make unto you, neither fulfil the promises which ye expect at my hands, saith the Lord;

48. For instead of blessings, ye, by your own works, bring cursings, wrath, indignation, and judgments upon your own heads, by your follies, and by all your abominations, which you practise before me, saith the Lord.

49. Verily, verily I say unto you, That when I give a commandment to any of the sons of men, to do a work unto my name, and those sons of men go with all their might, and with

D&C 124:40—In these grand words is epitomized the design of God for the gathering of the Saints—to congregate them around holy and dedicated places where the higher truths and ordinances of the gospel of salvation and exaltation may be made available to the righteous and faithful of the fold of Jesus Christ. The Prophet Joseph Smith explained this principle in a Sunday sermon given on June 11, 1843:

The main object [of the gathering] was to build unto the Lord a house whereby He could reveal unto His people the ordinances of His house and the glories of His kingdom, and teach the people the way of salvation; for there are certain ordinances and principles that, when they are taught and practiced, must be done in a place or house built for that purpose.

It was the design of the councils of heaven before the world was, that the principles and laws of the priesthood should be predicated upon the gathering of the people in every age of the world. Jesus did everything to gather the people, and they would not be gathered, and He therefore poured out curses upon them. Ordinances instituted in the heavens before the foundation of the world, in the priesthood, for the salvation of men, are not to be altered or changed. All must be saved on the same principles.

It is for the same purpose that God gathers together His people in the last days, to build unto the Lord a house to prepare them for the ordinances and endowments, washings and anointings, etc. One of the ordinances of the house of the Lord is baptism for the dead. God decreed before the foundation of the world that that ordinance should be administered in a font prepared for that purpose in the house of the Lord. (HC 5:423–424.)

The cooking area behind the Joseph Smith Homestead in Nauvoo.

all they have, to perform that work, and cease not their diligence, and their enemies come upon them, and hinder them from performing that work, behold, it behooveth me to require that work no more at the hands of those sons of men, but to accept of their offerings.

50. And the iniquity and transgression of my holy laws and commandments, I will visit upon the heads of those who hindered my work, unto the third and fourth generation, so long as they repent not, and hate me, saith the Lord God.

51. Therefore for this cause have I accepted the offerings of those whom I commanded to build up a city and a house unto my name, in Jackson county, Missouri, and were hindered by their enemies, saith the Lord your God:

52. And I will answer judgment, wrath, and indignation, wailing, and anguish, and gnashing of teeth upon their heads, unto the third and fourth generation, so long as they repent not and hate me, saith the Lord your God.

53. And this I make an example unto you, for your consolation concerning all those who have been commanded to do a work, and have been hindered by the hands of their enemies, and by oppression, saith the Lord your God;

54. For I am the Lord your God, and will save all those of your brethren who have been pure in heart, and have been slain in the land of Missouri, saith the Lord.

55. And again, verily I say unto you, I command you again to build a house to my name, even in this place, that you may prove yourselves unto me that ye are faithful in all things whatsoever I command you, that I may bless you, and crown you with honor, immortality, and eternal life.

56. And now I say unto you, as pertaining to my boarding house which I have commanded you to build for the boarding of strangers, let it be built unto my name, and let my name be named upon it, and let my servant Joseph, and his house have place therein, from generation to generation;

57. For this anointing have I put upon his head, that his blessing shall also be put upon the head of his posterity after him,

58. And as I said unto Abraham concerning the kindreds of the earth, even so I say unto my servant Joseph: In thee and in thy seed shall the kindred of the earth be blessed.

59. Therefore, let my servant Joseph and his seed after him have place in that house, from generation to generation, for ever and ever, saith the Lord,

60. And let the name of that house be called Nauvoo house, and let it be a delightful habitation for man, and a resting place for the weary traveler, that he may contemplate the glory of Zion, and the glory of this, the corner-stone thereof;

61. That he may receive also the counsel from those whom I have set to be as plants of renown, and as watchmen upon her walls.

62. Behold, verily I say unto you, let my servant George Miller, and

D&C 124:49, 53—As the Saints were forced from Missouri, a comforting revelation from the Lord taught an eternal truth: All that the Lord expects of us is to do our very best. He will accept our offering as if we had completed the task even though prevented by the evil designs of men. President Charles W. Penrose clarified this doctrine as follows: "If God gives a commandment, and we do not obey it, why he revokes it, and he revokes the blessings. If he gives us a commandment to do certain things, and we find ourselves unable to do them, either by restricted laws or any other obstacles in the way of physical force, the Lord requires them no more but accepts our offering, and he will visit his wrath and indignation upon those who prevent his people from accomplishing that which he required at their hands" (CR, April 1924, 13–14).

D&C 124:55— For a brief but shining moment, the work of the House of God in Nauvoo proved to be the consummation of the Saints' labor of love in obeying the voice of the Lord to build unto Him a house worthy of all acceptation. Elder James E. Talmage gives the chronology:

The cornerstones of the Nauvoo Temple were laid 6 April 1841, and the capstone was placed in position 24 May 1845; each event was celebrated by a solemn assembly and sacred service. Though it was evident that the people would be forced to flee again, and though they knew that the temple would have to be abandoned soon after completion, they labored with might and diligence to finish and properly furnish the structure. It was dedicated 30 April 1846, though certain portions, such as the baptistry, had been previously dedicated and used in ordinance work. Many of the Saints received their blessings and holy endowments in the Nauvoo Temple, though, even before the completion of the building, the exodus of the people had begun. The temple was abandoned by those who in poverty and by sacrifice had reared it. In November 1848 it became a prey to incendiary flames, and in May 1850 a tornado demolished what remained of the blackened walls. ("History of Temples," official LDS Website, www.lds.org.)

On June 27, 2002, the rebuilt Nauvoo Temple was dedicated as a memorial to the mission of Joseph Smith, the Prophet of the Restoration, and as a glorious monument in praise to the Lord Jesus Christ, from whom all blessings flow.

D&C 124:60—The Lord gives directions for erecting a boarding house in Nauvoo, including the raising of capital through stockholdings assigned to specified brethren, the rights to which would be perpetuated through the coming generations. As mentioned earlier, the project could not be completed because of rising persecution and the urgency of focusing on the building of the temple.

my servant Lyman Wight, and my servant John Snider, and my servant Peter Haws, organize themselves, and appoint one of them to be a president over their quorum for the purpose of building that house.

63. And they shall form a constitution whereby they may receive stock for the building of that house.

64. And they shall not receive less than fifty dollars for a share of stock in that house, and they shall be permitted to receive fifteen thousand dollars from any one man for stock in that house;

65. But they shall not be permitted to receive over fifteen thousand dollars stock from any one man;

66. And they shall not be permitted to receive under fifty dollars for a share of stock from any one man in that house;

67. And they shall not be permitted to receive any man, as a stockholder in this house, except the same shall pay his stock into their hands at the time he receives stock;

68. And in proportion to the amount of stock he pays into their hands, he shall receive stock in that house; but if he pays nothing into their hands, he shall not receive any stock in that house.

69. And if any pay stock into their hands, it shall be for stock in that house, for himself and for his generation after him, from generation to generation, so long as he and his heirs shall hold that stock, and do not sell or convey the stock away out of their hands by their own free will and act, if you will do my will, saith the Lord your God.

70. And again, verily I say unto you, if my servant George Miller, and my servant Lyman Wight, and my servant John Snider, and my servant Peter Haws, receive any stock into their hands, in moneys, or in properties wherein they receive the real value of moneys, they shall not appropriate any portion of that stock to any other purpose, only in that house;

71. And if they do appropriate any portion of that stock any where else, only in that house, without the consent of the stockholder, and do not repay fourfold for the stock which they appropriate any where else, only in that house, they shall be accursed, and shall be moved out of their place, saith the Lord God, for I, the Lord, am God, and cannot be mocked in any of these things.

72. Verily I say unto you, Let my servant Joseph pay stock into their hands for the building of that house, as seemeth him good; but my servant Joseph cannot pay over fifteen thousand dollars stock in that house, nor under fifty dollars; neither can any other man, saith the Lord.

73. And there are others also who wish to know my will concerning them, for they have asked it at my hands.

74. Therefore I say unto you concerning my servant Vinson Knight, if he will do my will, let him put stock into that house for himself, and for his generation after him, from generation to generation.

75. And let him lift up his voice long and loud, in the midst of the people, to plead the cause of the poor and the needy, and let him not fail, neither let his heart faint, and I will accept of his offerings, for they shall not be unto me as the offerings of Cain, for he shall be mine, saith the Lord.

76. Let his family rejoice and turn away their hearts from affliction, for I have chosen him and anointed him, and he shall be honored in the midst of his house, for I will forgive all his sins, saith the Lord. Amen.

77. Verily I say unto you, let my servant Hyrum put stock into that house as seemeth him good, for himself and his generation after him, from generation to generation.

78. Let my servant Isaac Galland put stock into that house, for I, the Lord, love him for the work he hath done, and will forgive all his sins; therefore, let him be remembered for

The rebuilt Nauvoo Temple, constructed under the direction of President Gordon B. Hinckley. The original Nauvoo Temple—which was built for a total cost of $750,00—was 128 feet long, 88 feet wide, and 65 feet high, with a spire that rose 165 feet from the ground.

The exterior of the original Nauvoo Temple featured both sunstones and starstones, which the Prophet Joseph Smith saw in vision before the temple was built. This is one of the thirty original sunstones, now on display in Nauvoo.

an interest in that house from generation to generation.

79. Let my servant Isaac Galland be appointed among you, and be ordained by my servant William Marks, and be blessed of him, to go with my servant Hyrum, to accomplish the work that my servant Joseph shall point out to them, and they shall be greatly blessed.

80. Let my servant William Marks pay stock into that house, as it seemeth him good, for himself and his generation, from generation to generation.

81. Let my servant Henry G. Sherwood pay stock into that house, as seemeth him good, for himself and his seed after him, from generation to generation.

82. Let my servant William Law pay stock into that house, for himself and his seed after him, from generation to generation.

83. If he will do my will let him not take his family unto the eastern lands, even unto Kirtland; nevertheless, I, the Lord, will build up Kirtland, but I, the Lord, have a scourge prepared for the inhabitants thereof.

84. And with my servant Almon Babbitt, there are many things with which I am not well pleased; behold, he aspireth to establish his counsel instead of the counsel which I have ordained, even that of the Presidency of my church, and he setteth up a golden calf for the worship of my people.

85. Let no man go from this place who has come here essaying to keep my commandments.

86. If they live here let them live unto me; and if they die let them die unto me; for they shall rest from all their labors here, and shall continue their works.

87. Therefore let my servant William put his trust in me, and cease to fear concerning his family, because of the sickness of the land. If ye love me, keep my commandments, and the sickness of the land shall redound to your glory.

88. Let my servant William go and proclaim my everlasting gospel with a loud voice, and with great joy, as he shall be moved upon by my Spirit, unto the inhabitants of Warsaw, and also unto the inhabitants of Carthage, and also unto the inhabitants of Burlington, and also unto the inhabitants of Madison, and await patiently and diligently for further instructions at my general conference, saith the Lord.

89. If he will do my will let him from henceforth hearken to the counsel of my servant Joseph, and with his interest support the cause of the poor and publish the new translation of my holy word unto the inhabitants of the earth;

90. And if he will do this, I will bless him with a multiplicity of blessings, that he shall not be forsaken, nor his seed be found begging bread.

91. And again, verily I say unto you, Let my servant William be appointed, ordained, and anointed, as a counselor unto my servant Joseph, in the room of my servant Hyrum, that my servant Hyrum may take the office of Priesthood and Patriarch, which was appointed unto him by his father, by blessing and also by right,

92. That from henceforth he shall hold the keys of the patriarchal blessings upon the heads of all my people,

93. That whoever he blesses shall be blessed, and whoever he curses shall be cursed; that whatsoever he

D&C 124:84—Almon Babbitt tried to circumvent the authority of the Prophet and tried to persuade the Saints to leave Nauvoo. As this verse indicates, he was blinded by greed: his chief interest was making money. As Heber C. Kimball pointed out, Babbitt pocketed money that was supposed to be used for facilitating the gathering of the Saints.

D&C 124:87—The William in this verse is William Law, a member of the First Presidency who eventually became one of the most bitter enemies of the Church. He later tried to start his own church with a group of other apostates.

D&C 124:91, 94—Hyrum was honored with two grand callings—to be a patriarch (succeeding his father, Joseph Smith Sr.) and to be a prophet, seer, and revelator in conjunction with his brother Joseph. President Joseph Fielding Smith comments on this dual responsibility:

> Joseph Smith, Sr., was succeeded in this office [Patriarch to the Church] by his faithful son, Hyrum, who was ordained to this position, January 24, 1841. . . .
>
> This blessing pertains to the office and calling of the man who holds the keys of the Patriarchal Priesthood. The Lord conferred upon Hyrum Smith, however, another important and special honor, in making him as well as Joseph Smith a holder of the keys of authority in this Dispensation of the Fulness of Times. . . .
>
> This was a special blessing given to Hyrum Smith, and in accepting it he took the place of Oliver Cowdery, upon whom these keys had previously been bestowed. . . .
>
> . . . the Lord opened to the vision of Hyrum Smith and showed to him those things which were necessary to qualify him for this exalted position, and upon him were conferred by Joseph Smith all the keys and authorities by which he, Hyrum Smith, was able to act in concert with his younger brother as a prophet, seer and revelator, and president of the Church, "as well as my servant Joseph" [D&C 124:94]. (*Utah Genealogical and Historical Magazine,* April 1932, 5:51–52.)

The Nauvoo House, intended to be a more luxurious home than the Joseph Smith Homestead, was not completed at the time the Prophet Joseph Smith was martyred. The widowed Emma Smith married Lewis Bidamon in December 1847, and he finished building the Nauvoo House for his wife. He also built the stables shown here.

shall bind on earth shall be bound in heaven; and whatsoever he shall loose on earth shall be loosed in heaven;

94. And from this time forth I appoint unto him that he may be a prophet, and a seer, and a revelator unto my church, as well as my servant Joseph,

95. That he may act in concert also with my servant Joseph, and that he shall receive counsel from my servant Joseph, who shall show unto him the keys whereby he may ask and receive, and be crowned with the same blessing, and glory, and honor, and Priesthood, and gifts of the Priesthood that once were put upon him that was my servant Oliver Cowdery;

96. That my servant Hyrum may bear record of the things which I shall show unto him, that his name may be had in honorable remembrance from generation to generation, for ever and ever.

97. Let my servant William Law also receive the keys by which he may ask and receive blessings; let him be humble before me, and be without guile, and he shall receive of my Spirit, even the Comforter, which shall manifest unto him the truth of all things, and shall give him in the very hour, what he shall say.

98. And these signs shall follow him; he shall heal the sick, he shall cast out devils, and shall be delivered from those who would administer unto him deadly poison;

99. And he shall be led in paths where the poisonous serpent cannot lay hold upon his heel, and he shall mount up in the imagination of his thoughts as upon eagles' wings;

100. And what if I will that he should raise the dead, let him not withhold his voice.

101. Therefore, let my servant William cry aloud and spare not, with joy and rejoicing, and with hosannas to him that sitteth upon the throne for ever and ever, saith the Lord your God.

102. Behold, I say unto you, I have a mission in store for my servant William, and my servant Hyrum, and for them alone; and let my servant Joseph tarry at home, for he is needed: the remainder I will show unto you hereafter. Even so. Amen.

103. And again, verily I say unto you, if my servant Sidney will serve me and be counselor unto my servant Joseph, let him arise and come up and stand in the office of his calling, and humble himself before me;

104. And if he will offer unto me an acceptable offering, and acknowledgments, and remain with my people, behold, I, the Lord your God, will heal him that he shall be healed; and he shall lift up his voice again on the mountains, and be a spokesman before my face.

105. Let him come and locate his family in the neighborhood in which my servant Joseph resides,

106. And in all his journeyings let him lift up his voice as with the sound of a trump, and warn the inhabitants of the earth to flee the wrath to come;

107. Let him assist my servant Joseph; and also let my servant William Law assist my servant Joseph, in making a solemn proclamation unto the kings of the earth, even as I have before said unto you.

108. If my servant Sidney will do my will, let him not remove his family unto the eastern lands, but

D&C 124:102—The lives of these two brethren provide compelling case studies of contrasting substance and outcome. Hyrum was one of the grand exemplars of boundless charity and enduring discipleship in the restored Church. In August of 1842, Hyrum would be among a group of family members and close associates who helped rescue the maligned Prophet from his enemies, causing Joseph to declare: "There was Brother Hyrum who next took me by the hand—a natural brother. Thought I to myself, Brother Hyrum, what a faithful heart you have got! Oh may the Eternal Jehovah crown eternal blessings upon your head, as a reward for the care you have had for my soul! O how many are the sorrows we have shared together; and again we find ourselves shackled with the unrelenting hand of oppression. Hyrum, thy name shall be written in the book of the law of the Lord, for those who come after thee to look upon, that they may pattern after thy works" (*HC* 5:107–108).

By contrast, William Law was to perish spiritually through deceit and contempt for his covenants. William fell from his position within a short period of time and became a ruthless conspirator bent on destroying the Church and the Prophet. His anti-Mormon publication, the *Nauvoo Expositor*—together with the foment caused when the city fathers took action to suppress it—resulted in a sequence of events leading directly to the martyrdom of Joseph and Hyrum at Carthage on June 27, 1844.

D&C 124:103—The Lord knew the heart and mind of His servant Sidney Rigdon. Sidney had witnessed firsthand the unfolding of the Restoration in the latter days. He had received an abundance of heavenly blessings to confirm the grandeur and glory of the cause of Zion. But his spiritual fiber was unwinding as he yielded to the enticements of pride and conceit.

> . . . he was no longer the great leader in the Church that he had been. Joseph Smith rejected him as a counselor because of his unfaithfulness. The Prophet later remarked that if Sidney led the Church, he would lead the Church to destruction in less than five years. After the death of the Prophet Joseph Smith, Sidney returned to Nauvoo from Pittsburgh, where he had gone in spite of the Lord's counsel (D&C 124:108). Sidney claimed he should be the guardian for the Church. When he secretly began plotting against the Twelve, after originally agreeing to support them, he was excommunicated. These events show that Sidney Rigdon chose to allow his trials and tribulations to make him a bitter man, finally losing his testimony, faith, and honor.
>
> If we say that suffering and trials were the ruin of Sidney Rigdon, we could say that tribulations were the making of Joseph Smith. (*HO*, 279.)

let him change their habitation, even as I have said.

109. Behold, it is not my will that he shall seek to find safety and refuge out of the city which I have appointed unto you, even the city of Nauvoo.

110. Verily I say unto you, even now, if he will hearken unto my voice, it shall be well with him. Even so. Amen.

111. And again, verily I say unto you, Let my servant Amos Davies pay stock into the hands of those whom I have appointed to build a house for boarding, even the Nauvoo House;

112. This let him do if he will have an interest, and let him hearken unto the counsel of my servant Joseph, and labor with his own hands that he may obtain the confidence of men;

113. And when he shall prove himself faithful in all things that shall be entrusted unto his care, yea, even a few things, he shall be made ruler over many;

114. Let him therefore abase himself that he may be exalted. Even so. Amen.

115. And again, verily I say unto you, if my servant Robert D. Foster will obey my voice, let him build a house for my servant Joseph, according to the contract which he has made with him, as the door shall be open to him from time to time;

116. And let him repent of all his folly, and clothe himself with charity, and cease to do evil, and lay aside all his hard speeches;

117. And pay stock also into the hands of the quorum of the Nauvoo House, for himself and for his generation after him, from generation to generation.

118. And hearken unto the counsel of my servants Joseph, and Hyrum, and William Law, and unto the authorities which I have called to lay the foundation of Zion, and it shall be well with him for ever and ever. Even so. Amen.

119. And again, verily I say unto you, Let no man pay stock to the quorum of the Nauvoo House, unless he shall be a believer in the Book of Mormon, and the revelations I have given unto you, saith the Lord your God;

120. For that which is more or less than this cometh of evil, and shall be attended with cursings and not blessings, saith the Lord your God. Even so. Amen.

121. And again, verily I say unto you, Let the quorum of the Nauvoo House have a just recompense of wages for all their labors which they do in building the Nauvoo House, and let their wages be as shall be agreed among themselves, as pertaining to the price thereof;

122. And let every man who pays stock bear his proportion of their wages, if it must needs be, for their support, saith the Lord; otherwise, their labors shall be accounted unto them for stock in that house. Even so. Amen.

123. Verily I say unto you, I now give unto you the officers belonging to my Priesthood, that ye may hold the keys thereof, even the Priesthood which is after the order of Melchizedek, which is after the order of mine Only Begotten Son.

124. First, I give unto you Hyrum Smith to be a patriarch unto you, to hold the sealing blessings of my church, even the Holy Spirit of promise, whereby ye are sealed up

D&C 124:116—The "folly" and "evil" in this verse refer to the fact that Robert D. Foster had Joseph Smith indicted on false charges and conspired to bring about the Prophet's death.

D&C 124:119—The directives given to various individuals concerning their participation in the construction enterprise at Nauvoo make clear that their qualification for being part of this central group was conditioned on a *spiritual* measure—whether they had a testimony of the Book of Mormon and the revelations given (in other words, the Doctrine and Covenants). Their business acumen, their resources, their commitment to the project—all these factors played a role. But the core ingredient for being part of the group was their *testimony*. Then as now, it is one's spiritual core, one's anchor in the truths of the word of God, that qualify him for the work. The Nauvoo House referred to in this verse was to be used as a hotel.

D&C 124:124—According to John Taylor, the patriarch is mentioned first here, but the patriarch is under the prophet. The president of the Church presides over all patriarchs, presidents, and councils of the Church (see D&C 107:91).

Being Accepted of the Lord

What does it mean to be accepted of the Lord? We remember that the Lord commanded us to be perfect (see 3 Ne. 12:48). Can we be accepted of the Lord even while we struggle up the long path towards perfection? Or must we wait for that acceptance until we arrive at the designated destination?

Many people feel frustration and failure because they don't understand they can be accepted of the Lord in their imperfect state. The reason for their frustration is that they have not yet accomplished or performed their tasks of life consistent with the performance level that they know is attainable.

The Lord has revealed that His acceptance of the work of imperfect mortals is not based on perfect performance only, but also on faithful and diligent efforts towards the accomplishment of any God-given task (see D&C 124:49). With this understanding, then, we need not be confused. Anyone who is accepted of the Lord is not a failure. He is, as Moroni taught, "perfect in Christ" (Moroni 10:32–33) (*STDC* 2:316).

unto the day of redemption, that ye may not fall notwithstanding the hour of temptation that may come upon you.

125. I give unto you my servant Joseph to be a presiding elder over all my church, to be a translator, a revelator, a seer and prophet.

126. I give unto him for counselors my servant Sidney Rigdon and my servant William Law, that these may constitute a quorum and First Presidency, to receive the oracles for the whole church.

127. I give unto you my servant Brigham Young, to be a president over the Twelve traveling Council,

128. Which Twelve hold the keys to open up the authority of my kingdom upon the four corners of the earth, and after that to send my word to every creature.

129. They are—Heber C. Kimball, Parley P. Pratt, Orson Pratt, Orson Hyde, William Smith, John Taylor, John E. Page, Wilford Woodruff, Willard Richards, George A. Smith;

130. David Patten I have taken unto myself; behold, his Priesthood no man taketh from him; but, verily I say unto you, another may be appointed unto the same calling.

131. And again, I say unto you, I give unto you a High Council, for the corner stone of Zion;

132. Viz., Samuel Bent, H. G. Sherwood, George W. Harris, Charles C. Rich, Thomas Grover, Newel Knight, David Dort, Dunbar Wilson; (Seymour Brunson I have taken unto myself; no man taketh his priesthood, but another may be appointed unto the same Priesthood in his stead; and verily I say unto you, let my servant Aaron Johnson be ordained unto this calling in his stead;) David Fullmer, Alpheus Cutler, William Huntington.

133. And again, I give unto you Don C. Smith, to be a president over a quorum of High Priests;

134. Which ordinance is instituted for the purpose of qualifying those who shall be appointed standing presidents or servants over different Stakes scattered abroad,

135. And they may travel also if they choose, but rather be ordained for standing presidents, this is the office of their calling, saith the Lord your God.

136. I give unto him Amasa Lyman, and Noah Packard, for counselors, that they may preside over the quorum of High Priests of my church, saith the Lord.

137. And again, I say unto you, I give unto you John A. Hicks, Samuel Williams, and Jesse Baker, which Priesthood is to preside over the quorum of elders, which quorum is instituted for standing ministers, nevertheless they may travel, yet they are ordained to be standing ministers to my church, saith the Lord.

138. And again, I give unto you Joseph Young, Josiah Butterfield, Daniel Miles, Henry Herriman, Zera Pulsipher, Levi Hancock, James Foster, to preside over the quorum of seventies,

139. Which quorum is instituted for traveling elders to bear record of my name in all the world, wherever the traveling High Council, mine apostles, shall send them to prepare a way before my face.

140. The difference between this quorum and the quorum of elders is, that one is to travel continually, and the other is to preside over the

D&C 124:126—Through the First Presidency is revealed the will of God for His Church and Kingdom. Said the Prophet Joseph Smith: "There are certain ordinances which belong to the Priesthood, from which flow certain results; and the Presidents or Presidency are over the Church; and revelations of the mind and will of God to the Church are to come through the Presidency" (HC 2:477).

While there are three members of the First Presidency, there is only one "presiding President" for the Church (see D&C 43:1–5). John A. Widtsoe provides this confirming information:

> The question as to whether the Counselors held the same power as the President was soon debated among the people. What could the counselors do without direct appointment from the President? These questions were answered in a meeting on January 26, 1836. The prophet there said, "The Twelve are not subject to any other than the First Presidency . . . and where I am not, there is no First Presidency over the Twelve." (JS, 303.)

Do the counselors in the First Presidency need to be Apostles? President Joseph F. Smith said: "It does not follow and never has followed that the members of the first presidency of the Church are necessarily to be ordained apostles. They hold by virtue of their rights as presidents of the Church all the keys and all the authority that pertains to the Melchisedek Priesthood. . ." (CR, April 1913, 4).

D&C 124:127–128—Under the direction of the First Presidency, the Twelve have full authority to perform any and all ordinances in the Church. The Twelve are "special witnesses of the name of Christ in all the world . . . And they form a quorum, equal in authority and power" to the First Presidency (D&C 107:23–24); "ordain and set in order all the other officers of the Church" (D&C 107:58); hold "the keys to open up the authority of my [God's] kingdom upon the four corners of the earth" (D&C 124:128); and "are a Traveling Presiding High Council, to officiate in the name of the Lord, under the direction of the Presidency of the Church, agreeable to the institution of heaven; to build up the church, and regulate all the affairs of the same in all nations, first unto the Gentiles and secondly unto the Jews" (D&C 107:33).

D&C 124:131—The first high council of the Church was established in Kirtland by the Prophet Joseph Smith at a conference on February 17, 1834 (see HC 2:28–31), with a second high council being organized in Missouri later that year. Other high councils were organized in sequence with the growth of the Church. Such councils do indeed serve as "the cornerstone of Zion" in the various stakes, for they accomplish important administrative, consultative, and judicial functions under the direction of the local stake presidency by which they are organized.

churches from time to time; the one has the responsibility of presiding from time to time, and the other has no responsibility of presiding, saith the Lord your God.

141. And again, I say unto you I give unto you Vinson Knight, Samuel H. Smith, and Shadrach Roundy, if he will receive it, to preside over

the bishopric; a knowledge of said bishopric is given unto you in the Book of Doctrine and Covenants.

142. And again, I say unto you, Samuel Rolfe and his counselors for priests, and the president of the teachers and his counselors, and also the president of the deacons and his counselors, and also the president of the stake and his counselors;

143. The above offices I have given unto you, and the keys thereof, for helps and for governments, for the work of the ministry and the perfecting of my saints;

144. And a commandment I give unto you that you should fill all these offices and approve of those names which I have mentioned, or else disapprove of them at my general conference,

145. And that ye should prepare rooms for all these offices in my house when you build it unto my name, saith the Lord your God. Even so. Amen.

SECTION 125

1. "What is the will of the Lord, concerning the saints in the Territory of Iowa?"

2. Verily, thus saith the Lord, I say unto you, if those who call themselves by my name, and are essaying to be my saints, if they will do my will and keep my commandments concerning them; let them gather themselves together, unto the places which I shall appoint unto them by my servant Joseph, and build up cities unto my name, that they may be prepared for that which is in store for a time to come.

3. Let them build up a city unto my name upon the land opposite the city of Nauvoo, and let the name of Zarahemla be named upon it.

4. And let all those who come from the east, and the west, and the north, and the south, that have desires to dwell therein, take up their inheritance in the same, as well as in the city of Nashville, or in the city of Nauvoo, and in all the Stakes which I have appointed, saith the Lord.

D&C 124:143—Concerning the extraordinary priesthood organization of the Church, President Joseph F. Smith observed:

It [the Church] has been organized by the wisdom of the Almighty, and not by the wisdom of man. It has been organized to accomplish the purposes that the Lord has in view to be accomplished by it. The people are organized that they may be taught righteousness; that they may be faithful before the Lord in keeping the covenants that they have made with Him in righteousness . . . that the people of God may be a light unto this generation and unto the world; that men may see your good works and glorify your Father which is in heaven. (CR, Oct. 1904, 4.)

Section 125 Background—Given at Nauvoo, Illinois, March 1841 (see *HC* 4:311–312). The Prophet explained: "About this time I received a revelation, given in the City of Nauvoo, in answer to the following interrogatory— 'What is the will of the Lord, concerning the Saints in the Territory of Iowa?'" (*HC* 4:311).

D&C 125:2—The master plan was to gather the Saints to the Rocky Mountains in due time. Meanwhile, Nauvoo was the central venue for the Saints to gather, and the migration also brought settlements to Iowa for a period of time. According to Hyrum M. Smith and Janne M. Sjodahl: "When the Saints left Missouri, a large number of fugitives found their way into the Territory of Iowa. Large tracts of land were purchased, and several settlements were built up in the southeastern portion of that Territory. Before the arrival of the Saints, there were only 2,839 inhabitants in Lee County. In 1846 the population was estimated at 12,860. So rapidly did the County develop, when touched by the magic wand of 'Mormon' industry" (*DCC*, 795).

A current monument at Montrose, Iowa, to the Mormon Trail, the "Mormon Sojourn in Lee County 1839–1846," and Fort Des Moines, in use by the Saints from 1834 to 1837.

SECTION 126

1. Dear and well-beloved brother Brigham Young, verily thus saith the Lord unto you, my servant Brigham, it is no more required at your hand to leave your family as in times past, for your offering is acceptable to me;
2. I have seen your labor and toil in journeyings for my name.
3. I therefore command you to send my word abroad, and take special care of your family from this time, henceforth, and for ever. Amen.

SECTION 127

1. Forasmuch as the Lord has revealed unto me that my enemies, both in Missouri and this State, were again in the pursuit of me; and inasmuch as they pursue me without a cause, and have not the least shadow or coloring of justice or right on their side, in the getting up of their prosecutions against me; and inasmuch as their pretensions are all founded in falsehood of the blackest dye, I have thought it expedient and wisdom in me to leave the place for a short season, for my own safety, and the safety of this people. I would say to all those with whom I have business, that I have left my affairs with agents and clerks, who will transact all business in a prompt and proper manner, and will see that all my debts are canceled in due time, by turning out property, or otherwise, as the case may require, or as the circumstances may admit of. When I learn that the storm is fully blown over, then I will return to you again.
2. And as for the perils which I am called to pass through, they seem but a small thing to me, as the envy and wrath of man have been my common lot all the days of my life; and for what cause it seems mysterious, unless I was ordained from before the foundation of the world for some good end, or bad, as you may choose to call it. Judge ye for yourselves. God knoweth all these things, whether it be good or bad. But nevertheless, deep water is what I am wont to swim in. It all has become a second nature to me, and I feel like Paul, to glory in tribulation, for to this day has the God of my fathers delivered me out of them all, and will deliver me from henceforth; for behold, and lo, I shall triumph over all my enemies, for the Lord God hath spoken it.
3. Let all the saints rejoice, therefore, and be exceedingly glad, for Israel's God is their God, and he will mete out a just recompense of reward upon the heads of all their oppressors.

Section 126 Background—Given in the house of Brigham Young in Nauvoo, July 9, 1841 (*HC* 4:382). At the time of this revelation, Brigham Young was serving as president of the Quorum of the Twelve Apostles.

D&C 126:1—From the time of his conversion in 1832, Brigham Young had served the cause of Zion indefatigably—often not knowing from hour to hour where his next penny would come from to sustain his labors in his homeland or overseas. On the occasion of receiving the vision of the celestial kingdom on January 21, 1836 (Section 137), several years before Brigham Young and his fellow Apostles left for their missions in England, the Prophet foresaw them laboring in conditions of meekness and poverty: "I saw the Twelve Apostles of the Lamb, who are now upon the earth, who hold the keys of this last ministry, in foreign lands, standing together in a circle, much fatigued, with their clothes tattered and feet swollen, with their eyes cast downward, and Jesus standing in their midst, and they did not behold Him. The Savior looked upon them and wept" (*HC* 2:381).

Few of Lord's servants were more devout and responsive than Brigham Young, who journeyed vast distances not a few times on the Lord's errand. From this passage of scripture we gain an inkling of the Lord's love for His righteous and obedient servants, and we sense the deep charity with which the Lord now commissions Brigham to labor closer to home and more directly nurture his family.

Section 127 Background—The Prophet Joseph Smith gave this introductory statement to his inspired epistle, written in the hand of William Clayton and dated September 1, 1842, concerning baptism for the dead: "During the forenoon in the Assembly Room, and in the afternoon at home, attending to business. Wrote the following" [then appears the letter that is now Section 127] (see *HC* 5:142–144). This first letter was followed by a second one, dated September 6, 1842 (Section 128)—both of them giving important information about the ordinance of baptism for the dead. At this time the Prophet was making few public appearances because of threats to his life.

D&C 127:2—The Prophet had faith in deliverance, and, indeed, he would live long enough to complete his mission of the Restoration of the gospel for mankind. The attitude we cultivate in dealing with our adversities will result in either our humility and growth or our having a hardened heart and rebelling (see Alma 62:41).

4. And again, verily thus saith the Lord, Let the work of my temple, and all the works which I have appointed unto you, be continued on and not cease; and let your diligence, and your perseverance, and patience, and your works be redoubled, and you shall in nowise lose your reward, saith the Lord of Hosts. And if they persecute you, so persecuted they the prophets and righteous men that were before you. For all this there is a reward in heaven.

5. And again, I give unto you a word in relation to the baptism for your dead.

6. Verily, thus saith the Lord unto you concerning your dead: When any of you are baptized for your dead, let there be a Recorder, and let him be eye witness of your baptisms; let him hear with his ears, that he may testify of a truth, saith the Lord;

7. That in all your recordings it may be recorded in heaven; whatsoever you bind on earth, may be bound in heaven; whatsoever you loose on earth, may be loosed in heaven;

8. For I am about to restore many things to the earth, pertaining to the Priesthood, saith the Lord of Hosts.

9. And again, let all the records be had in order, that they may be put in the archives of my Holy Temple, to be held in remembrance from generation to generation, saith the Lord of hosts.

10. I will say to all the saints, that I desired, with exceedingly great desire, to have addressed them from the stand, on the subject of baptism for the dead, on the following sabbath. But inasmuch as it is out of my power to do so, I will write the word of the Lord from time to time, on that subject, and send it to you by mail, as well as many other things.

11. I now close my letter for the present, for the want of more time; for the enemy is on the alert, and as the Savior said, the prince of this world cometh, but he hath nothing in me.

12. Behold, my prayer to God is, that you all may be saved. And I subscribe myself your servant in the Lord, Prophet and Seer of the Church of Jesus Christ of Latter-day Saints.

Joseph Smith.

D&C 127:6–7—The law of witnesses (see D&C 6:28) was to apply as well to ordinance work in the temple (see also D&C 128:2–4). At a meeting of the Relief Society in Nauvoo on August 31, 1842, the Prophet Joseph Smith said:

> I have one remark to make respecting the baptism for the dead to suffice for the time being, until I have opportunity to discuss the subject at greater length—all persons baptized for the dead must have a recorder present, that he may be an eyewitness to record and testify of the truth and validity of his record. It will be necessary, in the Grand Council, that these things be testified to by competent witnesses. Therefore let the recording and witnessing of baptisms for the dead be carefully attended to from this time forth. If there is any lack, it may be at the expense of our friends; they may not come forth. (HC 5:141.)

D&C 127:12—The love of the Prophet Joseph for his Heavenly Father, the Lord Jesus Christ, and the Saints of the Church is confirmed once again in verse 12. Joseph—though prophet and seer of the Church—thinks of himself as "your servant in the Lord" (verse 12). Despite the abundance of persecution and suffering experienced by the Saints, this was a season of joy in the glories of the Restoration.

BAPTISMS FOR THE DEAD: WITNESSES AND RECORDINGS

In this dispensation, the Lord has revealed again that "in the mouth of two or three witnesses shall every word be established" (D&C 6:28). This law of witnesses was to be observed in the performance of the ordinance of baptism for the dead (see D&C 127:5–7, 9; 128:2–4).

The functions of a witness are:

1. To verify that the ordinance was performed, which provides protection for the one who receives the ordinance.

2. To verify that the ordinance was performed by an authorized priesthood holder; this protects against deception.

3. To verify that the ordinance was performed properly, which protects against an error in performance.

4. To verify the time and place that the ordinance was performed.

The Prophet Joseph Smith said that if there was not a witness to baptisms for the dead, "it may be at the expense of our friends; they may not come forth" (HC 5:141) (STDC 2:329–330).

SECTION 128

1. As I stated to you in my letter before I left my place, that I would write to you from time to time, and give you information in relation to many subjects, I now resume the subject of the baptism for the dead, as that subject seems to occupy my mind, and press itself upon my feelings the strongest, since I have been pursued by my enemies.
2. I wrote a few words of revelation to you concerning a recorder. I have had a few additional views in relation to this matter, which I now certify. That is, it was declared in my former letter that there should be a recorder, who should be eye witness, and also to hear with his ears, that he might make a record of a truth before the Lord.
3. Now, in relation to this matter, it would be very difficult for one recorder to be present at all times, and do all the business. To obviate this difficulty, there can be a recorder appointed in each ward of the city, who is well qualified for taking accurate minutes; and let him be very particular and precise in taking the whole proceedings, certifying in his record that he saw with his eyes, and heard with his ears, giving the date, and names, &c., so forth, and the history of the whole transaction; naming also some three individuals that are present, if there be any present, who can at any time when called upon, certify to the same, that in the mouth of two or three witnesses, every word may be established.
4. Then let there be a general recorder, to whom these other records can be handed, being attended with certificates over their own signatures, certifying that the record they have made is true. Then the general church recorder can enter the record on the general church book, with the certificates and all the attending witnesses, with his own statement that he verily believes the above statement and records to be true, from his knowledge of the general character and appointment of those men by the church. And when this is done on the general church book, the record shall be just as holy, and shall answer the ordinance just the same as if he had seen with his eyes, and heard with his ears, and made a record of the same on the general church book.
5. You may think this order of things to be very particular, but let me tell you, that it is only to answer the will of God, by conforming to the ordinance and preparation that the Lord ordained and prepared before the foundation of the world, for the salvation of the dead who should die without a knowledge of the gospel.
6. And further I want you to remember that John the Revelator was contemplating this very subject in relation to the dead, when he declared, as you will find recorded in Revelations xx. 12—"And I saw the dead, small and great, stand before God; and the books were opened; and another book was opened, which was the book of life; and the dead were judged out of those things which were written in the books, according to their works."
7. You will discover in this quotation, that the books were opened; and another book was opened, which was the book of life; but the dead were judged out of those things which were written in the books, according to their works; consequently the books spoken of must be the books which contained the record of their works; and refer to the records which are kept on the earth. And the book which was the book of life, is the record which is

Section 128 Background—An inspired epistle to the Church written by the Prophet Joseph Smith and containing additional directions on baptism for the dead, dated September 6, 1842 (see *HC* 5:148–153).

D&C 128:1—The Prophet, under acute pressure from his enemies, must have sensed that his time on earth was growing shorter—that it was incumbent upon him to complete the urgent work of laying the foundation for temple work. Temple work affords the faithful and devoted Saints of God the supreme opportunity to partake of the nature of redeeming, saving love in doing for their progenitors what these deceased persons could not do for themselves. In this way, those who come to the temples of the Most High with the records of their dead to participate in vicarious ordinances are a fulfillment of the view of the ancient prophet Obadiah, who declared, in relationship to the unfolding work of the Lord: "And saviours shall come up on mount Zion . . ." (Oba. 1:21). Said the Prophet Joseph Smith:

> The doctrine of baptism for the dead is clearly shown in the New Testament; and if the doctrine is not good, then throw the New Testament away; but if it is the word of God, then let the doctrine be acknowledged; and it was the reason why Jesus said unto the Jews, "How oft would I have gathered thy children together, even as a hen gathereth her chickens under her wings, and ye would not!" [See Matt. 23:37.]—that they might attend to the ordinances of baptism for the dead as well as other ordinances of the priesthood, and receive revelations from heaven, and be perfected in the things of the kingdom of God—but they would not. This was the case on the day of Pentecost: those blessings were poured out on the disciples on that occasion. God ordained that he would save the dead, and would do it by gathering his people together. (*HC* 5:425.)

D&C 128:7—The records kept on earth by the agents of the Lord form the witness of righteousness and obedience that factor into the process of eternal judgment. From the foundation of the world it was decreed that the history of mankind—the deeds and works of all individuals—would be memorialized as a chronicle to factor into the ultimate judgments of God. Through latter-day revelation, much additional light has been shed on the importance of record-keeping as a key priesthood practice in the kingdom of God (see D&C 85:9–12).

The records of the Church are kept in compliance with the principle of there being a parallel and simultaneous heavenly monitoring and recording of events that transpire in the temporal sphere. The faithful and obedient are thus motivated to cultivate a "godly walk and conversation" (D&C 20:69) in order to please God and be found worthy, based on the records of remembrance, of taking their places at the right hand of the Lord through the power of the Atonement and in keeping with the harmonizing of justice and mercy.

kept in heaven; the principle agreeing precisely with the doctrine which is commanded you in the revelation contained in the letter which I wrote to you previously to my leaving my place—that in all your recordings it may be recorded in heaven.

8. Now the nature of this ordinance consists in the power of the Priesthood, by the revelation of Jesus Christ, wherein it is granted, that whatsoever you bind on earth, shall be bound in heaven, and whatsoever you loose on earth, shall be loosed in heaven. Or, in other words, taking a different view of the translation, whatsoever you record on earth, shall be recorded in heaven; and whatsoever you do not record on earth, shall not be recorded in heaven; for out of the books shall your dead be judged, according to their own works, whether they themselves have attended to the ordinances in their own propria persona, or by the means of their own agents, according to the ordinance which God has prepared for their salvation from before the foundation of the world, according to the records which they have kept concerning their dead.

9. It may seem to some to be a very bold doctrine that we talk of—a power which records or binds on earth, and binds in heaven. Nevertheless in all ages of the world, whenever the Lord has given a dispensation of the Priesthood to any man by actual revelation, or any set of men, this power has always been given. Hence, whatsoever those men did in authority, in the name of the Lord, and did it truly and faithfully, and kept a proper and faithful record of the same, it became a law on earth and in heaven, and could not be annulled, according to the decrees of the great Jehovah. This is a faithful saying! Who can hear it?

10. And again, for the precedent, Matthew 16:18, 19, "And I say also unto thee, that thou art Peter: and upon this rock I will build my church; and the gates of hell shall not prevail against it; and I will give unto thee the keys of the kingdom of heaven, and whatsoever thou shalt bind on earth, shall be bound in heaven; and whatsoever thou shalt loose on earth, shall be loosed in heaven."

11. Now the great and grand secret of the whole matter, and the summum bonum of the whole subject that is lying before us, consists in obtaining the powers of the Holy Priesthood. For him to whom these keys are given, there is no difficulty in obtaining a knowledge of facts in relation to the salvation of the children of men, both as well for the dead as for the living.

12. Herein is glory and honor, and immortality and eternal life. The ordinance of baptism by water, to be immersed therein in order to answer to the likeness of the dead, that one principle might accord with the other. To be immersed in the water and come forth out of the water is in the likeness of the resurrection of the dead in coming forth out of their graves; hence this ordinance was instituted to form a relationship with the ordinance of baptism for the dead, being in likeness of the dead.

13. Consequently the baptismal font was instituted as a simile of the grave and was commanded to be in a place underneath where the living are wont to assemble, to show forth the living and the dead and that all things may have their likeness, and that they may accord one with another—that which is earthly

D&C 128:11—The foundation of the Church is comprised of the keys of the holy priesthood by means of which divine revelation is unlocked for the salvation of mankind. Such a flow of revelation enables the priesthood to take correct and authorized action using the binding and sealing ordinances for the blessing and exaltation of the faithful and obedient.

D&C 128:12—Baptism is an ordinance reflecting symbolism of great beauty and vitality—to be cleansed of the old and reborn into a state of newness, just as the dead come forth in the resurrection to a state of immortality. President Joseph Fielding Smith observed:

> The Lord has placed the baptismal font in our Temples below the foundation, or the surface of the earth. This is symbolical, since the dead are in their graves, and we are working for the dead when we are baptized for them. Moreover, baptism is also symbolical of death and the resurrection, in fact, is virtually a resurrection from the life of sin, or from spiritual death, to the life of spiritual life. (See D. & C. 29:41–45.) Therefore when the dead have had this ordinance performed in their behalf they are considered to have been brought into the presence of God, just as this doctrine is applied to the living. Other ordinances of the endowment and sealings therefore do not have to be performed below the surface of the earth as in the case of baptism. (CHMR 4:137–138.)

SALVATION FOR THE LIVING AND THE DEAD

All children of God who have lived or who will yet live on this earth will have come here to a state of probation. Many leave mortality and enter the spirit world still in a probationary condition. For instance, those who have not had full opportunity to hear and accept the gospel of Jesus Christ still must make proper decisions in order to have access to the fullness of the blessings promised to righteous Saints. The ordinance work necessary for those in the spirit world who accept and desire salvation must be performed by righteous Saints in mortality.

Members of the Church have been given the authority and responsibility to perform the ordinances for and in behalf of the departed dead. Our obligation is to share the benefits of the gospel with both the living and the dead. God is no respecter of persons, and neither should we be. Salvation for both the living and the dead depends in part on the faithful obedience of God's covenant children in discharging their sacred responsibilities toward their brothers and sisters who are still without covenant blessings in our Heavenly Father's kingdom. Until all people have had the opportunity to hear and accept the gospel and its covenants, their period of probation is not over (STDC 2:331).

conforming to that which is heavenly, as Paul hath declared, 1 Corinthians 15:46, 47, and 48.

14. "Howbeit that was not first which is spiritual, but that which is natural, and afterwards that which is spiritual. The first man is of the earth, earthy; the second man is the Lord, from heaven. As is the earthy, such are they also that are earthy; and as is the heavenly, such are they also that are heavenly." And as are the records on the earth in relation to your dead, which are truly made out, so also are the records in heaven. This, therefore, is the sealing and binding power, and, in one sense of the word, the keys of the kingdom which consist in the key of knowledge.

15. And now, my dearly beloved brethren and sisters, let me assure you that these are principles in relation to the dead, and the living, that cannot be lightly passed over, as pertaining to our salvation. For their salvation is necessary, and essential to our salvation, as Paul says concerning the fathers, "that they without us cannot be made perfect;" either can we without our dead be made perfect.

16. And now, in relation to the baptism for the dead, I will give you another quotation of Paul, 1 Corinthians 15:29, "Else what shall they do which are baptized for the dead, if the dead rise not at all; why are they then baptized for the dead?"

17. And again, in connection with this quotation, I will give you a quotation from one of the prophets, who had his eye fixed on the restoration of the Priesthood, the glories to be revealed in the last days, and in an especial manner this most glorious of all subjects belonging to the everlasting gospel, namely, the baptism for the dead; for Malachi says, last chapter, verses 5th and 6th, "Behold, I will send you Elijah the prophet, before the coming of the great and dreadful day of the Lord; and he shall turn the heart of the fathers to the children, and the heart of the children to their fathers, lest I come and smite the earth with a curse.

18. I might have rendered a plainer translation to this, but it is sufficiently plain to suit my purpose as it stands. It is sufficient to know, in this case, that the earth will be smitten with a curse, unless there is a welding link of some kind or other, between the fathers and the children, upon some subject or other, and behold what is that subject? It is the baptism for the dead. For we without them cannot be made perfect; neither can they without us be made perfect. Neither can they nor we, be made perfect, without those who have died in the gospel also; for it is necessary in the ushering in of the dispensation of the fulness of times; which dispensation is now beginning to usher in, that a whole and complete and perfect union, and welding together of dispensations, and keys, and powers, and glories should take place, and be revealed from the days of Adam even to the present time; and not only this, but those things which never have been revealed from the foundation of the world, but have been kept hid from the wise and prudent, shall be revealed unto babes and sucklings in this the dispensation of the fulness of times.

19. Now, what do we hear in the gospel which we have received? "A voice of gladness! A voice of

D&C 128:15—As we seek out our dead and do the vicarious work for them in the temple, we will be blessed, along with our kindred dead. It is, in effect, a divine partnership. The work for the dead is of a vicarious nature; it is something that they cannot do for themselves. We become saviors on Mount Zion (see Oba. 1:21; D&C 103:9). As with service of the highest order, it is always of a vicarious nature, just like our beloved Savior's atoning sacrifice for us. Our exaltation depends on our willingness to serve others—and especially our dead.

D&C 128:16—The reality of the resurrection substantiates the need for vicarious temple ordinances on behalf of the dead. Said the Prophet Joseph Smith:

> Every man that has been baptized and belongs to the kingdom has a right to be baptized for those who have gone before; and as soon as the law of the Gospel is obeyed here by their friends who act as proxy for them, the Lord has administrators there to set them free. (HC 6:365.)

D&C 128:17–18—The spirit of Elijah is the consummate power of binding unification among fathers and sons, mothers and daughters, the living and the dead—so that the family of God can be sealed His according to the covenants, principles, and saving ordinances of the gospel of Jesus Christ. The Prophet Joseph Smith explained:

> I wish you to understand this subject, for it is important; and if you receive it, this is the spirit of Elijah, that we redeem our dead, and connect ourselves with our fathers which are in heaven, and seal up our dead to come forth in the first resurrection; and here we want the power of Elijah to seal those who dwell on earth to those who dwell in heaven. This is the power of Elijah and the keys of the kingdom of Jehovah. (TPJS, 337–338.)

D&C 128:19—What is the tone of the Prophet's message, sent from isolation and reclusion in the shadows of obscurity, away from the destructive designs of the enemies of the Church? Is it a tone of anguish and embitterment, dejection and sorrow? To the contrary. It is a message of joy and glory—for the triumph of God's designs was imminent. It is an anthem of glory in celebration of the milestones of the Restoration.

"Oh, how lovely was the morning!" begins the beloved hymn recounting Joseph Smith's first uttered prayer in the shady grove that was to become sacred to generations of truth-seekers everywhere. What occurred that spring morning in 1820 changed the history of the world, but it was no accident that he participated in that glorious opening event of the Restoration of the gospel of Jesus Christ. From the foundations of the world this moment had been planned and anticipated as an essential step in Heavenly Father's design. The First Vision ended generations of spiritual darkness fostered by the great apostasy—that general falling away from truth as foreseen by prophets of old and foretold by the Savior and His Apostles.

mercy from heaven; and a voice of truth out of the earth; glad tidings for the dead; a voice of gladness for the living and the dead; glad tidings of great joy; how beautiful upon the mountains are the feet of those that bring glad tidings of good things; and that say unto Zion; behold! thy God reigneth. As the dews of Carmel, so shall the knowledge of God descend upon them."

20. And again, what do we hear? Glad tidings from Cumorah! Moroni, an angel from heaven, declaring the fulfilment of the prophets—the book to be revealed. A voice of the Lord in the wilderness of Fayette, Seneca county, declaring the three witnesses to bear record of the book. The voice of Michael on the banks of the Susquehanna, detecting the devil when he appeared as an angel of light. The voice of Peter, James, and John in the wilderness between Harmony, Susquehanna county, and Colesville, Broome county, on the Susquehanna river, declaring themselves as possessing the keys of the kingdom, and of the dispensation of the fulness of times.

21. And again, the voice of God in the chamber of old father Whitmer, in Fayette, Seneca county, and at sundry times, and in divers places through all the travels and tribulations of this Church of Jesus Christ of Latter-day Saints. And the voice of Michael, the archangel; the voice of Gabriel, and of Raphael, and of divers angels, from Michael or Adam, down to the present time, all declaring their dispensation, their rights, their keys, their honors, their majesty and glory, and the power of their Priesthood; giving line upon line, precept upon precept; here a little, and there a little—giving us consolation by holding forth that which is to come, confirming our hope.

22. Brethren, shall we not go on in so great a cause? Go forward and not backward. Courage, brethren; and on, on to the victory! Let your hearts rejoice, and be exceedingly glad. Let the earth break forth into singing. Let the dead speak forth anthems of eternal praise to the King Immanuel, who hath ordained before the world was, that which would enable us to redeem them out of their prison; for the prisoners shall go free.

23. Let the mountains shout for joy, and all ye valleys cry aloud; and all ye seas and dry lands tell the wonders of your Eternal King. And ye rivers, and brooks, and rills flow down with gladness. Let the woods and all the trees of the field praise the Lord; and ye solid rocks weep for joy. And let the sun, moon, and the morning stars sing together, and let all the sons of God shout for joy. And let the eternal creations declare his name for ever and ever. And again I say, how glorious is the voice we hear from heaven, proclaiming in our ears, glory, and salvation, and honor, and immortality,

D&C 128:22—Thus did the Prophet Joseph Smith express his joy at the unfolding of the principles and doctrines of mercy and grace underlying the work for the dead as it was to be carried out in the temples of the Most High. The words of this revelation flow with sublime poetic majesty. Among all the doctrines and practices that distinguish The Church of Jesus Christ of Latter-day Saints and set it apart from all other churches of the world, the vast, encompassing work of the temples of God is perhaps the most unique and compelling. Temple work is the evidence that God has extended to every individual who has ever lived upon the earth, and who will ever be born into this mortal experience, the blessings and opportunities of salvation, immortality, and eternal life.

D&C 128:24—John A. Widtsoe comments on this passage as follows: "The 'offering in righteousness' is here identified with temple work for the salvation of the dead, which encompasses all the principles of the plan of salvation. When, therefore, the sons of Levi accept Christ and His gospel, subject themselves to the ordinances of the Church, and become active in gospel requirements, they will offer the offering in righteousness of which has been spoken" (ER, 247).

The commission laid upon the shoulders of the Saints is evident: We were preserved to come forth in these days to build temples, seek after our dead, and perform their temple work, that they too might partake of the blessings of our Heavenly Father. The record of these life-saving ordinances will be presented to the Lord in righteousness. Elder Orson Pratt characterized the motivation and determination of the Saints regarding temple work as follows:

> We are willing to go the earth over to save the living; we are willing to build temples and administer in ordinances to save the dead; we are willing to enter the eternal worlds and preach to every creature who has not placed himself beyond the reach of mercy. We are willing to labour both in this world and in the next to save men.
>
> . . . Let all rejoice that the great day of the dispensation of the fulness of times has come. Let the living rejoice; let the dead rejoice; let the heavens and the earth rejoice; let all creation shout hosannah! glory to God in the highest! for he hath brought salvation, and glory, and honour, and immortality, and eternal life to the fallen sons of men. Amen. (JD 7:91.)

and eternal life; kingdoms, principalities, and powers.

24. Behold the great day of the Lord is at hand, and who can abide the day of his coming, and who can stand when he appeareth; for he is like a refiner's fire, and like fuller's soap; and he shall sit as a refiner and purifier of silver, and he shall purify the sons of Levi, and purge them as gold and silver, that they may offer unto the Lord an offering in righteousness. Let us therefore, as a church and a people, and as Latter-day Saints offer unto the Lord an offering in righteousness; and let us present in his holy temple, when it is finished, a book containing the records of our dead, which shall be worthy of all acceptation.

25. Brethren, I have many things to say to you on the subject; but shall now close for the present, and continue the subject another time. I am, as ever, your humble servant and never deviating friend.

Joseph Smith.

SECTION 129

1. There are two kinds of beings in heaven, namely: Angels, who are resurrected personages, having bodies of flesh and bones—

2. For instance, Jesus said, "Handle me and see, for a spirit hath not flesh and bones, as ye see me have."

3. Secondly: the spirits of just men made perfect, they who are not resurrected, but inherit the same glory.

4. When a messenger comes, saying he has a message from God, offer him your hand, and request him to shake hands with you.

5. If he be an angel, he will do so, and you will feel his hand.

6. If he be the spirit of a just man made perfect, he will come in his glory; for that is the only way he can appear—

7. Ask him to shake hands with you, but he will not move, because it is contrary to the order of heaven for a just man to deceive; but he will still deliver his message.

8. If it be the Devil as an angel of light, when you ask him to shake hands, he will offer you his hand, and you will not feel anything; you may therefore detect him.

9. These are three grand keys whereby you may know whether any administration is from God.

Section 129 Background—This revelation includes *"Three Grand Keys by which Good or Bad Angels or Spirits may be Known—Revealed to Joseph the Prophet, at Nauvoo, Illinois, February 9, 1843"* (HC 5:267).

D&C 129:1—The Prophet distinguishes between embodied (resurrected) beings and disembodied beings (spirits prior to their resurrected state). The reference to "the spirits of just men made perfect" (verse 3) concerns the state of those beings who will eventually inherit the highest degree of the celestial kingdom as resurrected beings: "These are they who have come to an innumerable company of angels, to the general assembly and church of Enoch, and of the Firstborn. . . . These are they who are just men made perfect through Jesus the mediator of the new covenant, who wrought out this perfect atonement through the shedding of his own blood. These are they whose bodies are celestial" (D&C 76:67, 69–70). Prior to this exalted and resurrected condition, the unembodied spirits of "just men made perfect" can be commissioned of the Lord as emissaries to perform missions to God's children. The same applied to the Savior following His crucifixion and prior to His resurrection. At a general conference of the Church held in Nauvoo on Sunday, October 3, 1841, the Prophet said:

Translated bodies cannot enter into rest until they have undergone a change equivalent to death. Translated bodies are designed for future missions.

The angel that appeared to John on the Isle of Patmos was a translated or resurrected body [personage]. Jesus Christ went in body after His resurrection, to minister to resurrected bodies. There has been a chain of authority and power from Adam down to the present time. (HC 4:425.)

D&C 129:9—Joseph, the Prophet of the Restoration, was more knowledgeable concerning these principles than any other individual on the earth. His counsel concerning the discerning of messengers can speak for itself. Orson F. Whitney observed:

To those in quest of spiritual light, this word of counsel: Seek it only in the Lord's appointed way. Follow the advice of the Apostle James [James 1:5] and the example of Joseph the Prophet. Never go upon the Devil's ground. Keep away from all deceptive influence. . . . Go not after them; and if they come to you, put them to the test. "Try the spirits." [1 Jn. 4:1.] If they speak not according to revealed truth, if they conform not to divine standards, "it is because there is no light in them." (Orson F. Whitney, *Saturday Night Thoughts* [1921], 312.)

SECTION 130

1. When the Savior shall appear, we shall see him as he is. We shall see that he is a man like ourselves;

2. And that same sociality which exists among us here will exist among us there, only it will be coupled with eternal glory, which glory we do not now enjoy.

3. John 14:23—The appearing of the Father and the Son, in that verse, is a personal appearance; and the idea that the Father and the Son dwell in a man's heart, is an old sectarian notion, and is false.

4. In answer to the question, "is not the reckoning of God's time, angel's time, prophet's time, and man's time according to the planet on which they reside?"

5. I answer, yes. But there are no angels who minister to this earth but those who do belong or have belonged to it.

6. The angels do not reside on a planet like this earth.

7. But they reside in the presence of God, on a globe like a sea of glass and fire, where all things for their glory are manifest—past, present, and future, and are continually before the Lord.

8. The place where God resides is a great Urim and Thummim.

9. This earth, in its sanctified and immortal state, will be made like unto crystal and will be a Urim and Thummim to the inhabitants who dwell thereon, whereby all things pertaining to an inferior kingdom, or all kingdoms of a lower order, will be manifest to those who dwell on it; and this earth will be Christ's.

10. Then the white stone mentioned in Revelations ii. 17, will become a Urim and Thummim to each individual who receives one, whereby things pertaining to a higher order of kingdoms, even all kingdoms will be made known;

11. And a white stone is given to each of those who come into the celestial kingdom, whereon is a new name written, which no man

Section 130 Background—The section head pertaining to these materials in the *History of the Church* states: "Important Items of Instruction given by Joseph the Prophet at Ramus, Illinois, April 2nd, 1843" (see *HC* 5:323–325). On this day, at a morning Church meeting in Ramus, a small town east of Nauvoo, the Prophet Joseph Smith listens to Orson Hyde preach a sermon in which he says, "It is our privilege to have the Father and Son dwelling in our hearts" (*HC* 5:323). Afterwards, during a luncheon at the home of the Prophet's sister, Sophronia McCleary, the Prophet tells Elder Hyde that he is going to offer some corrections to his sermon. Orson Hyde replies, "They shall be thankfully received." The Prophet then shares with him the important insights included in Section 130. Later on that day, the Prophet makes public this and many additional items of instruction now part of Section 130 concerning the true nature of God and His laws.

D&C 130:4–8—Peter declared "that one day *is* with the Lord as a thousand years, and a thousand years as one day" (2 Pet. 3:8). The Lord revealed to Abraham by the Urim and Thummim "that Kolob [the star nearest to the throne of God] was after the manner of the Lord, according to its times and seasons in the revolutions thereof; that one revolution was a day unto the Lord, after his manner of reckoning, it being one thousand years according to the time appointed unto that whereon thou standest. . . ." (Abr. 3:4). Such references may impart an equivalency formula for understanding the time of the Lord relative to our own, or they may convey the fact that the Lord's reckoning of time is vastly different from our own—or perhaps both.

D&C 130:9–11—Each individual who comes into the celestial kingdom will be given a "white stone," a personalized Urim and Thummim revealing things of a higher order. We begin to have a small inkling concerning the potential for such a celestial tool—the heavenly "white stone"—just by considering our own modern computer systems. Do they not operate through the technical capability of "stones"—microchips enabled and empowered through silicon-based transistors? What if the modest breakthroughs of modern science were magnified a billion times within the framework of celestial laws and divine principles? Then the workings of the "white stone" would begin to take on contours better understood by our limited minds and hearts.

The meetinghouse in Ramus, Illinois, a small town east of Nauvoo, where Orson Hyde preached a sermon that was later clarified by the Prophet Joseph Smith. The meetinghouse was built by the nearly 600 members of the Ramus Branch of the Church in the 1840s. The Prophet taught the doctrines found in Sections 130 and 131 in this meetinghouse.

knoweth save he that receiveth it. The new name is the key word.

12. I prophesy, in the name of the Lord God, that the commencement of the difficulties which will cause much bloodshed previous to the coming of the Son of Man will be in South Carolina.

13. It may probably arise through the slave question. This a voice declared to me, while I was praying earnestly on the subject, December 25th, 1832.

14. I was once praying very earnestly to know the time of the coming of the Son of Man, when I heard a voice repeat the following—

15. "Joseph, my son, if thou livest until thou art eighty-five years old, thou shalt see the face of the Son of Man: therefore let this suffice, and trouble me no more on this matter."

16. I was left thus, without being able to decide whether this coming referred to the beginning of the millennium or to some previous appearing, or whether I should die and thus see his face.

17. I believe the coming of the Son of Man will not be any sooner than that time.

18. Whatever principle of intelligence we attain unto in this life, it will rise with us in the resurrection;

19. And if a person gains more knowledge and intelligence in this life through his diligence and obedience than another, he will have so much the advantage in the world to come.

20. There is a law, irrevocably decreed in heaven before the foundations of this world, upon which all blessings are predicated;

21. And when we obtain any blessing from God, it is by obedience to that law upon which it is predicated.

22. The Father has a body of flesh and bones as tangible as man's; the Son also; but the Holy Ghost has not a body of flesh and bones, but is a personage of Spirit. Were it not so, the Holy Ghost could not dwell in us.

23. A man may receive the Holy Ghost, and it may descend upon him and not tarry with him.

D&C 130:12—On December 25, 1832, the Prophet prophesied of the beginning of hostilities leading to the American Civil War (see Section 87). This theme is now sounded once again, eleven years later.

D&C 130:14—The Savior taught: "But of that day, and hour, no one knoweth; no, not the angels of God in heaven, but my Father only" (JS–Matthew 1:40). We know not the hour of the Second Coming—but the signs only. The Prophet Joseph Smith reminds us:

> Judah must return, Jerusalem must be rebuilt, and the temple, and water come out from under the temple, and the waters of the Dead Sea be healed. It will take some time to rebuild the walls of the city and the temple, &c.; and all this must be done before the Son of Man will make His appearance. There will be wars and rumors of wars, signs in the heavens above and on the earth beneath, the sun turned into darkness and the moon to blood, earthquakes in divers places, the seas heaving beyond their bounds; then will appear one grand sign of the Son of Man in heaven. But what will the world do? They will say it is a planet, a comet, &c. But the Son of Man will come as the sign of the coming of the Son of Man, which will be as the light of the morning cometh out of the east. (HC 5:336–337.)

D&C 130:18—Elder Bruce R. McConkie has written that "intelligence" is much more than simply knowing and understanding: it is the truth and light that comes from Christ (see MD, 386).

D&C 130:20—The law of the harvest is simple: we are blessed by practicing true principles and obeying the commandments of God.

D&C 130:22—This simple statement of fact, confirmed by the experience of the First Vision, resolves millennia of controversy and disputation on the nature of God. Said President Marion G. Romney regarding the First Vision:

> When [Joseph Smith] came out of that sacred interview he knew with certainty the nature of God. He had seen and conversed with him. From him he had received a personal introduction to his resurrected Son Jesus Christ.
>
> In after years Joseph referred to God as an "exalted man," and said that both he and the Son were personages of flesh and bone, as tangible as man. (CR, Oct. 1958, 95–96.)

SECTION 131

1. In the celestial glory there are three heavens or degrees;

2. And in order to obtain the highest, a man must enter into this Order of the Priesthood; (meaning the new and everlasting covenant of marriage;)

3. And if he does not he cannot obtain it.

4. He may enter into the other, but that is the end of his kingdom: he cannot have an increase.

5. (May 17th, 1843.) The more sure word of prophecy (mentioned by Peter) means a man's knowing that he is sealed up unto eternal life, by revelation and the spirit of prophecy, through the power of the Holy Priesthood.

6. It is impossible for a man to be saved in ignorance.

7. There is no such thing as immaterial matter. All spirit is matter, but it is more fine or pure, and can only be discerned by purer eyes.

8. We cannot see it; but when our bodies are purified, we shall see that it is all matter.

SECTION 132

1. Verily, thus saith the Lord unto you, my servant Joseph, that inasmuch as you have inquired of my hand, to know and understand wherein I, the Lord, justified my servants Abraham, Isaac and Jacob; as also Moses, David and Solomon, my servants, as touching the principle

Joseph Smith's Red Brick Store on the banks of the Mississippi River. Many important events happened here: the Relief Society was organized here on March 17, 1842; the first endowments in this dispensation were administered on the third floor of the store on May 4, 1843; Joseph Smith finished the translation of the Book of Abraham here; and Joseph Smith asked the Twelve to investigate the possibility of moving west during a meeting here. The Red Brick Store served as the social, economic, and educational center of Nauvoo, and was also the bank for the city of Nauvoo. The first floor held a general store and the office for Bishop Newel K. Whitney, and the second floor was a large assembly hall that served as Church headquarters.

Section 131 Background—Inspired instructions given by the Prophet Joseph Smith at Ramus, Illinois, east of Nauvoo, on May 16 and 17, 1843 (see *HC* 5:293–393).

D&C 131:1–2—In order to obtain the highest of these heavens or degrees of glory, it is necessary for the faithful to enter into the covenant of marriage for time and all eternity. The kingdom of God, at its fundamental level, is made up of families. Celestial marriage, through the priesthood, is the divinely commissioned structure of family governance and perpetuity, so ordained of God in order to maximize the opportunities for eternal blessings to be poured out upon His children at the highest level possible in this life and in the life to come.

D&C 131:5–6—In the ascending range of knowledge available to mankind, knowledge about salvation is of highest worth. James E. Talmage explains:

> Not all knowledge is of equal worth. The knowledge that constitutes the wisdom of the heavens is all embraced in the Gospel as taught by Jesus Christ; and willful ignorance of this, the highest type of knowledge, will regulate its victim to the inferior order of intelligences. . . . If a man be ignorant of the terms on which salvation is predicated he is unable to comply therewith, and consequently fails to attain what otherwise might have been his eternal gain. The ignorance that thus condemns is responsible ignorance, involving wilful and sinful neglect. (*VM*, 1919, 278.)

D&C 131:7—Temporal vision is limited; spiritual vision is boundless. When we attain to a fullness of purity in our spiritual unfolding, then we will behold the eternal world in all its glory, and spirit matter will become discernible in overpowering radiance and magnificence.

Section 132 Background—Given at Nauvoo, Illinois, and recorded on July 12, 1843 (see *HC* 5:501–507). The revelation contains important doctrine on the subject of celestial marriage and plural marriage. Hyrum M. Smith and Janne M. Sjodal summarize the background as follows:

> This was not the first mention of the subject [plural marriage] among the Saints. Sarah Ann Kimball and many others knew of it in 1842, and Joseph B. Noble heard of it in the fall of 1840. Orson Pratt says that the Prophet Joseph, in the forepart of 1832, while he was living at the house of Father Johnson at Hiram, Ohio, told Church members that he had enquired of the Lord concerning this doctrine, and received the answer that it was true, but that the time to practice it had not come (*Discourse by Orson Pratt*, Salt Lake City, Oct. 7, 1869). Consequently, the Law of the Church remained as stated in Doctrine and Covenants 42:22, and as it is to-day, "Thou shalt love thy wife with all thy heart, and shall cleave unto her and none else." (*DCC*, 820–821.)

and doctrine of their having many wives and concubines:

2. Behold! and lo, I am the Lord thy God, and will answer thee as touching this matter:

3. Therefore, prepare thy heart to receive and obey the instructions which I am about to give unto you; for all those who have this law revealed unto them must obey the same;

4. For behold! I reveal unto you a new and an everlasting covenant; and if ye abide not that covenant, then are ye damned; for no one can reject this covenant, and be permitted to enter into my glory;

5. For all who will have a blessing at my hands, shall abide the law which was appointed for that blessing, and the conditions thereof, as were instituted from before the foundation of the world:

6. And as pertaining to the new and everlasting covenant, it was instituted for the fulness of my glory; and he that receiveth a fulness thereof, must and shall abide the law, or he shall be damned, saith the Lord God.

7. And verily I say unto you, that the conditions of this law are these—All covenants, contracts, bonds, obligations, oaths, vows, performances, connections, associations, or expectations, that are not made, and entered into, and sealed, by the Holy Spirit of promise, of him who is anointed, both as well for time and for all eternity, and that too most holy, by revelation and commandment through the medium of mine anointed, whom I have appointed on the earth to hold this power, (and I have appointed unto my servant Joseph to hold this power in the last days, and there is never but one on the earth at a time, on whom this power and the keys of this Priesthood are conferred) are of no efficacy, virtue or force, in and after the resurrection from the dead; for all contracts that are not made unto this end, have an end when men are dead.

8. Behold! mine house is a house of order, saith the Lord God, and not a house of confusion.

9. Will I accept of an offering, saith the Lord, that is not made in my name!

10. Or, will I receive at your hands that which I have not appointed!

11. And will I appoint unto you, saith the Lord, except it be by law, even as I and my Father ordained unto you, before the world was!

12. I am the Lord thy God, and I give unto you this commandment, that no man shall come unto the Father but by me, or by my word, which is my law, saith the Lord;

13. And everything that is in the world, whether it be ordained of men, by thrones or principalities, or powers, or things of name, whatsoever they may be, that are not by me, or by my word, saith the Lord, shall be thrown down, and shall not remain after men are dead, neither

D&C 132:1—Concubines were secondary wives; because of the caste system, they did not have equal standing with primary wives.

D&C 132:3–6—In these verses, the Lord underscores the importance of the new and everlasting covenant, including the covenant of celestial marriage. We are told that:
• We must obey the covenant (verse 3)
• If we don't obey the covenant, we will be damned (verse 4)
• No one will be permitted to enter the Lord's glory unless he obeys the covenant (verse 4)
• In order to have a blessing at the Lord's hands, we must obey the covenant (verse 5)
• In order to receive a fullness of glory, we must obey the covenant (verse 6)

D&C 132:4—Our relationship with Deity is defined in covenant terms. Blessings flow on the basis of covenant obedience (see D&C 130:20–21), and covenants were instituted for the good of mankind from "before the foundation of the world" (verse 5). What is termed "a new and an everlasting covenant" (verse 4, meaning eternal marriage) belongs to the full program of the Lord restored as "the new and everlasting covenant" (verse 6). As Elder Bruce R. McConkie explains, "The gospel is the *everlasting* covenant because it is ordained by Him who is Everlasting and also because it is everlastingly the same" (MD, 529).

D&C 132:7—The one "anointed" is the president of the Church, being the only one on whom "this power and the keys of this priesthood are conferred" (verse 7) under direction of the Lord. President Joseph Fielding Smith explains the term *Holy Spirit of Promise:*

> *The Holy Spirit of Promise is the Holy Ghost* who places the stamp of approval upon every ordinance: baptism, confirmation, ordination, marriage. *The promise is that the blessings will be received through faithfulness.*
>
> If a person violates a covenant, whether it be of baptism, ordination, marriage or anything else, the Spirit withdraws the stamp of approval, and the blessings will not be received. (DS, 1:45.)

An ordinance sealed by the Holy Spirit of Promise is ratified by the Holy Ghost, justified by the Spirit, and approved of the Lord.

D&C 132:13—Man-made laws and institutions not founded on divine law will cease to exist with death, and there will be no trace of them in eternity.

in nor after the resurrection, saith the Lord your God;

14. For whatsoever things remain are by me; and whatsoever things are not by me, shall be shaken and destroyed.

15. Therefore, if a man marry him a wife in the world, and he marry her not by me, nor by my word; and he covenant with her so long as he is in the world, and she with him, their covenant and marriage are not of force when they are dead, and when they are out of the world; therefore, they are not bound by any law when they are out of the world;

16. Therefore, when they are out of the world, they neither marry, nor are given in marriage; but are appointed angels in heaven, which angels are ministering servants, to minister for those who are worthy of a far more, and an exceeding, and an eternal weight of glory;

17. For these angels did not abide my law, therefore, they cannot be enlarged, but remain separately and singly, without exaltation, in their saved condition, to all eternity, and from henceforth are not Gods, but are angels of God, for ever and ever.

18. And again, verily I say unto you, if a man marry a wife, and make a covenant with her for time and for all eternity, if that covenant is not by me, or by my word, which is my law, and is not sealed by the Holy Spirit of promise, through him whom I have anointed and appointed unto this power—then it is not valid, neither of force when they are out of the world, because they are not joined by me, saith the Lord, neither by my word; when they are out of the world, it cannot be received there, because the angels and the Gods are appointed there, by whom they cannot pass; they cannot, therefore, inherit my glory, for my house is a house of order, saith the Lord God.

19. And again, verily I say unto you, if a man marry a wife by my word, which is my law, and by the new and everlasting covenant, and it is sealed unto them by the Holy Spirit of promise, by him who is anointed unto whom I have appointed this power, and the keys of this Priesthood; and it shall be said unto them, ye shall come forth in the first resurrection; and if it be after the first resurrection, in the next resurrection; and shall inherit thrones, kingdoms, principalities, and powers, dominions, all heights and depths—then shall it be written in the Lamb's Book of Life, that he shall commit no murder whereby to shed innocent blood, and if ye abide in my covenant, and commit no murder whereby to shed innocent blood, it shall be done unto them in all things whatsoever my servant hath put upon them, in time, and through all eternity, and shall be of full force when they are out of the world; and they shall pass by the angels, and the Gods, which are set there, to their exaltation and glory in all things, as hath been sealed upon their heads, which glory shall be a fulness and a continuation of the seeds for ever and ever.

20. Then shall they be Gods, because they have no end; therefore shall they be from everlasting to everlasting,

D&C 132:16—According to Elder James E. Talmage, there will be no marriage in the resurrection; questions of marital status must be settled before then.

D&C 132:19–20—The divine plan for the spirit children of our Father in Heaven to come to earth to receive mortal tabernacles essential for their ongoing progression involves a sacred partnership with the heavens. The Lord provides the system of life, with its sustaining vitality, and we provide the family relationships within which pure souls can come to earth to be nurtured and cared for in love. The power to call forth new life in this way is a solemn and beautiful commission from God that requires purity, devotion, courage, and a constant commitment to remember the covenants in faith and gratitude.

Honoring the sacred covenants of temple marriage brings magnificent blessings. All blessings of God relating to eternal marriage are bestowed by covenant, conditioned upon our faithfulness and obedience to the principles pertaining thereto. The greatest commission from God to us as His children is to raise up our families in righteousness and truth.

D&C 132:19–22—Having a marriage sealed by the Holy Spirit of Promise does not occur with the sealing itself; it generally takes years and requires a lifelong commitment to righteousness. These verses explain how to obtain a fullness of God's glory. The Lamb's Book of Life is a record kept in heaven that contains the names of the faithful and an account of their righteous covenants and deeds—the names of those who will inherit eternal life and be sanctified. Elder Bruce R. McConkie said that having one's calling and election made sure is an addition to celestial marriage and results from an undeviating and perfect devotion to righteousness. Elder Richard G. Scott encouraged us to live for that blessing and prepare our hearts for it.

THE REVOCATION OF PLURAL MARRIAGE

A fundamental truth evident in the functioning of the kingdom of God is that the Lord commands and revokes as He sees fit. Any commandment or revocation of a commandment that comes from the Lord will be made known through His living prophet.

The Lord revealed to the prophet Wilford Woodruff that the practice of plural marriage should cease in that no additional plural marriages would be sanctioned by the Lord. An official statement was issued by the Church in 1890 announcing the revocation of plural marriage (see D&C Official Declaration 1).

Just as the implementation of plural marriage was of divine origin, just as certainly was the revocation of the practice given by the Lord. Just as those who obeyed His command to practice plural marriage stood approved by Him, so do those who violate His revocation stand condemned before Him (*STDC* 2:356–357).

because they continue; then shall they be above all, because all things are subject unto them. Then shall they be Gods, because they have all power, and the angels are subject unto them.

21. Verily, verily I say unto you, except ye abide my law, ye cannot attain to this glory;

22. For strait is the gate, and narrow the way that leadeth unto the exaltation and continuation of the lives, and few there be that find it, because ye receive me not in the world, neither do ye know me.

23. But if ye receive me in the world, then shall ye know me, and shall receive your exaltation, that where I am, ye shall be also.

24. This is eternal lives, to know the only wise and true God, and Jesus Christ, whom he hath sent. I am he. Receive ye, therefore, my law.

25. Broad is the gate, and wide the way that leadeth to the deaths, and many there are that go in thereat; because they receive me not, neither do they abide in my law.

26. Verily, verily I say unto you, if a man marry a wife according to my word, and they are sealed by the Holy Spirit of promise, according to mine appointment, and he or she shall commit any sin or transgression of the new and everlasting covenant whatever, and all manner of blasphemies, and if they commit no murder, wherein they shed innocent blood—yet they shall come forth in the first resurrection, and enter into their exaltation; but they shall be destroyed in the flesh, and shall be delivered unto the buffetings of Satan unto the day of redemption, saith the Lord God.

27. The blasphemy against the Holy Ghost, which shall not be forgiven in the world, nor out of the world, is in that ye commit murder, wherein ye shed innocent blood, and assent unto my death, after ye have received my new and everlasting covenant, saith the Lord God; and he that abideth not this law, can in no wise enter into my glory, but shall be damned, saith the Lord.

28. I am the Lord thy God, and will give unto thee the law of my Holy Priesthood, as was ordained by me, and my Father before the world was.

29. Abraham received all things, whatsoever he received, by revelation and commandment, by my word, saith the Lord, and hath entered into his exaltation, and sitteth upon his throne.

30. Abraham received promises concerning his seed, and of the fruit of his loins,—from whose loins ye

D&C 132:21–24—The gate is "strait" and the way "narrow" in verse 22, providing another reminder that "many are called, but few are chosen" (D&C 121:40). The word *strait* derives from a Latin verb meaning "to draw tight." Thus a "strait" gate is one that is restricted and narrow—a reference to the qualifying conditions placed on those who enter therein. A "strait" gate is in fact a *covenant* gate, one that requires abiding by eternal laws and principles in order to pass through. Once admitted, the traveler proceeds by way of a "narrow" pathway, one that is defined by the strict fundamentals of the gospel. To veer from the pathway is to go into detours and sideways, much like the wayward travelers in Lehi's vision who "fell away into forbidden paths and were lost" (1 Ne. 8:28).

D&C 132:26—President Joseph Fielding Smith clarifies the meaning of this passage:

> Verse 26, in Section 132, is the most abused passage in any scripture. The Lord has never promised any soul that he may be taken into exaltation without the spirit of repentance. While repentance is not stated in this passage, yet it is, and must be, implied. . . .
>
> The Lord said by his own mouth: ". . . *And no unclean thing can enter into his kingdom; therefore nothing entereth into his rest save it be those who have washed their garments in my blood, because of their faith, and the repentance of all their sins, and their faithfulness unto the end*" [3 Nephi 27:19].
>
> So we must conclude that those spoken of in verse 26 are those who, having sinned, have *fully repented* and are willing to pay the price of their sinning, else the blessings of exaltation will not follow. Repentance is absolutely necessary for the forgiveness, and the person having sinned must be cleansed. . . . (*DS* 2:94–96.)

THE LORD'S LAW OF CELESTIAL MARRIAGE

Here, the Lord described three different kinds of marriage and the conditions and promises associated with each:

Marriage for mortality only. The law under which this kind of marriage is contracted is valid only to the extent that man has authority or power to control the affairs of life. It is limited to mortal life and does not extend beyond the grave. Such a law of marriage is not of the Lord. Spouses in this marriage will be alone throughout eternity, and will serve as angels to those who have received higher degrees of exaltation (see D&C 132:16–17).

A counterfeit celestial marriage. Marriage can endure for eternity when people comply with the conditions the Lord has set. Some have assumed that the power to perform such a marriage is available through sources not authorized by the Lord. When a marriage is performed by those who do not have authority from the Lord to do so, the marriage will also have an end when men are dead (see D&C 132:18).

Celestial marriage. Unique among the doctrines and practices of this world is the Lord's concept of marriage as provided in the Lord's Church and kingdom upon the earth (see D&C 132:19, 131:1–4). He has revealed that His law provides eternal relationships for families that have been created under His law of marriage. He referred to this law as a gate, and it is only by entering this gate that a couple gains access to eternal marriage blessings. The conditions and promises related to this marriage depend on proper authority, worthiness, and the sealing of the Holy Spirit of Promise. These spouses will be sealed up to eternal life (with their calling and election made sure), will inherit all powers and dominions, will have a continuation of children forever, and will inherit all that God has (*STDC* 2:357–358).

are, namely, my servant Joseph—which were to continue so long as they were in the world; and as touching Abraham and his seed, out of the world they should continue; both in the world and out of the world should they continue as innumerable as the stars; or, if ye were to count the sand upon the sea shore, ye could not number them.

31. This promise is yours, also, because ye are of Abraham, and the promise was made unto Abraham; and by this law is the continuation of the works of my Father, wherein he glorified himself.

32. Go ye, therefore, and do the works of Abraham; enter ye into my law, and ye shall be saved.

33. But if ye enter not into my law ye cannot receive the promise of my Father which he made unto Abraham.

34. God commanded Abraham, and Sarah gave Hagar to Abraham to wife. And why did she do it? Because this was the law, and from Hagar sprang many people. This, therefore, was fulfilling, among other things, the promises.

35. Was Abraham, therefore, under condemnation? Verily, I say unto you, Nay; for I, the Lord, commanded it.

36. Abraham was commanded to offer his son Isaac; nevertheless, it was written, thou shalt not kill. Abraham, however, did not refuse, and it was accounted unto him for righteousness.

37. Abraham received concubines, and they bear him children, and it was accounted unto him for righteousness, because they were given unto him, and he abode in my law, as Isaac also, and Jacob did none other things than that which they were commanded; and because they did none other things than that which they were commanded, they have entered into their exaltation, according to the promises, and sit upon thrones, and are not angels, but are Gods.

38. David also received many wives and concubines, and also Solomon and Moses my servants, as also many others of my servants, from the beginning of creation until this time; and in nothing did they sin, save in those things which they received not of me.

39. David's wives and concubines were given unto him, of me, by the hand of Nathan, my servant, and others of the prophets who had the keys of this power; and in none of these things did he sin against me, save in the case of Uriah and his wife; and, therefore he hath fallen from his exaltation, and received his portion: and he shall not inherit them out of the world; for I gave them unto another, saith the Lord.

40. I am the Lord thy God, and I gave unto thee, my servant Joseph, an appointment, and restore all things; ask what ye will, and it shall be given unto you according to my word:

41. And as ye have asked concerning adultery—verily, verily I

D&C 132:30–34, 38—Under provisions of the Abrahamic covenant, Abraham was to be blessed with a progeny as enumerable as the stars (see Abr. 2:9). Joseph Smith, of the lineage of Abraham, received the same promise (verse 31). Through the Restoration, the Abrahamic covenant is again enacted and operative, with the gathering and ministry of Israel to serve the purpose of spreading the gospel to the four corners of the earth. Orson Hyde expounded on this theme:

> If Abraham was to be a prince and a ruler, and his posterity become numerous, may we not, if faithful to our God and to our covenants, be as Abraham? Shall there be any end to our posterity? May they not be as numerous as the stars in the firmament, and as the sands upon the seashore? Abraham may be in advance of us; he lived in an earlier period; but we are following up in the same track. Although we may not be called upon to yield up an only son, as Abraham was, yet, may we not enjoy through faithfulness the blessings, and honors, and privileges that he did? I see nothing in the way of it. I believe it is [according] to the goodness, and generosity, and loving kindness of our Father in heaven. (JD 11:151–52.)

THE BLESSINGS AND WORKS OF ABRAHAM

In this revelation, the Lord made known to Joseph Smith that the blessings of Abraham would be made available to this dispensation. The full realization of these blessings is contingent upon entering into the law of celestial marriage and being true to the conditions of that marriage covenant.

When this revelation on the law of celestial marriage was given to the Prophet Joseph Smith, it was a unique doctrine among the religious organizations of the earth. No other people in the world understood such a beautiful concept as the potential eternal relationships of husbands and wives.

Expressing his overwhelming delight at being taught such a doctrine of heaven, Parley P. Pratt recorded:

> It was from [Joseph Smith] that I learned that the wife of my bosom might be secured to me for time and all eternity; and that the refined sympathies and affections which endeared us to each other emanated from the fountain of divine eternal love. It was from him I learned that we might cultivate these affections, and grow and increase in the same to all eternity; while the result of our endless union would be an offspring as numerous as the stars of heaven, or the sands of the sea shore. . . . I had loved before, but I knew not why. But now I loved—with a pureness—an intensity of elevated, exalted feeling. . . . the wife of my bosom was an immortal eternal companion; a kind ministering angel, given to me as a comfort, and a crown of glory for ever and ever (APPP, 297–298) (STDC 2:360–362).

say unto you, if a man receiveth a wife in the new and everlasting covenant, and if she be with another man, and I have not appointed unto her by the holy anointing, she hath committed adultery, and shall be destroyed.

42. If she be not in the new and everlasting covenant, and she be with another man, she has committed adultery;

43. And if her husband be with another woman, and he was under a vow, he hath broken his vow, and hath committed adultery,

44. And if she hath not committed adultery, but is innocent, and hath not broken her vow, and she knoweth it, and I reveal it unto you, my servant Joseph, then shall you have power, by the power of my Holy Priesthood, to take her, and give her unto him that hath not committed adultery, but hath been faithful; for he shall be made ruler over many;

45. For I have conferred upon you the keys and power of the Priesthood, wherein I restore all things, and make known unto you all things in due time.

46. And verily, verily I say unto you, that whatsoever you seal on earth, shall be sealed in heaven; and whatsoever you bind on earth, in my name, and by my word, saith the Lord, it shall be eternally bound in the heavens; and whosesoever sins you remit on earth shall be remitted eternally in the heavens; and whosesoever sins you retain on earth, shall be retained in heaven.

47. And again, verily I say, whomsoever you bless, I will bless, and whomsoever you curse, I will curse, saith the Lord; for I, the Lord, am thy God.

48. And again, verily I say unto you, my servant Joseph, that whatsoever you give on earth, and to whomsoever you give any one on earth, by my word, and according to my law, it shall be visited with blessings, and not cursings, and with my power, saith the Lord, and shall be without condemnation on earth, and in heaven;

49. For I am the Lord thy God, and will be with thee even unto the end of the world, and through all eternity; for verily, I seal upon you your exaltation, and prepare a throne for you in the kingdom of my Father, with Abraham your father.

50. Behold, I have seen your sacrifices, and will forgive all your sins; I have seen your sacrifices in obedience to that which I have told you; go, therefore, and I make a way for your escape, as I accepted the offering of Abraham, of his son Isaac.

51. Verily, I say unto you, a commandment I give unto mine handmaid, Emma Smith, your wife, whom I have given unto you, that she stay herself, and partake not of that which I commanded you to offer unto her; for I did it, saith the Lord, to prove you all, as I did Abraham; and that I might require an offering at your hand, by covenant and sacrifice;

52. And let mine handmaid, Emma Smith, receive all those that have

D&C 132:41—God Himself will execute the judgment for adultery (a sin that is defined in verses 41–44).

D&C 132:45, 49—Joseph Smith held the keys of the kingdom, by which he could seal on earth and have that seal honored in heaven; similarly, he could remit sins on earth and have that remittance honored in heaven.

D&C 132:46—Temple sealings can be canceled, but the approval of the president of the Church must be given for such a sealing to be canceled. This verse refers to sins remitted on earth: only our Father in Heaven can forgive sins. The bishop acts on His behalf and extends forgiveness on behalf of the Church as He is inspired to do so. Revelation is *always* required in such a case.

D&C 132:49—This verse verifies that Joseph Smith's calling and election was made sure.

D&C 132:51—We don't know exactly what this verse is referring to. Whatever was involved was obviously a test of faith that was not actually required at Joseph's hand or at Emma's hand. Because we are not given clear information about it, it is useless for us to speculate about what it was.

been given unto my servant Joseph, and who are virtuous and pure before me; and those who are not pure, and have said they were pure, shall be destroyed, saith the Lord God;

53. For I am the Lord thy God, and ye shall obey my voice; and I give unto my servant Joseph, that he shall be made ruler over many things, for he hath been faithful over a few things, and from henceforth I will strengthen him.

54. And I command mine handmaid, Emma Smith, to abide and cleave unto my servant Joseph, and to none else. But if she will not abide this commandment, she shall be destroyed, saith the Lord; for I am the Lord thy God, and will destroy her, if she abide not in my law;

55. But if she will not abide this commandment, then shall my servant Joseph do all things for her, even as he hath said; and I will bless him and multiply him and give unto him an hundred-fold in this world, of fathers and mothers, brothers and sisters, houses and lands, wives and children, and crowns of eternal lives in the eternal worlds.

56. And again, verily I say, let mine handmaid forgive my servant Joseph his trespasses; and then shall she be forgiven her trespasses, wherein she has trespassed against me; and I, the Lord thy God, will bless her, and multiply her, and make her heart to rejoice.

57. And again, I say, let not my servant Joseph put his property out of his hands, lest an enemy come and destroy him; for Satan seeketh to destroy; for I am the Lord thy God, and he is my servant; and behold, and lo, I am with him, as I was with Abraham, thy father, even unto his exaltation and glory.

58. Now, as touching the law of the Priesthood, there are many things pertaining thereunto.

59. Verily, if a man be called of my Father, as was Aaron, by mine own voice, and by the voice of him that sent me; and I have endowed him with the keys of the power of this Priesthood, if he do anything in my name, and according to my law, and by my word, he will not commit sin, and I will justify him.

60. Let no one, therefore, set on my servant Joseph; for I will justify him; for he shall do the sacrifice which I require at his hands, for his transgressions, saith the Lord your God.

61. And again, as pertaining to the law of the Priesthood: If any man espouse a virgin, and desire to espouse another, and the first give her consent; and if he espouse the second, and they are virgins, and have vowed to no other man, then is he justified; he cannot commit adultery, for they are given unto him; for he cannot commit adultery with that that belongeth unto him and to no one else;

62. And if he have ten virgins given unto him by this law, he cannot commit adultery, for they belong to him, and they are given unto him, therefore is he justified.

63. But if one or either of the ten virgins, after she is espoused, shall be with another man; she has committed adultery, and shall be destroyed; for they are given unto him to multiply and replenish the earth, according to my commandment, and

D&C 132:52–56—Emma Smith was required to do four things: 1) Accept all those who had been given to Joseph Smith, women who were virtuous and pure before the Lord; 2) Obey the Lord's voice; 3) Abide and cleave unto Joseph, and to none else; and 4) Forgive Joseph of his trespasses. In these verses are stated the blessings to Emma if she obeys these commandments (she will be forgiven her trespasses and the Lord will cause her to rejoice) as well as the punishment to Emma if she rejects these commandments (she will be destroyed).

D&C 132:56—Concerning plural marriage, Elder Bruce R. McConkie wrote that a man can have only one wife at a time unless the Lord otherwise commands through revelation. The principle of plural marriage was instituted during the early days of this dispensation as part of the restitution of all things, and the Prophet Joseph Smith and certain other Church leaders were commanded to enter into the practice of plural marriage, which was openly taught and practiced after Brigham Young led the Saints to the Salt Lake Valley. In 1890, the Lord *by revelation* withdrew the command to practice plural marriage, and President Wilford Woodruff issued the Manifesto. According to Elder McConkie, "Plural marriage is not essential to salvation or exaltation. . . . *All who pretend or assume to engage in plural marriage in this day, when the one holding the keys has withdrawn the power by which they are performed, are guilty of gross wickedness*" (MD, 577–579).

D&C 132:59—What human law regards as a crime may or may not be a sin from a divine point of view, according to the law of the priesthood. That law states that whatever is done in the name of God, according to His law and by His direction, cannot be considered sin.

The Lord can command and revoke according to His will. Such has been the case at different times here upon the earth and in this instance, regarding the plurality of wives. A statement in the *Deseret News* in 1933 reiterated the official Church position on this doctrine:

The members of the Church are reminded that the practice of polygamous or plural marriage is not the only law whose suspension has been authorized by the Lord and adopted by the people. The law of animal sacrifice, in force in ancient Israel, has been suspended, but the Prophet Joseph asserted it would be again restored, and such is the effect of the statement made by John the Baptist when restoring the Aaronic Priesthood. The law of the United Order has likewise been suspended, to be reestablished in the due time of the Lord. Other laws might be mentioned. . . . (*Deseret News Church Section*, June 17, 1933, 19–20.)

to fulfil the promise which was given by my Father before the foundation of the world; and for their exaltation in the eternal worlds, that they may bear the souls of men; for herein is the work of my Father continued, that he may be glorified.

64. And again, verily, verily I say unto you, if any man have a wife, who holds the keys of this power, and he teaches unto her the law of my Priesthood, as pertaining to these things, then shall she believe, and administer unto him, or she shall be destroyed, saith the Lord your God, for I will destroy her; for I will magnify my name upon all those who receive and abide in my law.

65. Therefore, it shall be lawful in me, if she receive not this law, for him to receive all things, whatsoever I, the Lord his God, will give unto him, because she did not administer unto him according to my word; and she then becomes the transgressor; and he is exempt from the law of Sarah, who administered unto Abraham according to the law, when I commanded Abraham to take Hagar to wife.

66. And now, as pertaining to this law, verily, verily I say unto you, I will reveal more unto you, hereafter; therefore, let this suffice for the present. Behold, I am Alpha and Omega. Amen.

SECTION 133

1. Hearken, O ye people of my church, saith the Lord your God, and hear the word of the Lord concerning you:

2. The Lord who shall suddenly come to his temple; the Lord who shall come down upon the world with a curse to judgment; yea, upon all the nations that forget God, and upon all the ungodly among you.

3. For he shall make bare his holy arm in the eyes of all the nations,

Section 133 Background—Given on November 3, 1831, at Hiram, Ohio, at the close of a three-day conference (see HC 1:229–234). Given two days after Section 1 (the "Preface"), it was called the "Appendix" because it followed the revelation approving the publication of all the revelations. Because it has been called the "Appendix," it has always been near the end of the Doctrine and Covenants instead of being placed in chronological order.

The Prophet wrote in his journal: "It had been decided by the conference that Elder Oliver Cowdery should carry the commandments and revelations to Independence, Missouri, for printing, and that I should arrange and get them in readiness by the time that he left, which was to be by—or, if possible, before the—15th of the month [November]. At this time there were many things which the Elders desired to know relative to preaching the Gospel to the inhabitants of the earth, and concerning the gathering; and in order to walk by the true light, and be instructed from on high, on the 3rd of November, 1831, I inquired of the Lord and received the following important revelation [Section 133], which has since been added to the book of Doctrine and Covenants, and called the Appendix" (HC 1:229).

As the Lord's appendix to the D&C, Section 133 was added to amplify, emphasize, make stronger, or better explain its contents. Elder John A. Widtsoe said that this material supplements the Lord's preface (Section 1), and that together these two sections encompass the contents of hte book in condensed form.

Interestingly, this section contains many concepts that presuppose knowledge of other scriptures. These include the Lord coming to His temple (see verse 2), concepts surrounding Babylon (see verses 4–7 and 14), the parable of the ten virgins (see verse 10), Lot's wife (see verse 15), the Lamb on Mt. Zion (see verse 18), and Jesus on the Mount of Olives (see verse 20).

D&C 133:2—This verse begins with a reference to the Lord suddenly coming to His temple. This will occur as part of the Second Coming, when the Lord will bless and minister to His people.

D&C 133:3—The Lord making "bare his holy arm" refers to the fact that He will reveal His strength to all the world. All the people in all the nations of the world will see God's victory and deliverance on behalf of His people.

and all the ends of the earth shall see the salvation of their God.

4. Wherefore, prepare ye, prepare ye, O my people; sanctify yourselves; gather ye together, O ye people of my church, upon the land of Zion, all you that have not been commanded to tarry.

5. Go ye out from Babylon. Be ye clean that bear the vessels of the Lord.

6. Call your solemn assemblies, and speak often one to another. And let every man call upon the name of the Lord;

7. Yea, verily I say unto you again, the time has come when the voice of the Lord is unto you, go ye out of Babylon; gather ye out from among the nations, from the four winds, from one end of heaven to the other.

8. Send forth the elders of my church unto the nations which are afar off; unto the islands of the sea; send forth unto foreign lands; call upon all nations, firstly, upon the Gentiles, and then upon the Jews.

9. And behold, and lo, this shall be their cry, and the voice of the Lord unto all people: Go ye forth unto the land of Zion, that the borders of my people may be enlarged, and that her Stakes may be strengthened, and that Zion may go forth unto the regions round about;

10. Yea, let the cry go forth among all people: Awake and arise and go forth to meet the Bridegroom: behold and lo, the Bridegroom cometh, go ye out to meet him. Prepare yourselves for the great day of the Lord.

11. Watch, therefore, for ye know neither the day nor the hour.

12. Let them therefore, who are among the Gentiles, flee unto Zion.

13. And let them who be of Judah flee unto Jerusalem, unto the mountains of the Lord's house.

14. Go ye out from among the nations, even from Babylon, from the midst of wickedness, which is spiritual Babylon.

15. But verily, thus saith the Lord, Let not your flight be in haste, but let all things be prepared before you; and he that goeth, let him not look back, lest sudden destruction shall come upon him.

16. Hearken and hear, O ye inhabitants of the earth. Listen ye elders of my church together, and hear the voice of the Lord, for he calleth upon all men, and he commandeth all men everywhere to repent;

17. For, behold, the Lord God hath sent forth the angel crying through the midst of heaven, saying, Prepare ye the way of the Lord, and make his

D&C 133:4, 9—From the eternal perspective of the Lord it is revealed that the vast upheavals of the last days will bring commotion and anguish to the nations of the earth, while those who are prepared and sanctified will be preserved in places of safety and holiness. When will these events transpire? ". . . of that day and hour knoweth no man, no, not the angels of heaven, but my Father only" (Matt. 24:36).

D&C 133:4—Because no unclean thing can dwell in the presence of the Lord, all those who are caught up to meet Him at His Second Coming must be sanctified, or made pure before Him. The prophets of this dispensation and the scriptures repeatedly say we must do three important things as we prepare for the Second Coming: 1) We must prepare by learning to know God the Father and His Son, Jesus Christ, and by developing our own testimony of Joseph Smith and the Restoration. 2) We must become sanctified (in other words, pure and clean). 3) We must gather—in other words, we must be in areas where we can receive the blessings of the temple.

D&C 133:5—Babylon is a symbol of sin, evil, and the wickedness present in the world. Priesthood holders ("ye" in this verse) must make certain that they themselves are clean and free from the influences of the world.

D&C 133:8—The Jews will receive the gospel last because they rejected the Savior during His mortal ministry. President Spencer W. Kimball, in referring to this verse, asked if we have possibly underestimated its meaning: the Lord specifically asks us to call on *all* nations, and He means every nation on earth.

D&C 133:11—Elder Bruce R. McConkie taught that we will not know the day nor the hour, but through revelation and a careful observation of the signs, we can know the generation.

D&C 133:12–13—During the Millennium, there will be two equal centers of government: one in Zion (Jackson County, Missouri) and one in Palestine (Jerusalem). Likewise, two great temples will be built: one in Jackson County and one in Jerusalem.

D&C 133:14–15—The Saints among the Gentiles are to flee to Zion, and those of Judah to Jerusalem. All are to flee out of the grip of the spiritual depravity of Babylon and migrate in an orderly fashion to places of safety—"unto the mountains of the Lord's house" (verse 13). Our commitment to maintaining our forward motion in the cause of Zion is to be unflinching and unshakable. We cannot look back as we flee Babylon. There is no comprising the standards of salvation and exaltation. The theme of the hour prior to the coming of the Son of God is repentance.

paths straight for the hour of his coming is nigh,

18. When the Lamb shall stand upon Mount Zion, and with him a hundred and forty-four thousand, having his Father's name written on their foreheads:

19. Wherefore, prepare ye for the coming of the Bridegroom; go ye, go ye out to meet him,

20. For behold, he shall stand upon the mount of Olivet, and upon the mighty ocean, even the great deep, and upon the islands of the sea, and upon the land of Zion;

21. And he shall utter his voice out of Zion, and he shall speak from Jerusalem, and his voice shall be heard among all people,

22. And it shall be a voice as the voice of many waters, and as the voice of a great thunder, which shall break down the mountains, and the valleys shall not be found;

23. He shall command the great deep, and it shall be driven back into the north countries, and the islands shall become one land,

24. And the land of Jerusalem and the land of Zion shall be turned back into their own place, and the earth shall be like as it was in the days before it was divided.

25. And the Lord, even the Savior, shall stand in the midst of his people, and shall reign over all flesh.

26. And they who are in the north countries shall come in remembrance before the Lord, and their prophets shall hear his voice, and shall no longer stay themselves, and they shall smite the rocks, and the ice shall flow down at their presence.

27. And an highway shall be cast up in the midst of the great deep.

28. Their enemies shall become a prey unto them,

29. And in the barren deserts there shall come forth pools of living water; and the parched ground shall no longer be a thirsty land.

30. And they shall bring forth their rich treasures unto the children of Ephraim my servants.

31. And the boundaries of the everlasting hills shall tremble at their presence.

32. And there shall they fall down and be crowned with glory, even in Zion, by the hands of the servants of the Lord, even the children of Ephraim;

33. And they shall be filled with songs of everlasting joy.

34. Behold, this is the blessing of the everlasting God upon the tribes

D&C 133:18–35—Concerning the 144,000 referenced in verse 18, Orson Pratt observed:

> On that occasion he [John the Revelator] saw one hundred and forty-four thousand standing upon Mount Zion, singing a new and glorious song; the singers seemed to be among the most happy and glorious of those who were shown to John. They, the one hundred and forty-four thousand, had a peculiar inscription in their foreheads. [Rev. 14:1.] What was it? It was the Father's name. What is the Father's name? It is God—the being we worship. (*JD* 14:242–243.)

The geological dislocations prior to the Second Coming will be of immense scope and magnitude. The Prophet Joseph Smith observed:

> There shall be famine, and pestilence, and earthquake in divers places; and the prophets have declared that the valleys should rise; that the mountains should be laid low; that a great earthquake should be, in which the sun should become black as sack-cloth of hair and the moon turn into blood; yea, the Eternal God hath declared that the great deep shall roll back into the north countries and that the land of Zion and the land of Jerusalem shall be joined together, as they were before they were divided in the days of Peleg. [Gen. 10:25.] No wonder the mind starts at the sound of the last days. (*Evening and Morning Star*, Feb. 1835.)

The return of the Lost Tribes will be a literal event—separate from the gathering of the elect from the four quarters of the earth through missionary work. James E. Talmage explains:

> I have found elders in Israel who would tell me that the predictions relating to the Lost Tribes are to be explained in this figurative manner—that the gathering of those tribes is already well advanced and that there is no hiding place whereto God has led them, from which they shall come forth, led by their prophets to receive their blessings here at the hands of gathered Ephraim, the gathered portions that have been scattered among the nations. Yea, let God be true, and doubt we not his word, though it makes the opinions of men appear to be lies. The tribes shall come; they are not lost unto the Lord; they shall be brought forth as hath been predicted; . . . . the records of the Lost Tribes of Israel . . . shall be made one with the record of the Jews, or the Holy Bible, and the record of the Nephites, or the Book of Mormon, even as the Lord hath predicted; and those records, which the tribes lost to man but yet to be found again shall bring, shall tell of the visit of the resurrected Christ to them, after He had manifested Himself to the Nephites upon this continent. For, as not one jot or tittle of the law has been permitted to fail, so surely no jot or tittle of the Gospel shall go unfulfilled. (*CR*, Oct. 1916, 76.)

of Israel, and the richer blessing upon the head of Ephraim and his fellows.

35. And they also of the tribe of Judah, after their pain, shall be sanctified in holiness before the Lord to dwell in his presence, day and night, for ever and ever.

36. And now, verily saith the Lord, That these things might be known among you, O inhabitants of the earth, I have sent forth mine angel, flying through the midst of heaven, having the everlasting gospel, who hath appeared unto some, and hath committed it unto man, who shall appear unto many that dwell on the earth;

37. And this gospel shall be preached unto every nation, and kindred, tongue, and people,

38. And the servants of God shall go forth, saying, with a loud voice, Fear God and give glory to him, for the hour of his judgment is come:

39. And worship him that made heaven, and earth, and the sea, and the fountains of waters,

40. Calling upon the name of the Lord day and night, saying, O that thou wouldst rend the heavens, that thou wouldst come down, that the mountains might flow down at thy presence.

41. And it shall be answered upon their heads, for the presence of the Lord shall be as the melting fire that burneth, and as the fire which causeth the waters to boil.

42. O Lord thou shalt come down to make thy name known to thine adversaries, and all nations shall tremble at thy presence.

43. When thou doest terrible things—things they look not for;

44. Yea, when thou comest down, and the mountains flow down at thy presence, thou shalt meet him who rejoiceth and worketh righteousness, who remembereth thee in thy ways;

45. For since the beginning of the world have not men heard nor perceived by the ear, neither hath any eye seen, O God, besides thee, how great things thou hast prepared for him that waiteth for thee.

46. And it shall be said, Who is this that cometh down from God in heaven with dyed garments; yea, from the regions which are not known, clothed in his glorious apparel, traveling in the greatness of his strength?

47. And he shall say, I am he who spake in righteousness, mighty to save.

48. And the Lord shall be red in his apparel, and his garments like him that treadeth in the wine vat,

49. And so great shall be the glory of his presence, that the sun shall hide his face in shame; and the moon

D&C 133:35—When the Savior appears on the Mount of Olives as part of His Second Coming, the Jews who are there will see the wounds from the nails in His hands and feet, and they will recognize Him as the Messiah who was crucified in Israel. At that time the Savior will forgive the Jews and will sanctify them.

D&C 133:37, 48—The emissaries of the Lord will carry the gospel to the ends of the earth in the final period of the earth's history prior to the Second Coming. They will sound the theme of repentance and gather the elect from the shadows. But their work will not succeed in turning all the hearts to the Lord—for many will be caught in their wickedness and folly when He returns. Joseph Fielding McConkie summarizes the state of affairs at the final hour:

> The scriptures describe a state of wickedness that will usher in the Millennium, not a state of righteousness. Malachi speaks of the time of Christ's return as "the great and dreadful day" (Malachi 4:5), one in which the proud and the wicked shall be burned as stubble . . . it will be a wicked, not a righteous, world that greets the returning Christ. . . . Though a state of wickedness will usher in the Millennium and the return of Christ, a sizable number of faithful Saints will be prepared to meet him. (ASA, 120–122.)

D&C 133:48—The red color of the Savior's garments at the time of His Second Coming represents the wine, which in turn represents the blood that was shed as part of the Atonement. It is actually literal, not figurative.

D&C 133:49—Other indications of the Savior's glory at His Second Coming are that the mountains will flow down (see D&C 133:40), the waters on earth will boil (see D&C 133:41), the nations will tremble (see D&C 133:42), and the wicked will be burned by the brightness of His glory (see Malachi 4:1–3).

shall withhold its light; and the stars shall be hurled from their places;

50. And his voice shall be heard, I have trodden the wine-press alone, and have brought judgment upon all people; and none were with me;

51. And I have trampled them in my fury, and I did tread upon them in mine anger, and their blood have I sprinkled upon my garments, and stained all my raiment; for this was the day of vengeance which was in my heart.

52. And now the year of my redeemed is come, and they shall mention the loving kindness of their Lord, and all that he has bestowed upon them according to his goodness, and according to his loving kindness, for ever and ever.

53. In all their afflictions he was afflicted. And the angel of his presence saved them; and in his love, and in his pity, he redeemed them, and bear them, and carried them all the days of old;

54. Yea, and Enoch also, and they who were with him; the prophets who were before him; and Noah also, and they who were before him; and Moses also, and they who were before him;

55. And from Moses to Elijah; and from Elijah to John, who were with Christ in his resurrection, and the holy apostles, with Abraham, Isaac, and Jacob, shall be in the presence of the Lamb.

56. And the graves of the saints shall be opened; and they shall come forth and stand on the right hand of the Lamb, when he shall stand upon Mount Zion, and upon the holy city, the New Jerusalem, and they shall sing the song of the Lamb, day and night, for ever and ever.

57. And for this cause, that men might be made partakers of the glories which were to be revealed, the Lord sent forth the fulness of his gospel, his everlasting covenant, reasoning in plainness and simplicity,

58. To prepare the weak for those things which are coming on the earth, and for the Lord's errand in the day when the weak shall confound the wise, and the little one become a strong nation, and two should put their tens of thousands to flight;

59. And by the weak things of the earth the Lord shall thresh the nations by the power of his Spirit.

60. And for this cause these commandments were given; they were commanded to be kept from the world in the day that they were

D&C 133:52—The colossal magnitude of the Great Judgment, with its ultimate cleansing operation that brings finality to the reign of wickedness on the earth, will stand in stark contrast to the celebration of glory among the redeemed, whose endless testimonies will dissipate the atmosphere of evil and anguish spewing forth from those caught unprepared for the Second Coming. The lesson that emerges from these passages of scripture is this: to live worthy of a joyful reunion with our Redeemer, our Lord, our Savior, our King. Said Elder Bruce R. McConkie:

Of all the resurrections that ever have been or ever will be upon this earth, the most glorious—the one that transcends all others in power, grandeur, and might—will be the resurrection that attends the return of the Lord Jesus. He will come with ten thousands of his saints, all of them resurrected persons from ages past. He will call forth from their graves and from the watery deep ten thousands of his other saints, all of them righteous persons who have lived since his mortal ministry. Those among his saints on earth who are faithful will be caught up to meet him in the clouds of glory, and they will then return to earth with him to live out their appointed days on the new earth with its new heavens. (MMSC, 627.)

D&C 133:57, 62—President Wilford Woodruff places these themes in the context of urgency as well as opportunity:

We live in one of the most important dispensations that God ever gave to man, namely, the great and last dispensation of the fulness of times, the dispensation of all dispensations, and the one in which the whole flood of prophecy in the holy Bible will be fulfilled. . . . I wish to have the Latter-day Saints understand their appointment, position, and responsibility before the God of heaven, and their responsibilities to both Jew and Gentile, living and dead, on this and the other side of the [veil]. . . .

The Lord has chosen a royal Priesthood and a holy people from among the weak things of the world, in fulfillment of his revelations; and we have been commanded to go forth and bear record of these things, and we have done it. . . . The Millennium is dawning upon the world, we are at the end of the sixth thousand years, and the great day of rest, the Millennium of which the Lord has spoken, will soon dawn and the Savior will come in the clouds of heaven to reign over his people on the earth one thousand years. The Lord has a great work ahead and he is preparing a people to do it before his coming. (JD 18:110, 113–14.)

given, but now are to go forth unto all flesh.

61. And this according to the mind and will of the Lord, who ruleth over all flesh.

62. And unto him that repenteth and sanctifieth himself before the Lord, shall be given eternal life;

63. And upon them that hearken not to the voice of the Lord, shall be fulfilled that which was written by the Prophet Moses, that they should be cut off from among the people.

64. And also that which was written by the prophet Malachi; for, behold, the day cometh that shall burn as an oven, and all the proud, yea, and all that do wickedly, shall be stubble; and the day that cometh shall burn them up, saith the Lord of hosts, that it shall leave them neither root nor branch.

65. Wherefore, this shall be the answer of the Lord unto them—

66. In that day when I came unto mine own, no man among you received me, and you were driven out.

67. When I called again, there was none of you to answer, yet my arm was not shortened at all, that I could not redeem, neither my power to deliver.

68. Behold, at my rebuke I dry up the sea. I make the rivers a wilderness; their fish stinketh, and dieth for thirst.

69. I clothe the heavens with blackness, and make sackcloth their covering.

70. And this shall ye have of my hand, ye shall lie down in sorrow.

71. Behold and lo, there are none to deliver you, for ye obeyed not my voice when I called to you out of the heavens; ye believed not my servants, and when they were sent unto you ye received them not;

72. Wherefore they sealed up the testimony and bound up the law, and ye were delivered over unto darkness;

73. These shall go away into outer darkness where there is weeping, and wailing, and gnashing of teeth.

74. Behold the Lord your God hath spoken it. Amen.

D&C 133:63–64—These two verses give important information about what will be going on with the wicked when the Lord appears in his glory. First, the wicked will see the judgments of God, but the Lord will not allow them to share the inheritance of the righteous. As indicated in verse 64, "it shall leave them neither root nor branch," meaning that the wicked will have no family inheritance or patriarchal lineage. In essence, they won't inherit celestial glory.

D&C 133:71–72—President Spencer W. Kimball said that the most common excuses for rejecting the prophets were that the prophets came from obscurity and many seemed slow of speech. The real problem, of course, was with the people themselves: they had their hearts set too much upon the things of the world, were too intent upon following the philosophies of men, and were too often looking beyond the mark. But by far the most common cause, he taught, was that the hearts of the people had become hardened.

D&C 133:73—The "outer darkness" referred to in this verse is not the place to which sons of perdition will be banished, but hell, or the telestial kingdom. In this verse it is so called because it is a place of darkness that hates truth.

THE SECOND COMING

It is folly to assume that we know the specific time or sequence of the events associated with the Lord's Second Coming. Suffice it to say that they will take place in connection with the ushering in of the Lord's millennial reign. Some of the specific events mentioned by the Lord in this revelation are (see D&C 133:17–35, 56, 62–64):

- The 144,000 high priests will appear
- The voice of the Lord will be heard throughout the earth
- The earth's surface will be changed
- The lost tribes will return from the north countries
- The tribe of Judah will be sanctified
- The Saints will be resurrected and will appear with the Lord
- The wicked will be cleansed from the earth

This list is not exhaustive, but it provides a glimpse of some of the magnificent events that we can look forward to with great anticipation. The Second Coming is among the greatest and most significant events in the earth's history. With all the signs, there are two absolute truths we should remember: 1) the Savior is coming, and 2) the Savior's Church is the only way whereby mankind can obtain the saving principles of the gospel and thus be adequately prepared for that great day (STDC 2:368–369).

SECTION 134

1. We believe that governments were instituted of God for the benefit of man, and that he holds men accountable for their acts in relation to them, either in making laws and administering them, for the good and safety of society.

2. We believe that no government can exist in peace, except such laws are framed and held inviolate as will secure to each individual the free exercise of conscience, the right and control of property, and the protection of life.

3. We believe that all governments necessarily require civil officers and magistrates to enforce the laws of the same, and that such as will administer the law in equity and justice, should be sought for and upheld by the voice of the people (if a republic,) or the will of the sovereign.

4. We believe that religion is instituted of God, and that men are amenable to him, and to him only, for the exercise of it, unless their religious opinions prompt them to infringe upon the rights and liberties of others; but we do not believe that human law has a right to interfere in prescribing rules of worship to bind the consciences of men, nor dictate forms for public or private devotion; that the civil magistrate should restrain crime, but never control conscience; should punish guilt, but never suppress the freedom of the soul.

5. We believe that all men are bound to sustain and uphold the respective governments in which they reside, while protected in their inherent and inalienable rights by the laws of such governments; and that sedition and rebellion are unbecoming every citizen thus protected, and should be punished accordingly; and that all governments have a right to enact such laws as in their own judgment are best calculated to secure the public interest, at the same time, however, holding sacred the freedom of conscience.

6. We believe that every man should be honored in his station: rulers and magistrates as such, being placed for the protection of the innocent, and the punishment of the guilty; and that to the laws, all men owe respect and deference, as without them peace and harmony would be supplanted by anarchy and terror; human laws being instituted for the express purpose of regulating our interests as individuals and nations, between man and man, and divine laws given of heaven, prescribing rules on spiritual concerns, for faith and worship, both to be answered by man to his Maker.

Section 134 Background—At a general assembly of the priesthood held at Kirtland on August 17, 1835, the material for the forthcoming "Book of Doctrine and Covenants of the Church of the Latter-day Saints" (*HC* 2:244) was reviewed and approved. The committee charged with the responsibility of preparing these materials consisted of Joseph Smith, Sidney Rigdon, Oliver Cowdery, and Frederick G. Williams. "President Oliver Cowdery then read the following article on 'Governments and Laws in General' [Section 134], which was accepted and adopted and ordered to be printed in said book, by a unanimous vote" (*HC* 2:247). This section served to contravene salacious lies by the enemies of the Church that the Saints were adopting principles and institutions that opposed law and order.

D&C 134:1—Covenant-abiding Saints are also law-abiding citizens of the land where they reside. The Lord has counseled us to participate in the enterprise of serving our communities and country as we engage in building the kingdom of God. This combination of consistent and devoted service to God, country, and our fellow men furthers the work of the ministry and supports the cause of missionary work throughout the world.

D&C 134:2–4—President Heber J. Grant said: "One of the fundamental articles of faith promulgated by the Prophet Joseph Smith was: 'We claim the privilege of worshiping Almighty God according to the dictates of our own conscience; and allow all men the same privilege, let them worship how, where, or what they may.' But we claim absolutely no right, no prerogative whatever, to interfere with any other people" (*CR*, April 1921, 203).

D&C 134:5—The First Presidency—Brigham Young, Heber C. Kimball, and Willard Richards—no strangers to the actions of injustice and unlawful attacks against the Church, counseled:

> Sustain the government of the nation wherever you are, and speak well of it, for this is right, and the government has a right to expect it of you so long as that government sustains you in your civil and religious liberty, in those rights which inherently belong to every person born on the earth; and if you are persecuted in your native land, and denied the privilege of worshiping the true God in spirit and in truth, flee to the land of Zion, to America—to the United States, where constitutional rights and freedom are not surpassed by any nation—where God saw fit, in these last days, to renew the dispensation of salvation, by revelations from the heavens, and where all, by the Constitution and laws of the land, when executed in righteousness, are protected in all the civil and religious freedom that man is capable of enjoying on earth. . . . (*Millennial Star*, July 17, 1852; 14:325.)

7. We believe that rulers, states, and governments, have a right, and are bound to enact laws for the protection of all citizens in the free exercise of their religious belief; but we do not believe that they have a right in justice, to deprive citizens of this privilege, or proscribe them in their opinions, so long as a regard and reverence are shown to the laws, and such religious opinions do not justify sedition nor conspiracy.

8. We believe that the commission of crime should be punished according to the nature of the offense; that murder, treason, robbery, theft, and the breach of the general peace, in all respects, should be punished according to their criminality, and their tendency to evil among men, by the laws of that government in which the offense is committed; and for the public peace and tranquility, all men should step forward and use their ability in bringing offenders against good laws to punishment.

9. We do not believe it just to mingle religious influence with civil government, whereby one religious society is fostered, and another proscribed in its spiritual privileges, and the individual rights of its members as citizens, denied.

10. We believe that all religious societies have a right to deal with their members for disorderly conduct according to the rules and regulations of such societies, provided that such dealings be for fellowship and good standing; but we do not believe that any religious society has authority to try men on the right of property or life, to take from them this world's goods, or to put them in jeopardy of either life or limb, neither to inflict any physical punishment upon them, they can only excommunicate them from their society, and withdraw from them their fellowship.

11. We believe that men should appeal to the civil law for redress of all wrongs and grievances, where personal abuse is inflicted, or the right of property or character infringed, where such laws exist as will protect the same; but we believe that all men are justified in defending themselves, their friends, and property, and the government, from the unlawful assaults and encroachments of all persons, in times of exigency, where immediate appeal cannot be made to the laws, and relief afforded.

12. We believe it just to preach the gospel to the nations of the earth, and warn the righteous to save themselves from the corruption of the world; but we do not believe it right to interfere with bond servants, neither preach the gospel to, nor baptize them, contrary to the will and wish of their masters, nor to meddle with or influence them in the least, to cause them to be dissatisfied with their situations in this life, thereby jeopardizing the lives of men; such interference we believe to be unlawful and unjust, and dangerous to the peace of every government allowing human beings to be held in servitude.

D&C 134:6–7—James E. Talmage provides this articulate summary of the Church's position with respect to the laws of the land:

> In the case of a conflict between the requirements made by the revealed word of God, and those imposed by the secular law, which of these authorities would the members of the Church be bound to obey? In answer, the words of Christ may be applied—it is the duty of the people to render unto Caesar the things that are Caesar's, and unto God the things that are God's. . . . Pending the overruling by Providence in favor of religious liberty, it is the duty of the saints to submit themselves to the laws of their country. Nevertheless, they should use every proper method, as citizens or subjects of their several governments, to secure for themselves and for all men the boon of freedom in religious service. (*AF*, 422–423.)

D&C 134:9—A statement more than a century ago by the First Presidency—Joseph F. Smith, John R. Winder, and Anthon H. Lund—confirmed this principle: "The Church of Jesus Christ of Latter-day Saints holds to the doctrine of the separation of church and state; the non-interference of church authority in political matters; and the absolute freedom and independence of the individual in the performance of his political duties. If, at any time, there has been conduct at variance with this doctrine, it has been in violation of the well settled principles and the policy of the Church" (*CR*, April 1907, 14). In terms of disciplinary action brought by the Church, a member can be disfellowshipped or excommunicated, but any further punishment is in the hands of the civil courts.

D&C 134:11—Concerning this principle, President John Taylor declared: "We shall abide all constitutional law, as we always have done; but while we are God-fearing and law-abiding, and respect all honorable men and officers, we are no craven serfs, and have not learned to lick the feet of oppressors, nor to bow in base submission to unreasoning clamor. We will contend inch by inch, legally and constitutionally, for our rights as American citizens" (*The Life of John Taylor*, 1882, 363).

D&C 134:12—Said Joseph Smith:

> Remember that your business is to preach the Gospel in all humility and meekness, and warn sinners to repent and come to Christ. Avoid contentions and vain disputes with men of corrupt minds, who do not desire to know the truth. [D&C 10:62–63.] Remember that "it is a day of warning, and not a day of many words." [D&C 63:58.] If they receive not your testimony in one place, flee to another, remembering to cast no reflections, nor throw out any bitter sayings. If you do your duty, it will be just as well with you, as though all men embraced the Gospel. (*HC* 1:468.)

SECTION 135

1. To seal the testimony of this book and the Book of Mormon, we announce the Martyrdom of Joseph Smith the Prophet, and Hyrum Smith the Patriarch. They were shot in Carthage jail, on the 27th of June, 1844, about five o'clock p.m., by an armed mob, painted black—of from 150 to 200 persons. Hyrum was shot first and fell calmly, exclaiming, "I am a dead man?" Joseph leaped from the window, and was shot dead in the attempt, exclaiming, "O Lord my God!" They were both shot after they were dead in a brutal manner, and both received four balls.

2. John Taylor, and Willard Richards, two of the Twelve, were the only persons in the room at the time; the former was wounded in a savage manner with four balls, but has since recovered; the latter, through the providence of God, escaped, "without even a hole in his robe."

3. Joseph Smith, the Prophet and Seer of the Lord, has done more (save Jesus only) for the salvation of men in this world, than any other man that ever lived in it. In the short space of twenty years, he has brought forth the Book of Mormon, which he translated by the gift and power of God, and has been the means of publishing it on two continents; has sent the fulness of the everlasting gospel which it contained to the four quarters of the earth; has brought forth the revelations and commandments which compose this Book of Doctrine and Covenants, and many other wise documents and instructions for the benefit of the children of men; gathered many thousands of the Latter-day Saints, founded a great city, and left a fame and name that cannot be slain. He lived great, and he died great in the eyes of God and his people, and like most of the Lord's anointed in ancient times, has sealed his mission and his works with his own blood—and so has his brother Hyrum. In life they were not divided, and in death they were not separated!

4. When Joseph went to Carthage to deliver himself up to the pretended requirements of the law, two or three days previous to his assassination, he said, "I am going like a lamb to the slaughter; but I am calm as a summer's morning; I have a conscience void of offense towards God, and towards all men. I shall die innocent, and it shall yet be said of me—he was murdered in cold blood." The same morning, after Hyrum had made ready to go—shall it be said to the slaughter? Yes, for so it was,—he read the following paragraph, near the close of the twelfth chapter of Ether, in the Book of Mormon, and turned down the leaf upon it—

5. "And it came to pass that I prayed unto the Lord that he would give unto the Gentiles grace, that they might have charity. And it came to pass that the Lord said unto me, if they have not charity, it mattereth not unto you,

Section 135 Background—This moving and inspired memorial was written by John Taylor of the Council of the Twelve, a personal witness to the martyrdom of Joseph and Hyrum on June 27, 1844, at the hands of a lawless mob (see *HC* 6:629–631).

D&C 135:3—Joseph Smith was the mighty instrument of the Restoration in the hands of the Lord. What Joseph did—though in parallel with the sacrifice of all the gospel martyrs throughout history—was unique, for it was he of whom the Lord spoke, saying: "Unto whom I have committed the keys of my kingdom, and a dispensation of the gospel for the last times; and for the fulness of times, in the which I will gather together in one all things, both which are in heaven, and which are on earth" (D&C 27:13).

What did the Lord Himself say concerning the Prophet Joseph? "The ends of the earth shall inquire after thy name. . . . The pure in heart, and the wise, and the noble, and the virtuous, shall seek counsel, and authority, and blessings constantly from under thy hand. . . . Thy voice shall be more terrible in the midst of thine enemies than the fierce lion, because of thy righteousness; and thy God shall stand by thee forever and ever" (D&C 122:1–4).

D&C 135:4—There is tragedy in the treacherous and sordid circumstances that cost Joseph Smith his life at the hands of an evil mob; yet there is triumph in his martyr's witness that the gospel is true and that no hand can stay the advance of the stone, cut from the mountain without hands, that would roll forth in glory to fill the entire world (see Dan. 2:35, 44–45).

Elder Bruce R. McConkie clarified that simply laying down one's life does not mean one is a gospel martyr—both the wicked and the righteous have sacrificed their lives for country or friends without being what we know to be "martyrs." A martyr—one who receives eternal life—is one who has the truth and who could escape death by denying that truth (see *MD*, 470).

"The Prophet's Last Ride," commemorating the ride of the Prophet Joseph Smith and his brother Hyrum Smith to Carthage Jail, where both were martyred.

thou hast been faithful; wherefore thy garments are clean. And because thou hast seen thy weakness, thou shalt be made strong, even unto the sitting down in the place which I have prepared in the mansions of my Father. And now I———bid farewell unto the Gentiles; yea and also unto my brethren whom I love, until we shall meet before the judgment-seat of Christ, where all men shall know that my garments are not spotted with your blood." The testators are now dead, and their testament is in force.

6. Hyrum Smith was 44 years old in February, 1844, and Joseph Smith was 38 in December, 1843, and henceforward their names will be classed among the martyrs of religion; and the reader in every nation will be reminded that the "Book of Mormon" and this book of Doctrine and Covenants of the church, cost the best blood of the nineteenth century to bring them forth for the salvation of a ruined world: and that if the fire can scathe a green tree for the glory of God, how easy it will burn up the "dry trees" to purify the vineyard of corruption. They lived for glory; they died for glory; and glory is their eternal reward. From age to age shall their names go down to posterity as gems for the sanctified.

7. They were innocent of any crime, as they had often been proved before, and were only confined in jail by the conspiracy of traitors and wicked men; and their innocent blood on the floor of Carthage jail, is a broad seal affixed to "Mormonism" that cannot be rejected by any court on earth; and their innocent blood on the escutcheon of the State of Illinois, with the broken faith of the State as pledged by the Governor, is a witness to the truth of the everlasting gospel, that all the world cannot impeach; and their innocent blood on the banner of liberty, and on the magna charta of the United States, is an ambassador for the religion of Jesus Christ, that will touch the hearts of honest men among all nations; and their innocent blood, with the innocent blood of all the martyrs under the altar that John saw, will cry unto the Lord of hosts till he avenges that blood on the earth. Amen.

SECTION 136

1. The word and will of the Lord concerning the Camp of Israel in their journeyings to the West.

2. Let all the people of the Church of Jesus Christ of Latter-day Saints, and those who journey with them, be organized into companies, with a covenant and promise to keep all

D&C 135:6—The great example of the Prophet Joseph and his brother Hyrum will ever stand as a witness to the world of the truthfulness of the gospel of Jesus Christ and His kingdom once again established here upon the earth. We will probably not be required to die for the kingdom, but rather to live to build up the kingdom of God—this is our joy and our glory (see D&C 84:85–88; 100:5–6).

D&C 135:7—The Prophet Joseph and his beloved brother Hyrum sealed their testimony with their innocent blood as martyrs for the kingdom of God. Through the inspiration of the Lord, John Taylor declared that their martyrdom surely "cost the best blood of the nineteenth century" in bringing forth the truth to a wicked world (see D&C 135:6).

Section 136 Background—"The Word and Will of the Lord," as identified in verse 1, given through Brigham Young at Winter Quarters, Nebraska, on the west bank of the Missouri River, near Council Bluffs, Iowa (see *Journal History of the Church*, January 14, 1847). The Saints had departed from Nauvoo in 1846 and established themselves in settlements across Iowa and on the west bank of the Missouri in Nebraska. Church leaders were concerned about organizing the people for the westward migration, and thus members of the Twelve convened on January 14, 1847, at Heber C. Kimball's house to consider the matter. It was on that occasion, as well as during the course of the day at other nearby locations, that Brigham Young received and dictated what is now known as Section 136, setting forth divine counsel to prepare for, and carry out, the journey to the Salt Lake Valley.

Orson F. Whitney later expressed this view of the circumstances: "In 1847 the Latter-day Saints, under the leadership of President Brigham Young began to fulfill the prediction of the Prophet Joseph who had declared, two years before his death, that the Saints would 'become a mighty people in the midst of the Rocky Mountains.' In the book of Doctrine and Covenants there is a revelation entitled 'The Word and Will of the Lord,' to a people encamped upon the Missouri river. . . . That 'Word and Will of the Lord' commanded the people of The Church of Jesus Christ of Latter-day Saints to organize themselves into companies of hundreds, fifties, and tens preparatory to the long and wearisome ox-team journey to Salt Lake Valley" (CR, Oct. 1916, 54–55).

D&C 136:1—The Latter-day Saint exodus to the valleys of the Mountain West is among the great historical events of American history. Enormous sacrifice attended this mass movement, and were it not for the inspired leadership and meticulous preparation involved, the suffering and adversity would have been much greater than it was. Indeed, the Saints journeyed under the merciful hand of the Lord and in His strength, much as ancient Israel crossed the wilderness guided by the cloudy pillar during the day and the heralding fire at night (see Neh. 9:12).

the commandments and statutes of the Lord our God.

3. Let the companies be organized with captains of hundreds, captains of fifties, and captains of tens, with a president and his two counselors at their head, under the direction of the Twelve Apostles;

4. And this shall be our covenant, that we will walk in all the ordinances of the Lord.

5. Let each company provide themselves with all the teams, wagons, provisions, clothing, and other necessaries for the journey that they can.

6. When the companies are organized, let them go to with their might, to prepare for those who are to tarry.

7. Let each company with their captains and presidents decide how many can go next spring; then choose out a sufficient number of able-bodied and expert men, to take teams, seeds, and farming utensils, to go as pioneers to prepare for putting in spring crops.

8. Let each company bear an equal proportion, according to the dividend of their property, in taking the poor, the widows, the fatherless, and the families of those who have gone into the army, that the cries of the widow and the fatherless come not up into the ears of the Lord against this people.

9. Let each company prepare houses, and fields for raising grain, for those who are to remain behind this season, and this is the will of the Lord concerning his people.

10. Let every man use all his influence and property to remove this people to the place where the Lord shall locate a Stake of Zion;

11. And if ye do this with a pure heart, in all faithfulness, ye shall be blessed; you shall be blessed in your flocks, and in your herds, and in your fields, and in your houses, and in your families.

12. Let my servants Ezra T. Benson and Erastus Snow organize a company;

13. And let my servants Orson Pratt and Wilford Woodruff organize a company.

14. Also, let my servants Amasa Lyman and George A. Smith organize a company;

15. And appoint presidents, and captains of hundreds, and of fifties, and of tens,

16. And let my servants that have been appointed go and teach this, my will, to the saints, that they may be ready to go to a land of peace.

17. Go thy way and do as I have told you, and fear not thine enemies; for they shall not have power to stop my work.

18. Zion shall be redeemed in mine own due time,

19. And if any man shall seek to build up himself, and seeketh not my counsel, he shall have no power, and his folly shall be made manifest.

20. Seek ye, and keep all your pledges one with another, and covet not that which is thy brother's.

21. Keep yourselves from evil to take the name of the Lord in vain, for I am the Lord your God, even the God of your fathers, the God of Abraham, and of Isaac, and of Jacob.

D&C 136:3—The pattern described in this verse was the one used by Zion's Camp on their march from Kirtland to Missouri. As they began to plan for the trek west, the Saints were destitute; they had been robbed of their possessions and run off their land. They needed guidance and direction on their journey to the west, and it was essential that they walk by covenant.

D&C 136:5—The planning and organization required to move the Saints West was enormous. It is noted that having the Saints care for one another in charity was and is among the foremost concerns of the Lord. In this context, what could a family take on its journey—given the limitations of space and resources? They had to leave behind whatever wouldn't fit in their wagons—and they had to take those items that were essential not only for the trek, but for survival both while on the trail and once at their journey's end. They also had to take those things that would enable them to build homes and plant crops when they arrived at their destination.

In addition to a strong wagon box, two to three yoke of oxen, three cows (for milk), and at least three sheep, it is estimated that a family of five would have needed 1,000 pounds of flour, 100 pounds of sugar, cornmeal, 5 pounds of dried beef or bacon, 1 bushel of beans, 20 pounds of pumpkin, 15 pounds of dried apples, 15 pounds of dried peaches, molasses, 25 pounds of salt, 1 pound of cinnamon, half a pound of cloves, 1 pound of cayenne pepper, 12 nutmegs, plenty of lard, medicines, and 25 pounds of seeds. As far as equipment goes, they would have needed a tent, bedding, clothing, ax, hammer, plow, scythe, shovel, hook, pulley, fish hooks and lines, block and tackle, rope, rifle, 1 pound of gunpowder, 4 pounds of lead, water barrel, dipper, copper washtub, 20 pounds of soap, candle mold, Dutch oven, large skillet, grinder, butter churn, knives, forks, spoons, and tin cups and plates.

D&C 136:11, 24—At the outset, the Lord enjoins the Saints to be pure and edify one another. Language is a gift of God. Our ability to use words—both spoken and written—derives from our divine provenance. We honor our Father in Heaven by cultivating language that is worthy of heavenly acceptation. We live up to our potential when we foster thoughts and discourse that invite the Holy Ghost to dwell within us. Paul preached: "Let no corrupt communication proceed out of your mouth, but that which is good to the use of edifying, that it may minister grace unto the hearers" (Eph. 4:29). Furthermore, we are told: "Wherefore, let all men beware how they take my name in their lips—For behold, verily I say, that many there be who are under this condemnation, who use the name of the Lord, and use it in vain, having not authority" (D&C 63:61–62).

D&C 136:18—The Saints had become discouraged; this was their reassurance that the Lord had not forgotten Zion.

22. I am he who led the children of Israel out of the land of Egypt, and my arm is stretched out in the last days, to save my people Israel.

23. Cease to contend one with another, cease to speak evil one of another.

24. Cease drunkenness, and let your words tend to edifying one another.

25. If thou borrowest of thy neighbor, thou shalt restore that which thou hast borrowed; and if thou canst not repay, then go straightway and tell thy neighbor, lest he condemn thee.

26. If thou shalt find that which thy neighbor has lost, thou shalt make diligent search till thou shalt deliver it to him again.

27. Thou shalt be diligent in preserving what thou hast, that thou mayest be a wise steward; for it is the free gift of the Lord thy God, and thou art his steward.

28. If thou art merry, praise the Lord with singing, with music, with dancing, and with a prayer of praise and thanksgiving.

29. If thou art sorrowful, call on the Lord thy God with supplication, that your souls may be joyful.

30. Fear not thine enemies, for they are in mine hands, and I will do my pleasure with them.

31. My people must be tried in all things, that they may be prepared to receive the glory that I have for them, even the glory of Zion, and he that will not bear chastisement, is not worthy of my kingdom.

32. Let him that is ignorant learn wisdom by humbling himself and calling upon the Lord his God, that his eyes may be opened that he may see, and his ears opened that he may hear,

33. For my Spirit is sent forth into the world to enlighten the humble and contrite, and to the condemnation of the ungodly.

34. Thy brethren have rejected you and your testimony, even the nation that has driven you out;

35. And now cometh the day of their calamity, even the days of sorrow, like a woman that is taken in travail; and their sorrow shall be great, unless they speedily repent; yea, very speedily;

36. For they killed the prophets,

D&C 136:27—On our journey together as a people striving to be a Zion society, we at times encounter circumstances that try our patience and challenge our understanding. It was no different with the pioneers. The Lord's counsel to be charitable in all things is part of the great commandment—to love God. Then, if we love God, we will also love our fellow men, for this is the second great commandment (see Mark 12:31). Love is expressed in the way we treat others and behave toward them.

D&C 136:28–29—In the spirit of the Psalms, this counsel of the Lord invokes cheer and praise—despite the tribulations and pains of the journey. The Lord knew the Saints would be weary and discouraged, and He knew that music and dancing would lift and revive their spirits. Who can read the words of these verses without thinking of William Clayton's celebrated hymn of the exodus: "Come, Come, Ye Saints" (*Hymns*, no. 30)?

THE ORGANIZATION OF THE CAMP OF ISRAEL

The Lord's house is a house of order, even while sojourning in the wilderness. In order for the Saints to travel most effectively to their western abode, the Lord instructed them to organize in companies with captains over groups of tens, fifties, and hundreds. There was to be a presidency over each company, and those were in turn directed by the Quorum of the Twelve (see D&C 136:2–3).

Each company had certain responsibilities, some of which were to 1) provide their own wagons, provisions, clothing, and other necessities (see verse 5); 2) take care of the needs of those who remained behind (see verses 6, 9); 3) send men as an advance party to plan spring crops (see verse 7); and 4) bear equal portion of the responsibility of caring for the poor, widows, and fatherless children (see verse 8).

Several lessons loom large. First, the Lord always provides adequate leadership for His people to accomplish whatever tasks they may be given. Their success is contingent on their trusting the Lord by following His appointed representatives. Second, whether situations are temporary or permanent, the Lord expects His people to conduct the affairs of their lives in an orderly fashion. Third, all Saints are important to God. The Church looks after the temporal and spiritual needs of all its members, and regardless of economic or other status distinctions, all worthy Saints are alike unto God. All will move forward together.

and them that were sent unto them, and they have shed innocent blood, which crieth from the ground against them:

37. Therefore marvel not at these things, for ye are not pure; ye can not yet bear my glory; but ye shall behold it if ye are faithful in keeping all my words that I have given you from the days of Adam to Abraham; from Abraham to Moses; from Moses to Jesus and his apostles; and from Jesus and his apostles to Joseph Smith, whom I did call upon by mine angels, my ministering servants; and by mine own voice out of the heavens, to bring forth my work,

38. Which foundation he did lay, and was faithful and I took him to myself.

39. Many have marveled because of his death, but it was needful that he should seal his testimony with his blood that he might be honored, and the wicked might be condemned.

40. Have I not delivered you from your enemies, only in that I have left a witness of my name?

41. Now, therefore, hearken, O ye people of my church; and ye elders listen together; you have received my kingdom.

42. Be diligent in keeping all my commandments, lest judgments come upon you, and your faith fail you, and your enemies triumph over you—So no more at present. Amen, and Amen.

SECTION 137

1. The heavens were opened upon us, and I beheld the celestial kingdom of God, and the glory thereof, whether in the body or out I cannot tell.

2. I saw the transcendent beauty of the gate through which the heirs of that kingdom will enter, which was like unto circling flames of fire;

3. Also the blazing throne of God, whereon was seated the Father and the Son.

4. I saw the beautiful streets of that kingdom, which had the appearance of being paved with gold.

5. I saw Father Adam and Abraham;

D&C 136:37—The trek west was to be marked with trials and miracles as the Saints followed the directions of their inspired leader—the successor to the martyred Prophet Joseph. Sacrifice upon sacrifice, endurance upon endurance, faith upon faith—these are the witnesses and triumphs of a people tested by trial and tragedy, refined by affliction and reversal, sustained by faith and hope, sanctified by refulgent light from God, and drawn onward by an irrepressible conviction to do the will of the Lord. We can be reminded through the words of Section 136 to remember our covenants as the essential preparation for our own mortal journey.

Section 137 Background—Given through the Prophet Joseph Smith in the temple at Kirtland, Ohio, on January 21, 1836 (see *HC* 2:380–381). This revelation and vision came as the First Presidency and other leaders gathered in Joseph Smith's office at the west end of the third (or attic) floor of the temple two months before its dedication. On this occasion, these leaders instituted the first ordinance in our dispensation performed in a temple: anointing with holy oil. Oliver Cowdery said, "[We] were annointed with the same kind of oil and in the man[ner] that were Moses and Aaron, and those who stood before the Lord in ancient days." Then referring to the vision described in this revelation, Oliver said, "The heavens were opened to many, and great and marvelous things were shown" (Oliver Cowdery/1836 Diary, *BYU Studies*, Vol. 12, No. 4, 419). As these leaders participated in this ordinance, a glorious vision burst upon them. The first half of this section describes this vision. Joseph made particular mention that he could not distinguish whether he was in the body or out of it. The second half reports the words of the Lord as the revelation continued.

D&C 137:1–3—What an august and resplendent view awaits those who live worthy to see the dwelling place of God. The words of this revelation inspire us to live day by day at the peak of righteousness in order to realize this most cherished of all outcomes—being invited into the presence of the Father and the Son. There is no gift so great as eternal life in the glories of heaven. John the Beloved also beheld the city of God, which he described, in part, with these words:

> And the twelve gates *were* twelve pearls; every several gate was of one pearl: and the street of the city *was* pure gold, as it were transparent glass.
> And I saw no temple therein: for the Lord God Almighty and the Lamb are the temple of it.
> And the city had no need of the sun, neither of the moon, to shine in it: for the glory of God did lighten it, and the Lamb *is* the light thereof. (Rev. 21:21–23.)

Alvin Smith grave, with its restored marker.

and my father and my mother; my brother Alvin, that has long since slept;

6. And marveled how it was that he had obtained an inheritance in that kingdom, seeing that he had departed this life before the Lord had set his hand to gather Israel the second time, and had not been baptized for the remission of sins.

7. Thus came the voice of the Lord unto me, saying: All who have died without a knowledge of this gospel, who would have received it if they had been permitted to tarry, shall be heirs of the celestial kingdom of God;

8. Also all that shall die henceforth without a knowledge of it, who would have received it with all their hearts, shall be heirs of that kingdom.

9. For I, the Lord, will judge all men according to their works, according to the desire of their hearts.

10. And I also beheld that all children who die before they arrive at the years of accountability are saved in the celestial kingdom of heaven.

SECTION 138

1. On the third of October, in the year nineteen hundred and eighteen, I

ALVIN SMITH

Alvin was born February 11, 1798 (or 1799), at Tunbridge, Orange County, Vermont, son of Joseph Smith Sr. and Lucy Mack Smith. He had a strong work ethic and was of great help to his family in their years of financial struggle, including arranging to build a frame home for them across the street from their log home in the Palmyra area. He likewise encouraged his younger brother Joseph as the work of the Restoration commenced. Regretfully, Alvin became seriously ill in November 1823. The attending physician administered a medication that resulted in unanticipated lethal side effects, and Alvin expired on November 19, 1823. On January 21, 1836, the Prophet Joseph beheld his brother once again as a resident of the celestial kingdom (D&C 137:5–6). Of Alvin, the Prophet said:

Alvin, my oldest brother—I remember well the pangs of sorrow that swelled my youthful bosom and almost burst my tender heart when he died. He was the oldest and the noblest of my father's family. He was one of the noblest of the sons of men. Shall his name not be remembered in this book [Joseph's Book of the Law of the Lord]? Yes, Alvin, let it be had here and be handed down on these sacred pages for ever and ever (HC 5:126).

D&C 137:7—The Prophet sees his brother Alvin (who passed away in 1823) within the walls of the heavenly kingdom. He also sees his parents in vision, both of whom were still living (his father, in fact, was in the room at the time of the vision). Thus, in this vision of the future, the glorious truths of work for the dead begin to emerge after long centuries of eclipse. Those who do not have the opportunity to embrace the gospel in this life will yet learn of its exalting power in the hereafter—and will be judged "according to men in the flesh, but live according to God in the spirit" (1 Pet. 4:6). The Lord knows our hearts and dispositions. He will judge based on our character. All will have a chance to exercise their agency and come into the fold of Christ. Children who pass away before becoming accountable before God will be "saved in the celestial kingdom of heaven" (verse 10; see also D&C 18:42; 20:71; Moroni 8).

Section 138 Background—Given through President Joseph F. Smith on October 3, 1918, in Salt Lake City, Utah, and recorded following the conclusion of the 89th semi-annual conference of the Church that month. Historian Lyndon W. Cook has summarized the circumstances:

Section 138, known as the "Vision of the Redemption of the Dead" [see D&C 138:60], was received by Joseph F. Smith six weeks before his death, during his final illness. President Smith alluded to this vision in his opening remarks at the Eighty-Ninth Semiannual Conference of the Church on 4 October 1918. In this short talk he stated, "I will not, I dare not, attempt to enter upon many things that are resting upon my mind this morning, and I shall postpone until some future time, the Lord being willing, my attempt to tell you some of the things that are in my mind, and that dwell in my heart. I have not lived alone these five months. I have dwelt in the spirit of prayer, of supplication, of faith and of determination; and I have had my communication with the Spirit of the Lord continuously."

Concerning the occasion, James E. Talmage—a member of the Quorum of the Twelve—recorded the following:

Attended meeting of the First Presidency and the Twelve. Today President Smith, who is still confined to his home by illness, sent to the Brethren the account of a vision through which, as he states, were revealed to him important facts relating to the work of the disembodied Savior in the realm of departed spirits, and of the missionary work in progress on the other side of the veil. By united action the Council of the Twelve, with the Counsellors in the First Presidency, and the Presiding Patriarch accepted and enforced the revelation as the Word of the Lord. President Smith's signed statement will be published in the next issue (December) of the Improvement Era. . . . (RPJS, 306.)

sat in my room pondering over the scriptures;

2. And reflecting upon the great atoning sacrifice that was made by the Son of God, for the redemption of the world;

3. And the great and wonderful love made manifest by the Father and the Son in the coming of the Redeemer into the world;

4. That through his atonement, and by obedience to the principles of the gospel, mankind might be saved.

5. While I was thus engaged, my mind reverted to the writings of the apostle Peter, to the primitive saints scattered abroad throughout Pontus, Galatia, Cappadocia, and other parts of Asia, where the gospel had been preached after the crucifixion of the Lord.

6. I opened the Bible and read the third and fourth chapters of the first epistle of Peter, and as I read I was greatly impressed, more than I had ever been before with the following passages:

7. "For Christ also hath once suffered for sins, the just for the unjust, that he might bring us to God, being put to death in the flesh, but quickened by the Spirit:

8. "By which also he went and preached unto the spirits in prison;

9. "Which sometime were disobedient, when once the long suffering of God waited in the days of Noah, while the ark was a preparing, wherein few, that is, eight souls were saved by water." (1. Peter 3:18-20.)

10. "For, for this cause was the gospel preached also to them that are dead, that they might be judged according to men in the flesh, but live according to God in the spirit." (1. Peter 4:6.)

11. As I pondered over these things which are written, the eyes of my understanding were opened, and the Spirit of the Lord rested upon me, and I saw the hosts of the dead, both small and great.

12. And there were gathered together in one place an innumerable company of the spirits of the just, who had been faithful in the testimony of Jesus while they lived in mortality;

13. And who had offered sacrifice in the similitude of the great sacrifice of the Son of God, and had suffered tribulation in their Redeemer's name.

14. All these had departed the mortal life, firm in the hope of a glorious resurrection, through the grace of God the Father and his Only Begotten Son, Jesus Christ.

15. I beheld that they were filled with joy and gladness, and were rejoicing together because the day of their deliverance was at hand.

D&C 138:1—An often-neglected part of our gospel study and personal worship is meditation and pondering. Nephi's great sequence of visions (see 1 Ne. 11–14) concerning the plan of salvation and the destiny of God's peoples began with pondering (see 1 Ne. 11:1). The risen Lord counseled the people at Bountiful in the New World: "Therefore, go ye unto your homes, and ponder upon the things which I have said, and ask of the Father, in my name, that ye may understand, and prepare your minds for the morrow, and I come unto you again" (3 Ne. 17:3).

D&C 138:10—Undoubtedly, Peter and his companions were taught personally by the risen Lord concerning His mission to the spirit realm between the time of His crucifixion and the time of His resurrection. Peter was present on the Mount of Transfiguration when priesthood keys were delivered by anointed prophets of old to carry on the work of salvation among the children of men (see Matt. 17). Now, more than two millennia later, a modern prophet of God—a successor to Joseph Smith, the founding Prophet of the Restoration—is blessed with a vision of the work being conducted in the spirit realm among the departed spirits—the righteous as well as the wicked.

D&C 138:11–22—The spirit world comprises two vast realms—one of light and one of darkness; one for the righteous and obedient who were "faithful in the testimony of Jesus" (verse 12), and one for the wicked and those who rejected the testimony of the prophets of the Lord. These latter were not favored to "behold his presence, nor look upon his face" (verse 22). But those of the realm of light had the transcendent privilege of looking upon the face of the Redeemer and hearing from His mouth the glorious confirmation of the hope and faith that deliverance was nigh.

Those who ponder these passages of scripture discern that the blessings of a righteous life allow us the privilege of being with the Savior in the world to come. Those who choose to ignore Him or His prophets will not have the privilege of His presence.

D&C 138:14—We can be confident of gaining exaltation if we gain a testimony, chart a course of righteousness, obey the commandments, keep our covenants, overcome the world, and put first the kingdom of God.

D&C 138:15—These people knew they were about to be resurrected. The great principle of happiness consists in having a body, and a fullness of joy is found only among those who have been resurrected and thus have been give their bodies once again.

16. They were assembled awaiting the advent of the Son of God into the spirit world, to declare their redemption from the bands of death.

17. Their sleeping dust was to be restored unto its perfect frame bone to his bone, and the sinews and the flesh upon them, the spirit and the body to be united never again to be divided, that they might receive a fulness of joy.

18. While this vast multitude waited and conversed, rejoicing in the hour of their deliverance from the chains of death, the Son of God appeared, declaring liberty to the captives who had been faithful;

19. And there he preached to them the everlasting gospel, the doctrine of the resurrection and the redemption of mankind from the fall, and from individual sins on conditions of repentance.

20. But unto the wicked he did not go, and among the ungodly and the unrepentant who had defiled themselves while in the flesh, his voice was not raised;

21. Neither did the rebellious who rejected the testimonies and the warnings of the ancient prophets behold his presence, nor look upon his face.

22. Where these were, darkness reigned, but among the righteous there was peace;

23. And the saints rejoiced in their redemption, and bowed the knee and acknowledged the Son of God as their Redeemer and Deliverer from death and the chains of hell.

24. Their countenances shone, and the radiance from the presence of the Lord rested upon them and they sang praises unto his holy name.

25. I marveled, for I understood that the Savior spent about three years in his ministry among the Jews and those of the house of Israel, endeavoring to teach them the everlasting gospel and call them unto repentance;

26. And yet, notwithstanding his mighty works, and miracles, and proclamation of the truth, in great power and authority, there were but few who hearkened to his voice, and rejoiced in his presence, and received salvation at his hands.

27. But his ministry among those who were dead was limited to the brief time intervening between the crucifixion and his resurrection;

28. And I wondered at the words of Peter—wherein he said that the Son of God preached unto the spirits in prison, who sometime were disobedient, when once the long-suffering of God waited in the days of Noah—and how it was possible for him to preach to those spirits and perform the necessary labor among them in so short a time.

The Righteous in the Spirit World from Adam to Christ

From this vision, there are several things to be learned about the condition and experience of the righteous spirits when the Savior visited the spirit world.

Joyful condition of celestial saints (see D&C 138:12–18). All of these people had lived in obedience to celestial law while in mortality. This vast multitude had died firm in their testimony of Jesus Christ, and consequently were filled with joyful anticipation of the Savior's advent into the spirit world. They knew that His coming meant the end of the separation of their spirits from their bodies. They were to be resurrected in conjunction with the Savior's own resurrection, never again to suffer death.

The Savior's delcaration and preaching (see D&C 138:18–19). Of all the children of God who have walked in mortality, only One has conquered death and could declare liberty from the death that held all others captive. That One was Jesus Christ, the Son of God. The announcement of liberty was first declared to the celestial saints in the spirit world at the time Jesus appeared there.

Rejoicing of the righteous (see D&C 138:23–24). It is one thing to be taught the blessings of the Atonement; it is quite another to experience those blessings. When the Savior stood in the midst of righteous spirits in the spirit world, they rejoiced over their freedom from both sin and death—something that had become a living experience and a reality in their lives.

Great and mighty ones (see D&C 138:38–49). In this vision, President Joseph F. Smith was privileged to see many great and mighty saints of the past who were faithful to Jesus Christ. Several testimonies come to us as a result: those people are not just characters in a book, but are living sons and daughters of God who lived on this earth in ages past; the Lord had living prophets on this earth in ages past who testified of Jesus Christ; the flood was not a myth or a figment of someone's imagination, but was real; the testimony of these prophets has been preserved in scripture, which is available to us today; and the ancient prophets foretold of the restoration of the kingdom of God in the last days, with all its teachings and ordinances.

Immortality and eternal life (see D&C 138:50–52). Regardless of the level of righteousness of the individual, life in the spirit world constitutes bondage. People are living there without a body, and they cannot be released from that bondage without the Atonement of the Savior. When the Savior appeared among the people there, He gave them the power, or keys, of resurrection, that they might follow Him through the process of resurrection so they could be crowned with immorality and eternal life. These keys are not found on earth among mortals (*STDC* 2:395–397).

29. And as I wondered, my eyes were opened, and my understanding quickened, and I perceived that the Lord went not in person among the wicked and the disobedient who had rejected the truth, to teach them;

30. But behold, from among the righteous, he organized his forces and appointed messengers, clothed with power and authority, and commissioned them to go forth and carry the light of the gospel to them that were in darkness, even to all the spirits of men; and thus was the gospel preached to the dead.

31. And the chosen messengers went forth to declare the acceptable day of the Lord and proclaim liberty to the captives who were bound, even unto all who would repent of their sins and receive the gospel.

32. Thus was the gospel preached to those who had died in their sins, without a knowledge of the truth, or in transgression, having rejected the prophets.

33. These were taught faith in God, repentance from sin, vicarious baptism for the remission of sins, the gift of the Holy Ghost by the laying on of hands.

34. And all other principles of the gospel that were necessary for them to know in order to qualify themselves that they might be judged according to men in the flesh, but live according to God in the spirit.

35. And so it was made known among the dead, both small and great, the unrighteous as well and the faithful, that redemption had been wrought through the sacrifice of the Son of God upon the cross.

36. Thus was it made known that our Redeemer spent his time during his sojourn in the world of spirits, instructing and preparing the faithful spirits of the prophets who had testified of him in the flesh.

37. That they might carry the message of redemption unto all the dead, unto whom he could not go personally, because of their rebellion and transgression, that they through the ministration of his servants might also hear his words.

38. Among the great and mighty ones who were assembled in this vast congregation of the righteous were Father Adam, the Ancient of Days and father of all,

39. And our glorious Mother Eve, with many of her faithful daughters who had lived through the ages and worshiped the true and living God.

40. Abel, the first martyr, was there, and his brother Seth, one of the mighty ones, who was in the express image of his father, Adam.

41. Noah, who gave warning of the

D&C 138:30–34—The vision of the vast enterprise of missionary work moving forward apace in the spirit world is one of the most glorious of revelations. More than one million have been called into active missionary service in the kingdom of God on earth since the organization of the restored Church in 1830. Perhaps the figure is much greater in the spirit realm as the work of proclaiming the gospel unfolds with power and priesthood authority, established and blessed by the Lamb of God in His eternal role as Redeemer.

The Wicked in the Spirit World from Adam to Christ

When the Savior went into the spirit world, he did not go among the wicked, who constituted two classes of people: those who participated in the defilement of their mortal bodies and who were not clean (see D&C 138:20) and those who rejected the testimony of Jesus Christ and warnings from His authorized representatives (see D&C 138:21).

Even though these unrighteous people had rejected the Savior or had not complied with His teachings, still He did not forget them. He provided a way for them to be taught truths that would bless their lives beyond their current state of misery. He sent messengers to them to declare the principles and ordinances of the gospel. Their compliance with these teachings would serve as a means to an inheritance of a degree of glory. Their hope of redemption would also come through the Atonement of the Savior, regardless of the level of glory they attained (see D&C 138:29–37).

Every knee will bow and every tongue confess that redemption for souls in every kingdom of glory will only be achieved through the Atonement of Jesus Christ (*STDC* 2:397).

flood; Shem, the great high priest; Abraham, the father of the faithful; Isaac, Jacob, and Moses, the great law-giver of Israel;

42. And Isaiah, who declared by prophecy that the Redeemer was anointed to bind up the broken-hearted, to proclaim liberty to the captives, and the opening of the prison to them that were bound, were also there.

43. Moreover, Ezekiel, who was shown in vision the great valley of dry bones, which were to be clothed upon with flesh, to come forth again in the resurrection of the dead, living souls;

44. Daniel, who foresaw and foretold the establishment of the kingdom of God in the latter days, never again to be destroyed nor given to other people;

45. Elias, who was with Moses on the Mount of Transfiguration;

46. And Malachi, the prophet who testified of the coming of Elijah—of whom also Moroni spake to the Prophet Joseph Smith, declaring that he should come before the ushering in of the great and dreadful day of the Lord—were also there.

47. The Prophet Elijah was to plant in the hearts of the children the promises made to their fathers.

48. Foreshadowing the great work to be done in the temples of the Lord in the dispensation of the fulness of times, for the redemption of the dead, and the sealing of the children to their parents, lest the whole earth be smitten with a curse and utterly wasted at his coming.

49. All these and many more, even the prophets who dwelt among the Nephites and testified of the coming of the Son of God, mingled in the vast assembly and waited for their deliverance,

50. For the dead had looked upon the long absence of their spirits from their bodies as a bondage.

51. These the Lord taught, and gave them power to come forth, after his resurrection from the dead, to enter into his Father's kingdom and there to be crowned with immortality and eternal life.

52. And continue thence forth their labor as had been promised by the Lord, and be partakers of all blessings which were held in reserve for them that love him.

53. The Prophet Joseph Smith, and my father, Hyrum Smith, Brigham Young, John Taylor, Wilford Woodruff, and other choice spirits who were reserved to come forth in the fulness of times to take part in laying the foundations of the great latter-day work,

54. Including the building of the temples and the performance of ordinances therein for the redemption of the dead, were also in the spirit world.

55. I observed that they were also

D&C 138:51–52—The great work on behalf of those who have passed beyond the mortal veil is unfolded in glorious terms in this section of the Doctrine and Covenants, as well as in several other sections treating this theme, including 2, 110, 127, and 128. The eminent prophets and servants of God enumerated in Section 138 as belonging to the "vast congregation of the righteous" each had a significant role to play in establishing the kingdom of God on earth and laying the groundwork that was to be fulfilled through the Restoration of the gospel in the dispensation of the fullness of times. Elijah, to cite one example, restored the sealing powers essential to the operation of the temples of God when he visited the Kirtland Temple on April 3, 1836, in fulfillment of the prophecy of Malachi (see D&C 110:13–15; Malachi 4:5–6; D&C 2). This event inaugurated the magnificent, all-encompassing work to bind together worthy families of all generations into the glorious and eternal family of our Father in Heaven. Elijah was "to plant in the hearts of the children the promises made to their fathers" (D&C 138:47), foreshadowing the magnificent latter-day work of the temples of God on behalf of His children.

D&C 138:55–56—This remarkable passage confirms the continuity of the process by which pure knowledge of a saving kind is bestowed upon the elect who are to perform mighty service on behalf of God's children. Spiritual enlightenment began in the premortal realm and continues in this world. It will be perpetuated in the world to come as an eternal quest for glorious truth and eternal wisdom. Those who labor in the vineyard of the Lord "for the salvation of the souls of men" (verse 56)—and this would logically include all Saints acting in valor and obedience—attended what could be deemed a missionary preparation course of the highest caliber prior to their embarking on their mortal journey. Indeed, we made covenants in that premortal realm to come forward in these days for the salvation of mankind. We were there "When the morning stars sang together, and all the sons of God shouted for joy" (Job 38:7).

People in the Spirit World from This Dispensation

President Smith was shown people in the spirit world who had lived in mortality during the dispensation of the fullness of times. First, he saw departed presiding leaders of the Church. They were not leaders by chance; they had been chosen for this noble calling in the premortal spirit world before coming to earth to labor for the souls of men (see D&C 138:53–56). This vision provides further testimony of the foreordination and approval of the Lord of the ministries of prophets of this dispensation.

Secondly, President Smith observed the labors of departed faithful elders of this dispensation. They continue to teach and labor for the souls of the departed dead. They declare that redemption comes only through the Atonement of the Jesus Christ. They teach that eternal rewards are dependent on the degree of compliance with the truths of the gospel (see D&C 138:57–59).

among the noble and great ones who were chosen in the beginning to be rulers in the Church of God.

56. Even before they were born, they, with many others, received their first lessons in the world of spirits and were prepared to come forth in the due time of the Lord to labor in his vineyard for the salvation of the souls of men.

57. I beheld that the faithful elders of this dispensation, when they depart from mortal life, continue their labors in the preaching of the gospel of repentance and redemption, through the sacrifice of the Only Begotten Son of God, among those who are in darkness and under the bondage of sin in the great world of the spirits of the dead.

58. The dead who repent will be redeemed, through obedience to the ordinances of the house of God.

59. And after they have paid the penalty of their transgressions, and are washed clean, shall receive a reward according to their works, for they are heirs of salvation.

60. Thus was the vision of the redemption of the dead revealed to me, and I bear record, and I know that this record is true, through the blessing of our Lord and Savior, Jesus Christ, even so, Amen.

OFFICIAL DECLARATION—1

To Whom It May Concern:

Press dispatches having been sent for political purposes, from Salt Lake City, which have been widely published, to the effect that the Utah Commission, in their recent report to the Secretary of the Interior, allege that plural marriages are still being solemnized and that forty or more such marriages have been contracted in Utah since last June or during the past year, also that in public discourses the leaders of the Church have taught, encouraged and urged the continuance of the practice of polygamy—

I, therefore, as President of the Church of Jesus Christ of Latter-day Saints, do hereby, in the most solemn manner, declare that these charges are false. We are not teaching polygamy or plural marriage, nor permitting any person to enter into its practice, and I deny that either forty or any other number of plural marriages have during that period been solemnized in our Temples or in any other place in the Territory.

One case has been reported, in which the parties allege that the marriage was performed in the Endowment House, in Salt Lake City, in the Spring of 1889, but I have not been able to learn who performed the ceremony; whatever was done in this matter was without my knowledge. In consequence of this alleged occurrence the Endowment House was, by my instructions, taken down without delay.

Inasmuch as laws have been enacted by Congress forbidding plural marriages, which laws have been pronounced constitutional by the court

D&C 138:57—Missionary work continues beyond the veil—and will be carried forth until the process of resurrection leaves the spirit world without tenants. How important, therefore, is the work of the temples of God as a means to accomplish the proxy ordinance work for those in the spirit realm. The modern-day program to extend temple blessings into all corners of the kingdom of God is a miraculous undertaking that demonstrates the wisdom of having a living prophet of God as an emissary of the Almighty in bringing about the plan of salvation on behalf of all—both living and deceased. Everything in the gospel and kingdom of God points to the temple as the crowning blessing here upon the earth.

OFFICIAL DECLARATION—1 Background—Commentators Hyrum M. Smith and Janne M. Sjodahl provide the following details:

> . . . the doctrine of plural marriage was made known to the Prophet in 1831, or 1832, although the Revelation on the subject was not committed to writing until the year 1843. It should be noted that even then it was not given to the *Church*. This step was taken on the 29th of August, 1852, when the Revelation was read to a General Conference in the "Old Tabernacle," Salt Lake City, and accepted by the assembly as a revelation from God and part of the law of the Church. In voting for the Revelation, the Saints firmly believed that they were only exercising their legal right as American citizens. They believed that, as a majority, they had the indisputable constitutional right to regulate their domestic affairs, within the boundaries of their own territory, and that the Supreme Court of the United States would uphold this view, even if Congress should be of a different opinion. And they were strengthened in their position by the fact that not until ten years after the action taken by the Church in 1852 was any effort made by Congress to stamp plural marriage as illegal.
>
> The first Congressional enactment against plural marriage, passed in 1862, remained a dead letter for twenty years. By that time, the anti-Mormons had evidence that the Supreme Court would uphold legislation of that kind, and the laws more drastic than the first were passed by Congress. The Church leaders appealed to the Supreme Court, as was their prerogative. For years there was a legal conflict. At last, when the Supreme Court had declared the anti-polygamy laws constitutional and there was no prospect that there would be a reversal of this decision, the Church loyally and gracefully accepted it. President Wilford Woodruff issued his Manifesto against the practice of plural marriage, and this was accepted by a unanimous vote of the General Conference assembled in Salt Lake City, Oct.

of last resort, I hereby declare my intention to submit to those laws, and to use my influence with the members of the Church over which I preside to have them do likewise.

There is nothing in my teachings to the Church or in those of my associates, during the time specified, which can be reasonably construed to inculcate or encourage polygamy; and when any Elder of the Church has used language which appeared to convey any such teaching, he has been promptly reproved. And I now publicly declare that my advice to the Latter-day Saints is to refrain from contracting any marriage forbidden by the law of the land.

WILFORD WOODRUFF
President of the Church of Jesus Christ
of Latter-day Saints.

President Lorenzo Snow offered the following:

"I move that, recognizing Wilford Woodruff as the President of the Church of Jesus Christ of Latter-day Saints, and the only man on the earth at the present time who holds the keys of the sealing ordinances, we consider him fully authorized by virtue of his position to issue the Manifesto which has been read in our hearing, and which is dated September 24th, 1890, and that as a Church in General Conference assembled, we accept his declaration concerning plural marriages as authoritative and binding."

The vote to sustain the foregoing motion was unanimous.

Salt Lake City, Utah, October 6, 1890.

EXCERPTS FROM THREE ADDRESSES BY PRESIDENT WILFORD WOODRUFF REGARDING THE MANIFESTO

The Lord will never permit me or any other man who stands as President of this Church to lead you astray. It is not in the programme. It is not in the mind of God. If I were to attempt that, the Lord would remove me out of my place, and so He will any other man who attempts to lead the children of men astray from the oracles of God and from their duty. (Sixty-first Semiannual General Conference of the Church, Monday, October 6, 1890, Salt Lake City, Utah. Reported in Deseret Evening News, October 11, 1890, p. 2.)

It matters not who lives or who dies, or who is called to lead this Church, they have got to lead it by the inspiration of Almighty God. If they do not do it that way, they cannot do it at all. . . . I have had some revelations of late, and very important ones to me, and I will tell you what the Lord has said to me. Let me bring your minds to what is termed the manifesto . . .

The Lord has told me to ask the Latter-day Saints a question, and He also told me that if they would listen to what I said to them and answer the question put to them, by the Spirit and power of God, they would all answer alike, and they would all believe alike with regard to this matter.

The question is this: Which is the wisest course for the Latter-day Saints to pursue—to continue to attempt to practice plural marriage, with the laws of the nation against it and the opposition of sixty millions of people, and at the cost of the confiscation and loss of all the Temples, and the stopping of all the ordinances therein, both for the living and the dead, and the imprisonment of the First Presidency and Twelve and the heads of families in the Church, and the confiscation of personal property of the people (all of which of themselves would stop the practice); or, after doing and suffering what we have through our adherence to this principle to cease the practice and submit to the law, and through doing so leave the Prophets, Apostles and fathers at home, so

6th, 1890. This was done by divine revelation to President Wilford Woodruff. . . .

By this action the Church voted to conform to the laws of the land as interpreted by the highest tribunal, and to leave the issue with God. Since that conference, and, in fact, for some time previous to the acceptance of the Manifesto, no plural marriage has been performed anywhere with the sanction of the Church, or the approbation of the First Presidency, or anyone representing them, as was fully proved during the so-called Smoot investigation in the United States Senate, which commenced January 16, 1904.

"I want to say to this congregation, and to the world, that never at any time since my presidency in the Church of Jesus Christ of Latter-day Saints have I authorized any man to perform plural marriage, and never since my presidency of the Church has any plural marriage been performed with my sanction or knowledge, or with the consent of the Church of Jesus Christ of Latter-day Saints; and therefore such unions as have been formed unlawfully, contrary to the order of the Church, are null and void in the sight of God, and are not marriages." (President Joseph F. Smith, at the General Conference of the Church, Oct. 4th, 1918)." (DCC, 836–837.)

Manifesto—What is the meaning of the word *manifesto*? It is not just something manifested to the world by the Church; rather, it is that which is manifested to the living prophet by the Lord. In this sense, all scripture is a "manifesto"—for it reveals the will of the Lord through His servant, the authorized prophet-leader of the Church, having all the keys and rights of presidency. President Wilford Woodruff declares: "I will tell you what the Lord has said to me." An alternative formulation would be "Thus saith the Lord"—a statement that appears in the standard works no fewer than 517 times.

The approach used by the Lord in this case is especially compelling, for the Lord reasons with His Saints by asking a question. He asks, in effect: What would happen if the practice of plural marriage were not suspended? The answer: The work and forward motion of the Church and Kingdom would be destroyed. What should the Saints do? Whatever is necessary to carry out the will of the Lord. Thus a decision had to be reached—and it was, as evidenced by the Manifesto of 1890. To paraphrase the words of an angel to Nephi on another occasion it is better that one divine practice should be suspended than that the work of the Church and kingdom should dwindle and perish in confusion (see 1 Ne. 4:13).

How widespread was the practice of plural marriage prior to the Manifesto? Commentator Richard Cowan indicates:

It is impossible to state exactly how many were involved in the practice of plural marriage.

that they can instruct the people and attend to the duties of the Church, and also leave the Temples in the hands of the Saints, so that they can attend to the ordinances of the Gospel, both for the living and the dead?

The Lord showed me by vision and revelation exactly what would take place if we did not stop this practice. If we had not stopped it, you would have had no use for . . . any of the men in this temple at Logan; for all ordinances would be stopped throughout the land of Zion. Confusion would reign throughout Israel, and many men would be made prisoners. This trouble would have come upon the whole Church, and we should have been compelled to stop the practice. Now, the question is, whether it should be stopped in this manner, or in the way the Lord has manifested to us, and leave our Prophets and Apostles and fathers free men, and the temples in the hands of the people, so that the dead may be redeemed. A large number has already been delivered from the prison house in the spirit world by this people, and shall the work go on or stop? This is the question I lay before the Latter-day Saints. You have to judge for yourselves. I want you to answer it for yourselves. I shall not answer it; but I say to you that is exactly the condition we as a people would have been in had we not taken the course we have.

. . . I saw exactly what would come to pass if there was not something done. I have had this spirit upon me for a long time. But I want to say this: I should have let all the temples go out of our hands; I should have gone to prison myself, and let every other man go there, had not the God of heaven commanded me to do what I did do; and when the hour came that I was commanded to do that, it was all clear to me. I went before the Lord, and I wrote what the Lord told me to write . . .

I leave this with you, for you to contemplate and consider. The Lord is at work with us. (Cache Stake Conference, Logan, Utah, Sunday, November 1, 1891. Reported in Deseret Weekly, November 14, 1891.)

Now I will tell you what was manifested to me and what the Son of God performed in this thing. . . . All these things would have come to pass, as God Almighty lives, had not that Manifesto been given. Therefore, the Son of God felt disposed to have that thing presented to the Church and to the world for purposes in his own mind. The Lord had decreed the establishment of Zion. He had decreed the finishing of this temple. He had decreed that the salvation of the living and the dead should be given in these valleys of the mountains. And Almighty God decreed that the Devil should not thwart it. If you can understand that, that is a key to it. (From a discourse at the sixth session of the dedication of the Salt Lake Temple, April 1893. Typescript of Dedicatory Services, Archives, Church Historical Department, Salt Lake City, Utah.)

Reliable estimates vary from 2 to 3 percent if only married men are counted, or about 10 to 15 percent if men, women, and children are included. Church leaders enforced strict standards in connection with authorizing plural marriages. Even though there were some abuses which attracted publicity, most plural families enjoyed rich spiritual blessings and a variety of other advantages if they were willing to put forth the requisite effort to live in this system of marriage. . . .

It was agreed by Church leaders and non-Mormon officials that new polygamous marriages would not be allowed, but that those who had entered plural marriage before the Manifesto was issued could continue to live with these families without fear of prosecution. It was under these terms that Utah was admitted as one of the United States in 1896. In 1904, President Joseph F. Smith again upheld the principles set forth in the Official Declaration and stressed that the Church would not sanction plural marriages anywhere in the world. Since that time, a few small groups have gained notoriety by their practice of polygamy, but such persons are subject to excommunication from the Church. (DCOMS, 210–213.)

OFFICIAL DECLARATION—2

On June 8, 1978, an announcement of a revelation was made by the First Presidency—Spencer W. Kimball, N. Eldon Tanner, and Marion G. Romney—restoring the priesthood to all worthy male members of the Church without regard for race or color.

On September 30, 1978, President N. Eldon Tanner read the revelation to those assembled at the 148th Semiannual General Conference of The Church of Jesus Christ of Latter-day Saints; by a show of hands, those assembled unanimously accepted the revelation as the word and will of the Lord.

The revelation was subsequently added to the 1981 edition of the Doctrine and Covenants as Official Declaration—2.

OFFICIAL DECLARATION—2 Background—Richard O. Cowan provides the following details concerning the historic announcement by the President of the Church:

Over a period of several months the General Authorities discussed at length in their regular temple meetings the matter of extending the blessings of the priesthood. In addition to these deliberations, President Kimball frequently went to the temple, particularly on Saturdays and Sundays when he could be in that holy place alone in order to plead for guidance. . . .

On 1 June 1978, nearly all the General Authorities gathered, fasting, for their regular monthly meeting in the temple. After this three-hour session which was filled with spiritual uplift and enlightenment, President Kimball invited his counselors and the Twelve to remain while the other General Authorities were excused. When the First Presidency and the Twelve were alone, he again brought up the possibility of conferring the priesthood on worthy brethren of all races. He expressed the hope that there might be a clear answer received one way or the other. . . . After a two-hour discussion, President Kimball asked the group to unite in formal prayer . . . .

It was during this prayer that the revelation came. The Spirit of the Lord rested mightily upon us all; we felt something akin to what happened on the day of Pentecost and at the dedication of the Kirtland Temple. From the midst of eternity, the voice of God, conveyed by the power of the Spirit, spoke to his prophet. . . . And we all heard the same voice, received the same message, and became personal witnesses that the word received was the mind and will and voice of the Lord (Bruce R. McConkie, "The New Revelation on Priesthood," 128).

Reflecting on this experience, President Spencer W. Kimball and President Ezra Taft Benson and others of the Twelve concurred that none "had ever experienced anything of such spiritual magnitude and power as was poured out upon the Presidency and the Twelve that day in the upper room in the house of the Lord" (McConkie, "The New Revelation on Priesthood," 128). . . . (Richard O. Cowan, "Official Declarations 1 and 2," in SSDC, 567–569.)

D&C Official Declaration 2—Extending the reach of priesthood blessings to all worthy male members is a primary instance in the ongoing process of modern-day, continuing revelation through God's living prophets. President James E. Faust said: "In our lifetime we have been favored with ongoing communication from the heavens, which have been open to the prophets of our time. . . . Surely one of the greatest divine disclosures came in 1978 when the blessings of the priesthood and temple became available to all worthy male members (*RUL*, 111).

There was rejoicing across the kingdom of God when this milestone in priesthood administration was announced. Hearts were warmed; spirits lifted; gratitude kindled. Something of the spirit of the times is reflected in these words of scholar Richard Holzapfel: " . . . the work that was begun among a comparative handful of people in the eastern United States more than a century and a half ago, which then spread to neighboring nations, Europe, and the Pacific, now has the potential to touch every land and people. . . . " (Richard Neitzel Holzapfel, "The Incomparable Blessings of the Priesthood," *Ensign*, Oct. 1997, 44).